Adobe® Premiere®
Pro 2 Bible

Adobe® Premiere® Pro 2 Bible

Adele Droblas and Seth Greenberg

WILEY

Wiley Publishing, Inc.

Adobe® Premiere® Pro 2 Bible

Published by
Wiley Publishing, Inc.
111 River Street
Hoboken, N.J. 07030-5774
www.wiley.com

Copyright © 2006 by Wiley Publishing, Inc., Indianapolis, Indiana

Published simultaneously in Canada

Library of Congress Cataloging-in-Publication Data: 2005936639

ISBN13: 978-0-471-75175-5
ISBN10: 0-471-75175-8

Manufactured in the United States of America

10 9 8 7 6 5 4 3 2 1

1O/QU/QR/QW/IN

About the Authors

Adele Droblas is an artist. For more information about Adele, go to www.BonitaVida.com.

Seth Greenberg is a computer consultant, programmer, and author. He has worked as an interactive project manager, television producer and scriptwriter.

Credits

Acquisitions Editor
Mike Roney

Project Editor
Martin V. Minner

Technical Editor
Bill Lyon

Copy Editor
Gwenette Gaddis Goshert

Editorial Manager
Robyn Siesky

Vice President and Executive Group Publisher
Richard Swadley

Vice President and Publisher
Barry Pruett

Project Coordinator
Ryan Steffen

Graphics and Production Specialists
Carrie Foster
Lauren Goddard
Denny Hager
Joyce Haughey
Jennifer Heleine
Alicia B. South

Quality Control Technicians
John Greenough

Permissions Editor
Laura Moss

Media Development Specialist
Kate Jenkins

Proofreading and Indexing
TECHBOOKS Production Services

Cover Illustration
Daniela Richardson

To our family and to Angelique and Laurence,
the stars of our videos,
who make every day and every night shine.

Foreword

As a Worldwide Product Evangelist for Adobe, it is my job to enlighten, inspire, and essentially "proselytize" the Adobe video and audio products to their fullest extent across the globe. How ironic then, when I was asked to write the foreword for the *Adobe Premiere Pro 2 Bible*. An evangelist touting a Bible? Sounds complicated...and a bit edgy. But literal nomenclature aside, my mission is really about spreading the word about Adobe products and the better references that support them.

After all, what we're really talking about is the necessity for an ideal printed reference; a companion to get you from point A to point B with a learning curve that is easy enough to handle at your own pace, while providing you with lots of tips and tricks to start making your productions come alive in ways you never thought possible.

With the introduction of Adobe Premiere Pro 2.0, Adobe has enhanced its already powerful feature set with a plethora of new tools that elevate your ability to create in a variety of formats (HD, HDV, DV), edit and cut between multiple cameras in your timeline (with the new native MultiCam feature), and even do quick exports of your video and audio using Adobe PDF technology, for fast and efficient client commentary and digital daily distribution through a new feature known as Clip Notes. That's just the beginning. Premiere Pro 2.0 also boasts a new three-way color corrector, as well as fantastic new menu templates for DVD authoring directly from the timeline. In addition, for sound editing and creation, you'll find even tighter integration with Adobe Audition, giving you the ability to edit, restore, and replace audio from any video source file.

Couple this with enhanced integration between the existing Adobe Production Studio applications (Adobe After Effects, Audition, Encore DVD, Illustrator CS2, and Photoshop CS2) and suddenly you find yourself in high-end production territory with everything at your fingertips. Consider the new Timewarp, HDR Color Support, and Graph Editing features in After Effects; Flowcharting and Dynamic Slideshows in Adobe Encore DVD; and the fantastic Low-latency Mixer and new Spectral Editing tools in Adobe Audition.

That's where the Adobe Premiere Pro 2 Bible comes in. From basic instructions on getting started , through cutting video and adding transitions in the timeline, to applying audio effects, restoration tools, and creating motion graphics and authoring DVDs, you'll find the information herein is both informative and pertinent to anyone working with digital video on a PC.

If you happen to own the entire Adobe Production Studio, you'll be able to take advantage of our latest integration technology known as "Dynamic Link," which elevates your workflow to a whole new level with the ability to import and play "Live" After Effects compositions in Premiere Pro, all without the need to render. The flexibility of Dynamic Link can also be found between After Effects and Adobe Encore DVD, allowing you to create your motion menus in After Effects and dynamically link them to an Adobe Encore DVD project without rendering.

Dynamic Link is just one of the many new features that you'll find in the Adobe Production Studio. The most obvious change is the new, unified interface design. Whether you're working in Premiere Pro, After Effects, Audition, or Encore DVD, all four applications share a unified, docking "panel" scheme (panels have replaced palettes) that allows you to customize and save your layouts while maximizing screen real estate and optimizing your workflow. If you're in need of templates, music beds, and royalty free artwork, look no further. After Effects, Audition, and Encore DVD all ship with additional content including animation and behavior presets along with template projects and backgrounds (After Effects), radio-ready music beds (Audition), and animated motion menus and additional menus, buttons, and background layers in lots of new styles (Encore DVD), enabling you to author extremely professional, sleek looking DVDs. Just as with the previous *Adobe Premiere Pro Bible,* Adele Droblas and Seth Greenberg have done a fantastic job of taking you beyond editing with Adobe Premiere Pro 2.0 and explaining how the result of your efforts can be enhanced by the other powerful Adobe software tools.

I hope you enjoy all of the new features that Adobe Premiere Pro 2.0 has to offer. There is an enormous amount of information to ingest, but with this book by your side, you can follow along at your own speed. Just remember to sit back, take it all in, and spread the word (through your productions, that is). Spoken like a true product evangelist, indeed.

Jason Levine
Senior Worldwide Product Evangelist — Digital Video and Audio
Adobe Systems Incorporated

Preface

As you read these words, a revolution in desktop video is taking place. One of the main causes of the revolution is the advent of the digital video camera, which digitizes high-quality video directly in the camera. After the signal has been digitized, it can be transferred directly over a cable to a personal computer. After your computer gets hold of the video, you need Adobe Premiere Pro to help you creatively shape it into a compelling desktop video production.

Adobe Premiere Pro combines power and ease of use to provide a complete authoring environment for producing desktop digital video productions. By using Premiere Pro, you can capture video directly from your camcorder into Premiere Pro's capture window. After you've captured or imported video and sound, you can assemble your clips into a production by simply clicking and dragging a video clip from one window to another. Placing clips and reassembling them is almost as easy as snapping together the cars in a child's toy railroad train set. Creating transitions that dissolve one scene into another or wipe one scene away to reveal another is simply a matter of dragging an icon representing the transition between the two clips. To fine-tune your work, Premiere Pro provides numerous digital-editing tools—some similar to those available in professional editing studios, others only possible through digital magic. After you've finished editing, you can output your digital movie with settings for the Web, videotape, or DVD. If you've ever tried creating a video production by using traditional videotape hardware, Adobe Premiere Pro will revolutionize the way that you work.

Who Should Read This Book

The *Adobe Premiere Pro 2 Bible* is for video producers, video editors, filmmakers, multimedia producers, Web designers, graphic designers, artists — anyone interested in using his or her computer to create desktop video productions or to output desktop video to videotape, DVD, or the Web. As you read through the *Adobe Premiere Pro 2 Bible*, you soon see that it is more than just a reference to virtually all the features in Adobe Premiere Pro. The book is filled with short tutorial exercises that help you understand concepts and put into practice the key Premiere Pro features covered in a chapter. You'll find this book indispensable as you learn to use Adobe Premiere Pro (and a useful reference book after you've mastered Premiere Pro's key features). So don't wait another moment — start reading and learning what you can do with your creative visions.

How This Book Is Organized

If you read the *Adobe Premiere Pro 2 Bible*'s chapters in order, you'll gradually become an expert at using Adobe Premiere Pro. However, we expect that most readers will jump in and out of chapters as needed or as their interest moves from subject to subject. Throughout the book, we've included numerous step-by-step tutorials to guide you through the process of creating video sequences by using many Adobe Premiere Pro features. As you work, you'll find many clips on the DVD that will aid you in quickly and efficiently creating short examples that illustrate and help explain chapter topics.

Note For updated information on Adobe Premiere Pro, be sure to visit Adobe's Web site at www.adobe.com.

The *Adobe Premiere Pro 2 Bible* is divided into seven main parts, each described in the following sections.

Part I: Getting Started with Premiere Pro

Part I provides an introduction to as well as an overview of Adobe Premiere Pro. Chapter 1 includes a getting-started tutorial that introduces you to the basics of creating a desktop video production using Adobe Premiere Pro. Chapter 2 provides an overview of the Premiere Pro interface, menus, palettes, and tools. Chapter 3 takes a look at how to customize Premiere Pro so that you can save time when creating projects. Chapter 4 introduces you to Premiere Pro's basic project settings. Chapter 5 shows you how to capture video directly into Premiere Pro from a digital video camcorder or an analog camcorder.

Part II: Editing with Premiere Pro

Part II provides a thorough look at the basics of putting together a digital video production. Chapter 6 shows you how to use Premiere Pro's Timeline and sequences to assemble a video production. It also reviews many features to ease production project management. Chapter 7 provides the basics of editing using the Timeline panel and Source Monitor. Chapters 8 and 9 provide a look at Premiere Pro's audio features. Chapter 10 rounds out this part with a discussion of how to use transitions to smooth changes from one clip to another.

Part III: Working with Type and Graphics

Part III is dedicated to type and graphics. This part shows you how to use the Title Designer panel and titling tools. You learn how to create titles with styles, templates, and logos; how to create rolling and scrolling credits; and how to create titles with drop shadows. You also learn how to create graphics using the Title Designer, Adobe Illustrator, and Adobe Photoshop. Chapters 11 and 12 cover creating type and graphic effects.

Part IV: Advanced Techniques and Special Effects

Part IV covers advanced editing techniques and special effects. Chapter 13 covers sophisticated editing features in Premiere Pro, such as three-point and four-point edits. It also provides a discussion on how to use Premiere Pro's Rolling Edit and Ripple Edit tools as well as using its Slip and Slide editing tools. Chapter 13 also covers precise frame-by-frame editing by using the Trim panel. Chapter 14 reviews the video effects in the Effects panel, while Chapter 15 covers the program's transparency effects (found in the Keying bin of the Effects panel). Chapter 16 provides you with information on how to create color mattes and backgrounds using Premiere Pro, Photoshop, and Illustrator. If you want to create motion effects in Premiere Pro, check out Chapter 17, which provides a thorough look at Motion effects. Chapter 18 shows you how to enhance your video using Premiere Pro's color correction tools.

Part V: Outputting Digital Video from Premiere Pro

After you've learned how to create a digital video production in Premiere Pro, your next concern is how to output your work in the best possible manner. This part covers all the bases. Chapter 19 reviews Premiere Pro's settings for exporting QuickTime, AVI, and MPEG movies. It also shows you how to use Premiere Pro's DVD markers as the basis for interactive buttons in DVD templates. Chapters 20 and 21 describe how to obtain the best possible quality when outputting a movie to the Web. Chapter 22 provides a discussion of outputting to videotape, while Chapter 23 covers outputting to CD-ROM as well as using Premiere Pro with Macromedia Director and Flash.

Part VI: Premiere Pro and Beyond

The chapters in this section provide a look at using Premiere Pro with different software packages, such as Adobe Audition, Adobe Encore, Adobe Photoshop, Adobe Illustrator, and Adobe After Effects. Chapter 24 reviews using Adobe Audition. Chapters 25 and 26 take you on a tour of how to use Adobe Encore to create a DVD. Chapter 27 provides a look at how to trim clips using Adobe After Effects. Chapter 28 shows you how to create alpha channels in Photoshop that can be used in Premiere Pro; it also shows you how to edit Premiere Pro frames in Photoshop and export them back into Premiere Pro. Chapter 29 shows how to create graphics and text using Adobe Illustrator. These graphics and texts are then imported and used in Adobe Premiere Pro, many times as masks. Chapters 30 and 31 deal with working with Adobe After Effects. In Chapter 30, you learn how to create and animate masks using After Effects Bezier masks. In Chapter 31, you learn how to use After Effects to animate Photoshop and Illustrator files, how to use After Effects' powerful motion paths, and how to create composite video clips.

Part VII: Appendixes

The *Adobe Premiere Pro 2 Bible* appendixes provide a hardware overview geared to non-technical users, a resource guide, and a guide to the *Adobe Premiere Pro 2 Bible* DVD. The hardware overview appendix provides a look at computer systems and IEEE 1394/FireWire ports, and it also provides a short guide to DV camcorders and audio. The resource appendix provides a Web guide for digital video and sound equipment as well as the Web addresses for magazines and publishers specializing in video, audio, and lighting.

Things to Note

The *Adobe Premiere Pro 2 Bible* runs only on Windows XP Pro and XP Home Edition. The program's target user is the video professional.

Key combinations

Here are some conventions in this book that you should note. To save your file, press Ctrl+S. When keyboard instructions call for pressing several keys simultaneously, the keys are separated by a plus sign. For example, to deselect all clips in the Timeline, press Ctrl+Shift+A.

Mouse instructions

When the text specifies to click an item, move the mouse pointer over the item and click once. Windows users always click the left mouse button unless otherwise instructed. If the text specifies that you double-click, click the mouse twice without moving it.

Menu commands

When the text specifies steps for executing a menu command, the menu and the command are separated by an arrow symbol, such as File⏵Import. When submenus are specified, you often see an arrow separating each menu command. For example, to export a project from Premiere Pro, you'll see the instructions written as File⏵Export⏵Movie.

Acknowledgments

Thanks to Adobe Systems for creating products that allow us to express our creative visions. A special thanks to the entire Adobe team for doing such a good job in coming out with great products. Thanks in particular to these people at Adobe Systems: Jason Levine, Bruce Bowman, Steve Kilisky, Vishal Khandpur, Wendy Kuramoto, Charat Maheshwari, Kevin Coleman, Jill Devlin, Peter Green, and Ron Day.

Thanks to everyone at Wiley Publishing, Inc., especially Mike Roney who helped get the *Adobe Premiere Pro 2 Bible* off the ground and who always kept us on schedule. Thanks to publishers Richard Swadley and Barry Pruett. Thanks also to Project Editor Martin V. Minner for keeping the editorial process well organized and flowing smoothly. Thanks to copy editor Gwenette Gaddis Goshert for doing such a careful and meticulous job. Thanks, too, to Ryan Steffen, the production coordinator, and the graphics department for their help with the book. For their help in putting the DVD together, we thank Laura Moss and Kate Jenkins. Thanks especially to Bill Lyon for his job in tech editing the *Adobe Premiere Pro 2 Bible*.

Thanks to Thomas Smith from Digital Vision for supplying us with digital stock clips for use on the DVD that accompanies the book.

Thanks to all the people (family; friends, especially our musician and computer friends; the children of today, who are the future; and to all those people we have met who radiate peace and happiness for all) who have touched our lives and inspired us to want to capture those wonderful moments that life has to offer. Hopefully, the *Adobe Premiere Pro 2 Bible* will help capture those special moments in your life and allow you to share them with friends and loved ones.

We hope you enjoy the *Adobe Premiere Pro 2 Bible*.

Contents at a Glance

Contents

Part II: Editing with Premiere Pro   105

Chapter 6: The Timeline, Sequences, and Clip Management 107

Chapter 7: Basic Editing with the Source Monitor and Timeline Panels . . 129

Part III: Working with Type and Graphics   227

Part IV: Advanced Techniques and Special Effects   307

Part VII: Appendixes 739

Getting Started with Premiere Pro

Premiere Pro Quick Start

Welcome to the world of Adobe Premiere Pro and digital video. For both experts and beginners alike, Adobe Premiere Pro packs the power you need to create sophisticated digital video productions. You can create digital movies, documentaries, sales presentations, and music videos directly from your desktop computer or laptop. Your digital video production can be output to videotape to the Web or to DVD, or you can integrate it into projects in other programs, such as Adobe After Effects, Adobe Encore DVD, Macromedia Director, and Macromedia Flash.

This chapter introduces you to the basics of Adobe Premiere Pro: It helps you understand what it is and what you can do with it. This chapter also provides a simple Quick Start project to get you acquainted with the Premiere Pro production process. You'll see how easy it is to load digital video clips and graphics into an Adobe Premiere project and edit them into a short presentation. After you've completed the editing the project, you'll export the movie as either a QuickTime or Windows Media file for use in other programs.

Knowing What You Can Do with Premiere Pro

Whether you need to create a simple video clip for the Web, a sophisticated documentary, rock video, or a video of an artistic event or wedding, Premiere Pro has the tools you need to create a dynamic video production. In fact, the best way to think about Premiere Pro is to visualize it as a complete production facility. You would need a room full of videotape and special effects equipment to do everything that Premiere Pro can do.

Here's a short list of some of the production tasks that you can accomplish with Premiere Pro:

✦ Edit digital video clips into a complete digital video production.

✦ Capture video from a camcorder or videotape recorder.

✦ Capture audio from a microphone or audio playback device.

✦ Load stock digital graphics, video, and audio clips.

✦ Create titles and animated title effects, such as scrolling or rolling titles.

✦ Integrate files from different sources into your production. Premiere Pro can import not only digital video and audio files, but also Adobe Photoshop, Adobe Illustrator, JPEG, and TIFF graphics.

✦ Create special effects, such as distortions, blurring, and pinching.

✦ Create motion effects in which logos or graphics fly or bounce across the screen.

✦ Create transparency effects. You can superimpose titles over backgrounds or use color, such as blue or green, to mask the background from one image so that you can super-impose a new background.

✦ Edit sound. Premiere Pro enables you to cut and assemble audio clips as well as create sophisticated audio effects, such as cross fades and pans.

✦ Create transitions. Premiere Pro can create simple dissolves from one scene to another, as well as a host of sophisticated transition effects, such as page curls and curtain wipes.

✦ Output files in a variety of digital formats. Premiere Pro can output QuickTime, Windows Media, and Video for Windows files. These files can be imported into other multimedia application, as well as viewed on the Web.

✦ Output files to videotape and DVD.

Understanding How Premiere Pro Works

To understand the Premiere Pro production process, you need a basic understanding of the steps involved in creating a conventional videotape production in which the production footage is *not* digitized. In traditional, or *linear*, video production, all production elements are trans-ferred to videotape. During the editing process, the final production is electronically edited onto one final or *program* videotape. Even though computers are used while editing, the linear or analog nature of videotape makes the process very time-consuming; during the actual editing session, videotape must be loaded and unloaded from tape or cassette machines. Time is wasted as producers simply wait for videotape machines to reach the correct editing point. The production is usually assembled sequentially. If you want to go back to a previous scene and replace it with one that is shorter or longer, all subsequent scenes must be rerecorded to the program reel.

Nonlinear editing programs (often abbreviated as NLE) such as Premiere Pro have revolution-ized the entire process of video editing. Digital video and Premiere Pro eliminate many of the time-consuming production chores of traditional editing. When using Premiere Pro, you don't need to hunt for tapes or load and remove them from tape machines. When producers use Premiere Pro, all production elements are digitized to disk. Icons in Premiere Pro's Project panel represent each element in a production, whether it is a video clip, a sound clip, or a still image. The final production is represented by icons in a panel called the *Timeline.* The focal points of the Timeline are its video and audio tracks, which appear as parallel bars that stretch from left to right across the screen. When you need to use a video clip, sound clip, or still image, you can simply select it in the Project panel and drag it to a track in the Timeline. You can place the items of your production down sequentially or drag them to different tracks. As you work, you can access any portion of your production by clicking with the mouse in the desired portion of the Timeline. You can also click and drag on the beginning or end of a clip to shorten or extend its duration.

To fine-tune your edits, you can view and edit the clips frame by frame in Premiere Pro's Source and Program Monitors. You can also set in and out points in the Source Monitor panel. Setting an *in point* determines where a clip starts playing, and setting an *out point* specifies where a clip stops playing. Because all clips are digitized (and no videotape is involved), Premiere Pro can quickly adjust the final production as you edit.

This list summarizes some of the digital-editing magic that you can perform in Premiere Pro by simply dragging clips in the Timeline:

✦ **Rolling edit:** As you click and drag to the right on a clip edge in the Timeline, Premiere Pro automatically subtracts from the frames in the next clip. If you click and left drag to remove frames, Premiere Pro automatically adds back frames from the next clip in the Timeline.

✦ **Ripple edit:** As you click and drag left or right on the edge of a clip, you add or subtract frames to the clip. Premiere Pro automatically adds to or subtracts from the entire program's duration.

✦ **Slip edit:** Dragging a clip between two other clips to the left or right automatically changes both in and out points of the clip without changing the program duration.

✦ **Slide edit:** Dragging a clip between two other clips to the left or right keeps the clip's duration intact but changes the in or out points of the preceding or succeeding clip.

Cross-Reference   Chapters 7 and 13 both provide in-depth discussion of Premiere Pro editing techniques.

As you work, you can easily preview edits, special effects, and transitions. Changing edits and effects is often a simple matter of changing in and out points. There's no hunting down the right videotape or waiting for the production to be reassembled on tape. When all your editing is completed, you can export the file to videotape or create a new digital file in one of several formats. You can export it as many times as you want, in many different file formats at different frame sizes and frame rates. Furthermore, if you want to add more special effects to your Premiere Pro projects, you can easily import them into Adobe After Effects. You can also integrate your Premiere Pro movie into a Web page or to Adobe Encore DVD to create a DVD production.

Cross-Reference   Adobe After Effects is covered in Chapters 27, 30 and 31. Adobe Encore DVD is covered in Chapters 25 and 26.

Creating Your First Video Production

The following sections provide a Quick Start editing session that leads you step-by-step through the process of creating a very short video production in Premiere Pro. As you work through the tutorial, you learn how to place clips in the Timeline, edit clips in the Source Monitor, apply transitions, and fade video and audio.

In this project, you create a simple video sequence called Nite Out. Figure 1-1 shows frames of the production in Premiere Pro's Timeline window. The clips used to create the project are from Digital Vision's NightMoves CD-ROM. The production begins with a title created in Premiere Pro's Title Designer, viewed over an opening scene of people walking in the city. After a few seconds, a dissolve transitions to a scene of diners in a restaurant. Soon the dining scene dissolves into one showing kitchen workers preparing food. The project ends with another title superimposed over the last scene.

The video clips (705008f.mov, 705009f.mov, and 705029f.mov) used in the Nite Out project are QuickTime files from Digital Vision's NightMoves CD. You must have QuickTime installed on your computer to access these files. The sound clip (705001.aif) used in the Nite Out project is also from Digital Vision's NightMoves CD. The Nite Out folder is in the Chapter 1 folder in the Tutorial Projects folder on the DVD that accompanies this book. For best performance, copy the Chapter 1 folder to your hard drive.

Starting a Premiere Pro project

A Premiere Pro digital video production is called a *project* instead of a video production. The reason for this is that Premiere Pro not only enables you to create the production, but it also enables you to manage production assets as well as create and store titles, transitions, and effects. Thus, the file you work in is much more than just a production — it's truly a project.

Your first step in creating a digital video production in Premiere Pro is to create a new project. Follow these steps:

1. **To load Premiere Pro, double-click the Adobe Premiere Pro icon (or click it in the Windows Start menu).** When you load Premiere Pro, the program automatically assumes that you want to create a new project or open one previously created.

2. 🖼 **To create a new project, click the New Project icon.** If Premiere Pro is already loaded, you can create a new project by choosing File ➪ New Project.

If Premiere Pro is already loaded and you already have a project onscreen, you need to close that project because you can only have one project open at a time.

Specifying project settings

Before you can start importing files and editing, you must specify video and audio settings for the project. The New Project dialog box, shown in Figure 1-2, appears whenever you create a new project. This dialog box enables you to quickly choose predetermined video and audio settings. The most important project settings determine the frame rate (frames per second) and the frame size (viewing area) of your project as well as how the digital video is compressed.

For a detailed description of project settings, see Chapter 4.

Figure 1-1: Scenes from the Nite Out project

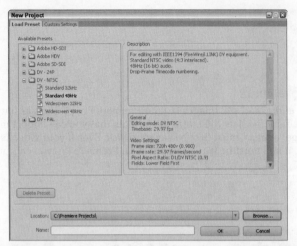

Figure 1-2: Use the New Project dialog box to quickly choose project settings.

As a general rule, choose project settings that match your source footage. The footage used for this tutorial conforms to a video standard called NTSC D1. The frame size is 720 × 486.

1. **To work with the tutorial footage, choose the DV NTSC Standard 48 kHz.** After you click, Premiere Pro displays information about the project settings.

   Notice that the Frame Size is 720 × 480, the standard DV frame size that is close enough to our 720 × 486 footage. Also note that under Video Settings, the display reads D1/DV Pixel Aspect Ratio (0.9). This indicates that you are creating a project for footage with non-square pixels. Because the tutorial footage uses non-square pixels, this is the correct choice for the project.

Cross-Reference   To learn more about Pixel Aspect Ratio and choosing project settings, see Chapter 4.

Tip   If you are creating projects for the Web or for multimedia application, you often will export your project at a smaller frame size, slower frame rate, and lower resolution audio then your original project settings. Typically, you export your project after you have edited it using project settings that match your source footage.

2. **Select a location to store your file.** If you want to change the default file location, click Browse and use the mouse to navigate to the folder where you want to store your project.

3. **Enter a name such as Nite Out in the name field.**

4. **To open your new project, click OK.**

Setting a workspace

Before you start editing, you may want to set your workspace so that you can easily view the most important Premiere Pro windows used in editing. This is easily accomplished by picking an editing workspace. Choose Window ➪ Workspace ➪ Editing. This opens the Project, Source Monitor, Program Monitor, and Timeline panels as well as the Info and History panels. In this tutorial, you use the Project panel as your home for source footage. You'll edit your clips in the Timeline and Source Monitor panels, and you'll view the edited project in the Program Monitor.

Importing production elements

You can place and edit video, audio, and still images in your Premiere Pro projects as long as they are in a digital format. Table 1-1 lists the major file formats that you can import into Premiere Pro. All media footage, or *clips*, must first be saved to disk. Even if your video is stored on a digital camcorder, it still must be transferred to disk. Premiere Pro can capture the digital video clips and automatically store them in your projects. Analog media such as motion picture film and videotape must first be digitized before Premiere Pro can use it. In this case, Premiere Pro, in conjunction with a capture board, can capture your clips directly into a project.

 For more information about capturing video and audio, see Chapter 5.

Table 1-1: Supported Files in Adobe Premiere Pro

Media	File Formats
Video	Video for Windows (AVI Type 2) QuickTime (MOV) (Apple's QuickTime must also be installed), MPEG-1, MPEG-2, and Windows Media (.wmv, .wma)
Audio	AIFF, WAV, AVI, MOV, and MP3
Still images and Sequences	TIF, JPEG, BMP, PNG, EPS, GIF, Filmstrip, Illustrator, and Photoshop

After the Premiere Pro panels open, you're ready to import the various graphic and sound elements that will comprise your digital video production. All the items that you import appear in a list in the Project panel. An icon represents each item. Next to the icon, Premiere Pro displays whether the item is a video clip, an audio clip, or a graphic.

When importing files into Premiere Pro, you can choose whether to import one file, multiple files (by pressing and holding Ctrl as you click the file), or an entire folder. If desired, you can even import one project into another, using the File ➪ Import ➪ Project command.

Follow these steps to load the production elements for the Nite Out project:

1. **Choose File ➪ Import.**

2. **If you want to load the files, select the Nite Out folder in the Chapter 1 folder and click Import Folder.** The Nite Out folder now appears in the Project panel. (If you didn't copy the Chapter 1 folder to your hard drive, you need to open the Tutorial Projects folder on the *Adobe Premiere Pro 2 Bible* DVD-ROM.)

3. **To view the titles, video clips, and audio clips, double-click the Nite Out folder in the Project panel.**

4. **Rename each clip.** Because the names of imported clips may not clearly describe their footage, you can rename them in the Project panel. To rename a clip, click it in the Project panel and choose Clip ➪ Rename. (As a shortcut, you can also right-click the clip and rename it.) Here are the filenames and the new names to use:

- Name the 705001.aif audio clip **Background Music**.

- Name the 705008f clip **Diners**.

- Name the 705009f clip **Chefs**.

- Name the 705029f clip **Walkers**.

Figure 1-3 shows the Project panel with all the clips needed to create the Nite Out project clip. Notice that the Project panel displays the Start and Stop time of each clip as well as its duration.

Figure 1-3: The Project panel with the items needed to create the Nite Out project

The Nite Out project requires the following files:

✦ A video clip showing shadows of people walking in the city (Walkers)

✦ A video clip of people out in a restaurant (Diners)

✦ A video clip of chefs working in a restaurant (Chefs)

✦ Two title files created using templates in Premiere Pro's Title Designer

✦ A sound clip of background music

Note   The video footage was captured at 30 frames per second. Although not necessary for this tutorial, you can change footage frame rate to the Project frame rate by selecting the footage in the Project window and choosing File ➪ Interpret Footage. In the Interpret Footage dialog box, you can enter a new frame rate for the footage.

Cross-Reference   Creating titles in Premiere Pro is discussed in Chapter 11.

Viewing clips in the Project panel

Before you begin assembling your production, you may want to view a clip or graphic, or listen to an audio track. You can see a thumbnail preview of any of the clips in the Project panel by clicking the clip. The preview appears at the upper-left corner of the Project panel. A small triangle (Play button) appears to the left of the thumbnail preview area. Click the Play button to see a preview of a video clip or to hear an audio clip. If you prefer, you can click and drag the tiny slider below the thumbnail preview to gradually view the clip.

 Note   Double-clicking the clip in the Project panel opens the clip in the Source Monitor. You can preview the clip there by clicking the Play button.

Assembling production elements

After you import all your production elements, you need to place them in a sequence in the Timeline panel so that you can start editing your project. A sequence is a sequential assembly of video, audio, effects, and transitions that comprise part of your production.

 Note   If you are working on long projects in Premiere Pro, you probably want to break your work into multiple sequences. After you've edited the sequences, you can drag them into another Timeline panel, where they appear as nested sequences. Using nested sequences is discussed in Chapter 6.

Placing clips in the Timeline

To move a clip or graphic from the Project panel to the Timeline panel, you can simply click it in the Project panel and then drag the item to a track in the Timeline. The item then appears in the Timeline as an icon. The duration of the clip or graphic is represented by the length of the clip in the Timeline.

 Note   You can place clips directly in the Timeline by opening them in the SourceMonitor panel and clicking the Insert or Overlay button. This technique is discussed in Chapter 7.

Selecting clips in the Timeline

You'll spend a great deal of time positioning clips in the Timeline while editing your production. Premiere Pro's Selection and Range Select tools help you assemble your program's clips in the order you want.

Here's how to select and move clips:

✦ **Single clip:** Click the Selection tool (the arrow icon in the upper-left corner of the Timeline). Next, click in the middle of the clip in the Timeline. (To quickly activate the Selection tool, press V on your keyboard.) With the clip selected, click and drag it to the desired location.

✦ **Entire track:** Click the Track Select tool (the dotted-line square icon in the toolbox located to the right or below the Selection tool) on a clip. The Track Select tool selects the entire track from the point where you click.

Figure 1-4 displays the Timeline panel for the Nite Out project. The title appears in the Video 2 track. We put it here because it enables us to create a transparency effect in which we fade in the title text over background video. The Walkers video clip appears in the Video 1 track, as does the next clip (the Diners clip). Between the two tracks is a transition: a dissolve created by dragging it from the Video Effects panel. The project also ends with a transition to a scene of chefs working in a kitchen, before the final title appears and then fades out.

Trying out the Timeline panel

As mentioned earlier, the Timeline provides a graphical overview of your project. Before continuing, try changing zoom settings, clicking and dragging on the current-time indicator, and expanding a video track. Doing so will help familiarize you with the Timeline controls you'll be working with in this chapter.

Changing the zoom level

Most Premiere Pro users create their video projects at 29.97 frames per second. Viewing all these frames on the Timeline quickly consumes valuable screen real estate. As you work, you probably want to zoom in and out between close-up and bird's-eye views of your work. When you zoom in, you see fewer frames, which may make fine-tuning your project easier, particularly because the space between time intervals in the Timeline expands. When you want to see an overview of your entire project, you may want to zoom out.

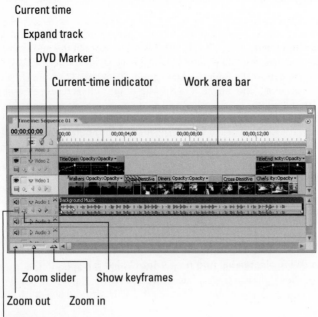

Figure 1-4: The Timeline panel with the clips for the Nite Out video project

To zoom in and out, click the Timeline zoom level slider in the lower-left corner of the Timeline. Figure 1-4 shows the Timeline zoom slider as well as the zoom in and zoom out buttons. Clicking and dragging left (zooming out) shows more footage in the Timeline; clicking and dragging right (zooming in) shows less footage.

For example, if you zoom out, a one-minute clip takes up less space in the Timeline, which means you can see many different clips as well as your one-minute clip. If you zoom in, a one-minute clip occupies more space in the Timeline, which means that it may be the only clip visible.

Moving the current-time indicator

The current-time indicator (sometimes referred to as CTI) is the blue triangular icon at the top of the ruler area in the Timeline. If you click and drag the current-time indicator, you move the red edit line. The edit line shows you the current editing position in the Program Monitor. Try clicking and dragging the current-time indicator. Notice that as you drag, the blue current time readout changes, showing your current position in the Timeline. In Figure 1-4, the edit line is at the very beginning of Timeline, and the current time reads 00;00;00;00. If you want to quickly jump to an area in the Timeline, just click in the ruler area. If you want to slowly move through the Timeline one frame at a time, select the Timeline and then press the right or left arrow keys.

Expanding tracks

By default, you see three video tracks in the Timeline. If you expand a track, you can see video frames in the track and video effects. Later, you'll change the display style to show frames in the video tracks and volume in audio tracks. The white dots in the audio and video tracks in Figure 1-4 are keyframes, which indicate a change in volume or opacity. By default, Video 1track and Audio 1 track are expanded. In this project, you also use Video 2 track. Try expanding it now by clicking the right-pointing triangle to the left of Video 2 track.

Adding the title to the Timeline

Start the production process by adding the opening title to the Timeline. The title includes an *alpha channel*, which allows the background video to be seen beneath the title. The title was created from a template in Premiere Pro's Title Designer. In this section, you place the title in the Video 2 track because it enables you to easily fade in the text over the video in lower tracks.

Cross-Reference

You can edit a title in the Title Designer by double-clicking it in the Project panel. See Chapter 11 to learn more about the Title Designer.

Follow these steps to add the title to the Timeline:

1. **Click TitleOpen in the Project panel and drag it into Video 2 track.**

2. **If you would like to see more of the title in the Timeline, zoom in by clicking and dragging the zoom slider to the right.**

3. **Expand Track 2 by clicking the triangle to the left of the words *Video 2*.** This allows you to access the Set Display Style drop-down menu.

4. **Now view the footage as individual frames in the Timeline. In Video 2 track, click the Set Display Style drop-down menu and choose Show Frames.** (This drop-down menu is a tiny frame icon directly below the Eye icon in the track.)

5. **Reduce the length of the title to 4 seconds by clicking and dragging left with the Selection tool on the right edge of the title clip.** When you move the mouse over the clip's edge, the pointer changes to a bracket with left and right pointing arrows. As you drag, the clip's duration is displayed beneath the lower-right side of the Program Monitor. You can also use the time readout at the top of the Timeline as a guide.

Tip

This technique will allow you to work more precisely in the Timeline: Click and drag the current-time indicator to the 4-second mark. Then use the red edit line as a stopping point when you click and drag the end of the title clip.

Fading in the title

Next, you fade in the titles. In Figure 1-4, the diagonal line immediately in the track represents the fade-in effect. The diagonal line indicates that the title fades in gradually over the first second. In this section, you create the fade-in effect by changing the opacity of the title clip in the Effect Controls panel. Figure 1-5 shows the Effect Controls panel and the Opacity slider. The diamonds to the right of the panel are called *keyframes*. When you make opacity setting changes over time, Premiere Pro creates a keyframe; it gradually changes the opacity between the keyframes.

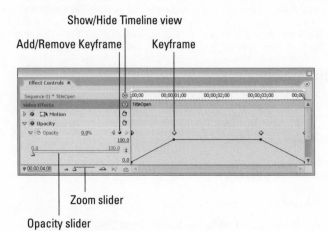

Figure 1-5: Opacity creates a fade-in effect

Follow these steps to change opacity:

1. **Select the TitleOpen file in the Timeline by clicking it.**

2. **Open the Effect Controls panel by choosing Window ➪ Effect Controls.**

3. **Expand the Effect Controls panel, so you can see the panel's Timeline and zoom slider, by clicking the Show/Hide Timeline view icon (the chevron to the right of the TitleOpen).** Before continuing, note that the Effect Controls panel includes a Zoom slider in the lower left and a current-time indicator. Both function exactly as they do in the Timeline panel.

4. **Set the current-time indicator to the 00;00;00 in the Effect Controls or Timeline panel.**

5. **Now expand the Opacity effect by clicking the right-pointing triangle button (to the left of the word *Opacity*).** The Opacity control expands. You can easily change opacity by clicking and dragging the Opacity slider. To view the slider, click the right-pointing arrow to the left of the stopwatch in the Opacity section.

6. **Lower the opacity to 0.** To lower opacity, click and drag the Opacity slider control left until the display reads 0%, as shown in Figure 1-5.

7. **Now drag the current-time indicator in the Effect Controls panel to the 1-second mark.** As you click and drag, you see the time display change in the lower-left corner. Stop when you reach 1 second.

Tip

You can also move the current-time indicator by clicking and dragging left or right over the time readout in the Effect Controls panel.

8. **Now raise the opacity back to 100 percent by clicking and dragging the slider to the right.** As you drag, the percentage increases. The change in opacity creates two keyframes, one at the start of the clip and another one second later. Between the two keyframes, Premiere Pro adjusts opacity to gradually increase from 0 to 100 percent.

9. **Now create a fade-out at the 3-second mark. Click and drag the current-time indicator to the 3-second mark, then click the Add/Remove Keyframe button.** Then drag the Timeline indicator slider to the 4-second mark. Click and drag the Opacity slider to set it to 0%. After you make the change, Premiere Pro adds another keyframe. When you're finished, the Effect Controls panel should resemble Figure 1-5.

Note

You can also change video opacity directly in the Timeline with the Pen or Selection tool. Ctrl-clicking the Opacity graph line in the Timeline creates keyframes. After you create keyframes, you can adjust opacity by clicking and dragging with the Pen or Selection tool.

Tip

If you need to delete a keyframe, right-click it in the Effect Controls panel and then choose Clear in the drop-down menu.

Trimming clips in the Timeline panel

You can edit video and audio clips in several ways. We'll start simply: editing the first clip by clicking and dragging its out point in the Timeline. Before editing a clip, you may want to play it in the Source Monitor panel. To play any clip, double-click it in the Project panel. When the clip appears in the Source Monitor panel, click the Play button to view the clip, as shown in Figure 1-6.

Play In to Out   Play

Figure 1-6: The Monitor panel's Play button

Follow these steps to add the first video clip (the Walkers clip) to the Timeline and edit it (the clip is 14 seconds long, but you need only the first 4 seconds of it):

1. **Drag the Walkers clip from the Source Monitor into the Video 1 track.** Position the clip so that it starts where the title fade-in ends — about 1 second on the Timeline. If you want to be precise, drag the Timeline indicator to the 1-second mark and then drag the Walkers clip to the current-time indicator edit line. When the clip touches the edit line, it snaps to it.

2. **Position the mouse pointer at the end of the Walkers clip.** The cursor changes to a bracket.

3. **Click and drag to the left to shorten the clip.** Make the clip about 4 seconds long so that it ends on the 5-second mark (00;00;05;00) on the Timeline. Again, you may want to drag the current-time indicator to the 5-second mark first (the position of the current-time indicator is displayed in the left side of the Program Monitor) and then adjust the clip by clicking and dragging the right edge of the clip to the left so it snaps on the edit line. As you drag to the left, notice that the clip's duration is displayed in the Program Monitor.

Tip   If you get lost in the Timeline and inadvertently move out of the edited area, zoom out so that you can see the clips you've placed in the Timeline, move the current-time indicator into the edited area, and then zoom in.

Previewing in the Program Monitor

To view the video production so far, you can play the program in the Program Monitor panel. The Program Monitor displays the program being edited in the current sequence in the Timeline window. The Source Monitor shows source clips. To play from the beginning to the end of your project, click the Play In to Out button at the bottom of the Program Monitor window.

As soon as you click, the video clip rewinds and begins playing in the Monitor. As it plays, you see the clip fade in and the Walkers clip superimposed beneath the opening title. The Walkers clip appears only in the black area of the Title clip.

Tip   If you want to play your production in the Program Monitor from the current-time indicator position, press the spacebar or click the Play/Stop toggle button in the Program Monitor. To stop playback using the keyboard, press the spacebar again.

Editing in the Source Monitor

The Source Monitor panel provides precise controls for editing clips. Using the Source Monitor, you can easily navigate to specific frames and then mark in and out points. After you set the in and out points, you can drag the clip directly to the Timeline. Now you'll set the in and out points in the Source Monitor panel. To learn about the different ways to edit a video clip, see Chapters 7 and 13.

Note   You can also click the Insert button or Overlay button in the Source Monitor panel to place a clip in the Timeline. This technique is described in Chapter 7.

Note   By default, Premiere Pro automatically snaps two adjacent clips together. You can also turn snap on or off by clicking the Snap icon (magnet) in the Timeline panel.

1. **Double-click the clip in the Project panel.** This opens the clip in the Source Monitor, shown in Figure 1-7. As discussed earlier, the Source Monitor displays source clips, and the Program Monitor displays the edited sequence in the Timeline window. If the current-time indicator is on the Walkers clip, you see it in the Program Monitor.

2. **Play the clip by clicking the Play button in the Source Monitor.** The scene eventually shows a waitress handing out menus. Before you edit the clip's in and out points, you need to go to the precise frame that you want to edit.

3. **Before editing the clip, jump back to its first frame by clicking the Go to In Point button.**

4. **Now you want to be able to slowly move through the clip to set the in point. Here are several options:**

   • Click the current-time indicator in the Source Monitor and drag. As you drag, you'll move or scrub through the clip frame by frame.

   • Click and drag in the jog tread at the bottom of the Monitor panel. As you click and drag, you'll move through the clip frame by frame.

   • Click and hold down the shuttle control to move in slow or fast motion. Speed is controlled by how far left or right you move the shuttle. Moving right moves forward through the clip. Dragging the shuttle to the left moves backward.

   • Click the Step Backward or Step Forward button to move one frame at a time forward or backward.

Current-time indicator

Set In point   Step backward

Time display   Set Out point   Step forward

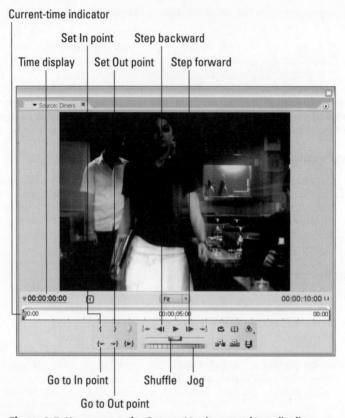

Go to In point   Shuffle   Jog

Go to Out point

Figure 1-7: You can use the Source Monitor panel to edit clips.

5. **Now click and drag the jog tread to the right, or drag the current-time indicator in the Source Monitor to the right.** After about 6 seconds, the scene switches to a long shot of the waitress handing out menus.

6. **Either by clicking and dragging or by typing this precise location into the Time display, position the current-time indicator at 00;00;06;00.**

7. **Click the Set Out Point button (refer to Figure 1-7).**

Note   To clear an in or out point, press Alt while clicking the Set In Point or Set Out Point button.

8. **Now drag the clip to the Timeline so that it snaps to the Walkers clip.**

Tip   To move a clip in the Timeline one frame at a time to the right, select it and press Alt +.
To move the selected clip left one frame at a time, press Alt+,.

Note Although you edited the Walkers clip, the original clip on your hard disk is untouched. At any point in time, you can re-edit the clip.

Creating a transition

Now view your production by previewing it in the Program Monitor. To start the preview from the beginning of the Timeline, click the Play In to Out button in the Program Monitor. As you watch the preview, notice that the cut from the Walkers clip to the Diners clip is quite abrupt. To smooth the flow of the production, you add a *transition* between the two clips.

Cross-Reference For more information on using transitions, see Chapter 10.

Follow these steps to add a Cross Dissolve transition to your project:

1. **Click the Effects panel tab to display the panel contents. If the Effects panel is not open, choose Window ⇨ Effects.**

2. **In the Effects panel, open the Video Transitions bin by clicking its triangle icon.**

3. **Open the Dissolve bin by clicking its triangle icon.**

 Note Folders with effects and clips are referred to as Bins in Premiere Pro.

4. **To add the transition to your project, click and drag the Cross Dissolve transition over the beginning of the Diners clip in the Timeline.**

5. **To open the Cross Dissolve controls, double-click the Cross Dissolve icon in the Timeline.** This opens the transition in the Effect Controls panel.

6. **Adjust the position and length of the transition.** You can adjust the position and the duration of the transition by clicking and dragging the mouse on the transition icon in the Effect Controls panel. However, the fastest technique is to enter a value in the Duration readout and change settings in the Alignment drop-down menu. Set the Duration to 2 seconds by changing the time readout to 00;00;02;00. Then choose Center at Cut in the Alignment drop-down menu, as shown in Figure 1-8.

7. **View a thumbnail preview.** Preview the final transition by clicking the Play Transition button in the Effect Controls window. To see a preview of the effect with the footage, select the Show Actual Sources check box.

Previewing the transition

Premiere Pro includes a real-time preview feature that enables you to view transitions and video effects as you work. To play your project from the current frame, press the spacebar. To render the project from the beginning, press Enter.

A Note about Rendering and Playback Quality

As Premiere Pro plays your program in the Program Monitor, it attempts to adjust the output to deliver the highest quality possible. If possible, it tries to play back at the project's full frame rate. If a portion of your program cannot be properly displayed, a red preview bar appears onscreen. This indicates that the area must be rendered to disk. After rendering, Premiere Pro uses the rendered disk file to properly display the effect. If you want to render your entire project, press Enter. If you want to render only a portion of your project, first adjust the work area bar so that it encompasses only the area that you want to render, and then press Enter. If you want to lower the processing requirements so that you can see effects at a lower quality setting without rendering, you can change to Draft Quality in the Monitor panel menu.

You should also note that despite the Quality Setting in the Program Monitor panel, playback quality in the Program Monitor is not as high as that of exported video. When Premiere Pro processes video in the Monitor window, it uses *bilinear pixel resampling*. When Premiere Pro exports, it uses *cubic resampling*, a higher quality method that also produces higher quality sound.

Play button

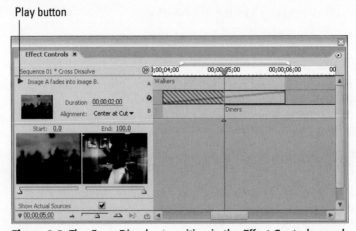

Figure 1-8: The Cross Dissolve transition in the Effect Controls panel

Editing the Chefs clip

Next, you add the Chefs clip to the program and edit it in the Monitor window:

1. **Double-click the Chefs clip in the Project panel.** This opens the clip in the Source Monitor.

2. **Set the in point.** Click and drag the current-time indicator in the Source Monitor (in the area below the Monitor preview and above the Play button) to choose a frame at a little more than 3 seconds into the clip. Click the Set In Point button.

3. **Set the out point.** Click and drag the Source Monitor current-time indicator to find a point about 6 seconds and 15 frames into the clip. Watch the time display at the bottom-right of the window to pick the frame. When you have found the frame you want, click the Set Out Point button.

4. **After you've set the in and out points, drag the clip directly from the Source Monitor or the Project panel to the Timeline.**

Adding another dissolve

Now create another transition — this time between the Diners clip and the Chefs clip:

1. **Open the Dissolve bin in the Effects panel.**

2. **Drag the Cross Dissolve transition over the Chefs clip.**

3. **Double-click the transition icon between the Diners and Chefs clips in the Timeline.**

4. **In the Effect Controls window, set the Alignment drop-down menu to Center of Cut.** If you want to change the duration of the transition, edit the Duration time display.

Adding the last title

Your next step is to add the end title to the Video 2 track:

1. **Drag the end title image (TitleEnd) from the Project panel to the Video 2 track.** Position the title clip so that it begins where the Chefs clip starts.

2. **Drag the clip's end edge to make its duration 3 seconds long, or select the title and choose Clip ➪ Speed/Duration.** In the Clip Speed Duration dialog box, set the display to 00;00;03;00 and click OK.

3. **Create the fade-in and fade-out using the Opacity effect, as you did for the opening title.** Remember to select the clip in the Timeline and open the Effect Controls panel by choosing Window ➪ Effect Controls. Use Figure 1-4 as a reference.

4. **To render and preview your work, press Enter.**

Adding and fading-in the audio track

Now that the majority of editing is complete, it's time to add the audio track. Fortunately, Premiere Pro treats audio much the same as it does video. In this section, you drag the music track to the Timeline and then see how you can use the Pen tool to create keyframes in an audio track:

1. **Listen to the Background Music clip by double-clicking it in the Project panel.** After the clip opens in the Monitor panel, click the Play button.

2. **Drag the Background Music clip from the Project panel to the Audio 1 track in the Timeline.** Line up the beginning of the audio track with the beginning of the video track.

3. **If the Audio 1 track is not expanded, expand it by clicking the triangle icon at the far left of the track.**

4. **Click the Audio track's Show keyframes drop-down menu, and choose Show Clip Volume.**

5. **Activate the Pen tool in the tool panel.**

6. **With the Pen tool activated, Ctrl-click at the beginning of the audio to create a keyframe. Note you can also Ctrl-click with the Selection tool.**

7. **Create another keyframe about 2 seconds into the track by Ctrl-clicking again with the Pen tool.**

8. **Use the Pen tool to drag down the start of the volume line.**

9. **Use the Pen tool to create a keyframe toward the end of the audio.** About 12 seconds into the Project, use Ctrl-click with the Pen tool to create a keyframe.

10. **Create a keyframe at the very end of the audio.** Then drag the final keyframe down to create the fade-out.

11. **Press Enter to Preview your entire project and hear the fade-out.** If you want to fine-tune the effect, use the Pen tool to adjust the volume line in the audio track.

Note   Audio fade-ins can also be created using the Crossfade audio transition. You can also fade audio in and out using the Volume effect in the Effect Controls panel. See Chapter 8 to learn more about audio effects. Also note that Premiere Pro allows you to change the volume of the entire audio track as well as individual clips.

Fine-tuning the project

The project you've worked on is an introduction to basic editing in Premiere Pro. Feel free to enhance, change, and re-edit as you desire. If you want, you can also create a fade to black from the Chefs clip. The easiest way to fade video to black is to use the Dip to Black transition in the Dissolve bin in the Video Effects panel. You can also create pure black video and place it in a video track. To create black, choose File ➪ New ➪ Black Video. This command places the black video clip into the Project panel. From there, you can drag it into the Timeline. If you want to fade in or out to the black video, place it in Video 2 track.

Exporting your first movie

When you finish editing your movie, you can export it as a new file in a variety of formats. Premiere Pro enables you to export movies in video formats such as QuickTime, RealVideo, and Advanced Windows Media, as well as formats for DVD. As mentioned earlier, if your video's final destination is the Web or a multimedia application, you can change frame size and frame rate and lower audio resolution when exporting.

Here is a summary of Premiere Pro's export commands:

✦ If you want to export your file in a format for Web or DVD use, select the Timeline panel and choose File ➪ Export ➪ Adobe Media Encoder. The Media Encoder allows you to create MPEG-2, Windows Media, Real Video, and QuickTime streaming files.

✦ If you want to export your movie as an AVI, QuickTime, or animated GIF file, select the Timeline panel and choose File ➪ Export ➪ Movie.

✦ If you want to export your movie to videotape, select the Timeline panel and choose File ➪ Export to Tape.

✦ If you want to embed your movie in an Adobe Acrobat PDF file for workgroup review, select the Timeline panel and choose Sequence ➪ Export for Clip Notes.

✦ If you want to burn a DVD directly from Premiere Pro, you can create DVD markers to use as the basis for interactive DVD menu buttons in Premiere Pro DVD menu templates. To pick a menu template, choose Window ➪ DVD Layout. Creating a DVD menu is described in the next section.

Exporting to DVD

If you want to turn your Premiere Pro project into an interactive DVD, you can set DVD Timeline markers that link to buttons on Premiere Pro's DVD menu templates. Figure 1-9 shows buttons that Premiere Pro automatically creates in a DVD menu template. The menu template not only creates buttons from the Nite Out project but displays thumbnails of the video in the buttons. To create buttons, set DVD scene markers along the Timeline and then choose a DVD template. The menu, shown in Figure 1-9, is the second of a two-part menu template. The first menu screen includes a Play Movie button and a Scene Selection button that allow the user to jump to the menu screen shown in Figure 1-9.

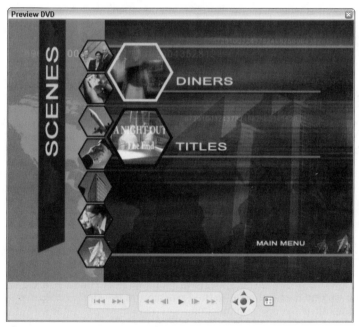

Figure 1-9: DVD Menu created from DVD Timeline marker

This section shows you how to create a DVD menu from DVD markers that you add to this chapter's tutorial project. It gives you a brief look at Premiere Pro's ability to quickly create interactive DVDs.

Cross-Reference Undoubtedly, if you are creating an interactive DVD, you want to create it from a much longer video project and edit the DVD buttons. For more information about choosing DVD menu templates and editing them, see Chapter 19.

Before you get started, note the DVD marker symbol in the Timeline. In the following steps, you create DVD markers at the beginning of the Diners and end title scenes. Later, you pick a DVD template that automatically links the DVD markers to interactive buttons. Follow these steps:

1. **Move the current-time indicator to the start of the Diners scene (so that you see the first frame of the Diners clip in the Program Monitor).**

2. **Create a DVD marker by clicking the DVD marker icon in the Timeline.**

3. **In the DVD Marker dialog box, type** Diners **in the Name field, as shown in Figure 1-10.** Make sure that the Marker Type is set to Scene Marker, and click OK.

When the DVD Marker dialog box closes, you see that a DVD marker is added to the Timeline. Notice also that a DVD marker is automatically created at the start of the Timeline as well. Premiere Pro uses this first marker as the basis for a Play Movie button that appears in the template.

Figure 1-10: Creating a DVD Marker

4. **Drag the current-time indicator to the first frame of the closing title.** You should see the closing title in the Program Monitor.

5. **Create another DVD maker by clicking the DVD marker icon in the Timeline.**

6. **In the DVD Marker dialog box, enter Titles in the Name field and click OK.**

Now that you've created markers, you can choose a DVD template, which links your markers to DVD buttons. Here's how:

1. **To pick a DVD template, choose Window ➪ DVD Layout.**

2. **In the DVD Layout dialog box, click Change Template.**

3. **In the DVD Templates dialog box, make sure that Apply a Template for a DVD with Menus is selected, as shown in Figure 1-11.** Then click a thumbnail of a template. We picked the Numbers template in the Corporate Theme section. Click this template or another template, and then click OK to return to the DVD Layout dialog box.

Note If you don't click a DVD Template thumbnail in the DVD Templates dialog box, the OK button does not activate.

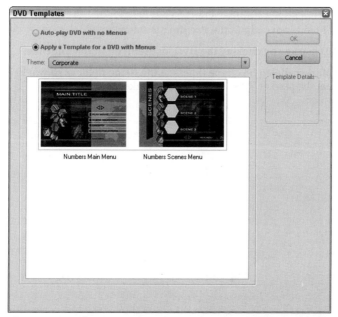

Figure 1-11: Select a DVD template in the DVD Templates dialog box.

4. Now that you've chosen a template, view a live version of the template by clicking Preview in the DVD Layout dialog box.

The Preview screen includes DVD control buttons as well as Play Movie and Scene Selection buttons. In this menu, click the Scene Selection button, and the second menu with your Chefs and Titles button should appear. Click either button to play the scene. After you close the DVD preview, you can click Burn to burn a DVD directly from Premiere Pro.

Exporting a Windows Media file

Windows Media files are commonly used on the Web and can be imported into multimedia programs such as Macromedia Director. To export your movie in Windows Media format, follow these steps:

1. Select the Timeline panel that houses the project you want to export.

2. Choose File ⇨ Export ⇨ Adobe Media Encoder. The Export Settings dialog box appears.

3. In the Format drop-down menu, choose Windows Media (if it isn't already selected), shown in Figure 1-12.

4. Choose a preset in the preset drop-down menu. For example, if you have a streaming media server and want to export your file for multiple Web audiences, including those with a high-speed Internet connections, you can choose the WM9 NSTC streaming format. When you pick the preset, the Summary area in the Export Settings dialog box displays frame height, frame rate, and other exporting details for the slowest video stream. The WM9 NSTC streaming preset includes different streams at different frame rates and different frame sizes for different Web connections from 28.8 kbps modem to Broadband/Cable/DSL (visible by clicking the panel menu button). To continue with the export, click OK.

5. **In the Save File dialog box, select a destination folder in which to store the finished Windows Media file, and enter a filename.**

6. **To start the export, click Save.**

Figure 1-12: Use the Adobe Media Encoder to create a Windows Media file for the Web.

Note   For an in-depth review of the Adobe Media encoder, see Chapter 21.

Exporting a QuickTime movie

Apple's QuickTime is widely used on the Web and in most multimedia applications. Depending on the final destination of your project, you may want to change the frame size and frame rate of your video before exporting. For example, if you want to export a file to a multimedia project, you want to reduce the DV frame size from 720 × 480 to a smaller size that fits comfortably into your production.

Follow these steps for exporting your project as a QuickTime movie:

1. **Select the Timeline panel.**

2. **Choose File ➪ Export ➪ Movie.** The Export Movie dialog box appears.

3. **Click the Settings button.** The Export Movie Settings dialog box appears, where you can view export settings.

4. **Choose QuickTime from the File Type drop-down list, as shown in Figure 1-13.**

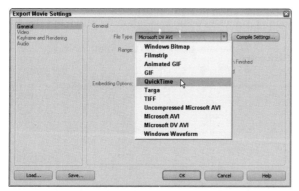

Figure 1-13: Choose QuickTime in the File Type drop-down menu.

5. **To switch frame size and frame rate, choose Video from the list box at the upper-left of the dialog box.** The Video Settings dialog box appears. These settings are covered in detail in Chapter 4.

6. **If you are creating a multimedia project that will play on a computer, select Sorenson as the compressor.** You can change the frame size to 320 × 240 and change the frame rate, if desired. If you are outputting the file for CD-ROM, you probably want to change the data rate. Doing so slows the data rate to prevent frames from being dropped during playback. See Chapter 19 for more details.

7. **After you make your changes, click OK.** Premiere Pro returns you to the Export Movie dialog box.

8. **In the Export Movie dialog box, type a name for your file.**

9. **Click Save.** Premiere Pro builds the export file and soon opens it in the Program Monitor for viewing.

Summary

This chapter gave you a chance to experiment with the basic concepts of editing in Premiere Pro. You learned how to do the following:

✦ Create a project by choosing File ⇨ New Project

✦ Add clips to the Timeline by dragging them from the Project or Source Monitor panel

✦ Edit clips in the Source Monitor panel by clicking the Set In and Set Out point buttons

✦ Change clip opacity by selecting the clip and adjusting the Opacity effect in the Effect Controls panel

✦ Create a transition by dragging a transition from the Effects panel over the edge of two clips in the Timeline panel

✦ Preview your production in the Program Monitor panel

✦ Fade in and out audio by creating keyframes in the Timeline

✦ Export your production using the Adobe Media Encoder

✦ Create a DVD menu using DVD markers and the DVD Layout panel

✦ ✦ ✦

Premiere Pro Basics

The Adobe Premiere Pro user interface is a combination of a video-editing studio and an electronic image-editing studio. If you're familiar with film, video editing, or audio editing, you'll feel right at home working within Premiere Pro's Project, Monitor, and Audio panels. If you've worked with such programs as Adobe After Effects, Adobe Live Motion, Macromedia Flash, or Macromedia Director, Premiere Pro's Timeline, digital tools, and panels will seem familiar. If you're completely new to video editing and computers, don't worry; Premiere Pro panels, windows, and menus are efficiently designed to get you up and running quickly.

To help get you started, this chapter provides an overview of Premiere Pro windows and menus. Consider it a thorough introduction to the program's workspace and a handy reference for planning and producing your own digital video productions.

Premiere Pro's Panels

After you first launch Premiere Pro, several panels automatically appear onscreen, each vying for your attention. Why do you need more than one panel opened at once? A video production is a multifaceted undertaking. In one production, you may need to capture video, edit video, and create titles, transitions, and special effects. Premiere Pro windows help keep these tasks separated and organized for you.

Each of Premiere's panels is accessible by clicking its name in the Windows menu. For example, if you want to open the Timeline, Monitor, Audio Mixer, History, Info, or Tools panels, choose the Window menu and then click the desired panel name. If you have more than one video sequence on the screen, you see them listed in the Window ➪ Timelines submenu.

This section provides an overview of the windows that enable you to create the various elements of your digital video project.

Manipulating Premiere Pro panels

Before you begin exploring Premiere Pro's panels, you can help ensure that you work efficiently if you know how to group and dock them. Grouping and docking panels helps ensure that you're making the best use of available screen real estate.

All of Premiere Pro's video-editing tools reside in panels that can be grouped or docked together in virtually any combination. When panels are docked, they are attached to each other, so resizing one panel resizes another. Figure 2-1 shows the Source Monitor being resized. Notice in the second frame of Figure 2-1 that enlarging the Source Monitor reduces the size of the Project panel.

Figure 2-1 shows the Project panel grouped with the Effects and Audio Mixer tabs peeking out in the same panel group. You can easily add to or remove panels from a grouped panel by simply clicking and dragging the panel tab (click the indented dots to the left of the tab name).

If you want a panel to appear as a standard window that floats above others, you can drag a panel out from behind others. Try adjusting a few panels as you read through the following sections that explain how to resize, group, and separate panels.

Resizing docked panels

Windows that are grouped together are referred to as "panels." To resize a panel, move the cursor over the dividing line between panels. When the cursor changes to two arrows, as shown in Figure 2-1, click and drag. You can drag left or right, on the vertical separator between panels, or up and down when clicking on the horizontal border between two panels. If you want to resize the panel both horizontally and vertically, position the mouse cursor over a panel corner. When the mouse pointer changes to four arrows, click and drag.

Figure 2-1: Resizing panels

Docking and grouping panels

If you want to dock one panel to another one (the target panel), click and drag it over to the top, bottom, left, or right portion of the target panel. Before releasing the mouse, wait for the dim preview of the docked panel to appear. If you're satisfied with the results, release the mouse; otherwise, press Esc.

If you want to place one panel into another panel, click and drag the panel's tab lip. Drag it into the target panel, and then release the mouse. The new panel's tab appears on the far right of all existing tabs.

Creating floating windows

To separate a panel so it floats on the screen independently like a standard window, press Ctrl while clicking the panel's tab. Release the mouse to create the new floating window, then release Ctrl. Alternatively, you can click and drag the panel outside of Premiere Pro — provided you have the screen space. Note that once you create a new floating window, you can create a panel group by clicking and dragging other panels to it.

Closing and saving workspaces

Although Premiere Pro's primary windows open automatically onscreen from time to time, you may want to close one of them. To close a window, simply click its close window *X* icon.

If you've organized your windows and panels in specific positions at specific sizes, you can save this configuration by choosing Window ➪ Workspace ➪ Save Workspace. After you name your workspace and save it, the name of the workspace appears in the Window ➪ Workspace submenu. Anytime you want to use that workspace, simply click its name.

The Project panel

If you've ever worked on a project with many video and audio clips as well as other production elements, you'll soon appreciate Premiere Pro's Project panel, shown in Figure 2-2. The Project panel provides a bird's-eye view of your production elements (often called assets) and even enables you to preview a clip by clicking on its play button.

As you work, Premiere Pro automatically loads items into the Project panel. When you import a file, the video and audio clips are automatically loaded into the Project panel.. If you import a folder of clips, Premiere Pro creates a new bin (a folder) for the clips, using the folder name as the bin name. When you capture sound or video, you can quickly add the captured media to a Project panel bin before closing the clip. Later, you can create your own bins by clicking the Bin button, at which point you can drag production elements from one bin to another. The New Item button (refer to Figure 2-2) enables you to quickly create a new title or other production element, such as a transparent video clip (often used with Premiere Pro's Timecode video effect to overlay timecode over other clips), color matte (covered in Chapter 13), or bars and tone (used to calibrate color and sound when editing). The New Item button also allows you to add new sequences, offline files, black video, and universal counting leaders. If you click the Icon button, all production elements appear as icons onscreen rather than in list format. Clicking the List button returns the display of the Project panel to List view. If you want to quickly add Project panel elements to the Timeline, you can simply select them and then click the Automate to Sequence button.

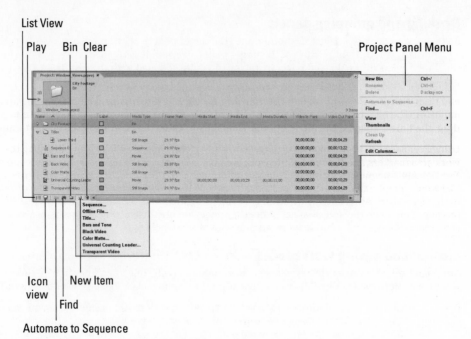

Figure 2-2: Premiere Pro's Project panel stores production elements.

If you expand the Project panel by clicking and dragging the panel border, you see that Premiere Pro lists the Start and Stop times as well as the in and out points and the duration of each clip. If you click the Project panel's menu, you can choose to add or remove columns from the Project panel.

In the Project panel, production assets are grouped according to the current sort order. You can change the order of production elements so that they are arranged by any of the column headings. To sort by one of the column categories, simply click it. The first time you click, production items are sorted in ascending order. To sort in descending order, click the column heading again. The sort order is represented by a small triangle. When the arrow points up, the sort order is ascending. When it points down, the sort order is descending.

To keep your production assets well organized, you can create bins to store similar elements. For example, you may create a bin for all sound files or a bin for all interview clips. If the bin gets stuffed, you can see more elements at one time by switching from the default Thumbnail view to List view, which lists each item but doesn't show a thumbnail image.

If you want to play a clip in the thumbnail monitor in the Project panel, click the clip and then click the Play button — the small triangle next to the thumbnail monitor.

If you want to preserve space and hide the Project panel's thumbnail monitor, choose View ➪ Preview Area in the Project panel menu. This toggles the monitor display off and on.

Tip   You can change the speed and duration of a clip by right-clicking the clip in the Project panel and choosing Speed/Duration. You can also quickly place the clip in the Source Monitor by right-clicking the clip and choosing Open in Source Monitor.

The Timeline panel

The Timeline panel, shown in Figure 2-3, is the foundation of your video production. It provides a graphic and temporal overview of the video sequences, effects, titles, and transitions that comprise your project. Fortunately, the Timeline is not for viewing only — it's interactive. Using your mouse, you can build your production by dragging video and audio clips, graphics, and titles from the Project panel to the Timeline. By clicking and dragging on the current-time indicator (the blue triangle), you can jump to any part of your production. As you click and drag, the time display at the top left of the Timeline indicates the position of the current frame.

Using Premiere Pro tools, you can arrange, cut, and extend clips. By clicking and dragging the work area markers at either end of the work area bar — edges of the light gray bar at the top of the Timeline — you specify the portion of the Timeline that Premiere Pro previews or exports. The thin, colored bar beneath the work area bar indicates whether a preview file for the project exists. A red bar indicates no preview, and a green bar indicates that a video preview has been created. If an audio preview exists, a thinner, light green bar appears. (To create the Preview file, choose Sequence ➪ Render Work Area or press Enter to render the work area.)

Tip   Rendering the work area helps ensure that your project plays back at the project frame rate. If you create video and audio effects, the Preview file stores the rendered effects. Thus, the next time you play back the effect, Premiere Pro does not have to process the effect again.

Set Display Style

Toggle Track Output   Current-time indicator

Time Display   Viewing Area bar   Work Area bar

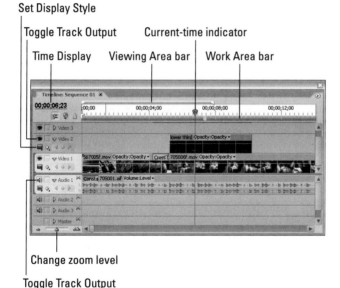

Change zoom level

Toggle Track Output

Figure 2-3: The Timeline panel provides an overview of your project and enables you to edit clips.

Note In Figure 2-3, the first video clip in Video 1 track is from Digital Vision's CityMix CD (567005f.mov). It is found in the Chapter 28 folder (which is in the Tutorial Projects folder) on the DVD that accompanies this book. The second clip is from Digital Vision's NightMoves CD (705008f.mov). This clip is in the Chapter 1 folder. The sound clip is from Digital Vision's NightMoves CD (705001.aif). This clip is also in the Chapter 1 folder.

Undoubtedly, the most useful visual metaphor in the Timeline panel is its representation of video and audio tracks as parallel bars. Premiere Pro provides multiple, parallel tracks so that you can both preview and conceptualize a production in real time. For example, parallel video and audio tracks enable you to view video as audio plays. The Timeline also includes icons for hiding or viewing tracks. Clicking the video Toggle Track Output button (Eye icon) hides a track while you preview your production; clicking it again makes the track visible. Clicking the audio Toggle Track Output button (Speaker icon) turns audio tracks on and off. Beneath the Eye icon is another icon that sets the display mode for clips in the track. Clicking the Set Display Style icon allows you to choose whether you want to see frames from the actual clip in the Timeline or only the name of the clip. At the bottom left of the window, the Time Zoom Level slider enables you to change the Timeline's time intervals. For example, zooming out shows your project over less Timeline space, and zooming in shows your work over a greater area of the Timeline. Thus, if you are viewing frames in the Timeline, zooming in reveals more frames. You can also zoom in and out by clicking the edges of the Viewing Areabar at the top of the Timeline. To learn more about the many features of the Timeline panel, see Chapter 6.

The Monitor panels

The Monitor panels, shown in Figure 2-4, are primarily used to preview your production as you create it. When previewing your work, click the Play button to play in the Source or Program Monitor. As you work, you can also click and drag in the *tread area* (serrated lines just below the clip) to *jog*, or slowly scroll, through your footage. Below the tread area is a triangular icon called the *shuttle slider*. You can click and drag the shuttle slider to jump to a specific clip area. As you click, the time display in the Monitor panel indicates your position in the clip. The Monitor panels can also be used to set in and out points. As discussed in Chapter 1, the in and out points determine which part of a clip appears in your project.

Note In Figure 2-4, the video clip in the Source Monitor panel is from Digital Vision's NightMoves CD (705009f.mov). The video clip in the Program Monitor is from Digital Vision's NightMoves CD (705008f.mov). Both video clips are found in the Nite Out folder in the Chapter 1 folder (which is in the Tutorial Projects folder) on the DVD that accompanies this book.

Premiere Pro provides five different monitors panels: the Source Monitor, the Program Monitor, the Trim Monitor the Reference Monitor, and Multi-Camera monitor. The Trim, Reference and Multi-Camera monitors are accessed from the Program Monitor's panel menu.

✦ **Source Monitor:** The Source Monitor shows source footage that has not yet been placed on the video sequence in the Timeline. You can use the Source Monitor to the set in and out points of clips and then insert or overlay them into your production. The Source Monitor can also display audio waveforms of audio clips. (To display the audio waveform, set the Take Audio/Video button to audio or double-click un-linked audio. See Chapter 8 for more details.)

✦ **Program Monitor:** The Program Monitor displays your video program: the clips, graphics, effects, and transitions that you've assembled in a video sequence in the Timeline window. You can use the Lift and Extract buttons on the Program Monitor to remove footage as well. To play a sequence in the Program Monitor, you can either click the window's Play button or press the spacebar.

✦ **Trim Monitor:** The Trim Monitor allows you to precisely fine-tune edits. The Trim is accessed from the Program Monitor, either by clicking Trim in the Program Monitor panel menu or by clicking the Trim button.

In the Trim panel, the left and right sides of an edit are shown on either side of the window. To edit, you can click and drag between the two monitor views of the edit to add or subtract frames from either side of the edit (refer to Figure 2-4). You can also click and drag in the left or right monitor to edit only the left or right side of the edit. You can also choose to edit one frame or five frames at a time by simply clicking a button. Using the Trim Monitor is covered in Chapter 13.

✦ **Reference Monitor:** In many respects, the Reference Monitor is a second Program Monitor. Many Premiere Pro editors use it when making color and tonal adjustments because it allows them to view video scopes (which display hue and saturation levels) in the Reference Monitor while simultaneously viewing the actual footage in the Program Monitor. The Reference monitor can be *ganged* or set to play in sync with the Program Monitor, or it can be unganged. Using the Reference Monitor is discussed in Chapter 18.

✦ **Multi-Camera Monitor:** The Multi-Camera Monitor allows you to view four different clips simultaneously in one monitor. As footage plays in the monitor, use the mouse or keyboard to pick a scene to insert into your program sequence. The Multi-Camera Monitor is most helpful when editing event footage shot simultaneously from different cameras. See Chapter 13 to learn more about using the Multi-Camera Monitor.

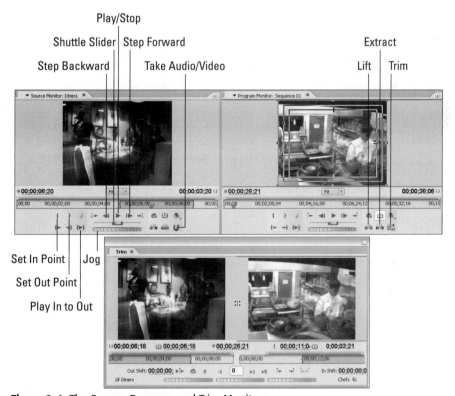

Figure 2-4: The Source, Program, and Trim Monitors

The Audio Mixer panel

The Audio Mixer panel, shown in Figure 2-5, enables you to mix different audio tracks, create audio effects, and record narration. The Audio Mixer's capability of working in real time gives you the advantage of mixing the audio tracks and applying audio effects while viewing the accompanying video.

Using the panel controls, you can raise and lower audio levels for tracks by clicking and dragging the volume fader controls with the mouse. The round knob-like controls enable you to pan or balance audio. You can change the settings by clicking and dragging the knob icon. The buttons below the balance controls let you play all tracks, pick the tracks that you want to hear, or pick the tracks that you want to mute.

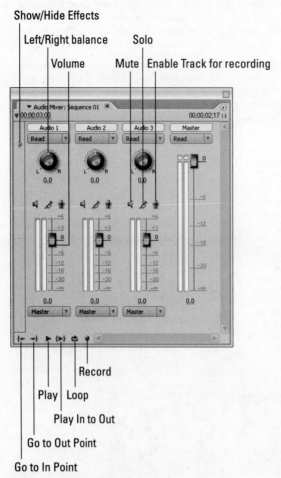

Figure 2-5: Use the Audio Mixer to mix audio and create audio effects.

The familiar controls at the bottom of the Audio Mixer panel enable you to start and stop recording changes while the audio runs. Chapter 5 covers how to record audio using the Audio Mixer. Chapter 9 provides an in-depth discussion of how to mix and apply effects using the Audio Mixer.

The Effects panel

The Effects panel allows you to quickly apply audio, video effects, and transitions. The Effects panel provides a grab bag of useful effects and transitions. For example, the Video Effects bin (folder) includes effects that correct color, change an image's contrast, and distort and blur images. As you can see from Figure 2-6, the effects are organized into bins. For example, among the many bins in the Effects window is the Distort bin, which features effects that distort clips by bending or pinching them.

Applying an effect is simple: Just click and drag the effect over a clip in the Timeline. You can then edit the effect using controls in the Effect Controls panel.

New Custom folder

Delete

Figure 2-6: Use the Effects panel to apply transitions and special effects.

Tip   The Effects panel allows you to create your own bins and move effects into them so that you can quickly access the effects you want to use in each project.

Premiere Pro's Video Transitions bin, which also appears in the Effects panel, features more than 70 transitional effects. Some transitions, such as the Dissolve group, can provide a smooth transition from one video clip to another. Other transitions, such as page peel, can be used as a special effect to dramatically jump from one scene to another.

If you are using the same transitions throughout a production, you can create a bin, name it, and keep the transitions in the custom bin for quick access.

Cross-Reference   See Chapter 10 for more information on creating transitions; see Chapter 14 for more information on using video effects.

The Effect Controls panel

The Effect Controls panel, shown in Figure 2-7, allows you to quickly create and control audio and video effects and transitions. For example, you can add an effect to a clip by selecting it in the Effect panel and then dragging the effect over the clip in the Timeline or directly into the Effect Controls panel. As you can see in Figure 2-7, the Effect Controls panel includes its own version of the Timeline as well as a slider control for zooming into the Timeline. By clicking and dragging the Timeline and changing effect settings, you can change effects over time. As you change settings, you create keyframes (indicated by diamond icons) in the Effect Controls panel and in the Timeline.

If you create multiple effects for one clip, you can see the settings for the different effects by selecting the clip and opening the Effect Controls panel.

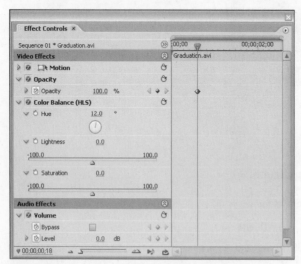

Figure 2-7: The Effect Controls panel enables you to quickly display and edit video and audio effects.

The Tools panel

The tools in Premiere Pro's Tools panel, shown in Figure 2-8, are primarily used to edit clips in the Timeline. Activate each tool by clicking it in the tool panel. Here's a brief summary of the tools:

✦ The Selection tool is often used for selecting and moving clips on the Timeline.

✦ The Track Select tool selects all items on a track. Pressing Shift while clicking the Track Select tools selects multiple tracks.

✦ The Ripple Edit, Rolling Edit, Slip, and Slide tools, covered in Chapter 13, are used to adjust edits on the Timeline.

✦ The Razor tool allows you to cut a clip simply by clicking on it. Pressing Shift while clicking the Razor tool cuts footage in multiple tracks.

✦ The Rate Stretch tool allows you to change the speed of a clip by clicking and dragging a clip edge with the tool.

✦ The Pen tool allows you to create keyframes on the Timeline when adjusting video and audio effects. Audio effects are covered in Chapter 8. Video effects are covered in Chapter 14.

✦ The Hand tool enables you to scroll through different parts of the Timeline without changing the Zoom level.

✦ The Zoom tool provides yet another means of zooming in and out in the Timeline. With the Zoom tool activated, click to zoom in and Ctrl-click to zoom out.

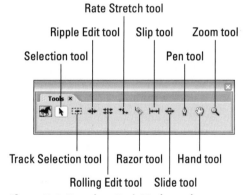

Figure 2-8: Premiere Pro's Tool panel

The History panel

Premiere Pro's History panel, shown in Figure 2-9, lets you perform virtually unlimited Undo operations. As you work, the History panel records your production steps. To return to a previous version of your project, just click that history state in the History panel. After you click and begin working again, you rewrite history — all past steps following the state you returned to are removed from the panel as new ones appear. If you want to clear all history from the panel, choose Clear in the History panel's panel menu (launched by clicking the right triangle). To delete a history state, select it and then click the Delete button (trash can icon) in the panel.

Figure 2-9: The History panel provides virtually unlimited Undo operations.

Caution   If you click a history state in the History panel to undo an action and then begin to work, all steps after the one you clicked are removed from your project.

The Info panel

The Info panel provides important information about clips and transitions, and even about gaps in the Timeline. To see the Info panel in action, click a clip, transition, or empty gap in the Timeline. The Info window shows the clip's (or gap's) size, duration, and starting and ending points, as shown in Figure 2-10.

Figure 2-10: The Info panel displays information about clips and transitions.

The Info window can be very handy when editing because the window displays starting and ending points of the clips as you edit them in the Timeline panel.

The Event panel

The Event panel lists errors that might occur when using third-party video and audio plugins. Selecting the error message in the Event panel, and then clicking Details, provides more information about the specific error.

The DVD Layout panel

Premiere Pro's DVD Layout panel, shown in Figure 2-11, allows you to create an interactive DVD directly from Premiere Pro. Using the DVD Layout panel, you can choose from a number of pre-designed DVD templates. After you've chosen a template, you can edit the text of the buttons, preview the material, and burn a DVD. Navigation from scene to scene is determined by DVD markers created in the Timeline menu or from Premiere Pro's Marker menu. For more details about using DVD templates in Premiere Pro, see Chapter 19.

Figure 2-11: Choose a template in the DVD Layout panel to create an interactive DVD.

The Title Designer

Premiere Pro's Title Designer panel allows you to quickly create titles for video projects. The Title Designer can be used to create animated title effects. To aid title placement, the Title Designer can display video behind the titles you are creating. Tools and other options for creating titles can be opened onscreen from the Title Designer's panel menu, or by choosing Window ⇨ Title Tools, Title Styles, Title Actions, or Title properties. In Figure 2-12, the Title tools are upper left, displayed vertically; the Title Actions are lower left, also displayed vertically.

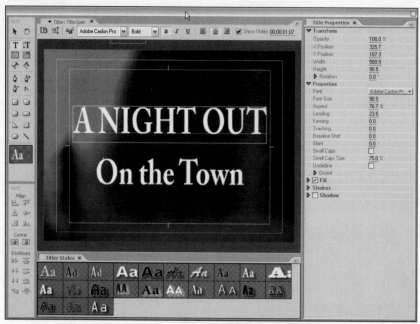

Figure 2-12: The Title panel with tools and options for editing titles

The Menus

Premiere Pro features seven main menus: File, Edit, Project, Clip, Sequence, Marker, Title, Window, and Help. The following sections provide an overview of the different menus and include tables that summarize each menu's commands.

The File menu

The File menu consists of standard Windows commands such as New, Open, Close, Save, Save as, Revert, and Quit. The menu includes commands for loading movie clips and folders full of files. The File New Sequence command can be used to add Timelines to a project. Table 2-1 summarizes the File menu commands.

Table 2-1: File Menu Commands

Command	Shortcut	Description
New ⇨ Project	Ctrl+Alt+N	Creates new file for new digital video production
New ⇨ Sequence	Ctrl+N	Adds new sequence to the current project
New ⇨ Bin	Ctrl+/	Creates new bin in Project panel
New ⇨ Offline File		Creates new file entry in Project panel that can be used for footage to be captured

Command	Shortcut	Description
New ➪ Title	F9	Opens Title Designer for creating text and graphic titles
New ➪ Photoshop File		Creates new blank Photoshop file using project dimensions
New ➪ Bars and Tone		Adds color bar and sound tone to bin in Project panel
New ➪ Black Video		Adds pure black video clip to bin in Project panel
New ➪ Color Matte		Creates new color matte in Project panel
New ➪ Universal Counting Leader		Automatically creates countdown clip
Open Project	Ctrl+O	Opens Premiere Pro project files
Open Recent Project		Loads recently used Premiere Pro movie
Browse	Ctrl+Alt+O	Opens Adobe Bridge
Close	Ctrl+W	Closes Project
Save	Ctrl+S	Saves project file to disk
Save as	Ctrl+Shift+S	Saves project file under new name or saves to different disk location; leaves user in newly created file
Save a Copy	Ctrl+Alt+Shift	Creates a copy of the project on disk, but user remains in original
Revert		Reverts project to previously saved version
Capture		Captures clips from videotape
Batch Capture		Automatically captures multiple clips from the same tape; requires device control
Adobe Dynamic		Allows you to create a new Adobe After Effects Composition
Link ➪ New After Effects Composition		linked to Premiere Pro Project
Adobe Dynamic Link ➪ Import After Effects Composition		Creates link and imports file from After Effects
Import	Ctrl+I	Imports video, audio clip, or graphic
Import Recent File		Imports files that have been recently used into Premiere Pro
Export ➪ Movie		Exports movie to disk according to Export Movie settings dialog box
Export ➪ Frame		Exports frame to be used as still image
Export ➪ Audio		Exports Timeline audio to disk according to settings in Audio Settings dialog box
Export ➪ Title		Exports title from Project panel
Export ➪ Export to Tape		Exports Timeline to videotape

Continued

Table 2-1 (continued)

Command	Shortcut	Description
Export ➪ Export to DVD		Burns DVD from Timeline
Export ➪ Export to EDL		Exports Edit Decision List
Export ➪ Adobe Media Encoder		Exports in different formats: MPEG1,MPEG-2, Real Media, QuickTime, Windows Media
Get Properties for ➪ File		Provides size, resolution, and other digital info about a disk file
Get Properties for ➪ Selection		Provides size, resolution, and other digital info about selection in Project panel
File Info for ➪ File		Opens description dialog box; allows creation of metadata for file
File Info for ➪ Selection		Opens description dialog box for selected file in Project panel; allows creation of metadata for file
Reveal in Bridge		Opens info about file in Adobe Bridge
Interpret Footage		Changes frame rate and pixel aspect ratio of selected item in Project window; also inverts and ignores alpha channel
Timecode		Sets timecode starting point of selected clip in Project panel
Exit	Ctrl+Q	Quits Premiere Pro

The Edit menu

Premiere Pro's Edit menu consists of standard editing commands, such as Copy, Cut, and Paste, which can be used throughout the program. The Edit menu also provides special paste functions for editing, as well as preferences for Premiere Pro's default settings. Table 2-2 describes the Edit menu commands.

Table 2-2: Edit Menu Commands

Command	Shortcut	Description
Undo	Ctrl+Z	Undoes last action
Redo	Ctrl+Shift+Z	Repeats last action
Cut	Ctrl+X	Cuts selected item from screen, placing it into clipboard
Copy	Ctrl+C	Copies selected item into clipboard
Paste	Ctrl+V	Changes out point of pasted clip so it fits in paste area
Paste Insert	Ctrl+Shift+V	Pastes and inserts clip
Paste Attributes	Ctrl+Alt+V	Pastes attributes of one clip to another
Clear	Backspace	Cuts item from screen without saving it in clipboard
Ripple Delete	Ctrl+Shift+Delete	Deletes selected clips without leaving gap in Timeline

Command	Shortcut	Description
Duplicate	Ctrl+Shift+/	Copies selected element in Project panel
Select All	Ctrl+A	Selects all elements in Project panel
Deselect All	Ctrl+Shift+A	Deselects all elements in Project panel
Find	Ctrl+F	Finds elements in Project panel (Project window must be panel).
Label		Allows choice of label colors in Project panel
Edit Original	Ctrl+E	Loads selected clip or graphic from disk in its original application
Edit in Adobe Audition		Opens audio file for editing in Adobe Audition
Edit in Adobe Photoshop		Opens graphic file for editing in Photoshop
Keyboard Customization		Assigns keyboard shortcuts
Preferences		Allows you to access a variety of setup preferences

The Project menu

The Project menu provides commands that change attributes for the entire project. The most important commands enable you to set compression, frame size, and frame rate. Table 2-3 describes the Project menu commands.

Table 2-3: Project Menu Commands

Command	Description
Project Settings ➪ General	Sets video movie, timebase, and time display; displays video and audio settings
Project Settings ➪ Capture	Provides settings for capturing audio and video
Project Settings ➪ Video Rendering	Sets options for rendering video
Project Settings ➪ Default Sequence	Sets Timeline defaults for video and audio tracks
Link Media	Replaces offline file in Project panel with captured file on disk
Make Offline	Makes clip offline, so it is unavailable in project
Automate to Sequence	Sequentially places contents of project panels files into Timeline
Import Batch List	Imports Batch list into Project panel
Export Batch List	Exports Batch list from Project panel as text
Project Manager	Opens Project Manager; allows creation of trimmed version of project
Remove Unused	Removes unused assets from Project panel
Export Project as AAF	Exports Project in Advanced Authoring Format for use in other applications

The Clip menu

The Clip menu provides options that change a clip's motion and transparency settings. It also includes features that aid in editing clips in the Timeline. Table 2-4 describes the Clip menu commands.

Table 2-4: Clip Menu Commands

Command	Shortcut	Description
Rename	Ctrl+H	Renames the selected clip
Make Subclip		Creates subclip from clip edited in Source Monitor
Edit Subclip		Allows editing of in and out points of subclip
Capture Settings ⇨ Set Capture Settings		Sets capture settings for offline files
Capture Settings ⇨ Clear Capture Settings		Clears capture settings for offline files
Insert		Automatically inserts clip into Timeline at current-time indicator
Overlay		Drops clip into area at current-time indicator position, overlaying any existing footage
Enable		Allows clips in Timeline to be enabled or disabled. Disabled clips are not viewed in Program Monitor and are not exported
Link/Unlink		Unlinks audio from video clip/links audio to video
Group	Ctrl+G	Places Timeline clips in a group so they can be manipulated together
UnGroup	Ctrl+Shift+G	Ungroups clips
Synchronize		Lines up clip on Timeline according to clip start, end, or timecode
Multicamera ⇨ Camera 1, 2, 3 or 4		Replaces footage created in multicamera edit with footage from different camera
Video Options ⇨ Frame Hold		Specifies settings for making still frame from clip
Video options ⇨ Field Options		Sets interlace options; also sets reverse field dominance
Video options ⇨ Frame Blend		Smoothes motion of clips whose speed or frame rate has been changed
Video options ⇨ Scale to Frame Size		Scales clip or graphic to project size
Audio Options ⇨ Audio gain		Allows change of audio level

Command	Shortcut	Description
Audio Options ➪ Source		Allows mapping mono audio clip as stereo Channel Mappings
Audio Options ➪ Render and Replace		Replaces selected audio clip with new clip and maintains effects
Audio Options ➪ Extract Audio		Creates new audio clip from selected clip
Speed/Duration		Allows changing speed and/or duration

The Sequence menu

The Sequence menu enables you to preview the clips in the Timeline panel and to change the number of video and audio tracks that appear in the Timeline panel. Table 2-5 describes the Sequence menu commands.

Table 2-5: Sequence Menu Commands

Command	Shortcut	Description
Render Work Area	Enter	Creates preview of work area; stores preview file on disk
Delete Render Files		Removes render files from disk
Razor at Current-time Indicator	Ctrl+K	Cuts project at current-time indicator in Timeline
Lift	;	Removes frames from in to out points set in Program Monitor and leaves gap in Timeline
Extract	'	Removes frames from sequence from in to out points set in Program Monitor without leaving gap in Timeline
Apply Video Transition	Ctrl+D	Applies default video transition between two clips at current-time indicator
Apply Audio Transition	Ctrl+Shift+D	Applies default audio transition between two clips at current-time indicator
Zoom in	=	Zooms into Timeline
Zoom out	-	Zooms back from Timeline
Snap	S	Turns on/off snap to edges for clips
Add tracks		Adds tracks to Timeline
Delete tracks		Deletes tracks from Timeline
Export for Clip Notes		Exports for electronic review in PDF format
Import Clip Note Comments		Imports comments of reviewed file

*When using the keys in the Shortcut column, first press and hold Ctrl.

The Marker menu

Premiere Pro's Edit menu provides commands for creating and editing clip and sequence markers. Markers are designated by pentagon-like shapes just below the Timeline ruler or within a clip in a Timeline. You can use Markers to quickly jump to a specific area of the Timeline or to a specific frame in a clip. Table 2-6 summarizes the Marker menu.

Table 2-6: Marker Menu Commands

Command	Description
Auto Generate DVD Markers	Creates new DVD markers at new scenes or at time intervals
Set Clip Marker	Sets clip marker for clip in Source Monitor at point specified in submenu
Go to Clip Marker	Goes to clip marker at point specified in submenu
Clear Clip Marker	Clears selected clip marker
Set Sequence Marker	Sets sequence Marker specified in submenu
Go to Sequence Marker	Goes to sequence marker specified in submenu
Clear Sequence Marker	Clears sequence marker specified in submenu
Set DVD Marker	Creates DVD marker at current-time indicator position
Go to DVD Marker	Sends current-time indicator to DVD marker
Clear DVD Marker	Removes DVD marker
Edit DVD Markers	Allows editing of DVD marker
Edit Sequence Marker	Allows editing of Timeline markers

The Title menu

Most of Premiere Pro's Title menu is activated after you create a new title in Premiere Pro's Title Designer. The commands in the Title menu alter text and graphics created in the Title Designer. Table 2-7 summarizes the Title menu commands.

Table 2-7: Title Menu Commands

Command	Shortcut*	Description
New Title ⇨ Default Still		Creates new title screen with options for creating still titles
New Title ⇨ Default Roll		Creates new title screen with options for creating rolling titles
New Title ⇨ Defaut Crawl		Creates new title screen with options for creating crawling titles
New Title ⇨ Based on Current Title		Creates new title screen from current tiles

✦ Use the Effect Controls panel to create video and audio effects and audio transitions.

✦ The Monitor panels allow you to edit and preview your production.

✦ Use the DVD Layout panel to choose DVD templates and to preview and burn DVDs.

✦ The Audio Mixer enables you to mix audio and create audio effects.

✦　　✦　　✦

Customizing Premiere Pro

After you become familiar with Premiere Pro, you're certain to appreciate its many timesaving features. Nevertheless, as you edit and fine-tune your work, you'll undoubtedly want to save as much time as possible. Fortunately, Premiere Pro provides numerous utilities for keyboard and program customization. This chapter takes a look at how you can create your own keyboard shortcuts to customize Premiere Pro to respond to your every touch. The chapter also provides an overview of Premiere Pro's default settings, which you can also customize to your own specifications. For example, you can customize the brightness of Premiere Pro's background interface color, the frame length of graphic and still images, and the preroll time needed when capturing video with an external device such as a camcorder or VCR.

Creating Keyboard Shortcuts

Keyboard shortcuts can help take the drudgery out of repetitive tasks and speed up your production work. Fortunately, Premiere Pro provides keyboard shortcuts for activating its tools, opening all its panel, and accessing most of its menu commands. As you'll soon see, these commands are preset but can easily be altered. If a keyboard command does not exist for a Premiere Pro operation, you can create your own.

To change keyboard shortcuts, open the Keyboard Customization dialog box by choosing Edit ⇨ Keyboard Customization. The Keyboard Customization dialog box, shown in Figure 3-1, is divided into three sections: Application, Windows, and Tools.

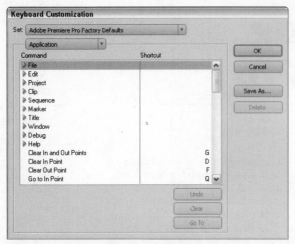

Figure 3-1: The Keyboard Customization dialog box allows you to customize keyboard commands.

Changing Application keyboard preferences

To change Application keyboard commands, choose Application in the Set drop-down menu. To change or create a keyboard setting, click the triangle to open the menu heading that contains the command. For example, suppose that you want to create a keyboard short-cut to use for the Revert command, which allows you to immediately return to the previously saved version of your work. Use the following steps as a guide for changing or creating your own keyboard commands:

1. **Click the triangle icon to open the File menu commands**.

2. **Click in the Shortcut column in the Revert line.** When the Revert command line is activated, dotted lines appear around it, as shown in Figure 3-2.

3. **To create the keyboard command, simply press a function key or a modifier key combination.** Use any unassigned shortcut, such as Ctrl+Shift+R, or Alt+Shift+R.

4. **To create the new keyboard command, click OK.**

   If you want to save your keyboard command in a new keyboard command set, click Save As. Then name it in the Name Key Set dialog box, shown in Figure 3-5. If you make a mistake or want to cancel the command, simply click Clear.

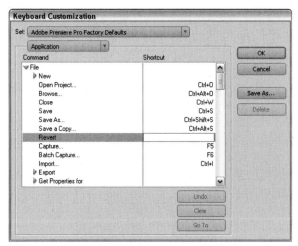

Figure 3-2: Creating a keyboard shortcut for the Revert command

Changing Premiere Pro Windows keyboard preferences

Premiere Pro's keyboard customization of its Window commands is quite extensive. To access Premiere Pro's Windows keyboard commands, choose Windows from the drop-down menu in the Keyboard Customization dialog box. The keyboard commands found here provide shortcuts for many commands that would normally require one click or clicking and dragging the mouse. Thus, even if you are not going to create or change the existing keyboard commands, examining the Windows keyboard commands to see the many timesaving shortcuts that Premiere Pro offers is worth your time. For example, Figure 3-3 shows the keyboard shortcuts for Timeline operations. Notice that you can use a few simple keystrokes to nudge a clip left or right one or five frames. If you want to change a keyboard command, follow the same procedures described in the preceding section: Click in the shortcut column of the command line and press the command keys you want to use for the shortcut.

Changing Tools keyboard preferences

Premiere Pro provides keyboard shortcuts for each of its tools. To access the Tools keyboard shortcuts, shown in Figure 3-4, choose Tools from the drop-down menu in the Keyboard Customization dialog box. To change a keyboard command in the Tools section of the dialog box, simply click in the shortcut column in a tool's row and enter your keystroke shortcut on the keyboard.

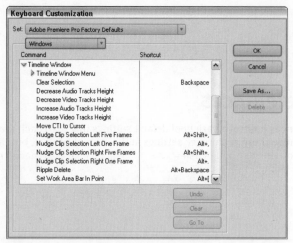

Figure 3-3: Keyboard shortcuts for Timeline commands

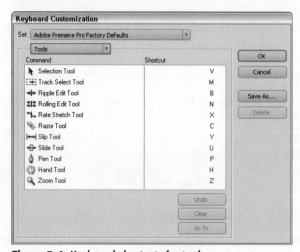

Figure 3-4: Keyboard shortcuts for tools

Saving and loading custom commands

As you change keyboard commands, Premiere Pro automatically adds a new custom set to the Set menu. This prevents you from overwriting Premiere Pro's factory default settings. If you want to provide a name for the custom set or create multiple custom sets, click Save As in the Keyboard Customization window. This opens the Name Key Set dialog box, shown in Figure 3-5, where you can enter a name. After you save the name, it appears in the Set drop-down list, along with Adobe's factory default settings. If you want to delete the custom set, select it from the drop-down list and click Delete.

Figure 3-5: Name a custom setting in the Name Key Set dialog box.

Setting Program Preferences

Premiere Pro's Program preferences control a variety of default settings that load each time you open a project. You can change these preference settings in the current project, but the changes aren't activated until you create or open a new one. You can change the defaults for capture devices and the duration of transitions and still images, as well as the label colors in the Project menus. This section provides an overview of the many default settings that Premiere Pro offers. You access each of the settings by choosing Edit ➪ Preferences and then selecting a choice from the Preferences submenu, shown in Figure 3-6. This section provides a review of the different sections of Premiere Pro's Preferences dialog box.

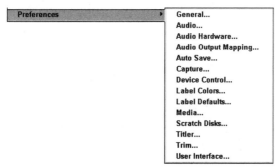

Figure 3-6: Use Edit Preferences submenu to change default settings.

General

The General preferences, shown in Figure 3-7, provide settings for a variety of Premiere Pro default preferences. The commands control Timeline and clip settings:

✦ **Preroll and Postroll:** These settings control the footage Premiere plays before and after the current-time indicator location when you click Play Around. (To Play Around in the Source or Program Monitor, Alt-Click the Play In to Out button). If you click Play Around in the Source, Program, or Multi-Camera Monitor, the current-time indicator backs up to the preroll position and plays to the postroll position. Set the time in seconds in the Preroll and Postroll fields.

✦ **Video Transition Default Duration:** This setting controls the duration of transitions when you first apply them. By default, this field is set to 30 frames — approximately 1 second.

✦ **Audio Transition Default Duration:** This setting controls the duration of audio transitions when you first apply them. The default setting is 1 second.

✦ **Still Image Default Duration:** This setting controls the duration of still images when first placed on the Timeline. The default setting is 150 frames (5 seconds at 30 frames per second).

✦ **Timeline Scrolling:** This setting allows you to choose whether to scroll on the Timeline panel on a page-by-page basis, to scroll smoothly (with the current-time indicator in the middle of the visible area of the Timeline), or to turn off scrolling completely.

✦ **Play work area after rendering previews:** By default, Premiere Pro plays the work area after rendering. Deselect this option if you do not want playback after rendering previews.

✦ **Default scale to frame size:** By default, Premiere Pro does not shrink or enlarge footage that does not match the project frame size. Select this option if you want Premiere Pro to scale imported footage automatically. Note that if you choose to have Premiere Pro scale to frame size, imported images not created at your project frame size may appear distorted.

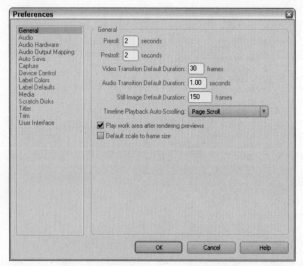

Figure 3-7: The General section in the Preferences dialog box

Audio

Premiere Pro's Audio preferences, shown in Figure 3-8, control settings for Premiere Pro's Audio mixer:

✦ **Automatch Time:** This setting is used in conjunction with the Touch option in the Audio Mixer. When you choose Touch in the Audio Mixer window, Premiere Pro returns to the previous values used before changes were made — but only after a specific number of seconds. For example, if you changed audio levels for Track 1 during a mix, after making the change the level would revert back to its previous setting — to those just before the changes were recorded. The Automatch setting controls the time interval before Premiere Pro returns to the previous values before audio changes were made.

Cross-Reference For more information about using the Audio Mixer, see Chapter 9.

✦ **5.1 Mixdown Type:** These settings control 5.1 surround-sound track mixes. A 5.1 track is composed of these essential channels: left, center, and right channels (the first three of five main channels), with left- and right-rear channels (two more channels make five), plus a low frequency channel (LFE). The 5.1 Mixdown Type drop-down menu allows you change settings for the channels used when mixing, which reduces the number of audio channels.

✦ **Play audio while scrubbing:** This setting controls whether audio plays while scrubbing in the Timeline or Monitor panels.

✦ **Automatically mute input during timeline recording:** This setting turns off audio while recording using Audio mixer. Selecting this option can prevent audio feedback when speakers are connected to your computer.

✦ **Automatic Keyframe Optimization:** This setting helps prevent the Audio Mixer from creating too many keyframes — which can result in performance degradation. The choices are:

  • **Linear Keyframe Thinning:** Attempts to create keyframes only at the end points of a straight line. For example, a diagonal line indicating a change in volume would have one keyframe at either endpoint.

  • **Minimal Time Interval Thinning:** Use this setting to control the minimum time between keyframes. For example, if you set the interval time to 20 milliseconds, keyframes will be created only after an interval of 20 milliseconds.

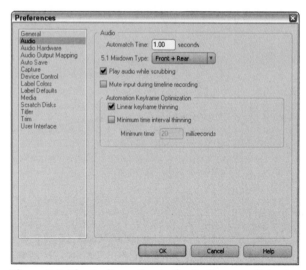

Figure 3-8: The Audio section in the Preferences dialog box provides options relating to audio editing.

Audio Hardware

The Audio Hardware preferences, shown in Figure 3-9, provide details and options about installed audio hardware. Figure 3-9 shows ASIO (Audio Stream Input/Output cards) for audio input and output ports. The options that appear are based on the specific hardware installed in your computer.

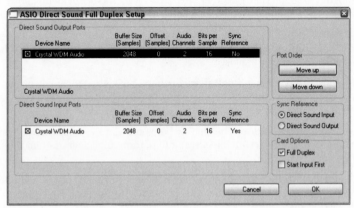

Figure 3-9: The ASIO dialog box provides settings for audio hardware.

Audio Output mapping

Audio Output mapping provides a display of speaker output for Stereo and 5.1 surround sounds. Darkened speakers in the stereo display and black dots in the 5.1 display indicate how the audio is mapped out to sound devices.

Auto Save

If you're worried about forgetting to save your projects as you work, don't worry too much. By default, Premiere Pro's Auto Save preference is turned on. When this option is activated, Premiere Pro saves your project every 20 minutes and creates five different versions of your work. In the Auto Save section, shown in Figure 3-10, you can change the time interval for saving. You can also change the number of different versions that Premiere Pro saves. When you enlist Auto Save, Premiere Pro saves your work along this path: MyDocuments/Adobe/Adobe Premiere Pro/2.0/Adobe Premiere Pro Auto-Save.

Note   Don't worry about consuming massive amounts of disk space with Auto Save. When Premiere Pro saves, it only saves references to the media files. It doesn't resave the files each time it creates a new version of your work.

Capture

Premiere Pro's default Capture settings provide options for Video and Audio capture. The Capture preferences are self-explanatory. You can choose to abort the capture when frames are dropped. You can choose to view a report onscreen about the capture process and dropped frames. The Generate batch log file option saves a log file to disk, listing the results of an unsuccessful batch capture.

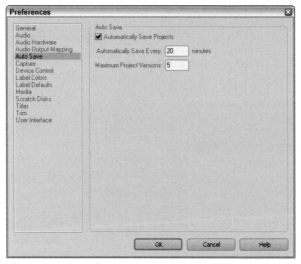

Figure 3-10: Premiere Pro's Auto Save preferences saves multiple versions of your work automatically.

Device Control

The Device Control preferences section, shown in Figure 3-11, lets you choose a current capture device such as a camcorder or VCR. The Preroll setting allows you to set the interval between the times the tape rolls and capture begins. This lets the camcorder or VCR get up to speed before capture. The Timecode Offset option allows you to specify an interval in quarter-frames that provides an offset between the timecode of the captured material and the actual tape. This option allows you to attempt to set the timecode of the captured video so that it matches frames on the videotape.

Clicking the Options button in the dialog box opens the DV Device Control options dialog box where you can choose the brand of your capture device, set the timecode format, and check to see whether the device is online or offline.

Cross-Reference   For more information about capturing video and the DV Device Control Options dialog box, see Chapter 5.

Label Colors and Label Defaults

The Label Colors default setting allows you to change colors of the labels that appear in the Project panel. As discussed in Chapter 2, you can assign specific colors to different media types in the Project panel. To change colors, click the colored label swatch. This opens Premiere Pro's Color Settings dialog box. Here you can change colors by clicking and dragging the vertical slider and by clicking in the rectangular colored box. You can also change colors by entering numbers into the numeric fields. After you change colors, you can edit the color names in the Label Colors section of the Preferences dialog box.

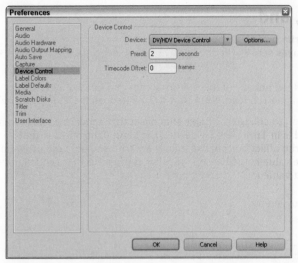

Figure 3-11: Premiere Pro's Device Control preferences allow you to choose preroll time and a capture device.

In the Label Defaults preference section, you can change label colors assigned to assets such as Video, Audio, Bins, and Sequences labels that appear in the Project panel. If you don't like the choices that Adobe made when assigning label colors to different media types, you can change color assignments. For example, to change the Label color of video, click the pop-up menu in the Video line and choose a different color.

Media

Premiere Pro's Media preferences allow you to set the location of its Media Cache database, which keeps track of cached media used in your production. A computer uses a cache to quickly access data that has been recently used. Cached data files in Premiere Pro can be recognized as: .pek (Peak audio files), .cfa (conformed audio files), and MPEG video index files. Clicking the Clean button removes these unnecessary cache files on your computer. After you click Clean, Premiere Pro surveys original files, compares them to cached files, and removes files that are no longer needed.

The Media preferences also sets timecode to be displayed using the source footage's frame rate. If you de-select this option, the project frame rate is used instead. (The project frame rate is set in the Timebase field in the Custom Settings tab when you create a new project.) The In/out points show media offset choice provides a display of the clip's in and out points in relation to the clip's timecode.

Scratch Disks

The Scratch Disks section allows you to set the default disks for a variety of files that Premiere Pro uses while you edit. These include Captured Video, Captured Audio, Video Previews, Audio Previews, Proxies, Media Cache, and DVD Encoding. To set a specific disk and folder, click the Browse button and navigate to the storage device and folder that you want to use.

Still Images, Titler, and Trim

The Still Images, Titler, and Trim preferences provide a variety of default settings for still images and clips. The Still Images setting allows you to set the duration of still images that you insert into a production.

The Titler preferences control the display of the style swatches and fonts browser that appear in the Adobe Title Designer (choose File ⇨ New ⇨ Title to open the Title Designer).

The Trim preferences allow you to change the Large trim offset that appears in the Monitor panel when the Monitor panel is in Trim view. By default, the Large Trim offset is set to 5 frames. When you click the Trim offset button, five frames are trimmed from the program's in or out point. If you change the value in the Large Trim offset field in the Trim section, the next time you create a project, that value appears as a button in the Monitor panel.

See Chapter 13 for a discussion on how to edit in Trim view in the Monitor panel.

User Interface

The User Interface Brightness preference controls the brightness of Premiere Pro's windows. Click and drag the slider to the left to create a dark gray background; click and drag to the right to lighten the window background.

Summary

Premiere Pro provides many options for customizing its commands and features. Many of these options can be used to help streamline your workflow:

✦ Use the Edit ⇨ Keyboard Customization command to customize keyboard commands for the tools and other windows.

✦ To edit default settings in Premiere Pro, choose Edit ⇨ Preferences.

✦　　✦　　✦

Working with Project Settings

✦   ✦   ✦   ✦

In This Chapter

Using analog versus digital video

Understanding video compression

Understanding frame size and pixel aspect ratio

Understanding compression

Using Project Settings

✦   ✦   ✦   ✦

When you first begin creating projects in Premiere Pro, digital video terminology and numerous settings for video, compression, capturing, and exporting can seem overwhelming. If you're just getting started with Premiere Pro and are primarily interested in learning the basics of the program, you needn't worry too much about understanding all the options in all the project-settings dialog boxes. However, if you don't understand such terms as *frame rate*, *frame size*, and *pixel aspect ratio* — terms used in Premiere Pro's project-settings dialog boxes — you're likely to be frustrated when you attempt to output your production.

This chapter provides an overview of key digital video concepts. It also provides a guide to the different dialog boxes in which you designate the startup settings for Premiere Pro projects. For the most part, these are settings that Premiere Pro uses while you are editing in Premiere Pro. Settings for capturing video are covered in Chapter 5. Project settings for exporting video are covered later in Part V of this book.

What Is Digital Video?

In the past few years, the term *digital video* has taken on a variety of new meanings. To the consumer, digital video may simply mean shooting video with the latest video camera from Canon, JVC, Panasonic, or Sony. A digital video camera is named as such because the picture information is stored as a digital signal. The camera translates the picture data into digital signals and saves it on tape in much the same way that your computer saves data to a hard drive.

Some video-recording systems store information in an analog format on tape. In analog format, information is sent in waves rather than as specific individual bits of data.

In Premiere Pro, a digital video *project* usually contains video, still images, and audio that has been *digitized*, or converted from analog to digital format. Video and audio information stored in digital format from digital video cameras can be transferred directly to a computer through an IEEE 1394 port. (Although Apple Computer's trade name for the IEEE port is *FireWire* and Sony's is i.Link, the specifications are identical.) Because the data is already digitized, the IEEE 1394 port provides a fast means of transferring the data. Using video footage shot on an analog video camera or recorded on an analog video deck, however, requires the additional step of first digitizing the footage. Analog-to-digital capture boards that can be installed in PCs generally handle this process. These boards digitize both audio and video. Other types of visual media, such as photographs and slides, also need to be converted to a digital format before Premiere Pro can use them. Scanners digitize slides and still photos, but you can also digitize slides and photos by photographing them with a digital still camera. Once digitized and saved to the computer's hard drive, these images can be loaded directly into Premiere Pro. After your project has been fine-tuned, the last step of the digital video production process is to output it to your hard drive, a DVD, or to videotape.

Note The abbreviation *DV* refers to a distinct digital video format used in consumer and "prosumer" camcorders. DV (also known as DV25) utilizes a specific frame size and frame rate, which are discussed in the section "Digital video essentials" later in this chapter.

Digital video provides numerous advantages over traditional analog video. In digital video, you can freely duplicate video and audio without losing quality. With analog video, on the other hand, you "go down a generation" each time you copy a clip on videotape, thus losing a little quality.

One major advantage of digital video is that it enables you to edit video in a *nonlinear* fashion. Traditional video editing requires the editor to assemble a videotape production piece by piece from start to finish in a *linear* manner. In linear editing, each video clip is recorded after the previous clip onto a *program* reel. One problem with a linear system is the time it takes to re-edit a segment or to insert a segment that is not the same duration as the original segment to be replaced. If you need to re-edit a clip in the middle of a production, the entire program needs to be reassembled. The process is similar to creating a necklace with a string of beads. If you want to add beads to the middle of the necklace, you need to pull out all the beads, insert the new ones, and put the old beads back in the necklace, all the while being careful to keep everything in the same order.

In a nonlinear video system, you can freely insert, remove, and rearrange footage. If you reconsider the bead necklace analogy, nonlinear editing enables you to magically pop the beads on the necklace wherever you want, as if the string didn't exist. Because the image is made up of digital pixels that can be transformed and replaced, digital video enables you to create numerous transitions and effects that are not possible on a purely analog system. To return to the necklace analogy, a digital system lets you not only insert and replace beads freely, but it also allows you to change their color and shape at will.

Digital video essentials

Before you begin creating a digital video project, it's important to understand some basic terminology. Terms such as *frame rate, compression,* and *frame size* abundantly populate Premiere Pro's dialog boxes. Understanding these terms helps you make the right decisions as you create new projects and export them to videotape, to your hard drive, to the Web, or to DVD.

Video frame rates

If you take a strip of motion picture film in your hand and hold it up to the light, you can see the individual picture frames that comprise the production. If you look closely, you can see how motion is created: Each frame of a moving image is slightly different than the previous frame. A change in the visual information in each frame creates the illusion of motion.

If you hold up a piece of videotape to light, you won't see any frames. However, the video camera does electronically store the picture data into individual video frames. The standard DV NTSC (North American and Japanese standard) frame rate in video is 29.97 frames per second; in Europe, the standard frame rate is 25 frames per second. Europe uses the PAL system (Phase Alternate Line). The standard frame rate of film is 24 frames per second. Newer high definition video camcorders can also record at 24 frames per second (23.976 to be exact).

Frame rate is extremely important in Premiere Pro because it helps determine the smoothness of the motion in your project. Typically, the frame rate of your project matches the frame rate of your video footage. For example, if you capture video directly into Premiere Pro using DV equipment, the capture rate is set to 29.97 frames per second, which matches Premiere Pro's DV project setting frame rate. Although you want the project frame rate to be the same rate as the source footage, you may want to export at a lower frame rate if you are preparing the project for the Web. By exporting at a lower frame rate, you enable the production to quickly download to a Web browser. Exporting to the Web is covered in Chapter 21.

Interlaced and progressive scanning

Filmmakers who are new to video may wonder why all camcorders don't record and play back at the film rate of 24 frames per second. The answer is rooted in the basics of early television display technology. Video engineers devised a scanning technique of creating images by shooting electron beams one line at a time across the internal phosphor screen of the video display. To prevent the top lines from fading as the scan reached the bottom, engineers divided the video frame into two sets of scanned lines: the even lines and the odd lines. Each scan (called a video field) darts down the screen at one sixtieth of a second. During the first scan, the odd lines of the video screen are drawn from right to left (lines 1, 3, 5, and so on). During the second pass, the even lines are scanned. The scan is so fast that your eye isn't supposed to see the flicker. This process is known as interlacing. Because each field is displayed at a sixtieth of a second, one video frame appears each thirtieth of a second; thus, the video frame rate is 30 frames per second. Video recording equipment was designed around this process of creating interlaced fields at a sixtieth of a second.

Newer and more expensive video cameras can render a complete video frame in one pass. Thus, there is no need for interlacing. Each video frame is drawn progressively from line 1 to line 2 to line 3 and so on. This process is known as progressive scan. Some video cameras that record using progressive scan can record at 24 frames per second and deliver a higher quality image than interlaced video. Premiere Pro has presets for progressive scan equipment. The future undoubtedly will see more and more video shot on progressive scan equipment. Once progressive scan video is edited in Premiere Pro, producers can export to programs like Adobe Encore DVD, where they can create progressive scan DVDs. A progressive scan DVD viewed on progressive scan DVD players and high definition monitors is certain to mean a further drop in movie-house attendance.

Frame size

The frame size of a digital video production determines the width and height of your production onscreen. In Premiere Pro, frame size is measured in *pixels*. A pixel is the smallest picture element displayed on a computer monitor. If you are working on a project that uses DV footage, you typically are using the DV standard frame size of 720 × 480 pixels. HDV video camcorders (Sony and JVC) can record at 1280 × 720 and 1440 × 1080. More expensive high definition (HD) equipment can shoot at 1920 × 1080.

Note High definition video camcorders can record either interlaced or progressive video; some can record both. In video specifications, *720 p* indicates progressive video at a frame size of 1280 × 720. High definition formats of 1920 × 1080 can be either progressive or interlaced. In video specifications, *1080 60i* designates interlaced video at a frame height of 1080 pixels. The number 60 refers to the number of fields per second, thus indicating a recording rate of 30 frames per second.

To view a white paper on high definition cameras and tape formats, go to http://www.adobe.com/products/premiere/pdfs/hdprimer.pdf.

Non-square pixels and pixel aspect ratio

Before the advent of DV, the standard frame size used in most desktop computer video systems was 640 × 480 pixels. Computer images are composed of square pixels, so frame size of 640 × 480 and 320 × 240 (for multimedia) conformed nicely to the aspect ratio (width to height) of television, which is 4:3 (for every four square horizontal pixels, there are three square vertical pixels).

But when you're working with a DV frame size of 720 × 480 or 720 × 486, the math isn't so clean. The problem: If you create a 720 × 480 the aspect ratio is 3:2, not the television standard of 4:3. How do you squeeze 720 × 480 pixels into a 4:3 ratio? The answer is to use rectangular pixels, essentially non-square pixels that are taller than they are wide. [In PAL DV systems (720 × 576), the pixels are horizontally longer than they are wide.]

If the concept of square versus non-square pixels seems a bit confusing, remember that 640 × 480 provides a 4:3 aspect ratio. One way of viewing the problem presented by a 720 × 480 frame size is to ask how the width of 720 is converted down to 640. A little high school math comes in handy here: 720 times what number equals 640? The answer is .90 — 640 is 90 percent of 720. Thus, if each square pixel is kind enough to shave its width to 9/10 of its former self, you can translate 720 × 480 into a 4:3 aspect ratio. If you're working with DV, you may frequently see the number 0.9 (short for 0.9:1). This is called the *pixel aspect ratio.*

When you create a DV project in Premiere Pro, you will see that the DV pixel aspect ratio is set to 0.9 instead of 1 (for square pixels). Furthermore, if you import footage with a frame size of 720 × 480 into Premiere Pro, the pixel aspect ratio is automatically set to 0.9.

Tip You can calculate the pixel aspect ratio for an image by using this formula: frame height / frame width × aspect ratio width / aspect ratio height. Thus, for a 4:3 aspect ratio 480 / 640 × 4 / 3 = 1 and 720 / 480 × 4 / 3 = .9. For PAL systems, the calculation would be 576 / 720 × 4 / 3 = 1.067.

When you create a DV project in Premiere Pro, the pixel aspect ratio is chosen automatically. Premiere Pro also adjusts the computer display so that images created from non-square pixel footages are not distorted when viewed on your square pixel computer display. Nonetheless, it's helpful to understand the concept of square versus non-square pixels because you may need to export a DV project to the Web or a multimedia application (both of which display square pixels because they are viewed on computer monitors). You might also need to work in a project with source material created from both square and non-square pixels. For example, if you import footage digitized with an analog video board (which digitizes using square pixels) or import images created in a computer graphics program that uses square pixels into a DV project with DV footage, you'll have two flavors of pixels in your video stew. To prevent distortion, you may need to use Premiere Pro's Interpret Footage command to properly set frame sizes of imported graphics and footage. (For more information, see the sidebar "Preventing Display Distortion.")

Preventing Display Distortion

When non-square pixels that haven't been altered are viewed on a computer monitor (which displays square pixels), images may appear distorted. The distortion does not appear when the footage is viewed on a video monitor instead of on a computer display. Fortunately, Premiere Pro adjusts non-square pixel footage on a computer display and, thus, does not distort non-square footage when imported into a DV project. Furthermore, if you export a project for the Web using Premiere Pro's Adobe Media Encoder (covered in Chapter 21), you can adjust the pixel aspect ratio to prevent distortion. However, if you create a graphic at 720 × 480 (or 720 × 486) in a square pixel program such as Photoshop 7 and then import it into an NTSC DV project, the graphic may appear distorted in Premiere Pro. The figure shows an image of a circle in a square created at 720 × 480 in Photoshop 7. Notice that the image appears distorted in Premiere's Pro's Monitor panel. The graphic is distorted because Premiere Pro automatically converts it to a non-square 0.9 pixel aspect ratio.

If you create a graphic at 720 × 576 in a square pixel program and import it into a PAL DV project, Premiere Pro also converts it to a non-square pixel aspect ratio. Distortion can occur because Premiere Pro interprets any digital source file created at a DV frame size as non-square pixel data. (This file import rule is specified in a text file called "Interpretation Rules.txt." The file is found in Premiere Pro's Plug-ins folder [in the en_US folder] and can be edited so that Premiere Pro interprets graphic and video files differently.)

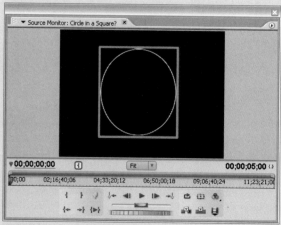

Distorted graphic created with square pixels imported in DV project.

Fortunately, if you are creating graphics in Photoshop CS, it can help you avoid distorted graphics. Photoshop CS features a 720 × 480 DV preset that sets the pixel aspect ratio in a file to 0.9. If you use this preset, you can preview graphics before importing them into a DV project. If Photoshop CS is installed on the same computer as Premiere Pro, you can create a Photoshop file in Premiere Pro by choosing File ➪ New ➪ Photoshop file. The file is configured to match the pixel aspect ratio of your Premiere Pro project. If you are using Photoshop CS, you can even set the Pixel Aspect Ratio of an image to match the Pixel Aspect Ratio of your Premiere project. First choose Image ➪ Image Size to set the frame size to match that of your Premiere project. Next choose Image ➪ Pixel Aspect Ratio and choose the Pixel Aspect Ratio that matches your project.

Continued

Continued

However, If you are *not* using Photoshop CS, you should create full-screen graphics for DV projects at 720 × 534 (DV/DVD) or 720 × 540 and 768 × 576 for PAL (note that Photoshop 7 does include presets for these sizes). For widescreen projects, choose 864 × 480 (DV/DVD) or 1024 × 576 (PAL). After creating your graphics, import them into Premiere Pro by selecting them in the Project panel and then choosing Clip ➪ Video Options ➪ Scale to Frame Size. This squeezes graphics to fit into your DV project without distortion.

If you do create a graphic file at 720 × 480 in a square pixel program and import it into a Premiere Pro DV project, you may notice distortion because Premiere Pro displays the file as though it were created with non-square pixels. Fortunately, you can "fix" the image in Premiere Pro using its Interpret Footage command. Note that, if you use this technique, Premiere Pro must interpolate (adding about 10 percent more pixels to the image), which may make it appear less sharp.

Here's how to convert your graphics back to square pixels using Premiere Pro's Interpret Footage command to correct distorted images:

1. **Select the graphic image in the Project panel Note that the Project panel indicates that the pixel aspect ratio is not set to 1.0.**

2. **To change the pixel aspect ratio back to square pixels, choose File ➪ Interpret Footage.**

3. **In the Pixel Aspect Ratio section of the Interpret Footage dialog box, click Conform to.** Then choose Square Pixels (1.0) in the drop-dwon menu. Click OK.

After you click OK, the listing in the Project panel indicates that the image has been converted to square pixels.

RGB color and bit depth

A color image on the computer screen is created from the combination of red, green, and blue color phosphors. The combination of different amounts of red, green, and blue light enables you to display millions of different colors. In digital imaging programs, such as Premiere Pro and Photoshop, the red, green, and blue color components are often called *channels*. Each channel can provide 256 colors (2^8 — often referred to as 8-bit color because 8 bits are in a byte), and the combination of 256 red colors × 256 green colors × 256 blue colors results in over 17.6 million colors. Thus, when creating projects in Premiere Pro, you see most color depth options set to millions of colors. A color depth of millions of colors is often called *24-bit color* (2^{24}). Some new high definition cameras can record at 10 bits per pixel, providing 1024 colors per each red, green, and blue pixel. That's quite a bit more than 256 for each red, green, and blue color channel. Nevertheless, most video gets sampled down to 8 bits per pixel, so 10-bit color may not offer a great production advantage over 8-bit.

Note   Although television uses a monitor very much like a computer display, it does not use RGB color. Instead, television uses a color system called YCbCr. The Y stands for *luminance*, which essentially controls brightness levels. Both C channels are chroma (hue and saturation) channels. YCbCr was created when television was transitioning between black-and-white and color systems to enable those with black-and-white systems as well as those with color systems to view the TV signal. YCbCr is a form of the YUV color system, which also uses luminance and two chroma channels. The two terms are often used synonymously.

Compression

Larger frame sizes provide greater bit depth, and 24 to 30 frames a frames per second produce a high quality Premiere Pro digital video project. Unfortunately, a full-frame, 24-bit color, 30-frames-per-second video production requires vast amounts of storage space. You can easily calculate how much hard drive space a full-frame production would require. Start by multiplying the frame dimensions. Assume that you are creating a project at 720×480 pixels. Each pixel needs to be capable of displaying red, green, and blue elements of color, so multiply $720 \times 480 \times 3$. Each frame is more than 1MB. Thus, one second of video at 30 frames per second is more than 30MB. (This doesn't even include sound.) A five-minute uncompressed production consumes more than 8GB of storage space. Obviously, uncompressed HD formats would consume even more space.

To store more data in less space with a minimum loss of quality, software engineers have created a variety of video compression schemes. The two primary compression schemes are spatial and temporal. Here's a brief description of each:

✦ **Spatial compression (also known as intra-frame):** In spatial compression, computer software analyzes the pixels in an image and then saves a pattern that simulates the entire image. The compression is handled within individual frames without processing other frames (that's why this compression scheme is also called intra-frame compression). DV camcorders primarily use intra-frame compression. Because all the compression information for the frame is within one frame, the CPU works less when editing in programs like Premiere Pro.

✦ **Temporal compression (inter-frame compression):** Temporal compression works by analyzing the pixels in video frames for screen areas that don't change. Rather than creating many frames with the same image, temporal compression works by creating one keyframe for image areas that don't change. The system calculates the differences between frames to create the compression. For example, in a video that consists of frames of a flower that sometimes blows in the wind, the computer needs to store only one frame for the flower and record more frames only when the flower moves. Without temporal compression, different frames would need to be saved to disk for each second of video, whether or not the image onscreen changes.

MPEG-2 (named after the Motion Picture Engineering Group, which oversees the creation of different MPEG file formats) uses inter-frame compression. In this compression scheme, Groups of Pictures (GOP) are analyzed and compressed into one frame. For example, in MPEG-2, as many as 15 frames may be grouped together (12 frames in PAL). The GOP consists of *I frames*, *B frames*, and *P frames*. An *I frame* is a keyframe of the entire frame data, and a *P frame* is a predictive frame that can be a small percentage of the size of the I frame. Finally, a *B frame* is a frame that can use a portion of the I frame and the P frame. Because compression data is stretched over several frames, the CPU is taxed to pull all the pieces together when you edit. That is why many desktop editing systems do not edit using MPEG-2 source material.

When you work with compression in Premiere Pro, you don't have to choose spatial or temporal compression. Instead, depending upon your project settings, you choose compression settings by specifying an editing compression format or *CODEC*. CODEC stands for compression and decompression. For example, if you are using DV, you are using a DV codec. When you work with Premiere Pro, you're not actually looking at the compressed video. You are viewing the video after the CODEC has decompressed. When you've completed your project, you can export it using another compression format.

Note   A DV camera compresses video before it is transferred to your computer. The standard compression ratio used is 5:1, which makes the transferred video signal five times smaller than the original video signal. The DV video data rate is 25 megabits; DV camcorders primarily use intra-frame compression. Newer DV50 formats such as DVCPro and DVCam have a 50-megabit data rate.

If you wish to read a very technical discussion on how a DV camera compresses video, see the Video Signal Processing section of the DVCAM1 Overview brochure at www.sony.ca/dvcam. Click the Reference menu, and choose brochures.

QuickTime, Video for Windows, and MPEG

In order for your computer to use a video compression system, software and sometimes hardware must be installed. Both Macs and PCs usually have video compression software built into their operating systems. QuickTime is the digital video compression system automatically installed with the Macintosh operating system; Video for Windows (AVI) is the digital video compression system automatically installed in the Windows operating system. Both QuickTime and AVI utilize a variety of CODECs. QuickTime can also be installed on PCs. Because QuickTime is cross-platform, it is one of the more popular digital video systems for CD-ROM and Web digital video.

When you export a movie from Premiere Pro, you can access the QuickTime (if installed on your PC) or AVI compression settings, enabling you to choose from a list of QuickTime or AVI CODECs. You can also use the Adobe Media Encoder to export in MPEG, QuickTime, RealMedia, and Windows Media formats. If you have a capture board installed in your computer, the capture board typically provides a set of CODECs from which to choose.

Both QuickTime and AVI video clips can be imported into Premiere Pro and integrated into a Premiere Pro project. Premiere supports the following file formats: Type 2 AVI, MOV (QuickTime), Open DML, and WMV (Windows Media). Premiere also supports MPEG (including MPG and MPE). However, because MPEG-2 uses inter-frame compression, the CPU is heavily taxed when using MPEG-2 source files.

When you export, you can export your file in a variety of compression formats. You can export in Windows Media, QuickTime, Real, or MPEG-1 (sometimes used in multimedia and for Web needs), as well as MPEG-2. Outputting in MPEG formats is covered in Chapter 19. MPEG-2 compression is used to create DVDs, which can provide up to two hours of video with eight tracks of audio. MPEG-1 compression, which can be used on the Web or on CD-ROMs, provides VHS-quality video. The newest MPEG standard, MPEG-4 (available in QuickTime 6), provides even better compression than MPEG-2.

Digital format overview

If you haven't dealt extensively with the concepts of video formats, frame sizes, and aspect ratios, you may find seeing these formats organized in tabular format helpful. Table 4-1 provides an overview of DV formats for NTSC and PAL. As you view the chart, you can see the difference between standard and widescreen DV formats, as well as the difference in frame size between *HDV* and standard definition DV. HDV has five times as much picture information as standard DV. HDV camcorders are substantially cheaper than HD cameras. The format is called HDV because the format uses the horizontal line resolution of high definition, but it's compressed to fit on mini-DV tapes. Most video reviewers have praised the high quality of HDV footage. But the advantage of HDV will be most important when a high definition DVD format becomes standardized. Because the current standard DVD frame size matches the DV frame size (not the HD frame size), DVD viewers aren't yet getting the full benefit of viewing material shot on HD or HDV systems (at least at the time of this book's publication).

Table 4-1: Digital Video Specs

Format	Frame Size	Aspect Ratio/Pixel Aspect Ratio	Frames per Second[1]
D1[2] / DV NTSC	720 × 486 / 720 × 480	4:3 / 0.9	29.97
DV NTSC (Widescreen)	720 × 480	16:9 / 1.2	29.97
D1 / DV (PAL)	720 × 576	4:3 / 1.067	25
DV Widescreen (PAL)	720 × 576	16:9 / 1.422	25
HDV 720	1280 × 720	16:9 / 1	29.97
HDV 1080	1440 × 1080	16:9 / 1.33	25 / 29.97
HD 1080	1920 × 1080	16:9/1	25/29.97/23.97
HD 720	1280 × 720	16:9/1	59.94

[1] Note that frames per second for HD and HDV video depends upon manufacturer and whether the video is interlaced or progressive.

[2] D1 is an expensive broadcast-quality uncompressed digital format introduced in 1986 by Sony.

Understanding Project Settings

After you gain a basic understanding of frame rate, frame size, and compression, you can better choose settings when you create a project in Premiere Pro. If you choose your project settings carefully, you can produce the best quality video and audio. Figure 4-1, shows Premiere Pro's New Project dialog box, which appears when you create a new project in Premiere Pro.

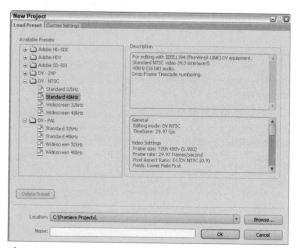

Figure 4-1: The New Project dialog box includes project presets.

The New Project dialog box appears when you click New Project after starting Premiere Pro or when you choose File ➪ New Project. The creators of Premiere Pro have streamlined the process of choosing project settings. To get started, you simply need to click one of the available presets. Notice that Premiere Pro provides DV (Digital Video format) presets for NTSC television and the PAL standards. If you are working with HDV or HD, you can also choose presets.

How do you decide which preset to choose? If you are working on a DV project and your video is not going to be in a widescreen format (16:9 aspect ratio), you can choose the Standard 48 kHz option. The 48 kHz indicates the sound quality, which should match the sound quality of your source footage. The 24 P Preset folder is for use with footage shot at 24 frames per second progressively scanned at a frame size of 720 × 480 (Panasonic and Canon make cameras that shoot in this mode). If you have a third-party video capture board, you may see other presets specifically created to work with your capture board.

Clicking one of the presets displays the its settings for Compression, Frame Size, Pixel Aspect Ratio (discussed later in this chapter), Frame Rate, and Bit Depth, as well as for audio settings. If you are working with DV footage, you probably do not need to change the default settings. If you need to alter the presets, click the Custom Settings tab. This opens the General section of the New Project dialog box.

Tip　If you create a custom preset in the Custom Tab of the New Project dialog box, you can save it for use in other projects by clicking Save Preset. Saved presets can be loaded from a folder called Custom that appears in the Load Preset tab in the New Project dialog box.

Video and audio project settings are divided into four categories: General, Capture, Video Rendering, and Default Sequence. The sections that follow describe the General, Video Rendering, and Default Sequences settings. All these sections of the New Project dialog box are accessible when you first create a project. If you want to view project settings after creating a project, choose Project ➪ Project Settings ➪ General. Note, however, that after you create a project, most settings cannot be changed.

Cross-Reference　You can find out more about audio settings in Chapter 8 and capture settings in Chapter 5. See Chapter 19 for more information about exporting Premiere Pro projects.

General settings

The General settings section of the New Project dialog box, shown in Figure 4-2, provides a summary of the individual project settings.

You can access this dialog box by choosing File ➪ New Project (or by clicking the New Project button) and then clicking the Custom Settings tab. To access this dialog box after creating a project, choose Project ➪ Project Settings ➪ General.

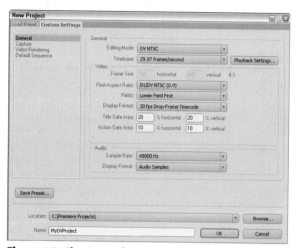

Figure 4-2: The General settings section of the New Project dialog box

These are your choices:

✦ **Editing Mode:** The editing mode is determined by the chosen preset in the Load Preset tab of the New Project dialog box. The editing mode choice sets the Timeline playback method as well as compression settings. When you choose a DV preset, the editing mode is automatically set to DV NTSC or DV PAL. If you don't pick a preset, you can choose a variety of editing modes from the Custom Settings tab. These choices are shown in Figure 4-3.

If you are working with analog video that uses square pixels, you can change the editing mode to Desktop, which allows you to access frame size options which can be changed to match the footage you will be using.

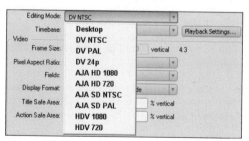

Figure 4-3: The Custom video editing choices

✦ **Timebase:** The timebase determines how Premiere Pro divides video frames each second when calculating editing precision. In most projects, the timebase should match the frame rate of captured footage. For DV projects, the timebase is set to 29.97 and cannot be changed. The timebase for PAL projects should be set to 25; film projects should be set to 24. The timebase setting also determines which choices are available in the Display Format field. Both the Timebase and the Display Format fields determine the positions of the ruler tick marks in the Timeline window.

Note

By default, Source footage timecode is displayed using the frame rate of the source footage, not the frame rate specified in the Timebase field. In previous versions of Premiere, Source footage timecode was displayed using the Project frame rate. You can choose to have Source footage timecode displayed using the project frame rate by choosing Preferences ⇨ Media. In the Preferences dialog box, deselect Display Media Timecode in Source Frame Rate.

✦ **Frame Size:** The frame size of your project is its width and height in pixels. The first number represents the frame width, and the second number represents the frame height. If you choose a DV preset, the frame size is set to the DV defaults (720 × 480). If you are using the DV editing mode, you cannot change the project frame size. However, frame size can be changed if you create a project using the Desktop editing mode. If you do need to change the frame size, use a frame size that matches your video footage. If creating a project for the Web or CD-ROM, you can reduce its frame size when exporting your project (discussed in Part V later in the book).

✦ **Pixel Aspect Ratio:** This setting should match the shape of the image pixels — the width to height of one pixel in your image. For analog video and images created in graphics programs or scanned, choose square pixels. The default setting for D1/DV project is 0.9. The pop-up menu allows you to choose different settings depending upon the editing mode choice. For example, if you pick DV NTSC, you can choose from 0.9 or 1.2 for widescreen footage. Desktop AJA HD 720 and HDV 720 are square pixel formats. If you choose Desktop as the editing mode, you can freely choose pixel aspect ratio, although this most likely will be used by those who need to work with square pixels.

Choose the Anamorphic 2:1 choice if the video was shot on film with an anamorphic lens. These lenses squeeze the images during shooting, but when projected, an anamorphic projection lens reverses the compression to create a widescreen effect.

Tip

If you need to change the frame rate of an imported clip or the pixel aspect ratio (because either one doesn't match your Project settings), select the clip in the Project panel and choose File ⇨ Interpret Footage. To change frame rate, in the Interpret Footage dialog box, click Assume this frame rate. Then enter the new frame rate in the field. To change pixel aspect ratio, click Conform to. Then choose from a list of pixel aspect ratios. After you click OK, the Project panel indicates the changes.

Tip

If you need to import widescreen footage (16:9) aspect ratio into a project that uses a 4:3 aspect ratio, you can scale or manipulate widescreen footage using the Position and Scale options of the Motion video effect. See Chapter 17 for more information about using the Motion video effect.

✦ **Fields:** Fields are relevant when working on a project that will be exported to videotape. Each video frame is divided into two fields that appear for one-sixtieth of a second. In the PAL standard, each field is displayed every one-fiftieth of a second. Choose either the Upper or Lower setting in the fields section depending upon which field your system expects. (See Chapter 22 for more information.)

✦ **Display Format:** This setting determines the number of frames Premiere Pro uses when it plays back from the Timeline and whether drop frame or non-drop frame timecode is used. In Premiere Pro, time for video projects is displayed in the Timeline and other panels using SMPTE (Society of Motion Picture Television Engineers) video time readouts called *timecode.* In non-drop frame timecode, colons are used to separate hours, minutes, seconds, and frames. At 29.97 or 30 frames per second in non-drop frame timecode, the frame following 1:01:59:29 is 1:02:00:00.

In drop frame timecode, semicolons are used to separate hours, minutes, seconds, and frames. For example, the frame after 1;01;59;29 is 01;02;00;02. The visual frame display drops numbers each minute to compensate for the fact that the NTSC video frame rate is 29.97, not 30 frames per second. Note that video frames are not dropped; only numbers in the timecode display are dropped.

If you are working on a film project at 24 frames per second, you can choose options for either 16mm or 35mm.

The difference between drop frame and non-drop frame timecode is discussed in more detail in Chapter 5.

✦ **Title Safe Area and Action Safe Area:** These two settings are important if your project will be viewed on a video monitor. The settings help you compensate for monitor *overscan*, which can cause a TV monitor to cut off the edges of the pictures. The settings provide a warning border, showing the limits where titles and actions can safely be viewed. You can change the percentages for the title safe and action safe zones. To view the safe areas in the Monitor window, choose Safe Margins from the Monitor window menu. When the safe areas, shown in Figure 4-4, appear, make sure that all titles appear within the first boundary and all actions appear within the second boundary. The clip in Figure 4-4 is 705008f from Digital Vision's NightMoves CD.

✦ **Sample Rate:** The audio sample rate determines audio quality. Higher rates provide better quality audio. It's best to keep this setting at the rate your audio was recorded. If you change this setting to another rate, more processing is required, and quality may be adversely affected.

✦ **Display Format:** When working with audio clips, you can change the Timeline or Monitor window display to show Audio units instead of video frames. The audio display format allows you to set audio units to be in milliseconds or audio samples. (Like a frame in video, an audio sample is the smallest increment that can be used in editing.)

For more information about Audio sample rates and audio display formats, see Chapter 8.

Because DV projects use industry standard settings, you should not change settings for pixel aspect ratio, time base, frame size, or fields.

Action safe area   Title safe area

Figure 4-4: Title safe (inner rectangle) and action safe areas (outer rectangle) viewed in the Monitor panel

If you are working with a DV, HD, or HDV editing mode, you can click the Playback Settings button, which opens the Playback Settings dialog box shown in Figure 4-5.

✦ **RealTime Playback:** In this section, select how you want to view your project as you edit. You can select an online camcorder or VCR from the External Device drop-down as your playback output. If you will be exporting your project to videotape, outputting to a video monitor or to your camcorder monitor (rather than to your computer display) provides the best preview of your project. If you're not outputting to video, choose Desktop Video.

✦ **Aspect Ratio Conversion:** This choice allows you to choose whether your system's hardware or software controls pixel aspect ratio conversion.

✦ **Export:** If you will be exporting to an external device such as a camcorder or VCR, choose it from the Export External Device drop-down menu.

✦ **The 24p Conversion Method:** This section allows you to specify how Premiere copes with displaying 24 frames per second progressive video in a 30 fps video. To accomplish this, Premiere must generate a new frame out of thin air to compensate for the difference between 24 frames per second and 30 frames per second. In other words, for every 4 frames at 24 frames per second, Premiere must make 5 frames. In order to understand the choices, first assume that the 4 frames of your 24 fps footage are labeled A, B, C, and D. The ABBCD option simply repeats when needed to make the 5 frames. The 2:3:3:2 Interlaced choice uses interlacing to create an extra frame. It taxes the computer's CPU more then the ABBCD choice but provides smoother playback. Here's how 2:3:3:2 works: We start with Frames A, B, C, and D and end up with Frames 1, 2, 3, 4, and 5.

- **New Frame 1:** From first field of **A** and second field of **A**

- **New Frame 2:** From first field of **B** and second field of **B**

- **New Frame 3:** From 2nd field of **B** and first field of **C** **(Shares fields from B and C)**

- **New Frame 4:** From first field of **C** and second field of **C**

- **New Frame 5:** From first field of **D** and second field of **D**

If you count the fields used, you get two As, three Bs, three Cs, and two Ds. Thus, the abbreviation 2:3:3:2.

Note

You can simulate a "telecine" video-on-film look with 24p footage by selecting it in the Project panel and choosing File ➪ Interpret Footage. In the Frame Rate section, choose Remove 24P DV Pulldown.

✦ **Desktop Display Mode:** Choose the option that matches your graphics display. Select Standard if your display does not support Direct 3D 9.0 acceleration. This provides the slowest performance. Select Standard if your display card supports Direct 3D 9.0 acceleration. This setting provides accelerated display video. Select Accelerated GPU mode if have a new generation Direct 3D 9.0 card, which accelerates video playback and effects.

✦ **Disable Video Output When Premiere Pro is in the Background:** Selecting this option disables output to a video monitor when Premiere Pro is not the active application.

Note

Third-party software plug-ins may also allow different playback options.

Figure 4-5: Use the DV Playback Settings dialog box to select playback options for DV camcorders and VCRs.

Video rendering

The Video Rendering section of the New Project dialog box, shown in Figure 4-6, specifies settings for playing back video. You can access the Video Rendering Section by choosing File ⇨ New Project (or by clicking the New Project button), clicking the Custom Settings tab, and clicking Video Rendering. To access this dialog box after creating a project, choose Project ⇨ Project Settings ⇨ Video Rendering.

Maximum Bit Depth

The Maximum Bit Depth option instructs Premiere Pro to display video at the maximum bit depth available based on project settings. The highest bit depth is 32 bits.

Previews

The Previews section of the Video Rendering settings specifies how video is previewed when using Premiere Pro. Most of the choices are governed by the project Editing Mode and cannot be changed. For instance for DV projects, you cannot change any options. If you choose the Desktop Editing Mode, you can pick a CODEC in the Compressor drop down menu. If you choose an HD Editing Mode, you can choose a File Format. If options are available in the Previews section, choose the combination of File Format, Compressor, and Color Depth that provide the best balance between playback quality, rendering time, and file size.

Choosing the Optimize Stills option instructs Premiere Pro to use fewer frames when rendering still images. For example, instead of creating 30 frames of video to render a one-second still image, Premiere Pro can optimize output by creating one frame that is one second long. If still images are not cleanly displayed with this option selected, deselect it and export your video again.

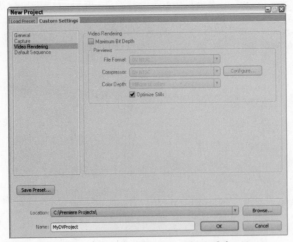

Figure 4-6: The Video Rendering section of the New Project dialog box provides settings for video output.

Default Sequence

The Default Sequence section of the New Project dialog box, shown in Figure 4-7, provides options for setting up Timeline defaults for new projects, including the number of video and audio tracks in the Timeline panel. You can access Default Sequence settings when you create a new project by choosing File ➪ New Project (or by clicking the New Project button). Next click the Custom Settings tab, and then click Default Sequence. To access this dialog box after creating a project, choose Project ➪ Project Settings ➪ Default Sequence.

Changing settings in this dialog box section does not alter the current Timeline. However, if you create a new project or a new sequence (by choosing File ➪ New Sequence), the next Timeline added to the project displays the new settings. Options in the dialog box allow you change the number of video and audio tracks. You can also choose whether to create submix tracks and Dolby Digital tracks. The audio submix and Dolby 5.1 choices are covered in Chapters 8 and 9.

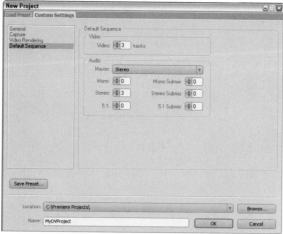

Figure 4-7: Use the Default Sequence section of the New Project dialog box to set Timeline defaults.

Summary

Premiere Pro provides a nonlinear system of creating desktop video projects. A nonlinear system lets you edit video quickly and efficiently. You can easily edit and insert clips without reassembling your entire project. When you create a new project, you need to specify project settings. This chapter covered the following topics:

✦ When creating a new project, the easiest way to pick project settings is to choose a preset from the New Project dialog box.

✦ If you are creating a DV project, you shouldn't need to change most DV presets.

✦ To change project settings in a new project, click the Custom Settings tab in the New Project dialog box.

✦ Use the Default Sequence section of the New Project or Project Settings dialog box to change the number of video and audio tracks in new projects.

✦   ✦   ✦

Capturing Video and Audio

The quality of video clips in a Premiere Pro project can often mean the difference between a production that attracts viewers and firmly holds their attention or one that sends them looking for other sources of information or entertainment. Undoubtedly, one of the primary factors in determining the quality of source material is how the video is captured. Fortunately, Premiere Pro provides extremely efficient and reliable capture options.

If you have a capture board or peripheral card that digitizes analog video, you may be able to access the capture board directly from Premiere Pro to digitize video. If you have an IEEE 1394 port, you may also be able to use Premiere Pro's Capture window to transfer clips directly from your DV camera. Depending upon the sophistication of your equipment and the quality requirements of your production, you may be able to capture all your video source material by using Premiere Pro.

This chapter focuses on the process of capturing video and audio using Premiere Pro. It leads you step-by-step through the process of using Premiere Pro's Capture window to capture videotape to your computer's hard disk. If your equipment enables device control, you can start and stop a camcorder or tape deck directly from Premiere Pro. You may also be able to set up a batch capture session in which Premiere Pro automatically uses list clip in and out points to capture multiple clips during one session.

Getting Started

Before you start capturing video for a production, you should first realize that the quality of the final captured footage depends on the sophistication of your digitizing equipment and the speed of the hard drive that you are using to capture the material. Much of the equipment sold today can provide quality suitable for the Web or in-house corporate video. However, if your goal is to create very high-quality video productions and transfer them to videotape, you should analyze your production needs and carefully assess exactly what hardware and software configuration best suits your needs.

Fortunately, Premiere Pro can capture audio and video using low-end and high-end hardware. Capture hardware, whether high-end or low-end, usually falls into three categories:

✦ **FireWire/IEEE1394:** Apple Computer created the IEEE 1394 port primarily as a means of quickly sending digitized video from video devices to a computer. In Apple computers, the IEEE 1394 board is called a FireWire port. Several PC manufacturers, including Sony (Sony calls its IEEE 1394 port an i.Link port) and Dell, sell computers with IEEE pre-installed. If you are shopping for an IEEE 1394, hardware should be OHCI (Open Host Controller Interface) compliant. OHCI is a standard interface that allows Windows to work with and recognize the card. If Windows has no problems recognizing the card, most DV software applications can utilize the card without problems.

If your computer has an IEEE 1394 port, you can transfer digitized data directly from a DV camcorder to your computer. As mentioned in Chapter 4, DV and HDV camcorders actually digitize and compress the signal as you shoot. Thus, the IEEE 1394 port is a conduit between the already digitized data and Premiere Pro. If your equipment is Premiere Pro-compatible, you can use Premiere Pro's Capture window to start, stop, and preview the capture process. If you have an IEEE 1394 board in your computer, you may be able to start and stop a camcorder or tape deck from within Premiere Pro; this is called *device control*. With device control, everything is controlled from Premiere Pro. You can cue up the video source material to specific tape locations, record timecode, and set up batch sessions, enabling you to record different sections of videotape automatically in one session.

Note To ensure high-quality capture, your hard disk should be able to sustain a 3.6 data rate — the DV data rate.

✦ **Analog to digital capture cards:** These cards take an analog video signal and digitize it. Some computer manufacturers have sold models with these boards built directly into the computer. On the PC, most analog-to-digital capture boards are add-ins that must be installed in the computer. More expensive analog-to-digital capture boards permit device control, enabling you to start and stop a camcorder or tape deck as well as cue it up to the tape location that you want to record. If you are using an analog-to-digital capture card, you must realize that not all cards are designed with the same standards, and some may not be compatible with Premiere Pro. To check video card compatibility, see www.adobe.com/products/premiere/dvhdwrdb.html.

✦ **HD or SD Capture Card with SDI input:** If you are capturing HD footage, you need an Adobe Premiere Pro-compliant HD capture card installed in your system. The card must have a Serial Device Interface (SDI). Adobe Premiere Pro internally supports the AJA's HD SDI card. For more information about AJA cards, visit the Windows section of www.aja.com. Adobe Premiere Pro also supports SD (Standard Definition) SDI cards as well.

Making the Right Connection

Before you begin the process of capturing video or audio, make sure that you've read all relevant documentation supplied with the hardware. Many boards include plug-ins so that you can capture directly into Premiere Pro (rather than first capturing in another software application and then importing into Premiere). This section provides a brief description of the connection requirements for analog to digital boards and IEEE 1394 ports:

✦ **The IEEE/FireWire connection:** Making the connection from a DV or HDV camera to your computer's IEEE 1394 port is easy. Simply plug the IEEE 1394 cable into the DV In/Out jack of your camcorder, and plug the other end into the IEEE 1394 jack of your computer. Despite the simplicity, be sure to read all documentation. The connection may not work unless you supply external power to your DV/HDV camera. The transfer may not work on the DV/HDV camera's batteries alone.

Note

IEEE 1394 cables for desktop and laptop computers are usually different and are not inter-changeable. Furthermore, an IEEE 1394 cable that connects an external FireWire hard drive to a computer may be different from an IEEE 1394 cable that connects a computer to a cam-corder. Before purchasing an IEEE 1394 cable, make sure you have the right cable for your computer.

✦ **Analog to digital:** Most analog-to-digital capture boards use Composite Video or S-Video systems. Some boards provide both Composite and S-Video. Hooking up a Composite system usually entails connecting a cable with three RCA jacks from the video and sound output jacks of your camcorder or tape deck to the video and sound input jacks of your computer's capture board. The S-Video connection provides video output from your camcorder to the capture board. Typically, this means simply con-necting one cable from the camcorder or tape deck's S-Video output jack to the com-puter's S-Video input jack. Some S-Video cables have an extra jack for sound as well.

✦ **Serial device control:** Adobe Premiere allows you to control video to professional VTR equipment through your computer's serial communications (COM) port. (A computer's serial port is often used for modem communication and printing). Serial control allows transport and timecode information to be sent over the computer's serial port. Using serial device control, you can capture playback and record video. Because serial con-trol exports only timecode and transport signals, you need a hardware capture card to send the video and audio signals to tape. Premiere supports the following standards: nine-pin serial port, Sony RS-422, Sony RS-232, Sony RS-232 UVW, Panasonic RS-422, Panasonic RS-232, and JVC-232.

Starting the Capture Process

Many settings in Premiere Pro depend upon the actual equipment you have installed in your computer. The dialog boxes that appear when capturing change depending upon the hard-ware and software installed in your computer. The dialog boxes that appear in this chapter may vary from what you see on your computer, but the general steps for capturing video and audio are pretty much the same. However, if you have a capture board that digitizes analog video, the setup process is different than if you have an IEEE 1394 port installed in your com-puter. The following sections describe how to set up Premiere Pro for both systems.

Note

To ensure that your capture session is successful, be sure to read all manufacturers' read-me files and documentation. Know exactly what is installed in your computer.

Reviewing capture settings

Before you begin the capture process, review Premiere Pro's project and default settings, which affect the capture process. After the defaults are set, they remain saved when you reload the program. Defaults that affect capture include scratch disk settings and device control settings.

Setting scratch disk preferences

Whether you are capturing digital video or digitizing analog video, one of your first steps should be to ensure that Premiere Pro's capture *scratch disk* locations are set up properly. The scratch disk is the disk used to actually perform the capture. Make sure that the scratch disk is the fastest one connected to your computer and that the hard drive is the one with the most free space. In Premiere, you can set different scratch disk locations for video and audio. To check scratch disk settings, choose Edit ⇨ Preferences ⇨ Scratch Disks. If you want to change settings for captured video or audio, click the appropriate Browse button and set a new capture path by navigating to a specified drive and folder with your mouse.

In the Capture Locations section, click the Browse button to choose the hard disk or disks that you want to use for capturing video and audio.

Note   During the capture process, Premiere Pro also creates a conformed high-quality audio file that Premiere Pro uses to quickly access audio. The Scratch Disk section of the Preferences dialog box (Edit ⇨ Preferences) also allows you to set a scratch disk location for conformed audio.

Setting Capture preferences

Premiere's Pro's Capture preferences allow you to specify whether you want to stop the capture session if frames are dropped, report the dropped frames, or generate a batch log file if the capture is unsuccessful. The batch file is a text file listing the clip information about the failed capture. To view Capture preferences, shown in Figure 5-1, choose File ⇨ Preferences ⇨ Capture. In the Capture dialog box, choose Device Control timecode if you want to use the timecode created by an external device rather than the timecode of the source material.

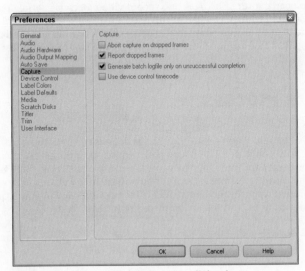

Figure 5-1: The Capture Preferences dialog box

Using device control default settings

If your system allows device control, you can start and stop recording and set in and out points using onscreen buttons in Premiere. You also can perform batch capture operations in which Premiere captures multiple clips automatically. To access the default settings for device control, choose Edit ➪ Preferences ➪ Device Control. As discussed in Chapter 3, the Device Control section of the Preferences dialog box, shown in Figure 5-2, allows you to set Preroll and Timecode settings, as well as choose your video/audio source device.

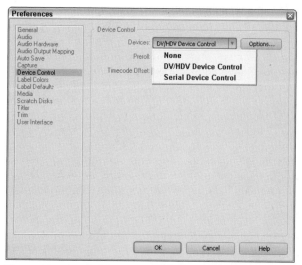

Figure 5-2: Set device control defaults in the Device Control section of the Preferences dialog box.

The Device Control section contains the following options:

✦ **Devices:** If you are using device control, use this drop-down menu to choose DV/HDV Device Control or a device control choice provided by your board manufacturer. If you are not using device control, you can set this option to None. If you are using Serial Device Control, choose this option. See "Using Serial Device Control" later in this chapter.

✦ **Preroll:** Set a preroll time to enable your playback device to back up and get up to speed before the capture starts. Refer to camcorder and tape deck instructions for specifics.

✦ **Timecode Offset:** This setting allows you to alter the timecode recorded on the captured video so that it accurately matches the same frame on the source videotape.

✦ **Options:** Clicking the Options button opens up the DV Device Control Options dialog box, shown in Figure 5-3. Here you can set your preferred video standard (NTSC or PAL), the Device Brand, Device Type, and Timecode Format (Drop-Frame or Non-Drop-Frame). If your device is properly connected to your computer, is turned on, and is in VCR mode, the status readout should be "Online." If you can't get your device online and you have an Internet connection, try clicking Go Online for Device Info. You'll be taken to an Adobe Web page with compatibility information.

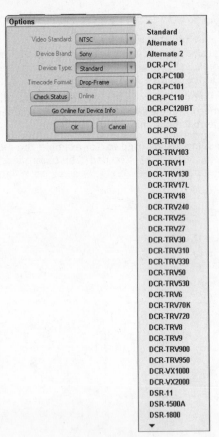

Figure 5-3: Choose your video source and check its status in the DV Device Control Options dialog box.

Capture project settings

The Capture settings for a project determine how video and audio are captured. The Capture settings are determined by project presets. If you want to capture video from a DV camera or DV tape deck, the capture process is straightforward. Because DV cameras compress and digitize, very few settings need to change. However, to ensure the best quality capture, you must create a DV project before the capture session.

Review these general project setup steps before capturing:

1. **Create a new project by choosing File ➪ New Project.** If you are capturing from a DV source, choose a DV project preset. If you are capturing from an analog card, you may need to pick a non-DV preset or one recommended by your card manufacturer.

2. **Set Capture Project Settings.** Open the Capture Project Settings dialog box by choosing Project ➪ Project Settings ➪ Capture. Click the setting in the Capture Format drop-down menu, shown in Figure 5-4, that matches your source footage: Adobe HD SDI Capture, DV Capture, or HDV Capture. If you are using a third-party board, you may see settings for frame rate, frame size, compressor, format [or bit depth], and number of audio channels. If you want to turn off desktop previews of audio and video, click the Settings button.

Drop-Frame versus Non-Drop-Frame Timecode

SMPTE (Society of Motion Picture and Television Engineers) timecode is "striped" (recorded) on tape on a track separate from the video track. Video producers use the timecode as a means of specifying exact in and out points during edit sessions. When previewing footage, producers often create a "window dub "of the timecode so that the timecode appears in a window. This enables the producers to view the tape and the timecode at the same time. By default, Premiere Pro uses SMPTE timecode to display times in this format: hour: minute: second: frame.

If you're new to video or Premiere, this can take some getting used to. For example, the next readout after 01:01:59:29 is 01:02:00:00 (when using 30 frames per second). This timecode format code is called *non-drop-frame*. However, professional video producers typically use a time-code format called *drop-frame*.

Drop-frame timecode is necessary because the NTSC professional video frame rate is 29.97 (not 30 frames a second). Over a long duration, the .03 time difference between 30 frames and 29.97 frames begins to add up, resulting in inaccurate program times. To solve the problem, professional video producers created a timecode system that would actually visually drop frames in the code without dropping frames in the video. When SMPTE non-drop-frame is striped, two frames of every minute are skipped — except for the tenth minute. In drop-frame timecode, the frame after 01;01;59;29 is 01;02;00;02. Notice that semicolons are used to designate drop-frame from non-drop-frame.

If you are not creating video where exact time duration is important, you do not need to use drop-frame timecode. You can capture and use 30 frames per second instead of the 29.97 project setting. Furthermore, non-drop-frame was created for NTSC video. Do not use it for PAL or SECAM, which use 25 frames per second.

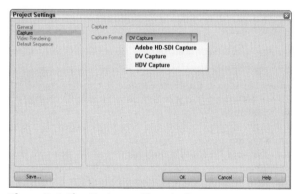

Figure 5-4: The Capture settings in the Project Settings dialog box

3. **Check connections.** Check all connections from video equipment to your computer. Turn on your video/audio source. If you're using a camcorder, set it to VCR mode.

Note

To prevent dropped frames during a DV capture session, your hard drive should be able to sustain a 3.6MB per second data rate. Also note that the system requirements for HDV and HD are different from those for DV. See Appendix C for details.

Timecode Troubles

If you are using device control and are capturing a videotape with recorded timecode, you just ensure that the timecode is continuous — that no timecode is repeated. If you start and stop recording timecode while shooting, two or more frames on one tape may have the same timecode. For example, two different frames on the tape may have 01;02;00;02 as their recorded code. This creates a problem for Premiere Pro. When Premiere Pro captures video using device control and batch processing, it seeks out a specific frame of recorded timecode for the in point and captures until a frame of timecode is designated as the out point. If the same timecode appears on the tape at different points, Premiere Pro gets confused and does not capture the correct sequence.

One solution to this problem is to stripe all tape with continuous timecode before shooting. Simply record black (with the lenscap on) while you record timecode on the entire tape. Use the same settings that you will use when shooting video, but don't record audio.

Alternatively, you can try a sort of rhythm method of shooting that prevents timecode numbers from being re-recorded. To do so, shoot an extra 5 to 10 seconds of video after the scene that you want recorded ends. When you start recording again, first rewind the tape so it begins at a location that already has timecode recorded on it. If you see the timecode starting again at 00;00;00, rewind until you reach a section of previously recorded timecode.

4. **If your equipment supports device control, check settings by choosing Edit ⇨ Preferences ⇨ Device Control.** If you are capturing using DV/HDV, choose DV/HDV Device Control in the Devices drop-down menu. If you are capturing using serial device control, choose Serial Device Control.

   To set device control for a DV device, click Options. In the DV Device Control Options dialog box, choose your brand and Device Type. If your camcorder is already attached to your computer and is set to VCR mode, it should appear online (you can also check this later in the Capture window).

   If you are capturing using serial device control, see the section "Capturing with Serial Device Control" later in this chapter.

5. **Choose Project ⇨ Project Settings ⇨ Capture.** Choose the appropriate Setting: Adobe HD SDI, DV, or HDV. Those with third-party boards may be able to change frame size and frame rate and audio settings.

Tip   Before beginning a capture session, make sure that no other programs besides Premiere Pro are running. Also, be sure that your hard disk is not fragmented. Windows XP Pro users can defragment and test for hard drive errors by right-clicking their hard drives and then clicking Properties. Next, click the Tools tab to access hard drive maintenance utilities.

Capture window settings

Before you start capturing, become familiar with the Capture window settings. The settings determine whether video and audio are captured together or separately. The window also allows you to change scratch disk and device control settings.

To open the Capture window, shown in Figure 5-5, choose File ➪ Capture. To view capture settings, click the Settings tab. If the Settings tab isn't visible, click the Capture window menu and choose Expand Window (which changes to Collapse window after the window is expanded, as shown in Figure 5-5). The following sections describe different areas of the Capture window: the Capture window menu and the Capture Settings, Capture Locations, and Device Control sections.

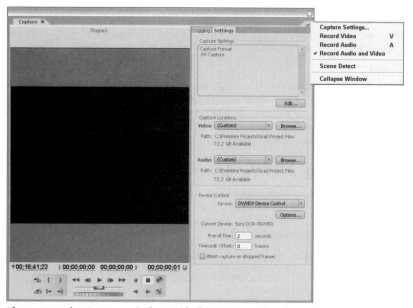

Figure 5-5: The Capture window with the Settings tab selected

Capture window menu

The following sections describe the key areas of the Capture Settings menu shown at the upper-right corner in Figure 5-5.

✦ **Capture Settings:** Clicking this menu item opens the Project Settings Capture dialog box, where you can check or change capture settings.

✦ **Record Audio and Record Video:** Here you can choose whether to capture Audio only or Video only. The default setting is Audio and Video.

✦ **Scene Detect:** This menu item turns on Premiere's automatic scene detection available with device control. When Scene Detect is on, Premiere Pro automatically breaks up the capture into different clips when Premiere Pro detects a change in the video timestamp, which occurs when the Pause button is pressed on a camcorder.

Note   As of the publication of this book, Scene Detect was not implemented in Premiere Pro for HDV capture.

✦ **Collapse Window:** This command removes the Settings and Logging tabs from the Window. When the window is collapsed, the menu command changes to Expand Window.

Capture Settings

This section of the Capture window displays the selected capture settings from the Project Settings dialog box. Clicking the Settings tab opens the Capture Settings dialog box. As mentioned earlier, if you are capturing DV, you cannot change frame size or change audio options because all capture settings conform to the IEEE standard. Those Premiere Pro users with a third-party board may see settings that allow them to change frame size, frame rate, and audio sample rates.

Capture Locations

The Capture Locations section displays the default settings for Video and Audio. You can change locations for Video and Audio by clicking either of the Browse buttons.

Device Control

The Device Control section displays defaults from the Device Control Preferences dialog box. You can change the defaults here as well, and click the Options button to choose your playback device and see whether it is online. In this section, you can also choose to abort the session if any frames are dropped during capture.

Capturing Video in the Capture Window

If your system does not allow device control, you can capture video by turning on your tape deck or camera and viewing the footage in the Capture window. By manually starting and stopping the camera or tape deck, you can preview the source material. Follow these steps to capture video without device control:

1. **Make sure that all cables are properly connected.**

2. **Choose File ➪ Capture.** You can change the window size by clicking and dragging the lower-right edge of the window.

3. **If you want to capture only video or only audio, change settings in the Capture window menu.** You can also change settings by clicking the Logging tab and choosing Video (only) or Audio (only) from the drop-down list.

4. **Set the camera or tape deck to Play mode.** You should see and hear the source clip in the Capture window as the tape plays.

5. **Click the Record button in the Movie Capture window 5 to 7 seconds before the section that should be recorded appears.** At the top of the capture screen, you see a display of the capture progress, including whether any frames were dropped during the recording.

6. **To stop recording, press Esc.** When the recording is paused, the Filename dialog box appears.

7. **Type a filename for the clip.** Optionally, you may type additional comments in the Comments box.

8. **Click OK to save the file.** The captured clip appears in the Project panel.

9. **Press the Stop button on your playback device.**

Tip   To view clip information about dropped frames, data rate, and file location, right-click the clip in the Project window and choose Properties from the drop-down menu that appears. Alternatively, select the clip and choose File ➪ Properties ➪ Selection.

Where's My Audio?

If you've captured video and audio and don't hear the audio, you may need to wait until Premiere Pro finishes creating an audio conforming file for the captured segment. When an AVI video file is created, the audio is interleaved with the video. By creating a separate high-quality conforming audio file, Premiere Pro can access and process audio faster as you edit. The downside of a conforming file is that you must wait for it to be created, and it takes up extra hard disk space. However, the advantages of faster audio processing outweigh the disadvantages.

Capturing with Device Control

During the capture session, device control enables you to start and stop a camera or tape deck directly from Premiere. If you have an IEEE 1394 connection and are capturing from a camcorder, chances are good that you can use device control. Otherwise, to work with device control, you need a capture board that supports device control as well as a frame-accurate tape deck (that is controlled by the board). If you do not have a DV board, you probably need a Premiere Pro-compatible plug-in to use device control. If device control is supported by your system, you may also be able to import the timecode and automatically generate a batch list to batch capture clips automatically.

The device control buttons provided at the bottom of the Capture window magically control your camcorder or VCR. The buttons and callouts for them are shown in Figure 5-6. Using these buttons, you can start and stop and set in and out points for the video.

Note   Premiere's Scene Detect button attempts to automatically break up sequences into separate files based upon the Time/Date stamp. It can be very helpful when capturing an entire tape as described in the section "Capturing a Tape with Scene Detection." Scene detection can be activated by clicking Scene Detect in the device control area, or by clicking Scene Detect in the Capture area of the Capture window.

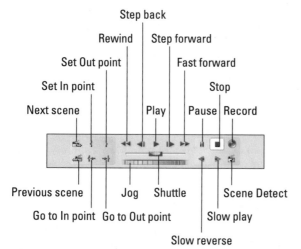

Figure 5-6: The Capture window Device Control buttons

Tip

Clicking the Fast Forward button when the tape is either playing or paused allows you to fast forward while previewing the video; clicking the Rewind button when the tape is either playing or paused allows you to rewind while previewing the video.

You may also want to review the default keyboard commands for the Capture window:

Eject	E
Fast Forward	F
Go to In Point	Q
Go to Out Point	W
Record	G
Rewind	R
Set Out Point	O
Set In Point	I

When you are ready to capture with device control, follow these steps:

1. **Choose File ⇨ Capture.**

2. **Check Capture Settings by clicking the Settings tab.** In the Device Control area, make sure that the Device drop-down menu is set to Device Control. If you need to check the status of your playback device, click Options.

    If you want to change settings, you can change project settings by clicking the Edit button in the Capture Settings area. If you want to change the location of video or audio scratch disks, click the Browse button(s) in the Capture Locations area.

3. **Click the Logging tab.** The Logging section of the Capture window includes buttons for automatically capturing from a clip's in point to its out point. It also includes a Scene Detect check box, another method of turning on Premiere Pro's Scene Detect option.

4. **Click the controls onscreen to move to the point from which you want to start capturing video.**

Tip

Click and drag the jog control area to the left to rewind one frame; click and drag to the right to advance one frame. Drag the shuttle control to change speed as you view the footage.

5. **Click either the Set In Point icon or the Set In button in the Timecode section of the Logging tab, shown in Figure 5-7.**

6. **Click the controls onscreen to move to the point at which you want to stop capturing video.**

7. **Click either the Set Out Point icon or the Set Out button in the Timecode section of the Logging tab.** At this point, you can review your in and out points by clicking the Go to In Point button or Go to Out Point button.

Note

If Scene Detection is on, Premiere Pro may break a clip between specified in and out points.

8. **If you want to add frames before the in point and after the out point of the captured clips, enter the number of frames in the Handles field in the Capture area.**

9. **To begin capturing, click the In/Out button in the Capture section of the Logging tab.** Premiere Pro starts the preroll. After the preroll, your video appears in the Capture window, as shown in Figure 5-7. Premiere Pro starts the capture session at the in point and ends it at the out point.

10. **When the Filename dialog box appears, type a name for the clip.** If a project is open onscreen, the clip automatically appears in the Project window.

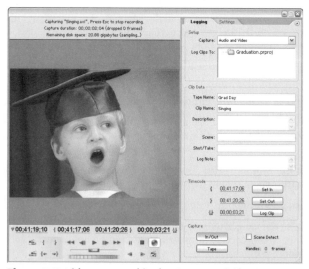

Figure 5-7: Video captured in the Capture window

Note If you don't want to set in and out points for recording, you can just click the Play button and then click Record to capture the sequence that appears in the Capture window.

Capturing a Tape with Scene Detection

The bottom Capture section of the Capture dialog box provides options for capturing an entire tape with scene detection. Follow these steps for capturing an entire tape with scene detection.

1. **Insert the tape that you want to capture into your playback device.**

2. **When prompted by Premiere Pro, name the tape.**

3. **If necessary, rewind the tape.**

4. **If you want Premiere Pro to automatically break up the tape into separate scenes, click the Scene Detection button.** If you want to add frame frames before the in point and after the out point of the captured clips, enter the number of frames in the Handles field.

5. **To start recording, click Tape in the Capture section.**

Using Serial Device Control

Serial Device control allows you to precisely control videotape decks and camcorders through your computer's serial port. To use Serial device control, choose Serial Device control as your Device Control preference and then calibrate for serial device control. This section describes these steps. After you've completed them, you can capture video using the steps discussed earlier in the section "Capturing with Device Control."

Setting up Serial Device Control

Before you can capture or export video using serial device control, you must set up Premiere's Serial Device Control preference. Before you begin, read your equipment manuals, connect your recording equipment to your computer's Com port, and then follow these steps in Premiere:

1. **Open the Device Control Preference dialog box by choosing Edit ➪ Preferences ➪ Device Control.**

2. **In the Device Control dialog box, choose Serial Device Control in the Control Device drop-down menu.**

3. **In the Serial Device Control dialog box, shown in Figure 5-8, choose from the following options:**

   - **Protocol:** In the Protocol drop-down menu, choose the serial protocol specified by your recording equipment manufacturer.

   - **Port:** Choose your Com port from the Port drop-down menu.

   - **Use VTRs Internal Cue:** This may be necessary if your equipment cannot properly cue to specific timecode numbers. (It should be not necessary if you are using high-end equipment).

   - **Use 19.2 Baud for RS-232:** This is a high-speed communication option that can improve editing accuracy. This option is available only for RS-232 mode equipment.

   - **Time Source:** Choose the time source used by your source videotape. If you want your equipment to choose, select the LTC+VITC choice. Otherwise, choose LTC (Longitudinal Timecode), or VITC (Vertical Interval Timecode).

   - **Timebase:** In the Timebase drop-down menu, select the Timebase that matches your source videotape.

Figure 5-8: Set Serial Device options in the Serial Device Control dialog box.

Calibrating for Serial Capture

To help ensure accuracy when capturing with serial control, you should compare captured timecode with the timecode on the original tape. Follow these steps to calibrate with serial control:

1. **Capture a clip using the steps described in the "Capturing with Device Control" section.** Do not close the Capture panel.

2. **Compare the timecode of the clip (in the Source Monitor) with the timecode in the original tape.** If the two codes do not match, follow these steps:

   a. **Calculate the offset difference in frames.** If the captured clip in the Source Monitor is greater than the original source clip, the offset is positive. If the captured clip in the Source Monitor is less than the original source clip, the offset is negative.

   b. **Click the Settings tab in the Capture panel, and type the offset frame value in the Timecode Offset field.**

   c. **Repeat from Step 1 until the captured timecode matches the source timecode.**

Performing a Batch Capture

If your capture board supports device control, you can set up a *batch capture list* that appears in the Project panel, as shown in Figure 5-9. The checks in the Capture Settings column indicate which offline clips will be captured. Note that the icon for the offline clips is different than the normal online icon in the Project panel. Other columns in the Project panel indicate the in and out points for the clips that will be captured. After creating the list, you can have Premiere Pro capture each of the clips automatically while you go off and take a coffee break. You can create a batch capture list manually or by using device control. If you create a batch list manually, you need to type the timecode in and out points for all clips. If you use device control, Premiere Pro enters the start and stop times after you click the Set In and Set Out buttons in the Timecode section of the Logging tab in the Capture window.

Tip   When Adobe Premiere Pro captures from a batch capture list, it automatically captures using the settings of the current project. Although you most likely want to batch capture clips using the frame size and other settings of the current project, you can select a clip to be captured in the Project panel and choose a capture setting for it by choosing Clip ⇨ Capture Settings ⇨ Set Capture Settings. This places an X next to the clip in the Capture Settings column in the Project Panel. To clear capture settings for a clip, select the clip, and choose Clip ⇨ Capture Settings ⇨ Clear Capture Settings.

Figure 5-9: A batch capture list in the Project panel

Creating a batch capture list manually

To create a batch capture list of clips that you specify manually, follow these steps:

1. **If you want the batch list to appear in a bin in the Project panel, open the bin or create one by clicking the Folder button at the bottom of the panel.**

2. **To create the batch file listing, choose File ➪ New Offline File (or click the New Item icon and choose New Offline file).** The Offline File dialog box, shown in Figure 5-10, opens.

Figure 5-10: Use the Offline File dialog box to manually log clips.

3. **Type an in point, an out point, and a filename for the clip. Add other descriptive notes, such as a reel name.**

4. **Click OK.** The clip's information is added to the Project panel.

5. **For each clip that you want captured, repeat Steps 2 through 4.**

Note

You can edit the in and out points of offline files by clicking in the Video In and Out Point column for the specific clip and changing the timecode readouts.

6. **If you want to save the batch list to disk so that you can capture the clips at another time, or so that you can load the list into another computer application, choose Project ⇨ Export Batch list.** You can reload the list later when you want to begin the capture session by choosing Project ⇨ Import Batch list.

Creating a batch capture list with device control

If you want to create a batch capture list but do not want to type the in and out points of all clips, you can use Premiere Pro's Capture window to do the job for you. Follow these steps:

1. **Open the Movie Capture window by choosing File ⇨ Capture.**

2. **Click the Logging tab. In the Clip Data section, enter a Tape Name and the Clip Name that you want to see in the Project panel. Add other comments as desired.**

3. **Use the capture control icons to locate the portion of the tape that includes the section you want to capture.**

4. **Click the Set In button.** The in point appears in the Logging tab's In field.

5. **Use the capture control icons to locate the clip's out point.**

6. **Click the Set Out button.** The out point appears in the Out field.

7. **Click the Log Clip button and enter a filename for the clip (unless you want to use the default name provided).** If desired, type comments in the dialog box and then click OK.

8. **For every clip you want to capture, repeat Steps 4 through 8.**

9. **If you want to save the batch list to disk, so that you can capture the clips at another time or so that you can load the list into another computer application, choose Project ⇨ Export Batch list.** You can reload the list later when you want to begin the capture session by choosing Project ⇨ Import Batch list.

10. **Close the Movie Capture window.**

Capturing using a batch list

After you've created a batch list of clips that you want to capture, you can have Premiere Pro capture the clips automatically from a list in the Project panel. In order to complete the following steps, you need to create a batch list as described in the previous section.

Note

Batch lists can be automatically captured only by systems that support device control.

1. **If your batch list of offline files is saved and not loaded into the Project panel, load the list by choosing Project ➪ Import Batch list.** This loads the list of files into the Project panel.

2. **To specify which clips you want captured, select the offline clips in the Project panel and then choose File ➪ Batch Capture.** This opens the Batch Capture dialog box where you can change capture settings by clicking override clip settings, if desired; otherwise, click OK.

3. **When the Insert Tape dialog box appears, make sure that the correct tape is in your camcorder/playback device and then click OK.** The Capture window opens, and the capture process begins.

4. **Check to see the capture status.** When the batch process is over, an alert appears, indicating that the clips have been captured. In the Project panel, Premiere Pro changes the icons of the filenames to indicate that they are now linked to files on disk. To see the status of the captured clips, scroll right in the Project panel. You'll see check marks for captured clips in the Capture Settings column. The status for the clips should be "Online," another indication that the clips are linked to disk files.

Note   If you have offline files in the Project panel and you want to link them to files that have already been captured, right-click the clip in the Project panel and then choose Link Media. You then need to navigate with the mouse to the actual clip on your hard disk.

Adding Timecode to a Clip

High-end video cameras and mid-range DV cameras can record timecode to videotape (often called SMPTE timecode, for the Society of Motion Picture and Television Engineers). The timecode provides a frame-accurate readout of each videotape frame in Hour:Minute:Second:Frame format. Timecode is used by video producers to move to specific locations on tape and also to set in and out points. During an edit session, broadcast equipment uses the timecode to create frame-accurate edits of the source material onto the final program tape.

When capturing with device control, Premiere Pro captures the timecode along with the video. However, for project management purposes you may want to reset the timecode. Follow these steps:

1. **Select the clip in the Project panel.** If you don't want the timecode to start at the beginning of the clip, double-click it to open it in the Source Monitor panel. Then move to the frame at which you want to begin the timecode.

2. **Choose File ➪ Timecode.**

3. **In the Timecode dialog box, shown in Figure 5-11, enter the starting timecode that you want to use.**

4. **If you moved to a specific frame and want to start the timecode at that point, click Set at Current Frame.**

5. **Enter a Tape Name.**

6. **Click OK.**

Figure 5-11: Use the Timecode dialog box to set the timecode for a clip.

Tip

To help review footage, you can use the Timecode video effect to overlay timecode on footage. The Timecode video effect can be found in the Video bin in the Video Effects bin in the Effects panel.

Capturing Audio

You can capture audio independently of video using Premiere Pro's Audio Mixer panel. Using the audio mixer, you can record directly into Premiere Pro from an audio source such as a microphone or tape recorder. You can even record narration while viewing video in the Program monitor. When you capture audio, quality is based on the sample rate and bit depth set for your audio hardware. To view these settings, choose Edit ➪ Preferences ➪ Audio Hardware and click the ASIO (Audio Stream Input Output) button. Hardware details most likely will include information about audio sample rates and bit depth. The sample rate is the number of samples taken each second. The bit depth is the number of bits (8 bits are in a byte of data) per each sample of the actual digitized audio. The minimum bit depth of most audio CODECs is 16.

To record using the audio mixer, follow these steps:

1. **Connect the tape recorder, microphone, or other audio source to the sound port or sound card of your computer.**

Note

If you want to create a new audio track for audio capture, choose Sequence ➪ Add Track. In the Audio track section, enter **1** in the Add Audio Track field. If you are using a monophonic microphone, choose Mono in the Track Type drop-down menu and enter **0** in the Add Video Track and Add Submix tracks fields.

2. **Open the Audio Mixer, shown in Figure 5-12, by choosing Window ➪ Audio Mixer.** (In Figure 5-12, the word Narration appears in Audio track 1 because the track was renamed "Narration." You can rename a track by right-clicking on the Track name and choosing Rename in the drop-down menu that appears.)

3. **If you have video on the Timeline and want to record narration for the video, move the Timeline about 5 seconds before you want the audio to begin.**

Record Enable button

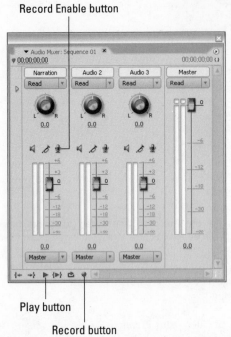

Play button

Record button

Figure 5-12: Use the Audio Mixer to record analog audio directly into Premiere Pro.

4. **To prepare for recording, click the Record Enable button (microphone) in the Audio Mixer panel in the track section for the track you are recording.** The Record Enable button turns red. If you are recording voice-over narration, you may want to click the Solo button for the track to mute output from other audio tracks.

5. **Click the Record button at the bottom of the Audio Mixer window.** The record button starts to blink.

6. **Test audio levels. In the Audio Mixer panel menu, choose Meter Input(s) Only.** When this option is selected a checkmark appears in the panel menu and a VU meter replaces the volume control to display hardware input for any track being recorded. Note that when Meter Input(s) Only is activated, you can still view track levels for those tracks that you aren't recording.

7. **Speak into the microphone.** As you speak, sound levels should be near 0 db without entering the red zone.

8. **If necessary, adjust levels for your microphone or your recording input device.** For example, in most systems with a microphone directly connected to a computer, you can change recording levels in the Audio tab of the Sounds and Audio Properties Control Panel (click the Start Menu, and then Choose Control panel to access the Sounds and Audio Properties Control panel).

9. **To start recording, click the Play button at the bottom of the Audio Mixer panel.**

10. **Play the tape recorder or begin speaking into the microphone to record the narration.**

11. **When the narration or audio is complete, click the Record button to stop recording in the Audio Mixer.**

Cross-Reference

Chapter 9 covers mixing audio using the Audio Mixer panel.

Summary

Premiere Pro enables you to capture video and audio directly from a video camera or video-tape recorder. You can also capture audio from a tape recorder or other sound device. This chapter covered these topics:

✦ Before starting a capture session, read all documentation related to your capture hardware.

✦ Be sure to set up cables properly before the capture session.

✦ Set up default settings for capturing video by choosing Edit ⇨ Preferences ⇨ Capture and Edit Preferences ⇨ Device Control.

✦ If you are capturing video, create a project before the capture session. Use settings recommended by your computer or board manufacturer.

✦ If your equipment allows device control, you can set up a batch capture session.

✦ To capture analog audio, use Premiere Pro's Audio Mixer.

✦   ✦   ✦

Editing with Premiere Pro

The Timeline, Sequences, and Clip Management

Undoubtedly, the Timeline is Premiere Pro's most versatile panel. The Timeline not only provides a graphical overview of clips, transitions, and effects, but it also provides a practical framework for managing projects. Using the Timeline, you can edit and assemble digital footage and control transparency and audio volume. You can add keyframes for both audio and video effects. With all this power packed in one Timeline, you'll want to take full advantage of all it has to offer. If you do, you're sure to be working as efficiently as possible in Premiere Pro.

To get you started, this chapter provides a thorough review of Timeline panel features and options. It shows you how to navigate through footage in the Timeline, add tracks, lock tracks, and change viewing modes. The chapter also includes a section on how to use *sequences*. In Premiere Pro, a sequence is the assembled footage that is placed in the Timeline panel. As you'll soon see, Premiere Pro allows you to create multiple sequences in a Timeline panel, separate sequences into different Timeline panels, and drag one sequence into another to create a "nested" sequence.

After covering the Timeline panel, this chapter concludes with a look at a variety of features for managing Premiere Pro projects, including trimming projects, using subclips, and using Adobe Bridge.

Touring the Timeline

At first glance, trying to decipher all the Timeline buttons, icons, sliders, and controls may seem like an overwhelming task. But after you start using the Timeline, you'll gradually learn what each feature does and how to use it. To make the process of exploring the Timeline easier, this section is organized according to three specific Timeline locales: the ruler area and icons that control the ruler, the Video tracks, and the Audio tracks. Before you get started, you may want to place a video and audio clip from the Chapter 1 or Chapter 6 folder of the *Adobe Premiere Pro 2 Bible* DVD into the Timeline panel. This allows you to experiment with the different viewing options discussed in this section. To load the video and audio clip from the Chapter 1 or Chapter 6 folder of the *Adobe Premiere Pro 2 Bible* DVD, choose File ➭ Import. After the clip appears in the Project panel, click and drag the video footage to Video 1 track. Click and drag the audio file into Audio 1 track. (The video clip in Chapter 1 is 705008f.mov; the audio clip is 705001.aif; both are from Digital Vision's NightMoves CD. The clip in the Chapter 6 folder is 625005f.mov from Digital Vision's SkyRider CD.)

Tip   If the Timeline panel is not visible onscreen, you can open it by double-clicking a Sequence in the Project panel.

Timeline ruler options

The Timeline ruler icons and controls determine how footage is viewed and what areas are rendered and exported by Premiere Pro. Figure 6-1 provides a look at the Timeline ruler icons and controls.

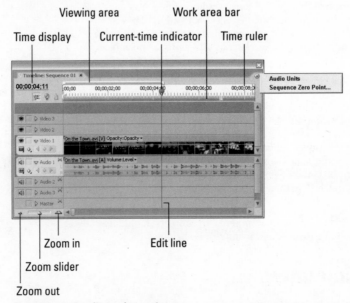

Figure 6-1: Timeline ruler options

Here is a description of the Timeline ruler controls:

✦ **Time ruler:** The Time ruler is a visual display of time intervals divided into frames per second, which corresponds to your project frame rate. The actual number of tick marks between numbers that appear on the ruler is controlled by the current zoom level, which you can adjust by dragging the viewing area bar or zoom slider.

Tip

By default, the Timeline ruler displays time intervals in frames per second. If you are editing audio, you can change the ruler to display audio units in milliseconds or audio samples. To switch to audio units, choose Audio units in the Timeline menu (refer to Figure 6-1). Choose either milliseconds or audio samples in the Audio section of the Project Settings dialog box (Project ➪ Project Settings ➪ General).

✦ **Current-time indicator:** The current-time indicator (CTI) is the blue triangular icon that appears in the ruler. You can click and drag the CTI to gradually move through your footage. You can click in the Ruler area to move the CTI to a specific frame, or you can type a time in the Time display and press Enter to move to that position. You can also click and drag left or right in the Time display to move the current-time indicator left or right along the ruler.

✦ **Time display:** As you move the current-time indicator through the Timeline, the Time display indicates the position of the current frame. You can quickly jump to a specific frame by clicking the Time display and entering a time. When you type, you do not need to enter semicolons or colons. For example, you can move to frame 02:15:00 by clicking in the Frame readout area, typing **215**, and pressing Enter. If you set a project's Display Format to be drop-frame, time is displayed with semicolons. If you set a project's Display Format to be non-drop-frame, time is displayed with colons. To view or change the Display Format for a project, choose Project ➪ Project Settings ➪ General.

✦ **Viewing area bar:** Clicking and dragging the viewing area bar changes the zoom level in the Timeline. The zoom level determines ruler increments and how much footage appears in the Timeline panel. You can click and drag either end of the viewing area bar to change the zoom level. Clicking and dragging the right viewing endpoint of the viewing area bar to the left displays fewer frames on the Timeline. Consequently, this increases the distance on the ruler between tick marks as shorter time intervals are displayed. Dragging right shows more footage and decreases the time intervals on the Timeline. To summarize: To zoom in, click and drag left on the viewing area bar; to zoom out, click and drag right. As you click and drag, notice that the zoom slider in the lower-left corner changes accordingly. Figure 6-2 shows the Timeline footage zoomed in. Note the difference between the zoomed-out view in Figure 6-1 and the zoomed-in view in Figure 6-2.

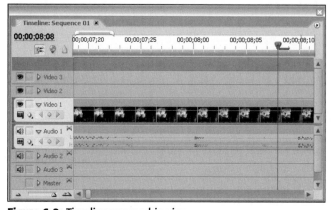

Figure 6-2: Timeline zoomed-in view

✦ **Work area bar:** Beneath the Timeline ruler is Premiere Pro's work area bar, which can be used to designate a work area for exporting or rendering. You can click and drag either endpoint of the work area bar or drag the entire bar from left to right. Why would you change the work area bar? When you render your project, Premiere Pro renders only the area defined by the work area bar. Furthermore, when you export your file, you can choose to export only the work area section of the selected sequence in the Timeline.

Tip   You can quickly adjust the width and position of the work area bar by resetting its endpoints with keyboard shortcuts. To set the left endpoint, move the current-time indicator to a specific frame and press Alt+[; to set the right endpoint, move the current-time indicator to a specific frame and press Alt+]. You can also expand or contract the work area bar to encompass the footage in the current sequence or the width of the Timeline window (whichever is shorter) by double-clicking the work area bar.

✦ **Preview indicator:** The preview indicator displays which portion of your program has been rendered. After footage is rendered, transitions and effects appear at their highest quality (if Highest Quality or Automatic Quality is set as the display choice in the Source Monitor or Program Monitor panel menu). As a sequence is rendered, Premiere Pro saves the rendered work file to disk. Green areas in the Preview indicator area indicate footage that has been rendered. Red indicates non-rendered footage. To render the work area, press Enter or choose Sequence ➪ Render Work Area.

✦ **Zoom slider:** Clicking and dragging the zoom slider serves the same purpose as clicking and dragging the viewing area bar. Clicking and dragging left zooms out (you can also click the zoom out button). As you zoom out, more tick marks are displayed on the Timeline, allowing you to see more of your footage within the boundaries of the Timeline panel. Clicking and dragging right to zoom in increases the distance between tick marks and shows less of your footage in the Timeline panel.

✦ **Set Unnumbered Marker button:** Sequence markers allow you to set points on the Timeline to which you can quickly jump. Sequence markers can also help you divide up your work in the Timeline as you edit. Markers can also be used as chapter headings when you export Premiere Pro projects to Encore DVD. To set an unnumbered marker, drag the current-time indicator to the frame where you want the marker to appear and then click the Set Unnumbered Marker button (the pentagon icon to the right of the DVD icon).

✦ **DVD marker:** DVD markers are used to create menu items in DVD templates. DVD markers are divided into three categories: Scene markers, Chapter markers, and Stop markers. To set a DVD marker, drag the current-time indicator to the frame where you want the marker to appear and click the DVD Marker button (to the right of the magnet icon). For more information about using DVD markers, see Chapter 19.

Timeline track icons and options

Undoubtedly, the most important areas of the Timeline are its video and audio tracks, which provide a visual representation of your video and audio footage, transitions, and effects. Using the Timeline track options, you can add and delete tracks and control how tracks are displayed. You can control whether specific tracks are output when you export your project. You can also lock tracks and specify whether to view video frames in video tracks.

Show Keyframes/Opacity handles

Set Display Style

Target Track

Toggle Track

Toggle Track Lock

Output Snap

Collapse/Expand Track

Add/Remove Keyframe

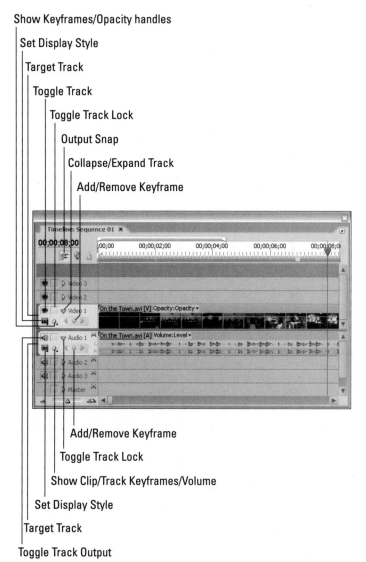

Add/Remove Keyframe

Toggle Track Lock

Show Clip/Track Keyframes/Volume

Set Display Style

Target Track

Toggle Track Output

Figure 6-3: Timeline track options

The following is a review of the icons and track options shown in Figure 6-3:

✦ **Snap:** The Snap icon toggles Premiere Pro's Snap to Edges command. When Snap is on, frames from one sequence snap to touch frames from the next sequence. This electronic magnetic effect helps ensure that no gaps appear in your production. To enable Snap, you can simply click the Snap icon or choose Sequence ➪ Snap. When Snap is on, the magnet in the upper-left corner of the Timeline appears as though it is pressed down.

✦ **Target:** When you edit footage using the Source, Program, or Trim Monitors, Premiere Pro alters the footage in the current target track in the Timeline. To specify a target track, simply click in the far-left area of the track. The target track changes to display rounded edges, as shown in track 1 in Figure 6-3.

✦ **Collapse/Expand:** To view all the options available for a track, click the Collapse/Expand track button. If you are not using a track, you might as well leave the track in its unexpanded mode so that it doesn't consume too much screen space. If you've expanded a track and want to collapse it, simply click the Collapse/Expand icon again.

✦ **Toggle Track Output:** Clicking the eye icon toggles on and off track output, which prevents the track from being viewed in the Program Monitor panel during playing or when exporting. To turn output on again, click the button again, and the eye icon returns, indicating that the track will be viewed in the Monitor window and output when exporting.

✦ **Toggle Track Lock:** Clicking the Toggle Track Lock icon locks the track. When a track is locked, no changes can be made to the track. When you click the Lock track icon, a lock appears indicating that the track is locked. To unlock the track, click the icon again.

✦ **Set Display Style:** Clicking this pop-up menu allows you to choose how and whether thumbnail images appear in the Timeline tracks. The choices are Head and Tail, Show Head Only, Show Frames, and Show Name only. To view footage in the frames throughout a clip, choose Show Frames.

✦ **Show Keyframes/Opacity Handles:** Clicking this pop-up menu allows you to view keyframes or opacity handles in the Timeline's effects graph line. Keyframes denote control points for special effects chosen in the Effects panel. Opacity indicates transparency in frames. After you've created effects with keyframes, the effect names appear in a pop-up menu in the effects graph line in the Timeline. After selecting an effect in this pop-up menu, you can adjust it by clicking and dragging its keyframes in the Timeline. If you are working with opacity handles, dragging down lowers opacity, and dragging up raises opacity.

✦ **Add/Remove keyframe:** Clicking this button allows you to add or remove a keyframe from a track's effects graph line. To add a keyframe, move the current-time indicator to where you want the keyframe to appear and click the Add/Remove keyframe button. To remove a keyframe, move the current-time indicator to the keyframe and click the Add/Remove keyframe button. To move from keyframe to keyframe, click either the left or right arrow icon.

Since the Timeline's effects graph line can show only one control for an effect at a time, you should create and edit most effects in the Effect Controls panel. In the Effects Panel you can see all controls for each effect. However, effects such as Opacity, which have one control that changes only one value, can easily be managed in the Timeline.

You can also create and remove keyframes by Ctrl-clicking with the Selection or Pen tool.

Audio track icons and options

Audio track Timeline controls are similar to video track controls. Using the audio track Timeline options, you can adjust audio volume, choose which tracks are exported, and show and hide keyframes. Premiere Pro provides a variety of different audio tracks: standard audio,

Submix tracks, Master tracks, and 5.1 tracks. Use the standard audio track for .wav and .aif clips. Submix tracks allow you to create effects with a subset of your tracks rather than all of them. Audio is placed in the Master and Submix tracks using Premiere Pro's Audio Mixer. The 5.1 tracks are special tracks used only for surround sound audio. Figure 6-3 shows the audio section of the Timeline with a Master, Submix, and 5.1 track.

Cross-Reference   Chapter 8 covers using audio in the Timeline and creating audio effects. Chapter 9 covers the Audio Mixer, Master, and Submix tracks.

Note   If you drag a video clip that contains audio to a video track, the audio automatically is placed in the corresponding audio track. Otherwise, you can simply drag music audio to an audio track; as the Timeline plays, the video and corresponding audio will play.

The following describes many of the audio icons and options seen in Figure 6-3:

✦ **Target:** As you edit, Premiere Pro alters the target track. The target track in Figure 6-3 is Audio 1. Note that audio has rounded corners. To select a target track, click it.

✦ **Enable Track Output:** Clicking this icon turns audio output off and on for the track. When output is off, audio is not output when played in the Monitor panel or when the project is output.

✦ **Toggle Lock:** This option locks the track so it cannot be altered. Clicking the Toggle Lock track icon toggles track locking on or off. When a track is locked, a lock icon appears.

✦ **Set Display Style:** Click this drop-down menu to choose whether audio clips are displayed by name or as a waveform.

✦ **Show Clip/Track keyframe/Volume:** This drop-down menu allows you to choose to view keyframes or volume settings for audio clips or for the entire track. Keyframes in the audio track indicate changes in audio effects. If you choose to show volume settings for clips or the entire track, you can adjust the volume in the Timeline using the Pen or Selection tool. After you've created audio effects with keyframes, the effect names appear in a pop-up menu in the audio effects graph line in the Timeline. After selecting an effect in this pop-up menu, you can adjust it by clicking and dragging its keyframes in the Timeline.

✦ **Add/Remove keyframe:** Clicking this button allows you to add or remove a keyframe from a track's volume or audio effect's graph line. To add a keyframe, move the current-time indicator to where you want the keyframe to appear and click the Add/Remove keyframe button. To remove the keyframe, move the current-time indicator to the keyframe and click the Add/Remove keyframe button.

✦ **Show Track Keyframes/Volume:** This drop-down menu allows you to choose whether audio keyframe and volume for an audio track are displayed. If you display keyframes and volume, you can click and drag to move keyframes and change volume settings.

✦ **Master track:** The Master track is used in conjunction with the Audio Mixer (see Chapter 9). Like other audio tracks, the Master track can be expanded; you can show keyframes and volume; and you can set or remove keyframes.

Track Commands

As you work with the Timeline, you may want to add or remove or rename audio and video tracks. This section reviews the commands for renaming, adding, and removing tracks, as well as for changing the Snap options and the starting point of a sequence, the sequence zero point. Some of the commands described are activated by right-clicking in the Timeline panel; others are activated through menu commands.

✦ **Rename Track:** To rename an audio or video track, right-click its name. After you release the mouse, you can edit the track's name.

✦ **Add Tracks:** To add a track, choose Sequence ➪ Add Tracks (or right-click a track name and choose Add Track). This opens the Add Tracks dialog box, shown in Figure 6-4. Here you can choose what type of track to create and where to place it.

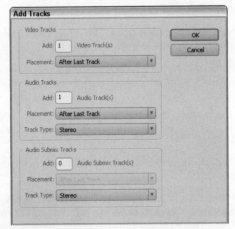

Figure 6-4: Use the Add Tracks dialog box to specify options for new tracks.

✦ **Delete Track:** Before deleting a track, decide whether you want to delete a target track or empty tracks. If you want to delete a target track, click at the left side of the track to select it and choose Sequence ➪ Delete Tracks (or right-click the track name and choose Delete Track). This opens the Delete Tracks dialog box, where you can choose to delete empty tracks, the target tracks, or Submix tracks.

✦ **Snap:** The Snap icon (magnet) toggles Premiere Pro's Snap Edges command. When activated, clips snap together automatically when you click and drag one near the other. This prevents Timeline gaps between edits. To enable Snap, you can also choose Sequence ➪ Snap.

✦ **Sequence Zero Point:** You can change the zero point of a sequence by moving the current-time indicator to the position where you want the sequence timecode to start and choosing Sequence Zero Point from the Timeline panel menu. Why change the sequence zero point? You may start your production with a countdown, or other sequence, but not want the duration of this opening sequence to be added to Timeline frame count.

✦ **Display Audio Units:** By default, Premiere Pro shows Timeline intervals in frames. You can change the Timeline interval to display audio samples by choosing Audio Units in the Timeline panel menu. If you choose Audio Units, the display shows audio units in milliseconds or audio samples. You specify the audio unit to be either milliseconds or samples in the Project Settings dialog box, when you first create a project or new sequence.

Using Multiple Sequences

An assembled production in a Timeline is called a *sequence*. Why differentiate between the Timeline and the sequence within it? The answer is that you can place multiple sequences within a Timeline, each sequence featuring different footage. Furthermore, each sequence has a name and can be renamed. You may want to use multiple sequences to divide your project into smaller elements. After you've completed editing in the smaller sequences, you can then combine them into one sequence before exporting. You may also want to copy and paste footage from one sequence into another to experiment with different edits, effects, or transitions. Figure 6-5 shows a Timeline panel with two sequences within it.

Note   If you import one Premiere Pro project into another Premiere Pro project, the imported project is displayed in a separate sequence that Premiere Pro places in a bin (folder) in the Project panel. The bin name is the name of the imported project.

Creating a new sequence

When you create a new sequence, it is automatically added to the active Timeline panel as a new tab in the panel, as shown in Figure 6-5. Creating a sequence is easy; simply choose File ➪ New ➪ Sequence. This opens the New Sequence dialog box, shown in Figure 6-6. Here you can rename the sequence and choose how many tracks to add. Clicking OK creates a new sequence and adds it to the currently selected Timeline. After you've placed two sequences onscreen, you can cut and paste from one to the other or edit a sequence and nest it into another sequence.

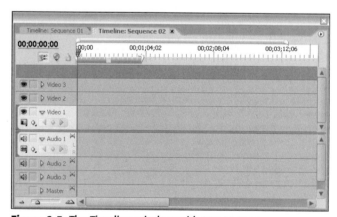

Figure 6-5: The Timeline window with two sequences

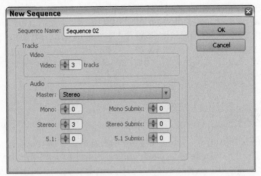

Figure 6-6: The New Sequence dialog box controls how tracks are created in new sequences.

To move from one sequence to another in the Timeline panel, click the sequence's tab. If you want to separate a sequence into a separate window, click its tab and then press Ctrl and drag it away from the Timeline panel. Next release the mouse and then the Ctrl key. If you've opened multiple windows onscreen, you can activate a window with a sequence in it by choosing Window ➪ Timelines and choosing the sequence name in the submenu.

Nesting sequences

After you create a new sequence to a project, you can place footage in it and add effects and transitions. Later, if desired, you can embed or nest it into another sequence. You can use this feature to gradually create a project in separate short sequences, and then assemble them all into one sequence (with the short sequences nested within the one sequence).

One advantage of nesting is that you can reuse an edited sequence again and again by simply nesting it several times in another Timeline. Each time you nest one sequence in another, you can trim it or change the transitions surrounding it in the Timeline. When you apply an effect to a nested sequence, Premiere Pro applies the effect to all the clips in the sequence, saving you from having to apply the same effect to multiple clips.

If you are going to nest sequences, be aware that nested sequences always refer to their original source clips. If you change the original source clips, the change is reflected in the sequences in which it is nested.

Figure 6-7 shows how a nested sequence appears in the Timeline panel. In this figure, Sequence 02 was nested within Sequence 01, and audio and video transitions were added between the two sequences.

On the DVD-ROM

The nested sequence in Figure 6-7 includes an image from the Skyrider folder from Digital Vision's SkyRider CD-ROM. The clip, 652005f.mov, is included in the Chapter 6 folder of the *Adobe Premiere Pro 2 Bible* DVD. Figure 6-7 also includes two video clips called diners.mov and chefs.mov. These clips are from the Nite Out project in Chapter 1. The clips are Digital Vision's NightMoves 705008f.mov and 705009f.mov.

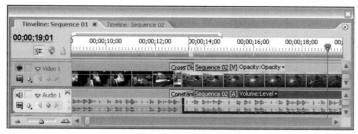

Figure 6-7: Sequence 02 nested within Sequence 01

Follow these steps to nest one sequence within another:

1. **Create a new sequence by choosing File ➪ New ➪ Sequence.**

2. **In the new sequence, create edits, transitions, and effects as needed.**

3. **To nest one sequence in another sequence, click and drag the sequence from the Project panel or from the Source section of the Monitor window into the track of another sequence.**

Tip To open a sequence in the Source Monitor, Ctrl+double-click it in the Project panel or in the Timeline panel.

Tip To quickly return to the original sequence of a nested sequence, double-click the nested sequence in the Timeline panel

Clip Project Management

Although the Timeline keeps program footage organized in a consistent linear structure, if you want to work efficiently, you also need to keep your source footage organized as well. Fortunately, Premiere Pro provides several features to keep your source clips organized while you work. The following sections review a variety of menu commands and options that can help you work efficiently with clips. Here's a summary of the primary topics in this section.

✦ **Project Manager:** Creates a new version of your project and can remove unused footage and extraneous frames from clips.

✦ **Subclips:** Allows you divide up longer clips into multiple shorter clips.

✦ **Clip Notes:** Allow you to create PDF versions of a project for workgroup review. Members of the workgroup can view the video in Adobe Acrobat Reader.

✦ **Adobe Bridge:** An asset management application included with Adobe Premiere Pro that allows you to drag and drop files from Bridge directly into a project.

Using the Project Manager

Premiere Pro's Project Manager provides the fastest method to reduce the file size of a project and remove extraneous clips. The Project Manager can save lots of disk space by creating a new trimmed version of your work by removing files that aren't being used in a project and by removing extra frames before in points and after out points. When the Project Manager creates a new project, you have two options: to create a new trimmed project or to copy all or some of the project files to a new location.

To use the Project Manager, choose Project ➪ Project Manger. This opens the Project Manager dialog box shown in Figure 6-8, where you can choose from the following options:

Figure 6-8: Project Manager options

✦ **Exclude Unused Clips:** This option removes unused clips from the new project.

✦ **Make Offline:** Select this option to take project clips offline so that you can recapture them using Premiere Pro's Batch capture command. (Choose File ➪ Batch Capture.) This option can be very useful if you are using low-resolution versions of footage. (See Chapter 5 for more information about batch capturing.)

✦ **Include Handles:** This option allows you to choose the number of extra frames before the in point and after the out point of project clips.

✦ **Include Preview Files:** This option allows preview files of rendered footage to be included in the new project. If you deselect this option, you create a smaller project, but need to re-render effects to view the effects in the new project. This option can be selected only if you choose Collect Files and Copy to New Location.

✦ **Include Audio Conform Files:** This option keeps conformed audio files in the new project. If you do not select this option, the new project consumes less disk space; however,

Premiere Pro must conform the audio files in the new project — which may prove time-consuming. (For more information about audio files, see Chapter 8.) This option can be selected only if you choose Collect Files and Copy to New Location.

✦ **Rename Media Files To Match Clip Names:** If you renamed clips in the Project panel, this option ensures that those new names are maintained in the new project. Note that if you rename a clip and then set its status to offline, the original file name is maintained.

✦ **Project Destination:** This option allows you to specify a location for the project folder that contains the trimmed project material. Click Browse to choose the location.

✦ **Disk Space:** This option compares the file size of the original project and the new trimmed project. Click Calculate to update file sizes.

Tip

If you want to remove only unused clips from your project, choose Project ➪ Remove Unused.

Managing clips

If you are working on a long video project, organizing video and audio clips efficiently can help ensure that you are working productively. Premiere Pro provides a variety of handy features for clip management. You can rename clips, create subclips out of longer clips, and take clips that you no longer need offline. However, before you begin to use these features, you should understand the relationship among master clips, clip instances, and subclips.

✦ **Master clip:** When you first import a clip, it appears as a master clip in the Project panel. The master clip is a screen representation of the media disk file. You can rename and delete the master clip in the Project panel without affecting the original disk file.

✦ **Instance:** When you place a clip in the Timeline, you create an *instance* of the master clip. Premiere Pro allows you to create multiple instances of the master clip in the Timeline. If you delete the instance from the Timeline, the master clip remains in the Project panel. However, if you remove a master clip from the Project panel, all instances disappear from the Timeline.

✦ **Subclip:** A subclip is a shorter, edited version of a master clip that is independent of the master clip. For example, if you've captured a long interview, you could divide different topics into multiple subclips and quickly access them in the Project panel. When editing, working with shorter clips is more efficient than taking one longer clip and using different instances of it in the Timeline. If you delete a master clip from the project, its subclips still remain in the project. Subclips can be recaptured from the Project panel using Premiere's batch capture options.

✦ **Duplicate Clip:** A duplicate clip is another instance of the master clip in the Project panel. It exists independently of the original and can be renamed. If the master clip is deleted from the Project panel, the duplicate remains. In the current version of Premiere Pro, most users will use subclips instead of duplicate clips. In previous versions of Premiere, many users would use duplicate clips in a similar fashion to Premiere Pro's subclips. But subclips are more efficient because they do not contain all of the master clip footage.

Creating subclips

After you understand the relationship between master clips, clip instances, and subclips, you'll undoubtedly want to start using subclips in your projects. As mentioned, Premiere Pro allows you to reproduce parts of footage from one long clip in one or more shorter clips called subclips. This feature allows you to work with shorter child clips that exist independently of the master clip. Follow these steps to create a subclip:

1. **Double-click the master clip's icon in the Project panel.** This opens the clip in the Source Monitor. Alternatively, drag the clip from the Project panel to the Source Monitor.

2. **Set in and out points for the clip.** To set the in point, move the Source Monitor's current-time indicator to the desired frame and then click the Set In Point button. Next, move the current-time indicator to the desired out point and click the Set Out Point button.

3. **If you don't want the audio of a master clip to be included in a subclip, click the Toggle Take Audio and Video icon in the Source Monitor and choose the Toggle Take Video icon (or click Take Video in the Source Monitor panel menu).**

4. **Choose Clip ➪ Make Subclip, or drag the clip from the Source Monitor to an empty area of the Project panel.** This opens the Make Subclip dialog box, shown in Figure 6-9.

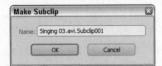

Figure 6-9: The Make Subclip dialog box

5. **In the Make Subclip dialog box, enter a name for the subclip.** This creates a new subclip in the Project panel.

Tip   If you want to create a subclip from an edited clip that has already been inserted in the Timeline, you can quickly place the clip in the Source Monitor by viewing it in the Program Monitor and pressing T. After the clip appears in the Source Monitor, you can edit its in and out points and then drag it to an empty area in the Project panel to create a subclip.

Editing a subclip

After you create a subclip, you can edit its in and out points, or you can convert it to a master clip. To edit a subclip, select the subclip in the Project panel and choose Edit ➪ Subclip. In the Edit Subclip dialog box, shown in Figure 6-10, edit the in and out points. To convert the clip to a master clip, select Convert to Master clip and click OK. After the master clip is created, its icon in the Project panel changes to a full clip, rather than a clip within a clip.

Note   If you use the Edit Subclip command to change the in and out points of a clip that is not a subclip, Premiere Pro converts it into a subclip.

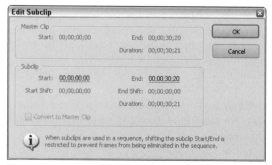

Figure 6-10: The Edit Subclip dialog box

Offline and online clips

As you work with master and subclips, you may want to take a clip offline. This removes the link from a clip in the Project panel to its disk file. If you remove the link, Premiere Pro no longer attempts to access the footage when the project is open. After a clip is offline, it can be re-linked to disk media and can be recaptured in a batch capture session.

To take a clip offline, right-click it in the Project panel and choose Make Offline in the drop-down menu. This opens the Make Offline dialog box, where you can specify whether to delete the original file footage from your disk media.

If you want to later link the files to another disk file, right-click the offline file in the Project panel and choose Link media. In the Link Media dialog box, navigate to the file to which you want to link.

Tip   You can replace one or more offline files with captured footage on disk by first selecting the offline files in the Project panel and then choosing Project ➪ Link Media.

Master and subclip relations

Because subclips are children of parent master clips and both can inhabit a project simultaneously, you must understand their relationship to the original source footage and what happens if either clip is offline. Here are some tips for managing master clips and subclips:

✦ **If you take a master clip offline or delete it in the Project panel, but don't delete the clip's file from disk, the subclip and subclip instances stay online.**

✦ **If you take a clip offline and delete the clip's file from disk, the subclip and its master clip are taken offline.**

✦ **If you delete a subclip from a project, the master clip is not affected.**

✦ **If you take a subclip offline, instances of the subclip are taken offline in Timeline sequences, but duplicates of the subclip remain online.** Other subclips based on the master clip also remain online.

✦ **If you recapture a subclip, the subclip becomes a master clip. Instances of the subclip in sequences are linked to the new subclip footage.** They are no longer linked to the old subclip material. (See Chapter 5 to learn more about batch capture.)

Duplicating, renaming, and deleting clips

Although using subclips is more efficient than duplicating and renaming clips, from time to time you may want to duplicate an entire clip so you have another instance of the master clip in the Project panel.

To duplicate and rename a clip, follow these steps:

1. **Select the clip in the Project panel.**

2. **Choose Edit ⇨ Duplicate.** A duplicate of the clip appears in the Project panel with the word *copy* following the original clip name.

3. **Rename the clip by choosing Edit ⇨ Rename.**

Tip   You can duplicate a master clip in the Project panel by pressing Ctrl and dragging it below the last item in the panel. Release the mouse, and then release the Ctrl key. If you want to delete a clip from the Project panel or from the Timeline, select it and press Backspace, or choose Edit ⇨ Cut or Edit ⇨ Clear. (Edit ⇨ Cut places the clip in the clipboard, so that it can be pasted into Premiere Pro again.) You can also delete a clip by right-clicking it and choosing Edit ⇨ Cut or Edit ⇨ Clear.

Enabling and disabling clips

While editing, you may decide that you don't want to see a clip's video when you play your project in the Program Monitor. Rather than deleting the clip, you can disable it — which also prevents it from being exported. To disable the clip, select the clip and choose Clip ⇨ Enable. This toggles the clip to a disabled state, and a check mark is removed from the Enable menu item. To re-enable the clip, choose Clip ⇨ Enable. This toggles the clip back to its original enabled state.

Using Clip Notes for workgroup review

If you are working as a member of a production team, Premiere Pro's Clip Notes option allows you to share your project with co-workers who aren't video editors. Clip Notes are exported from Premiere Pro as an Adobe PDF, and thus can be read in Adobe Acrobat Reader. When you export your project using a Clip Note, Premiere Pro embeds either the entire project or the work area into the PDF file. When team members open the PDF file, they can review your project by clicking the Play button, shown in Figure 6-11. Reviewers can later export comments that can be imported into your Premiere Pro project.

To export a clip note file in PDF format, follow these steps:

1. **Select the Timeline panel that includes the sequence that you want to export.**

2. **Choose Sequence ⇨ Export for Clip Notes.**

3. **In the Export for Clip Notes dialog box, enter the format, range, and video preset in the Export Settings section.**

4. **Click OK.**

5. **In the Save dialog box, enter a name for your file, specify a location for the file, and then click Save.**

After you create the PDF file, it can be opened in Adobe Acrobat Reader, as shown in Figure 6-11. In the PDF file, team members can enter comments and then click Export to export the file in .xfdf (XML Forms Data Format) format. You can import the .xfdf file into the Premiere project by choosing File ⇨ Import. When imported, the comments appear as marker comments in the Timeline. To view a reviewer's comments, you need only double-click the marker icon in the Timeline.

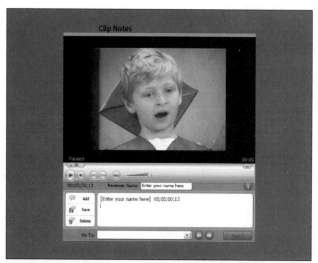

Figure 6-11: Premiere Pro project viewed in Adobe Acrobat Reader

Timecode for Workgroup Review

If you want different members of your workgroup to review footage and edits, you can temporarily place timecode over video footage. To do this, you can add transparent video to a track above your footage and then apply the timecode video effect to the transparent video. The result is timecode overlaying your footage, simulating what is often called a *window dub*. This allows everyone in your workgroup to refer to the same timecode as they view footage and compile editing comments.

To create Transparent video, choose File ⇨ New ⇨ Transparent Video. After the Transparent video appears in the Project panel, drag it to a track above your footage in the Timeline. Next, extend the transparent video by clicking and dragging on the clip edge or by selecting it and choosing Clip ⇨ Speed/Duration (In the Speed/Duration dialog box, enter the duration for the transparent video). After you've laid down the Transparent video, drag the timecode effect over it. (The Timecode effect can be found in the Video bin, in the Effects bin in the Effects panel.) Once you've completed reviewing the project, you can remove the timecode by deleting the transparent video track or turning off track output for the transparent video track. To learn more about applying Video Effects, see Chapter 14.

Adding metadata to project files

Metadata is descriptive text information that can be embedded in video and project files. Typically, metadata includes copyright information, author name, title, and other information. Because metadata remains with project files, it can help you keep your files organized and can be viewed by others who may load your project. Premiere Pro uses XMP metadata file format, a format used by other Adobe applications as well as applications created by other vendors.

To add metadata to a project file, select the project file in the Project panel and then choose File ➪ File Info For ➪ Selection. In the dialog box shown in Figure 6-12, click a category in the left column and enter the data. Click Save to save the metadata.

If you will be typing the same entries into metadata for different files, you can save your metadata text entries in a template for use with other files. To create a template from your description choices, choose Save Metadata Template from the dialog box's menu. This opens the Save Metadata Template dialog box where you can name your template. After you save a template, it appears in the menu where it can be loaded by clicking its name. After you pick a template, the data is loaded onscreen. You can also load the template data into a metadata field by clicking from the drop-down menu arrows to the right of the metadata fields.

Tip   You can add metadata to a file that is not in the current project by choosing File ➪ File Info For ➪ File.

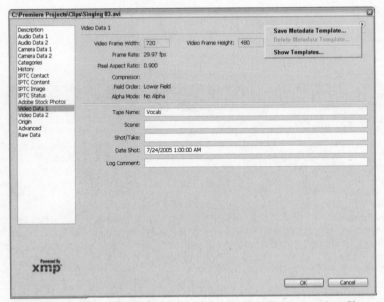

Figure 6-12: Adding metadata information to a Premiere Pro project file

Using Adobe Bridge

Adobe Bridge is a file and asset management application directly accessible from Premiere Pro. You can use Adobe Bridge to organize project files, add metadata, and preview video files. You can also import files directly from Adobe Bridge into Premiere Pro by double-clicking the file or dragging it into Premiere's Project panel.

Although using Bridge is certainly not a necessity for creating Premiere Pro projects, it can prove helpful, particularly when organizing media before you create your projects. For example, you can add metadata to all files you will be using in a project, and quickly search for them in Adobe Bridge. After files are found, you can place them in an Adobe Bridge Collection. By clicking an Adobe Bridge Collection icon, you can immediately access the files in the collection. This section provides an overview of features that Premiere Pro users may find useful when planning and editing projects.

Opening Adobe Bridge

Premiere Pro provides two options for opening Adobe Bridge directly from a project:

✦ **To open Adobe Bridge from Premiere, choose File ➪ Browse.** Figure 6-13 shows files being displayed in Adobe Bridge.

✦ **If you want to quickly find an online file's location on your disk and view it in Adobe Bridge, select the file in Premiere's Project panel and choose File ➪ Reveal in Bridge.**

Viewing files in Bridge

The best way to get familiar with Adobe Bridge is to start by navigating through your hard disk using Bridge. Here are few techniques for navigating and viewing files:

✦ **To view the contents of any folder, simply double-click on the folder.** (If you double-click a file, it is imported into Premiere Pro.) When you double-click, the main viewing area of Bridge reveals the contents of the folders. To jump one level back to the previous folder, click the Go Up folder at the top of the screen (shown in Figure 6-13).

✦ **To quickly jump to a folder, click in the drop-down menu at the top of the Bridge screen.** As you work, folders that you use are automatically added to the drop-down menu.

✦ **If you want to zoom in to view the images displayed in the Bridge file area, you can click and drag the zoom slider at the bottom of the screen, or pick a view from the Window menu.**

✦ **Premiere Pro users who want to access Bridge and use it while working in Premiere most likely will prefer to work in Compact mode.** Compact mode shrinks the Bridge window so that you can view Adobe Premiere Pro panels and Bridge at the same time. To switch to compact mode, click the Compact Mode icon in the top right of the Adobe Bridge screen.

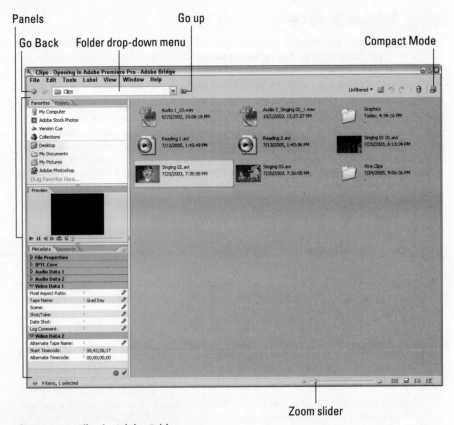

Panels

Go Back   Folder drop-down menu   Go up   Compact Mode

Zoom slider

Figure 6-13: Files in Adobe Bridge

Bridge panels

After you start using Adobe Bridge, you'll see that it provides a visual alternative to Windows Explorer. Its panels also provide another graphic interface to help keep you organized. These panels, which appear along the left side of Adobe Bridge (see Figure 6-13), allow you to create keywords, view metadata, and copy files into favorites. To open a panel, click the View menu and then choose the panel that you want to open. Bridge Panels include the following:

✦ **Favorites:** This panel shows commonly used folders and files. To add to the favorites list, drag a file or folder from the main file area into the Favorites panel.

✦ **Preview:** Use this panel to preview audio and video files. Click and drag a file into the Preview panel, and then click the Play button to play video.

✦ **Keywords:** This panel allows you to view and add keywords to a file. Keywords can be used to describe a file, which can later be used for searching. Keywords are primarily used with Adobe's Photo Collection and images from Adobe's Creative Suite. Premiere users who want to embed descriptive attributes in a file should use metadata.

✦ **Metadata:** This panel allows you to add metadata to a file. Metadata provides descriptive information about a file that remains with the file when used in different applications.

Tip   If you want to remove or view the panels quickly, click Show/Hide Panels in the lower-left corner.

Using metadata in Bridge

Using Bridge's metadata capabilities, you can tag files with metadata information and search using metadata criteria. Some common fields for metadata include: Title, Author, Description, and Copyright Information. Several video data metadata fields are show in Figure 6-13. To add metadata, simply click the pencil icon adjacent to the field name and enter the appropriate information. After you finish entering metadata, click the check mark icon at the bottom of screen to save the changes, or click the circle bar icon to cancel.

The fields in the metadata section are controlled by the Metadata preferences. To change preferences, click Preferences in the flyout menu and select which fields you want to include in the metadata panel.

Note   In the metadata panel, you can specify metadata according to the International Press Telecommunications Council (IPTC) standards.

Finding files using metadata criteria

If you begin embedding metadata to files, you can find and group your files based upon metadata criteria. To find data in Bridge based upon metadata criteria, start by choosing Edit ⇨ Find. In the Find dialog box, specify the search folder in the Look in drop-down menu.

Choose metadata in the Criteria drop-down menu, as shown in Figure 6-14. Enter the search criteria in the search field. If you want to have the search results displayed in a new window, select the check box by Show find results in a new browser window. To execute the search, click Find.

Figure 6-14: Finding using metadata criteria

After the data is found, a dialog box allows you to save the pictures in a collection. After you name the collection, a Collections icon appears in the Favorites panel. When you click the Collections icon, you can see the files you've stored in the collection.

Other Bridge options

Bridge provides numerous other features for renaming and organizing files using ratings and labels. These features are easily accessed from Bridge's View. However, despite all Bridge has to offer, Premiere Pro users should generally not move and rename files after importing them into Premiere Pro. Otherwise, Premiere Pro cannot find them when you first load your project. Your best bet is to arrange and rename source files before you import them.

Summary

Premiere Pro provides numerous project management features. Its Timeline panel controls how clips are viewed and exported. In the Timeline panel you can work with multiple sequences and embed one sequence in another. This chapter covered these topics:

✦ Use Timeline ruler options to change zoom levels.

✦ Select a track by clicking at the head of the track to make it the target track.

✦ Tracks can be locked and hidden.

✦ You can view keyframe and opacity settings in video tracks.

✦ To create a new sequence, choose File ➪ New ➪ Sequence.

✦ To nest one sequence in another, click and drag the sequence from the Project panel into a track in the Timeline window of another sequence.

✦ Use the Project Management dialog box to trim projects.

✦ Use subclips to create shorter source clips from master clips.

✦ You can export a project for review using Premiere Pro's Clip Notes option.

✦   ✦   ✦

Basic Editing with the Source Monitor and Timeline Panels

Editing drives a video program. The careful assembly of sound and video clips can control excitement, tension, and interest. Fortunately, Premiere Pro makes this crucial element of digital video production a logical, creative, and rewarding process rather than a tedious and frustrating one. Premiere Pro's interface — which features its Timeline and Monitor panels — combines with its track selection and editing tools to provide a fully integrated and powerful working environment.

This chapter introduces the basic techniques of editing in Premiere Pro. It begins with an overview of the editing process and provides details on creating insert and overlay edits using the Source Monitor and Timeline panels. The chapter concludes with a discussion of how to create lift and extract edits in the Timeline. Premiere Pro's advanced editing techniques are discussed in Chapter 13.

On the DVD-ROM   The clips used in the figures in this chapter are from 705008f.mov from Digital Vision's Night Moves CD-ROM. This clip and others can be found in the Chapter 1 folder on the *Adobe Premiere Pro 2 Bible* DVD-ROM.

Basic Editing Concepts and Tools

Before you begin editing video in Premiere Pro, you need a basic idea of different techniques that you can use to edit a digital video production. Premiere Pro provides two main areas for editing clips and assembling them — the Monitor panels and the Timeline panel. As discussed earlier in this book, the Timeline provides a visual overview of your project. You can begin creating a rough edit by simply dragging clips from the Project panel into the Timeline. Using the selection tools in the Timeline, you begin arranging the clips in a logical order. You can work even more efficiently by editing a clip's in and out points in the Source Monitor panel.

The Source Monitor displays clips that are not in a sequence in the Timeline, while the Program Monitor plays clips already edited in a Timeline sequence. Using controls in the Source Monitor panel, you can change the in and out points of clips, and then use an insert or overlay edit to place the clip in the Timeline. The steps and examples in this chapter show you how to create, insert, and overlay edits.

To further fine-tune your editing work, you can use Premiere Pro's editing tools to perform ripple, slide, and slip edits. These and more sophisticated editing techniques that can be performed in the Source Monitor panel — such as three- and four-point editing — are discussed in Chapter 13.

Note   When you are performing edits, you may find that using keyboard shortcuts saves time. To display the keyboard commands, choose Edit ⇨ Keyboard Customization. Choose Windows in the pop-up menu, and then open the section for Monitor and Trim panels.

The workspace

An important consideration before actually editing a project is to plan how you want your workspace set up. To pick a predefined workspace, choose Window ⇨ Workspace and then choose from the four choices presented: Editing, Audio, Effects, and Color Correction.

In the Editing workspace, shown in Figure 7-1, the Project, Monitor, Effects, Tools, and Timeline panels consume the entire screen. These are the most important panels you use as you assemble a project. You can drag clips from the Project panel into the Source Monitor panel, or you can drag them directly from the Timeline. As explained later in this chapter, you can edit the clips in either the Timeline panel or Monitor panel.

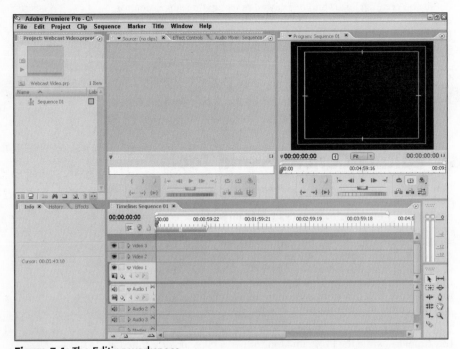

Figure 7-1: The Editing workspace

At any point in time, you can change the arrangement of panels onscreen and save your workspace by choosing Window ➪ Workspace ➪ Save Workspace. This command allows you to save a workspace to disk. It then adds the workspace name to the top of the Windows ➪ Workspace submenu. When you want to reload your workspace, simply choose Window ➪ Workspace and select your workspace name from the menu.

Getting started

After you import your video, audio, and still footage into the Project panel, you may be tempted to immediately start dragging clips to the Timeline to begin the process of editing your production. If you're working on a long project with many production elements, you undoubtedly want to plan your production on paper beforehand. If you work from a script that describes the video elements and includes all narration, you can save yourself hours of time when you begin to edit your production. To help you visualize your production or various parts of it, you may also want to create a storyboard, which contains drawings or printouts of the video. After you load the various production elements into bins in the Project panel, you also may find it helpful to double-click each clip in the Project panel and click the play button in the Source Monitor panel to view each clip before editing.

For beginners who are working on new projects, another good idea is to practice editing short video and audio sequences so that you become familiar with the basic techniques of creating a production. In Premiere Pro, you can edit clips in either the Source Monitor panel or the Timelime panel. Beginners may be tempted to drag all clips into the Timeline and click and drag to edit them there. But for precision editing, the Source Monitor panel provides better controls for fine-tuning your work. After you've edited a clip's in and out points in the Source Monitor, you can then drag the clip to a sequence in the Timeline, or you can click the Source Monitor's Insert button or Overlay button to place the clip in the sequence.

Working with the Monitor Panels

The Source, Program, and Trim Monitor panels are not only used for previewing your production as you work, but they can also be used for precise editing and trimming. You can use the Source Monitor panel, shown in Figure 7-2, to trim clips before placing them in a video sequence. You can use the Program Monitor, shown in Figure 7-3, to edit footage already placed on the Timeline. You can also open the Trim Monitor panel, shown in Figure 7-4, to fine-tune your edits. In the Trim Panel, the frame to the right and the frame to the left of the current-time indicator are represented in separate sections to provide greater precision for setting in and out points. To open the Trim Monitor panel (covered later in this chapter), you can either click the Trim button in the Program Monitor panel or choose Trim from the Program Monitor's panel menu.

In most editing situations, you want to keep the Source Monitor and Program Monitor open onscreen. This enables you to view source clips (clips to be used in the program) and the program material (the clips already placed in a sequence in the Timeline panel) at the same time. Before you use more sophisticated editing techniques, you should become familiar with both panels. Beneath the Source Monitor's video area is the source controller, which enables you to play source clips that haven't been added to the Timeline. The Set In Point and Set Out Point buttons enable you to set in and out points of source clips.

Beneath the Program Monitor's video area is the program controller, which enables you to play the program that exists on the Timeline. Clicking the In Point and Out Point icons in the Program Monitor changes the in and out points of the sequence already on the Timeline. You use the sequence Set In Point and Set Out Point icons when performing lift and extract edits, which remove footage from the current sequence, and when you create three-point edits. (Three-point edits are covered in Chapter 13.)

Figure 7-2: The Source Monitor panel

Current-time indicator   Lift   Extract

Figure 7-3: The Program Monitor panel

Both the Source Monitor and the Program Monitor allow you to view safe zones. Monitor-safe margins enable you to show the video-safe zones for movement and for titles. These margins indicate that the image area is safely within the Monitor viewing area, as well as the image area that might be overscanned. A safe zone is needed because television screens overscan images, thus expanding portions of them beyond the screen. To view the safe-margin markers in the Monitor panel, choose Safe Margins from the Monitor's panel menu or click the monitor's Safe Margins icon. When the safe-zone margins appear in the Monitor window, the inner safe zone is the title-safe area, and the outer is the action-safe area.

Left frame of edit   Right frame of edit

Figure 7-4: The Monitor panel in Trim View

Trimming clips in the Source Monitor panel

Before placing clips in a video sequence in the Timeline, you may want to first trim them (set the in and out points) in the Source Monitor panel, because captured clips invariably contain more footage than needed. If you trim a clip before placing it in a video sequence in the Timeline, you'll probably find that you save time that would otherwise be spent clicking and dragging clip edges in the Timeline. Follow these steps for setting the in and out points of a clip in the Source Monitor panel:

Tip   To practice, import a clip into your project or load a clip from the Chapter 1 folder on the *Adobe Premiere Pro 2 Bible* DVD. To import the clip, choose File ➪ Import and then select the clip from your hard drive or DVD. (You can work faster if you copy clips from the DVD-ROM to your hard drive.)

1. **To display a clip in the Source Monitor panel, double-click it in the Project panel.** Alternatively, you can click and drag a clip from the Project panel to the Source Monitor.

Note   If you double-click footage that is already placed in a sequence in the Timeline panel, the video portion appears in the Source Monitor. If you double-click an unlinked audio track, Premiere Pro displays audio part In the Source Monitor. (See Chapter 8 for more information about editing audio.)

When the clip appears in the Source Monitor panel, you can use the controls shown in Figure 7-1 to play the clip.

2. **Click the Play button to play the entire clip. (You play the clip continuously by clicking the Loop button.)** When you find a section you want to edit, you can stop it by clicking the Stop button. When you stop the clip, look at the time display in the left side of the Source Monitor to see at which frame you have stopped. This can help you when setting in and out points and when setting markers.

3. **To precisely access the frame that you want to set as your in point, start by clicking and dragging the blue triangle current-time indicator (CTI) over the ruler area in the Monitor panel.** As you click and drag, the Source Monitor's time display indicates your frame location. If you don't stop at the correct frame, you can click the Step forward and Step backward buttons to slowly move one frame at a time forward or backward. You can also click and drag the shuttle (refer to Figure 7-2) or the jog tread area to move back and forth through your clip. If you prefer to use the keyboard, press the left or right arrow keys to move back and forth frame by frame.

You can jump to a specific frame in a clip by double-clicking over the Time display in the bottom-left corner of the Source Monitor. Make sure that the entire timecode readout is selected (you might need to double-click twice), and then type a specific timecode position. You do not need to type colons or semicolons. For instance, typing 50 is read as 50;00. If you type +50, the current-time indicator jumps forward 50 frames; type -50 and the CTI jumps back 50 frames. These shortcuts also work in the Timeline panel.

If you want to enlarge the time ruler intervals in the Source Monitor, click and drag on its Viewing Area bar. The Viewing Area Bar is the gray bar with curved edges above the panel's time ruler.

4. **When you reach the in point, click the Set In Point button or press I, or choose Marker ⇨ Set Clip Marker ⇨ In.** A left brace appears in the ruler area.

5. **Now locate the frame that you want to set as the out point, and click the Set Out button or press O, or choose Marker ⇨ Set Clip Marker ⇨ Out.** A right brace appears in the ruler area. After you set the in and out points, you can easily edit their positions by simply clicking and dragging on one of the brace icons. After you've set the in and out points, note the time display on the right side of the Monitor. This number indicates the duration from the in point to the out point.

6. **Play the edited sequence in the Source Monitor by clicking the Play In to Out button**.

If you want to play a short video segment near the current-time indicator, press Alt while clicking the Play In to Out button. (This converts the Play In Out button to a Play Around button).The footage backs up to the Preroll time set in the General Preferences dialog box and plays to the Postroll time. You can set the Preroll and Postroll times by choosing Edit ⇨ Preferences ⇨ General.

After you edit a clip in the Source Monitor, you can insert it or overlay it in the Timeline. Insert and Overlay edits are discussed in the "Creating Insert and Overlay Edits" section later in this chapter.

Shuttle Keyboard Commands

You can use these keyboard combinations to shuttle through footage:

Forward frame by frame	Hold K, while tapping L
Reverse frame by frame	Hold K, while tapping J
Play forward at 8fps	Press K and L simultaneously
Reverse at 8 fps	Press K and J simultaneously
Forward 5 frames	Shift+right arrow
Back 5 frames	Shift+left arrow

Choosing clips in the Source Monitor panel

After you start working with clips in the Source Monitor panel, you can easily return to previously used clips. When you first work with a clip in the Source Monitor, the clip's name appears in the tab at the top of the Source Monitor. If you want to return to a clip that you previously used in the Source Monitor, simply click the tab's down arrow. This opens a drop-down menu in which you can pick previously used clips. After you choose the clip in the drop-down menu, it appears in the Source window.

"Taking" audio and/or video

When working with clips in the Source Monitor, you can specify whether to use both audio and video, video only, or audio only. If the clip that you are editing in the Source Monitor includes both video and audio, you can use the Take Audio and Video button to "take" audio only or video only. If you want to edit using only a clip's video, click the Toggle Take Audio and Video icon in the Monitor panel (refer to Figure 7-3) until it changes to the Take Video icon. If you want to edit using only audio from the clip, click the Toggle Take Audio and Video icon until the Take Audio icon appears. (If your clip doesn't include an audio track, the audio icon does not appear.) When you perform an insert or overlay edit, Premiere Pro creates the edit using the audio and video, the video only, or the audio only, depending on the setting of the Toggle Audio and Video icons.

Note You can also choose Take Audio and Video, Take Video, and Take Audio from the Source Monitor's panel menu.

Creating Insert and Overlay Edits

Once you've edited the in and out points of a clip, you probably want to place it into a sequence on the Timelime. Once the clip is in the Timeline, it plays in the Program Monitor. As you place clips in the Timeline, you can insert clips between other footage or you can overlay it. When you create an overlay edit, you replace old footage with new footage; when you insert, the new footage is added to the Timeline, but no footage is replaced.

For example, assume that footage in the Timeline includes a galloping horse. You want to edit a three-second close-up of the jockey on the horse into the footage. If you perform an insert edit, the clip is split at the current edit point, and the jockey is inserted into the clip. The entire Timeline sequence is three seconds longer. If you perform an overlay edit instead, the three-second jockey footage replaces three seconds of horse footage. An overlay enables you to continue using the audio track that is linked to the galloping horse clip.

Inserting and overlaying from the Source Monitor

Creating an insert edit or overlay edit from the Source Monitor is quite easy. First choose the clip you want to edit in the Source monitor. If the clip isn't already in the Source Monitor, double-click it or drag it from the Project panel to the Source Monitor. Once the clip is in the Source Monitor, set the in and out points (as described in "Trimming Clips in the Source Monitor Panel"). If you only want to insert or overlay video without audio, set the toggle Audio and Video to Take Video (or choose Take Video from the Source Monitor panel menu). Then follow these steps to insert or overlay a clip in the timeline:

1. **Select the Target track in the Timeline.** The target track is where you want the video to appear. To select a target track, click the left edge of the track. After you select it, it displays rounded edges.

2. **Move the current-time indicator to the point where you want the clip to appear in the sequence in the Timeline.**

3. **Create the insert or overlay edit.**

   • To create an insert edit, click the Insert button in the Source Monitor panel or choose Clip ➪ Insert.

   • To create an insert edit, click the Overlay button in the Source monitor panel or choose Clip ➪ Overlay.

Inserting and overlaying by clicking and dragging

If you enjoy using the mouse, you can create insert and overlay edits by dragging clips directly to the timeline.

✦ To create an insert edit, press and hold Ctrl and then click and drag a clip from the Source Monitor Project panel over a clip in the Timeline. As you move one clip over the other, the mouse pointer changes to an Insert icon (an arrow pointing to the right). When you release the mouse (make sure Ctrl is still pressed), Premiere Pro inserts the new clip in the Timeline and pushes the footage at the insert point to the right. Figure 7-5 shows the Timeline before and after an insert edit.

   In Figure 7-5, the frames from the Diners clip now appear after the inserted Chefs clip. The arrows in the middle of the figure indicate that the edit affects all tracks (a gap is inserted into other tracks). To insert only into the target track, press Ctrl+Alt while clicking and dragging. Release the mouse before releasing the keys.

✦ To create an overlay edit on the Timeline, click and drag a clip from the Source Monitor window or Project panel over a clip in the Timeline. As you drag one clip over the other, the mouse pointer changes to an Overlay icon (an arrow pointing downward). When you release the mouse, Premiere Pro places one clip over the other and removes the underlying video. Figure 7-6 shows the Timeline before and after an overlay edit.

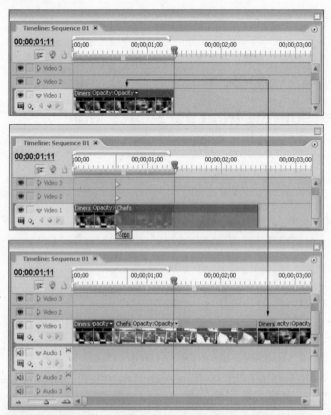

Figure 7-5: Sequence in Timeline panel before and after an insert edit

Using Clip Markers

If you want to return to a particular frame in a clip, you can set a marker as a reference point.

Markers appear as triangles in the Source Monitor panel or in sequences in the Timeline panel. To set a marker for a source clip, move the Source Monitor's current-timeline indicator to the frame where you want to create the marker, and then click the Marker button in the Source Monitor. To return to a clip marker, you can jump to it by clicking the Go to Next Marker icon or Go to Previous Marker icon in the Source Monitor panel.

If you'd like to place a numbered or unnumbered marker on a clip in the Timeline, select the Timeline and then move the current-time indicator to the frame where you want the marker to be. Next choose Marker ➪ Set Marker ➪ Unnumbered or Marker ➪ Set Marker ➪ Next Available Marker. Markers appear in the Time Ruler/Work Area bar portion of the Timeline.

To jump to a marker a sequence, select the Sequence and then choose Marker ➪ Go to Clip Marker ➪ Next or Clip ➪ Go to Clip Marker ➪ Previous. If you choose Marker ➪ Go to Clip Marker ➪ Numbered, a dialog box appears listing all clip markers. You can then click an item in the list to go to a specific marker. To clear a clip marker, choose Marker ➪ Clear Clip Marker and then choose the type of marker that you want to clear from the Clip Marker submenu.

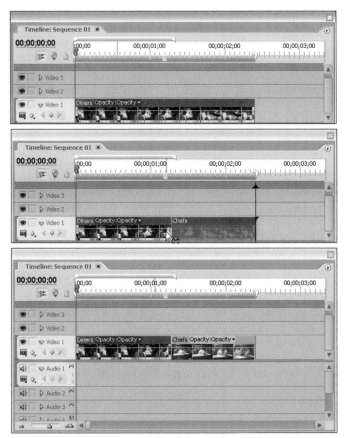

Figure 7-6: Sequence in Timeline panel before and after an overlay edit

Tip   You can add a video or audio track to the Timeline by clicking and dragging a clip from the Timeline or the Source Monitor panel above the top video track or below the last audio track.

Editing in the Timeline

As discussed in Chapter 6, Premiere Pro's Timeline provides a graphical representation of your project. By simply analyzing the effects and transitions in a video sequence in the Timeline, you can get a visual sense of your production without actually viewing the footage. Premiere Pro provides a variety of ways to place clips into the Timeline:

✦ Click and drag the footage or image from the Project panel into the Timeline.

✦ Select a clip in the Project panel, and then choose Clip ➪ Insert or Clip ➪ Overlay. The clip is inserted or overlaid into the target track at the current-time indicator. When a clip is inserted, it is dropped into the sequence and pushes footage to the right. When a clip is overlaid, it replaces footage.

✦ Double-click the clip in the Project panel to open it in the Source Monitor window. After setting in and out points, click the Insert or Overlay buttons in the Source Monitor window (or Clip ⇨ Insert or Clip ⇨ Overlay). Alternatively, drag the clip from the Source Monitor panel to the Timeline. As discussed earlier, pressing Ctrl inserts footage into the Timeline, dragging without Ctrl overlays footage.

✦ If you want to place multiple clips in the Timeline to create a rough cut of your work, you can use the Automate to Sequence command described in the next section.

Note   To make a track the target track, click in the track's header area.

Automate to Sequence

Premiere Pro's Automate to Sequence command provides a fast way to assemble a project in the Timeline. Automate to Sequence not only places clips from the Project panel into the Timeline; it can also add default transitions between clips as well. Thus, you may view this command as an efficient means of creating a quick rough cut. However, if the clips in the Project panel contain too much extraneous footage, your best bet is to trim the clips in the Source Monitor panel before executing Automate to Sequence. Follow these steps for using Automate to Sequence:

Tip   Automate to Sequence places clips in the first non-locked track in the Timeline. If you want to place clips in tracks other than Video 1 track, lock the preceding tracks. Be sure to re-select the Project panel before executing Automate to Sequence.

1. **Move the current-time indicator to the location in the Timeline where you want the footage to begin.**

2. **Select the clips in the Project panel that you want to place in the Timeline.** To select a group of adjacent clips, click the first clip you want to include in the sequence and press Shift. While holding Shift, click the last clip you want in the sequence.

Tip   To select non-adjacent clips, Ctrl-click different clips in the Project panel.

3. **To add the selected clips to the Timeline, choose Project ⇨ Automate to Sequence or click the Automate to Sequence button in the Project panel.** This opens the Automate to Sequence dialog box, shown in Figure 7-7.

4. **In the Automate to Sequence dialog box, choose the options to control how the clips are placed on the Timeline.** These are your choices:

   • **Ordering:** This option allows you to choose to have the clips placed in their sorted order in the Project panel or according to the order in which you selected them in the Project panel.

   • **Placement:** You can choose to have the clips ordered sequentially or at each unnumbered marker in the Timeline. If you choose the Unnumbered Marker option, Premiere Pro disables the Transitions option in the dialog box.

- **Method:** This option allows you to choose Insert or Overlay edit. If you choose Insert, clips already in the Timeline are pushed to the right. If you choose Overlay, clips from the Project panel replace clips in the Timeline.

- **Clip Overlap:** This option allows you to specify how many seconds or frames are used for the default transition. In a 30 frame long transition, 15 frames overlap from two adjacent clips.

- **Apply Default Audio/Video Transition:** This option applies the currently set default transition between clips.

- **Ignore Audio:** If this option is selected, Premiere Pro doesn't place the audio linked to clips.

- **Ignore Video:** If this option is selected, Premiere Pro doesn't place the video in the Timeline.

 5. **To execute the Automate to Sequence command, click OK.**

Figure 7-7: Use Automate to Sequence to create a rough cut.

Selecting and moving clips in the Timeline

After you place clips in the Timeline, you may need to reposition them as part of the editing process. You can choose to move one clip at a time, or you can move several clips at the same time. (You can also move either the video or audio of a clip independently. To do this, you need to temporarily unlink the clip.)

Using the Selection tool

The simplest way to move a single clip is to click it with the Selection tool and move it in the Timeline panel. If you want the clip to snap to the edge of another clip, make sure that the Snap to Edges command is selected. You may either choose Sequence ⇨ Snap or click the Snap icon (a magnet) in the upper-left corner of the Timeline panel. After clips are selected, you can move them by clicking and dragging or delete them from a sequence by pressing Delete. These tips will help you select clips and tracks using Premiere Pro's Selection tool:

✦ To select a clip, activate the Selection tool and click the clip.

✦ To select more than one clip, press and hold Shift and then click the clips that you want to select. Alternatively, you can also click and drag to create a marquee selection around the clips that you want to select. After you release the mouse, the clips within the marquee are selected. You can also use this technique to select clips that are on different tracks.

✦ If you want to select the video without the audio portion of a clip, or the audio without the video, Alt+click the video or audio track.

✦ To add or subtract a clip or a selection of clips to or from a selection, press Shift and then click and drag a marquee selection around the clip or clips.

Tip   You can move a clip a specific number of frames right or left in the Timeline by selecting the clip and then pressing + or - on the numeric keyboard. Next, enter the number of frames to move and press Enter.

Using the Track Select tool

If you want to quickly select several clips on a track or to delete clips on a track, use the Track Select tool. The Track Select tool does not select all clips on the track. It selects all clips from the point at which you click. Thus, if you place four clips on the Timeline and want to select the last two, click the third clip. Figure 7-8 shows clips selected with the Track Select tool.

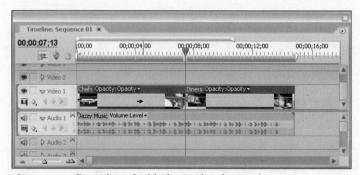

Figure 7-8: Clips selected with the Track Select tool.

If you want to quickly select multiple clips on different Timeline tracks, press and hold Shift while you click in a track with the Track Select tool. This selects all clips on all tracks starting at the point where you first click.

Grouping clips

If you know you need to select and reselect the same clips again and again, you should place them in a group. After you create a group of clips, you can select every member of the group by clicking any group member. You can also delete all clips in a group by selecting any member of the group and pressing Delete.

To create a group of clips, start by selecting the clips and then choose Clip ➪ Group. To ungroup the clips, choose Clip ➪ Ungroup.

If you move a clip on the Timeline that is grouped to another clip — such as a video clip that is linked to its audio clip — the linked clips move together.

Setting In and Out Points in the Timeline Panel

After you're familiar with the how to select clips in the Timeline, you can easily perform edits. You can edit by using the Selection tool or by setting in and out points using markers.

Using the Selection tool to set in and out points

One of the simplest ways to edit in the Timeline panel is to set in and out points using the Selection tool. To edit an in or out point with the Selection tool, follow these steps:

1. **Click the Selection tool in the Tools panel.**

2. **To set a clip's in point, move the Selection tool over the left edge of the clip in the Timeline.** The Selection tool changes to an Edge icon.

3. **Click and drag the edge of the clip to where you want the clip to start.** As you click and drag, a timecode readout appears next to the clip showing the editing change. The display in the Program Monitor panel changes to show the in point of the clip.

4. **To set a clip's out point, move the Selection tool over the right edge of the clip in the Timeline.** The Selection tool changes to an Edge icon.

5. **Click and drag the edge of the clip to where you want the clip to end.** As you click and drag, a timecode readout appears next to the clip showing the editing change. The display in the Program Monitor panel shows the out point of the clip.

Note   If you don't want the Program Monitor to display timecode as you edit clips, deselect Timecode Overlay During Edit in the Program Monitor panel menu.

Cutting clips with the Razor tool

 If you want to create an in or out point quickly, you can literally slice a clip in two with the Razor tool. Move the current-time indicator to the frame that you want to slice, and then click the frame with the Razor tool. Alternatively, choose Sequence ➪ Razor at Current Time Indicator. To slice footage in multiple tracks simultaneously, press Shift while clicking a frame with the Razor Tool.

Rearranging clips

As you edit, you may want to grab a clip in the Timeline and place it into another area. If do this, you're left with a gap where you've removed footage. This is called a *lift edit*. The opposite of a lift edit is an *extract edit*, which closes the gap after you remove footage. Premiere

Pro provides a timesaving keyboard command that combines an extract edit with either an insert or overlay edit:

✦ To rearrange footage using an extract edit (which closes the gap) and an insert edit, press Ctrl as you drag a clip or a group of selected clips to a new location. Release the mouse and then release Ctrl.

✦ To rearrange footage using an extract edit (which closes the gap) and an overlay edit, press Ctrl as you drag a clip or a group of selected clips to a new location. Release Ctrl and, then release the mouse.

Editing with Sequence Markers

You also can perform basic editing in the currently selected sequence by setting in and out points using the Marker ➪ Set Sequence Marker ➪ In and Marker ➪ Set Sequence Marker ➪ Out commands. These commands set in and out points for the beginning and end of the Timeline sequence. After you create Sequence Markers, you can use them as in and out points for lift and extract edits, which remove frames from the Timeline panel (described in the next section).

Setting in and out points

Follow these steps to set in and out points on the Timeline using menu commands:

1. **Click and drag the current-time indicator to where you want to set the Sequence in point.**

2. **Choose Marker ➪ Set Sequence Marker ➪ In.** An In Point icon appears at the ruler line on the Timeline at the position of the current-time indicator.

3. **Click and drag the current-time indicator to where you want to set the out point.**

4. **Choose Marker ➪ Set Sequence Marker ➪ Out.** An Out Point icon appears on the Timeline at the Current Time Indicator position.

Note   After you create the in and out points, you can easily move them by clicking and dragging them in the Timeline panel.

Tip   You can also set in and out points for the current sequence by clicking the Set In Point and Set Out Point icons in the Program Monitor.

Clearing in and out points

After creating Sequence Markers, you can easily clear them with the following menu commands:

✦ To clear both the in and out points and start all over again, choose Marker ➪ Clear Sequence Marker ➪ In and Out.

✦ To clear just the in point, choose Marker ➪ Clear Sequence Marker ➪ In.

✦ To clear just the out point, choose Marker ➪ Clear Sequence Marker ➪ Out.

Performing lift and extract edits at Sequence Markers

You can use Sequence Markers to easily remove clip segments from the Timeline by executing the Sequence Lift command or the Sequence Extract command. When you perform a lift edit, Premiere Pro lifts a segment off the Timeline and leaves a blank space where the deleted clip existed. When you perform an extract edit, Premiere Pro removes a section of the clip and then joins the frames of remaining clip sections together so no blank area exists.

 To perform a lift edit using Sequence Markers, follow these steps:

1. **Set in and out Sequence Markers at the section that you want to delete.** The top of Figure 7-9 shows in and out points created with Sequence Markers in the Timeline panel. See the earlier section "Setting in and out points" for information on creating in and out points.

2. **To perform a lift edit, choose Sequence ➪ Lift, or click the Lift icon in the Program Monitor.** Premiere Pro removes the section bordered by the in and out markers and leaves a blank area in the Timeline, as shown at the bottom of Figure 7-9.

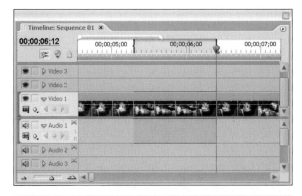

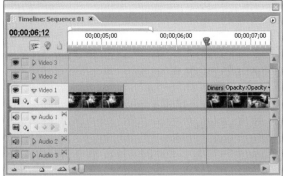

Figure 7-9: Sequence in Timeline panel before and after a lift edit

Adding Sequence Markers

You can add numerical markers to a sequence and use them as visual landmarks that you want to quickly return to later. These are especially useful with longer projects. To add a marker, move the current-time indicator in the Timeline panel to where you want to add a marker and then choose Marker ⇨ Set Sequence Marker ⇨ Next Available Numbered.

You can jump to a marker by choosing Marker ⇨ Go To Sequence Marker ⇨ Next or Marker ⇨ Go To Sequence Marker ⇨ Numbered. As mentioned earlier, you can also select a clip on a sequence and set a clip marker by moving the current-time indicator to a frame and then choosing Marker ⇨ Set Clip Marker.

 To perform an extract edit using Sequence Markers, follow these steps:

1. **Set in and out Sequence Markers at the section that you want to delete.** See the earlier section "Setting in and out points" for steps on creating in and out points.

2. **To perform an extract edit, choose Sequence ⇨ Extract, or click the Extract icon in the Program Monitor.** Premiere Pro removes the section bordered by the in and out markers and joins the edited sections together.

Summary

Premiere Pro provides graphical tools to aid in editing a digital video production. The Timeline, the Selection tools, and the Monitor panel all come into play when you begin to assemble and fine-tune your production. When you edit in Premiere Pro, you can do the following:

✦ Drag clips to a sequence in the Timeline from the Project panel.

✦ Use the Selection tools to select and move clips in a sequence in the Timeline.

✦ Set in and out points in a sequence in the Timeline.

✦ Set in and out points in the Source Monitor panel.

✦ Perform lift and extract edits using the menu commands or the controls in the Program Monitor panel.

✦   ✦   ✦

Editing Audio

Just as a picture is worth a thousand words, sound can create a mood that could take a thousand words to describe. Sound can be used to capture your audience's attention. The right background music can create a feeling of intrigue, comedy, or mystery. Sound effects can add realism and suspense to the visual elements that you present. Undoubtedly, the success of many of the best video productions and movies is related to the sound underlying the video.

Fortunately, Premiere Pro provides a wealth of features that enable you to integrate sound into your video projects. When you place a video clip in the Timeline, Premiere Pro automatically takes the sound along with it. If you want to fade in or fade out background music or narration, Premiere Pro's Effect Controls panel provides the tools. If you want to add an audio effect that enhances an audio clip or add a special effect, you can simply drag it from the Effects panel to the clip. If you want to mix audio into a master track, Premiere Pro's Audio Mixer does the job.

This chapter focuses on audio track basics. It provides a look at how to use Premiere Pro's audio tracks and how to create effects in the Timeline. The chapter also includes an overview of Premiere Pro's many audio effects and concludes with a look at how to export audio.

 Cross-Reference Chapter 9 covers creating audio effects and mixing tracks with the Audio Mixer. Audition, Adobe's audio editing and composition program, is covered in Chapter 24.

What Is Sound?

Before you begin to use Premiere Pro's audio features, you need to have a fundamental idea of what sound is and the terms used to describe it. Understanding exactly what type of sound you're working with and its quality is helpful. Terms such as *sample rate* of 48,000 kHz and *16-bit* appear in the Custom Settings dialog boxes, Export dialog boxes, and in the Project panel, as shown in Figure 8-1.

Figure 8-1: Audio information shown in the Project panel

Audio sample rate and bit rate

To understand digital sound, we must start in the analog world, where a sound such as someone beating on a drum or playing a musical instrument in a concert hall travels to us through waves. We hear sounds because of the vibrations the waves create. The rate of this vibration is the sound's pitch. Thus, a high-pitched sound vibrates more than a low-pitch sound. How frequently this wave vibrates between high and low points during a specific period of time is the sound's frequency. Sound frequency is measured in hertz (Hz). Humans can generally hear within a range from 20 Hz to about 20,000 Hz (20 kHz).

The size of a sound wave curve — or its amplitude — is measured in *decibels*. The greater the curve, the greater its amplitude is and the louder the sound.

Sound bits and sampling

When sound is digitized, thousands of numbers represent *amplitude*, or the height and depth of waves. During this process, the sound is sampled and recreated digitally into a series of 1s and 0s, or *bits*. If you use Premiere Pro's Audio Mixer to record narration, the waves of sound from your voice are processed by a microphone and then digitized by your sound card. When you play back the narration, the sound card converts the 1s and 0s back to analog sound waves.

Higher-quality digital recording uses more bits. CD-quality stereo uses a minimum of 16 bits. (Older multimedia software sometimes used 8-bit sound rates, which provided poorer-quality sound, yet produced smaller digital sound files.) Thus, one sample of CD-quality sound could be digitized into a series of sixteen 1s and 0s to look like this:

    1011011011101010

If the concept of bit rate is confusing, visual artists may find it easiest to think of a sound's bit rate as somewhat similar to image resolution: A higher bit rate produces a smoother-looking sound curve, just as higher image resolution produces smoother images.

In digital sound, the frequency of the digital waves is determined by the *sample rate*. Many camcorders record sound at a sample rate of 32 kHz, thus recording 32,000 samples every second. The higher the sample rate, the greater the frequency range that the sound can reproduce.

To reproduce a specific frequency, sound generally should be sampled at double that frequency. Consequently, to reproduce the highest frequency of human hearing of 20,000 kHz, a sample rate of at least 40,000 samples is required (CDs are recorded at a sample rate of 44,100).

Figure 8-2 shows a spectral depiction of a low-frequency bass recording compared to the audio frequencies of a portion of Beethoven's 9th Symphony. As you'll see later in this chapter, you can use several of Premiere Pro's Audio Effects to hone into specific frequency ranges to fine-tune and alter sound. The screen shots were taken in Adobe Audition, Adobe's audio-editing and composition application.

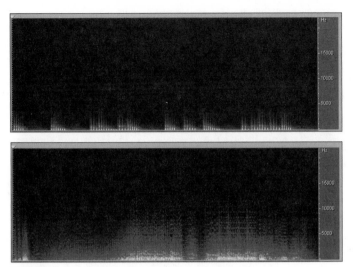

Figure 8-2: Audio frequency of bass recording, above; audio frequencies of Beethoven's 9th, below

Digitized sound file sizes

As you might imagine, the larger a sound's bit depth and the larger its sample rate, the larger the sound's file size is. Because sound files, like video, can be very large, it can be important to estimate how large a sound is. You can estimate a sound file's size, by multiplying the bit rate by the sample rate. Thus, one second of one track mono at 16 bits with a sample rate of 44,100 (16-bit × 44,100) produces 705,600 bytes per second, over 4 megabytes a minute. A stereo clip would be twice as large.

Timeline Audio Tracks

When you edit in Premiere Pro, its Timeline panel provide a bird's eye view of the audio that accompanies your video. As you can see from Figure 8-3, audio tracks are grouped together beneath video tracks. If you click in the Set Display style pop-up menu, you can choose to show an audio clip's name or its waveform. As with video clips, if you place audio clips into a sequence in the Timeline, you can click and drag to move them, use the Razor tool to slice audio, and use the Selection tool to adjust in and out points.

As you'll soon see, you can also edit the in and out points of audio clips in the Source Monitor and store subclips of audio clips in the Project panel.

When you place a video clip into the Timeline, Premiere Pro automatically places its audio into the corresponding audio track. Thus, if you place a video clip with audio in Video 1 track, the audio comes along for the ride, automatically placed into Audio track 1. If you slice a video clip with the Razor tool, the linked audio is sliced along with it.

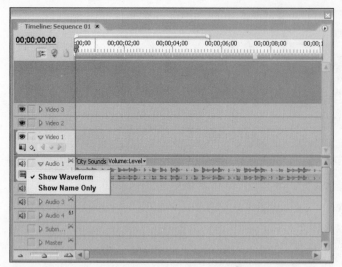

Figure 8-3: Audio tracks with 5.1, submix, and master tracks

As discussed in Chapter 6, you can expand and compress audio track views by clicking the Collapse/Expand icon. After the track is expanded, you can choose from the following display options:

✦ You can view the audio by name or by waveform by choosing from the Set Display Style pop-up menu in the Timeline window (refer to Figure 8-3).

✦ You can view changes in audio levels for the clip or the entire track by choosing Show Clip Volume or Show Track Volume in the Show Keyframes pop-up menu, as shown in Figure 8-4.

✦ You can view audio effect keyframes by choosing Show Clip Keyframes or Show Track Keyframes in the Show Keyframes pop-up menu (see Figure 8-4). The Show Keyframe mode also shows volume as an effect as well as other effects. Effects appear in a pop-up menu along the keyframe graph line.

As you work with audio in Premiere Pro, you'll encounter different types of audio tracks. The Standard audio track allows for either Mono or Stereo (two-channel sound). The other tracks available include the following:

✦ **Master track:** This displays keyframes and volume for the master track. You can mix sound from other tracks onto the master track using Premiere Pro's Audio Mixer.

✦ **Submix tracks:** These are mixed tracks used by the Audio Mixer to mix a subset of other audio tracks.

✦ **5.1 track:** 5.1 tracks are used in Dolby's Surround Sound. 5.1 tracks are used often for DVD movies in surround sound. In 5.1 sound, the left, right, and center channels are in front of the audience, with ambient sounds produced from two speakers behind. This is a total of five channels; the extra .1 channel is a subwoofer that produces sudden explosive-type sounds.

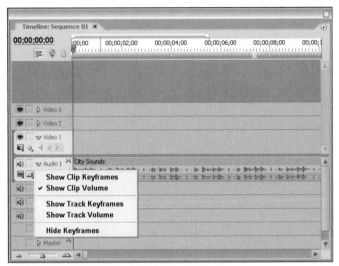

Figure 8-4: Choices from the Show Keyframes pop-up menu

Playing a Sound Clip

After you import a sound clip using Premiere Pro's standard File ⇨ Import command, you can play it in the Project panel or Monitor panel.

On the DVD-ROM

The DVD-ROM includes practice sound clips from Digital Vision's royalty-free CD Acoustic Chillout. The filename of the sound clip used in this chapter is 730009aw.wav. We renamed it citysounds to keep our files organized. You can locate the sound clip in the Chapter 8 folder on the *Adobe Premiere Pro 2 Bible* DVD-ROM. You can also use the audio clip used in Chapter 1 (705001.aif from Digital Visions NightMoves CD).

Here are the steps:

1. **Choose File ⇨ Import ⇨ File to import a sound file into your new project.**

2. **At this point, you can play the clip in the Project panel by clicking the Play button, as shown in Figure 8-5.** Alternatively, you can double-click the sound file in the Project window. The clip opens in the Source Monitor panel.

Play button

Figure 8-5: Click the Play button to play a clip in the Project window.

3. **If you opened the clip in the Source Monitor panel, you'll see the audio waveform in the Source Monitor.** Click the Source Monitor's Play button to play the clip.

Note   You can view the audio waveform of a video clip by choosing Audio Waveform in the Source Monitor panel menu.

Editing Audio

Depending upon your needs, you can take several approaches to editing audio in Premiere. You can slice the audio with the Razor tool in the Timeline as you edit video, clicking and dragging clips or clip edges as you work. If you need to work with the audio independently of the video, you can unlink the audio from the video. If you need to edit narration or sound effects, you can set in and out points for an audio clip in the Source Monitor. Premiere Pro also allows you to extract the audio from the video, so it appears in the Project panel as another content source. If you need to edit your audio more precisely, you can send an audio clip directly to Adobe Audition (if Audition is installed on your computer). When you edit the audio in Audition, the changes are reflected when you return to Premiere Pro. Finally, if you need to enhance, sweeten, or create transitions or audio effects, you can use the audio effects provided by Premiere Pro's Effects panel.

Using audio units

As you edit in the Monitor panels, the standard unit of measurement is the video frame. This is perfect for editing video where you can precisely set in or out points on a frame-by-frame basis. However, with audio, you may need more precision. For example, you may want to edit out an extraneous sound that is less than a frame long. Fortunately, Premiere Pro can display audio time in audio "units" as opposed to frames. You can view audio units in milliseconds or the smallest possible increment — the audio sample. These are your choices for working with audio units:

✦ To choose between milliseconds and audio samples, choose Project ➪ Project Settings ➪ General in the Audio Display Format drop-down menu, and then choose milliseconds or audio samples.

✦ To view the audio units in the time display sections of the Source or Program Monitor panels, choose Audio Units in the panel menu.

✦ To view audio units in the Timeline's time ruler and time display, choose Audio units in the Timeline's panel menu.

Editing audio on the Timeline

Although Premiere Pro is not a sophisticated audio-editing program, you can make simple edits in the Timeline panel. You can unlink audio from video and shift the audio so it accompanies a different section of audio. You can also execute audio edits by zooming into the audio clips waveform in the Timeline panel and slicing audio with the Razor tool. Here are the basic steps for setting up the timeline for audio editing:

1. **Click the Collapse/Expand button (the triangle in front of the audio track's name) to expand the audio track.**

2. **Click the Set Display Style icon in the Timeline, and choose Show Waveform.**

3. **Change units to audio samples by choosing Audio Units in the Timeline panel menu.** This changes the Timeline ruler display to audio units as either audio samples or milliseconds. (The default setting is audio samples; however, this can be changed by choosing Project ⇨ Project Settings and choosing Milliseconds in the Audio Section Display Format drop-down menu.)

4. **Zoom in by clicking and dragging toward the right on the Timeline zoom slider.** Figure 8-6 shows the ruler with audio units in view. Note that the time readout is shown in audio samples, and notice in the audio track how much audio exists between two adjacent video frames.

5. **Use editing tools to edit the audio.** You can also click and drag either clip edge to change in and out points. Or you can edit by activating the Razor tool in the Tools panel and clicking to slice the audio at a specific point.

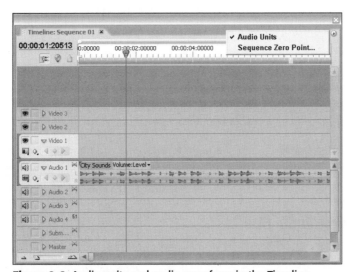

Figure 8-6: Audio units and audio waveform in the Timeline

Unlinking and linking

If you place a clip with audio in the Timeline, you can edit its audio separately from the video. To do this, you first need to unlink the audio from the video; then you can edit audio in and out points separate from the video. For example, you may want to create a *j-cut,* where audio begins playing before the next video scene, or an *l-cut,* where the audio extends over the next video scene. Follow these steps to unlink video from audio:

1. **Select the clip in the Timeline.**

2. **Unlink the clip by choosing Clip ⇨ Unlink (or you can right-click on either the audio or video clip and choose Unlink).**

3. **Deselect the audio and video tracks by clicking in an empty Timeline track.**

If you later want to re-link the audio and video, select the Audio and the Video and choose Clip ➪ Link.

> **Tip**   If you've edited two clips together and unlinked the audio, you can use the Rolling Edit tool to simultaneously adjust the out point of one audio clip and the in point of the next. The Rolling Edit tool can be helpful in creating j-cuts and l-cuts. Using the Rolling Edit tool is discussed in detail in Chapter 13.

Unlinking and resyncing audio

Premiere Pro provides a temporary method of unlinking audio and video. You can temporarily unlink audio and video by pressing Alt and then clicking and dragging on either the audio or video portion of the clip. When you release the mouse, the clips are considered linked, but are out of sync. If you use this temporary unlinking technique, Premiere Pro displays the out of sync frame difference at the in point of the clip on the Timeline. If you want to place the temporary unlinked clips back in sync, follow these steps:

1. Right-click the out of sync number at the in point of the clip.

2. ![Move into Sync / Slip into Sync menu] In the drop-down menu that appears, choose one of the following:

   - Choose Move into Sync to move the audio and video back into sync. Be aware that this can overwrite existing clips.

   - Choose Slip into Sync to sync the clips without moving them. This choice uses a slip edit to create a new sync point for the clip.

> **Note**   You can synchronize clips in multiple tracks to a clip in a target track by choosing Clip ➪ Synchronize. The Synchronize Clips dialog box allows you to synchronize clips at the start or end of a clip in the target track, at a numbered sequence marker, or by Timecode. See Chapter 13 for more information about using the Synchronize Clips command.

Linking multiple audio files

If you're working with multiple audio tracks that play simultaneously with video, you can link them all together. Later, if you need to apply effects, all tracks appear in the Effect Controls panel where you can selectively choose to which tracks you want to apply the effects. Here's how to link multiple audio tracks:

1. **Place the audio into separate audio tracks.**

2. **Select the tracks by Shift-clicking the audio to be linked. Note that you cannot mix track types. For example, you cannot link a stereo to a mono track.**

3. **Choose Edit ➪ Link.**

Later, if you need to unlink, select one of the linked tracks and choose Edit ➪ Unlink.

Editing source clips

Although you may find that editing audio in the Timeline meets most of your needs, you can also an audio clip's in and out points in the Source Monitor. You can also use the Source monitor to create subclips from one long audio clip, and then edit the subclips individually in the Source Monitor or in the Timeline. (As discussed in Chapter 6, you create a subclip by setting in and out points in the Source Monitor, selecting it in the Source monitor, and then choosing Clip ➪ Make Subclip. Alternatively, you can drag the edited clip from the Source Monitor into an empty area of the Project panel.)

Taking audio only

When editing a clip with audio and video, you may find that you want to use the audio without the video. If you choose Take Audio in the Source Monitor, the video image is replaced by the audio's waveform. Follow these steps to take audio only and set in and outpoints in the Source Monitor:

1. **Drag the video clip to the Source Monitor window, or double-click it in the Project panel.**

2. **Click the Toggle Take Audio and Video button, and choose the Take Audio icon. Alternatively, you can choose Take Audio in the Source Monitor panel menu.** The audio waveform for the clip appears in the Source Monitor as shown in Figure 8-7.

3. **Use the Set In Point and Set Out Point icons to edit the clip.** To set in and out points, in the Source Monitor, you can use the same techniques used for video. You can click and drag the current-time indicator, use the scrubbing bar, or press the left or right arrow keys on your keyboard. As you reposition the current-time indicator, Premiere Pro plays the audio. Click the Set In Point button. Move the current-time indicator to the out point and click the Set Out Point button.

4. **If you want to change or choose a target track for the audio, click the left track edge to select it.**

5. **To place the edited audio into the target track, set the current-time indicator in the Timeline to where you want to place the audio and then click the Insert or Overlay button in the Source Monitor panel.**

Figure 8-7: Audio waveform in the Source Monitor

Tip   If the display in the Source Monitor is set to Audio Units, use the Step Back or Step Forward button (or press the left or right arrow key) to step through the audio one audio unit at a time.

Tip   You can add an Audio In point and Audio Out point column to the Project panel. Choose Edit Columns in the Project panel menu, and then select Audio In point and Audio Outpoint in the Edit Columns dialog box.

Extracting audio from video

If you want to separate audio from its video so you can work with it as a separate media source in the Project panel, you can have Premiere strip the audio from the video. To create a new audio .wav file from a video clip that includes audio, select a clip or multiple clips in the Project window and then choose Clip ➪ Audio Options ➪ Extract Audio. The .wav file then appears in the Project panel.

Editing in Adobe Audition

If you have Adobe Audition installed on your computer, your best bet for tuning audio is to send your Premier audio clips to Audition for a quick visit. After you edit the clip in Audition, the changes are reflected in Premiere Pro. To edit a clip in Audition, select an audio clip or video clip that includes audio in the Project window and then choose Edit ➪ Edit in Audition. Alternatively, right-click the clip in the Timeline and then choose Edit in Audition. After you save the changes in Audition, the changes appear when you return to Premiere Pro.

Mapping audio channels

As you work with audio, you may want to disable one channel from a stereo track or select a mono audio clip and convert it into to one stereo clip. All these feats can be accomplished using Premiere's Source Channel Mapping command. Here are the steps to remap audio:

1. **Select an audio clip in the Project panel that hasn't previously been placed in a sequence on the Timeline.** If you want to select more than one clip, click the other clip while holding down the Shift key.

2. **Choose Clip ➪ Audio Options ➪ Source Channel Mappings.**

3. **In the Source Channel Mappings dialog box, shown in Figure 8-8, select the track format: Mono, stereo, Mono as Stereo, or 5.1 audio.** If you want to disable a Source channel, deselect it in the Enable column.

4. **Preview the sound by clicking the triangle at the bottom of the dialogue box.**

5. **Click OK to remap the sound.**

Tip   If you want to simply make separate mono tracks from a stereo track, select the audio in the Project panel and choose Clip ➪ Audio Options ➪ Breakout to Mono. Two audio subclips are added to the Project panel.

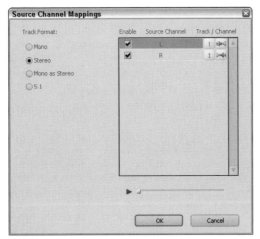

Figure 8-8: Remap audio tracks in the Source Channel Mappings dialog box.

Gaining, Fading, and Balancing

One of the most common sound effects is to slowly fade in audio at the beginning of a clip and fade out at the end. You can easily accomplish this in Premiere Pro by setting keyframes on the keyframe graph line that appears when you choose Show Clip Volume in the Audio Tracks Display pop-up menu. You can also change the balance of a sound in a stereo channel. When you balance, you redistribute sound, removing a percentage of the sound information from one channel and adding it to the other. Premiere Pro also allows you to pan to create sounds that appear to come from different areas of a room. To pan, you alter a mono track when outputting to a multi-channel master or submix track.

You can also change the entire volume of a sound clip by using Premiere Pro's Gain command. The following sections show you how to adjust audio gain, fade audio in and out, and balance stereo channels.

Normalizing and adjusting gain

The Gain command enables you to change the sound level of an entire clip by raising or lowering audio gain in decibels. Generally in audio recording, engineers raise or lower gain during recording. If sound levels dip, the engineer "riding the gain" raises the gain; if the levels go too high, he or she can lower the gain. Premiere's Gain command also allows you to click one button to normalize audio. This raises the level of the clip as high as possible without distortion. Normalizing is often an efficient technique of ensuring that audio levels remain constant throughout a production. Here's how to use the Premiere Pro Gain command, which adjusts the uniform volume of the clip:

1. **Choose File ➪ Import to import a sound clip or a video clip with sound.**

2. **Click the clip in the Project panel, or drag the sound clip from the Project panel to an audio track in the Timeline panel.**

3. **If the clip is in the Timeline, click the sound clip in the audio track in the Timeline panel.**

4. **Choose Clip ➪ Audio Options ➪ Audio Gain.** The Clip Gain dialog box appears as shown in Figure 8-9.

Figure 8-9: Use the Clip Gain dialog box to adjust audio gain for an entire clip.

5. **Type a value in the field in the Clip Gain dialog box.** The 0 setting is the original clip volume in decibels. A number greater than 0 increases the sound volume of the clip. A number less than 0 decreases the volume. If you click Normalize, Premiere Pro sets the maximum gain possible without audio distortion. Distortion can occur when an audio signal is too high, and it can result in distortion.

Tip   Click and drag the mouse over the dB value in the Clip Gain dialog box to increase or decrease audio gain. Clicking and dragging right increases the dB value; clicking and dragging left decreases it.

Fading sound

Premiere Pro provides a variety of options for fading in or out a clip's volume. You can fade a clip in or out and change its volume using the Volume audio effect in the Effect Controls panel, or you can fade a clip in or out by applying a crossfade audio transition to the beginning or end of the clip. As shown in the following steps, you can also change volume using the Pen or Selection tool to create keyframes in the Timeline. After the keyframes are set, you can adjust volume by clicking and dragging the keyframe graph line.

When you fade sound, you can choose to fade the track's volume or a clip's volume. Note, however that if you apply volume keyframes to a track (rather than a clip) and delete the audio in the track, the keyframes still remain in the track. If you apply keyframes to a clip and delete the clip, the keyframes are deleted as well.

Follow these steps to fade volume:

1. **Choose File ➪ Import ➪ File to import a sound clip or a video clip with sound.**

2. **Drag the sound clip from the Project panel to an audio track in the Timeline panel.**

3. **Expand the audio track, and choose Show Track Volume or Show Clip Volume from the Show Keyframes drop-down menu (refer to Figure 8-4).** A yellow graph line now appears in the middle of the audio track.

Note   You can also choose Show Clip Keyframes or Show Track Keyframes from the Show Keyframes drop-down menu. This causes a Volume drop-down menu to appear in the track. When Volume is selected in the drop-down menu, you can adjust volume in the keyframes graph line.

4. **If the Tools panel is not open, open it by choosing Window ➪ Show Tools.**

5. **Activate the Selection tool, or select the Pen tool in the Tool panel.**

6. **Set the current-time indicator to the Timeline location where you want the fade to end.**

7. **Move the Pen or Selection tool to the point where you want the fade to end. Then press Ctrl (a plus sign appears), while you click in the graph line to create a keyframe.** This keyframe icon serves as a placeholder for the sound to stay at 100 percent of its volume at the middle of the sound clip.

Note You can also create a keyframe by clicking the Add/Remove keyframe button on the left side of the track. When applying keyframes to clips, select the clip before clicking the Add/Remove keyframe button.

8. **Move the Pen or Selection tool to the beginning of the clip, and create another keyframe there by Ctrl-clicking.**

9. **Drag the handle at the beginning of the graph line downward.** This makes the audio clip fade in. Dragging it upward increases the sound. As you click and drag, a tiny readout shows the current Timeline position and the change in decibels. Figure 8-10 shows the Timeline with the adjusted volume keyframes.

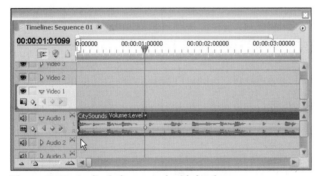

Figure 8-10: Audio fade created with keyframes

10. **To create a fade-out, repeat the preceding steps to create a keyframe at the end of the clip and a few seconds before the end of the clip. Drag the keyframe at the end of the graph line downward to make the audio clip fade-out.**

If desired, you can use the Pen or Selection tool to add more keyframes to the graph line. Adding more keyframes to the graph line enables you to fade a sound clip into different sections within the clip.

Note You can adjust overall volume for a clip or a track by showing track volume, and then clicking and dragging a track's volume graph line up or down with the Pen or Selection tool.

Creating a curve fade line

The previous example illustrates a linear fade, where the fade is created in a diagonal line. A curve fade line can produce a faster fade in or fade with less time spent at lower sound levels. The resulting fade is less likely to display noise inhabiting lower sound levels.

To create a curve on the Timeline keyframe line, follow these steps:

1. **Create at least two keyframes on the Keyframe line by Ctrl-clicking with either the Selection tool or the Pen tool.**

2. **Move the cursor over one of the keyframes and press Ctrl. When the cursor changes to a V-shaped symbol, click the mouse.** A small blue line appears.

3. **To create the curve, click and drag the blue line.** As you drag, a curve forms between the two keyframes.

If you later want to remove the curve, simply Ctrl-click on the keyframe handle and the smooth "corner" changes to a sharp corner.

Removing keyframes

As you edit audio in the Timeline, you may want to remove keyframes. The easiest way to do so is to have Premiere Pro jump to the specific keyframe and then click the Add/Remove Keyframe button in the Timeline. Here's how to remove a keyframe from an audio track in a sequence:

1. **Move the current-time indicator in front of the keyframe that you want to remove.**

2. **Click the Go to Next Keyframe button in the Timeline.**

3. **Click the Add/Remove keyframe button.** The keyframe is removed.

Tip   You can also delete a keyframe by clicking it, and then pressing Delete; or you can right-click it and choose Delete from the drop-down menu.

Balancing stereo in the Timeline

Premiere Pro enables you to adjust stereo channel balance in a stereo track. When you balance a stereo track, you redistribute the sound from one track to another. When balancing, as you add volume to one track, you subtract it from the other. Although balancing is also covered in Chapter 9, we include it here also because you can accomplish it simply in the Timeline panel.

Here's how to balance a stereo track:

1. **Expand the audio track if it isn't already expanded.**

2. **Choose Show Track Keyframes from the Show Keyframes drop-down menu at the head of the track.** A Volume drop-down menu appears in the track.

3. **In the Volume drop-down menu, choose Panner.** In the Panner drop-down menu, choose Balance, as shown in Figure 8-11.

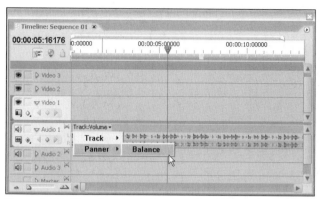

Figure 8-11: Choosing the Balance audio effect in the Timeline panel

4. **If the Selection tool is not selected, select it in the Tools panel.**

5. **To adjust stereo levels, click and drag with the Selection tool on the track keyframe graph line. (You can also use the Pen tool.)** If you want to set keyframes, Ctrl-click and drag to adjust the balance.

Creating Transitions Using Audio Effects

Premiere Pro's Audio Effects bin in the Effects panel provides audio effects and audio transitions that enable you to enhance and correct audio. The effects provided in the Audio Effects folder are similar to many found in professional audio studios.

To display the Effects window, as shown in Figure 8-12, choose Window ⇨ Effects. When the Effects panel opens, note that it includes folders for Mono, Stereo, and 5.1 tracks. In addition, note that the Audio Effects bin also includes audio transitions. To view the effects in the transitions or any other bin, click the triangle in front of the bin.

Creating bins in the Effects panel

In a project, you may need to apply effects that are in different bins again and again. If so, you may want to eliminate some unnecessary mouse clicks by creating a bin and placing these effects into it. To create a new bin, click the New Custom Bin icon at the bottom of the Effects panel, or choose New Custom Bin from the Effects panel menu. Premiere Pro adds the bin, naming it "Custom Bin" and assigning it a number. If you want to rename it, simply double-click the words Custom Bin and enter a new name. To populate the bin with effects, simply click and drag your favorite effects into it. Premiere Pro puts a copy of the effect into the new bin.

If you want to delete the bin or an effect within the bin, simply click it and click the Trash icon at the bottom of the panel. You can also right-click the item you wish to delete, and choose Delete from the drop-down menu.

Figure 8-12: The Effects panel includes audio transitions and audio effects.

Applying audio transitions

The Effects panel's Audio Transitions folder provides two crossfade effects that allow you to fade in and fade out audio. Premiere Pro provides two varieties of transitions: Constant Gain and Constant Power. Constant Power, the default audio transition, produces an effect that should sound like a gradual fading in and out to the human ear. Constant Gain produces a mathematical fade-in and fade-out.

Typically, crossfades are applied to create a smooth transition between two audio clips. However, when using Premiere Pro, you can place a crossfade transition at the front of an audio clip to create a fade-in or at the tail end of the audio clip to create a fade-out.

Note   Before creating a transition you must make sure that the Show Track/Clip keyframes pop-up menu is not set to Show Track Keyframes or Show Track Volume. Otherwise, you will not be able to apply a transition.

Here are the steps for creating an audio transition:

1. **Place two audio clips so that they are next to each other on the Timeline.**

2. **Open the Effects panel by choosing Window ⇨ Effects.**

3. **Open the Audio Transitions bin by clicking the small triangle to the left of the folder.**

4. **Open the Crossfade bin by clicking the small triangle to the left of the bin.**

5. **Drag the crossfade and drop it between the two clips in the audio track.** Don't worry if the transition does not drop directly over the middle of the two clips. You see the transition icon in the Timeline.

6. **If the Effect Controls panel is not open, chooseWindow ⇨ Effect Controls, or double-click the transition in the Timeline.**

7. **To center the transition between the two clips, choose Center at Cut from the Alignment drop-down menu in the Effect Controls panel, as shown in Figure 8-13.**

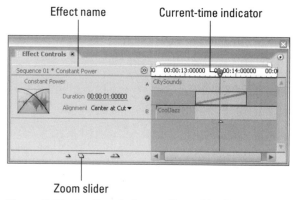

Effect name   Current-time indicator

Zoom slider

Figure 8-13: The Crossfade transition with Alignment set to Center at Cut

8. **To change the duration of the transition, click and drag either end of the transition icon or edit the time display in the Effect Controls window.**

Tip

The default audio transition duration can be set by altering the Default Audio Transition Duration setting found in the General Preferences dialog box. Choose Edit ⇨ Preferences ⇨ General. You can also change the default duration by choosing Default Transition Duration in the Effects panel menu.

9. **To play the transition, in the Effect Controls panel, set the current-time indicator before the transition and press the spacebar.**

Using the default audio transition

If you know that you will be using the same audio transition again and again, you can easily apply it using Premiere Pro's Apply Audio Transition command. If you want to set the default audio transition, select the transition in the Effects panel, and then choose Set Selected as Default Transition.

Follow these steps to apply the default audio transition:

1. **Place two audio clips so that they are next to each other in a track in the Timeline.**

2. **Select the left edge of the track to set it as the target track.**

3. Move the current-time indicator between the two audio clips.

4. Choose Sequence ➪ Apply Audio Transition.

Fading in and out using a crossfade transition

Earlier in this chapter, you saw how to manually create fade-in and fade-out effects using keyframes in the Timeline. You can also create a fade-in or fade-out by using a crossfade transition. Here's how to create a fade-in using a crossfade transition:

1. Drag a crossfade transition to the front of the in point of the audio clip.

2. In the Effect Controls panel, choose Start at Cut from the Alignment pop-up menu.

Here's how to create a fade-out using a crossover transition:

1. Drag a crossfade transition to the back of the out point of the audio clip.

2. In the Effect Controls window, choose End at Cut from the Alignment drop-down menu.

Applying an audio effect

Like transitions, you access audio effects from the Effects panel, and you can adjust them using controls in the Effect Controls panel. To display the Effect Controls panel, shown in Figure 8-14, choose Window ➪ Show Effect Controls.

To apply an audio effect to an audio clip, follow these steps:

1. Select the audio clip in the Timeline panel. If the clip is linked to video, unlink it by choosing Clip ➪ Unlink.

2. Select the effect in the Effects panel, either drag it into the Effect Controls panel or drag it over the audio in the audio track in the Timeline, and release the mouse.

Most audio effects provide settings that allow you to fine-tune them. If an audio effect provides settings that can be adjusted, the settings appear in the Effect Controls panel when the effect is expanded. To expand/collapse the effect, click the triangle in front of the effect's name.

You can adjust the effect in the Effect Controls panel either by dragging the sliders in the panel or by entering a value into a control's field. In Figure 8-12, the slider allows you to change the decibel level for the Volume effect. The panel also features a Play button, enabling you to play the sound.

Note   Volume is called a fixed effect because you do not need to drag it from the Effects panel. Other effects, called Standard effects, must be dragged over a clip or into the Effect Controls panel.

You delete an audio effect (other than the fixed Volume effect) from the Effects panel by right-clicking its name and choosing Clear from the pop-up menu. If you want to prevent an effect from playing, essentially turning it off, then click the *f* button next to the effect's name. To turn the effect back on, click the *f* again.

Cross-Reference   Audio effects can also be applied to audio tracks from Premiere Pro's Audio Mixer window. See Chapter 9 for details.

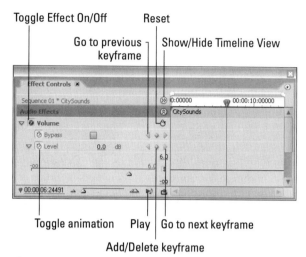

Figure 8-14: You can adjust audio effects in the Effect Controls panel.

Applying an audio effect over time

If you want to change the settings of an effect as an audio clip plays, you need to apply an effect over time and set keyframes where you want to make a change. A *keyframe* stores the effect at a specific point on the effects graph line in the Timeline in the Effect Controls panel.

To apply an audio effect over time, you should have a project open containing an audio clip in an audio track. If don't have an audio clip, use the audio clip in this chapter's folder in the Premiere Pro DVD, and try out a simple effect, such as Treble or Bass.

Then follow these steps:

1. **If the Effect Controls panel is not open, choose Window ⇨ Show Effect Controls to display the Effect Controls panel.** If the Effects panel is not open, choose Window ⇨ Show Effects.

2. **Select the clip in the Timeline to which you want to apply the effect.**

3. **Open the Audio Effects bin in the Effects folder by double-clicking it or by clicking the right-pointing triangle to the left of the bin.**

4. **Open a bin corresponding to the selected audio track (for example: Stereo) by double-clicking it or by clicking the triangle next to the bin name.**

5. **Drag an audio effect from the bin to the Effect Controls panels, or drop the effect over the clip.** (If you drop the effect over a clip, you don't need to select it first.)

6. **If Effect Controls panel's Timeline is not visible, click the Show/Hide Timeline View button.**

Note

If the Effect Controls panel's Timeline doesn't appear, the panel is not wide enough to display it. Click and drag on the right edge of the panel to widen it, and then click the Show/Hide Timeline View button.

7. **Turn on keyframe mode by clicking the Stopwatch icon.** The Add/Delete Keyframe button appears in the Effect Controls panel.

8. **Now click and drag the current-time indicator in the Effect Controls panel to a new position.**

9. **Adjust a setting for the effect in the Effect Controls panel.** This creates a keyframe.

10. **If needed, repeat the previous step to create new keyframes.** Figure 8-15 shows the Timeline in the Effect Controls window with various keyframes.

As you create keyframes, you can manipulate them and create curves using the same techniques used when working with keyframes in the Timeline. For example, you can also click and drag up or down on the keyframe graph line. You can Ctrl-click with the Selection or Pen tool on a keyframe in the graph line and drag it to create a curved line. You can also right-click on a keyframe above the graph line in the Effect Controls panel and choose Ease In or Ease Out in the drop-down menu (this changes the keyframe into a Bezier keyframe). For more information about editing effects in the Effects panel, see Chapter 14.

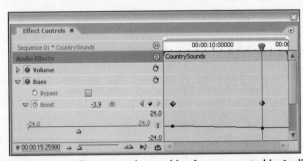

Figure 8-15: Effect Controls panel keyframes created in Audio Effects

11. **To delete a keyframe, move the current-time indicator over the keyframe that you want to delete, or click the Next or Previous Keyframe button and then click the Add/Delete Keyframes button. (You can also press Backspace on your keyboard.)**

12. **To play the effect, click the Play button in the Effect Controls panel.**

If you want to delete all keyframes for one of an effect's controls, click the Stopwatch icon for that control. To delete all effects for a clip, choose Delete All Effects from Clip in the Effect Controls panel menu.

You can copy and paste keyframes in the Effect Controls panel. First, select the keyframe or keyframes that you want to copy, and then move the current-timeline indicator in the Effect Control panel to where you want the keyframe or keyframes to appear. Then choose Edit ➪ Paste. Note also that you can select another clip before pasting the keyframes. If you need to view more of the Timeline in the Effect Controls panel, de-select Pin to Clip in the Effect Controls panel menu, and then widen the panel or scroll using the horizontal scroll bar.

Premiere Pro's audio effects

Premiere's audio effects provide an assortment of effects that can help you improve sound quality or create unusual sound effects. The following sections provide a review of Premiere Pro's audio effects. Because many effects from the Stereo bin also reside in the Mono and 5.1 folders, our audio effects overview is based on the contents of the Stereo folder. As you read through the overview of each effect, try them out. Remember that after you apply an audio effect, you can listen to it by clicking the Play button n the Effect Controls window.

In order to help you apply audio effects while you're working on a project, we grouped them according to functionality. We've based the effects groupings similarly to how audio effects are organized in Adobe Audition.

Note
Premiere Pro's audio effects conform to the Steinberg VST (Virtual Studio Technology) plug-in standard. This means that third-party VST audio effects can be applied from within Premiere Pro. They also appear in the Effects window with other plug-ins.

Amplitude

Amplitude measures the size of the sound wave. Effects that control Amplitude generally produce a change in volume or the balance among audio channels.

Balance

Balance changes the volume of the left and right stereo channels in a stereo clip. A positive number adds to the right channel and subtracts from the left. Negative values subtract from the right channel and add volume to the left. The controls for Balance are shown in Figure 8-16.

Figure 8-16: Balance audio effect options

Channel Volume

Use the Channel Volume effect to adjust channel volume in stereo or 5.1 clips or tracks. Unlike Balance, Channel Volume adjusts channels independently of other channels.

Fill Left

Fill Left copies the audio in the left stereo channel and fills the right channel with it — replacing the previous audio in the channel.

Fill Right

The Fill Right effect copies the audio in the right channel and fills the left channel with it — replacing the previous audio in the channel.

Swap Channels

This effect swaps or exchanges left and right channels in stereo tracks.

Volume

Use the Volume effect instead of Premiere's *fixed* Volume effect when you want to have volume rendered first. If you use Premiere's fixed volume effect, volume is rendered after other standard effects applied in the Effect Controls panel.

The Volume effect prevents distortion by preventing clipping when you increase volume. Increase volume with positive values, and decrease volume with negative values.

Delay effects

Delay effects pick repeat and play back sound after a delay. Although some delay effects repeat a sound or a word, others can transform the sound to seemingly bounce around a large room or echo through the Grand Canyon. A commonly used delay effect is Reverb, which creates room tone effects by simulating multiple sounds waves bouncing in a room.

Delay

Use Delay to create an echo effect that occurs after the time entered in the Delay field. Feedback is a percentage of the audio that is popped back into the delay. Use the Feedback option to create a series of delaying echoes. Use the Mix option to specify how much echo occurs in the effect.

Multitap Delay

The Multitap Delay Settings dialog box enables you to use four delays or taps (a *tap* is a delay effect) to control the overall delay effect. Use Delay 1 through Delay 4 controls to set the time of the delay. To create multiple delaying effects, use the Feedback 1 through Feedback 4 controls. The feedback controls add a percentage of the delayed signal back into the delay. Use the mix field to control the percentage of delayed to non-delayed echo.

Reverb

Reverberation refers to sound waves bouncing off an interior space. Reverb effects are commonly applied to simulate the sound or acoustics of a room. Thus, you can use Reverb to add ambience and a sense of humanity to dry electronic sound. Figure 8-17 shows the Reverb controls. Notice that a pop-up menu allows you to automatically generate settings for specific environments. Note that you can also control the effect by clicking and dragging the figures in the room area of the effect display. These choices are available in the Reverb panel:

✦ **PreDelay:** Use this control to simulate the time it takes for sound to hit a wall and bounce back to the audience.

✦ **Absorption:** Use to set sound absorption. This effect simulates a room that absorbs sound.

✦ **Size:** Use to set room size in percentage. The larger the percentage, the larger the room is.

✦ **Density:** Use to set the size or density of the "tail" of the reverberation.

✦ **Lo Damp:** Use to set low-frequency dampening.

✦ **Hi Damp:** Use to set high-frequency dampening.

✦ **Mix:** Use to set how much reverb effect is added to the sound.

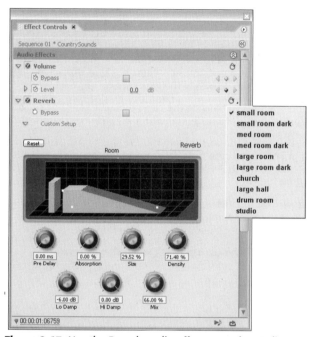

Figure 8-17: Use the Reverb audio effect controls to adjust room tone.

Filters

Filter effects are used to improve and restore sound by providing adjustments to specific frequencies. Thus, if you want to adjust just the bass or treble frequency of a sound, you could use the Bass or Treble filter to hone into the sound and raise or lower just the high or low frequency. Some filters, such as Notch, are used to filter out hiss and other noise from sounds.

Bandpass

Use the Bandpass filter to remove frequencies beyond a frequency band. The Center field indicates the center of the frequency band to keep. The Q settings indicate the frequency band range you want to preserve. To create a wide range of frequencies to preserve, use a low setting; to preserve a narrow band of frequencies, use a high setting.

Bass

Use the Bass filter to adjust lower frequencies (200 Hz and below). Use the Boost option to raise or lower decibels.

Treble

Use the Treble effect to adjust higher frequencies (4000 Hz and above). Use the Boost slider to adjust the effect. Dragging right increases the amount in decibels; dragging left decreases it.

Dynamics

The Dynamics effect provides a diverse set of options that can be used to adjust audio as shown in Figure 8-18.

✦ **AutoGate:** This option shuts the gate on unwanted audio signals. It removes the unwanted signal when its level drops below the dB setting for the Threshold control. When the signal goes beyond the Threshold, the Attack option determines the time interval for the gate to open. If the signal goes beyond the Threshold, the Release option determines the time interval for the gate to close. When the signal drops below the Threshold, the Hold time determines how long the gate stays open.

✦ **Compressor:** This option attempts to balance the clip's dynamic range by boosting soft sound levels and decreasing loud sound levels (*dynamic range* is the range from the highest level to the lowest level).

✦ **Expander:** This option produces a subtle AutoGate effect by dropping signals that are below the Threshold setting to the Ratio setting. A ratio setting of 2:1 would expand the decrease from 1 dB to 2 dB.

✦ **Limiter:** This option allows you to level out audio peaks to reduce clipping. Use the Threshold option to adjust the maximum signal level. Use the Release option to set the time necessary for gain to drop to its normal level after clipping.

✦ **SoftClip:** Like Limiter, SoftClip also reduces clipping when signals peak.

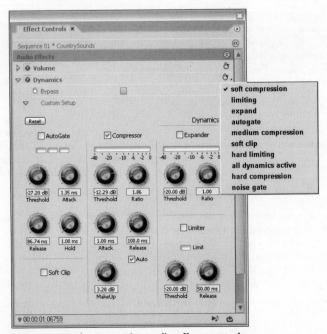

Figure 8-18: The Dynamics audio effect controls

EQ

EQ effects cut or boost specific frequency ranges. The EQ effect serves as a *parametric equalizer.* These equalizers allow you to precisely focus your audio corrections on specific frequencies. EQ controls frequency, bandwidth (called Q), and level using several bands: low, middle, and high. Figure 8-19 shows the EQ audio effect controls. Here is a summary of the controls:

✦ **Frequency:** Increases or decreases frequency between 20 and 2000 Hz.

✦ **Gain:** Adjusts the gain between –20 and 20 dB.

✦ **Cut:** Switches the low and high bands from a shelving filter that can boost or lower part of a signal to a cutoff filter, which excludes or cuts offs the signal at specified frequencies.

✦ **Q:** Specifies filter width between 0.05 and 5.0 octaves. This specifies the spectrum over which EQ adjustments are made.

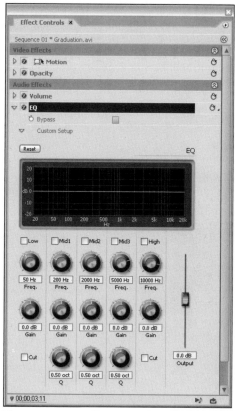

Figure 8-19: EQ effect controls

Notch

Use the Notch filter to remove hum and other extraneous "noises." Use the Center control to set the frequency that you want to exclude. Use the Q setting to control the bandwidth of the frequency.

Highpass

Use Highpass to remove frequencies above the Cutoff frequency.

Invert

Use Invert to invert the audio phase of each channel.

Lowpass

Use Lowpass to remove frequencies below the Cutoff frequency.

MultibandCompressor

Compressors are used to smooth out sound variations and maintain consistent volume

Use the MultibandCompressor, shown in Figure 8-20, for compressing sounds according to three bands that correspond to low-mid-high frequencies. Adjust the handles for controlling gain and frequency range. Use Band Select to select a band and Crossover Frequency to change the frequency range for the selected band. MultibandCompressor produces a softer effect than the Dynamics audio effect. This can apply to an individual stereo track.

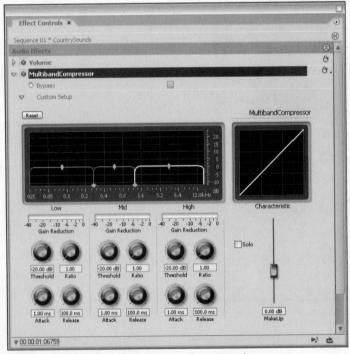

Figure 8-20: MultibandCompressor effect controls

Parametric EQ

Parametric EQ allows you to boost or lower frequency near a specified Center frequency. Use the Center control to set the frequency. Use the Q control to set the range of frequency (band-width) that you want to affect. A high setting affects a wide range; a low setting affects a low range. The Boost control allows you to specify how many decibels you want to boost or lower the frequency range — between –20 and 20 dB.

Restoration

Restoration effects are filter effects that restore audio. Some such as DeNoiser can be used to remove audio noise.

DeEsser

DeEsser removes "sss," or sibilant sounds that can occur in narration and singing. Use the Gain control to set the level of "SSS" reduction. Use the Male and Female controls to set DeEsser to remove the "SSS" based upon Male and Female voice frequencies.

DeHummer

The DeHummer effect removes hum from audio. The hum removal range is from 50 Hz (often found in European and Japanese audio) to 60 Hz, the frequency often found in the United States and Canada. Use the Reduction control to set the level of hum reduction. Adjust the Frequency setting to specify the center of the hum frequency range. The filter applies the DeHummer to harmonic frequencies that are multiples of the DeHummer Frequency setting.

DeNoiser

Use the DeNoiser effect to automatically remove noise from audio. Figure 8-21 shows the DeNoiser audio effect controls. In the Custom Setup area, you can click and drag the knob icons to adjust the effect. To set keyframes, use the Individual Parameters section.

- ✦ **Noisefloor:** This setting indicates the noise floor in decibels when the clip plays.
- ✦ **Freeze:** Click Freeze to halt the Noisefloor readout at its current decibel level.
- ✦ **Reduction:** Click and drag to indicate how much noise to remove. The range is –20 to 0 dB.
- ✦ **Offset:** This control sets an offset value or range for denoising between the Noisefloor and the values from –10 and +10 dB.

Pitch

Pitch effects change pitch. They often are used to change the pitch of a narrator or vocalist.

PitchShifter

As its name suggests, you can use the PitchShifter effect to alter pitch, particularly when you want to produce a change in voice. As you might expect, playing with pitches can also pro-duce special effects, particularly if you want your narrator to sound as if he or she is from outer space.

Use the Pitch control to alter pitch in semitones. Fine-tune the effect with the Finetune control. FormantPreserve prevents high-pitched voices from sounding like cartoon characters by preventing PitchShifter from altering formants (a *formant* is a resonant frequency). Try recording yourself singing with the Audio Mixer, and see whether the pitch shifter can put you back on key.

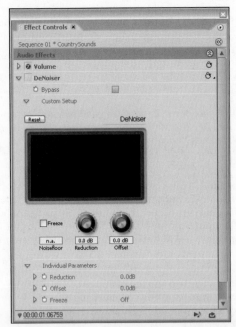

Figure 8-21: The DeNoiser audio effect controls

Exporting Sound Files

After you've edited and refined your audio tracks, you may want to export them as separate sound files so that they can be used in other software programs or other Premiere Pro projects. When you export a sound clip, you can export it in a variety of formats, such as Windows Waveform (.wav), QuickTime (.mov), Microsoft AVI (.avi). Follow these steps for exporting an audio file from Premiere Pro:

1. **Select the audio track with the audio clip you want to export by clicking the left edge of the Track.**

2. **Choose File ➪ Export ➪ Audio.** The Export Audio dialog box appears.

3. **Type a name for your audio file.**

4. **Click the Settings button.**

5. **In the Export Audio Settings dialog box General section, set the File Type drop-down menu to Windows Waveform, QuickTime, or the AVI choice.** You can set the Range drop-down menu to be either the entire sequence or only the work area.

6. **If you want to be able to open the project file by choosing File ⇨ Edit Original in another Adobe application, leave the Embedding Options choice set to Project;** otherwise choose None.

7. **Click the Audio listing to choose Sample Rate, Sample type, and Channels (for instance: Stereo or Mono).**

8. **If you want to compress the exported audio, choose from the Compressor drop-down menu.** Compressor choices are discussed in Chapter 22. Note that some applications do not support compressed audio.

9. **For most standard hard disks, leave the Interleave setting to 1/2 or 1 frame.** Higher settings consume more RAM. The interleave settings controls how often audio is slipped in between video frames.

10. **Click OK to close the dialog box.**

11. **Click Save to save audio file.**

Summary

Premiere Pro provides numerous features for adjusting and editing audio. You can control fade-ins and fade-outs in the Timeline panel. You can adjust and create professional audio effects using Premiere Pro's audio effects and transitions. This chapter covered these topics:

✦ You can edit audio in the Timeline with the Razor and Selection tools.

✦ In and out points for audio can be set in the Source Monitor panel.

✦ Using keyframes, you can fade in and fade out and adjust the volume of audio clips.

✦ You can adjust audio gain by choosing Clip ⇨ Audio Options ⇨ Gain.

✦ Use Premiere Pro's audio transitions to create crossfades.

✦ Use the effects in the Premiere Pro Effects panel to enhance and correct audio.

✦   ✦   ✦

Mixing and Creating Effects with the Audio Mixer

Creating the perfect blend of music, narration, and effects is certainly an audio art. The audio engineer who blends or mixes various tracks together into a master track must have a deft touch and sensitive ear. Music and narration can't be overpowering; sound effects must sound real. Mixing these together at the perfect sound levels produces audio that truly enhances the accompanying video.

In a recording studio, engineers use a mixing console to control the mixing of music tracks. In Premiere Pro, you can create a mix using its Audio Mixer. Using the Premiere Pro Audio Mixer, you can mix sound from a maximum of five tracks onto a master track, or you can apply effects to several tracks at once using a submix track, which can also be routed into the master track. Like a professional mixer, Premiere Pro allows you to adjust audio levels, fade in and fade out, balance stereo, control effects, and create effects "sends." Premiere Pro's Audio Mixer also allows you to record audio and isolate and listen to one "solo" track even while others play. You can even use it to add and adjust many of the audio effects found in the Effects panel.

This chapter provides a thorough look at the Audio Mixer and how to use it. After touring the Audio Mixer panel, this chapter covers the Audio Mixer's Automation settings, which allow you to adjust audio while it plays. After you learn how to create a mix, you then learn to balance and pan audio, add effects, and create submixes.

Audio Mixer Tour

Premiere Pro's Audio Mixer is undoubtedly one of its most complex and versatile utilities. To use it efficiently, you should become familiar with all its controls and functionality. If the Audio Mixer isn't open onscreen, open it by choosing Window ➪ Audio Mixer. If you would like to open the Audio Mixer in Premiere Pro's Audio Workspace, choose Window ➪ Workspace ➪ Audio. When the Audio Mixer, shown in Figure 9-1, opens onscreen, it automatically shows at least two tracks and the master track for the current active sequence. If you have more than two audio tracks in the sequence, click and drag the lower-right corner of the Audio Mixer panel to extend the panel.

Although the sight of so many knobs and levels probably wouldn't intimidate an audio engineer, you must understand and slowly examine the buttons and features. Note that the Audio Mixer offers two major views: the collapsed view (refer to Figure 9-1), which does not show the effects area, and the expanded view, which shows effects for the different tracks. To switch from one view to another, click the small triangle to the left of Audio track 1.

Note   The Audio Mixer shows only the current active sequence's audio tracks. If you want to show tracks from different sequences in the Audio Mixer panel simultaneously, you must nest the sequences in the current active sequence. Chapter 6 covers how to nest one sequence into another.

To become familiar with the Audio Mixer, start by examining the track area of the Audio Mixer. The vertical areas headed by Audio 1, Audio 2, and so on correspond to the tracks on the active sequence. When you are mixing, you can see audio levels in the displays in each track column and make adjustments using the controls in each column. As you make adjustments, the audio is mixed or blended together into a master track or submix track. Note that the drop-down menu at the bottom of each track indicates whether the current track signal is being sent to a submix track or the master track. By default, all tracks are output to the master track (refer to Figure 9-1).

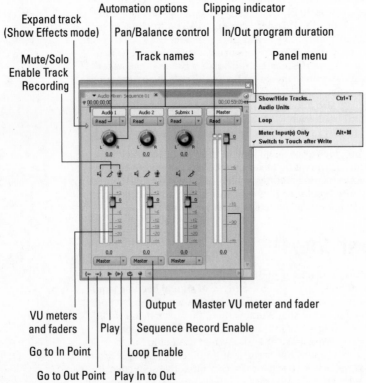

Figure 9-1: Audio Mixer collapsed view

Tracks versus Clips

Before you begin working with Premiere Pro's Audio Mixer, you must understand that the Audio Mixer affects the audio in an entire track. When you work in the Audio Mixer, you make audio track adjustments, not audio clip adjustments. When you create and alter effects in the Audio Mixer, you apply audio effects to tracks, not to specific clips. As discussed in Chapter 8, when you apply effects in the Effect Controls panel, you apply them to clips. The current sequence's Timeline panel can provide an overview of your work and shouldn't lose track (no pun intended) of whether clip or track keyframes are being displayed in the Timeline panel. Here's a review of audio track display options:

✦ To view audio adjustments for clips, choose Show Clip Volume or Show Clip Keyframes in the audio track's Show Keyframes pop-up menu. Note that the keyframe graph line for a clip extends from the in point to the out point of the clip, not to the entire track.

✦ To view audio adjustments for the entire track, choose Show Track Volume or Show Track Keyframes in the audio track's Show Keyframes pop-up menu. The graph line for keyframes in a track extends throughout the entire track. When you apply audio effects using the Audio Mixer, these Effects appear by name in a Track pop-up menu in the Audio track's graphline. If you choose the effect from the pop-up menu in the audio track graph line, the keyframes for the effect appear on the graphline.

For both clip and track graph lines, you can create keyframes by Ctrl-clicking with the Pen tool and making adjustments to keyframe placement by clicking and dragging with the Pen tool.

Note　You can set the master track to be mono, stereo, or 5.1 by choosing Master track settings in the Default Sequence Section of the New Project dialog box (you must first click the Custom Settings tab after creating a new project) or in the New Sequence dialog box (File ➪ New Sequence).

Below the track names are the track Automation options. In Figure 9-1, Automation is set to Read. When the Automation is set to Read, track adjustments written to the tracks with keyframes are read by the track. If you change Read to Write, Touch or Latch, keyframes are created in the current sequence's audio tracks, reflecting adjustments made in the Audio Mixer.

The following sections discuss the major controls and areas of the Audio Mixer, including the controls for Automation, Mute/Solo/Record, Pan/Balance, Volume, and Playback, as well as the Audio Effects menu and the Audio Sends area that appear in the expanded view (see "Effects and Sends options," later in this chapter).

Automation

The Automation options (Off, Read, Latch, Touch, and Write) determine whether Premiere Pro reads or saves the adjustments you make in the Audio Mixer as keyframes in the Timeline panel. A detailed description of each option is provided later in this chapter in "Mixing Audio."

The Mute, Solo, and Record buttons

The Mute and Solo buttons below the Automation options enable you to choose which audio tracks you want to work with and which ones you don't. The Record button allows you to record analog sound (which could be from a microphone attached to a computer audio input).

✦ Click the Mute button to mute or silence tracks that you don't want to hear during Audio Mixer playback. When you click Mute, no audio levels are shown in the Audio Mixer VU (audio level) meter for the track. Using Mute, you can set levels for one or more tracks without hearing others. For example, assume that your audio includes music and sound effects of footsteps nearing a pond of croaking frogs. You could mute the music and adjust levels for only the footsteps and frog croaking as the video shows the pond coming into view.

Note   If a track is in mute mode, its automation setting is not disabled. If you want to completely stop audio output from a track, click the track's speaker's icon in the Timeline panel. Automation settings are covered in the "Automation settings" section later in this chapter.

✦ Click the Solo button to isolate or work with one specific track in the Audio Mixer panel. When you click Solo, Premiere Pro mutes all other tracks, except the Solo track.

✦ Click the Record Enable Track Recording button to record to the enabled track. To record audio, you must then click the Sequence Record button at the bottom of the panel and then click Play. Using the Audio Mixer to capture sound is covered in Chapter 5.

Note   To completely turn off output for an audio track in the Timeline, click the Toggle Track Output button (speaker icon). After you click, the speaker icon disappears. Click again on the Toggle Track Output button to turn audio output back on.

The Pan and Balance controls

Panning allows you to control levels of mono tracks when outputting to stereo or 5.1 tracks. Thus, by panning, you can increase a sound effect like birds chirping in the right channel as trees come into view in the right side of your video monitor.

Balancing allows you to redistribute output in stereo and 5.1 tracks. So, as you add to the sound level in one channel, you subtract from another, and vice versa. Depending upon the type of track that you are working with, you control either balance or panning by using the Pan/Balance knob.

As you pan or balance, you can click and drag over the Pan/Balance knob or click and drag over the numeric readout below the knob. You can also click the numeric readout and type a value using your keyboard. (For more information, see "Panning and Balancing" later in this chapter.)

Volume

Dragging the Volume Fader control up or down adjusts track volume. Volume is recorded in decibels. The decibel volume is displayed in the field below the Volume Fader control. When the volume of an audio track is changed over time by clicking and dragging the Volume Fader control, Audio Mixer Automation settings can place keyframes in the track's audio graph line in the Timeline panel. You can further adjust the volume by dragging the keyframes on the graph line in the track with the Selection tool. Note that when the VU meter (to the left of the Volume Fader) turns red, it is a warning that clipping or sound distortion may be occurring. Also note that mono tracks display one VU meter, stereo tracks display two VU meters, and 5.1 tracks display 5 VU meters.

Tip   To view the VU meters without opening the Audio Mixer, choose Window Audio Master Meters.

Playback

Six icons appear at the lower-left side of the Audio Mixer panel. These icons are Stop, Play, Loop, Go to In point, Go to Out Point, and Play In to Out. Click the Play button to play an audio clip. To work with only a portion of the sequence in the Timeline panel, set in and out points and then jump to the in points by clicking the Go to In Point button. Next, click the Play In to Out button to mix only the audio between your in and out points. If you click the Loop button, playback is repeated so that you can continue to fine-tune the audio between the in and out points without starting and stopping playback.

Tip   You can set in and out points in a sequence by clicking the Set In Point and Set Out Point buttons in the Program Monitor or by moving the current-time indicator and choosing Marker ⇨ Set Sequence Marker ⇨ In or Marker ⇨ Set Sequence Marker ⇨ Out. You can also select a clip in the sequence and choose Marker ⇨ Set Sequence Marker ⇨ In and Out around Selection.

Audio Mixer menu

Because the Audio Mixer contains so many icons and controls, you may want to customize it to display just the controls and features you want to use. This list explains custom settings that are available in the Audio Mixer menu shown in Figure 9-1.

✦ **Show/Hide Tracks:** Shows or hides individual tracks.

✦ **Meter Input(s) Only:** Displays hardware (not track) input levels when recording. To display hardware input levels on the VU meters (not track levels in Adobe Premiere Pro), choose Meter Input(s) Only. When this option is on, you can still monitor audio in Adobe Premiere Pro for all tracks that aren't being recorded.

✦ **Audio Units:** Sets the display to audio units. If you want to display units in Milliseconds rather than Audio Samples, change this setting in the General tab of the Project Settings window (Project ⇨ Project Settings). The Audio setting changes the time display in the Timeline and Monitor panels as well.

✦ **Switch to Touch after Write:** Automatically switches the Automation mode from Write to Touch mode after using Write Automation mode.

Effects and Sends options

The Effects and Sends options that appear in the expanded view of the Audio Mixer are shown in Figure 9-2. To display the effects and sends, click the triangle to the left of the Automation options drop-down menus. To add an effect or send, click any of the triangles on the right side of the effects and sends lists. Figure 9-2 shows several of these triangles, which appear vertically down the effects and sends portion of each track.

Sends or effects option

Sends   Effects

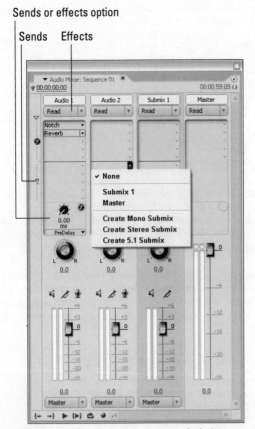

Figure 9-2: The Audio Mixer expanded view

Choosing Audio Effects

Clicking a triangle in the Audio Effects area allows you to choose an audio effect. You can place up to five effects in each track's Effects area. When an effect is loaded, you can adjust settings for the effect at the bottom of the Effects area. Figure 9-2 shows the Notch and Reverb effects loaded in the Audio Effects panel. The PreDelay adjustment for the Reverb effect is shown at the bottom of the Effects area.

Effects Sends area

Below the Effects area is the Effects Sends region. Figure 9-2 shows the pop-up menu that creates sends. Sends allow you to *send* a proportion of a track's signal to a submix track using a volume control knob. To learn more about sends, see the section "Creating Sends" later in this chapter.

Mixing Audio

When you use the Audio Mixer to mix audio, Premiere Pro can add keyframes in the Timeline panel for the currently selected sequence. As you add effects, they are also displayed in a track's pop-up menu in the Timeline panel. After you've placed all your audio clips in Premiere Pros' tracks, you're almost ready to start a trial mix. Before you begin, you should understand the Audio Mixer's Automation settings, because these control whether keyframes are created in audio track or not.

If you would like to practice using the Audio Mixer, you can use the audio clips in the Chapter 11 and Chapter 8 folders of the *Adobe Premiere Pro 2 Bible* DVD.

Automation settings

Premiere Pro's Audio Mixer uses the term "automation" because it allows you to automate audio track adjustments that are saved as keyframes. After you've made adjustments to one track, you can replay the audio sequence and adjust another track. As the Audio Mixer plays, you can hear the changes you made to the first track and see the fader handles move up and down in that track's section of the audio mixer.

You cannot successfully mix audio with Automation unless settings at the top of each track in the Audio Mixer are properly set. For example, in order to record your track adjustments with keyframes, you need the Automation drop-down menu set to Write, Touch, or Latch. After you make adjustments and stop audio playback, your adjustments are represented by keyframes in the Timeline panel (in the track graph line). Figure 9-3 shows the master track with the Automation pop-up menu exposed.

To see Audio Mixer keyframes in the Timeline panel, choose Show Track Keyframes in the audio track's Show Keyframe pop-up menu. You don't see the keyframes if you have the pop-up menu set to Show Clip Keyframes.

Here is a brief description of each Automation setting:

✦ **Write:** This setting immediately saves adjustments made for the track and creates keyframes in the Timeline panel that represent the audio adjustments. Write, unlike Latch and Touch, starts writing as soon as playback starts, even if changes are not made in the Audio Mixer. Thus, if you set a track to Write, change volume settings, and then start playing back the track, a keyframe is created at the start of the track — even if you do not make further adjustments.

You can right-click on a fader pan/volume or effect and choose Safe During Write to prevent changes to the setting while Write Automation is in effect. You can also have Write mode switch to Touch mode automatically when playback is finished by choosing Switch to Touch After Write in the Audio Mixer panel menu.

Figure 9-3: Automation pop-up menu choices

✦ **Latch:** Like Write, this mode saves adjustments and creates keyframes in the Timeline. But automation does not start until you begin to make adjustments. However, if you change settings (such as volume) when playing back a track that already has recorded automation, the settings do not return to their previous levels after current adjustments are made.

✦ **Touch:** Like Latch, Touch creates keyframes in the Timeline and does not make adjustments until you change control values. However, if you change settings (such as volume) when playing back a track that already has recorded automation, the settings return to their previous levels after current adjustments are made.

Note   The rate of return for values when Touch is the Automation setting is controlled by the Automatch Time audio preference. This preference can be changed by choosing Edit ➪ Preferences ➪ Audio. The default time is 1 second.

✦ **Read:** This setting plays each track's Automation setting during playback. If you adjust a setting (such as volume) during playback, you hear the change and see the change in the track's VU meters, and the entire track remains at that level.

If you previously made adjustments using an animation mode such as Write to record changes to a track and then play back in Read mode, settings return to the recorded values after you stop making adjustments in Read mode.

Like Touch, the rate of return is based on the Automatch Time preference.

✦ **Off:** This setting disregards the stored Automation settings during playback. Thus, if you adjust levels using an Automation setting such as Write and play back the track with the Automation mode set to Off, you don't hear the original adjustments.

The default minimum time for interval between keyframes created by automation in Premiere Pro 2.0 was increased to 2000ms. If you want to decrease the keyframes time interval, choose Edit ➪ Preferences. In the Preferences dialog box, click the Audio tab. In the Minimum Time Interval Thinning field, enter the desired value in milliseconds.

Creating a mix

After you review the Automation settings and are familiar with Audio Mixer controls, you're ready to try out a mix. The following steps outline how to do so. Before you begin, place audio in a minimum of two tracks in the current sequence in the Timeline panel. Choose Show Track Keyframes in each Audio track's Keyframe pop-up menu.

If you want to experiment with the audio mixer, place the narration track from the Chapter 9 folder of the *Adobe Premiere Pro 2 Bible* DVD into Audio Track 1, and place the music track into Audio Track 2. Start with changing sound levels with the Automation for the tracks set to Read, and then create keyframes by using the Touch Automation setting. Continue to experiment using Latch and Read, if desired.

As you experiment with the Audio Mixer, you can quickly undo your changes by clicking previous history states in the History panel.

1. **In the Audio Mixer panel or Timeline panel, set the current-time indicator to the position where you want to start the mix.**

2. **Preview the audio by clicking the Play button with automation set to Read. As the audio plays, you may want to see how changing levels with the fader controls affects the audio.** After previewing the audio, proceed to step three.

3. **At the top of the tracks for which you want to set automation, choose an Automation setting such as Touch, Latch, or Write.** If you want a keyframe to be created based upon the settings before changing them, set Automation to Write. If you want keyframes to be created when you start making adjustments, set Automation to Latch or Touch. Note that the drop-down menu at the bottom of the track indicates where the signal is being sent. By default, track output is routed to the master track, although it can be changed to a submix track (which can output to the master track).

If you don't want a control such as the Volume Fader to affect the track, right-click it and choose Safe During Write.

4. **Click the Play button in the Audio Mixer panel.** If you want to play from the sequence in point to out point, click the Play In to Out button.

5. **While the tracks play, make adjustments to the controls in the Audio Mixer.** If you work with the fader controls, you can see the changes in the meters for the different tracks.

6. **When you have completed making adjustments, click the Stop button in the Audio Mixer.** If the Timeline panel is open and the Show Keyframe pop-up menu set to Track Keyframes, you can click the Track pop-up menu to show Volume, Balance, or Panning keyframes.

7. **To play back the adjustments, return the current-time indicator to the beginning of the audio and click the Play button.**

8. **Repeat Steps 1 through 6 for each track that you want to adjust.**

Panning and Balancing

As you work a mix in the Audio Mixer, you can Pan or Balance. *Panning* allows you to adjust a mono track to emphasize it in a multitrack output. For example, as mentioned before, you could create a panning effect to increase the level of a sound effect in the right channel of a stereo track as an object appears in the right side of the video monitor. You can do this by panning as you output mono tracks to a stereo or 5.1 master track.

Balancing redistributes sound in multichannel tracks. For example, in a stereo track, you could subtract audio from one channel and add to the other. As you work, you must realize that the ability to pan or to balance depends upon the tracks you are playing back and outputting to. For example, you can pan a mono track if you are outputting to a stereo or 5.1 surround track. You can balance a stereo track if you are outputting to a stereo or 5.1 track. If you output a stereo track or 5.1 surround track to mono, Premiere Pro *downmixes*, or puts the sound tracks into fewer channels.

Note   You can set the Master track to be mono, stereo, or 5.1 by choosing master track settings in the Default Sequence Section of the New Project dialog box (you must first click the Custom Settings tab after creating a new project) or in the New Sequence dialog box (File ➪ New Sequence).

If you are panning or balancing a mono or stereo track, simply set up the Audio Mixer to output to a stereo submix or master track and use the round knob shown in Figure 9-4 to adjust the effect. If you are panning to a 5.1 submix or master track, the Audio Mixer replaces the knob with a "tray" icon. To pan using the tray, slide the puck icon within the tray area. The "pockets" along the edges of the tray represent the five surround sound speakers. You can adjust the center channel by clicking and dragging the Center percentage knob (upper-right area of the tray). You can adjust the sub-woofer channel by clicking and dragging the knob above the Bass Clef icon.

After you complete a panning or balancing session using the Audio Mixer, you can see recorded automation adjustments in the keyframe graph line for the adjusted audio tracks in the Timeline panel. To see the keyframes in the graph line, the Show Keyframe pop-up menu in the adjusted tracks should be set to Show Track Keyframes. In the Track pop-up menu that appears in the keyframe graph line, choose either Panner or Balance.

Tip   You can copy a stereo track into two mono tracks by selecting it in the Project panel and choosing Audio Options ➪ Breakout to Mono Clips. You can convert a mono audio clip to stereo by selecting it in the Project panel and choosing Treat as Stereo.

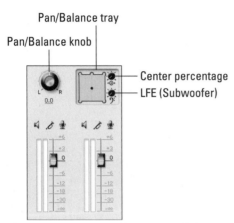

Pan/Balance tray

Pan/Balance knob

— Center percentage

— LFE (Subwoofer)

Figure 9-4: Panning/Balance controls for stereo and 5.1 surround track

You can pan or balance in the Timeline without using the Audio Mixer. To do this, set the Show Keyframes pop-up menu to Show Track Keyframes. In the Track pop-up menu, choose Panner ⇨ Pan or Panner ⇨ Balance. Use the Pen tool to adjust the graph line. If you want to create keyframes, Ctr+click with the Pen tool.

Applying Effects Using the Audio Mixer

After you become familiar with the Audio Mixer's powers of adjusting audio on the fly, you'll probably want to start using it to apply and adjust audio effects for audio tracks. Adding effects to the Audio Mixer is quite easy: You load the effects into the effects area and then adjust individual controls for the effect (a control appears as a knob). If you intend to apply many effects to a track, be aware that the Audio Mixer allows you to add only five audio effects. The following steps show you how to load an effect and adjust it:

1. **Place an audio clip in an audio track, or place a video clip that contains audio in a video track.**

2. **If the Effects section of the Audio Mixer is not open, open it by clicking the small expand/collapse triangle icon (refer to Figure 9-1).**

3. **In the track to which you want to apply the effect, click the down triangle in the effects area.** This opens a list of audio effects, as shown in Figure 9-5.

4. **Choose the effect that you want to apply from the list of effects.** After you select the effect, its name is displayed in the effects section of the Audio Mixer panel.

5. **If you want to switch to another control for the effect, click the down arrow to the right of the control name and choose another control. (The controls are near the Pan/Balance knob.)**

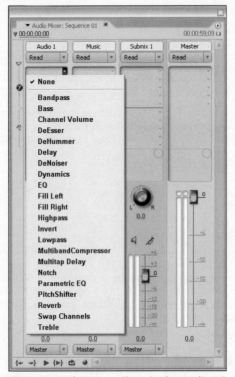

Figure 9-5: Choosing effects in the Audio Mixer panel

   6. Proceed to set Automation for the track.

   7. Click the Play button in the Audio Mixer panel, and adjust effect controls as desired.

Removing effects

If you want to remove an effect from an Audio Mixer track, select the triangle for the effect and choose None in the drop-down list.

Bypassing an effect

You can turn off or bypass an effect by clicking the *f* (Bypass icon) that appears to the right of the effects control knob. After you click, a slash appears in the icon. To turn the effect back on, simply click the Bypass icon again.

Trying out Fill Left and Swap Channels

The latest version of Premiere Pro adds Fill Left, Fill Right, and Swap Channels to the effects available in the Audio Mixer. As discussed in Chapter 8, Swap Channels puts the audio from the left channel in the right channel and vice versa; Fill Left fills the right stereo channel with audio from the Left, and Fill Right does the opposite.

If you want to quickly try out applying one of these effects in the Audio Mixer, you can experiment using the an audio file in the Chapter 8 folder on the *Adobe Premiere Pro 2 Bible* DVD.

1. **Create a New Project in Premiere Pro by choosing File ➪ New Project.** Alternatively, you can create a new sequence by choosing File ➪ New Sequence.

2. **If you don't have a stereo audio file to use, load one of the audio files from the Chapter 8 folder on the DVD by choosing File ➪ Import.**

3. **Remove the Right stereo track by selecting the audio file in the Project panel and choosing Clip ➪ Audio Options ➪ Source Channel Mappings.** In the Source Channel Mappings dialog box, de-select the Right channel checkbox and then click OK.

4. **Drag the audio file to Audio Track 1 in the new sequence.**

5. **Choose Window ➪ Audio Mixer, and choose the sequence containing your audio in the Submenu.**

6. **In the Audio Mixer, click the Show Effects button to switch to Effects View, as shown in Figure 9-5.**

7. **Click the Play or Play in to Out button in the Audio Mixer to play the audio and confirm that the narration is only in the left stereo channel.**

8. **From the Effects area of Track 1, click the Effects triangle to open the drop-down list of effects, and choose either Fill Left or Swap channels.**

9. **Switch out of Effects view in the Audio Mixer by clicking the Show Effects button.** This displays the VU meters and faders.

10. **Click the Audio Mixer's Play button.** As the audio plays, view the track meters to see how the audio that was in the left track has been switched to the right track. Note also that the clip itself hasn't been changed. The effect is applied to the track, not the clip.

Creating a Submix

Premiere Pro's Audio Mixer not only allows you to mix audio into a master track, but it also allows you to combine audio from different tracks into a submix track. Why use a submix track? Assume that you have four audio tracks and you want to apply the same effects to two of the tracks simultaneously. Using the Audio Mixer, you can route the two tracks to the submix track and apply the effect to this track, which could in turn output it to the master track. Applying the effect to one submix track instead of two standard audio tracks can be easier to manage and drains less resources from your computer.When using submix tracks, you can't manually drag clips into them in the Timeline. Their input is solely created from settings in the Audio Mixer. Follow these general steps for setting up a submix track:

1. **Create a submix by choosing Sequence ➪ Add track.** In the Add Tracks dialog box, shown in Figure 9-6, type **1** in the Add Audio Submix Track(s) field. In the Track Type drop-down menu, choose whether you want the submix track to be mono, stereo, or 5.1. You probably want to type **0** in other fields so that you do not add other audio or video tracks.

2. **In the Audio Mixer panel, set the output for the submix track if necessary. (You could output a submix track to another submix track, depending upon your track setup.)**

3. **Set the output for individual tracks that you want routed to the submix track in the output drop-down menu at the bottom of the track.**

4. **Choose effects for the submix track by clicking one of the effects triangles icons and selecting an effect.** Figure 9-7 shows one possible submix setup. After you choose an effect or effects, you can then set automation settings as needed.

Figure 9-6: Creating a submix track

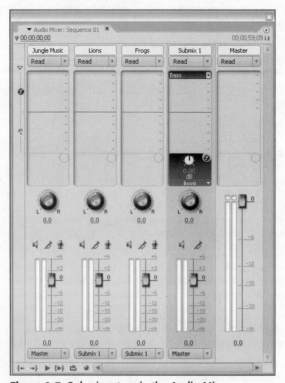

Figure 9-7: Submix set up in the Audio Mixer

Creating Sends

Premiere Pro's Audio Mixer allows you to create *sends*, which can be used to send a portion of a track's signal to a submix track. When a send is created, a control knob appears at the bottom of the track's area, as shown in Figure 9-8. (In Figure 9-8, the control knob is set to Volume. However by clicking the word Volume, you may be able to set the knob to Balance or Pan, depending upon whether you are working with mono or multichannel tracks.) This control knob allows you to adjust how much of a track's signal is duplicated to the submix track. In audio terminology, this is akin to the track portion of the signal being referred to as "dry," and the submix portion referred to as "wet." When you create a send, you can choose to set the send to be Pre-Fader or Post-Fader (the default choice). This allows you to control whether the signal is sent from the track before or after its fader control is adjusted. If you choose Pre-Fader, raising or lowering the send track's fader does not affect the send output. Choosing Post-Fader utilizes the control knob setting as you change volume in the send track. You can choose between Pre-Fader and Post-Fader settings by right-clicking the listed send in the Audio Mixer panel. In Figure 9-8, right-clicking Submix 1 opens the Pre-Fader/Post-Fader pop-up menu.

Follow these steps for creating a submix track in the Audio Mixer and then creating the effects send:

1. **If the effects/send area of the Audio Mixer is not open, expand it by clicking the expand/collapse triangle icon (refer to Figure 9-1).**

2. **Click one of the triangles in a track's Send area to open the send area pop-up menu.**

3. **If you haven't created a submix track, you can create it by choosing one of the create submix choices in the pop-up menu.** After you make the choice, a send is automatically created for the submix track. You can see the send in Audio Track 1 of Figure 9-8. If the submix track already exists in the Audio Mixer, choose it from the Send pop-up menu.

4. **When the send is created, a Volume knob appears, allowing you to control the proportion of the track signal that is sent to the submix track when you mix the tracks.**

5. **If desired, change send properties:**

   • Right-click the Send Properties pop-up menu, and choose Pre-Fader or Post-Fader.

   • Click the Mute button to mute the send.

   • Delete a send by choosing None in the Send Assignment pop-up menu.

Send Properties pop-up menu

Send Control knob

Send Assignment pop-up menu

Mute button

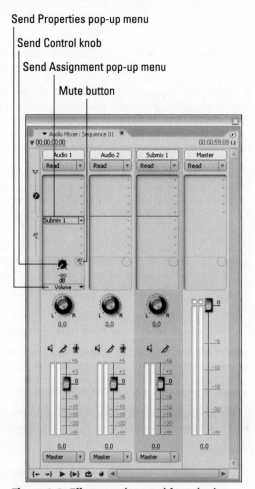

Figure 9-8: Effects send created for submix.

Audio Processing Order

With all the controls available for audio, you may wonder what order Premiere Pro uses to process audio. For example, are clip effects processed before track effects or vice versa? Here's an overview: First, Premiere Pro processes audio according to the audio settings you set in the New Project dialog box. When audio is output, Premiere Pro follows this general order:

1. **Clips adjusted with Premiere's Audio Gain command**

2. **Clip effects**

3. **Track effect settings such as Pre-Fader effects, fader effects, Post-Fader effects, and then pan/balance**

4. **Track volume from left to right in the Audio Mixer with output routed through any submix tracks to the master track**

You certainly don't need to memorize this, but having a general idea of the order in which audio is processed may prove helpful as you work on complex projects.

Summary

The Premiere Pro Audio Mixer provides a variety of utilities for mixing audio. After you set the Automation mode in the Automation pop-up menu, you can mix to a master or submix track during playback. These topics were covered in this chapter:

✦ Use the Audio Mixer automation controls to save changes to tracks when mixing.

✦ Use the Audio Mixer to pan and balance.

✦ Use a submix track to apply one effect to multiple tracks.

✦ You can add effects and adjust them in the Audio Mixer during playback.

✦ You can create effects sends in the Audio Mixer.

✦   ✦   ✦

Creating Transitions

A cut from one scene in your video production to another provides an excellent transition for action clips or for clips that move the viewer from one locale to another. However, when you want to convey the passage of time or create an effect in which a scene gradually transforms into the next, a simple cut just won't do. To artistically show passage of time, you may want to use a *cross dissolve,* which gradually fades one clip in over another. For a more dramatic and abrupt effect, you can use a *clock wipe,* in which one scene is rotated onscreen, as if it were swept into the frames by the hands of a clock.

Whether you're trying to turn night into day, day into night, youth into age — or simply wake up your audience with a startling special effect that bridges one scene to another — you should find what you're looking for with Adobe Premiere Pro's Video Transitions, and this chapter takes you on a tour of this feature.

Touring the Video Transitions Bin

The Video Transitions bin (folder) in the Effects panel stores more than 70 different transitional effects. To view the Video Transitions bin, choose Window ⇨ Effects. To see a list of the transition categories, click the triangle icon in front of the Video Transitions bin in the Effects panel. As shown in Figure 10-1, the Effects panel keeps all the video transitions organized into subfolders. To view the contents of a transition bin, click the triangle icon to the left of the bin. When the bin opens, the triangle icon points down. Click the downward-pointing triangle icon to close the bin.

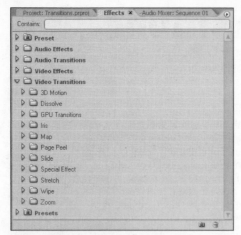

Figure 10-1: The Effects panel contains more than 70 different video transitions.

Navigating within the Video Transitions bin

The Effects panel can help you locate transitions and keep them organized. To find a video transition, click in the Contains field in the Effects panel and start typing the name of the transition. You needn't type the full name. For example, type the word **cross**, and Premiere Pro opens all the bins that have the name *cross* in the effects. Type the word **invert**, and Premiere Pro opens all the bins that have the word *invert* in the effects.

To organize your bin, you can create new custom bins to keep the transitions that you most often use grouped together. To create a new custom bin, click either the New Custom Bin at the bottom of the Effects panel or the triangle icon at the upper right of the panel and choose New Custom Bin. To rename a custom bin, first select the custom bin and then click the name of the bin. When the name is highlighted, begin typing the new name. To delete a custom bin, either click it to select it and click the Delete Custom Items icon, or choose Delete Custom Item from the panel menu. When the Delete Item dialog box appears, click OK to delete the bin.

The Effects panel also allows you to set a default transition. By default, the video transition is set to Cross Dissolve. The default transition has a red frame around its icon. The video transition default duration is set to 30 frames. To change the default transition duration, click the Default Transition Duration command, found in the Effects panel menu. In the Preferences dialog box, you can change the default video transition by entering a new number in the appropriate field. To select a new transition as the default, first select a video transition and then click Set Selected as Default Transition in the Effects panel menu.

Applying a transition

Premiere Pro allows you to apply transitions similar to traditional video editing: The transition is placed between two clips in the track. The transition uses the extra frames at the out point of the first clip and the extra clips at the in point of the second clip as the transitional area. When you use Single-Track editing, extra frames beyond the out point of one clip and the extra frames before the in point of the next clip are used as the transitional area. (If no extra frames are available, Premiere Pro enables you to repeat ending or beginning frames.)

Figure 10-2 shows a sample transition project with its panels. In the Timeline panel, you can see video clips with transitions. The Info panel shows information on the selected transition. The Effect Controls panel displays the options for the selected transition. In the Program Monitor panel, you can see a preview of the selected transition.

Tip

The Effects workspace helps organize all the windows and panels you need onscreen when working with transitions. To set your workspace to Effects, choose Window ➪ Workspace ➪ Effects.

Figures 10-3, 10-4, 10-5, and 10-6 show frames from the transition project that we created using Premiere Pro's new Single-Track editing features. We applied the Additive Dissolve, Cross Dissolve, Dither Dissolve, and Iris Points transitions. The clips we used to create the transition project are from Digital Vision. We used five video clips from Digital Vision's ComicCuts CD (891002f.mov, 891004f.mov, 891019f.mov, 891025f.mov, and 891033f.mov) and Digital Vision's Acoustic Chillout sound clip, 730001aw.wav. These clips are on the DVD that accompanies this book.

Figure 10-2: Premiere Pro's Effects workspace was used when applying transitions using Single-Track editing.

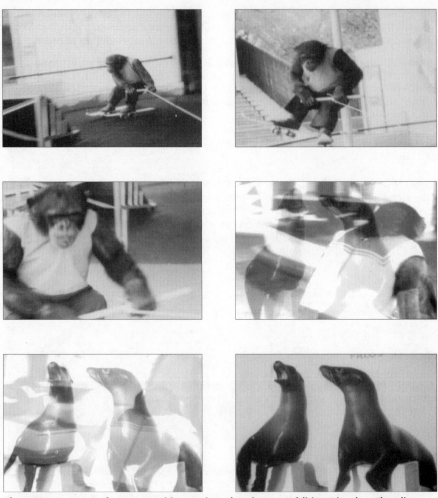

Figure 10-3: Frames from a transition project showing an Additive Dissolve. The clips used are Digital Vision's ComicCuts CD 891002f.mov and 891004f.mov.

Figure 10-4: Frames from a transition project showing a Cross Dissolve. The clips used are Digital Vision's ComicCuts CD 891004f.mov and 891019f.mov.

Figure 10-5: Frames from a transition project showing a Dither Dissolve. The clips used are Digital Vision's ComicCuts CD 891019f.mov and 891033f.mov.

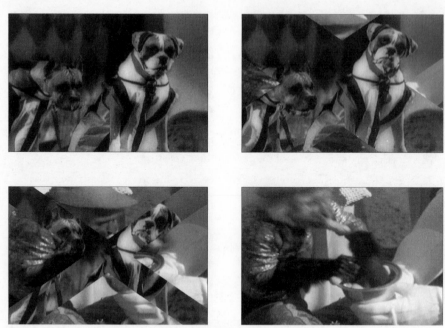

Figure 10-6: Frames from a transition project showing an Iris Points transition. The clips used are Digital Vision's ComicCuts CD 891033f.mov and 891025f.mov.

Here are the steps for creating a transition in Single-Track editing:

1. **Create a new project by choosing File ➪ New ➪ Project.** In the New Project dialog box, pick a preset or create a custom setting. Name your new project, and then click OK to create a new project.

2. **Choose Window ➪ Workspace ➪ Effects to set Premiere Pro's workspace to Effects mode.** In Effects workspace, all the necessary panels needed to apply and edit transitions are onscreen.

3. **Choose File ➪ Import to import video clips.** In the Import dialog box, select the clips you want to import. Then click Open to import a video clip into the Project panel. If you want to import a folder, click on the folder and then click on the Import Folder button in the Import dialog box.

On the DVD-ROM

The five video clips shown in Figures 10-2 through 10-6, from Digital Vision's ComicCuts CD (891002f.mov, 891004f.mov, 891019f.mov, 891025f.mov, and 891033f.mov) and Digital Vision's Acoustic Chillout sound clip, 730001aw.wav, are found in the Digital Vision folder in the Chapter 10 folder of the Tutorial Projects folder on the DVD that accompanies this book.

4. **Drag one video clip from the Project panel into Video 1 track of the Timeline. Then drag another clip next to it.** Set the out point of the first clip and the in point of the second clip. The first clip should have extra frames that extend beyond the out point. The second clip should have extra frames that extend beyond the in point. These extra

frames are used by Premiere Pro to determine the length of the transition. When you set the in and out points, each clip should have an equal number of extra frames. The extra frames determine the length of the transition. For example, to create a 30-frame dissolve, each clip should have 15 extra frames in each clip. You can set in and out points by using the Selection tool, Timeline markers, the Source Monitor, or the Program Monitor panel. For more information on setting in and out points, refer to Chapter 7.

5. **Another way to overlap two clips in the Timeline is to use the Snap option and the current-time indicator.** To do so, drag a clip to the Timeline panel and then move the current-time indicator toward the end of the first clip. Now drag the second clip to the current-time indicator. As you drag, notice that the second clip snaps to align at the left, right, or center of the current-time indicator.

6. **Now pick a transition from the Effects panel, and place it over the area where the two clips meet.** Premiere Pro highlights the area where the transition occurs and then places the transition within the track. If the number of extra frames for each clip is not sufficient to create the transition, a prompt appears saying "Insufficient media." This transition will contain repeated frames. You can either change the duration of the transition or click OK to have Premiere Pro repeat the last and first frames of the clips to accommodate the transition.

7. **You can edit a transition in the Timeline panel either by moving the clip to the right or left or by changing its duration by moving one of the transition's edges.**

Tip

If you move a transition edge, you may also move the edge of a clip. To move a transition edge without affecting any clips, press Ctrl while you click and drag the Transition edge.

8. **To see the overlapping areas and the transition displayed below the first clip and above the next clip (shown in Figure 10-7), double-click the transition in the Timeline panel.** Display the Effect Controls panel. To see the clips and transition in the Timeline of the Effect Controls panel, select the Show/Hide Keyframes option. You can edit the transition using either the Timeline features or the Duration and Alignment option in the Effect Controls panel. Using these features is discussed in the next section.

9. **To preview a transition in the Effect Controls panel (refer to Figure 10-7), click the Play the Transition button or select the Show Actual Sources checkbox and move the sliders below the Start and End previews.**

10. **To preview a transition in the Program Monitor panel (shown in Figure 10-7), either use the shuttle or jog slider or click the Play button.** You can also view the transition in the Program Monitor panel when you move the current-time indicator in the Timeline panel. By default, the Program Monitor panel displays the preview in Automatic Quality. To change the preview quality, click the Program Monitor panel menu and choose either Highest Quality or Draft Quality.

You may also import a sound clip and place it in Audio Track 1.

11. **To render the work area, choose Sequence ➪ Render Work Area.**

12. **Save your work by choosing File ➪ Save.**

13. **To make a movie from your Premiere Pro project, choose File ➪ Export ➪ Movie.**

Proceed to the next section to learn how to edit transitions.

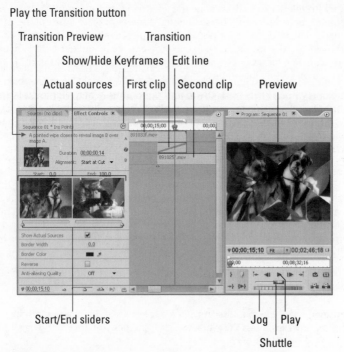

Figure 10-7: The Effect Controls panel and Program Monitor panel with a preview of a transition

Editing transitions

After you apply a transition, you can either edit it in the Timeline panel or use the Effect Controls panel. To edit a transition, you first need to select it in the Timeline panel. Then you can either move the transition's alignment or change its duration.

Changing a transition's alignment

To change a transition's alignment using the Timeline panel, click the transition and then drag it left or right or center it. When you drag left, you align the transition to the end of the edit point. When you drag right, you align the transition at the beginning or the edit point. When you center the transition, you align the transition so that it is centered within the edit point.

The Effect Controls panel allows you to make more editing changes. To change a transition's alignment using the Effect Controls panel, first double-click the transition in the Timeline panel. To view the clips and transition in the Timeline of the Effect Controls panel, the Show/Hide Keyframes option must be selected. Then choose an option from the Alignment pop-up menu to change the transition's alignment. To create a custom alignment, manually move the transition in the Timeline of the Effect Controls panel.

Changing a transition's duration

In the Timeline panel, you can increase or decrease the number of frames to which the transition is applied by dragging one of its edges. For accuracy, be sure to use the Info panel when making adjustments on the Timeline.

To change a transition's duration using the Effect Controls panel, first double-click the transition in the Timeline panel. To view the clips and transition in the Timeline of the Effect Controls panel, the Show/Hide Keyframes option must be selected. Then click and drag the Duration value to change the duration.

The alignment and duration of a transition work together. Changing the transition's duration is affected by its alignment. When the alignment setting is set to Center at Cut or Custom Start, changing the Duration value affects both the in and out points. When alignment is set to Start at Cut, changing the Duration value affects the out point. When alignment is set to End at Cut, changing the Duration value affects the in point. Besides using the Duration value to change the duration of a transition, you can also manually adjust the duration of the transition by clicking the right or left edge of the transition edge and dragging outward or inward.

Changing a transition's settings

Many of the transitions include setting options that enable you to change how a transition appears onscreen. After a transition is applied to a clip, you can find the settings for that transition at the bottom of the Effect Controls panel. To preview the settings for a transition (as shown in Figure 10-8), you may need to lengthen the Effect Controls panel.

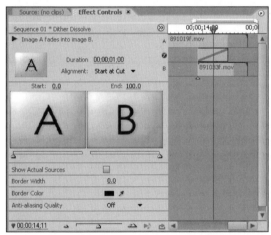

Figure 10-8: The Effect Controls panel with the Dither Dissolve settings

After you apply a transition, you can edit the transition direction by clicking the Reverse checkbox in the Effect Controls panel (refer to Figure 10-7). By default, a clip transitions from the first clip to the second (A to B). Occasionally, you may want to create a transition in which scene B transitions to scene A — even though scene B appears after scene A. To see a preview of the transition effect, click and drag the A or B slider. To see the actual clips previewed in the window, select the Show Actual Sources checkbox and then click and drag the sliders (refer to Figure 10-7). To preview the transition, you can also click the Play the Transition button.

Many transitions enable you to reverse the effect. For example, the Curtain Transition in the 3D Motion bin normally applies the transition with Clip A onscreen; the curtain opens to display clip B. However, by clicking the Reverse checkbox at the bottom of the Effect Controls panel, you can make the curtain close to reveal Clip B. The Doors Transition is quite similar. Normally the Doors open to reveal Clip B. If you click the Reverse checkbox, the doors close to reveal Clip A.

Several transitions also enable you to smooth the effect or create a soft-edge effect by applying anti-aliasing to the transitions. To smooth the effect, click the Anti-aliasing Quality pop-up menu (refer to Figure 10-8) and choose Anti-aliasing Quality. Some transitions also allow you to add a border. To do so, click and drag on the Border Width value to set the width of the border and then pick a border color. To pick a border color, use the Eyedropper or the swatch next to Border Color.

Creating a default transition

If you are applying the same transition many times throughout a project, you can set a default transition. After you've specified a default transition, you can easily apply it without having to drag it to the Timeline from the Effects panel.

Here are the steps for creating a default transition:

1. **If the Effects panel is not open, open it by choosing Window ➪ Effects.**

2. **In the Effects panel, click the transition that you want to set as the default.** By default, Premiere Pro sets the Cross Dissolve transition as the default transition.

3. **In the Effects panel menu, choose Set Selected as Default Transition.**

Note   The default transition remains the default transition for all Premiere Pro projects until you choose another default transition.

Applying a default transition

To use a default transition, organize the clips in Video 1 track as you would for a normal transition. You must position the clips so that the in and out points meet in the track. Follow these steps to apply the transition:

1. **Select the target track that includes the video clips by clicking on the left edge of the track.**

2. **Move the current-time indicator between the two clips.**

3. **Choose Sequence ➪ Apply Video Transition.** Alternatively, you can apply the default transition by pressing Ctrl+D.

Tip   You can create a keyboard shortcut for applying a default transition.

Replacing and deleting transitions

After you've created a transition, you may decide that it doesn't quite provide the effect you originally intended. Fortunately, replacing or deleting transitions is easy. You can do it in either of these ways:

✦ To replace one transition with another, simply click and drag one transition from the Effects panel over the transition that you want to replace in the Timeline. The new transition replaces the old transition.

✦ To delete a transition, simply select it with the mouse and then press the Delete or Backspace key.

Creating interesting animated graphic backgrounds using video transitions

You can create a simple graphic file in Photoshop using filters, import it into Premiere Pro, and apply video effects and video transitions to it to make a really interesting animated background. You can also take that simple graphic file and animate it using Photoshop filters and Adobe ImageReady. (For more information on using Adobe ImageReady, turn to Chapter 12.) An animated background can be used in any project as the backdrop of a title, or it can be superimposed onto another clip.

In Figure 10-9, we started with an animated graphic clip (Digital Vision's Ambient Space 434004f.mov). We used the same clip five times. Each time we dragged the clip to the Timeline panel, we made it overlap the previous clip. The overlapping area is where we applied a transition. We applied these transitions: Paint Splatter (shown in Figure 10-10), Multi-Spin (shown in Figure 10-11), Center Peel (shown in Figure 10-12), and Iris Star (shown in Figure 10-13). For the clip to look like a different clip, four different times, we applied the Color Balance video effect to change the clip's colors.

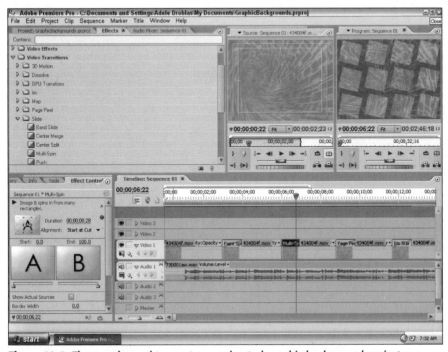

Figure 10-9: The panels used to create an animated graphic background project

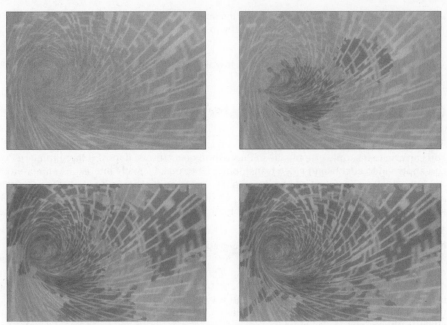

Figure 10-10: Various frames from the Paint Splatter transition (in the Wipe bin) in the animated graphic background project

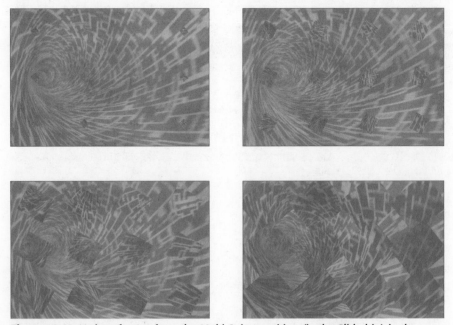

Figure 10-11: Various frames from the Multi-Spin transition (in the Slide bin) in the animated graphic background project

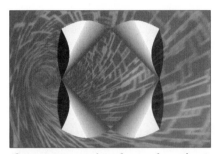 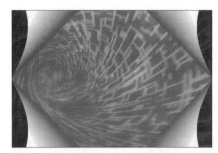

Figure 10-12: Various frames from the Center Peel transition (in the Page Peel) bin) in the animated graphic background project

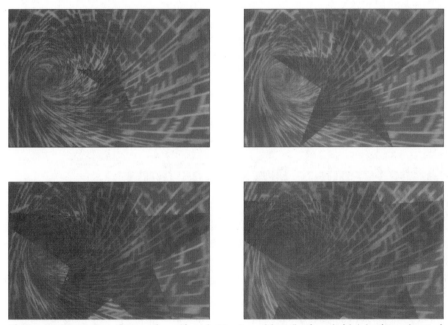

Figure 10-13: Various frames from the Iris Star transition (in the Iris bin) in the animated graphic background project

Here's how to use video transitions to animate a graphic background:

1. **Create a new project.**

2. **Import a still image or clip into the Premiere Pro Project panel.** Import a file that you created in Illustrator or Photoshop using graphics, paint tools, and filters, or import a generic-looking video clip, to which you can apply various Premiere Pro Video Effects to make it more interesting. We imported an animated graphic clip from Digital Vision's Ambient Space CD-ROM (434004f.mov).

On the DVD-ROM

The video clip shown in Figure 10-9 is from Digital Vision's Ambient Space CD (434004f.mov) and is found in the Digital Vision folder in the Chapter 10 folder that is in the Tutorial Projects folder on the DVD that accompanies this book. For this project, we also used Digital Vision's Acoustic Chillout sound clip, 730001aw.wav.

3. **Drag the imported clip from the Project panel to Video 1 track of the Timeline panel.** If you want apply a video effect to it, click and drag a video effect over the clip in the Timeline panel. For more information on using video effects, see Chapter 14.

4. **Drag the same imported clip from the Project panel so that it overlaps the clip already in Video 1 track.**

5. **Apply a video effect to the second clip so that it is not exactly the same as the first clip.** We used the Color Balance video effect to change the color of the clip. The Color Balance video effect is in the Image Control bin.

6. **Click and drag a video transition on the overlapping area of two clips in the Timeline panel.** For a more animated feel, you can try a transition from the Wipe, Slide, Page Peel, or Iris bin.

7. **Repeat Steps 5 and 6 as many times as you want.**

8. **Click the Play button in the Program Monitor panel to preview the project.**

9. **If you want, import a sound and place it in Audio Track 1.**

10. **Remember to save your work.**

Exploring Premiere Pro's Transitions

Premiere Pro's Video Transitions bin provides ten different transition bins: 3D Motion, Dissolve, Iris, Map, Page Peel, Slide, Special Effect, Stretch, Wipe, and Zoom. Each bin features its own set of eye-catching transitions. To view the video transitions in the Effects panel, choose Window ➪ Effects. In the Effects panel, click the triangle in front of the Video Transitions bin to display the video transition bins.

This section features a tour of virtually every transition in each bin, along with examples of some of the transitions. The examples shown in the figures use files created in Adobe Illustrator CS and Adobe Photoshop CS. These clips are in the Chapter 10 folder on the DVD that accompanies this book. When using Adobe Illustrator files, you may want to use the Scale to Frame Size command to scale the Illustrator file to the project frame size. To use the Scale to Frame Size command, first import an Illustrator file, and then click on it in the Project panel. Choose Clip ➪ Video Options ➪ Scale to Frame Size. The command immediately takes effect. When you are ready to use the Illustrator clip, drag it to a video track in the Timeline panel.

Note

To aid in describing the transitions, we call the first clip in the Video track *Clip A*; the second clip in the Video track is called *Clip B*. In the following sections, we describe how Clip A transitions to Clip B. However, note that many transitions can be reversed so that Clip B transitions to Clip A.

3D Motion

The 3D Motion bin features ten transitions: Cube Spin, Curtain, Doors, Flip Over, Fold Up, Spin, Spin Away, Swing In, Swing Out, and Tumble Away. Each one of the transitions includes motion as the transition occurs.

Cube Spin

The Cube Spin transition uses a spinning 3D cube to create the transition from Clip A to Clip B. In the Cube Spin settings, you can set the transition to be from left to right, right to left, top to bottom, or bottom to top. Drag the Border slider to the right to increase the border color between the two video tracks. Click the color swatch if you want to change the border color. You can see the Cube Spin controls in the Effect Controls panel and a preview of the effect in the Program Monitor panel, seen in Figure 10-14.

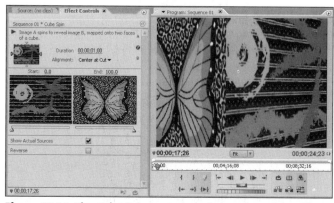

Figure 10-14: The Cube Spin controls and a preview of the effect

Curtain

The Curtain transition simulates a curtain that opens to reveal Clip B replacing Clip A. You can see the Curtain settings in the Effect Controls panel and a preview of the effect in the Program Monitor panel, seen in Figure 10-15.

Figure 10-15: The Curtain controls and a preview of the effect

Doors

The Doors transition simulates opening a door. What's behind the door? Clip B (replacing Clip A). You can have the transition move from left to right, right to left, top to bottom, or bottom to top. The Doors controls, shown in Figure 10-16, include a Border slider. Drag the Border slider to the right to increase the border color between the two video tracks. Click the color swatch if you want to change the border color.

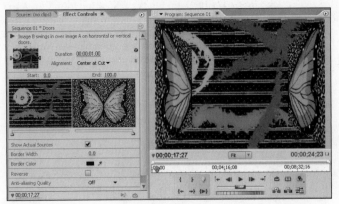

Figure 10-16: The Doors controls and a preview of the effect

Flip Over

The Flip Over transition flips Clip A along its vertical axis to reveal Clip B. Click the Custom button at the bottom of the Effect Controls panel to display the Flip Over Settings dialog box. Use this dialog box to set the number of bands and cell color. Click OK to close the dialog box.

Fold Up

The Fold Up transition folds up Clip A (as if it were a piece of paper) to reveal Clip B.

Spin

Spin is very similar to the Flip Over transition, except that Clip B spins onto the screen, rather than flipping, to replace Clip A.

Spin Away

In the Spin Away transition, Clip B spins onscreen similarly to the Spin transition. However, in Spin Away, Clip B consumes more of the frame than the Spin transition. The Spin Away controls in the Effect Controls panel and a preview of the effect in the Program Monitor panel are shown in Figure 10-17.

Swing In

In the Swing In transition, Clip B swings onto the screen from screen left, like a gate that is open and is being shut.

Swing Out

In the Swing Out transition, Clip B swings onto the screen from screen left, like a gate that is closed and is being opened.

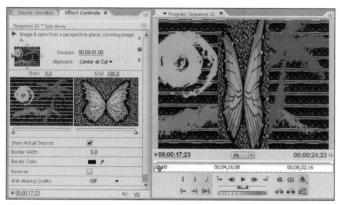

Figure 10-17: The Spin Away controls and preview of the effect

Tumble Away

In the Tumble Away transition, Clip A spins and gradually becomes smaller as it is replaced by Clip B. The Tumble Away controls in the Effect Controls panel and a preview of the effect in the Program Monitor panel are shown in Figure 10-18.

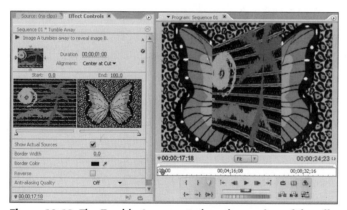

Figure 10-18: The Tumble Away controls and a preview of the effect

Dissolve

The Dissolve transition gradually fades in one video clip over another. Six dissolve transitions exist: Additive Dissolve, Cross Dissolve, Dip to Black, Dither Dissolve, Non-Additive Dissolve, and Random Invert.

Additive Dissolve

The Additive Dissolve transition creates a fade from one clip to the next.

Cross Dissolve

In this transition, Clip B fades in before Clip A fades out.

Dip to Black

In the Dip to Black transition, Clip A gradually fades to black, and then to Clip B.

Dither Dissolve

In the Dither Dissolve transition, Clip A dissolves to Clip B, as tiny dots appear onscreen.

Non-Additive Dissolve

In this transition, Clip B gradually appears in colored areas of Clip A.

Random Invert

In the Random Invert transition, random dot patterns appear as Clip B gradually replaces Clip A.

Iris

The Iris transitions all begin or end at the center point of the screen. The Iris transitions are Iris Box, Iris Cross, Iris Diamond, Iris Points, Iris Round, Iris Shapes, and Iris Star.

Iris Box

In this transition, Clip B gradually appears in an ever-growing square that gradually consumes the full frame.

Iris Cross

In this transition, Clip B gradually appears in a cross that grows bigger and bigger until it takes over the full frame.

Iris Diamond

In this transition, Clip B gradually appears in a diamond that gradually takes over the full frame. The Iris Diamond controls in the Effect Controls panel and a preview of the effect in the Program Monitor panel are shown in Figure 10-19.

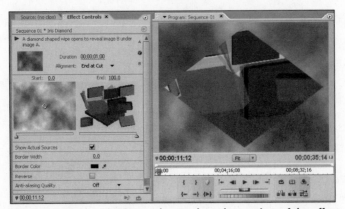

Figure 10-19: The Iris Diamond controls and a preview of the effect

Iris Points

In this transition, Clip B appears in the outer edges of a large cross, with Clip A in the cross. As the cross becomes smaller, Clip B gradually comes full screen.

Iris Round

In the Iris Round transition, Clip B gradually appears in an ever-growing circle that gradually consumes the full frame.

Iris Shapes

In this transition, Clip B gradually appears inside diamonds, ovals, or rectangles that gradually grow and consume the frame. When you choose this transition, you can click on the Custom button in the Effect Controls panel to display the Iris Shapes Settings dialog box. This dialog box allows you to pick the number of shapes and the shape type. The Iris Shapes Settings dialog box is shown in Figure 10-20. The Iris Shapes controls and a preview of the effect are shown in Figure 10-21.

Iris Star

In this transition, Clip B appears in an ever-growing star that gradually consumes the full frame.

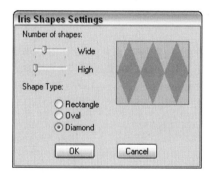

Figure 10-20: The Iris Shapes Settings dialog box allows you to choose a shape type.

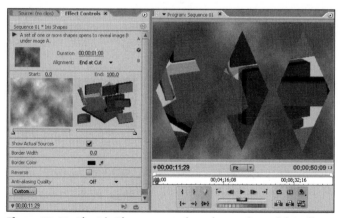

Figure 10-21: The Iris Shapes controls and a preview of the effect

Map transitions

The Map transitions remap colors during the transition. The Map transitions are Channel Map and Luminance Map.

Channel Map

The Channel Map transition enables you to create unusual color effects by mapping image channels to other image channels. When you use this transition, you can click on the Custom button in the Effect Controls panel to display the Channel Map Settings dialog box, as shown in Figure 10-22. In this dialog box, select the channel from the drop-down menu and choose whether to invert the colors. Click OK, and then preview the effect in the Effect Controls panel or Program Monitor panel.

Figure 10-22: The Channel Map Settings dialog box

Luminance Map

The Luminance Map transition replaces the brightness levels of one clip with another.

Page Peel

The transitions in the Page Peel bin simulate one page of a book turning to reveal the next page. On the first page is Clip A, and on the second page is Clip B. This transition can be quite striking, as Premiere Pro renders the image in Clip A curled onto the back of the turning page.

Center Peel

Center Peel creates four separate page curls that rip out of the center of Clip A to reveal Clip B.

Page Peel

This transition is a standard peel where the page curls from the upper left of the screen to the lower right to reveal the next page. Figure 10-23 shows the Page Peel settings.

Page Turn

With the Page Turn transition, the page turns, but it doesn't curl. As it turns to reveal Clip B, you see Clip A reversed on the back of the page.

Peel Back

In this transition, the page is peeled back from the middle to the upper left, then to the upper right, then the lower right, and then the lower left.

Figure 10-23: The Page Peel settings

Roll Away

In this transition, Clip A rolls from left to right off the page (with no curl) to reveal Clip B.

Slide

The Slide transitions enable you to slide clips in and out of the frame to provide transitional effects.

Band Slide

In this transition, rectangular bands appear from screen right and screen left, gradually replacing Clip A with Clip B. When you use this transition, you can click on the Custom button in the Effect Controls panel to display the Band Slide Settings dialog box. In this dialog box, type the number of band slides you want. The Band Slide controls in the Effect Controls panel and a preview of the effect in the Program Monitor panel are shown in Figure 10-24.

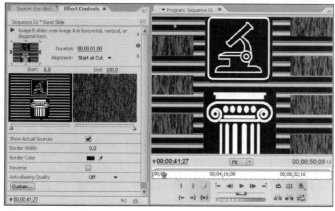

Figure 10-24: The Band Slide controls and a preview of the effect

Center Merge

In this transition, Clip A gradually shrinks and squeezes into the center of the frame as it is replaced by Clip B. Figure 10-25 shows the Center Merge controls in the Effect Controls panel and a preview of the effect in the Program Monitor panel.

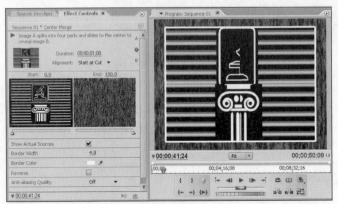

Figure 10-25: The Center Merge controls and a preview of the effect

Center Split

In the Center Split transition, Clip A is split into four quadrants and gradually moves from the center out as it is replaced by Clip B.

Multi-Spin

In the Multi-Spin transition, Clip B gradually appears in tiny spinning boxes that grow to reveal the entire clip. Click on the Custom button in the Effect Controls panel to display the Multi-Spin Settings dialog box to set the horizontal and vertical values. Click OK to close the dialog box.

Push

In this transition, Clip B pushes Clip A to one side. You can set the transition to push from West to East, East to West, North to South, or South to North.

Slash Slide

In this transition, diagonal slashes filled with pieces of Clip B gradually replace Clip A, as seen in Figure 10-26. You can set the slashes to move from Northwest to Southeast, Southeast to Northwest, Northeast to Southwest, Southwest to Northeast, West to East, East to West, North to South, or South to North. When you use this transition, the Slash Slide Settings dialog box appears. In the dialog box, set the number of slashes you want. Click the Custom button at the bottom of the Effect Controls panel to change the number of slashes.

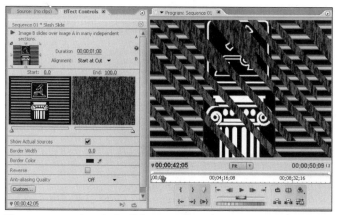

Figure 10-26: The Slash Slide controls and a preview of the effects

Slide

In the Slide transition, Clip B gradually slides over Clip A. You can set how the transition slides. The transition can slide from Northwest to Southeast, Southeast to Northwest, Northeast to Southwest, Southwest to Northeast, West to East, East to West, North to South, or South to North.

Sliding Bands

In this transition, Clip B begins in a compressed state and then gradually stretches across the frame to replace Clip A. The sliding bands can be set to move from North to South, South to North, West to East, or East to West.

Sliding Boxes

In the Sliding Boxes transition, vertical bands composed of Clip B gradually move across the screen to replace Clip A. When you use this transition, you can click on the Custom button in the Effect Controls panel to display the Sliding Boxes Settings dialog box. In the dialog box, set the number bands you want.

Split

In this transition, Clip A splits apart from the middle to reveal Clip B behind it. The effect is like opening two sliding doors to reveal the contents of a room.

Swap

In the Swap transition, Clip B swaps places with Clip A. The effect almost looks as if one clip moves left or right then behind the previous clip.

Swirl

In the Swirl transition, seen in Figure 10-27, Clip B swirls onto the screen to replace Clip A. When you use this transition, you can click on the Custom button in the Effect Controls panel to display the Swirl Settings dialog box. In this dialog box, set the horizontal, vertical, and rate amount.

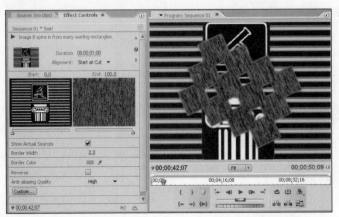

Figure 10-27: The Swirl controls and a preview of the effect

Special Effects

The transitions in the Special Effects bin are a grab bag of transitions that create special effects, many of which change colors or distort images. The Special Effects transitions are Direct, Displace, Image Mask, Take, Texturizer, and Three-D.

Direct

The Direct transition is actually a cut. Place the transition between two overlapping clips, and the scene cuts from A to B with audio from track A. By clicking and dragging on the transition edge, you can control the in and out points of Clip B without actually editing Clip B. This transition is most useful when you need to drop in a short piece of video. In other words, you can have Clip A play and use the Direct transition to create a short insert edit to Clip B before the program returns to Clip A.

Displace

In the Displace transition, the colors in Clip B create an image distortion in Clip A. When you use this transition, you can click on the Custom button in the Effect Controls panel to display the Displace Settings dialog box. This dialog box allows you to change the Scale settings. The lower the Scale, the larger the displacement is. If the displacement would cause the image to stretch beyond the frame, the Wrap Around option tells Premiere Pro to wrap the pixels to the other side of the frame. The Repeat Pixels option repeats the pixels along the image edges instead of wrapping them on the other side of the frame.

Image Mask

The Image Mask transition uses a black-and-white mask image to determine how the transition appears. When you apply this transition, you can click on the Custom button in the Effect Controls panel to display the Image Mask Settings dialog box. Click the Select Image button to select a black-and-white image to use as a mask. Click OK. You can see Clip B through white areas of the mask. You can see Clip A through black areas of the mask.

Note If you select a grayscale image to use as a mask, the transition converts all pixels below 50 percent black to white and all pixels above 50 percent black to black. This can result in a very aliased (jaggy) transition if the mask image is not carefully chosen.

Take

The Take transition is similar to Direct, providing a cut from Clip A to Clip B. If you click and drag the end of the transition beyond Clip B, Premiere Pro inserts black rather than returning to Clip A.

Texturizer

The Texturizer transition maps color values from Clip B into Clip A. The blending of the two clips can create a textured effect.

Three-D

The Three-D transition distorts the colors in Clips A and B creating a composite between the two images. The brightness values of Clip A applied to Clip B can create a three-dimensional effect.

Stretch transitions

The Stretch transitions provide a variety of effects that usually stretch at least one of the clips during the effect. These transitions are available under Stretch: Cross Stretch, Funnel, Stretch, Stretch In, and Stretch Over.

Cross Stretch

This transition is more like a 3D cube transition than a stretch. When the transition occurs, the clips appear as if on a cube that turns. As the cube turns, Clip B replaces Clip A.

Funnel

In this transition, Clip A is gradually transformed into a triangular shape and then sucked out the point of the triangle to be replaced by Clip B. The Funnel controls in the Effect Controls panel and a preview of the effect in the Program Monitor panel are shown in Figure 10-28.

Figure 10-28: The Funnel controls and a preview of the effect

Stretch

In the Stretch transition, Clip B starts compressed and then gradually stretches across the frame to replace Clip A.

Stretch In

Clip B appears over Clip A stretched but then gradually unstretches. When you use this transition, you can click on the Custom button in the Effect Controls panel to display the Stretch In Settings dialog box. In this dialog box, choose the number of bands you want.

Stretch Over

In this transition, Clip B appears over Clip A in a thin, elongated stretch but then gradually unstretches. Figure 10-29 shows the Stretch Over controls in the Effect Controls panel and a preview of the effect in the Program Monitor panel.

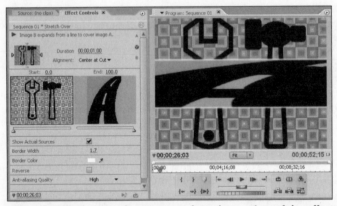

Figure 10-29: The Stretch Over controls and a preview of the effect

Wipe transitions

The Wipe transitions wipe away different parts of Clip A to reveal Clip B. Many of the transitions provide a very modern-looking digital effect. The choices include Band Wipe, Barn Doors, Checker Wipe, CheckerBoard, Clock Wipe, Gradient Wipe, Inset, Paint Splatter, Pinwheel, Radial Wipe, Random Blocks, Random Wipe, Spiral Boxes, Venetian Blinds, Wedge Wipe, Wipe, and Zig-Zag Blocks.

Band Wipe

In the Band Wipe transition, rectangular bands from screen left and screen right gradually replace Clip A with Clip B. When you use this transition, you can click on the Custom button in the Effect Controls panel to display the Band Wipe Settings dialog box appears. In the dialog box, type the number of bands you want. Click OK.

Barn Doors

In this transition, Clip A opens to reveal Clip B. The effect is more like sliding doors than barn doors that swing open.

Checker Wipe

In the Checker Wipe transition, a checkerboard pattern of square slices across the screen with Clip B in it. When you use this transition, the Checker Wipe Settings dialog box appears, allowing you to choose the number of horizontal and vertical slices. To change the number of slices, click the Custom button at the bottom of the Effect Controls panel. Figure 10-30 shows the Checker Wipe controls in the Effect Controls panel and a preview of the effect in the Program Monitor panel.

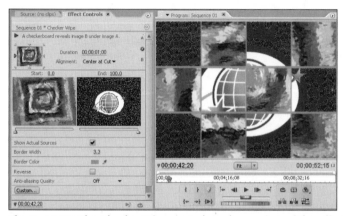

Figure 10-30: The Checker Wipe controls and a preview of the effect

CheckerBoard

In the CheckerBoard transition, a checkerboard pattern with Clip B in the pattern gradually replaces Clip A. This effect provides more squares than the Checker Wipe transition. When you use this transition, you can click on the Custom button in the Effect Controls panel to display the CheckerBoard Settings dialog box, allowing you to choose the number of horizontal and vertical slices. The CheckerBoard controls in the Effect Controls panel and a preview of the effect in the Program Monitor panel are shown in Figure 10-31.

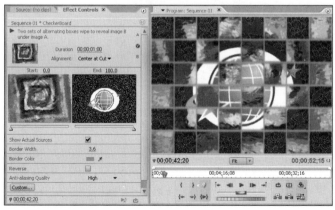

Figure 10-31: The CheckerBoard controls and a preview of the effect

Clock Wipe

In this transition, Clip B appears onscreen gradually revealed in a circular motion. It's as if the rotating hand of a clock is sweeping the clip onscreen.

Gradient Wipe

In this transition, Clip B gradually wipes across the screen using the brightness values of a user-selected grayscale image to determine which image areas in Clip A to replace. When you use this wipe, the Gradient Wipe Settings dialog box appears. In this dialog box, you can load a grayscale image by clicking the Select Image button. When the wipe appears, image areas of Clip B corresponding to the black areas and dark areas of Clip A show through first. In the Gradient Wipe Settings dialog box, you can also click and drag the softness slider to soften the effect. Click OK to apply the settings. To return to these settings, click the Custom button at the bottom of the Effect Controls panel.

Inset

In this transition, Clip B appears in a small rectangular box in the upper-left corner of the frame. As the wipe progresses, the box grows diagonally until Clip B replaces Clip A.

Paint Splatter

In the Paint Splatter transition, Clip B gradually appears in splashes that look like splattered paint.

Pinwheel

In this transition, Clip B gradually appears in a growing star that eventually consumes the full frame. When you use this transition, you can click on the Custom button in the Effect Controls panel to display the Pinwheel Settings dialog box. In the dialog box, choose the number of wedges you want. Figure 10-32 shows the Pinwheel controls in the Effect Controls panel and a preview of the effect in the Program Monitor panel.

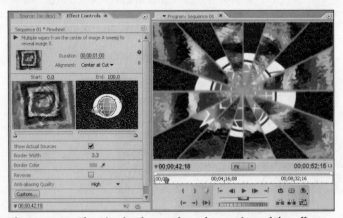

Figure 10-32: The Pinwheel controls and a preview of the effect

Radial Wipe

In the Radial Wipe transition, Clip B is revealed by a wipe that begins horizontally across the top of the frame and sweeps through an arc clockwise, gradually covering Clip A.

Random Blocks

In this transition, Clip B gradually appears in tiny boxes that appear randomly onscreen. When you use this transition, you can click on the Custom button in the Effect Controls panel to display the Random Blocks Settings dialog box. In the dialog box you can set the value for how wide and how high you want the boxes. Click OK to apply the changes.

Random Wipe

In this transition, Clip B gradually appears in small blocks that drop down the screen.

Spiral Boxes

In the Spiral Boxes transition, a rectangular border moves around the frame gradually replacing Clip A with Clip B. When you use this transition, you can click on the Custom button in the Effect Controls panel to display the Spiral Boxes Settings dialog box. In the dialog box, set the horizontal and vertical value. Click OK to apply the changes.

Venetian Blinds

In this transition, Clip B appears as if seen through Venetian blinds that open gradually to reveal Clip B's full frame. When you use this transition, you can click on the Custom button in the Effect Controls panel to display the Venetian Blinds Settings dialog box. In the dialog box, choose the number of bands you want to appear. Click OK to apply the changes. Figure 10-33 shows the Venetian Blinds controls in the Effect Controls panel and a preview of the effect in the Program Monitor panel.

Wedge Wipe

In the Wedge Wipe transition, Clip B appears in a pie wedge that becomes larger, gradually replacing Clip A with Clip B.

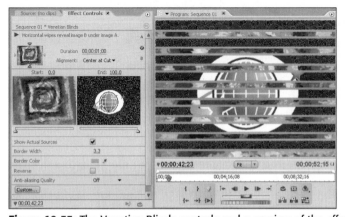

Figure 10-33: The Venetian Blinds controls and a preview of the effect

Wipe

In this simple transition, Clip B slides in from left to right replacing Clip A.

Zig-Zag Blocks

In this transition, Clip B gradually appears in horizontal bands that move from left to right and right to left down the screen. When you use this transition, you can click on the Custom button in the Effect Controls panel to display the Zig-Zag Blocks Settings dialog box. In the dialog box, choose the number of horizontal and vertical bands you want. Click OK to apply the changes.

Zoom transitions

The Zoom transitions provide effects in which the entire clip zooms in or out, or boxes zoom in and out to replace one clip with another. The choices are Cross Zoom, Zoom, Zoom Boxes, and Zoom Trails.

Cross Zoom

The Cross Zoom transition zooms into Clip B, which gradually grows to consume the full frame.

Zoom

In this transition, Clip B appears as a tiny dot and then gradually enlarges to replace Clip A. Figure 10-34 shows the Zoom controls in the Effect Controls panel and a preview of the effect in the Program Monitor panel.

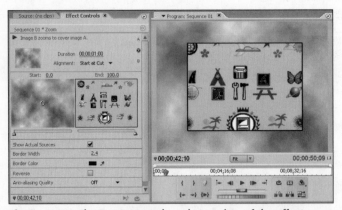

Figure 10-34: The Zoom controls and a preview of the effect

Zoom Boxes

In this transition, tiny boxes filled with Clip B gradually enlarge to replace Clip A. When you use this transition, you can click on the Custom button in the Effect Controls panel to display the Zoom Boxes Settings dialog box. In the dialog box, choose the number of shapes you want. Click OK to apply the changes.

Zoom Trails

In the Zoom Trails transition, Clip A gradually shrinks (a zoom-out effect), leaving trails as it is replaced by Clip B. When you use this transition, you can click on the Custom button in the Effect Controls panel to display the Zoom Trails Settings dialog box. In the dialog box, choose the number of trails you want. Click OK to close the dialog box. Figure 10-35 shows the Zoom Trails controls in the Effect Controls panel and a preview in the Program Monitor panel.

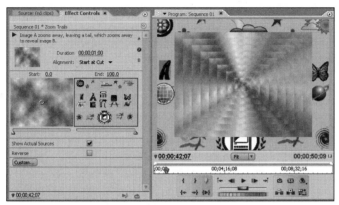

Figure 10-35: The Zoom Trails controls and a preview of the effect

Summary

Premiere Pro's video transitions provide a variety of transitions that you can use to smooth the flow from one clip to another. This chapter covered the following topics:

✦ To add a transition between two clips, drag the transition from the Effects panel and place it between two overlapping video clips.

✦ To edit a transition, use the Effect Controls panel or click the transition in the Timeline panel.

✦ To replace one transition with another, click and drag the new transition over the old transition.

✦ To specify a default transition, select the transition in the Effects panel and then choose Set Selected as Default Transition from the Effects panel menu.

✦   ✦   ✦

Working with Type and Graphics

Creating Titles and Graphics with Premiere Pro's Title Designer

Titles can help turn day into night, night into day, summer into fall, and fall into winter. Used effectively, titles at the beginning of a production can help build expectations, introduce a subject, establish a mood, and, of course, provide the title of the production. Throughout a video production, titles can provide transitions between one segment and another; they can help introduce speakers and locales, or reveal their names. Titles used with graphics can help convey statistical, geographical, and other technical information. At the end of the production, you can use titles to give yourself and your production crew the credit you so richly deserve for your creative efforts.

Although titles can be created in graphics programs, such as Adobe Photoshop and Adobe Illustrator, you may find that Premiere Pro's Title Designer offers all the titling capabilities you need for many productions without ever leaving the Premiere Pro environment. As you'll soon see, the Title Designer not only enables you to create text and graphics, but it also enables you to create drop shadows and animation effects with crawling and scrolling text.

This chapter provides a step-by-step look at how to create production titles using Premiere Pro's Title Designer. We then show you how to integrate your titles into your digital video productions.

Exploring the Title Designer

The Title Designer provides a simple and efficient means of creating text and graphics that can be used for video titles in Premiere Pro projects.

To display the Title Designer, you first need to load Premiere Pro and either create a new project or load a project. When creating a new project, make sure to use the frame size you want your title drawing area to have. The title drawing area takes on the frame size of the existing project.. By having the title and the output dimensions the same, your titles appear exactly where you want them to be in your final production.

To create a project using custom settings, choose File ➪ New ➪ Project. In the New Project dialog box, click on the Custom Settings tab. Click the Editing Mode drop-down menu and choose Desktop. To create a custom preset, type the appropriate Frame Size in the horizontal and vertical fields. To save the custom preset, click the Save Preset button. In the Save Project Settings dialog box, name the preset and give it a description, and then click OK. In the New Project dialog box, name the file project and click OK.

Creating a simple title

To familiarize you with the core tools and features of the Title Designer, use the following steps as a guide through the process of creating and saving a simple title clip for use in a Premiere Pro project:

1. **Choose File ➪ New ➪ Project to create a new project.** The New Project dialog box appears. Name your project, pick a preset, or create a custom preset. Click OK to create the new project. For more information on Premiere Pro digital video project settings, see Chapter 4. If you want, you can also load a Premiere Pro project.

2. **Choose File ➪ New ➪ Title or Title ➪ New Title ➪ Default Still to create a new title.** When the New Title dialog box appears, you can name your title in the Name field. Click OK to create the new title. The Title is placed in the current project's panel automatically and is saved with the project. The Titler panel appears onscreen, as shown in Figure 11-1. The drawing area of the Titler panel is the same size as the project frame size. If you plan to output your titles to film or videotape, you should display the safe title margin and safe action margin areas. By default, these options are already displayed. To view and hide these options, choose Title ➪ View ➪ Safe Title Margin and Title ➪ View ➪ Safe Action Margin. You can also select these options from the Titler panel menu. To have Premiere Pro display a video clip in the Timeline panel, either click the Show Video checkbox in the Titler panel or choose Show Video from the Titler menu. The Titler menu also allows you to display the Tools, Styles, Actions, and Properties panels.

   The tools in the Tools panel and drawing area in the Titler resemble those found in simple drawing and painting programs. Five panels make up the Title Designer: Titler, Title Tools, Title Styles, Title Actions, and Title Properties. The Title Designer panels can be displayed by selecting them from the Window menu. You can group some of the Title Designer panels to create a custom workspace. (To save a custom workspace, choose Window ➪ Workspace ➪ Save Workspace.) The Title Designer is divided into the following sections:

   • **Titler:** The Titler consists of the drawing area and the main toolbar. The main toolbar options allow you to specify whether you are creating still, crawling, or rolling text, or whether you're basing the title on a current title, and they allow you to pick a font and alignment. These options also allow you to show a video clip in the background.

   • **Title Tools:** The text and graphic tools are located in this panel. This panel also has a preview area displaying the current style.

   • **Title Properties:** The settings in this panel enable you to transform and stylize text and graphic objects.

   • **Title Actions:** The icons in this panel enable you to align and/or distribute text and graphic objects.

   • **Titler Styles:** The icons in this panel enable you to apply preset custom styles to text and graphic objects.

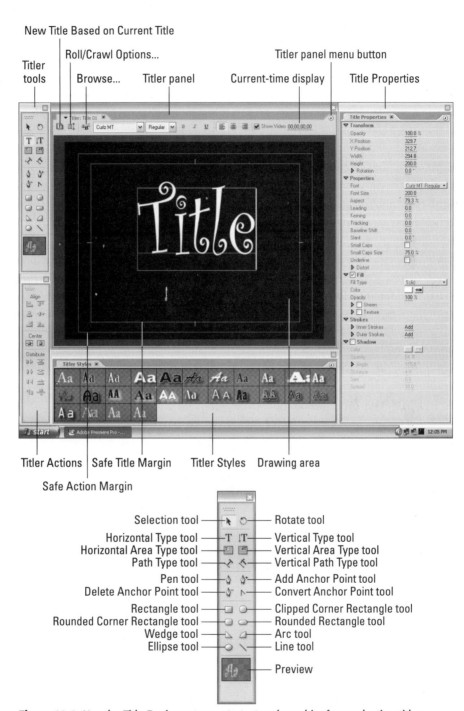

Figure 11-1: Use the Title Designer to create text and graphics for production titles.

3. **Click the Horizontal Title tool (the "T" next to the arrow), and move the mouse to the center of the drawing area.**

4. **Click the mouse, and type** Title.

5. **Format your text using the options in the Title Properties panel.** If you want to format just one letter, click and drag over the letter you want to format. The Title Properties panel contains the Font and Font Size, Fill, Strokes, and Shadow text options. You can change the following parameters:

   • **Font or font size:** Click the triangle beside the word Properties to expand the Properties section. Click the Font drop-down menu to change the font, and click and drag through the Font Size value to change the font size. For more information on stylizing type, see "Creating and Stylizing Type" later in this chapter.

   • **Font color:** Click the triangle beside the word Fill to expand the Fill section. Leave the Fill Type menu set to Solid, and click the Color Swatch next to the Color option. In the Color Picker dialog box that appears, click a color and then click OK. The new color is applied to the title text. For more information on working with color in the Title Designer, see "Using Color" later in this chapter.

6. **To add the title file to your project, close the Title Designer and then drag the title file from the Project panel to a video track in the Timeline panel.**

7. **To save the Title file to your hard drive, so that you can import it into other Premiere projects, click the Title in the Project panel and then choose File ⇨ Export ⇨ Title.** In the Save Title dialog box, you can rename your title using the File name drop-down menu. Locate a place on your hard drive to save your title, and then save it in .prtl format.

Touring the Title tools

The tools in the Title Tools panel enable you to create graphics and text. Table 11-1 reviews the tools and other graphic controls.

Table 11-1: Title Tools Panel Tool Items

Shortcut Key	Name	Description
V	Selection tool	Selects objects so that they can be moved or resized (stretched or shrunk); can also be used to select text before changing text attributes.
O	Rotation tool	Allows you to rotate text.
T	Horizontal Type tool	Creates type horizontally.
C	Vertical Type tool	Creates type vertically.
	Horizontal Area Type tool	Creates wrapped text horizontally.
	Vertical Area Type tool	Creates wrapped text vertically.
	Path Type tools	Creates text along a path.
P	Pen tool	Creates curved shapes using Bezier curves.

Shortcut Key	Name	Description
	Add Anchor Point tool	Adds anchor points to a path.
	Delete Anchor Point tool	Deletes anchor points from a path.
	Convert Anchor Point	Converts a curved point to a corner point, and vice versa.
R	Rectangle tool	Creates rectangles.
	Clipped Corner Rectangle tool	Creates rectangles with dog-eared corners.
	Rounded Corner Rectangle tool	Creates rectangles with round corners.
W	Wedge tool	Creates triangular shapes.
A	Arc tool	Creates curved shapes.
E	Ellipse tool	Creates ellipses.
L	Line tool	Creates lines.

Using the Title menu

Premiere Pro's Title menu enables you to change visual attributes of text and graphic objects. For example, you can use the Title menu to set the font, size, and style of the text that you create in the Title Designer. You can also use it to set the speed and direction of rolling title text. Table 11-2 summarizes the Title menu commands. The Title menu appears when the Title Designer is open onscreen.

Table 11-2: The Title Menu Commands

Menu Command	Description
New Title	Allows you to create a new still, roll, or crawl title.
Font	Changes typeface.
Size	Changes size of text.
Type Alignment	Sets text to flush left, flush right, or centered.
Orientation	Sets text to be horizontal or vertical.
Word Wrap	Sets text to wrap, when it reaches the safe title margin.
Tab Stops	Enables you to create tabs within a text box.
Templates	Enables you to apply, create, and edit templates.
Roll/Crawl Options	Provides options for setting direction and speed of rolling and crawling text.
Logo	Enables you to insert logos in the entire Title Designer drawing area as a background, in a portion of the drawing area, or within a text box.
Transform	Enables you to change the position, scale, rotation, and opacity of an object or text.

Continued

Table 11-2 *(continued)*

Menu Command	Description
Select	Enables you to select from a stack of objects, the first object above, next object above, next object below, or last object below.
Arrange	Enables you to bring selected objects to the front or forward, or to send selected objects to the back or backward in a stack of objects.
Position	Moves object so that it is either horizontally or vertically centered, or moves it to the lower third part of the Title Designer drawing area. The lower third position is frequently used for text that must be read without covering up the onscreen image.
Align Objects	Enables you to align selected objects horizontally left, right, or centered and vertically top, bottom, or centered.
Distribute Objects	Enables you to distribute selected objects horizontally left, right, centered, or even spacing and vertically top, bottom, centered, or even spacing.
View	Enables you to view safe title margin, safe action margin, text baselines, and tab markers.

Saving, Opening, and Copying a Title File

After you've created some stunning text and graphics with the Title Designer, you may want to reuse it in various other Premiere Pro projects. To do so, you need to export your title files, save them to your hard disk, and then import them into the projects you want to use them in.

Note   If you save your title to your hard disk, you can always load the title into any project.

To save your titles to your hard disk, click the title in the Project panel and then choose File ➪ Export ➪ Title. In the Save Title dialog box, you can rename your title using the File name drop-down menu. Locate a place on your hard drive to save your title, and then save it in .prtl format.

To import a saved title to a Premiere Pro project, choose File ➪ Import. In the Import dialog box, locate and select the title file you want to import and then click Open. The New Title dialog box that appears allows you to rename the title file. Rename the title, and then click OK. The imported title file appears in the Project panel ready to be placed in a video track in the Timeline panel.

Tip   Double-clicking a title clip in the Project panel opens that title in the Title Designer.

To edit the title file, double-click the title file in the Project panel. When the title appears in the Title Designer, make the changes. Making changes to the title replaces the old one. In order not to replace the current title, click the New Title Based on Current Title icon in the Titler panel. To make a copy of the current title, you can also choose Title ➪ New Title ➪ Based on Current Title. When the New Title dialog box appears, change the name of the title and click OK.

Note   You can even create one title as a template and then load it, edit the text and graphics, and save it under a new name.

Creating and Stylizing Type

Premiere Pro's horizontal and vertical Type tool works very much like Type tools in graphics programs. Creating text, selecting and moving it, and stylizing fonts works very much the same as most other Type tools. Changing type color and adding shadows is somewhat different but very simple when you get the hang of it. The Path Type tools even enable you to create text along a Bezier path.

Cross-Reference   Creating text along a path with the Path type tools, along with creating Bezier paths and shapes with the Pen tool, is covered later in this chapter in the section "Working with the Bezier Tools."

Using the Horizontal Type and Vertical Type tools

Text in video productions should be clear and easy to read. If viewers need to strain their eyes to read your titles, they'll either stop trying to read them or they'll ignore the video and audio as they try to decipher the text onscreen.

Premiere Pro's Type tools provide the versatility that you need to create clear and interesting text. Not only can you change size, font, and color by using the options in the Title Properties panel, but you also can create drop shadows and emboss effects.

Premiere Pro's Type tools enable you to place type anywhere in the Titler panel drawing area. As you work, Premiere Pro places each block of text within a text *bounding box* that you can easily move, resize, or delete.

Follow these steps to create horizontal and vertical text:

1. **Choose File ➪ New ➪ Project to create a new project.** Set the preset to the size of your title and production.

2. **Choose File ➪ New ➪ Title to create a new title.** In the New Title dialog box that appears, name your title and then click OK. The Title Designer window appears. Make sure the Title Type option is set to Still because you are creating still text rather than rolling or crawling text. To view the Title Type option, click the Roll/Crawl Options icon in the Titler.

Cross-Reference   To learn how to create rolling and crawling text, turn to the section "Rolling and Crawling Titles" later in this chapter.

3. **Click either the Horizontal Type or Vertical Type tool in the Title Tools panel.** The Horizontal Type tool creates text horizontally from left to right, and the Vertical Type tool creates text vertically.

4. **Drag the I-beam cursor to where you want your text to appear, and then click the mouse.** A blinking cursor appears.

Note Select the Horizontal Paragraph and Vertical Type Paragraph tool to create horizontal and vertical text that wraps.

5. **Type your title text.** If you make a mistake and want to delete the last character you typed, press Backspace. Figure 11-2 shows text being entered in a bounding box.

Note You can choose Edit ➪ Undo to undo your last entry.

Editing with the Type tools

If you want to edit text after you finish using the Type tool, you must reselect the text with the Type tool. Move the I-beam cursor over the characters that you want to edit and then click. The blinking cursor appears where you clicked; you can then edit your text. To select all the text within a text box, click the text with the Selection tool.

If you are using the Horizontal Type or Vertical Type tool and you want to create a new line, press Enter and then begin typing. Before you press Enter, make sure that the I-beam cursor is set to where you want the new line to begin.

Figure 11-2: Text created with Premiere Pro's Horizontal Type tool

Wrapping text

The Horizontal Type and Vertical Type tools do not automatically wrap text to the next line. If you want to have Premiere Pro automatically wrap text created with the Horizontal Type and/or Vertical Type tool, choose Title ➪ Word Wrap. The Horizontal Paragraph Type and Vertical Paragraph Type tools automatically wrap text to the next line. To use the Horizontal Paragraph Type and Vertical Paragraph Type tools, select the tool from the toolbox. Move the tool to the drawing area, click and drag to create a text box, and begin typing. Notice that as you type, the text automatically wraps to the next line.

Using tabs

You can add spacing between words and align them left, center, or right using tabs. Tabs can help make your titles (or rolling and crawling text) more readable. To apply tabs to your text, you need to use the tab ruler in the Tab Stops dialog box. Before you display the tab ruler, you may want to display the tab markers. When you display tab markers, Premiere Pro has lines appear where you set your tabs. By displaying the tab markers as lines, you can better visualize how your tabs will appear within your text. To display tab markers, choose Title ➪ View ➪ Tab Markers or choose Tab Markers from the Titler menu. To display the tab ruler, choose Title ➪ Tab Stops. To create a tab, just click the ruler with the left, center, or right tab selected. To move a tab, click and drag it. To apply the tab marks, click OK to close the Tab Stops dialog box. Then move the text beam in front of where you want to apply a tab, and press the Tab key on your keyboard. If you want to change the tabs after you've closed the Tab Stops dialog box, just reopen the Tab Stops dialog box and then click and drag the tab on the ruler to the desired location. The text is automatically updated. To delete tab markers, just click the tab and drag it off to either side of the ruler.

Moving text onscreen

You can move a text box by using the Selection tool, by choosing Title ➪ Transform ➪ Position or by changing the X and Y Position in the Transform section of the Title Properties panel. The Selection tool, the Title ➪ Transform ➪ Rotation menu, and the Transform options (in the Title Properties panel) can also be used to rotate the text box onscreen. You can also rotate text by moving the mouse over one of the corners of the text bounding box. When the mouse icon changes to a curved double-sided arrow, press and hold the mouse while you drag left or right.

Note   A quick way to display the Transform commands is to right-click the mouse while a text bounding box selected.

Manipulating text with the Selection tool

You can quickly move the type's bounding box by following these steps:

1. **In the Titler panel, click inside the text bounding box with the Selection tool.**

2. **Drag the text to a new location.** The X and Y Position values change in the Transform area in the Title Properties panel.

The Selection tool enables you to resize a text bounding box. To do so, follow these steps:

1. **Using the Selection tool, move the Selection tool over one of the bounding box handles.** The cursor changes to a small, straight line with two arrows at either end of it.

2. **Click and drag to increase or decrease the bounding box and font size.** Notice in the Transform section of the Title Properties panel that the Width, Height, X Position, and Y Position values change.

The Selection tool can also be used to rotate a bounding box. To do so, follow these steps:

1. **Move the Selection tool over one of the bounding box handles.**

2. **When the cursor icon changes to a small, curved line with two arrows at either end of it, click and drag to rotate the bounding box and text size.** Notice that the Rotation value in the Transform of the Title Properties panel changes.

Note   To rotate a bounding box, you can use the Rotation tool in the Title Tools panel. To use the Rotation tool, click it in the Title Tools panel. Then move it to the bounding box, and click and drag in the direction you want to rotate the text box.

Manipulating text with the Transform values

You can use the Transform values (located in the Title Properties panel) to move, resize, and rotate a bounding box. Before you can move, resize, or rotate a bounding box, you must select the bounding box by clicking inside it with the Type tool or the Selection tool. You can manipulate text in these ways:

✦ **Changing the opacity of a bounding box:** Click and drag to the right or left on the Opacity value to change it. Values less than 100 percent make the items in the bounding box translucent.

✦ **Moving a bounding box:** In the Transform section of the Title Properties panel, click and drag to the right or left on the X and Y Position values to change them. To move the text bounding box in increments of ten, press and hold the Shift key as you drag to the right or left on the X and Y Position values.

✦ **Resizing a bounding box:** In the Transform section of the Title Properties panel, click and drag to the right or left on the Width and Height values to change them. Pressing the Shift key as you drag left or right increases the values in increments of ten.

✦ **Rotating a bounding box:** In the Transform section of the Title Properties panel, click the Rotation value and drag to the right or left to change it. Dragging left rotates the box counterclockwise, and dragging right rotates the box clockwise.

Manipulating text with the Title menu

Before you can move, resize, or rotate a bounding box, you must select it. If it is not already selected, click inside the text bounding box with either the Type tool or the Selection tool. Here are some things you can do:

✦ **Moving the bounding box:** Choose Title ⇨ Transform ⇨ Position. In the Position dialog box, type a value for the X and Y Position and then click OK. The Title ⇨ Position command enables you to move the box horizontally center, vertically center, and to the lower third area.

✦ **Resizing the bounding box:** Choose Title ⇨ Transform ⇨ Scale. In the Scale dialog box, type a scale percentage. You can choose to scale uniformly or nonuniformly. Finally, click OK.

◆ **Rotating the bounding box:** Choose Title ➪ Transform ➪ Rotation. In the Rotation dialog box, type the degrees you want to rotate the text box and then click OK.

As you move, resize, and rotate the text bounding box, notice that the options in the Transform section in the Title Properties panel are updated to reflect the changes.

Changing text attributes

When you first type with the Type tool, Premiere Pro places the type onscreen in its default font and size. You can change type attributes by changing the Properties in the Title Properties panel or using the menu commands found in the Title menu. The Properties section in the Properties panel allows you not only to change font and font size, but also to set the aspect ratio, kerning, tracking, leading, baseline shift, slant, and small caps and to add an underline. You can use the Type menu to change font and size, and you can change the type orientation from horizontal to vertical, and vice versa.

Changing font and size attributes

You can use both the Title menu and the Properties options in the Title Properties panel to change the font and size of your type. The Title Designer offers three basic techniques for editing font and size attributes.

To change the font and size text attributes before typing, follow these steps:

1. **Click a Type tool.**

2. **Click where you want the text to appear.**

3. **Change the settings for font and size by using the Title ➪ Font command and the Title ➪ Size command.** You can also change the font and size from the Font drop-down menu in the Properties section in the Title Properties panel or by clicking on the Browse icon (which is next to the Roll/Crawl Options icon) at the top of the Titler panel. As you type, the new text you type features the attributes of the current font and size settings.

To change individual characters or words, try this:

1. **Select the text with the Type tool by clicking and dragging over the character.**

2. **Change type attributes using either the Title menu commands or the Properties options in Title Properties panel.**

Tip

To browse through the fonts available, choose Title ➪ Font ➪ Browse. In the Font Browser dialog box, click the down arrow to see a preview of the fonts. The character display in the Font Browser dialog box can be changed. To do so, choose Edit ➪ Preferences ➪ Titler. In the dialog box that appears, change the letters in the Font Browser field.

If you want to change all text in a text block, click the text with the Selection tool. Then change the font and size text attributes.

Changing spacing attributes

Typically, a typeface's default *leading* (space between lines), *kerning* (space between two letters), and *tracking* (space between various letters) provide sharp, readable type onscreen. If you begin using large type sizes, however, white space between lines and letters may look awkward. If this happens, you can use Premiere Pro's leading, kerning, and tracking controls to change spacing attributes.

Here's how to change leading (the spacing between lines):

1. **Use either the Horizontal Paragraph Type or Vertical Paragraph Type tool to create more than one line of text in the drawing area of the Titler panel.**

2. **Click and drag left or right on the Leading value.** Increase the leading value to add space between lines. Decrease the leading value to remove space between lines. If you want to reset spacing to its original leading, type **0** in the Leading field. The Leading field is in the Properties section of the Title Properties panel.

You can use the Baseline Shift property to move the baseline of a selected letter, word, or sentence up or down. Increasing the Baseline Shift value moves text down. Decreasing the Baseline Shift value moves text down. Here's how to change the Baseline Shift:

1. **Use the Horizontal Type or Vertical Type tool to create more than one line of text.**

2. **Click the triangle in front of the Properties section (in the Title Properties panel) to display the Properties.** The Baseline Shift property is located below the Tracking property.

3. **Click and drag the Baseline Shift value to change it.** Increasing the Baseline Shift moves the baseline of the text up. Decreasing the Baseline Shift moves the baseline of the text down.

Here's how to change kerning (the spacing between letters):

1. **Use a Type tool to create a word in the drawing area of the Titler panel.**

2. **Click between the two letters whose spacing you want to change.**

3. **Increase or decrease the kerning values in the Properties section of the Title Properties panel.** As you increase kerning value, the space between letters increases. If you decrease kerning value, the space between the letters decreases.

Here's how to change tracking (the spacing between words):

1. **Use a Type tool to create a word or two in the drawing area of the Title Properties panel.**

2. **Click and drag over the text with the Type tool.**

3. **Increase or decrease the tracking value in the Properties section of the Title Properties panel.** Increasing the tracking value increases the spacing between the letters. Decreasing the tracking value decreases the spacing between the letters.

Changing other text attributes

Some of the other text attributes allow you to change the look and feel of the text. These are the Aspect, Slant, Distort, Small Caps, and Underline attributes. Figure 11-3 shows text before and after changing the Aspect, Slant, and Distort attributes.

Figure 11-3: Text before and after changing the Aspect, Slant, and Distortion attributes

Here's how to change the look and feel of your text using some of the text attributes in the Properties section of the Title Properties panel:

1. **Select a font and font size.**

2. **Type a word using the Horizontal Type tool.**

3. **Click and drag to the right or left on the Aspect value to increase or decrease the horizontal scale of the text.**

4. **To slant the text to the right, click and drag the Slant value to the right. To slant the text to the left, click and drag the Slant value to the left.**

5. **To distort the text, click the X and Y values in the Distort section.**

6. **If you want to underline or convert the text to small caps, click the option's check box.** Doing so selects the option.

Using Color

The colors you choose for text and graphics can add to the mood and sophistication of your video project. Using the Premiere Pro color tools, you can pick colors as well as create gradients from one color to another. You can even add transparency effects that show background video frames through text and graphics.

How do you know what colors to pick when creating titles? The best guide is to use colors that stand out from background images. When watching broadcast television, pay special attention to titles. Many television producers simply use white text against a dark background, or they use bright text with drop shadows to prevent the titles from looking flat. If you are creating a production that includes many titles — such as *lower thirds* (graphics at the bottom of the screen, often providing information such as the names of speakers), keep the text the same color throughout the production to avoid distracting the viewer.

Choosing color with the Color Picker

Anytime you select a color in Premiere Pro, you are using Premiere Pro's Color Picker. Picking colors in Premiere Pro can be as simple as clicking the mouse. To see how easy it is to pick a color in Premiere Pro, open the Color Picker, shown in Figure 11-4, by clicking the Solid Fill Color swatch. Click the Fill triangle to expand the Fill section and display the Color Swatch. (The Fill section is found below the Properties section in the Title Properties panel.) For the Solid Fill Color Swatch to appear, the Fill Type drop-down menu should be set to Solid.

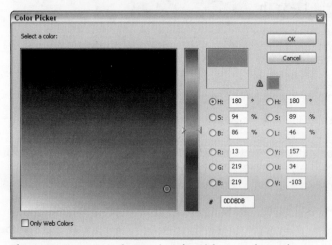

Figure 11-4: Use Premiere Pro's Color Picker to select colors.

You can pick colors for text and graphic objects in the Color Picker window by clicking in the main color area of the dialog box, or you can enter specific RGB values. As you work in the Color Picker, the color that you are creating is previewed in the bottom swatch in the upper-right of the Color Picker dialog box. The top swatch displays the original color. If you want to return to the original color, simply click the top color swatch.

If you pick a color that falls beyond the NTSC video color gamut, Premiere Pro displays a gamut warning signal that looks like a gray triangle with an exclamation mark in it (shown in Figure 11-4). To drop the color back to the nearest NTSC color, simply click the gamut warning signal. If you want to work with colors that are specifically for the Web, click the Only Web Colors option at the bottom left of the Color Picker dialog box.

Note   PAL and SECAM video feature larger color gamuts than NTSC video does. You can ignore the gamut warning if you are not using NTSC video.

Understanding RGB colors

Computer displays and television video monitors create colors by using the red, green, and blue color model. In this model, adding different values of red, green, and blue light creates millions of colors.

Premiere Pro's Color Picker simulates adding light by enabling you to enter values into its Red, Green, and Blue fields. The concept is illustrated in Table 11-3.

The largest number that can be entered into one of the color fields is 255, and the smallest is 0. Thus, Premiere Pro enables you to create over 16 million colors ($256 \times 256 \times 256$). When each RGB value equals 0, no light is added to create colors; the resulting color is black. If you enter 255 in each of the RGB fields, you create white.

To create different shades of gray, make all field values equal. Values of R 50, G 50, B 50 create a dark gray; values of R 250, G 250, B 250 create a light gray.

Table 11-3: The Color Values for RGB Colors

Color	Red Value	Green Value	Blue Value
Black	0	0	0
Red	255	0	0
Green	0	255	0
Blue	0	0	255
Cyan	0	255	255
Magenta	255	0	255
Yellow	255	255	0
White	255	255	255

Choosing color using the Eyedropper tool

Apart from the Color Picker, the most efficient way of picking colors is to click a color with the Eyedropper tool. The Eyedropper tool automatically copies the color you click into the Color swatch. Therefore, you can recreate a color with one click of the mouse, rather than wasting time experimenting with RGB values in the Color Picker.

You can use the Eyedropper tool to do the following:

✦ Select a color from a type or graphic object in the drawing area.

✦ Select a specific color from a logo, style, or template.

✦ Copy a specific color from a video clip in the background of the Titler panel.

The Eyedropper tool can be very handy for selecting colors from a video clip, logo, style, or template. Follow these steps to use the Eyedropper tool:

1. **Create a New Project using the presets you want your title to have.**

   If you want to use the Eyedropper tool to select a color from a video frame (shown in Figure 11-5), you need to import a video clip into your project by choosing File ➪ Import.

On the DVD-ROM

The video clip that appears in Figure 11-5 is in the Digital Vision folder in the Chapter 11 folder in the Tutorial Projects folder that is on the DVD that accompanies this book. The video clip is from Digital Vision's NightMoves (705018f.mov).

2. **Drag the video clip from the Project panel to a video track in the Timeline panel.**

3. **Choose File ➪ New ➪ Title to create a new title. When the New Title dialog box appears, name your title and click OK.**

4. **To display the video clip in the Titler panel, click the Show Video check box to display the video clip.**

5. **Click and drag in the Timeline location area to display the frame you want to appear in the background of the Titler drawing area.**

   Notice that the Fill, Strokes, and Shadow sections all have Eyedropper tools. Using the Fill Eyedropper tool changes the Fill Color Swatch. Using the Strokes Eyedropper tool changes the Strokes Color Swatch. Using the Shadow Eyedropper tool changes the Shadow Color Swatch. Click the Eyedropper tool you want to use.

Figure 11-5: Use the Eyedropper tool to select colors from a frame of a video clip.

Note To import a graphic file as the background or as a logo into the Titler panel drawing area, choose Title ⇨ Logo ⇨ Insert Logo. To insert a logo into text, choose Title ⇨ Logo ⇨ Insert Logo into Text. To import a template into the drawing area of the Titler panel, Title ⇨ Templates.

6. **Move the Eyedropper tool over the color you want to select, and click the mouse.** The Color Swatch changes to the new color.

Applying solid colors to text and graphics

After you've created a graphic object or some text, applying a solid fill color using Premiere Pro's Color Picker is quite simple. Here's how:

1. **Use a Type tool to create a text object, or use a Graphic tool to create a graphic object onscreen.** You can use the Selection tool to select a text or graphic object already onscreen.

2. **Verify that a check mark appears in front of the Fill option in the Title Properties panel.** Deselecting the Fill check box option removes the fill. Keep the Fill option selected.

3. **Click the triangle in front of the Fill option to display the options.**

4. **Set the Fill Type drop-down menu to Solid.**

5. **Click the Color Swatch to open the Color Picker.**

6. **Pick your new color, and close the Color Picker.** You can also use the Eyedropper tool to pick a color from an object in the drawing area or from a video clip in the background (see the preceding section).

7. **To make the color translucent so that you can see through it, reduce the Opacity percentage.** The lower the opacity, the more translucent the object is. You can change the opacity percentage by using either the Opacity field in the Object Style section or in the Transform section. You can also use the Title ⇨ Transform ⇨ Opacity command. By lowering the opacity in an object, you can create interesting graphic effects where portions of objects below show through the object above.

Applying highlights and textures with text and graphic objects

You can also add a highlight and/or a texture to the fill and stroke of text or a graphic object. To add a highlight, use the Sheen option. First click the triangle in front of Fill to display the Fill options. The Sheen option is located within the Fill section. To view the Sheen option, click in the box next to the Sheen option and then click the triangle in front of the Sheen option to display all the properties.

Adding a highlight

Follow these steps to create a sense of light and shadow in your text or graphic:

1. **In the Title Properties panel, with an object selected, click the triangle in front of the Fill property to display the Sheen option.** Then click the Sheen check box.

2. **Click the triangle in front of the Sheen check box to display the Sheen options.**

3. **Click the Color Swatch to pick a color.** You can also use the Eyedropper tool to pick a color from an object onscreen or from a background video clip.

4. **Click and drag over the Size value to change the size of the highlight.** Drag to the right to increase the size. Drag to the left to decrease the size.

5. **Click and drag over the Angle value to change the value of the highlight.**

6. **Click and drag over the Offset value to move the highlight up or down.** Increasing the offset value moves the highlight up, and decreasing the offset value moves the offset down.

7. **Change the Opacity value to make the highlight translucent.** Reducing the Opacity value makes the highlight more translucent.

Adding a texture to text or graphics

You can easily make text and graphics more realistic by applying a texture. Figure 11-6 shows the selected objects and text with a texture applied to it.

Follow these steps to learn how to apply textures:

1. **With an object selected in the Title Designer, click the triangle in front of the Fill property to display the Texture option.** Then click the Texture check box.

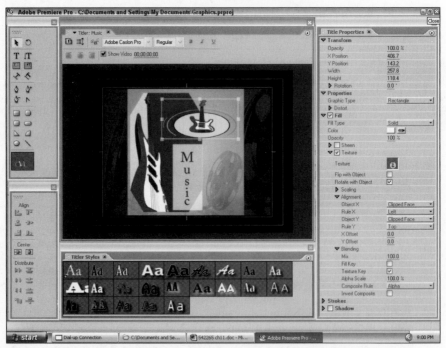

Figure 11-6: In the Title Designer, you can see textures applied to text and graphics.

2. **Click the triangle in front of the Texture check box to display the Texture options.**

3. **Click the Texture Swatch to display the Choose a Texture Image dialog box.**

4. **In the Choose a Texture Image dialog box, pick a texture from the Premiere Pro Textures folder.**

5. **Click Open to apply the texture to the selected object.**

Note You can create your own textures. You can use Photoshop to save any bitmap file as a PSD, JPEG, TARGA, or TIFF. Or you can use Premiere Pro to output a frame from a video clip.

6. **Specify optional settings.** These are your choices:

   - **Flip with Object or Rotate with Object:** Premiere Pro flips and/or rotates a texture with the object.

   - **Scaling:** Premiere Pro scales the texture. First, click the triangle in front of the option, and then click and drag over the Horizontal and Vertical values.

     The Scaling section also contains the Tile X and Tile Y option, which you use to specify whether you want the texture to be tiled to an object.

     You use the Object X and Object Y drop-down menu in the Scaling section to determine how the texture is stretched along the X and Y axes. The four choices from the drop-down menu are Clipped Face, Arbitrary, Face, and Extended Character. The choice you pick determines how the texture is stretched. By default, the Clipped Face option is selected.

   - **Alignment:** Use the Object X and Object Y drop-down menu in the section to determine how the texture aligns with the object. The four choices from the drop-down menu are Clipped Face, Arbitrary, Face, and Extended Character. The choice you pick determines how the texture is aligned. By default, the Clipped Face option is selected.

     You use the Rule X and Rule Y check boxes in the Alignment section to determine how the texture is aligned. Choose Top Left, Center, or Bottom Right.

     You use the X Offset and Y Offset values to move the texture within the selected object.

   - **Blending:** Use the Mix value in the Blending section to blend the texture with the fill color. Decreasing the Mix value increases the fill color and decreases the texture.

     The Fill Key and Texture Key check boxes in the Blending section allow for transparency of the object to be considered.

     Lowering the Alpha Scale value in the Blending section makes the object more translucent. The Composite Rule drop-down menu allows you to pick which channel is going to be used in determining the transparency. Clicking the Invert Composite check box inverts the alpha values.

Creating and applying gradients to text and graphics

Premiere Pro's color controls enable you to apply gradients to text and graphic objects created in the Title Designer. A *gradient*, which is a gradual blend from one color to another, can help add interest and depth to otherwise flat color. Used effectively, gradients can also help simulate lighting effects in graphics. The three types of gradients you can create in the Type Designer are Linear Gradient, Radial Gradient, and 4 Color Gradient. Linear and Radial Gradients are created from two colors. The 4 Color Gradient is created from four colors. Figure 11-7 shows a graphic created using gradients. To create the kite object shown in Figure 11-7, we used the 4 Color Gradient. To learn how to create a diamond shape using the Graphic tools in the Title Designer, turn to the "Working with the Bezier Tools" section in this chapter. The highlight area in the middle of the kite was created using the Sheen option. To the text inside the kite object, we applied a linear gradient.

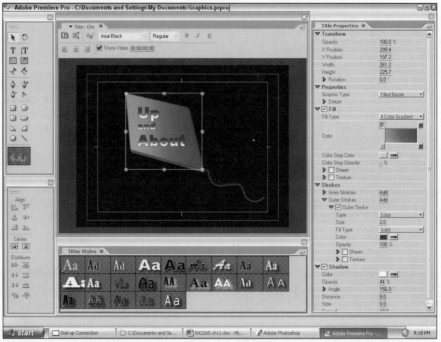

Figure 11-7: Graphic object and text created using gradients

Follow these steps to create a linear and radial gradient:

1. **In the Title Designer, create text or a graphic with the tools in the Title Tools panel or select text or a graphic with the Selection tool.**

Note

If you want to apply a gradient to specific letters in a text block, select the text by clicking and dragging over it with the Type tool.

Moving the Gradient Start and End Color Swatches

You can move the Gradient Start Color Swatch and the Gradient End Color Swatch. Moving the swatches changes how much color of each swatch is applied to the gradient.

The Color Stop Color Swatch allows you to change the color of the selected color swatch. The Color Stop Opacity allows you to change the opacity of the selected color swatch. The selected color swatch is the color swatch with a black triangle above it.

To change the angle in a linear gradient, click and drag over the Angle value.

To increase the number of repeats in the linear or radial blend, click and drag over the Repeat value.

 Note If you are outputting to video, gradients created in small text may make the text unreadable on a television monitor.

2. **The Fill check box should be selected, and the triangle in front of the check box should be facing downward.** Make these things so, if they aren't. The Fill option is found in the Title Properties panel.

3. **From the Fill Type drop-down menu, choose Linear Gradient, Radial Gradient, or 4 Color Gradient.**

4. **To set the start and ending colors of the gradients, use the Gradient Start and End Color Swatches.** The 4 Color Gradient has two start swatches and two end color swatches. In Linear Gradients and Radial Gradients, the Start and End Color Swatches are the two tiny rectangles below the gradient bar. In the 4 Color Gradient, the Color Swatches are two tiny rectangles below and above the gradient. Pick the starting gradient color by double-clicking the Gradient Start Color Swatch. When the Color Picker opens, pick a color. Double-click the Gradient End Color Swatch. When the Color Picker opens, pick an ending gradient color.

Creating and applying bevels to text and graphic objects

Premiere Pro enables you to create some really cool bevels in the Title Designer. You can add a three-dimensional effect to your text and graphic objects by beveling them, as shown in Figure 11-8.

Follow these steps to bevel an object:

1. **In the Title Designer, select either text or a graphic with the tools in the Title Tools panel or select text or a graphic with the Selection tool.**

2. **The Fill check box should be selected, and the triangle in front of the check box should be facing downwards.** Make these things so, if they aren't.

3. **From the Fill Type drop-down menu, choose Bevel.**

Figure 11-8: Text objects with a bevel

4. **Click the Highlight Color Swatch or use the Eyedropper tool to pick a highlight color.** Then click the Shadow Color Swatch or the Eyedropper tool to pick a shadow color.

5. **Click and drag the Size slider to the right to increase the bevel size.**

6. **To increase or decrease the highlight color, click and drag over the Balance value.** Increasing the highlight color decreases shadow color, and vice versa.

7. **To make your bevel look more decorative, click the Tube check box.** Notice that a tubular border appears between the highlight and shadow area.

8. **Click the Lit check box to increase the bevel effect and make the object more three-dimensional.** Click and drag over the Light Angle value to change the angle of the light. Click and drag over the Light Magnitude value to increase or decrease the amount of light.

9. **If you want to make the bevel translucent, click and drag to the left over either the Highlight Opacity or Shadow Opacity value.**

Applying shadows to text and graphics

To add a finishing touch to your text or graphic object, you may want to add a shadow to it. You can add either an inner or outer stroke to an object. Here's how:

1. **In the Title Designer, create text or a graphic with the tools in the Title Tools panel or select text or a graphic with the Selection tool.**

> **Note** If you want the selected object to fill but with a shadow, set the object's Fill Type to Ghost Fill.

2. **Click the Shadow check box to select it.**

3. **To see all the Shadow options, click the triangle in front of the Shadow option so that it is facing downward.**

4. **Click and drag over the Size value to set the size of the shadow.**

5. **Click and drag over the Distance and Angle values to move the shadow to the desired location.**

6. **Click and drag over the Spread value to soften the edges of the shadow.**

7. **Double-click the Color Swatch to change the color for the drop shadow.** You can also use the Eyedropper tool to pick a color from a background video clip or template.

8. **Reduce the Opacity value if you want to make the shadow translucent.**

> **Note** Don't let a shadow fool you. If you are changing the opacity of an object that has a solid shadow, the opacity effect you desire may not be possible until you remove the shadow or make the shadow transparent.

Applying strokes to text and graphics

To separate the fill color from the shadow color, you may want to add a stroke to it. You can add either an inner or outer stroke to an object. Here's how:

1. **In the Title Designer, create text or a graphic with the tools in the Title Tools panel or select text or a graphic with the Selection tool.**

> **Note** If you want the selected object to have a stroke, but no fill or shadow, set the object's Fill Type to Eliminate Fill. This way, you can use the selected object as a frame.

2. **Click the triangle in front of the Strokes option so that it is facing downward.**

3. **Click Add next to either the Inner Strokes and/or Outer Strokes option to add either inner and/or outer strokes to the selected object.**

> **Note** You can click the Object Style menu — the tiny circle with an arrow surrounding it — to add, delete, or move a stroke.

4. **Click the Stroke Type drop-down menu to pick a stroke type.**

5. **Click and drag over the Size value to change the stroke size.**

6. **Click and drag over the Angle value to change the angle of the Depth and Drop Face stroke type.**

7. **Click the Fill Type drop-down menu to pick a fill type.**

8. **Double-click the Color Swatch to pick a color for the drop shadow.** You can also use the Eyedropper tool to pick a color from a background video clip or template, and so on.

9. **Reduce the Opacity value if you want to make the stroke translucent.**

Using Styles

Although setting text attributes is quite simple, sometimes finding the right combination of font, size, style, kerning, and leading can be time-consuming. After you've spent the better part of an hour fine-tuning text attributes to one text block, you may want to apply the same attributes to other text in the Title Designer or to other text that you've previously saved. You can save attributes and color using styles.

The Premiere Pro Titler Styles panel enables you to save and load preset styles for text and graphics. Thus, instead of picking font, size, and color each time you create a title, you can apply a style name to the text and have all the attributes applied at once. Using one or two styles throughout your project helps ensure consistency. If you don't want to create your own styles, you can use the preset styles appearing in the Title Styles panel. To display the Title Styles, choose Window ➪ Title Styles or click the Titler panel menu and choose Styles. All you need to do to apply a style is to select some text and click the style swatch that suits your needs.

The choices for styles are hidden. They are within the Titler Styles panel. The style choices are accessible by clicking the Styles menu — the tiny circle with an arrow surrounding it. The Styles menu is shown in Figure 11-9. Clicking the Styles menu arrow opens up commands that allow you to create styles, save them to disk, and change the way styles appear onscreen.

Figure 11-9: The Styles menu displays styles and available style library options.

Follow these steps to create a style:

1. **Create the text using attributes that you have in the Title menu or the Title Properties panel.**

2. **Choose New Style from the Styles menu.**

3. **Enter a name for the style, and then click OK.** Either you see a swatch of the new style, or the style name appears in the Styles area.

Styles remain only during the current Premiere Pro project session. If you want to use a style again, you must save the styles into a styles file. Here's how to save a styles file:

1. **Select the name of the style you want to save, or select its thumbnail.**

You can also start by selecting each object containing the style that you want to save.

2. **Choose Save Style Library from the Styles menu.**

3. **Enter a name for the style, and designate its location on your hard drive.**

4. **Click Save.** Premiere Pro saves the file using a .prtl file extension.

You can replace a preexisting style name with a new style name by choosing Rename Style. To create a new style, choose New Style. To create a copy of the style, choose Duplicate Style.

Loading and applying styles

If you want to load a style from the hard drive to use in a new Premiere Pro session, you must load the style library before you can apply it.

Follow these steps to load styles from the hard drive:

1. **Click the triangle in the Styles section to display the Styles menu. Choose Load Style Library from the Styles menu.**

2. **Use the mouse to navigate to the hard drive location containing your style.**

3. **Select the style, and then click Open.** After styles are loaded, you can easily apply a style by clicking the text or object and then simply clicking the swatch for the style that you want to apply.

Renaming, deleting, and changing style swatches

You can duplicate styles and rename them. You can delete saved styles that you don't need to use anymore. You can also change the way the style swatches appear in the Title Designer.

Follow these steps to duplicate, rename, and delete styles:

1. **With a style selected, choose Duplicate Style from the Styles menu.**

2. **To rename a style, first select it and then choose Rename Style from the Styles menu.**

3. **In the dialog box that appears, type a new name.**

4. **To delete a style, select it from the Styles section.**

5. **With a style selected, choose Delete Style from the Styles menu. In the dialog box that appears, click OK to delete the selected style.**

If you feel the style swatches consume too much screen space, you can change the display of styles so that they appear as text or as small icons. To change the display, simply click the Styles menu and then choose either Text only, Large Thumbnails, or Small Thumbnails.

Note   To change the two characters that appear in the style swatch, choose Edit ➪ Preferences ➪ Titler. In the dialog box that appears, type the two characters that you want in the Style Swatches field.

Placing a Title in a Project

To use the titles you create in the Title Designer, you need to add them to a Premiere Pro project. When you save a title, Premiere Pro automatically adds the title to the Project panel of the current project. After the title is in the Project panel, you add titles to the Timeline panel in much the same way as you add video clips and other graphics — by dragging and dropping them from the Project panel to the Timeline panel. Titles can be placed either in a Video track above a video clip or in the same track as a video clip. Typically, you could add a title to the Video 2 track so that the title or title sequence appears over the video clips in the Video 1 track. If you want to have a Title file gradually transition into a video clip, you can place the Title file in the same Video track, so that the title overlaps the video clip at the beginning or at the end. The transition is applied to the overlapping section. For more information on working with video transitions, refer to Chapter 10.

You can add a pre-existing title to a project onscreen by importing it into a project. Here's how to add a title to the Project pane, by using the Import command:

1. **Choose File ➪ Open to open the project file that you want to work with.**

2. **Choose File ➪ Import to import the title file that you want to use. Choose File ➪ New ➪ Title to create a new title.**

   You should have the title file in the Project panel of the project file.

3. **Drag the title file from the Project panel to the Video 2 track of the Timeline panel.** If the Timeline panel is not open, you can open it by choosing Window ➪ Timelines or by double-clicking on Sequence 01 in the Project panel.

4. **After you add your title to a Video 2 track in the Timeline panel, you'll probably want to preview your project.** In the Timeline panel, move the current-time indicator over the area you want to preview. Then open the Monitor panel (choose Window ➪ Program Monitor ➪ Sequence 01). Press the Play button to have Premiere Pro play the clip in the Program Monitor panel. (For more information about previewing Premiere Pro projects, see Chapter 4.)

Tip   After you place a title file into a Premiere Pro project, you can edit the title file by double-clicking it. When you double-click, the Title Designer appears.

5. **Choose File ➪ Save to save your work.**

Adding a Background to a Title Clip

In this section, you create a new project. In the project, you import a video clip to use behind the title you create using the Premiere Pro Title Designer. Then you save the title and place it in your production. Figure 11-10 shows the Premiere Pro layout of a production created using a title superimposed over a video clip. In the Program Monitor panel, you can see the Title file superimposed over the video clip. In the Timeline panel, the Title file is selected. Premiere Pro creates titles files with transparent backgrounds, allowing you to see a video clip below the Title file. Notice that in the Timeline panel the Title file appears in the Video 2 track, the video clip appears in the Video 1 track (Digital Vision's CityMix 567023f.mov), and a sound clip (Digital Vision's Sounds from the Chill CD-ROM 665002aw.wav) appears in the Audio 1 track.

Follow these steps to create a title and to overlay it onto a video clip:

1. **Choose File ➪ New ➪ Project to create a project.** Make sure that you use the proper preset.

2. **Choose File ➪ Import to import the video clip you want to appear behind the title.**

If you want, you can use the video clip that appears in Figure 11-10. It is found in the Digital Vision folder, inside the Chapter 11 folder, in the Tutorial Projects folder that is on the DVD that accompanies this book. The video clip is from Digital Vision's CityMix CD-ROM (567023f.mov), and the sound clip is from Digital Vision's Sounds from the Chill CD-ROM (665002aw.wav).

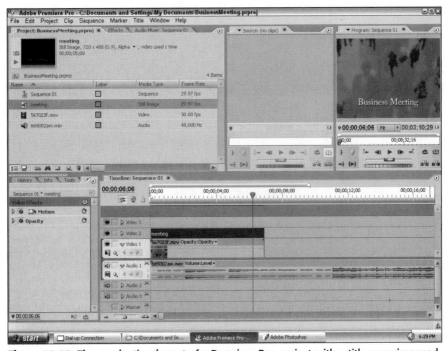

Figure 11-10: The production layout of a Premiere Pro project with a title superimposed over a video clip

3. **Drag the video clip from the Project panel to the Video 1 track in the Timeline panel.**

4. **Choose File ➪ New ➪ Title to create a new title. When the New Title dialog box appears, name your title and click OK.**

5. **Make sure to select the Show Video check box to display the video clip in the drawing area of the Titler panel.** Premiere Pro places the frame in the background where the current-time indicator is located. To use a different frame in the video clip, move the current-time indicator in the Timeline panel, or you can click and drag the Timeline values to the right of the Show Video check box.

Note

If you are outputting to video or film, you want to have the Safe Title Margin and Safe Action Margin displayed. If they are not displayed, choose Type ➪ View ➪ Safe Title Margins and Type ➪ View ➪ Safe Action Margins. If you are outputting to the Web, you don't need to select these options.

6. **Click the Type tool, move the I-beam cursor to the drawing area of the Titler panel, and type** Business Meeting **(as shown in Figure 11-11) or whatever else you prefer.**

7. **Choose a style.** You can change the text attributes, color, and shadow as desired using the Title Properties panel.

Figure 11-11: The Title Designer for the production shown in Figure 11-10

8. **Close the Title Designer.** The title is automatically in the Project panel of the project. If you want to save the title to your hard drive, click the Title in the Project panel and choose File ⇨ Export ⇨ Title. In the Save Title dialog box, click Save.

9. **Drag the title from the Project panel to the Video 2 track of the Timeline panel.** Move the title into position. We moved the title shown in Figure 11-10 so that it lines up with the video clip in the Video 1 track.

10. **If you need to extend the title so that it matches the length of the video clip, click the right side of the title in the Timeline panel and drag to the right.**

You can change the duration of a title by clicking the title in the Timeline panel and choosing Clip ⇨ Speed/Duration. In the Clip Speed/Duration dialog box, click the chain to unlink the speed and duration. Then type the new duration. Click OK to activate the changes.

11. **Display the Monitor panel, if it is not already open, by choosing Window ⇨ Program Monitor ⇨ Sequence.** Click the Play button to play the project.

You can animate your title by using either Perspective, the Basic 3D Video Effect, or by using the Motion options in the Effect Controls panel. Click the triangle in front of Motion in the Effect Controls panel to display the Motion options. The Motion options are Position, Scale, Rotation, and Anchor Point. For more information on using the Motion options, see Chapter 17.

12. **To add sound to your clip, choose File ⇨ Import.** Locate the sound you want to import. When the sound clip is in the Project panel, click and drag it to Audio 1 track of the Timeline panel. If the sound clip is too long, you can cut it using the Razor tool. For more information on editing sound, refer to Chapter 8.

13. **Choose File ⇨ Save to save the project. To preview the project with sound, click the Play button in the Program Monitor panel.**

Working with Logos

Logos can be imported into the Title Designer and used in a portion of the drawing area or in the entire area. A logo can be a graphic or a photograph. In Figure 11-12, we created the title by inserting two logos: a photograph of a sky into the background and a graphic of a sun into the center of the drawing area. The photograph is a Photoshop file, and the sun is an Illustrator file. To create the text, we used three different styles in using the Title Styles panel.

Follow these steps to import a logo into a title:

1. **Choose File ⇨ New ⇨ Project to create a new project.** In the New Project dialog box, choose a preset. Name your project, and click OK.

2. **Choose File ⇨ New ⇨ Title to create a new title. In the New Title dialog box that appears, name your title and click OK. Stylize the text as desired.**

Figure 11-12: A title created by inserting two logos into the Title Designer

3. **In the Title Designer, choose Title ➪ Logo ➪ Insert Logo.** In the Import Image as Logo dialog box, pick a file to import into the Titler drawing area. You can either use one of the logos in the Logo or Texture folder that comes with Premiere Pro or make your own by using Adobe Illustrator and/or Adobe Photoshop.

On the DVD-ROM

If you want, you can use the images that appear in Figure 11-12. They are found in the logo folder, inside the Chapter 11 folder, in the Tutorial Projects folder that is on the DVD that accompanies this book.

Note

To insert a logo in a text box, double-click the text box with the Selection tool. Then choose Title ➪ Logo ➪ Insert Logo into Text.

4. **To change the logo in the drawing area to a different graphic, click the box to the right of Logo Bitmap in the Properties section.** When the dialog box appears, pick a file.

5. **After the logo is in the drawing area, you can move, resize, and rotate it with the Selection tool.** You can also use the Transform commands in the dialog box or the Title menu.

6. **To restore the logo to its original settings, choose Title ➪ Logo ➪ Restore Logo Size or Title ➪ Logo ➪ Restore Logo Aspect Ratio.**

Using Templates

Creating titles using pre-existing styles and templates can help speed up the time it takes to create a Premiere Pro project. Creating a title using a template is easy.

Follow these steps to use a template:

1. **Choose File ➪ New ➪ Project to create a new project.**

2. **Choose File ➪ New ➪ Title to create a new title. When the New Title dialog box appears, name your title and click OK.**

3. **Choose Title ➪ Templates.** In the Templates dialog box that appears, pick a template from one of the folders. Then click Apply to apply the template to the drawing area.

You can use the Templates menu in the Templates dialog box to save a title as a template, rename a template, delete a template, plus other options. Here's how:

1. **Create a new title or open an existing title.**

2. **Choose Title ➪ Templates.**

3. **Click the triangle in the Templates dialog box to display the Templates menu, shown in Figure 11-13.**

Figure 11-13: The Templates menu enables you to save a title onscreen as a template.

4. **To save the title onscreen as a template, choose Save as Template.**

5. **To rename or delete a template, click the template you want to change and then pick Rename Template or Delete Template from the Templates menu.**

6. **To import a file as a template, select a file and then choose Import File as Template.**

7. **Click Apply to close the Templates dialog box.**

After the template is in the Title Designer, you can change it how you want. Click and drag over the text in the template with the Type tool to edit the text. If you want, you can also change the style of the text. You can select items in the template with the Selection tool and move them to a new position. You can also change the fill style and color.

Using a Title Created from a Template

In this section, you create a project using two different titles using templates. One title goes at the beginning of the project in the Video 2 track; the other title is at the end of the project, in Video 2 track. The first title template is used as an opening screen, which gradually fades out to the first video clip that is in the Video 1 track, and the second title template is used as a closing screen. The second template fades in and out over the video clip that is in Video 1 track. Figure 11-14 shows the Premiere Pro Timeline, Project, and Effect Controls panels for the project. Figure 11-15 shows frames from the Premiere Pro project created by using two template titles, two video clips, and a sound clip.

Figure 11-14: The Timeline, Project, and Effect Controls panels for a Premiere Pro project created using two titles that were created using templates

Figure 11-15: A Premiere Pro project created using two template titles, two video clips, and a sound clip

Follow these steps to create a project using two titles created from templates:

1. **Choose File ⇨ New ⇨ Project to create a project.** Make sure that you use the proper preset.

2. **Choose File ⇨ New ⇨ Title to create a new title. When the New Title dialog box appears, name your title and click OK.** The Title Designer appears.

3. **Choose Title ⇨ Templates.** In the Templates dialog box that appears, pick a template from one of the folders. For the project, you need to create two titles. The first template is used at the beginning of the project, and the second template is used at the end of the project. Start by creating the first title. The first title in the project has a title at the top and a subtitle at the bottom. Select a template. Click Apply for the template to appear in the drawing area of the Title Designer, as seen in Figure 11-16. We used the Business1 title template in the Business1 folder, which is in the Corporate folder in the Title Designer Preset folder.

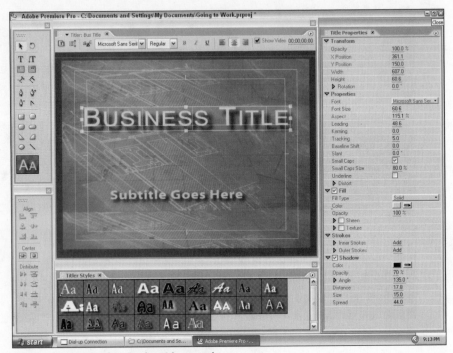

Figure 11-16: Template in the Titler panel.

4. **Use the Horizontal Type tool to type the heading, GOING TO WORK.** Use the Horizontal Type tool to type the subhead, **Make success your target**, as seen in Figure 11-17. In order to have the text fit within the drawing area, you might need to reduce the font size of the subtitle text. When you are finished, close the Title Designer. The Title appears in the Project panel of the project.

5. **Now that you've created the first title of your project (shown in the Video 2 track in Figure 11-14), create the second title (shown in the Video 2 track in Figure 11-14) by choosing Title ⇨ New Title ⇨ Based on Template.** In the Templates dialog box, select a template. Click OK for the template to appear in the drawing area of the Title Designer, as shown in Figure 11-18. We used the Business1 list template in the Business1 folder, which is in the Corporate folder in the Title Designer Preset folder.

6. **Use the Horizontal Type tool to type the heading, AFTER A SUCCESSFUL DAY, as seen in Figure 11-19.** You may need to reduce the size of the font of the Title text. Use the Horizontal Type tool to create the first bullet; type **Going to a Meeting** as shown in Figure 11-19. Create the second bullet and type **Going out to Dinner**. Create the third bullet and type **Going to the Movies**. Create the fourth bullet and type **Going to a Show**. Create the fifth bullet and type **Going Home**. When you are finished, close the Title Designer. The Title appears in the Project panel of the project.

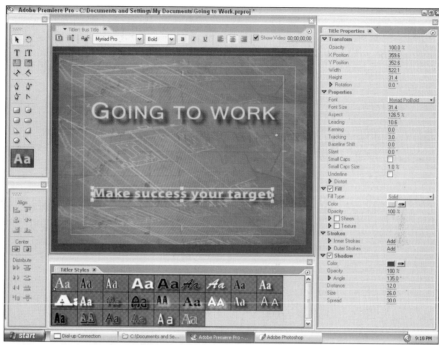

Figure 11-17: The template from Figure 11-16 after editing the text

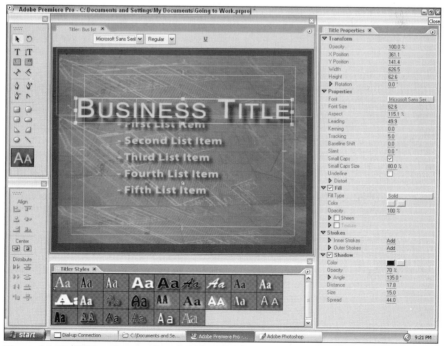

Figure 11-18: Editing the template in Titler panel

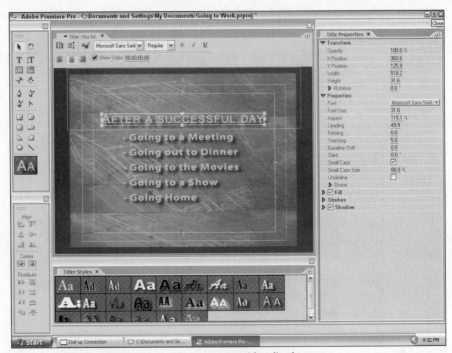

Figure 11-19: The template from Figure 11-18 with edited text

7. **Click and drag the first title you created at the beginning of the Video 2 track, as shown in Figure 11-14.** Then click and drag the second title to Video 2, as seen in Figure 11-14. The end of the second title lines up with the end of the last video clip in the Video 1 track. To extend the title duration, click and drag the end of the title left.

8. **Choose File ➪ Import to import the video clip that you want to appear at the beginning of the project.** Then import the video clip that you want to appear at the end of the project.

On the DVD-ROM

The video clips and sound clip that appear in Figure 11-14 are found in the Digital Vision folder, inside the Chapter 11 folder, in the Tutorial Projects folder that is on the DVD that accompanies this book. The video clips (567007f.mov and 567030f.mov) are from Digital Vision's CityMix. The sound clip (705005.aif) is from Digital Vision's NightMoves CD-ROM.

9. **Drag one video clip to the beginning of the Video 1 track and another video clip so that it overlaps the first video clip in the Video 1 track, as seen in Figure 11-14.** We put Digital Vision's video clip 567007f.mov at the beginning of Video 1 track and Digital Vision's video clip 567030f.mov in the Video 1 track so that it overlaps video clip 567007f.mov.

10. **In the Effects panel, click the triangle in front of the Video Transitions folder.** Click the triangle in front of the Iris folder, and click the Iris Cross transition. Drag the Iris Cross transition to Video 1 track, to where the two video clips overlap.

11. **For a quick preview of the transition, use the Effect Controls panel.** To open the Effect Controls panel (seen in Figure 11-14), choose Window ➪ Effect Controls. Next, click the transition in the Video 1 track. To preview the transition with the video clips, click the Show Actual Sources check box, and then click the Play the Transition button. You can also use the settings and the Timeline in the Effect Controls panel to edit the transition. For more information on using transitions, turn to Chapter 10.

12. **To fade the first title into the first video clip, click the first title to select it.** Then click the triangle in front of the words "Video 2" to expand the Video track. Next click the Show Keyframes icon, and choose Show Opacity Handles. To fade the title into the first video clip, you have to create two handles on the Opacity line and then drag the last handle downward. To create the first handle (shown in Figure 11-14), move the current-time indicator at the middle of the title. Then click the Add/Remove Keyframe button to add a handle. To create the last handle (seen in Figure 11-14), move the current-time indicator at the end of the title. Then click the Add/Remove Keyframe button to add a handle. Use the Selection tool to click and drag down on the last handle on the Opacity line.

13. **To preview the fade from the first title to the first video clip, click and drag the current-time indicator in the Timeline over the areas.**

14. **To gradually fade the last title into the last video clip, you must add two handles to the second title's Opacity line.** First, select the last title in the Timeline window. Move the current-time indicator at the beginning of the second title, and then click the Add/Remove Keyframe button to add the first handle. Move the current-time indicator toward the middle of the second title, and then click the Add/Remove Keyframe button to create a second handle. Use the Selection tool to click and drag down on the first handle on the Opacity line. To gradually fade the last title out, you need to create two more handles. Move the current-time indicator to the right of the second handle, and then click the Add/Remove Keyframe button to add a third handle (as shown in Figure 11-14). Move the current-time indicator to the end of the last title, and then click the Add/Remove Keyframe button to add a fourth handle. Use the Selection tool to click and drag down on the last handle on the Opacity line. For more information on fading video clips, turn to Chapter 15.

15. **To preview your project, click the Play button in the Program Monitor panel.**

16. **To add sound to your project, click and drag the sound clip from the Project panel to Audio 1 of the Timeline panel.** For more information on working with sound clips, refer to Chapter 8.

17. **To build a preview, press Enter on the keyboard. Press the Play button in the Program Monitor panel to play the project. Choose File ➪ Save to save your project.**

Rolling and Crawling Titles

If you are creating production credits or a long sequence of text, you probably want to animate the text so that it scrolls up or down or crawls left or right across the screen. Premiere Pro's Title Designer provides just what you need — it enables you to create smooth attractive titles that stream across the screen.

Follow these steps for creating scrolling or crawling text:

1. **Create a new project, or load a project.**

2. **Create a new title by choosing File ➪ Title ➪ Default Crawl or File ➪ Title ➪ Default Roll. To roll text vertically up or down, choose Default Roll. To make the text crawl across the screen, choose Default Crawl.**

3. **In the New Title dialog box, name your title and click OK.** The Title Designer appears.

Note   If you want to place a graphic in the background of the scrolling titles, you can choose Title ➪ Logo ➪ Insert Logo or Title ➪ Logo ➪ Insert Logo into Text.

4. **Select a Type tool.** Position the cursor in the area where you want the titles to appear, and then click. Start typing the text that you want to scroll across the screen. For scrolling text, press Enter to add new lines. Figure 11-20 shows scrolling text.

5. **Use the techniques described earlier in this chapter to stylize the text that you want to Roll or Crawl.** If you want to reposition or resize the bounding box, click in the middle and drag it to reposition it onscreen. To resize the box, click one of the four handles and drag with the mouse.

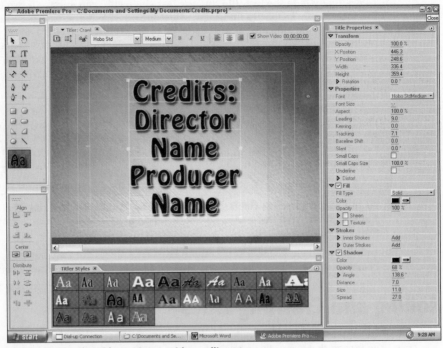

Figure 11-20: The Title Designer with scrolling text

6. **Set the Rolling and Crawling options by clicking the Roll/Crawl Options icon at the top of the Titler panel.** In the Roll/Crawl Options dialog box, the options provide choices to customize the roll or crawl.

   The options provide the following effects:

   - **Start Off Screen:** Choose this option to have the roll/crawl effect begin with the text offscreen.

   - **End Off Screen:** Choose this option to have the roll/crawl effect end with the text offscreen.

   - **Preroll:** If you want the text to appear motionless before the animation begins, enter the number of static frames in this field.

   - **Ease-In:** Enter the number of frames that you want to ramp up, or gradually accelerate, until normal playing speed.

   - **Ease-Out:** Enter the number of frames that you want the titles to ramp down, or gradually slow down, to a complete stop.

   - **Postroll:** If you want the text to appear motionless after the animation ends, enter the number of static frames in this field.

7. **Choose a Rolling and Crawling option from the Roll/Crawl Options dialog box, and click OK to close the dialog box.**

You can create templates from your rolling and scrawling text. To save the rolling or scrawling title onscreen as a template, choose Titles ➪ Templates. In the Templates dialog box, click the triangle to display the Templates menu. Choose Save as Template, and then click Apply to save the title onscreen as a template.

8. **After you create the rolling and scrawling title, close the Title Designer.** Notice that the icon for the Title in the Project panel is a video clip rather than a still clip. You can preview the rolling and scrawling title by clicking the Play button next to the Title preview in the Project panel. To put the scrolling or rolling type into action, drag the Title from the Project panel to a Video Track in the Timeline panel.

To save the rolling and scrawling text to the hard disk, click the Title in the Project panel and choose File ➪ Export ➪ Title. In the Save Title dialog box, click Save to save the Title file as a .prtl file.

Creating Basic Graphics

Premiere Pro's graphics tools enable you to create simple shapes such as lines, squares, ovals, rectangles, and polygons. You can find these basic graphic tools in the Title Tools panel. They are the Rectangle, Clipped Corner Rectangle, Rounded Corner Rectangle, Wedge, Arc, Ellipse, and Line tools.

Follow these steps to create a rectangle, a rounded rectangle, an ellipse, or a line:

Note   Before you go to Step 1, you need to have a project open with a Title and with the Title Designer onscreen.

1. **Select one of Premiere Pro's basic graphic tools, such as the Rectangle, Rounded Rectangle, Ellipse, or Line tool.**

2. **Move the pointer into the Title Designer drawing area where you want to have the shape appear, and click and drag onscreen to create the shape.** To create a perfect square, rounded square, or circle, press the Shift key as you click and drag. To create a line at 45-degree increments, press the Shift key while dragging with the Line tool. Press and hold the Alt key to create an object from its center out.

3. **As you drag, the shape appears onscreen.** Release the mouse after you finish drawing the shape.

4. **To change a graphic from one shape to another, click the Graphic Type drop-down menu and make a selection.** The Graphic Type drop-down menu is located in the Properties section of the Title Properties panel.

5. **To distort a graphic shape, change the X and Y values in the Distort section.** The Distort section is located below the Graphic Type section.

6. **Click the triangle in front of the Distort option to display the X and Y values. Adjust the X and Y values as needed.**

Transforming Graphics

After you create a graphic shape in Premiere Pro, you may want to resize or move it. The following sections provide step-by-step instructions on how to move and resize graphic shapes.

Moving graphic objects

To move a graphic object, follow these steps:

1. **Click the Selection tool, and click a graphic shape to select it.**

Note   If you have various shapes onscreen overlapping each other and are having difficulty selecting a specific shape, you may want to use one of the Title ⇨ Select commands and/or the Title ⇨ Arrange commands.

2. **With the Selection tool activated, click and drag the shape to move it.** As you move the graphic, notice the X and Y position in the Transform section of the Title Properties panel.

3. **If you want, you can change the position of a graphic shape by changing either the X position or the Y position in the Transform section of the Designer Type window or by using the Title ⇨ Transform ⇨ Position command.**

4. **To center a graphic horizontally, vertically, or in the lower-third section of the Titler drawing area, choose one of the Title ⇨ Position commands.**

Note If you have various shapes selected onscreen and are having difficulty distributing or aligning them horizontally or vertically, you may want to use one of the Title ⇨ Align Objects commands or the Title ⇨ Distribute Objects commands.

Resizing graphic objects

Follow these steps to resize and rotate an object:

1. **Click the Selection tool.**

2. **Resize the shape by moving the mouse pointer to one of the shape's handles.** When the icon changes to a line with arrows at either end of it, click and drag the shape's handle to enlarge or reduce the graphic shape. As you resize the graphic, notice that the X and Y position and the Width and Height values in the Transform section of the Title Properties panel change.

 Note Pressing and holding the Shift key while resizing a shape with the Selection tool keeps the shape's proportions. Press and hold Alt as you resize with the Selection tool to create an object from its center out.

3. **If you want, you can change the size of a graphic shape by changing the Width or Height in the Transform section of the Title Properties panel or by using the Title ⇨ Transform ⇨ Scale command.**

4. **Rotate the shape by moving the mouse pointer to one of the shape's handles.** When the icon changes to a curved line with arrows at either end of it, click and drag the shape's handle to rotate the graphic shape. As you rotate the graphic, notice that the Rotation value in the Transform section of the Title Properties panel changes.

5. **If you want, you can change the rotation of a graphic shape by changing the Rotation in the Transform section of the Title Properties panel, or by using the Title ⇨ Transform ⇨ Rotation command, or by using the Rotate tool in the toolbox.**

Stylizing Graphic Objects

After you've created a graphic object, you may want to change the attributes and stylize it. You can change the fill color, fill style, opacity, stroke, and size, and you can apply a shadow to it. You can also change the shape of a graphic. All these effects can be changed using the options in the Title Properties panel.

Changing the fill color

Follow these steps to change the fill color of an object:

1. **Use the Select tool to select the graphic shape you want to change.**

2. **Click the Fill Type drop-down menu, and pick a fill style.**

Note For more information on picking a color and fill style, see the section "Using Color."

3. **Click the Color Swatch, and pick a color from Premiere Pro's Color Picker.**

4. **If desired, you can change the opacity to make your object translucent.** Decreasing the Opacity value makes your object more translucent.

5. **You can also add a sheen (a highlight) or texture to your object.** You can add sheen by clicking the Sheen check box. You can add texture by clicking the Texture check box. Then click the triangle before the Sheen and/or Texture section to display the options.

Adding a shadow

Follow these steps to add a shadow to your object:

1. **Use the Select tool to select the graphic shape you want to change.**

2. **Click the Shadow box to add a check mark.** Then click the triangle in front of the check box to expand the Shadow section.

3. **By default, the shadow color is black. If you want to change the shadow color, click the Shadow Color Swatch to change the color.** If you have either a video clip or a graphic in the background of the Title Designer, you can use the Eyedropper tool to change the shadow color to one of the colors in the background. Just click the Eyedropper tool, and click the color to which you want to change the Shadow Color Swatch.

4. **Use the Size, Distance, and Angle options to customize the magnitude and direction of the shadow.** To soften the edges of the shadow, use the Spread and Opacity options.

5. **To remove the shadow, click the Shadow check box to remove the check mark.**

Applying a stroke

Follow these steps to add a stroke to your object:

1. **Select the filled object with the Selection tool.**

2. **Click the triangle before Strokes to expand the Strokes section.**

3. **To add a stroke using the default settings, click Add after the words Inner Strokes and/or Outer Strokes.**

4. **To customize the inner stroke or outer stroke, click the triangle before Inner Stroke and Outer Stroke.**

5. **Pick a stroke type and size. Then pick a fill type and fill color.** If you want, you can add a sheen and pattern.

6. **To remove a stroke, click the Inner Stroke and/or Outer Stroke check box to remove the check mark.**

Working with the Bezier Tools

Premiere Pro features a Pen tool (as found in Adobe Illustrator), a curve-drawing tool that enables you to create freeform shapes with round and/or corner edges. These freeform polygon shapes are created from anchor points, lines, and curves. You can edit these Bezier shapes by using the Selection tool to move anchor points or by using the Add Anchor Point or Delete Anchor Point tools to add or delete anchor points. You can also use the Convert Anchor Point tool for rounding the corners of polygons or for making rounded corners into pointed corners. For example, you can transform large triangles into mountains or many small triangles into waves.

Follow these steps to use the Pen tool to create a line (before continuing, you should have the Title Designer open):

1. **Select the Pen tool.**

2. **Move the Pen tool to the left side of the Title Designer work area, and click the mouse to establish an anchor point.**

3. **To create a straight line, move the Pen tool to the right side of Title Designer work area and press and hold the Shift key as you click the mouse.** Now you have two anchor points connected by a straight line.

4. **If you click again, the Pen tool keeps creating anchor points and lines.** To have the Pen tool stop creating anchors, click the Select tool. If you accidentally created an extra anchor point, you can delete it by selecting it with the Delete Anchor Point tool.

Follow these steps to convert a rectangle into a diamond:

1. **Select the Rectangle tool.**

2. **Move the Rectangle to the Title Designer drawing area. Then click and drag to create a rectangle.**

3. **Notice that the Graphic Type drop-down menu is set to Rectangle; change it to Closed Bezier.** The rectangle now has four anchor points, one at each corner.

4. **Use the Pen tool to click the anchor points and drag them so that you are slowly converting the rectangle into a diamond, as shown in Figure 11-21.**

5. **To fill the diamond, click the Graphic Type drop-down menu and choose Filled Bezier.** Then use the Fill options to customize the fill. You can also add a shadow and strokes to the diamond using the Shadow and Stroke options.

6. **After you have finished creating and filling the diamond, you can use the Rotate tool to rotate it or use the Title ⇨ Transform commands to transform it.**

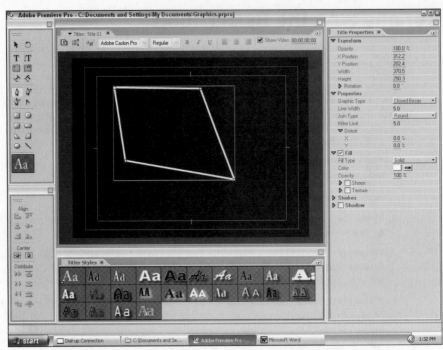

Figure 11-21: A rectangle converted to a diamond shape using the Pen tool

To convert a pointed corner to a rounded corner, follow these steps:

1. **Use the Pen tool to create four joining, small mountains (downward-pointing triangles), as shown in Figure 11-22. If you need to, you can use the Pen tool to edit the points so that the points at the top and bottom line up.**

2. **Select the Convert Anchor Point tool from the toolbox.**

3. **Click and drag the anchor points with the Convert Anchor Point tool to convert a pointed corner to a rounded corner, as shown in Figure 11-22.** Anytime you want to move a point, use the Pen tool.

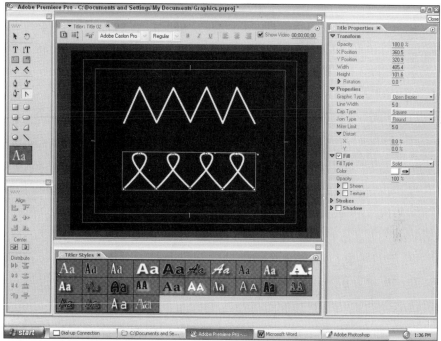

Figure 11-22: We created this path from pointed anchor points using the Pen tool and then converted to rounded anchor points using the Convert Anchor Point tool.

You can use the Add Anchor Point, Delete Anchor Point, and Pen tools to transform objects, as shown in Figure 11-23.

Follow these steps to learn how to transform an object:

1. **Start by creating a square using the Rectangle tool.** As you use the Rectangle tool, press and hold Shift to constrain the aspect ratios.

2. **To edit the object, choose Closed Bezier from the Graphic Type drop-down menu.**

3. **To turn the square into a house shape, you need to use the Add Anchor Point tool to add an anchor point in the middle of the top two anchor points.**

4. **Use the Pen tool to drag the anchor point up, as shown in Figure 11-23.**

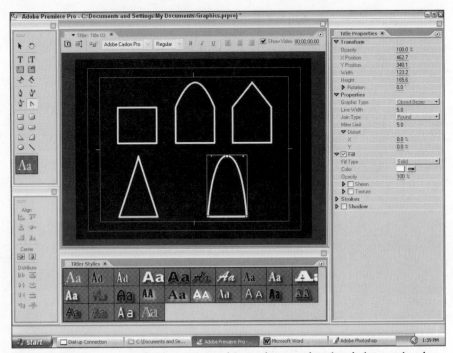

Figure 11-23: We converted a square into a house shape and a triangle into a triangle with a rounded point using the Add Anchor Point and Delete Anchor Point tools.

5. Now use the Convert Anchor Point tool to click the new anchor point to convert it from a curve anchor point to a corner anchor point.

6. To convert the house shape into a triangle (shown in Figure 11-23), use the Delete Anchor Point tool to delete the two anchor points below the newly added anchor point.

7. To convert the triangle into a dome shape (shown in Figure 11-23), use the Convert Anchor Point tool to click and drag the point of the triangle to convert it into a rounded anchor point.

8. To fill the shape, set the Graphic Type drop-down menu to Filled Bezier. Then use the Fill, Shadow, and Stroke options to customize the fill.

To create curves with the Pen tool, follow these steps:

1. Select the Pen tool from the toolbox.

2. Move the mouse to the left side of the Title Designer, and click to establish an anchor point. Don't release the mouse. Instead, drag straight up about half an inch (shown in Figure 11-24). Then release the mouse. The line that appears above and below the anchor point is called a *directional line.* The angle and direction at which the directional line is created determines the angle and direction of the curve being created. By extending the anchor point up rather than down, the first part of the curve bump points up rather than down.

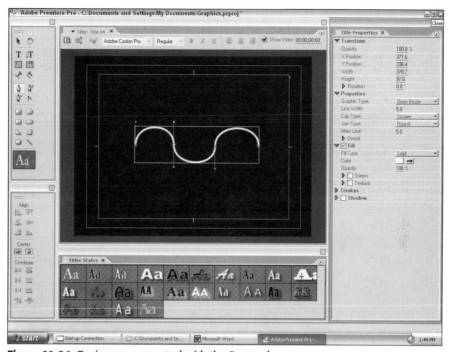

Figure 11-24: Bezier curves created with the Pen tool

3. **Move the mouse about half an inch to the right of the anchor you created in Step 2. Then click and drag straight down about half an inch.** As you drag down, notice that a new directional line appears. Release the mouse to create a curve that has the first part of the curve bump pointing up and the last part of the curve bump pointing down. Congratulations, you've just created your first curve.

4. **If you want, you can edit the curve. Use the Pen tool to move the curve's directional lines.** As you move the directional lines, the curve's shape alters.

5. **To continue drawing curves, move the mouse about half an inch to the right from the anchor point you created in Step 3.** Click and drag straight up about half an inch to create a curve pointing down.

6. **To draw another curve, pointing up, move the mouse about half an inch to the right from the anchor point you created in Step 5.** Then click and drag straight down about half an inch.

7. **To continue creating curves going down and up, repeat Steps 3 and 5.**

To create curves that connect to line segments, follow these steps:

1. **Select the Pen tool from the toolbox.**

2. **Now create a curve using the Pen tool.**

Move the mouse to the left side of the Title Designer, and click and drag straight up about half an inch. Move the mouse about an inch to the right of the anchor you just created. Then click and drag straight down about half an inch to create a curve. If you want your curve to point down instead of up, you need to reverse the dragging part of this step. Instead of starting by clicking and dragging up, you start by clicking and dragging down, and you finish by clicking and dragging up, instead of clicking and dragging down.

3. **Connect a line to the curve, as shown in Figure 11-25**. Move the mouse cursor over to the last anchor point you created in Step 2. Press and hold the Alt key, and notice that a tiny diagonal line appears at the bottom of the Pen tool icon. Click the anchor point to create a corner point. After you convert the point to a corner point, the shape of the curve may change. To adjust the shape of the curve, click the directional line above the corner point and move it to adjust the curve. To create the line segment, move the mouse pointer about an inch to the right and click the mouse. If you need to adjust the position of the line, use the Pen tool.

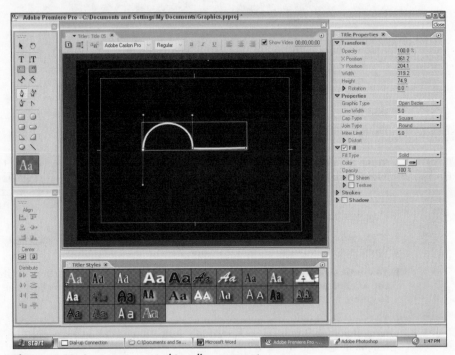

Figure 11-25: A curve connected to a line segment

To create lines that connect to curve segments, follow these steps:

1. **If you have the curve and line segment onscreen from the preceding section, click the Selection tool to deselect the curve and line segment.**

2. **Select the Pen tool so that you can create a line Bezier outline.**

3. **Use the Pen tool to create a line. To create a line, click in the middle of the screen, move the mouse over about an inch to the right, and click again.** Then press and hold the Alt key as you click the anchor point and drag up and to the right to establish a directional line.

4. **To connect a curve to the line you just created (shown in Figure 11-26), move the mouse straight to the right about an inch and then click and drag down about half an inch.** The curve you created is pointing up. If you want the curve to point down, make the directional line point down, rather than up; then click and drag up with the mouse, rather than down.

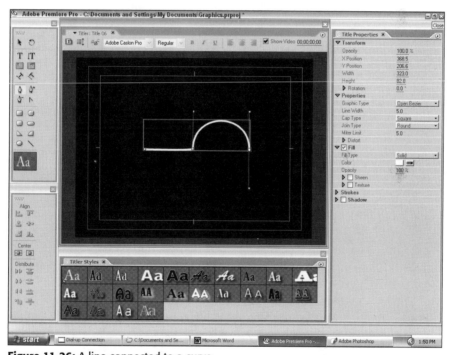

Figure 11-26: A line connected to a curve

Creating Text on a Bezier Path

To create text on a path, use the Path Type tools. To use the Path Type tool, you first need to create a path and then begin typing alongside it. Figure 11-27 shows text along a curve path.

Follow these steps to use the Path Type tool:

1. **In the Title Designer, select the Path Type tool from the toolbox.**

2. **Use the Path Type tool to create a path.** The Path Type tool creates paths the same way as the Pen tool. To review how to use the Pen tool, go to the preceding section.

3. **If you want to create a curved path and still don't feel confident in creating curves, create a path using the Path Type tool to create corner anchor points.** Then use the Convert Anchor Point tool to convert the corner anchor points to curve anchor points.

4. **Use the Pen tools to make the desired path.**

5. **Switch back to the Path Type tool, and start typing.**

6. **Use a Style to stylize your text. Use the Object Style options to edit the style.**

7. **If you want, use the Pen tools to create a shape below the text, as shown in Figure 11-27.** After you have finished creating the shape, choose Filled Bezier from the Graphic Type drop-down menu so that you can fill the shape with a color or gradient. Then use the Fill options to fill the shape.

If you want, you can edit the text or stylize it. As you edit the text and stylize it, you may find that you need to edit the path.

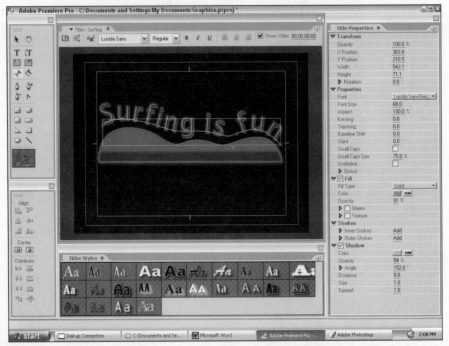

Figure 11-27: Text created along a curved path by using the Path Type tool

Creating a Logo

Logos may appear either at the beginning of a video clip, at the end of a video clip, or throughout a video clip. You can import a logo created in another program or create logos using the Premiere Pro Title Designer. Figure 11-28 shows a sample logo for a sailing school. The logo was created by using Premiere Pro's graphic tools and the Type tools in the Title Tools panel. The background video clip is from Digital Vision's Drifting Skies CD-ROM (386027f.mov).

Follow these steps to create the sailboat logo shown in Figure 11-28:

1. **Choose File ➪ New ➪ Project to create a new project.** Then choose File ➪ New ➪ Title to create a new title. In the New Title dialog box, name your title and click OK. The Title Designer appears.

2. **Use the Ellipse tool to create the circle surrounding the boat. Press Shift while clicking and dragging to create a perfect circle. Press Alt while clicking and dragging to create a circle from the center out.**

3. **Use the Rectangle tool to create the mast.**

4. **To create the sailboat shown in Figure 11-28, use the Wedge tool to create the sails.**

5. **Use the Pen tool to create the sailboat's hull.**

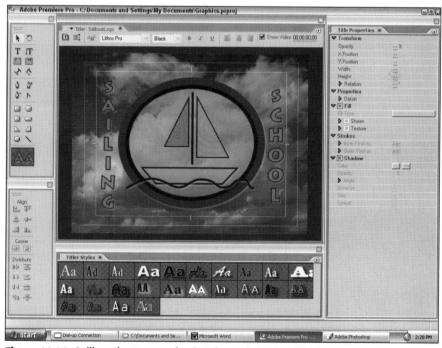

Figure 11-28: Sailboat logo created using the tools in the Title Designer

6. **Use the Pen tool to create small mountains (downward-pointing triangles). Use the Convert Anchor Point tool to turn the mountains into waves.**

Note   Use the Title ➪ Arrange commands to shift different shapes forward or backward as needed. Use the Title ➪ Position commands to horizontally and vertically center the geometric pieces.

7. **Color the objects with gradients and shadows.**

8. **To give the logo a layered look, use the Opacity field to reduce the opacity of the different shapes.**

9. **Use the Vertical Type tool to create the text. Set the attributes and color.**

10. **Close the Title Designer.**

11. **Drag and drop the logo from the Project panel to the Video 2 track in the Timeline panel of the Sailboat project.** Move the sailboat logo to the beginning if you want it to appear there. If not, drag it to the location where you want it. To stretch the logo over time, click and drag the edge of the clip outward.

12. **Choose File ➪ Import to import a video clip.** If you want, you can load a video clip from the DVD that accompanies this book. Drag the video clip to the Video 1 track. We imported a video clip of a sky background from Digital Vision's Drifting Skies CD-ROM (386027f.mov).

On the DVD-ROM   Digital Vision's Drifting Skies CD-ROM (386027f.mov) is in the Digital Vision folder that is in the Chapter 11 folder that is in the Tutorial Projects folder that is on the DVD that accompanies the book.

13. **Choose File ➪ Import to import a sound clip.** Then drag the sound clip from the Project panel to the Audio 1 track. We imported a sound clip from Digital Vision's Sounds from the Chill CD-ROM (665011aw.wav).

On the DVD-ROM   Digital Vision's Sounds from the Chill CD-ROM (665011aw.wav) is in the Digital Vision folder that is in the Chapter 11 folder that is in the Tutorial Projects folder that is on the DVD that accompanies the book.

14. **To preview the sailboat logo in the Sailboat project, display the Program Monitor panel (Window ➪ Program Monitor ➪ Sequence) and click the Play button to view the preview.**

15. **Choose File ➪ Save to save the changes to the Sailboat project to your hard drive.**

Summary

Premiere Pro's Title Designer provides an easy-to-use interface for creating digital video titles. By using the Title Designer, you can quickly create text and graphics to introduce video segments or to roll your final credits. This chapter covered the following topics:

✦ Using the tools in the Title Tools panel to create text and graphics.

✦ Editing object attributes by using the Title menu or the options in the Title Properties panel.

✦ Dragging titles from the Project panel to the Timeline panel.

✦ Creating titles using styles, templates, and logos.

✦ Creating rolling and scrolling text by using the Rolling and Crawling options.

✦ ✦ ✦

Creating Type and Graphic Effects

✦   ✦   ✦   ✦

In This Chapter

Using Photoshop to create text and graphics

Using Photoshop layers and ImageReady to create a QuickTime or AVI video clip

Creating Transparency text effects

Creating Illustrator text and graphic effects for Premiere Pro

Animating titles over graphics

✦   ✦   ✦   ✦

Adobe Premiere Pro packs enormous power as a digital video production tool. However, if you're creating a sophisticated project, designed to appeal to and impress viewers, you need to turn to other applications to create your text and graphics. During the course of production, many Premiere Pro producers turn to such graphics applications as Adobe Photoshop and Adobe Illustrator to create eye-catching text and graphics.

This chapter provides several tutorials to teach you how to create text and graphic effects in Adobe Photoshop and Adobe Illustrator. After you see how to create the graphics effects, you integrate them into Premiere Pro projects. After your graphics are loaded into Premiere Pro, you use Premiere Pro's effects to create some digital magic. Soon your Adobe Photoshop and Adobe Illustrator artwork appears with digital video in the background.

Creating and Importing Graphics from Adobe Photoshop

Adobe Photoshop is one of the most powerful digital imaging programs available for both PCs and Macs. Photoshop easily surpasses Premiere Pro in its capability to create and manipulate graphics. For example, by using Adobe Photoshop, you can quickly create three-dimensional text or grab a piece of text or graphics and bend, twist, or skew it. Because both Adobe Premiere Pro and Adobe Photoshop are friendly cousins in the Adobe family of graphics products, it's not surprising that you can create graphics, text, or photomontages in Photoshop and then import them to use as titles in Premiere Pro.

You can even use Adobe Photoshop's Web-application partner, Adobe ImageReady (free with Adobe Photoshop), to create animation for a Premiere Pro project. For example, you can import Photoshop layers into ImageReady, create animation from the individual layers, and then export the animation as a QuickTime or AVI movie. After you've created a QuickTime or AVI movie, you can import the file into Premiere Pro to make a slideshow presentation.

Creating a digital movie of warped text using Photoshop, ImageReady, and Premiere Pro

You can use Adobe Photoshop to create a layered file and then import the Photoshop layered file into Adobe ImageReady to create a QuickTime or AVI animation. The QuickTime or AVI animation can be imported into a Premiere Pro project to create a slideshow effect. Figure 12-1 shows a Photoshop file with a background layer and four layers with warped text. The following steps show you how to create a QuickTime or AVI movie of a Photoshop layer file.

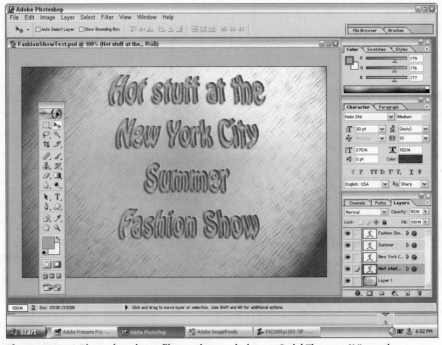

Figure 12-1: A Photoshop layer file can be made into a QuickTime or AVI movie.

1. **Load Adobe Photoshop, and choose File ⇨ New.**

2. **In the New dialog box, name your file,** TypeLayers. Because you probably will import the animation of this file into a Premiere Pro project, pick a frame size that will match your Premiere Pro project. As mentioned in Chapter 4, if you are creating full-screen graphics for an NTSC DV project (which uses non-square pixels), create your Photoshop CS file at 720 × 480 or 720 × 486 (D1). If you are using Photoshop 7, create your file at 720 × 534 or 720 × 540. When you import the file, Premiere Pro will scale down the image. (See Chapter 4 for more details.)

   When creating the file, set the Background mode to RGB Color and set the Contents to Background Color. Click OK to create the file.

Note If you create a graphic at 720 × 480 (or 720 × 486) in a square pixel program such as Adobe Photoshop 7 and then import it into a Premiere Pro NTSC DV project, the graphic may appear distorted in Premiere Pro. The graphic is distorted because Premiere Pro automatically converts it to a non-square 0.9 pixel aspect ratio. To convert the imported Photoshop graphic file back to square pixels, first select the graphic image in the Project window. Then choose File ➪ Interpret Footage. In the Pixel Aspect Ratio section of the Interpret Footage dialog box, click Conform to, and choose Square Pixels (1.0). Then choose Square Pixels (1.0) in the drop-down menu and click OK.

3. **Create your own background graphic using Photoshop's tools, colors, and filters to create an image onscreen.** To create the background in Figure 12-1, we started by first creating a white and gray gradient with the Gradient tool. Then we applied the Add Noise filter with the amount set to 17.95 and Distribution set to Uniform. Next, we applied the Artistic Colored Pencil filter. In the Colored Pencil dialog box, we set the Pencil width to 4, the Stroke Pressure to 8, and the Paper Brightness to 25. Lastly, we applied the Render Lighting Effects filter. In the Lighting Effects dialog box, we set the Style drop-down menu to 2 O'clock Spotlight.

Note Instead of creating your own graphic in Photoshop, you can use a photograph or create a photo collage as the background image. Open the file or files you want to use, and then drag and drop the digital image into the new file you created in Step 2. Photoshop automatically places the digital image in a new layer. If the image is too big for the file, you can scale it down by choosing Edit ➪ Transform ➪ Scale. Press Shift as you click and drag one of the handles. By pressing Shift, the image retains its proportions.

4. **Now you're ready to create some text.** Select the Horizontal Type tool from the Toolbox.

5. **Use the Horizontal Type tool to create some text, and then choose a font and size (we used the font Hobo with a font size of 30) either by using the Character panel or by using the options on the Type tab.** You can also change the color by using either the Colors panel or Swatches panel.

6. **To move the text onscreen, use the Move tool.**

7. **Choose Layer ➪ Layer Style ➪ Blending Options to stylize your text.** In the Layer Style dialog box, click the style you want and then customize it. Figure 12-2 shows the Layer Style dialog box with the settings we used to create the text shown in Figure 12-1. In Figure 12-1, we applied a drop shadow, an inner shadow, an outer glow, a white color overlay with 42 percent opacity, and a pattern overlay.

8. **Click the Warp button in the Type panel.** In the Warp Text dialog box, shown in Figure 12-3, pick a warp option to warp the text. Then click OK to close the dialog box and apply the effect.

9. **If Photoshop's Layer panel is not onscreen, open it by choosing Window ➪ Layers.** The text layer should be selected and at the top of the panel.

10. **Choose Duplicate Layer from the Layer menu to duplicate the text layer.** In the Duplicate Layer dialog box, name the layer and keep the Destination set to the document you are working on. Then click OK. When the layer is duplicated, the text appears on top of the previous one.

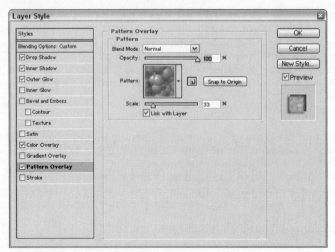

Figure 12-2: The Layer Style dialog box in Photoshop allows you to stylize text.

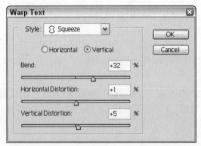

Figure 12-3: Photoshop's Warp Text dialog box allows you to warp type.

11. **Use the Move tool to move the text down.** Then use the Type tool to select the text and edit it.

12. **Repeat Steps 10 and 11 as many times as you need.**

13. **You may want to rearrange the layers in the Layers panel so that the bottom layer is the background, the second layer is the text first layer of your presentation, and the third layer is the second text layer of your presentation.** To move a layer in the Layers panel, click and drag it to move it either up or down.

14. **Choose File ➪ Save to save the file in Photoshop format.** Photoshop format saves a file with all its layers.

Note   The Photoshop TypeLayers file, seen in Figure 12-1, is found in the Chapter 12 folder of the DVD that accompanies this book.

Now you're ready to transform your Photoshop layers into a digital movie. Follow these steps:

1. **After you've saved your Photoshop file, choose File ➪ Jump to Adobe ImageReady.** ImageReady opens and automatically loads the Photoshop file.

Note

You may not have enough memory to have both Photoshop and ImageReady open at the same time. If not, first save your work and quit Photoshop. Then load ImageReady, and choose File ➪ Open to load the TypeLayers file.

2. **Open the Animation panel by choosing Window ➪ Show Animation.** Now you are ready to make frames from layers.

3. **To create frames from each layer and keep adding the background to each frame, you first need to hide all the layers except the text layers.** To do so, click the Eye icon next to the text layer in the Layers panel. Next click the New Frame command from the Animation panel. A second frame is created with the background. To add a text layer, click the Eye icon next to the text layer you want to display. To create a third frame, click the New Frame command. A third frame is created with both the background and the text from frame 2. To add another text layer, click another Eye icon to display the text layer in the frame. Continue creating new frames and displaying text layers until you have converted all the layers into frames. Figure 12-4 shows Photoshop layers converted to animation frames.

Note

To create a frame from each layer, you can choose Make Frames from Layers from the Animation panel window. After you execute the command, ImageReady creates a frame with each Photoshop layer in it. This command creates frames for each layer, but it doesn't duplicate the background into each layer. Note that when you create frames using this command, ImageReady uses the bottom layer for the first frame and the top layer for the last frame.

Note

The Photoshop TypeLayers QuickTime movie file seen in Figure 12-4 is found in the Chapter 12 folder of the DVD that accompanies this book.

4. **To set a delay between frames, click Sec. at the bottom of the frame you want to change and then choose a frame delay.** We set the delay to 2 seconds, except for the last frame, which we set to 5 seconds.

5. **Click the Play button in the Animation panel to preview the animation.**

6. **In ImageReady, choose File ➪ Export Original to export the file as a digital movie.** In the Export Original dialog box, choose QuickTime movie from the Save as Type drop-down menu. Name your file **TypeEffect**. Locate a place to save your file, and then click Save.

7. **In the Compression Settings dialog box that appears (shown in Figure 12-5), choose a type of compression.** To save each frame with no compression, choose the Animation setting and then set the slider to Best. If you're working with digital video, you may also want to choose Apple DV-NTSC so that the compression setting matches that of your project. Click OK to make a QuickTime movie.

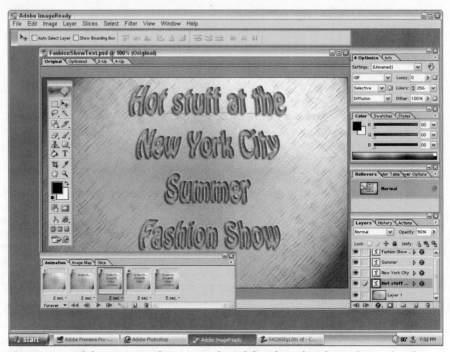

Figure 12-4: Adobe ImageReady converts the Adobe Photoshop layers into animation frames.

Figure 12-5: ImageReady's Compression Settings dialog box allows you to choose a compression setting.

After you've created a movie using Photoshop and ImageReady, you can import it into Premiere Pro. Follow these steps:

1. **Create a new Premiere project.** Make sure to use the same settings as the Photoshop and ImageReady files created in the previous sections.

2. **Choose File ⇨ Import.** In the Import dialog box, locate the ImageReady movie (TypeEffect) and click Open.

3. **Drag the movie from the Project panel to a video track in the Timeline panel.**

4. **Click the Play button in the Program Monitor panel to preview the movie.**

To have your presentation slowly fade into the first keyframe of the TypeEffect movie, follow these steps:

1. **In the Timeline panel, click the Expand/Collapse Track icon, click the Show Keyframes icon, and choose Show Opacity Handles.**

2. **Move the current-time indicator to the beginning of the clip, and click the Add/Remove Keyframe option to add a keyframe.**

3. **Move the current-time indicator to the right of the keyframe, and click the Add/Remove Keyframe option to add another keyframe.**

4. **Use the Selection tool to drag the first keyframe down, as shown in Figure 12-6.** The Selection tool can be activated from the Tools panel. Choose Window ⇨ Tools to display the Tools panel.

Cross-Reference   For more information on fading in and out, see Chapter 15.

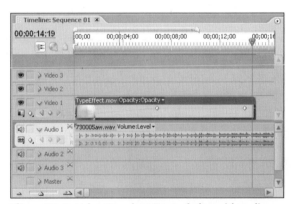

Figure 12-6: Using Premiere Pro to fade a video clip

5. **To preview the fade, click and drag the current-time indicator in the Timeline panel.**

To add sound to your movie, follow these steps:

1. **Choose File ⇨ Import. In the Import dialog box, locate a sound clip and click Open to import the clip into the Project panel.** We used Digital Vision's 730005aw.wav Acoustic Chillout sound clip.

2. **Drag the sound clip from the Project panel to Audio 1 of the Timeline panel.**

   If the sound clip is too long for the TypeEffect clip, click the end of the sound clip and drag left.

Cross-Reference   For more information on working with sound clips, see Chapters 8 and 9.

Digital Vision's 730005aw.wav Acoustic Chillout sound clip is in the Chapter 12 folder on the DVD that accompanies the book.

3. **Choose File ➪ Save to save your work.**

Creating a digital movie using Adobe Photoshop and ImageReady

Many users consider Adobe Photoshop to be one of the most powerful digital imaging programs available for personal computers. Its ability to manipulate images, colors, and text far surpasses Premiere Pro's. Therefore, you may want to use Adobe Photoshop to create or enhance graphics for eventual loading into Premiere Pro. The following project, called TimeFlies, leads you through the steps in manipulating and enhancing an Adobe Photoshop layer file. After you create it, you can animate the Adobe Photoshop file using Adobe ImageReady.

Follow these steps to create a Photoshop layered file using two photographs:

1. **Open the file with the photograph that you want to animate.** We used a clock image, shown in Figure 12-7. The clock image is in the Chapter 12 folder on the DVD that accompanies this book.

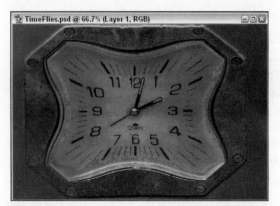

Figure 12-7: The clock image used to create the TimeFlies project

2. **Duplicate the layer with the photograph in it by choosing Duplicate Layer from the Layers panel drop-down menu or by clicking the digital image layer and dragging it over the Create a New Layer icon in the Layers panel.** The Create a New Layer icon is to the left of the Trash icon.

Remember that the more layers in an image, the larger the file. Make sure that your computer has enough RAM and hard drive space to handle all the layers you create.

3. **Choose Filter⇨Distort⇨Pinch. In the Pinch dialog box (shown in Figure 12-8), move the Amount slider to the right.** Click OK to apply the changes.

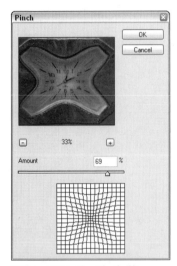

Figure 12-8: The Pinch filter dialog box

4. **Duplicate the Pinched layer, shown in Figure 12-9.**

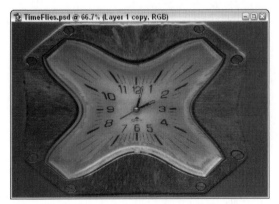

Figure 12-9: The clock image after applying the Pinch filter

Note

You may want to isolate (mask) part of your digital image from its background. This way, only the masked object is affected and not the background. You can use one of Photoshop's eraser tools to isolate the object from the background. If you are a Photoshop expert, you may want to use some of Photoshop's more advanced techniques.

5. **Use the Polygonal Lasso tool to select only the inner part of the clock (the x shape).**

6. **Choose Select ⇨ Save Selection.** Leave the default settings in the Save Selection dialog box, shown in Figure 12-10. By saving the selection, you can return to the same selection at any time.

Figure 12-10: The Save Selection dialog box allows you to save a selection.

7. **Choose Select ⇨ Inverse to invert the selection.**

8. **Set the Foreground color to blue and the Background color to white. Then choose Filter ⇨ Render ⇨ Clouds.** For a more interesting affect, apply another filter. We applied the Filter ⇨ Artistic ⇨ Film Grain command. Figure 12-11 shows the image after applying the Clouds and the Film Grain filters.

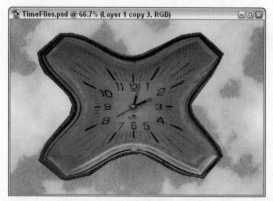

Figure 12-11: The clock image from Figure 12-7 after applying the Clouds and the Film Grain filters

9. **Duplicate the layer you are working on.**

10. **Choose Filter ⇨ Artistic ⇨ Colored Pencil.** The Colored Pencil dialog box is shown in Figure 12-12. The background of the clock image should now look similar to the one in Figure 12-13.

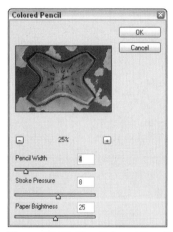

Figure 12-12: The Colored Pencil dialog box

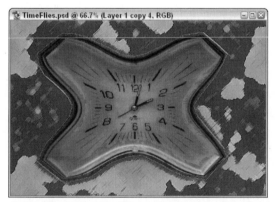

Figure 12-13: The clock image from Figure 12-11 after applying the Colored Pencil filter

11. **Duplicate the Colored Pencil layer.**

12. **Choose Select ➪ Deselect to deselect the selection.**

13. **Choose Filter ➪ Render ➪ Lighting Effects.** In the Lighting Effects dialog box (shown in Figure 12-14), click the Style drop-down menu and choose Soft Direct Lights. Then click OK to apply the effect.

14. **Choose Filter ➪ Distort ➪ Spherize.** In the Spherize dialog box (shown in Figure 12-15), set the Amount to **100** and choose Vertical from the Mode drop-down menu. Click OK to apply the effect. Figure 12-16 shows the clock image after applying the Spherize command.

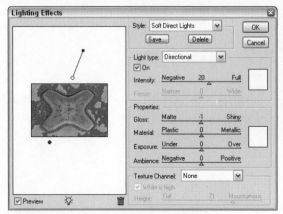

Figure 12-14: The Lighting Effects dialog box

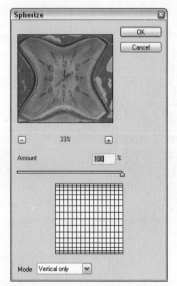

Figure 12-15: The Spherize dialog box

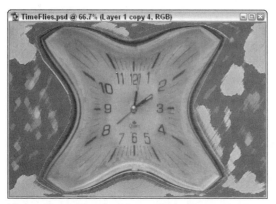

Figure 12-16: The clock image from Figure 12-13 after applying the Lighting Effects filter and the Spherize filter

15. **Choose File ➪ Save to save your file.** Now you are ready to animate your Photoshop layer file.

16. **Choose File ➪ Jump To ➪ ImageReady.**

17. **Open the Animation panel by choosing Window ➪ Show Animation.** Now you are ready to make frames from layers.

18. **To create a frame from each layer, you can choose Make Frames from Layers from the Animation panel window.** After you execute the command, ImageReady creates a frame with each Photoshop layer in it, as shown in Figure 12-17.

Figure 12-17: The Animation panel

19. **To set a delay between frames, click Sec. at the bottom of the frame you want to change and then choose a frame delay.** We set the delay to 2 seconds.

20. **Click the Play button in the Animation panel to preview the animation.**

21. **In ImageReady, choose File ➪ Export Original to export the file as a digital movie.** In the Export Original dialog box, choose QuickTime movie from the Save as Type drop-down menu. Name your file **TypeEffect**. Locate a place to save your file, and then click Save.

22. **Now choose a compression setting in the Compression dialog box.** To save each frame with no compression, choose the Animation setting and then set the slider to Best, or leave the default settings and click OK.

Creating Semitransparent Text

In Chapter 11, you created different title effects using Premiere Pro's Title Designer. Although the Adobe Title Designer provides many features for creating text effects, it can't compare with the text manipulation tools and filters that are available in Adobe Photoshop. In this section, you use Photoshop's Layer Styles to create a beveled text effect. You create an alpha channel out of the beveled text. When the text is loaded into Photoshop, the type appears semitransparent, allowing part of the background image to show through the highlighted areas of the text. To create color for the text in Premiere Pro, you use Premiere Pro's Color matte command and the Image Matte Key effect.

Creating beveled text in Photoshop

This section explains how to create the beveled text effect shown in Figure 12-18. If you're an experienced Photoshop user, feel free to vary any of the Photoshop effects.

Follow these steps to create a beveled text effect:

Figure 12-18: Beveled text created in Adobe Photoshop

1. **In Photoshop, create a new file that matches the pixel dimensions of your Premiere Pro project.**

2. **Using Photoshop's Type tool, create your title text.** We typed the word *Zoo* at 100 points. If you want to enlarge or stretch the text, choose Edit ➪ Free Transform and manually scale the text.

3. **Apply a beveled look to the text by choosing Layer ➪ Layer Style ➪ Bevel and Emboss.**

4. **In the Layer Style dialog box, choose the Inner Bevel from the Style menu and then use the dialog box controls to fine-tune the effect.** In the Technique drop-down menu, choose Chisel Soft and then edit the Gloss Contour.

5. **After you finish the effect, flatten the file by choosing Layer ➪ Flatten Image.**

6. **Now you need to create an alpha channel from the text, because Premiere Pro uses the alpha channel to create the transparency effect.** To quickly create an alpha channel, convert the image to Lab color mode and then duplicate the lightness channel. To convert to Lab mode, choose Image ➪ Mode ➪ Lab. The Lightness channel is essentially a grayscale version of the RGB color image. To turn it into an alpha channel, simply drag the Lightness channel over the New Channel icon in the Layers panel. After the alpha channel appears, convert the image back to RGB by choosing Image Mode ➪ RGB Color. (If you don't do this, Premiere Pro is not able to read the file.)

7. **Save your file in Photoshop format.**

Creating the Zoo project

Now that you've created the text in Photoshop, you're ready to import the text into Premiere Pro and create the Zoo project. Figure 12-19 shows a frame from the Zoo project.

Figure 12-19: A frame from the Zoo project

1. **Choose File ➪ New ➪ Project to create a new project in Adobe Premiere Pro.**

2. **In Premiere Pro, choose File ➪ New ➪ Color Matte to create a color matte that will be used later for the color of the text.** After the Color Picker dialog box opens, select a color. Click OK to close the Color Picker. Then name the color matte in the Color Matte dialog box.

3. **Drag the color matte from the Project panel to Video 2 track.** Click and drag to extend the length of the graphic in the Timeline to your desired duration.

4. **Choose File ➪ Import to import a video clip that you want to use.** We used Digital Vision's ComicCuts 891004f.mov.

On the DVD-ROM

The Digital Vision's ComicCuts 891004f.mov (shown in Figure 12-19) and the Zoo text file (shown in Figure 12-19) are in the Chapter 12 folder, inside the Tutorial Projects folder that is on the DVD that accompanies this book.

5. **Drag the video clip from the Project panel to Video 1 track.** If you use a short video clip as we did in Figure 12-19, you might want to select the video clip from the Project panel a second time and drag it next to the video clip that is already in Video 1 track of the Timeline panel, as seen in Figure 12-20.

Figure 12-20: The Timeline panel for the Zoo project

6. **Choose Window ⇨ Effect.** Then drag the Image Matte Key effect (found in the Keying folder, which is in the Video Effects folder) onto the color matte in Video 2 track.

7. **Choose Window ⇨ Effect Controls.** In the Effect Controls panel, click the Setup icon (next to the words Image Matte Key). When the Select a Matte Image dialog box appears, locate the Photoshop text graphic file that you want to use and click Open. The Zoo text file shown in Figure 12-19 is on the DVD that accompanies the book. In the Effect Controls panel, click the triangle in front of the Image Matte Key effect to display the controls. Select the Reverse option.

8. **Click the Play button in the Program Monitor panel.**

9. **If you want to add motion to the text, use the Motion settings in the Effect Controls panel.** For more information about using Motion, see Chapter 17.

Using Video Effects to Animate Adobe Illustrator Type and Graphics

Adobe Illustrator is known as a powerful digital drawing tool. By using Adobe Illustrator, you can create precision drawings and type effects. After creating graphics in Illustrator, you can apply Effects and Filters. You can also import them into Premiere Pro. (You can also import the graphics into Photoshop first, apply more filters, and then import into Premiere Pro.) This project (Hurricane Season) shows you how to create text on a curve in Adobe Illustrator and then use the text in a Premiere Pro project with video effects. The Timeline panel for Hurricane Season is shown in Figure 12-21. The Illustrator text is in Video 3 track, the Illustrator graphic is in Video 2 track, and a white matte is in Video 1 track.

Figure 12-21: Hurricane Season
Timeline panel

Creating curved text in Adobe Illustrator

Figure 12-22 shows type created on a curved path in Adobe Illustrator. We imported this illustration, along with a graphic created in Illustrator (shown in Figure 12-22), into Premiere Pro to create the Hurricane Season project. We created the distorted spiral graphic (shown in Figure 12-23) by applying filters to a spiral. This graphic was used as the background video track in the Hurricane Season project.

Figure 12-22: Curved text created in Adobe Illustrator

Figure 12-23: Graphic created in Adobe Illustrator

Follow these steps to create text on a curve by using Adobe Illustrator:

1. **Create a new file in Adobe Illustrator by choosing File ⇨ New.**

2. **In Adobe Illustrator, use the Pen tool or the Freeform tool to create a curved path.**

3. **Use the Path Type tool to type on the curved path.**

4. **Click the Path Type tool in the Toolbox.**

5. **Drag the Path Type tool to the far-left side of the curved path that you created, and then click.**

6. **When the blinking cursor appears, start typing.**

7. **After you've finished typing, select the text by clicking and dragging over it with the mouse and then choose a font and size from the Font menu.**

8. **Choose File ⇨ Save to save the file.**

Creating a graphic in Adobe Illustrator

Follow these steps to create the distorted spiral in Illustrator used as the background to create the Hurricane Season project:

1. **Pick Foreground and Background colors.**

2. **Click the Star tool in the Toolbox. The Star tool is in the same place as the Rectangle tool.**

3. **Create a star using the Star tool (Alt+click).** In the Star dialog box, increase the number of sides the star has. Click OK to close the dialog box and make a star. Feel free to experiment using various numbers of sides for your star.

4. **Distort the star by using the ZigZag and Twist filters in the Distort submenu.** Experiment with the settings in the dialog box for the desired effect.

5. **Save the file in Illustrator format.**

Creating the Hurricane Season project

In creating this project, we used the Effects panel to apply the Bend video effect to the background and the Strobe effect to the text. Figure 12-24 shows a frame from the Hurricane Season project.

Figure 12-24: A frame from the Hurricane Season project

You can create still images in other programs and then import them and animate them using Premiere Pro's Video Effects.

Follow these steps to animate Illustrator text and graphics using Premiere Pro:

1. **Choose File ➪ New Project to create a new project.**

2. **Choose File ➪ Import to import the text and graphic (created previously).** If you don't have Adobe Illustrator, you can import these two graphics from the *Premiere Pro 2 Bible* DVD. They are located in the Hurricane folder, found in the Chapter 12 folder.

On the DVD-ROM

To load the Hurricane text and graphic file (shown in Figure 12-21), choose File ➪ Import. Click Import Folder. Then locate the Hurricane folder, and click the Import Folder button. This folder is in the Chapter 12 folder in the Tutorial Projects folder on the DVD that accompanies this book.

3. Before you drag the Illustrator files from the Project panel to the Timeline panel, select one, and then choose Clip ➪ Video Options ➪ Scale to Frame Size. Then select the other file and apply the same command. This way, the Illustrator file takes on the Premiere Pro project file size. Drag the (Hurricane) text to Video 3 track and the (hurricane) graphic to Video 2 track.

4. **Choose File ➪ New ➪ Color Matte.** Select a white background (or any other color that you want) and click OK. Choose a name for your matte, and click OK. The color matte appears in the Project panel.

5. **Drag the color matte to Video 1 track.**

6. **Display the Effects panel by choosing Window ➪ Effects.** Open the Video Effects bin. Inside each bin are many effects. For more information on using the video effects in the Effects panel, see Chapter 14.

7. **Open the Stylize bin in the Effects panel.**

8. **Click a Strobe Light video effect, and drag it over the icon representation of the text in Video 3 track.**

9. **Click the background graphic icon in Video 2 track to select it.** In our example, we used the distorted spiral.

10. **Open the Distort bin in the Effects panel.**

11. **Click the Bend video effect, and drag it over the icon representation of the graphic in Video 2 track. Click the Setup icon (next to the word Bend in the Effect Controls panel) to display the Bend Settings dialog box.** In the Bend Settings dialog box, shown in Figure 12-25, select the options you want from the drop-down menus and sliders. Click OK to close the dialog box.

Figure 12-25: A preview of the Bend effect (in the Bend Settings dialog box) on the distorted graphic

12. **Choose File ➪ Save to save the project.**

13. **Click the Play button in the Program Monitor panel to preview the effect.**

Animating Titles over Graphics by Using Motion and the Alpha Adjust Invert Option

You can manipulate text within a video track so that it is semi-transparent and allows you to see the background clip through the text. The background clip appears in the video track below the video track with the text. You can also make the text move over the same background graphic.

This effect is shown in the frames from the Mosaic project in Figure 12-26. To create the moving, transparent text, we applied Premiere Pro's Motion effect and the Keying effect, Alpha Adjust Invert option to the word Mosaic. We created the mosaic text (shown in Figure 12-27) in Adobe Illustrator. The mosaic background (shown in Figure 12-28) was created using Corel Painter.

Figure 12-26: Frames from the Mosaic project

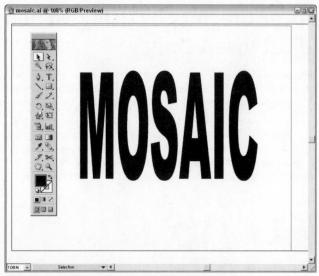

Figure 12-27: Mosaic text created using Adobe Illustrator

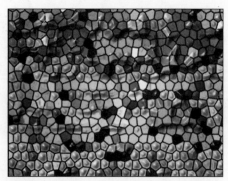

Figure 12-28: Mosaic background created
using Corel Painter

Follow these steps to animate using motion and a reverse alpha channel:

1. **In Premiere Pro, choose File ⇨ New ⇨ Project to create a new project.** In the New Project dialog box, choose a preset. Name your file and click OK.

2. **Choose File ⇨ Import to import a text graphic and background video clip.** You can create text using Premiere Pro's Title Designer or Adobe Illustrator, Adobe Photoshop, or Corel Painter. To create a background, use either Adobe Photoshop or Corel Painter.

On the DVD-ROM

To load the mosaic text (mosaic.ai) and mosaic background (stainedglass.psd) files seen in Figure 12-20, choose File ⇨ Import. Then locate the Mosaic folder and click the Import Folder button. The folder is in the Chapter 12 folder inside the Tutorial Projects folder on the DVD that accompanies this book.

3. **When the text and background files have been imported, they appear in the Project panel.** The text clip should be the same size as the project size. To have the Illustrator file take on the Premiere Pro project size, select the text clip in the Project panel and choose Clip ⇨ Video Options ⇨ Scale to Frame Size. Then drag the text file from the Project panel, to Video 3 track in the Timeline panel.

4. **Click the background file in the Project panel, and drag it to Video 1 track of the Timeline panel.** The background file should extend over the entire text area. To increase the duration of either clip, click the end of the clip and drag to the right.

5. **Move the Timeline indicator over the text clip in Video 1 track.** Notice that a preview of the text and the background clips appears in the Program Monitor panel.

6. **Choose File ⇨ New ⇨ Color Matte.** In the Color Picker dialog box, set the color to white and click OK. In the Choose Name dialog box, if you want, type a name, and then click OK. The Color Matte appears in the Project panel. Drag the color matte from the Project panel to the Video 2 track. The color matte should be between the clips in Video 1 track and Video 3 track in the Timeline panel. In order to see the video clip in Video 1 track, reduce the opacity of the white color matte to 70 percent. The Opacity control is found in the Effect Controls panel.

7. **To increase the size of the text clip, click the text clip (in Video 2 track) in the Timeline panel. To scale the clip, use the Motion Scale option.** Click the triangle in front of the word Motion in the Effect Controls panel to display the Scale option. Click and drag to the right on the Scale field to increase the scale.

8. **In the effects panel, click the Alpha Adjust Keying effect in the Keying bin (which is in the Video Effects bin) and drag it over the text clip in Video 2 track.** When the Alpha Adjust effect appears in the Effect Controls panel, click the triangle in front of the word Alpha Adjust to view the controls. Reduce the Opacity to 46 percent so that you can see the color matte in Video 2 track.

9. **Apply Motion to the text in Video 3 track by creating keyframes.** Start by moving the Timeline indicator (in either the Timeline panel or Effect Controls panel) to the beginning of the text clip in Video 3 track. Then click the stopwatch in front of the word Position in the Effect Controls panel. A keyframe is created.

   To create a second keyframe, move the Timeline indicator to the right and click the word Motion in the Effect Controls panel. Now move the text in the Monitor panel to the left as seen in Figure 12-26. Notice that a second keyframe is created.

   To create a third keyframe, move the Timeline indicator to the right. Now move the text in the Program Monitor panel to the right so that the text is centered as seen in Figure 12-26. Notice that a third keyframe is created.

   To create a fourth keyframe, again move the Timeline indicator to the right. Now move the text in the Program Monitor panel farther to the right, as seen in Figure 12-26. A fourth keyframe is created.

   To create a fifth keyframe, again move the Timeline indicator to the right. Now move the text in the Program Monitor panel back to the center. Notice that a fifth keyframe is created.

   To create a sixth keyframe, again move the Timeline indicator to the right. Now move the text in the Monitor panel up, as seen in Figure 12-26. Notice that a sixth keyframe is created. For more information on using the Motion Effect, see Chapter 17.

10. **Click the Play button in the Program Monitor panel to preview the project.** When the preview rolls, you should see the background graphic within the typed letters.

11. **Choose File ➪ Save to save your work.**

Summary

To create the most attractive and elaborate text and graphics effects, you may need to use the digital power of such programs as Adobe Photoshop, Adobe Illustrator, or Corel Painter in conjunction with Premiere Pro. This chapter covered these topics:

✦ Both Photoshop and Illustrator provide excellent text features that can be used in conjunction with Premiere Pro.

✦ Premiere Pro successfully interprets Photoshop transparency and alpha channels.

✦ Background transparent areas in Illustrator are automatically read as alpha channel masks in Premiere Pro.

✦ You can create a variety of different transparency effects using Premiere Pro and Photoshop or Illustrator.

✦　　✦　　✦

Advanced Techniques and Special Effects

✦   ✦   ✦   ✦

✦   ✦   ✦   ✦

Advanced Editing Techniques

Premiere Pro is so versatile that you can create and edit an entire project using little more than Premiere Pro's Selection tool. However, if you need to make precise edits, you want to explore Premiere Pro's advanced editing functions.

For example, Premiere Pro's Trim panel enables you to shave one frame at a time from the in or out point of a clip by simply clicking the mouse. As you click, you see the last frame of one out point in one side of the window, and the first frame of the adjacent in point in another side of the window. Premiere Pro also enables you to create sophisticated three-point edits where you can specify an in or out point to maintain in a source clip, and an in and or point for placement in your program. When you perform the edit, Premiere Pro calculates the precise section of the source clip to overlay into your program material.

This chapter provides a guide to Premiere Pro's intermediate and advanced editing features. It starts with a look at some basic editing utilities, such as copying and pasting clip attributes, and then proceeds to discuss Premiere Pro's toolbox editing tools — the Ripple Edit, Rolling Edit, Slip, and Slide tools. The chapter continues with a look at three-point and four-point editing, how to trim using the Trim Monitor, and how to edit using the Multi-Camera Monitor. The chapter has been designed to enable you to quickly move from subject to subject so that you can learn or review editing features and immediately put them to use.

Editing Utilities

From time to time, you may want to edit by simply copying clips from one section and pasting them in another. To aid in editing, you may want to unlink audio from video. This section provides a review of several different commands that can aid you as you edit your production. It starts with a discussion of the History panel, which enables you to quickly undo different stages of your work.

Undoing edits with the History panel

Even the best editors change their minds and make mistakes. Professional editing systems enable you to preview edits before actually recording the source material onto the program tape. However, professional editing systems can't provide as many levels of undo as Premiere Pro's History panel, shown in Figure 13-1.

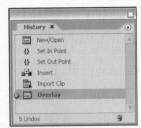

Figure 13-1: The History panel

As discussed in Chapter 2, the History panel records your editing activity while using Premiere Pro. Each step appears as a separate entry in the History panel. If you want to return to a previous step, simply click it in the History panel and you return to it. When you go forward with your work, the previously recorded steps (after the step you returned to) disappear.

If you haven't already tried the History panel, open it by choosing Window ➪ Show History. In a new or existing project, drag several clips to the Timeline. As you drag, watch how the states are recorded in the History panel. Now select one of the clips in the Timeline, and delete it by pressing Delete. Then delete another clip. Again, note how each state is recorded in the panel.

Now assume that you want to return the project to the state it was in before you deleted any clips. Just click in the History panel to the left of the first Delete state in the panel. The project returns to its state before any of the deletions. Now move one of the clips in the Timeline with the Selection tool. As soon as you move the clip, a new state is recorded in the History panel, removing the second Delete state in the History panel. After you return to one state in the History panel and begin to work, you can't go forward again.

Cutting and pasting clips

If you've ever used a word processor to edit text, you know that one of the easiest ways to rearrange your work is to copy and paste from one part of the text to another. In Premiere Pro, you can easily copy and paste, or cut and paste, a clip from one part of the Timeline panel to another. In fact, Premiere Pro provides three paste commands — Paste, Paste to Fit, and Paste Attributes.

Splitting a clip with the Razor and Multiple Razor tools

Before copying and pasting or moving a clip, you may want to splice it into two pieces and paste or move only a portion of the clip. An easy way to splice a clip is to use Premiere Pro's Razor tool. One click of the Razor tool splits a clip into two pieces. If you need to slice more than one track, press Shift while clicking the Razor tool. Here's how to use the Razor tool:

1. **If you want to splice one clip in one unlocked track into two pieces, select the Razor tool.** If you want to split all unlocked tracks into two separate pieces, press Shift and keep the Shift key pressed (the Razor tool icon changes to show two razors). To slice video without audio, or vice versa, press Alt.

Tip   Press C on the keyboard to activate the Razor tool.

2. **Move the current-time indicator to the frame that where you want to create a cut.**

3. **In the sequence that you want to edit, click the clip to cut it with the Razor tool, as shown in Figure 13-2.** (Or you can choose Sequence ➪ Razor at Current Time Indicator.) After you click with the Razor tool, you can move the cut portion of the clip independently of the rest of the clip.

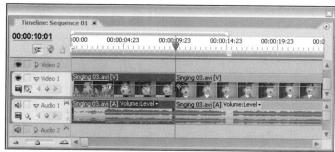

Figure 13-2: Cutting with either the Razor or Multiple Razor tool splits the clip into two sections.

Pasting clips

After you've split a clip, you may want to copy and paste it or cut and paste it to another location in the Timeline.

If the area into which you want to paste the clip already has clips within it, you can use Premiere Pro's Paste, Paste Insert, or Paste Attributes command. Premiere Pro's Paste command pastes a clip over any clip at the current-time indicator position, its Paste Insert command inserts the pasted clip in a Timeline gap, and its Paste Attributes command copies motion, opacity, volume, and color settings of one clip into another clip.

Using Paste to overlay clips

Premiere Pro's Paste command enables you to paste clips into gaps in the Timeline. It also provides options for how you want the inserted clips to fit within your production. Here's how to paste a clip so that it overlays or replaces clips in the current sequence in the Timeline:

1. **Select the clip or clips that you want to copy or paste.**

2. **Choose Edit ⇨ Cut or Edit ⇨ Copy.**

3. **Move the current-time indicator to where you want to overlay the clip.**

4. **Select the target track by clicking the track header (left end of the track).**

5. **Choose Edit ⇨ Paste.** Premiere Pro drops the new material over any clip at the current-time indicator.

Using Paste Insert to insert clips

Premiere Pro's Paste Insert command enables you to paste clips into gaps in the Timeline. It also provides options for inserting clips to fit within your production. Here's how to use Paste Insert to insert a clip:

1. **Select the clip or clips that you want to copy or paste.**

2. **Choose Edit ⇨ Cut or Edit ⇨ Copy.**

3. **Move the current-time indicator to where you want to insert the clip.**

4. **Select the target track by clicking the track header (left end of the track).**

5. **Choose Edit ⇨ Paste Insert.** Premiere Pro drops the clip at the current-time indicator and pushes all subsequent clips to the right.

Using Paste Attributes

Premiere Pro's Paste Attributes command allows you to copy one clip's attributes and apply them to another clip. For example, using Paste Attributes, you can copy the color settings, opacity, volume, and effects of one clip and apply them to another. To use the Paste Attributes command, follow these steps:

1. **Select the clip or clips that that have the attributes that you want to copy.**

2. **Choose Edit ⇨ Cut or Edit ⇨ Copy.**

3. **Select one or more clips.**

4. **Choose Edit ⇨ Paste Attributes.**

Removing sequence gaps

During the course of editing, you may purposely or inadvertently leave gaps in the Timeline. Sometimes the gaps aren't even visible because of the zoom level in the Timeline panel. Here's how to automatically remove a gap in the Timeline:

1. **Right-click the mouse in the gap in the Timeline.** You may need to zoom in to see small gaps.

2. **Choose Ripple Delete from the drop-down menu that appears in the sequence, as shown in Figure 13-3.** Premiere Pro removes the gap.

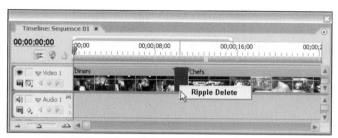

Figure 13-3: Right-click and choose Ripple Delete to remove gaps.

Unlinking and linking audio and video

While performing video edits, you may decide that you want to create audio effects where the audio from one clip plays over the next video clip (called a *split edit*). Although editing the video is a simple chore, you may find that you need to *unlink* the audio from the video to create the effect you want.

When you capture video using the Premiere Pro Capture command, Premiere Pro links the video information to the audio. This marriage is evident as you work. When you drag a clip to the Timeline, its audio automatically appears in an audio track. When you move the video, the audio moves with it. If you delete the video from the track, the audio is deleted. However, during editing, you may want to separate the video from its audio to create effects or to replace the audio altogether.

Tip

If you are trying to sync audio to video, viewing the audio's waveform in the audio track is helpful. To view the waveform, expand the audio track by clicking the triangle in front of the track. Next choose Show Waveform from the Set Display Style drop-down menu.

To unlink video from audio, follow these steps:

1. **Select the audio track that you want to unlink.** Note that the names of linked clips are underlined.

2. **Choose Clip ➪ Unlink.** You can also right-click the clip and choose Unlink from the pop-up menu, as shown in Figure 13-4. After unlinking, you can also delete the audio independently of the video, or vice versa.

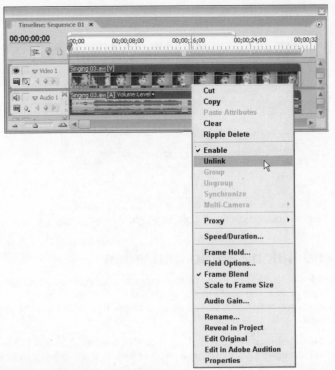

Figure 13-4: Right-click a linked clip, and choose Unlink Audio and Video to unlink it.

Cross-Reference   For more information about linking and unlinking audio and video, see Chapter 8.

Using a Reference Monitor

A Reference Monitor is a second Program Monitor that can display program footage independently of the Program Monitor. You may want to use the reference monitor to show footage just before or after the sequence you're editing in the Program Monitor to help you preview the effect of the edit. You can also use the Reference Monitor to display Premiere's scopes (vectorscope, YC Waveform, etc.) while the actual program footage runs. When doing this, you may want to *gang* the Reference Monitor and the Program Monitor so that each is displaying the same frames, with the Program Monitor showing the video and the Reference Monitor displaying the scopes.

To view the Reference Monitor, open the Program Monitor panel menu shown in Figure 13-5 and choose New Reference Monitor. To gang the Reference Monitor, choose Gang to Reference Monitor.

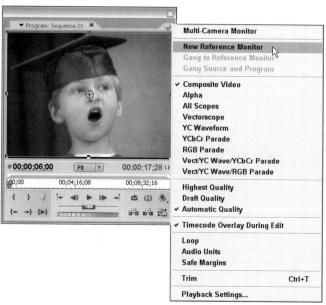

Figure 13-5: Right-click a clip, and choose Gang to Reference Monitor.

Using Keyboard Commands

As you work with Premiere Pro, you may find it difficult to fine-tune the movement of clips using the mouse. Fortunately, you can move clips a specific number of frames using the keyboard: Start by selecting the clip, pressing + or – on the numeric keypad, and then typing a number using the numeric keypad. Thus, +5 moves a clip forward five frames, and –5 moves a clip backward five frames. If the Timeline panel view is in Audio Units, the clip moves forward or backward in audio units. You can also move a selected clip one frame to the left by pressing Alt+,. You can move it five frames to the right by pressing Alt+Shift+,. You can move a selected clip one frame to the right by pressing Alt+. You can move it five frames to the right by pressing Alt+Shift+..

When working with the editing tools, keyboard commands can also speed your work. Pressing + zooms in, and pressing – zooms out. You can use the left-arrow key and right-arrow key to move forward and backward one frame at a time. You can also use the JKL keyboard combinations. Here's how:

Play forward frame by frame	Hold K, while pressing L
Play in reverse frame by frame	Hold K, while pressing J
Play forward at 8 fps	Press K and L simultaneously
Play in reverse at 8 fps	Press K and J simultaneously

Editing with the Tool Panel Tools

After you've edited two clips together in a sequence Timeline, you may want to fine-tune the edit by changing the out point of the first clip. Although you can use the Selection tool to change the edit point, you may prefer to use Premier Pro's editing tools, such as the Rolling Edit and Ripple Edit tools. Both tools enable you to quickly edit the out point of adjacent clips.

If you have three clips edited together, the Slip and Slide tools provide a quick means for editing the in or out point of the middle clip. The following sections describe how to use the Rolling Edit and Ripple Edit tools to edit adjacent clips and how to use the Slip and Slide tools to edit a clip between two other clips. As you try out these tools, keep the Program Monitor open. It provides an enlarged view of the clips. When using the Slip and Slide tools, the Monitor window also shows how many frames have been edited.

Figure 13-6 shows the Ripple Edit, Rolling Edit, Slip, and Slide tools.

Figure 13-6: The Ripple Edit, Rolling Edit, Slip, and Slide tools

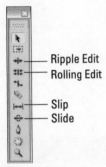

Ripple Edit
Rolling Edit

Slip
Slide

 On the DVD-ROM   The clips shown in this chapter use video footage from the Chapter 1 folder of the *Adobe Premiere Pro 2 Bible* DVD. The clips are 705008f and 705009f from Digital Vision's NightMoves CD.

Creating a rolling edit

The Rolling Edit tool enables you to click and drag the edit line of one clip and simultaneously change the in or out point of the next clip on the edit line. When you click and drag the edit line, the duration of the next clip is automatically edited to compensate for the change in the previous clip. For example, if you add five frames to the first clip, five frames are subtracted from the next. Thus, a rolling edit enables you to edit one clip without changing the duration of your edited program. Here's how to create a rolling edit:

1. **Onscreen you should have a project with at least two adjacent clips in a video track in the Timeline panel.** As a further aid, view the Program Monitor as you work, which previews the edit for you.

2. **Click the Rolling Edit tool to select it, or press N on the keyboard.**

3. **Move the Rolling Edit tool to the edit line between two adjacent clips.**

4. **Click and drag either left or right to trim the clips.** If you drag right, you extend the out point of the first clip and reduce the in point of the adjacent clip. If you click to the left, you reduce the out point of the first clip and extend the in point of the next clip. Figure 13-7 shows a rolling edit. In the figure, dragging the Rolling Edit tool right simultaneously changes the in point of the clip on the right and the out point of the clip on the left. The figure also shows how the Program Monitor previews the in and out points of the edit.

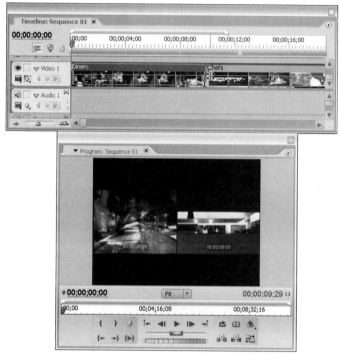

Figure 13-7: Simultaneously changing in and out points of two different clips with a rolling edit

Creating a ripple edit

The Ripple Edit tool enables you to edit a clip without affecting the adjacent clip. Performing a ripple edit is the opposite of performing a rolling edit. As you click and drag to extend the out point of a clip, Premiere Pro pushes the next clip to the right to avoid changing its in point — thus, creating a ripple effect throughout the production, changing its duration. If you click and drag to the left to reduce the out point, Premiere Pro doesn't change the in points of the next clips. To compensate for the change, Premiere Pro shortens the duration of the sequence. Here's how to perform a ripple edit with the Ripple Edit tool:

1. **Onscreen you should have a project with at least two clips touching side by side in a video track in the Timeline panel.** As a further aid, keep an eye on the Program Monitor, which previews the edit for you.

2. **Click the Ripple Edit tool to select it, or press B on the keyboard.**

3. **Move the Ripple Edit tool to the out point of the clip you want to trim.**

4. **Click and drag right to increase the clip's length or left to decrease the clip's length.** The duration of the next clip remains unchanged, but the duration of the sequence is changed. Figure 13-8 shows a ripple edit. In the figure, the in point of the Chefs clip remains unchanged, as the out point of the Diners clip (on the left) is extended.

Figure 13-8: The in point of the Chefs clip remains unchanged as a ripple edit is performed.

Tip   If you want to perform a ripple edit without affecting audio, press Alt while clicking and dragging the Ripple Edit tool.

Tip   To edit only the audio or video of a linked clip, Alt+drag with the Ripple Edit or Rolling Edit tool.

Creating a slip edit

A slip edit enables you to change the in and out points of a clip sandwiched between two other clips while maintaining the middle clip's original duration. As you click and drag the clip, the clip's neighbors to the left and right do not change, so neither does the sequence duration. Here's how to perform a slip edit with the Slip tool:

1. **Onscreen you should have a project with at least three clips side by side in a video track in the Timeline panel.** If you want to preview the edit as you work, pay close attention to the Program Monitor.

2. **Click the Slip tool to select it, or press Y on the keyboard.**

3. **With the Slip tool selected, click the clip that is in the middle of two other clips.**

4. **To change the in and out points without changing the duration of the sequence, click and drag left or right.** Figure 13-9 shows a slip edit. In the figure, the middle clip is dragged to the left, which changes its in and out points.

Figure 13-9: A slip edit changes the in and out points of the selected clip, but not the duration of the sequence.

Tip

Although the Slip tool is generally used to edit one clip between two others, you can edit the in and out points of a clip with the Slip tool even if it is not between other clips.

Creating a slide edit

Like the slip edit, the slide edit is performed on one clip placed between two others in a sequence. A slide edit maintains the in and out points of the clip that you are dragging while changing the duration of clips abutting it. When performing a slide edit, dragging right extends the out point of the previous clip as well as the in point of the next clip (making it occur later). Dragging left on a clip reduces the out point of the previous clip, as well as the in point of the following clip (causing it to occur earlier). As a result, the duration of the edited clip and the entire edited program do not change. Here's how to perform a slide edit with the Slide Edit tool:

1. **Onscreen you should have a project with at least three clips side by side in a video track in the Timeline window.** If you open the Program Monitor, you can preview the edit as you work.

2. **Click the Slide tool to select it, or press U on the keyboard.**

3. **Click and drag the clip that is in the middle of two other clips to move it.** Dragging left shortens the previous clip and lengthens the following clip. Dragging right lengthens the previous clip and shortens the following clip. Figure 13-10 shows a slide edit. In the figure, the Program Monitor shows the effect on all clips. As the Diners clip is dragged right, the out point of the Walkers clip (on the left) is extended, which causes the in point of the Chefs clip to occur later.

Figure 13-10: Dragging right to create a slide edit changes the out point of the clip on the left and the in point of the clip on the right.

Creating a Three-Point or Four-Point Edit

Three-point and four-point edits are commonly performed in professional video editing studios, using a monitor setup that is similar to Premiere Pro's Source and Program Monitor panels. As discussed in Chapter 7, the Source Monitor typically displays source clips that haven't been added to the Timeline, while the Program Monitor displays program material that has been added to the Timeline.

Performing a three-point edit

Typically, a three-point edit is used to overlay or replace a section of the program footage with a portion of the source clip. Before the edit is performed, three crucial points are specified. Usually the three points are as follows:

✦ **The in point of the source clip:** This is the first frame of the source clip that you eventually want to view in the program.

✦ **An in point of the program footage:** This is first frame of the program footage that you want replaced by the source footage.

✦ **An out point in the program footage:** This is the frame where you want the source replacement to end.

Note
You can perform a three-point edit with virtually any combination of three edit points. You could also set the in and out points of the source clip and the in point or out point of the program footage.

When the edit is performed, Premiere Pro automatically calculates the exact section of the source clip needed to replace the program footage. You could use a three-point edit in the following situation: Assume that you've placed sailboat footage in the Timeline and you want to replace two seconds of it with a clip of waves crashing. To set this up, you open the Waves clip in the Source Monitor and set its in point. Next, in the Program Monitor, you set in and out points within the Sailboat clip. When you perform the three-point edit, the Waves clip appears within the in and out points you just set in the Sailboat footage. Figure 13-11 shows a graphic depicting a three-point edit.

Follow these steps to perform a three-point edit. Before creating a three-point edit, you need a project onscreen containing at least one clip in the Timeline.

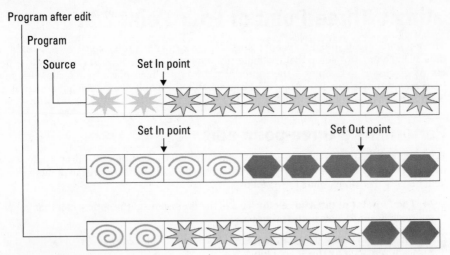

Figure 13-11: A three-point edit

If you want to practice using one of the tutorial files, start by importing the file 705008f.mov from the Chapter 1 folder of the *Adobe Premiere Pro 2 Bible* DVD. This clip shows a waitress leading diners to a table in a restaurant. After the file is imported, drag it into Video 1 track in the Timeline. This clip will appear in the Program section of the Monitor panel. Next, import clip 705009f.mov from the Chapter 1 folder of the DVD. This clip shows chefs working in the kitchen of a restaurant. Don't place this on the Timeline; Premiere Pro does it for you when you create the three-point edit. The three-point edit creates a cut-away from the restaurant diners to the chefs in the kitchen for a few seconds, before returning to the diners clip. Follow these steps to perform the three-point edit:

1. **Select the target track in the Timeline by clicking at the far left of the track.** As stated earlier, you should already have a clip in this track.

2. **Open a clip in the Source Monitor.** If you are using this book's DVD tutorial files, double-click clip 705009f.mov in the Project panel. The clip should appear in the Source Monitor, and its name should appear in the Source Monitor's tab. Note that you may be able to choose another clip from the Source Clip drop-down menu if you've already been working with clips in the Source Monitor.

3. **In the Source Monitor, set the in point for the source clip.** This is the first frame that you want overlaid into the program. If you are using the tutorial files, set the in point about 3 seconds and 25 frames, from the beginning of clip 705009b.mov. To move to the frame, click and drag in the jog tread control or the current-time indicator in the Source section and then use the Step Forward or Step Back buttons to navigate to the precise frame.

4. **Click the Set In Point button.**

5. **In the Program Monitor, move to the first frame that you want to replace with the source clip.** If you are using the tutorial files, move to about 2 seconds from the beginning of clip 7005008f.mov. To move to the frame, click and drag in the job tread or current-time indicator in the Program view and then use the Step Forward or Step Back buttons to navigate to the precise frame. Alternatively, you can click and drag the edit line in the Timeline window.

6. **Set the in point by clicking the Set In Point button in the Program Monitor.**

7. **In the Program Monitor, move to the last frame that you want replaced by the source clip.** If you are using the tutorial files, move about 4 seconds, and 18 frames, into clip 705008f. mov.

8. **Click the Set Out Point button.**

9. **To perform the edit, click the Overlay button in the Source Monitor, to the left of the Toggle Take Audio and Video button.**

Performing a four-point edit

Three-point edits are performed more frequently than four-point edits because you only need to specify three points. In a four-point edit, you specify the in and out points of the source clip as well as the in and out points of the program clip.

Before performing the edit, make sure that the target track is set. If not, choose the track that you want to have the clip dropped into on the Timeline by clicking at the far left of track.

Otherwise, performing a four-point edit, as shown in Figure 13-12, is identical to performing a three-point edit, except that you must set an out point as well as an in point in the Source Monitor. What happens if the source duration (the duration between in and out source points) does not match the duration between the program's in and out points? Premiere Pro opens an alert enabling you to choose whether you want to trim the source clip or change the speed of the source clip.

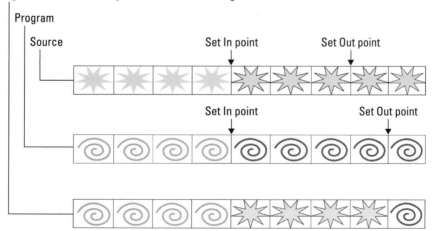

Figure 13-12: A four-point edit

Fine-Tuning Edits Using the Trim Monitor Panel

The Trim Monitor panel enables you to precisely change the edit points of clips on the Timeline. When you work in the Trim Monitor panel, shown in Figure 13-13, you can click to move from edit point to edit point, and then remove or add frames on either side of the edit line. The Trim Monitor panel enables you to create ripple edits and rolling edits by simply clicking and dragging in the panel itself. When you create a ripple edit, the project duration increases or decreases depending on whether frames are added to or subtracted from the edit. If you create a rolling edit, the project duration remains the same. Premiere Pro accomplishes this by adding frames from one side of the edit as it subtracts from the other and by subtracting from one side of the edit while it adds to the other.

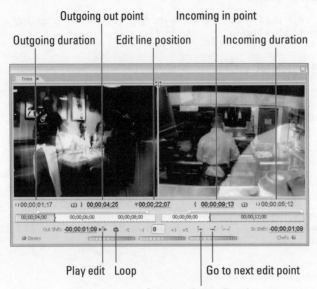

Figure 13-13: The Trim Monitor panel

Before you use the Trim Monitor panel, you should have at least two separate clips on the Timeline that are adjacent to each other. If you keep the Timeline panel open, you see the effects of the edit in the Timeline as you work. To use the Trim Monitor panel to trim an edit, follow these steps:

1. **Select the target track by clicking at the far left side of the track.**

2. **Move the current-time indicator close to the area that you want to fine-tune, or use the controls in the Program Monitor to move close to the area that you want to edit.**

3. **Open the Trim Monitor panel.** Click the Trim button in the Program Monitor (lower-right corner), or choose Trim in the Program Monitor panel menu.

4. **Click the Go to Next Edit Point button or the Go to Previous Edit Point button to move to the edit that you want to adjust.** The Out Shift section of the window shows the left side of the edit; the In Shift section of the window shows the right side of the edit (as if you were standing in the Timeline in the middle of a cut). Note that onscreen, the Trim window shows you the outgoing out point, the current edit point position, and the incoming in point.

5. **Edit the clip in one of the following ways:**

   - To create a ripple edit, follow these steps:

   a. **Click and drag either clip in the Trim Monitor panel.** If you click and drag left on the clip in the left window, you make this clip's duration shorter (changing its out point), without affecting the duration of the clip on the right. If you click and drag right on the clip in the right window, you delay its in point (causing it to be further into the clip), thereby shortening this clip, but not changing the duration of clip on the left.

   b. **After you start the process of creating a ripple edit, you can add or remove frames by clicking in the bordered frame (below and between the two clips) and entering a positive or negative number.** Enter a positive number of frames if you want to add frames to the last selected clip, or enter a negative number to subtract from the selected clip.

   Clicking the –5 or –1 button removes five frames or one frame from the last selected clip. Clicking the +5 or +1 button adds five frames or one frame to the last selected clip.

   You can also create a ripple edit by clicking the Jog In Point or Jog Out Point treads, clicking and dragging the In Point or Out Point icons, or clicking and dragging the timecode display of the incoming, outgoing, and current edit position.

   - To create a rolling edit, follow these steps:

   a. **Click and drag in the middle of the two clips.** If you click and drag right, you simultaneously change the in point of the clip on the right (making it later in the clip) and the out point of the clip on the left (making it later, as well). Clicking and dragging left produces the opposite effect.

   You can also create a rolling edit by clicking the Jog In Point and Jog Out Point treads.

   b. **After you start the process of creating a rolling edit, you can add or remove frames by clicking in the bordered frame (below and between the two clips) and entering a positive or negative number.** Enter a positive number to specify the number of frames that you want to add to both clips, or enter a negative number to specify the number of frames to delete from both clips.

   Clicking the –5 or –1 button removes five frames or one frame from both clips. Clicking the +5 or +1 button adds five frames or one frame to both clips.

6. **To play back the edit, click the Play Edit button.**

Note You can also edit in the Trim Monitor by clicking and editing jog controls, by clicking the Set In Point and Set Out Point buttons, or by editing the timecode numbers in the Incoming In Point and Outgoing Out Point timecode fields and then pressing Enter.

Tip To change the default trim amount (set to 5), choose Edit ⇨ Preferences ⇨ Trim.

Multi-Camera Editing

If you shoot footage from a live event such as a concert or a dance performance with several cameras, editing the footage together sequentially can be quite time-consuming. Fortunately, Premiere Pro's multi-camera editing feature can simulate some of the features of a video switcher (which allows you to choose shots from the cameras on the fly). Using Premiere Pro's Multi-Camera Monitor, you can view up to four video sources simultaneously and quickly select the best shot to record into a video sequence. As the video rolls, you can keep selecting from any of the four synchronized sources, making cuts from one source to the other. You can also choose to have the audio feed from different sources as well.

Although editing using the Multi-Camera Monitor is quite easy, the setup is somewhat involved: You synchronize your source footage in one Timeline sequence, embed this source sequence in a target Timeline sequence (where the edits are recorded), enable multi-camera editing, and start recording in the Multi-Camera Monitor.

After you've completed a multi-camera edit session, you can return to the sequence and easily substitute footage from one camera to another camera. The following sections detail these procedures.

Note Although Premiere Pro's multi-camera editing feature is primarily designed to allow edits from multi-camera shoots, you can use it to edit any footage, including graphics.

Setting up multi-camera clips

After you've imported your footage into Premiere Pro, you're ready to try out a multi-camera edit session. As mentioned earlier, you can create a multi-camera session from up to four video sources. Follow these steps to set up a multi-camera edit:

1. **Create a new sequence by choosing File ⇨ New Sequence.** In the New Sequence dialog box, choose the number of tracks you will need. You can have up to four tracks feeding the Multi-Camera Monitor.

2. **Place all footage on individual tracks so that they are parallel to one another.**

3. **Line up the footage in the tracks using the Clip ⇨ Synchronize command:**

   When you execute the Clip Synchronize command, Premiere Pro synchs all clips to the clip on the target track. Select a target track by clicking the left edge of a track. Next, Ctrl-click on each clip that you want to synchronize. Then choose Clip ⇨ Synchronize. The synchronize dialog box shown in Figure 13-14 provides the following options:

- **Clip Start:** This option synchs on the clip's in point.

- **Clip End:** This option synchs on the clip's out point.

- **Timecode:** Use this option by clicking and dragging in the timecode readout area, or entering a timecode from the keyboard. If you want to synch using only minutes, seconds, and frames, leave the Ignore Hour option selected.

- **Numbered Clip Marker:** This option synchs to a clip marker chosen.

When you click OK, Premiere Pro synchronizes the clips on the tracks.

Figure 13-14: Clips must be synchronized before they can be used as multi-camera sources.

4. **Create a new sequence to be the target sequence (for recording the final cuts) by choosing File ⇨ New Sequence.**

5. **Select the target sequence tab (from Step 4) so that it is visible in the Timeline.**

6. **Nest the source sequence into the target sequence.** Drag the source sequence (with the synchronized video) from the Project panel into a track in the target sequence (created in Step 4).

7. **Click to select the left area of the track header to designate it as the target track.**

8. **Click on the embedded sequence to select it in the target track.**

9. **Turn on multi-camera editing by choosing Clip ⇨ Multi-Camera ⇨ Enable. (**You will not be able to access this command unless the embedded sequence is selected in the timeline.)

Viewing multi-camera footage

After you've properly set up your source and target tracks and enabled multi-camera editing, you're ready to view your footage in the Multi-Camera Monitor. Follow these steps:

1. **Open the Multi-Camera Monitor by choosing Multi-Camera Monitor in the Program Monitor panel menu.** The Multi-Camera Monitor is shown in Figure 13-15.

2. **Play the footage in the Multi-Camera Monitor to view the clips simultaneously.** Here are some options for playing video:

   - **To view the footage, click any of the standard monitor transport controls: step forward, step backward, play, shuttle, and job.**

   - **Click the Play Around button, which backs up the current-time indicator to the preroll position and plays to the postroll position.**

Note   You can set the preroll and postroll settings in the General Preferences dialog box (Edit ⇨ Preferences ⇨ General).

> • **Press the spacebar to start and stop video; use the left-arrow key or right-arrow key to step forward or back; or use the JKL keyboard combinations.**

Note   If you click camera 1, 2, 3, or 4 while playing footage in the multi-camera monitor, the camera border turns red and the footage is automatically recorded to the Timeline.

Camera 1   Camera 2   Preview

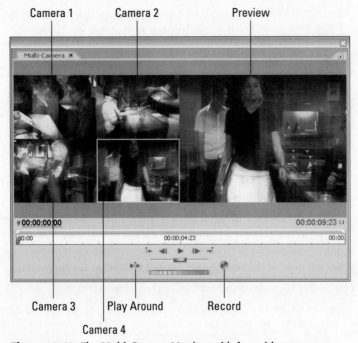

Camera 3   Play Around   Record

Camera 4

Figure 13-15: The Multi-Camera Monitor with four video sources

Recording multi-camera edits

After you've opened the Multi-Camera Monitor to display your footage, you're ready to start choosing shots to be recorded to the target sequence in the Timeline. When you record you can choose to record video and audio from the different source footage. Here's how to record multi-camera edits:

1. **Turn on recording by clicking the Record button.**

2. **Choose the first shot by clicking a camera in the Multi-Camera Monitor.**

3. **Set Audio as the audio source.** By default, multi-camera editing uses the Audio 1 track in the source footage. If you want audio to correspond to your camera-editing choices, choose Audio Follows Video from the Multi-Camera Monitor panel menu. Otherwise, make sure that Audio Follows Video is deselected.

4. **Play the sequence by pressing the spacebar or clicking the Play button in the Multi-Camera Monitor.**

5. **As the sequence plays, choose shots by clicking in the video from one of the cameras in the Multi-Camera Monitor or by pressing 1, 2, 3, or 4.**

6. **Stop recording by pressing the spacebar or clicking the Stop transport control.**

Replacing multi-camera scenes

After you have finished recording a multi-camera session, you may decide that you'd like to replace a scene from one camera with footage from a different camera. This is easily accomplished by simply selecting the footage in the target sequence, choosing Clip ➪ Multi-Camera, and then choosing one of the cameras from the Multi-Camera submenu. For example, you may select footage recorded from Camera 1 in the Timeline and then choose Clip ➪ Multi-Camera ➪ 2. Footage from Camera 2 replaces the selected footage in the target sequence.

Alternatively, you can also return to a specific area of the target sequence and record over it. To record over a sequence, set the current-time indicator at the point you want to start editing and then re-record using the recording steps described in the preceding section. Finally, you can also use the editing features described in this chapter to further enhance the multi-camera sequence.

Editing a Clip Using Clip Commands

When editing a production, you may find that you need to adjust a clip to maintain continuity in a project. For example, you may want to slow the speed of a clip to fill a gap in your production or to freeze a frame for a moment or two.

Various commands in the Clip menu enable you to edit a clip. Premiere Pro enables you to change the duration and/or the speed of a clip using the Clip ➪ Speed/Duration command. You can change the frame rate of a clip using the Clip ➪ Video Options ➪ Frame Hold command. Or you can use the Clip ➪ Video Options ➪ Frame Hold command to freeze a video frame.

Using the Duration and Speed commands

You can use the Clip ➪ Speed/Duration commands to change the length of a clip, to speed up or slow down a clip, or to play a clip in reverse.

Here's how to change the duration of a clip:

1. **Click the clip in a video track or in the Project panel to select it.**

2. **Choose Clip ➪ Speed/Duration.** The Clip Duration dialog box appears, as shown in Figure 13-16.

Figure 13-16: Use the Clip Speed/Duration dialog box to change a clip's speed or duration.

3. **Click the Link button to Unlink Speed and Duration.**

4. **Enter a duration.** You can't expand the clip to extend it past its original out point.

5. **Click OK to close the dialog box and set the new duration.**

> **Note** You can also change the duration of a clip by extending its edge with the Selection tool in the Timeline.

Here's how to change the speed of a clip (onscreen you should have a project with a clip in a video track in the Timeline window):

1. **Click the clip in the video track, or select it in the Timeline.**

2. **Choose Clip ⇨ Speed.** The Clip Speed/Duration dialog box appears.

3. **Type a value in the Speed field.** Type a value greater than 100 percent to speed up the clip, or type a value between 0 percent and 99 percent to slow down the clip. If you want to reverse the clip, click the Reverse Speed check box.

4. **Click OK to close the Clip Speed/Duration dialog box and apply the new speed.**

> **Tip** You also can change a clip's speed in the Timeline panel by clicking and dragging either edge of the clip with the Rate Stretch tool.

Using the Frame Hold command

Premiere Pro's Frame Hold command allows you to freeze one frame of a clip so that the frame appears from the in point to the out point of the clip. You can create a freeze frame from the in point, the out point, or at Marker point 0:

1. **Click the clip in a video track to select it.**

2. **If you want to freeze at a specific frame other than the in point or out point, set an unnumbered marker for the clip in the Source Monitor.**

3. **Choose Clip ⇨ Video Options ⇨ Frame Hold.** This opens the Frame Hold Options dialog box, shown in Figure 13-17.

4. **In the pop-up menu, choose whether to create the freeze frame on the In Point, on the Out Point, or at Marker 0.**

5. **Click the Hold On check box.**

6. **If you want to prevent keyframe effects from being viewed, click the Hold Filters check box.**

7. **To remove the effects of video interlacing, click the Deinterlace check box.** This deletes one of the fields and replaces it with a duplicate of the other field.

Figure 13-17: Use the Frame Hold Options dialog box to create a freeze frame.

More clip commands and utilities

As you edit in Premiere Pro, you're likely to use a variety of clip utilities, some of which have been described in preceding chapters. As a reminder, here is a summary of commands that may prove useful when editing:

✦ **Clip ➪ Group:** This command groups clips together, allowing you to move or delete several clips as one entity. Grouping clips can help you avoid inadvertently separating titles and unlinked audio in one track from footage in another. When clips are grouped, you can click and drag clip edges in the Timeline to edit all clips simultaneously. To group clips, select all the clips and then choose Clip ➪ Group. To ungroup, select one of the clips and choose Clip ➪ Ungroup. To select one member of a group independently of others, press Alt and click and drag the clip. Note that you can simultaneously apply commands from the Clip menu to clips that are in a group.

✦ **Clip ➪ Scale to Frame Size:** This command scales the selected clip to match the project frame size.

✦ **Clip ➪ Video Options ➪ Frame Blend:** The Frame Blend option prevents choppy video when you've changed speed or frame rate of clips. By default, Frame Blend is on.

✦ **Clip ➪ Video Options ➪ Field Options:** This command provides options for reducing flicker and removing interlacing in clips.

✦ **File ➪ Interpret Footage:** This command allows you to change the frames per second, pixel aspect ratio, and alpha channel use of the file selected in the Project panel.

✦ **File ➪ Get Properties for ➪ Selection:** This command provides data rate, file size, image size, and other file information about the selected file in the Project panel.

Summary

Premiere Pro provides numerous tools and commands that enable you to quickly and precisely edit a digital video production. Premiere Pro's editing tools can be found in the Timeline toolbox. Most other editing utilities reside in the Source, Program, Trim, and Multi-Camera Monitors. This chapter covered the following topics:

✦ Use the Ripple Edit and Rolling Edit tools to change the in and out points of clips in the Timeline. A ripple edit changes the project duration; a rolling edit does not.

✦ You can click and drag with the Slip or Slide tools to edit the in and out points of a clip in between two other clips. The Slip tool does not change project duration; the Slide tool does.

✦ Use the Source and Program Monitors to create three-point and four-point edits.

✦ Use the Trim panel to precisely shave frames from clips.

✦ Use the Multi-Camera Monitor to edit footage from up to four video sources.

✦ ✦ ✦

Using Video Effects

Adobe Premiere Pro's special effects can wake up even the dullest video production. Using the video effects in Premiere Pro's Effects panel, for example, you can blur or skew images and add bevels, drop shadows, and painterly effects. Some effects can correct and enhance video; others can make it seem as though the video is out of control. By changing controls for the effects, you can also create startling motion effects, such as making it appear as if an earthquake or tornado has struck your clip.

As this chapter illustrates, Premiere Pro's video effects work in sync with the keyframe track, enabling you to change effect settings at specific points on the Timeline. All you need to do is specify the settings for the start of an effect, move to another keyframe, and set the ending effect. When you create a preview, Premiere Pro does the rest: It interpolates the video effect, editing all the in-between frames to create a fluid effect over time.

If you haven't been adding effects to your video, this chapter provides everything you need to get up and running. You'll explore every video effect in the Effects panel and see how the Effect Controls panel enables you to change effect settings. You'll also have a chance to practice creating effects with keyframes and image mattes with sample clips from the DVD-ROM that accompanies this book.

If you've already started working with Premiere Pro effects, this chapter shows how to use Premiere Pro's keyframe track and provides a reference for every effect in the Effects panel.

Exploring the Video Effects

Premiere Pro's Effects panel is a storehouse of video effects. However, before you begin to use the effects, you should become familiar with the window interface. To display the Effects panel, choose Window ➪ Effects. The Effects panel, shown in Figure 14-1, not only contains the Video Effects, but also the Audio Effects, the Audio Transitions, and Video Transitions. To view the Video Effects, click the triangle to the left of the Video Effects Bin (folder) in the Effects panel. Within the Video Effects bin are 17 bins (folders) that contain different video effects.

Open a bin within the Video Effects bin to view a video effect. After the bin is open, a list of effects appears. An icon to the left of the video effect's name represents each effect. After you've opened a bin, you can apply a video effect to a video track by clicking and dragging it over a clip in the Timeline panel. To close a bin, click the triangle to the left of the bin.

Figure 14-1: Premiere Pro's Effects panel provides access to Premiere Pro's video effects.

Navigating within the video effects

The Effects panel features options that can help you keep organized while using Premiere Pro's many video effects. The following is a brief description of these options:

✦ **Find:** The Contains field at the top of the Effects panel helps locate effects. In the Contains field, type the name of the effect that you want to find. Premiere Pro automatically starts the search.

✦ **New Custom Bin:** When you create custom bins (folders), you can use them to organize effects. To create a custom bin, either click the bin icon at the bottom of the Effects panel or click the Effects menu and choose New Custom Bin. After you create a bin, drag the effects into it. With all your chosen effects in one bin, you'll find that they are easier to use and locate.

✦ **Rename:** You can change a name of a custom bin at any time by selecting the bin and then clicking the name. When the name of the bin is highlighted, type the name that you want in the Name field.

✦ **Delete:** If you have finished using a custom bin, you can delete it by selecting it and choosing the Delete Custom Item from the Effects menu or by clicking the Delete icon at the bottom of the panel. A prompt appears asking whether you want to delete the item. If you do, click Yes.

The Effect Controls panel

When you apply a video effect to an image, the effect appears in the Effect Controls panel, as shown in Figure 14-2.

Figure 14-2: The settings for a video effect appear in the Effect Controls panel after a video effect is applied to a clip.

At the top of the panel, the name of the selected clip appears. To the right of the clip name is a button that enables you to create and/or show or hide keyframes over a Timeline. At the bottom left of the Effect Controls panel is a time display showing you where the clip appears in the Timeline. To the right of the time display are options allowing you to zoom out or in.

Below the name of the selected sequence and clip name appear the Fixed Effects — Motion and Opacity. Below the Fixed Effects appear the Standard Effects. If a video effect has been applied to the selected clip, a Standard Effect is displayed below the Opacity option. All the video effects that have been applied to the selected clip are displayed below the Video Effects. The video effects appear in the order in which the effects have been applied. If you like, you can click and drag the standard video effects up or down to change the order. To the left of the Fixed Effects (Motion and Opacity) and a Video Effects name appears a box with an *f* in it. The *f* means that this effect is enabled. You can disable the effect by clicking the *f* or deselecting Effect Enabled in the Effect Controls menu. Also next to the effect name is a small triangle. If you click the triangle, the settings for that effect appear.

Many effects also feature a dialog box that includes a preview area. If the effect provides a dialog box, you see a little dialog box icon to the right of the name of the video effect in the Effect Controls panel. Click the icon to access the Setup dialog box. Many effects can be applied with Premiere Pro's keyframe and graph option. If so, a small stopwatch is shown in front of the name of the effect. To enable keyframing, click the small stopwatch icon. After you click, a small blue frame appears around the stopwatch icon. (Keyframing is explained later in this chapter.)

Note   You can copy and paste effects from one clip to another. In the Effect Controls panel, click the effect you want to copy. Shift-click to select more than one effect. Then choose Edit ⇨ Copy. In the Timeline panel, select the clip you want to apply the effects to and then choose Edit ⇨ Paste.

The Effect Controls menu

The Effect Controls menu provides control over all the clips in the panel. The menu enables you to turn previewing on and off and to select preview quality as well as to enable and disable effects. The following is a brief description of the Effect Controls menu commands:

✦ **Effect Enabled:** Click this command to disable or enable effects. By default, Effect Enabled is selected.

✦ **Delete Selected Effect:** This command removes the selected effect from the clip.

Note You can remove an effect from the panel by selecting it in the Effect Controls panel and pressing Delete.

✦ **Delete All Effects from Clip:** This command removes all effects from the clip.

Note The Audio commands in the Effect Controls menu are covered in Chapters 8 and 9.

Applying a Video Effect

You can apply one video effect or multiple video effects to an entire video clip by dragging the effect from the Effects panel to the Timeline. The video effects allow you to change the color of a clip, blur it, or even distort it.

Follow these steps to apply a video effect to a clip in the Timeline:

1. **Create a New Project, and call it VideoEffects.**

Note Refer to Chapter 4 for information on choosing a project preset.

2. **Choose Window ➪ Workspace ➪ Effects to display all the panels you need.**

3. **Choose File ➪ Import to import a video clip to use as the background.** If you want, you can use Digital Vision's Drifting Skies (386022f.mov) video clip as the background. It is located on the DVD that accompanies this book.

On the DVD-ROM Digital Vision's Drifting Skies 386022f.mov is in the Digital Vision folder in the Chapter 14 folder that is in the Tutorial Projects folder on the DVD that accompanies this book.

4. **Drag the background video clip from the Project panel to the Video 1 track of the Timeline panel.**

5. **To apply an effect to the background, you first need to select it in the Timeline panel.** Click the background clip in the Video 1 track.

6. **Choose an effect by clicking it.** For a simple effect, try the Directional Blur found in the Blur & Sharpen folder. We used the Lens Flare effect, which is found in the Render folder. Figure 14-3 shows the Lens Flare effect in the Program Monitor panel.

Note If you didn't choose the Directional Blur effect, the effect you chose may provide more settings in a dialog box. If a dialog box is provided for the effect, a Setup icon appears to the right of the effect in the Effect Controls panel. Click the Setup icon to open the dialog box and change the settings. Figure 14-4 shows the Lens Flare Settings dialog box.

Figure 14-3: The preview of the Lens Flare effect in the Program Monitor panel

Figure 14-4: The Lens Flare Settings dialog box

7. **To apply the effect, drag the effect from the Effects panel directly onto the clip in the Video 1 track or into the Effect Controls panel.** To adjust the settings of the effect, use the options found beneath the effect's name in the Effect Controls panel. To set an effect to its default settings, click the Reset button to the right of the effect's name. For a full discussion of the video effects and their options, read the "Touring Premiere Pro's Video Effects" section at the end of this chapter.

8. **Try different effects, such as those found in the Adjust, Distort, Image Control, Pixelate, Render, Stylize, Time, and Transform folders.** To turn the effect on or off, click the small *f* in front of the effect's name in the Effect Controls panel. To delete an effect, click the effect in the Effect Controls panel and press Delete, or click the menu and choose Delete Selected Effect. To remove all the effects from a clip, click the Effect Controls menu and choose Delete All Effects from Clip.

Note   You can add multiple effects to an image. You can also add the same effect with different effect settings to the same image.

9. **Click the Play button in the Program Monitor panel to see a preview of the effects.** As you work, watch the preview in the Program Monitor panel.

10. **Choose File ➯ Import to import a sound clip, and drag the sound clip to the Audio 1 track.** We used Digital Vision's Acoustic Chillout clip (730007aw.wav). This sound clip is located on the DVD that accompanies this book.

On the DVD-ROM   Digital Vision's Acoustic Chillout clip (730007aw.wav) is in the Digital Vision folder in the Chapter 14 folder that is in the Tutorial Projects folder on the DVD that accompanies this book.

11. **Choose File ➯ Save to save your project so that you can use it in the next section.**

Applying a video effect to a clip with an alpha channel

Not only can you apply an effect to a video clip, but you can also apply an effect to a still image that has an alpha channel. In a still image, an alpha channel is used to isolated an object from its background. To apply an effect to just an image and not its background, the image must have an alpha channel. You can use Adobe Photoshop to mask an image and save the mask either as an alpha channel or a layer. For more information on creating alpha channels using Photoshop, see Chapter 28.

Follow these steps to apply a video effect to a Photoshop file with an alpha channel:

On the DVD-ROM   If you want to apply an effect to an image with an alpha channel, you can apply video effects to the Airplane.psd image (shown in Figure 14-5) and use Digital Vision's Drifting Skies 386022f.mov as the background. These files are found in the Chapter 14 folder in the Tutorial Projects folder on the DVD that accompanies this book.

Before you start, load the video effects project from the previous section, or create a new project, import a video clip, and drag it into the Video 1 track. We used Digital Vision's Drifting Skies 386022f.mov as the background. It is found in the Chapter 14 folder in the Tutorial Projects folder on the DVD that accompanies this book.

1. **Choose Window ➯ Workspace ➯ Effects to display all the panels you need.**

2. **Choose File ➯ Import to load a Photoshop file with an alpha channel.**

3. **In the Import dialog box, locate a Photoshop file that has an alpha channel so that only the image and not the background is imported.** We used the Airplane.psd image (found on the DVD that accompanies this book). After you've located the file, click Open. In the Import Layered File dialog box, make sure Footage is selected in the Import As drop-down menu. In the Layer Options section, click the Choose Layer option. Set the drop-down menu to Alpha Channel or the appropriate channel.

4. **Click OK.** The Photoshop file and its alpha channel appear in the Project panel.

5. **Drag the still image with an alpha channel (the airplane image) from the Project panel to Video 2 track.** Place it directly above the background clip in the Video 1 track. The Timeline Marker should be over both clips.

6. **Double-click the airplane image in the Timeline panel to display it in the Program Monitor panel.** On one side of the Program Monitor panel, the Photoshop file (airplane image) appears on a black background. On the other side of the image, the Photoshop file (airplane image) appears over the selected background from the Video 1 track, as shown in Figure 14-5. The Photoshop file (airplane image) from the Video 2 track takes on the background of the clip from the Video 1 track because it has an alpha channel.

Figure 14-5: The Program Monitor panel on one side displays the Photoshop file with an alpha channel. On the other side, you can see the Photoshop file over a sky background. The background clip is in the Video 1 track of the Timeline panel, and the Photoshop file is in the Video 2 track.

7. **To see the Photoshop alpha channel, click the Program Monitor panel menu and choose Alpha.** Figure 14-6 shows the Photoshop alpha channel. To return to standard view, click Composite Video from the menu.

8. **Select the Photoshop file (airplane image) in the Video 2 track.**

9. **Drag the desired video effect from the Effects panel onto the Photoshop file (airplane image) in the Video 2 track or into the Effect Controls panel.** In our example, we applied the Emboss effect, which is found in the Stylize folder. We also applied the Drop Shadow and Bevel Edges effects found in the Perspective folder. In the next section, we apply the Basic 3D effect, found in the Perspective folder, by setting keyframes. By setting keyframes, you can change the effect over time. Proceed to the next section if you want to learn how to use video effects with keyframes.

10. **To preview your work, click and drag the shuttle or jog slider in the Program Monitor panel.** You can also move the Timeline Marker in the Timeline. To preview your entire clip, click the Play button in the Program Monitor panel.

Figure 14-6: The Photoshop alpha channel

11. **Choose File ➪ Import to import a sound clip, and then drag the sound clip to the Audio 1 track.** We used Digital Vision's Acoustic Chillout clip (730007aw.wav). This sound clip is located on the DVD that accompanies this book.

On the DVD-ROM

Digital Vision's Acoustic Chillout clip (730007aw.wav) is found in the Digital Vision folder in the Chapter 14 folder in the Tutorial Projects folder on the DVD that accompanies this book.

12. **Choose File ➪ Save to save your work so that you can use it in the next section.**

Applying video effects with markers

Premiere Pro allows you to go through your project and set markers in designated areas where you would like to add video effects to individual video clips. You can set In and Out markers, Unnumbered markers, Numbered markers, or Other Numbered markers. Markers are set using the Timeline ruler in either the Timeline panel or the Effect Controls panel. The Timeline ruler in the Effect Controls panel allows you to view and edit markers.

Follow these steps to set a marker:

1. **Click a video clip in one of the Video tracks in the Timeline panel.**

2. **Move the current-time indicator to the location where you want to set a marker.**

3. **Right-click in the Timeline ruler of either the Effect Controls panel or the Timeline panel.**

4. **In the drop-down menu that appears, choose Set Sequence Marker. Then select a type of marker.**

5. **If you made a mistake and want to delete a marker, right-click. In the drop down menu that appears, choose Clear Sequence Markers. Then choose the marker you want to delete.**

Note To display a clip beyond its In and Out points, deselect the Pin to Clip option from the Effect Controls menu.

After you've set markers, you can go to the markers and apply video effects to the location of the marker.

Follow these steps to go to a marker and apply an effect:

1. **Click a video clip in one of the Video tracks in the Timeline panel.**

2. **Right-click in the timeline ruler of either the Effect Controls panel or the Timeline panel.**

3. **In the drop-down menu that appears, choose Go to Sequence Marker. Then choose whether you want to go to the Next Marker, Previous, In, Out, or a Numbered marker.** Note that the current-time indicator moves to the spot of the designated marker.

4. **To apply an effect to the location of the marker, click and drag an effect to the Effect Controls panel. Then click the triangle in front of the name of the effect to display its controls. Make the necessary adjustments, and then click the Toggle Animation icon to set a keyframe at the location of the marker.**

5. **After you are finished applying effects to the markers you set, you may want to delete them.** To do so, right-click the Timeline ruler. In the drop-down menu that appears, choose Clear Sequence Markers and click All Markers.

Using Video Effects with Keyframes

Premiere Pro's keyframe feature enables you to change video effects at specific points in the Timeline. With keyframes, you can have Premiere Pro use the settings of an effect at one point on the Timeline, gradually changing to the settings at another point on the Timeline. When Premiere Pro creates the preview, it interpolates the effect over time, rendering all the frames that change in between the set points. Keyframing can be used to make video clips or stills more interesting. You can also import a still image of your logo and animate it using keyframes. If you want, you can use Premiere Pro's Title Designer to create a logo. To learn how to create a logo using Premiere Pro, see Chapter 11.

Figure 14-7 shows frames of the airplane image from the previous sections, animated over a sky background video clip. The airplane image is animated using the Basic 3D effect found in the Perspective folder. To make the airplane swivel and tilt to its original state, we set keyframes.

The keyframe track

Premiere Pro's keyframe track makes creating, editing, and manipulating keyframes quick, logical, and precise. The keyframe track is found in both the Timeline panel and the Effect Controls panel. Figure 14-8 shows the Timeline panel with the keyframe track. Figure 14-9 shows the Effect Controls panel with the keyframe track. To view the keyframe track in the Timeline panel, expand the track by clicking the track's Expand button. To view the keyframe track in the Effect Controls panel, make sure the Show/Hide Keyframes button is activated.

Figure 14-7: Frames from the airplane clip with the Basic 3D effect applied using keyframes

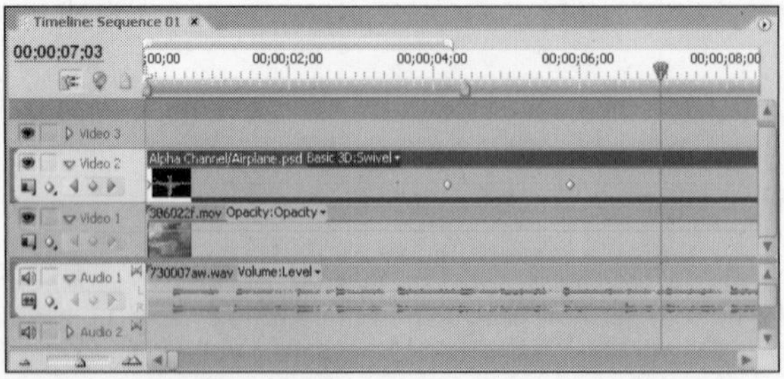

Figure 14-8: The Timeline panel with the Video 2 track expanded with keyframes

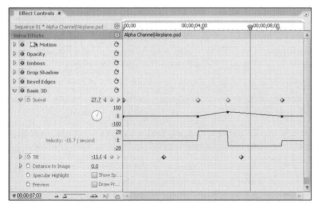

Figure 14-9: The Effect Controls panel with keyframes for the Video 2 track displayed

Note   The keyframe track does not appear if you do not have a clip in the track.

To enable keyframing, click the tiny stopwatch next to one of the settings for an effect in the Effect Controls panel. You can also turn keyframing on and off by clicking the Show Keyframes icon in the Timeline panel and choosing an effect setting from the video clip's menu. In the keyframe track, a circle or diamond indicates a keyframe exists at the current Timeline frame. Clicking the right arrow icon (Go to Previous Keyframe) jumps the Timeline Marker (current-time indicator) from one keyframe to the next. Clicking the left arrow (Go to Next Keyframe) moves the Timeline Marker backward from one keyframe to the next.

Follow these steps to apply an effect to a clip using keyframes:

1. **Before you start, load the Video Effects project from the previous section, or create a new project, import a background video clip for the Video 1 track, and import a still image or logo (that has an alpha channel) for the Video 2 track.** We used Digital Vision's Drifting Skies 386022f.mov as the background and the Airplane.psd for the Video 2 track. They are found in the Chapter 14 folder in the Tutorial Projects folder on the DVD that accompanies this book.

On the DVD-ROM   If you want, you can use the Airplane.psd image in the Video 2 track and use Digital Vision's Drifting Skies 386022f.mov as the background (the Video 1 track). They are found in the Chapter 14 folder in the Tutorial Projects folder on the DVD that accompanies this book.

2. **Choose Window ⇨ Workspace ⇨ Effects to display all the panels you need.**

Note   Using an image in the Video 2 track that has an alpha channel allows a background clip in the Video 1 tack to show through when previewed in the Program Monitor panel. To see a preview in the Program Monitor panel, click the Play button. To superimpose two video clips without alpha channels, you need to use the Keying Effects. The Keying Effects are briefly discussed in the next section. For a full description on these effects, see Chapter 15.

3. **Add an effect to the image in the Video 2 track by clicking an effect in the Effects panel and dragging it to the clip in the Timeline panel (or to the Effect Controls panel).** If you are animating a logo, for an unusual effect, you may want to try the Twirl effect. The Twirl effect is found in the Distort bin, in the Video Effects bin that is in the Effects panel. In Figures 14-7, 14-8, and 14-9, we used the Basic 3D effect.

4. **To create a keyframe for the effect you applied in Step 3 using the Timeline panel, move the Timeline Marker (edit line or current-time indicator) over the first frame of the image in the Video 2 track.**

5. **In the Timeline panel, click the Expand/Collapse Track icon (a triangle icon that appears before the track name) to expand the track.** Then click the Show keyframes icon to show the keyframe track.

6. **Click the clip's title bar menu, and choose an Effects control.**

7. **Click the Add/Delete Keyframe icon to add a keyframe.** A circle appears on the keyframe track.

8. **To add another keyframe, move the Timeline Marker (edit line) to a new position. Then click the Add Keyframe icon.** Change the settings for the effect by clicking the keyframe in the Timeline panel and moving it up or down.

9. **To add more keyframes using the Timeline panel, repeat Step 8 as many times as desired.** Figure 14-8 shows the Timeline panel with keyframes.

Note To delete a keyframe, click it and press Delete. You can move a keyframe by clicking and dragging it to a new location.

The keyframes that you created using the Timeline panel appear in the Effect Controls panel.

10. **You can also use the Effect Controls panel to adjust the settings for a keyframe.** In the Effect Controls panel, click the triangle in front of the effect to display the controls. Then move the Timeline Marker (edit line or current-time indicator) over the keyframe you want to edit. Then make the necessary changes.

11. **To create a keyframe for the effect you applied in Step 3 using the Effect Controls panel, move the edit line in the Timeline of the Effect Controls panel to the beginning of the clip.** Then click the Toggle Animation icon in front of the Effects control that you want to work with. A keyframe is added, and keyframing is enabled.

12. **Move the edit line in the Timeline of the Effect Controls panel to a new position, and adjust the control's setting.** As you adjust the control's setting, a keyframe is added.

13. **To add more keyframes using the Effect Controls panel, repeat Step 12 as many times as desired.** Figure 14-9 shows the Effect Controls panel with keyframes.

Note When keyframing is enabled for an effect's control, you can click the Toggle Animation icon to delete all the existing keyframes for that effect's control.

14. **To preview the video effect, choose Play from the Program Monitor panel.** You can also drag the Timeline Marker (current-time indicator) as you view the preview in the Program Monitor panel.

15. **Choose File ▷ Import to import a sound clip.** Then drag the sound clip to the Audio 1 track. We used Digital Vision's Acoustic Chillout clip 730007aw.wav. This sound clip is located on the DVD that accompanies this book.

On the DVD-ROM Digital Vision's Acoustic Chillout clip 730007aw.wav is found in the Digital Vision folder in the Chapter 14 folder in the Tutorial Projects folder on the DVD that accompanies this book.

16. **Choose File ▷ Save to save your project.**

Using Value and Velocity Graphs to change keyframe property values

Premiere Pro's Value and Velocity graphs allow you to fine-tune the smoothness of an effect and increase or decrease the speed of an effect. Most effects can have various graphs. Each control (property) of an effect can have a Value and Velocity graph. Note that some effects do not have any properties or controls, such as the Facet effect in the Pixelate bin.

When you make adjustments to a control of an effect with the Toggle Animation icon turned on, you add keyframes and points to the graph, as shown in Figure 14-10. Before you make any adjustments to the controls for an effect, the graph is a straight line. After you make adjustments to the effect's control, you add keyframes and alter the graph.

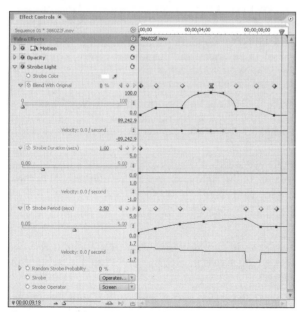

Figure 14-10: The Effect Controls panel with keyframes and Value and Velocity graphs for the Strobe Light effect

Value and Velocity graphs can be viewed and edited in the Effect Controls panel and the Timeline panel. You have limited editing power of the graph in the Timeline panel. Unlike the Timeline panel, the Effect Controls panel allows you to view and edit more than one graph at a time. To do so, you simply create keyframes for a control (property) in an effect. Then click the triangle in front of the name of the control (property). In the timeline of the Effect Controls panel, the Value graph appears above the Velocity graph. To view and edit a graph for an effect in the Timeline panel, click the Effect menu of a clip in a video track. Then select a property.

Note   The graphs for the properties of sound effects can be viewed in either the Effect Controls panel or the Timeline panel. The graphs for sound effects work basically the same as they do for video effects.

Follow these steps to work with Value and Velocity graphs using the Effect Controls panel:

1. **Create a new project.**

2. **Import a video clip. Drag the video clip from the Project panel to the Video 1 track of the Timeline panel.** If you want, you can use the sky background that we used — Digital Vision's Drifting Skies 386022f.mov. The sky background is on the DVD that accompanies the book.

3. **Drag an effect to the video clip in the Timeline panel.** We used the Strobe Light effect found in the Stylize bin.

4. **Click the triangle in front of the video effect to view all of its properties. Then click the triangle of the first property to view the controls.** In the case of the Strobe Light effect, click the triangle in front of Blend with Original. The control is set to 0 percent.

5. **Move the current-time indicator to the beginning of the Timeline. Then click the Toggle Animation icon to create a keyframe and display the control's Value and Velocity graph.** Note that the graphs are a straight horizontal line. This means there are no changes to the effect in the Timeline.

6. **To edit the graphs, move the current-time indicator to the right. Next, make adjustments to the control.** We moved the Blend with Original slider to the right. Note that another keyframe is created and a point on the graph is created, as shown in Figure 14-10.

7. **Continue editing the graph by creating new keyframes. To create a new keyframe, move the current-time indicator to the right and then make adjustments to the control.**

After you've created a graph, you can use the Selection tool to move the graph. Use one of these methods:

✦ To move the Value graph, place the mouse over the horizontal white line between the Value and Velocity graphs. When the mouse icon changes to an up and down arrow, click and drag either up or down.

✦ To move the Velocity graph, place the mouse over the horizontal white line below the Velocity graph. When the mouse icon changes to an up and down arrow, click and drag either up or down.

✦ To add a point on the Value graph, move the mouse pointer over the place on the graph that you want to add a point. When the mouse pointer changes to a Pen tool with a small plus sign, Ctrl-click. Note that a new keyframe is created above the new point on the graph.

✦ To turn a sharp corner point on the graph to a smooth curve, you can change the form of interpolation from Linear to Bezier. To change a Linear keyframe marker into a Bezier marker, either Ctrl-click and drag the point on the Value graph (below the Linear keyframe marker), or right-click the Linear keyframe marker. When a drop-down menu appears, choose Bezier. This changes the mode of interpolation from Linear to Bezier and also changes the icon of the keyframe. The Linear keyframe marker icon changes from a diamond-shaped icon to an hourglass-shaped icon. Also notice that the point on the graph now has directional handles and lines. The direction handles and lines can be used to adjust the effect.

Superimposing Video Clips Using the Keying Video Effects

To superimpose two video clips that don't have alpha channels, you need to use the Keying video effects. (For more detailed information on Keying video effects, see Chapter 15.) Figure 14-10 shows the panels we used to create a project using the Chroma Key effect. To create the project, we superimposed two video clips: a graphic video clip in the Video 2 track and a sky background in the Video 1 track. In the Video 3 track, we used an Adobe Photoshop file with an alpha channel so that you when we superimposed the clips in the Video 1 and the Video 2 tracks, you could see the background through them. Figure 14-11 shows the Program Monitor panel with a frame of the final result of the three clips from the three video tracks superimposed onto one another.

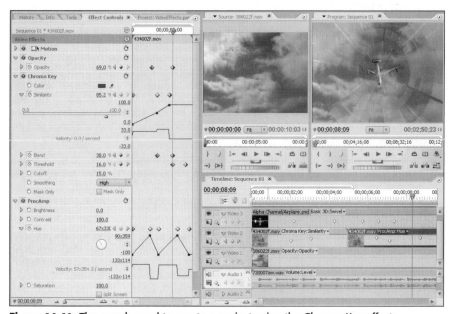

Figure 14-11: The panels used to create a project using the Chroma Key effect

In the project in Figure 14-11, we used the sky background and an Adobe Photoshop file with an alpha channel from the "the keyframe track" section. The sky background that we used is from Digital Vision's Drifting Skies 386022f.mov. To superimpose a video clip over the sky background, we moved the Adobe Photoshop file (Airplane.mov) from the Video 2 track to the Video 3 track. Then we imported a new video clip (Digital Vision's Ambient Space clip 434002f.mov) and dragged it into the Video 2 track, as shown in Figure 14-11. To jazz up our project, we added sound. The sound file we used is Digital Vision's Acoustic Chillout 730007aw.wav.

On the DVD-ROM

The video clips used to create the project shown in Figure 14-11 are found in the Chapter 14 folder in the Tutorial Projects folder located on the DVD that accompanies this book. The clips are Airplane.mov, Digital Vision's Drifting Skies 386022f.mov, Digital Vision's Ambient Space clip 434002f.mov, and Digital Vision's Acoustic Chillout clip 730007aw.wav.

Follow these steps to superimpose two video clips using the Chroma Key video effects:

1. **Choose File ➪ Open Project to open the project from the previous section, or choose File ➪ New ➪ Project to create a new project.**

2. **Your project onscreen should have two video clips and a third image with an alpha channel. Choose File ➪ Import to import the necessary clips.** If you are using a new project, you need to import three files. If you are using the project from the previous sections, you need to import one new video clip. We used Digital Vision's Ambient Space clip 434002f.mov. This video clip is located on the DVD that accompanies this book.

3. **Now you are ready to drag the clips from the Project panel to the Timeline panel.** If you are using a new project, you need to drag a background video clip from the Project panel to the Video 1 track. Then drag another video clip into the Video 2 track and the clip with an alpha channel into the Video 3 track. This clip should have an alpha channel so that the background shows through. If you are using the project from the previous section, move the airplane file with the alpha channel from the Video 2 track to the Video 3 track. Note that all the effects remain with the video clip as you move it. Then drag the new video clip (Digital Vision's Ambient Space clip 434002f.mov) into the Video 2 track. The video clip in the Video 2 track should be directly above the video clip in the Video 1 track. If the video clip in the Video 2 track is not as long as the one in the Video 1 track, you may want to copy the video clip in the Video 2 track and paste the copy next to it as shown in Figure 14-11.

4. **To superimpose the clips in the Video 1 and Video 2 tracks, we used the Chroma Key effect from the Keying bin and the ProcAmp video effect from the Adjust bin, and we reduced the Opacity option.** To apply the Chroma Key effect to the clip in the Video 2 track, select the Chroma Key effect from the Effects panel and drag it over the clip in the Video 2 track.

5. **Use the Effect Controls panel to adjust the settings of the video effect.** As you work, you can preview the video effect in the Program Monitor panel. To adjust the Chroma Key effect, click the triangle in front of the words *Chroma Key* to display the controls for the effect. Start by clicking the color swatch and picking a color that is similar to the color of the background clip in the Video 1 track. Then adjust the Similarity value and Blend value. If you need to, also adjust the Threshold and Cutoff values. If you want to animate the controls over time, you need to set keyframes. To create a keyframe, move the current-time indicator to the beginning of the video clip and click the stopwatch (Toggle Animation) icon. The first keyframe is created. Next move the current-time indicator to a

new location. As you adjust the control, a new keyframe is created. The keyframes are use to animate the control. To fine-tune the control, click the triangle in front of the control. This displays the graph for the control. Making adjustments to the graph changes the effect of the control.

Note

For more information on superimposing clips using the Video Keying effects and the Opacity option, see Chapter 15.

6. **To see more of the clip in the Video 1 track, reduce the opacity of the clip in the Video 2 track by using either the Opacity option in the Effect Controls panel or the Timeline panel.** To access the Opacity option in the Timeline panel, you need to expand the track, click the title bar of the track, and choose Opacity. A white line appears below the track's title bar. Drag this bar down to reduce the opacity.

7. **We made further adjustments to the colors of the clip in the Video 2 track by applying the ProcAmp video effect from the Adjust bin.** To use the ProAmp video effect, drag it over the clip in the Video 2 track.

8. **To have the colors of the clip in the Video 2 track change over time, you need to create keyframes for the ProcAmp Hue control.** Move the edit line (current-time indicator) to the beginning of the clip. Then click the Toggle Animation icon in front of the Hue control to enable keyframing and create your first keyframe. Then move the edit line (current-time indicator) to a new position, and adjust the Hue control to create another keyframe. Click the triangle in front of the word *Hue* to display the graph for this control. You can use the graph to fine-tune the effect.

9. **To jazz up your project, you can add a sound clip.** Choose File ➪ Import to import a sound clip. In the Import dialog box, locate a sound clip and click Open. We used Digital Vision's Acoustic Chillout clip 730007aw.wav. This sound clip is located on the DVD that accompanies this book.

10. **Drag the sound clip from the Project panel to the Audio 1 track.** If the sound clip is too long, click the left side of the clip and drag it inward. For more information on working with sound clips, see Chapter 8.

11. **Be sure to save your work.**

12. **Click the Play button in the Program Monitor panel to preview your work.**

13. **If you want, you can export your project as a movie.** Choose File ➪ Export ➪ Movie. In the Export Movie dialog box, name your movie. To change the settings, click the Settings button. Click Save to save the project as a movie.

Applying Effects to Different Image Areas Using the Image Matte Keying Effect

You can use an image matte to show an effect only in specific areas of a clip. When you apply a matte, Premiere Pro masks out the areas that you don't want shown.

An *image matte* is either a black-and-white image or a grayscale image. By default, Adobe Premiere Pro applies effects to the clip areas corresponding to white portions of the matte. (The effect does not appear in clip regions corresponding to black areas.) In gray areas, the effect is applied with some degree of transparency — which means that the areas where the effect is applied appear to be see-through to some extent.

You can use Adobe Photoshop, Adobe Illustrator, Procreate Painter, or even Adobe Premiere Pro's Title Designer to create an image matte. After you've created an image matte, you need two clips, one for the Video 1 track and one for the Video 2 track. If you don't have an image matte or video clips, you can use any of the sample files found on the DVD that accompanies this book. Figure 14-12 shows the panels used to create an Image Matte project. The clips used in Figure 14-12 are from Digital Vision's Electro clip 579020f.mov and Digital Vision's CityMix clip 567017f.mov.

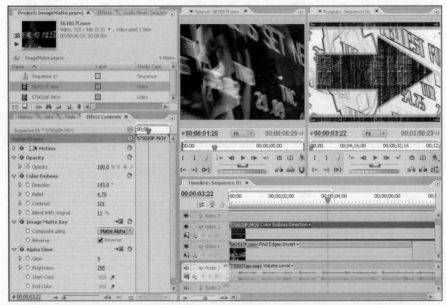

Figure 14-12: Frames from the sample image matte project using the emboss effect only on a certain area of the clip (outside the arrow)

Follow these steps to apply an effect using an image matte:

1. **Open an existing project, or create a new one.**

Note   Refer to Chapter 4 for information on choosing a project preset.

2. **Choose Window ➪ Workspace ➪ Effects to display all the panels you need.**

3. **Import two video clips into the Project panel.**

On the DVD-ROM   The clips used to create the project in Figure 14-12 are in the Digital Vision folder in the Chapter 14 folder in the Tutorial Projects folder located on the DVD that accompanies this book. The images are from Digital Vision's Electro clip 579020f.mov and Digital Vision's CityMix clip 567017f.mov. The matte image used in the project is called arrow.psd and is in the Chapter 14 folder.

4. **Click and drag one of the video clips from the Project panel to the Video 1 track of the Timeline panel.** The video clip in the Video 1 track is the clip that appears inside the matte. We used Digital Vision's CityMix clip 567017f.mov in the Video 1 track.

5. **Click and drag the other video clip to the Video 2 track.** The video clip in the Video 2 track is the clip that appears in the background of the matte. We used Digital Vision's Electro clip 579020f.mov in the Video 2 track.

6. **Apply an effect to the Video 2 track by dragging an effect from the Effects panel to the clip.** If you want, you can apply a different effect to the video clip in the Video 1 track. If you apply the effect to the Video 2 track, however, the effect can be seen only outside the matte image. If you apply the effect to the Video 1 track, the effect is seen only inside the matte image. We applied the Color Emboss effect (found in the Stylize bin) to the Video 2 track and the Find Edges effect (found in the Stylize bin) to the Video 1 track.

7. **To superimpose the Video 2 track over the Video 1 track, select the Video 2 track.**

8. **Choose Image Matte from the Keying bin in the Effects panel.** Then click and drag it over the Video 2 track.

9. **In the Effect Controls panel, click the Setup icon.** When the Select a Matte Image dialog box appears, browse to and load the matte image. (We used a file called arrow.psd for our matte image. The file can be found in the Chapter 14 folder on the DVD that accompanies the book.) Click OK to apply the image matte. The properties for the Image Matte effect appear in the Effect Controls panel. They are Composite Using and Reverse. We set the Composite Using drop-down menu to Matte Alpha and clicked the Reverse check box to reverse the effect.

10. **Drag the Alpha Glow effect from the Stylize bin to the Video 2 track.** This effect gives the arrow a three-dimensional look. If you want, you can also adjust the size and position of the clip in the Video 2 track by using the Motion effect. You can also reduce the Opacity effect to see more of the clip in the Video 1 track.

11. **Click the Play button in the Program Monitor panel to preview the effect.**

12. **Choose File ➪ Save to save your work.**

Touring Premiere Pro's Video Effects

Premiere Pro boasts over 100 video effects that are divided into 17 bins. The bins are Adjust, Blur & Sharpen, Channel, Color Correction, Distort, Image Control, Keying, Noise, Noise & Gain, Perspective, Pixelate, Render, Stylize, Time, Transform, Transition, and Video. That's lots of video effects to choose from. To help you deal with this overwhelming wealth of video effects, we've assembled a description of each effect according to its category folder.

Cross-Reference The Keying effects are discussed in detail in Chapter 15. The Color Correction effects are discussed in detail in Chapter 18.

Note Before undertaking a tour of the effects, remember that many effects provide previews in dialog boxes. If an effect provides a dialog box, click the Setup dialog box icon in the Effect Controls panel to see a preview.

Although most effects can be controlled by sliders that you click and drag, you can also click underlined values at the center of the slider to set effects. When you click the underlined value, a dialog box appears showing the largest and smallest values allowed in the slider setting.

If you want, you can experiment with the different video effects by applying them to one of the video clips in the Tutorial Projects folder located on the DVD that accompanies the book. In the figures within this section, we used various images that are located in the Chapter 14 folder.

The Adjust effect

The Adjust effect enables you to adjust the color attributes of selected clips, such as the brightness and contrast of an image. (For more information on adjusting a color clip, see Chapter 18.) If you are familiar with Adobe Photoshop, you'll find that several Premiere Pro video effects — such as Auto Color, Auto Contrast, Auto Levels, Channel Mixer, Levels, and Posterize — are quite similar to filters found in Adobe Photoshop.

Auto Color, Auto Contrast and Auto Levels

The Auto Color, Auto Contrast, and Auto Levels effects allow you to create quick, overall color corrections to a clip. These effects work on adjusting the midtones, shadows, and highlights. The Auto Color effect focuses on adjusting the colors. The Auto Contrast effect focuses on adjusting the shadows and highlights along with the overall color. The Auto Levels effect focuses primarily on adjusting the shadows and highlights. Each effect allows for you to fine-tune the effect by adjusting the effect's controls. Each effect allows you to adjust the result of the effect.

Each effect has five properties so you can adjust its controls. They are Temporal Smoothing, Scene Detect, Black Clip, White Clip, and Blend with Original. The Auto Color effect also has a Snap Neutral Midtones control. Here's how these properties work:

✦ The Temporal Smoothing control determines how many surrounding frames will be used to determine the amount of correction. When Temporal Smoothing is set to 0, Premiere Pro analyzes each frame independent of the others. When Temporal Smoothing is set to 1, Premiere Pro analyzes frames 1 second before the frame on display.

✦ When Temporal Smoothing is enabled, Scene Detect is displayed. When this option is selected, Premiere Pro ignores changes in scenes.

✦ Black Clip and White Clip controls adjust how much of the shadow and highlights are affected.

✦ The Blend with Original control can change how much of the effect is applied to the clip. When the percentage amount is set to 0, 100 percent of the effect is seen on the clip. When the percentage amount is set to 100, 0 percent of the effect is seen on the clip.

✦ The Snap Neutral Midtones control finds and adjusts the midtone (gray) colors.

Brightness and Contrast

Using the Brightness and Contrast effects is an easy way to adjust brightness and contrast in your image. Brightness controls how light or dark your image is. Contrast controls the difference between the brightest and darkest pixels in an image. In the Effect Controls panel, click and drag the Brightness slider to increase or reduce an image's brightness, and click and drag the Contrast slider to add or subtract contrast from an image.

Channel Mixer

The Channel Mixer effect enables you to create special effects by mixing colors from a clip's channels. With the Channel Mixer, you create color effects and turn a color image into a grayscale image or into an image with a sepia tone or tint effect.

To use the Channel Mixer, click and drag any Source Channel slider in the Effect Controls panel to the left to decrease the amount of color supplied to the image. Click and drag to the right to increase it.

To convert an image to grayscale, click the Monochrome button and adjust the sliders.

Color Balance

The Color Balance effect allows you to adjust the highlights, midtones, and shadows of the red, green, and blue colors. These controls allow you to create a unified color balance. Increasing the red, green, and blue color values increases the amount of that color in an image. Reducing these values increases the amount of that color's complement. Here's an example:

✦ Increasing the red values increases the red colors in an image and reduces the cyan. Reducing the red values reduces the red colors in an image and increases the cyan.

✦ Increasing the green values increases the green colors in an image and reduces the magenta. Reducing the green values in an image decreases the green colors in an image and increases the magenta.

✦ Increasing the blue values increases the blue color in an image and reduces the yellow. Reducing the blue values reduces the blue color in an image and increases the yellow.

Convolution Kernel

The Convolution Kernel effect uses mathematical *convolution* to change brightness values of clip. This effect can be used to increase sharpness or enhance image edges. The matrix of numbers in the Convolution Kernel Settings dialog box, shown in Figure 14-13, represents the pixels in the image. The center pixel text field is the pixel being analyzed. In the center box, enter the number that you want to use as the brightness multiplier. In other words, if you enter 2, the pixel's brightness values are doubled. The same concept applies for neighboring text fields. You can enter a brightness multiplier in the surrounding boxes — you can also enter 0 to have no increase in the brightness value.

Figure 14-13: The Convolution Kernel Settings dialog box

Values entered in the Scale box are used to divide the sum of the brightness values. If desired, enter a value in the Offset field, which is the same as the value added to the Scale field.

When using the Convolution Kernel filter, you can save settings by clicking the Save button; you can reload saved settings by clicking the Load button.

Extract

The Extract effect removes the color from a clip to create a black-and-white effect. The Input and Output sliders in the Extract Settings dialog box, shown in Figure 14-14, enable you to control which image areas are affected. The Softness slider softens the effect. The preview area provides a good idea of the result of the effect.

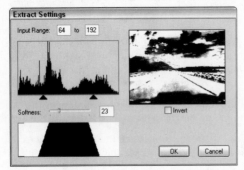

Figure 14-14: The Extract Settings dialog box

Levels

The Levels effect enables you to correct highlights, midtones, and shadows in an image. To apply the same levels to all color channels, leave the drop-down menu in the Levels Settings dialog box, shown in Figure 14-15, set to RGB. Otherwise, click to choose a red, green, or blue channel to apply the effect to.

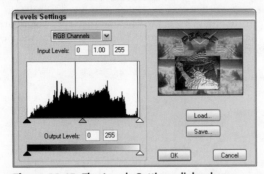

Figure 14-15: The Levels Settings dialog box

To complete your image correction, use the Input slider to increase contrast. Drag the middle slider to raise or lower midtone values. Drag the Output slider to decrease contrast.

Lighting Effect

The Lighting Effect allows you to apply up to five light effects to a clip. There are three different types of lights that you can apply: Spotlight, Omni, and Directional. You can also adjust the color for each light, the size, angle, intensity, the center of the light, and how far the light spreads. You can even apply a texture using the Bump controls. Figure 14-16 shows the Lighting Effects properties in the Effect Controls panel. Figure 14-17 shows the results of applying the Lighting effect to a clip.

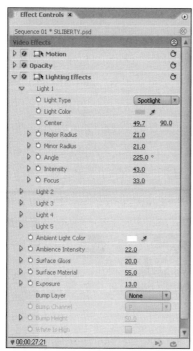

Figure 14-16: The Lighting Effects properties seen in the Effect Controls panel

Figure 14-17: A preview of the Lighting effects in the Program Monitor panel

Posterize

Posterize creates special color effects by reducing the tonal level in the red, green, and blue color channels. Click and drag the Levels amount in the Effect Controls panel to set how many levels of color are in an image.

ProcAmp

The Brightness and Contrast options for the ProcAmp effect allow for an easy way to adjust brightness and contrast in your image. Brightness controls how light or dark your image is. Contrast controls the difference between the brightest and darkest pixels in an image. In the Effect Controls panel, click and drag the Brightness option to the right to increase the image's brightness; click and drag to the left to reduce an image's brightness. Click and drag the Contrast option right or left to add or subtract contrast from an image. Click and drag the Hue values to change the color of your image. Click and drag the Saturation option to the right to make the colors more vibrant. Drag the Saturation option to 0 to take all the colors out of your image and make it a grayscale image. The Split Screen option allows you to apply the effect to only a portion of the image. The Split Percent value determines how much of the image is affected.

Shadow/Highlight

The Shadow/Highlight effect is a good effect to use if your image has a backlighting effect problem. The effect is meant to brighten shadows and reduce highlights. To manually adjust the Shadow Amount and Highlight Amount, you must deselect the Auto Amount property. By default, the Auto Amount property is selected. When this property is selected, Premiere Pro automatically adjusts the shadow or highlight areas.

The Temporal Smoothing control is used to determine how many surrounding frames will be used to determine the amount of correction. The Blend with Original control can change how much of the effect is applied to the clip.

The controls in the More Options section allow you to fine-tune the effect.

Threshold

The Threshold effect creates black-and-white images from color or gray images. The amount of black or white in an image can be adjusted by changing the Level control. The Level control can be adjusted from 0 to 255. Move the Level control to the right to add more black to your image. Setting the Level control to 255 turns the entire picture black. Move the Level control to the left to add more white to your image. Setting the Level control to 0 turns the entire picture white.

The Blur & Sharpen bin

The Blur effects contain options that allow you to blur images. Using blur effects, you can create motion effects or blur out a video track as a background to emphasize the foreground. The Sharpen effects enable you to sharpen images. Sharpening helps bring out image edges when digitized images or graphics appear too soft.

Anti-alias

The Anti-alias effect reduces jagged lines by blending image edges of contrasting colors to create a smooth edge.

Camera Blur

By using this effect with keyframes, you can simulate an image going in or out of focus. You can also simulate a "camera blur" effect. Use the Blur slider in the Camera Blur Settings dialog box, shown in Figure 14-18, to control the effect.

Figure 14-18: The Camera Blur Settings dialog box

Channel Blur

The Channel Blur effect enables you to blur an image using the red, green, blue channel or the alpha channel. By default, the Blur Dimension drop-down is set to Horizontal and Vertical. At the default setting, any blurring you do affects the image horizontally and vertically. If you want to blur only one dimension, set the drop-down menu to either Horizontal or Vertical. When the Edge Behavior/Repeat Edge Pixels option is deselected, the edges around the clip are blurred. When it is selected, they are not.

Compound Blur

The Compound Blur effect blurs images based on luminance values. The effect gives the image a smudged effect. The blur is based upon a Blur Layer. Click the Blur Layer drop-down menu to pick a video track. If you want, you can blur one video track with another to create a very interesting superimpose effect.

For another interesting effect, try superimposing the Sailing.psd and Power.psd images. These images are found in the Chapter 14 folder on the DVD that accompanies the book. Place the Sailing.psd file in the Video 2 track and the Power.psd file in the Video 1 track. Hide the Sailing.psd clip by clicking the Eye icon in the Timeline panel. Drag the Compound Blur effect onto the Power.psd clip in the Video 1 track. In the Effect Controls panel, set the Blur Layer drop-down menu to the Video 2 track. Then move the Maximum Blur control to about 16. If you want, click the Invert Blur check box to invert the blur. If the layer sizes differ, you can click the Stretch Map to Fit check box to stretch the blur layer to the clip where the blur effect is applied.

If you want to increase the contrast between the layers, you can use the Unsharp Mask effect. Turn to this effect's section, later in this chapter, for more information about this effect.

Directional Blur

The Directional Blur effect creates a motion effect by blurring an image in a specific direction. The sliders in the Effect Controls panel control the direction and the length of the blur.

Fast Blur

Use the Fast Blur effect to quickly blur a clip. Use the Blur Dimension drop-down menu in the Effect Controls panel to specify whether the blur should be vertical, horizontal, or both.

Gaussian Blur

The Gaussian Blur effect blurs video and reduces video signal noise. Similar to the Fast Blur effect, you can specify whether the blur should be vertical, horizontal, or both. The word *gaussian* is used because the filter uses a gaussian (bell-shaped) curve when removing contrast to create the blur effect.

Gaussian Sharpen

Apply the Gaussian Sharpen effect to create strong, overall sharpening. You can obtain similar results by applying the Sharpen filter several times. This effect provides no controls.

Ghosting

The Ghosting effect layers image areas from previous frames over one frame. Use this to show the path of a moving object — such as a speeding bullet or a pie thrown in the air.

Radial Blur

This effect creates a circular blurring effect. The Radial Blur dialog box, shown in Figure 14-19, lets you control the degree of blurring. To do so, increase the value in the Amount field by dragging the Amount slider to the right. In the Blur Method area, choose Spin to create a spinning blur; choose Zoom to create an outward blur. In the Quality section, choose Draft, Good, or Best. However, remember that the better the quality, the more processing time is needed to create the effect.

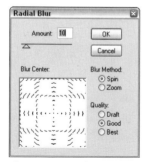

Figure 14-19: The Radial Blur dialog box

Sharpen

The Sharpen effect includes a value that enables you to control sharpening within your clip. Click and drag the Sharpen Amount value in the Effect Controls panel to the right to increase sharpening. The slider permits values from 0 to 100; however, if you click the underlined sharpen amount onscreen, you can enter values up to 4000 into the Value field.

Sharpen Edges

The Sharpen Edges effect applies sharpening effects on image edges.

Unsharp Mask

The Unsharp Mask works like the Unsharp Mask filter in Photoshop. This effect is used to increase detail in an image by increasing sharpness between colors. This effect has three controls that can be adjusted: Amount, Radius, and Threshold. Increase the Amount value to increase the amount of the effect. Increasing the Radius value increases the amount of pixels that are affected. The Threshold control can be set from 0 to 255. A smaller value creates a more dramatic effect.

The Channel bin

The Channel bin contains various effects that allow you to combine two clips, overlay a color on a clip, or adjust the red, green, and blue channels of a clip.

Use the Calculations effect to blend channels from different clips. Use Set Matte to replace the channel (matte) of one clip with another. Use the Blend effect to blend video clips based on color modes. Use Invert to invert the color values within a clip. Use Solid Composite to overlay a solid color over a clip.

3D Glasses

The 3D Glasses effect allows you to create a left and right 3D view effect. You can superimpose an image upon itself or superimpose two images. When using two different images, you may want to use images with the same dimensions.

To superimpose two different images, you can place one in the Video 1 track and another image above it in the Video 2 track. Then apply the effect to the clip in the Video 2 track. In the Effect Controls panel, click the Left and Right View drop-down menus and set one to the Video 1 track and the other to the Video 2 track. Then click the 3D View drop-down menu to choose a 3D View option.

To view the 3D effect, use either 3D glasses with red and green lenses or 3D glasses with red and blue lenses.

Arithmetic

The Arithmetic effect allows you to change the red, green, and blue values of a clip based on a mathematical operation. The method used to change the color values is determined by the option selected in the Operator drop-down menu.

To use the Arithmetic effect, click the Operator drop-down menu and adjust the red, green, and blue values.

Blend

The Blend effect allows you to blend video tracks using different modes: Crossfade, Color Only, Tint Only, Darken Only, and Lighten Only. The Blend with Original option is used to specify which clip you want to blend with. For example, if you apply the Blend effect to a clip in the Video 2 track and want to blend it with a clip below it in the Video 1 track, set the Blend with Layer drop-down menu to Video 1. For both clips to appear translucent, set the Blend with Original value to 50 percent. In order to see both clips in the Program Monitor panel, they must be selected with the Timeline Marker.

If you apply the Blend effect to a clip in Video 1 track and want to blend it with a clip directly above it in the Video 2 track, set the Blend with Layer drop-down menu to Video 2 track. Then hide Video 2 track by clicking on the Eye icon in the Timeline panel. In order to see both clips in the Program Monitor panel, they must be selected with the Timeline Marker and the Blend with Original value should be set to less than 90 percent.

The best way to understand the Blend effect is to try it out. If you want, you can use the SnowWhitetheCat.psd and the Highway.jpg files found in the Chapter 14 folder of the DVD that accompanies the book. Figure 14-20 shows the effects of applying the Blend effect to a clip (SnowWhitetheCat.psd) in the Video 1 track. Directly above the clip in the Video 1 track, we had another clip (Highway.jpg) in the Video 3 track. The clip in the Video 3 track was hidden, by clicking the Eye icon. In the Effect Controls panel the Blend with Layer drop-down menu was set to the Video 3 track, the Mode drop-down menu was set to Crossfade, and the Blend with Original value was set to 50 percent.

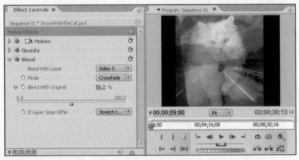

Figure 14-20: The Blend effect can be used to create interesting superimposition effects.

Calculations

The Calculations effect allows you to combine two video clips in separate tracks using the clips channels and various Blending modes. You can choose to overlay the clips using the composite channel (RGBA); the red, green, or blue channel; or the gray or alpha channel. The Blending modes are Copy, Darken, Multiply, Color Burn, Classic Color Burn, Add, Lighten, Screen, Color Dodge, Classic Color Dodge, Overlay, Soft Light, Hard Light, Linear Light, Vivid Light, Pin Light, Difference, Classic Difference, Exclusion, Hue, Saturation, Color, Luminosity, Stencil Alpha, Stencil Luma, Silhouette Alpha, Silhouette Luma, Alpha Add, and Luminescent Add.

To create the effect seen in the Program Monitor panel in Figure 14-21, we put a clip (SnowWhitetheCat.psd) in the Video 1 track and another clip (Sky.psd) in the Video 2 track. We applied the Calculations effect to the Video 1 track. The clip in the Video 2 track was hidden, by clicking the Eye icon. Figure 14-21 also shows the Effect Controls panel with the settings used for effect. In the Effect Controls panel, the Input Channel drop-down menu was set to RGBA, the Second Layer drop-down menu was set to Video 2, and the Second Layer Channel drop-down menu was set to RGBA. The Second Layer Opacity was set to 87 percent, and the Blending Mode drop-down menu was set to Multiply.

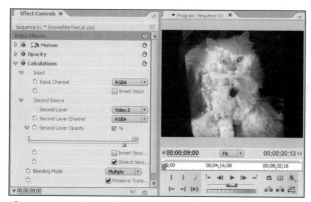

Figure 14-21: The Calculations controls can be seen in the Effect Controls panel, and a preview of the effect is seen in the Program Monitor panel.

Cineon Converter

The Cineon Converter effect allows you to convert the colors in a Cineon file. Cineon file format is often used when converting motion-picture film to digital. To use this effect, import a Cineon file into your project and place it in a video track in the Timeline panel. The controls for the Cineon Converter allow you to control how the clip is converted. Click the Conversion Type drop-down menu to pick a conversion method. Then specify a black and white point for the clip using the 10 Bit Black Point, Internal Black Point, 10 Bit White Point, and Internal White Point. Then specify midtone values using the Gamma control. If the highlight areas need adjusting, try using the Highlight Rolloff control.

Compound Arithmetic

The Compound Arithmetic effect is designed to be used with After Effects projects that use the Compound Arithmetic effect. This effect mathematically uses layers to create a combined effect. The controls for this effect determine how the original layer and the second source layer are blended together. The Second Source Layer drop-down menu allows you to choose another video clip to be used in the blending operation. The Operator drop-down menu allows you to pick from various modes to be used as the blending method. Adjusting these two controls greatly changes the outcome of the effect. You can also click the Operate on Channels drop-down menu and make a selection. Use the Blend with Original Layer control to adjust the opacity of the original layer and the second source layer.

Invert

The Invert effect inverts color values. You can turn black into white, white into black, and colors into their complements. In Figure 14-22, we turned a white cat into a black cat.

The Invert effect has two properties that control the outcome of the effect. They are Channel and Blend with Original. The Channel drop-down menu (found in the Effect Controls panel) enables you to choose a color model: RGB, HLS, or YIQ. YIQ is the NTSC color space. Y refers to luminance; I refer to inphase chrominance; Q refers to quadrature chrominance. The alpha choice enables you to invert the gray levels in an alpha channel. Use the Blend with Original slider if you want to blend the channel effect with the original image.

Figure 14-22: The Invert effect
converts a white cat into a black cat.

Set Matte

The Set Matte effect allows you to create traveling matte effects by combining two clips. The Track Matte effect is a better solution for creating traveling mattes. For more information on creating traveling mattes using the Track Matte effect, see Chapter 15.

To try out the Set Matte effect, place two video clips in the Timeline panel. Place one above the other. Then apply the effect to the clip in the first video track and hide the clip above it. The option you choose in the Use For Matte drop-down menu (seen in the Effect Controls panel) controls the results of the effect. To invert the effect, click the Invert Matte check box.

Figure 14-23 shows the effects of applying the Set Matte effect to a clip (SnowWhitetheCat.psd) in the Video 1 track. Directly above the clip in the Video 1 track, we had another clip (Highway.jpg) in the Video 3 track. The clip in the Video 3 track was hidden by clicking the Eye icon. In the Effect Controls panel, the Take Matte From layer drop-down menu was set to the Video 3 track and the Use For Matte drop-down menu was set to Luminance. Because layers differed in size, all the options in the If Layer Sizes Differ options were selected.

On the DVD-ROM   The SnowWhitetheCat.psd and Highway.jpg files are found in the Chapter 14 folder of the DVD that accompanies the book.

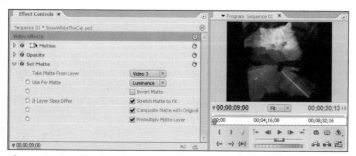

Figure 14-23: The Set Matte controls are seen in the Effect Controls panel, and the result of the effect is seen in the Program Monitor panel.

Solid Composite

The Solid Composite effect allows you to overlay a clip with a solid color. The way the color appears on the clip depends upon the Blending Mode selected. Both the opacity of the original clip and the solid color can be adjusted.

We used the Solid Composite to create a sepia effect, seen in Figure 14-24. To create the sepia effect, we set the Color Swatch to an orange-red color and the Blending Mode to Luminosity. We also reduced the opacity of the source clip and the solid color.

Figure 14-24: The Solid Composite controls are seen in the Effect Controls panel, and the result of the effect is seen in the Program Monitor panel.

The Color Correction bin

The Color Correction effects enable you to color correct the colors in a clip. Some of these commands are similar to the color correction filters found in Adobe Photoshop. The Color Correction effects are Fast Color Correction, Luma Correction, Luma Curve, RGB Color Corrector, RGB Curves, Three-Way Color Corrector, and Video Limitor. The Color Correction effects are discussed in detail in Chapter 18.

The Distort bin

The Distort commands, found in the Distort bin, enable you to distort an image either by twirling, pinching, or spherizing it. Many of these commands are similar to the distort filters found in Adobe Photoshop.

Bend

The Bend effect can bend your image in various directions. In the Bend Settings dialog box, which is shown in Figure 14-25, use the Intensity, Rate, and Width sliders to control effects for Horizontal and Vertical Bending. Intensity is the wave height, Rate is the frequency, and Width is the width of the wave. The Direction drop-down menu controls the direction of the effect. The Wave drop-down menu specifies the type of wave: sine, circle, triangle, or square.

Figure 14-25: The Bend Settings dialog box

Corner Pin

The Corner Pin effect allows you to distort an image by adjusting the Upper Left, Upper Right, Lower Left, and Lower Right values (corners).

Figure 14-26 shows controls for the Corner Pin in the Effect Controls panel, and the result of the effect is seen in the Program Monitor panel. In the figure, note that the Position of the clip was changed. The effect was applied to a clip in the Video 2 track. Below the clip in the Video 2 track, we had another clip. The clip seen in the background is the image from the Video 2 track, and the image in the foreground is the image from the Video 1 track. In the Video 2 track, we used the clip Bariloche.psd, and in the Video 1 track, we used the clip beach.psd. Both clips can be found in the Chapter 14 folder on the DVD that accompanies the book.

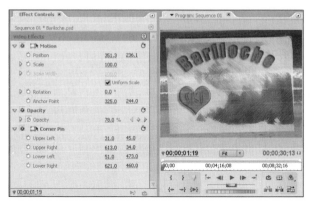

Figure 14-26: Image after applying the Corner Pin effect

Lens Distortion

Use the Lens Distortion effect to simulate video being viewed through a distorted lens.

Use the Curvature slider in the Lens Distortion Settings dialog box, shown in Figure 14-27, to change the lens curve. Negative values make the curvature more concave (inward); positive values make the curvature more convex (outward). Vertical and Horizontal Decentering sliders change the focal point of the lens.

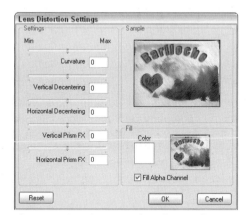

Figure 14-27: The Lens Distortion Settings dialog box

Vertical and Horizontal Prism FX creates effects similar to changing Vertical and Horizontal Decentering. Use the Fill color swatch to change the background color. Click the Fill Alpha Channel check box to make background areas transparent based on the clip's alpha channel.

Magnify

The Magnify effect allows you to magnify a certain portion of a clip or the entire clip.

Figure 14-28 shows controls for the Magnify effect in the Effect Controls panel, and the result of the effect as seen in the Program Monitor panel. In the figure, note that the Opacity of the clip has also been changed. In the figure, the Magnify effect was applied over the Corner Pin effect. The Magnify effect was applied to a clip in the Video 2 track. Below the clip in the Video 2 track, we had another clip. The clip seen in the background is the image from the Video 2 track, and the image in the foreground is the image from the Video 1 track. In the Video 2 track, we used the clip Bariloche.psd, and in the Video 1 track, we used the clip beach.psd. Both clips can be found in the Chapter 14 folder on the DVD that accompanies the book.

Figure 14-28: Image after applying the Magnify effect

Mirror

Mirror creates a mirrored effect. In the Effect Controls panel, click the Reflection center values to open the Edit Reflection Center dialog box to designate the X and Y coordinates of the reflection line. The reflection angle option enables you to choose where the reflection appears. The following degree settings should help orient you to how dragging the slider distorts the image:

✦ **0:** Left onto right side

✦ **90:** Right onto left side

✦ **180:** Top onto bottom

✦ **270:** Bottom onto top

Figure 14-29 shows the controls for Mirror effect in the Effect Controls panel, and the results of the effect can be seen in the Program Monitor panel. In the figure, note that the Position, Scale, and Opacity of the clip have also been changed. The effect was applied to a clip in the Video 2 track. Below the clip in the Video 2 track, we had another clip. The clip seen in the background is the image from the Video 2 track, and the image in the foreground is the image from the Video 1 track. In the Video 2 track, we used the clip Bariloche.psd, and in the Video 1 track, we used the clip beach.psd. Both clips can be found in the Chapter 14 folder on the DVD that accompanies the book.

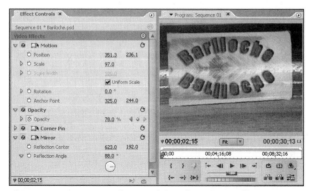

Figure 14-29: Image after applying the Mirror effect

Offset

The Offset effect allows you to shift a clip vertically and horizontally, creating a pan effect. Adjusting the Offset's Shift Center To controls can shift a clip vertically and/or horizontally. To blend some of the Offset effect with the original clip, adjust the Blend with Original clip control.

Polar Coordinates

Polar Coordinates can create a variety of unusual effects by changing the clip's X and Y coordinates to polar coordinates. In the polar coordinate system, the X and Y coordinates are distances radiating out from a focal point. By using this effect, you can transform a line into a half circle or horseshoe shape.

In the Effect Controls panel, the Interpolation value controls the amount of the distortion — 0 percent provides no distortion; 100 percent provides the most. In the Type of Conversion drop-down menu, Rect to Polar converts horizontal coordinates to Polar; Polar to Rect converts polar coordinates to rectangular ones. Figure 14-30 shows the Polar Coordinates effect with the Rect to Polar options selected.

Figure 14-30: The Polar Coordinates settings and a preview

Ripple

The Ripple effect turns a clip into rippled patterns. The Ripple Settings dialog box, shown in Figure 14-31, enables you to adjust the ripples on a horizontal and vertical plane and control the intensity and frequency of the ripples.

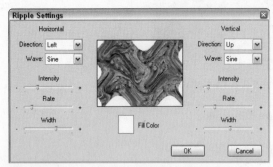

Figure 14-31: The Ripple Settings dialog box

Spherize

The Spherize effect can turn a flat image into a spherical one. Adjust the Radius property to control the spherizing effect. Dragging the slider to the right increases the Amount value, providing a larger sphere. Adjusting the Center of Sphere values changes the location of the sphere.

Figure 14-32 shows the results of applying the Spherize effect to a clip (America.psd) in the Video 2 track. Below the clip in the Video 2 track was another clip (CloudySky.psd). Both clips can be found in the Chapter 14 folder on the DVD that accompanies the book.

Figure 14-32: The Spherize controls are seen in the Effect Controls panel, and the effect is seen in the Program Monitor panel.

Transform

The Transform effect allows you to move an image's position, scale its height and weight, skew or rotate, and change its opacity, as shown in Figure 14-33. You can also use the Transform effect to change the position of a clip. To change the position of a clip, click the box next to the word *Position* in the Effect Controls panel. Then click in the Program Monitor panel where you want the clip to move to. Use the Anchor Point option to move a clip based on its anchor point.

Figure 14-33 shows the results of applying the Transform effect to a clip (America.psd) in the Video 2 track. Below the clip in the Video 2 track was another clip (CloudySky.psd). Both clips can be found in the Chapter 14 folder on the DVD that accompanies the book.

Figure 14-33: A preview of the Transform effect in the Program Monitor panel with the Transform properties in the Effect Controls panel

Turbulent Displace

The Turbulent Displace effect displaces a clip with the use of fractal noises. The effect can make an image feel like there is movement. The effect sometimes is used on waving flags or running water. Use the Displace drop-down menu to choose the type of displacement you want to occur. Then adjust the Amount, Size, Offset, Complexity, and Evolution controls to make the proper adjustments to the distortion you want to create.

Twirl

The Twirl effect can turn an image into twirling digital soup. Use the Angle values to control the degree of twirling. Larger angle settings create more twirling. Figure 14-34 shows a preview of the Twirl effect.

Figure 14-34 shows the results of applying the Twirl effect to a clip (America.psd) in the Video 2 track. Below the clip in the Video 2 track was another clip (CloudySky.psd).

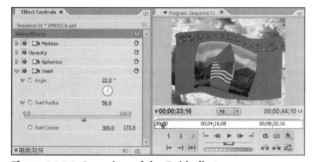

Figure 14-34: A preview of the Twirl effect

Wave Warp

The Wave effect creates wave-like effects that can make your clip look as if it were hit by a tidal wave. To control the effect, use the Wave Settings found in the Effect Controls panel, shown in Figure 14-35. In Figure 14-35, you can see the results of applying the Wave Warp effect to a clip (America.psd) in the Video 2 track. Below the clip in the Video 2 track was another clip (CloudySky.psd).

Figure 14-35: The Wave Warp controls and its effect

Following is a brief description of the controls for the Wave Warp effect:

✦ **Type:** Controls the type of wave crests: Sine (waving), Square, Triangle, Sawtooth, Circle, Semicircle, Uncircle, Noise, or Smooth Noise.

✦ **Wave Height:** Changes the distance between wave peaks. Controls the amount of vertical distortion.

✦ **Wave Width:** Changes the direction and wave length. Controls the amount of horizontal distortion.

✦ **Direction:** Controls the amount of horizontal and vertical distortion.

✦ **Wave Speed:** Randomizes the wavelength and amplitude.

✦ **Pinning:** Controls the amount of continuous waves. Selects image areas that will not have waves affect a certain area.

✦ **Phase:** Determines the point at which a wave cycle begins.

✦ **Antialiasing:** Determines the smoothness of the waves.

The GPU effects

The GPU effects are Page Curl, Refraction, and Ripple (Circular). The GPU effects appear if you have a Graphic Processing Unit card that supports Direct 3D, PS 1.3+, and VS 1.1+.

The Image Control bin

The Image Control bin contains a variety of color special effects.

Black & White

The Black & White effect produces a grayscale version of a selected clip.

Change Color

The Change Color effect adjusts a range of colors via its hue, saturation, and lightness.

On the DVD-ROM

You may want to use the Power.psd file found in the Chapter 14 folder of the DVD that accompanies the book to experiment with the Change Color effect. The file is full of lots of colors to change.

After you've applied the Change Color effect to a clip, you can get started.

1. **To start changing colors of a clip, you first need to pick a color to change. To do so, use either the color swatch or the eyedropper in the Color to Change section.**

2. **Click the View drop-down menu, and choose whether you want to view the color changes in the Corrected Layer or the Color Correction Mask.**

3. **Next click the Match Colors drop-down menu to determine the method to match colors.** There are three methods of matching colors: RGB, Hue, and Chroma. The RGB method chooses methods by using red, green, and blue colors. The Hue method uses hue colors to match the chosen color. The Chroma method uses saturation and hue but disregards lightness.

4. **Use the Hue Transform, Lightness Transform, and Saturation Transform controls to change the selected color.** Use the Matching Tolerance and Matching Softness to fine-tune the change of the selected color.

5. **To invert the selected color correction, click the Invert Color Correction Mask.**

Change to Color

The Change to Color effect allows you to change a color to another color by adjusting the color's Hue, Lightness, and Saturation (HLS) values.

After you've applied the Change to Color effect to a clip, you can start changing colors. Here's how:

1. **In the From and To section, use either the color swatch or the eyedropper to choose the color you want to change and pick the color you want to change it to.**

2. **Use the Change and Change By drop-down menus to choose a method in which to change colors.**

3. **Click the triangle in front of the Tolerance section to display the Hue, Lightness, and Saturation controls.** Use these controls to change the set colors.

4. **Use the Softness control to determine the smoothness of the color change.**

5. **If you want, you can click the View Correction Matte check box.**

Color Balance (HLS)

The Color Balance HLS effect enables you to change and adjust colors using Hue, Lightness, and Saturation sliders in the Effect Controls panel. Hue controls the color, Lightness controls how light and dark the color is, and Saturation controls the intensity of the color. For a full description of how to use this effect, see Chapter 18.

Color Balance (RGB)

The Color Balance RGB effect adds or subtracts red, green, or blue color values in a clip. Color values are easily added and subtracted by clicking the Red, Green, or Blue color sliders, shown in Figure 14-36. In the Effect Controls panel, dragging the sliders to the left reduces the amount of color; dragging the sliders to the right adds color. For a full description of how to use this effect, see Chapter 18.

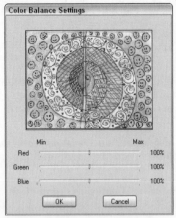

Figure 14-36: The Color Balance (RGB) Settings dialog box

Color Match

The Color Match effect allows you to match the colors of one clip to another. For a full description of how to use this effect, see Chapter 18.

Color Offset

The Color Offset effect enables you to create 3D images out of 2D artwork by enabling you to shift the red, green, and blue color channels up, down, left, and right. Use the Offset slider in the Color Offset Settings dialog box, shown in Figure 14-37, to control the distance between color channels. Using this effect, you can set up the image for viewing with 3D glasses.

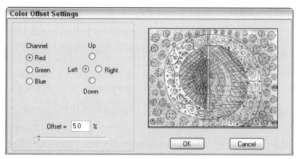

Figure 14-37: The Color Offset Settings dialog box

Color Pass

The Color Pass effect converts all but one color in a clip to grayscale — or it can convert just one color in a clip to grayscale. Use this effect to draw interest to specific items in a clip. For example, you may want to show a grayscale party scene in which a grayscale man or woman is wearing a colored hat or holding a colored balloon.

Follow these steps to set the Color Pass color and use the filter:

1. **In the Color Pass Settings dialog box clip area, shown in Figure 14-38, click the color that you want to preserve.** Alternatively, you can click the swatch area and choose a color in the Color Picker panel.

2. **To increase or decrease the color range, drag the Similarity slider to the right or left.**

3. **To reverse the color effect (in other words, make all colors normal and gray except the selected color), click Reverse.**

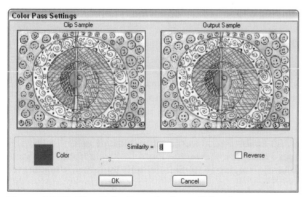

Figure 14-38: The Color Pass Settings dialog box

Color Replace

The Color Replace effect replaces one color or a range of colors with another color.

To choose a color or colors to replace, follow these steps:

1. **In the Color Replace Settings dialog box, shown in Figure 14-39, click the Target Color swatch area and choose a color in the Color Picker panel.**

2. **To choose the replacement color, click the Replace Color swatch.** Choose a color in the Color Picker panel.

3. **To increase or decrease the color range of the replacement color, drag the Similarity slider right or left.**

4. **Choose Solid Colors to replace the color with a solid color.**

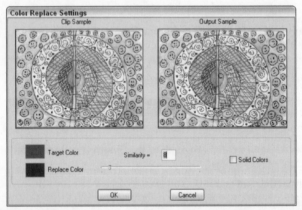

Figure 14-39: The Color Replace Settings dialog box

Equalize

The Equalize effect can be used to redistribute the brightness values in an image. To use the Equalize effect, first click the Equalize drop-down menu to pick an Equalize method. Then use the Amount to Equalize control to determine the amount to equalize.

Gamma Correction

The Gamma Correction effect enables you to adjust the midtone color levels of a clip. In the Gamma Correction Settings dialog box, shown in Figure 14-40, click and drag the Gamma slider to make the adjustment. Dragging to the left lightens midtones; dragging to the right darkens them.

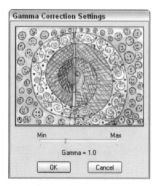

Figure 14-40: The Gamma Correction Settings dialog box

PS Arbitrary Map

The PS Arbitrary Map effect is primarily to be used with After Effects files that use the Arbitrary Map effect. The arbitrary map works by changing the brightness values.

Tint

Use the Tint effect to apply a color tint to your image. If desired, you can reassign the black-and-white portions of your clip with different colors by clicking the color swatch and choosing a color in the Color Picker panel. Choose color intensity by clicking and dragging the slider in the Color Picker panel.

The Keying bin

The Keying effects allow you to create a variety of interesting superimposing effects. The Keying consists of Alpha Adjust, Blue Screen Key, Chroma Key, Color Key, Difference Matte Key, Eight-Point Garbage Matte, Four-Point Garbage Matte, Green Screen Key, Image Matte Key, Luma Key, Multiply Matte, Non Red Key, RGB Difference Key, Remove Matte, Screen Key, Sixteen-Point Garbage Matte, and Track Matte Key. The Keying effects are discussed in detailed in Chapter 15.

The Noise bin

The Noise bin contains only one effect. The Noise effect is Median.

Median

The Median effect can be used to reduce noise. It creates the effect by taking the median pixel value of neighboring pixels and applying this value to pixels within the radius pixel area specified in the Effect Controls panel. If you enter large values for the radius, your image begins to look as if it were painted. Click the Operate on Alpha Channel option to apply the effect to the image's alpha channel as well as to the image.

The Noise & Gain bin

The effects in the Noise & Gain bin can be used to add noise to a clip.

Dust & Scratches

The Dust & Scratches effect changes pixels that are dissimilar and creates noise. Experiment with the Radius and Threshold controls for the desired effect. Click the Operate on Alpha Channel to have the effect applied to the alpha channel.

Noise Alpha

The Noise Alpha effect creates noise using the alpha channel of the effected clip.

Noise HLS and Noise HLS Auto

The Noise HLS effect and Noise HLS Auto effect allow you to create noise using Hue, Lightness, and Saturation. The noise can be animated.

The Perspective bin

You can use the effects in the Perspective bin to add depth to images, to create drop shadows, and to bevel image edges.

Basic 3D

The Basic 3D effect creates nice flipping and tilting effects. The Swivel slider in the Effect Controls panel controls rotation. The Tilt slider adjusts the tilt of the image. Dragging the Distance to Image slider creates an illusion of distance by reducing or enlarging the image. Click the Show Specular Highlight to add a tiny flare of light to your image (indicated by a red + sign). Draw Preview enables you to view a wireframe simulation of the effect, which provides a good idea of how the effect will look without waiting for Premiere Pro to render it.

Bevel Alpha

The Bevel Alpha effect can add a three-dimensional effect to a two-dimensional image by beveling the image's alpha channel. This filter is especially handy for creating beveled effects with text. Sliders in the Effect Controls panel enable you to fine-tune the effect by changing bevel edge thickness, light angle, and light intensity. Change the light color by clicking the color swatch and choosing a color in Premiere Pro's Color Picker panel.

Bevel Edges

The Bevel Edges effect bevels an image and adds lighting to give a clip a three-dimensional appearance. Image edges created with this effect are sharper than those created with the Bevel Alpha effect. To determine image edges, this filter also uses the clip's alpha channel. Similar to Bevel Alpha, sliders in the Effect Controls panel enable you to fine-tune the effect by changing bevel edge thickness, light angle, and light intensity. Change light color by clicking the color swatch and choosing a color in the Color Picker panel.

Drop Shadow

The Drop Shadow effect applies a drop shadow to a clip, using the clip's alpha channel to determine image edges. Sliders enable you to control the shadow's opacity, direction, and distance from the original clip. You can change the light color by clicking the color swatch in the panel and choosing a color from Premiere Pro's Color Picker panel.

Radial Shadow

The Radial Shadow effect can be used to create a shadow on a clip with an alpha channel. Try using the RocknRoll.psd file found in the Chapter 14 folder of the DVD that accompanies the book to experiment with this effect. To import the file with an alpha channel, the RocknRoll file, click the Choose Layer option in the Import Layered File dialog box that appears. Then click OK to import the file into the Project panel. Drag the file to the Video 2 track. Create a color matte by using the File ➪ New ➪ Color Matte command. Drag the file to the Video 1 track. Apply the effect to the RocknRoll.psd file in the Video 2 track. When you apply the effect, a shadow is automatically created.

Use the effects controls in the Effect Controls panel to change the way the shadow appears. Use the Shadow Color control to change the color of the shadow. Use the Opacity control to make the shadow more or less translucent. To soften the edges of the shadow, increase the value of the Softness control.

You can move the shadow either by using the Light Source control or by clicking the words *Radial Shadow* (in the Effect Controls panel) and moving the circle icon that appears in the Program Monitor panel. Increase the Projection Distance to move the shadow further away from the clip.

Click the Render drop-down menu to choose how the shadow will be rendered. The Color Influence control determines how much of the clip's color will appear in the shadow. To display only the shadow, click the Shadow Only check box.

The Pixelate bin

The effects found in the Pixelate bin create special effects by shifting, moving, and remapping pixels and their color values. These effects can create dramatic color distortions in your image.

Facet

The Facet effect creates a painterly effect by grouping similarly colored pixels together within a clip.

The Render bin

The Render bin features various interesting effects. Some of the effects will be familiar to you. For example, the Lens Flare effect is similar to Adobe Photoshop's Lens Flare filter. Other effects may be new to you, such as the 4-Color Gradient, Cell Pattern, Checkerboard, Circle, Ellipse, Eyedropper Fill, Grid, Lightning, Paint Bucket, and Ramp.

4-Color Gradient

The 4-Color Gradient effect can applied over a solid black video to create a four-color gradient or it can be applied to an image to create interesting blending effects.

Here's how the 4-Color Gradient works:

1. **Drag the effect over a video clip with an interesting image.** If you want, try using the 4-Color Gradient effect on the Highway.jpg file that is in the Chapter 14 folder on the DVD that accompanies the book.

2. **To blend the gradient and the video clip together, click the Blend drop-down menu and choose a blending mode (found in the Effect Controls panel).** Try experimenting with different modes.

3. **To move the position of the gradient, you can also click the words *4-Color Gradient* in the Effect Controls panel.** Notice that four circles with plus signs appear in the Program Monitor panel. Click one of the circle icons to move one of the gradients.

4. **If you want to reduce the opacity of the gradient, reduce the percentage value for the Opacity control.**

5. **To change the colors and the positions of the gradient, click the triangle in front of the Positions and Colors section.** Use the controls to create the desired effect.

6. **Use the Blend control to change the amount of blending between the gradients.** Use the Jitter control to control the amount of noise between the separate gradients.

Cell Pattern

The Cell Pattern effect can be used to create interesting background effects, or it can be used as a matte. Figure 14-41 shows the Cell Pattern properties in the Effect Controls panel and a preview in the Program Monitor panel. We applied the Cell Pattern effect to a black video that we created in Premiere Pro. It can also be applied to a solid color matte. To create a black video, select File ➪ New ➪ Black Video. A black video is automatically placed in the Project panel of your current project. To create a solid color matte, select File ➪ New ➪ Color Matte. In the Color Picker dialog box that appears, pick a color and click OK. When the Choose a Matte dialog box appears, click OK. The color matte you created appears in the Project panel.

Apply the Cell Pattern effect to either a solid color matte or a black video, and start experimenting with the Cell Pattern controls in the Effect Controls panel. To get started, click the Cell Pattern drop-down menu and pick a cell pattern.

To move the cell pattern, click the words *Cell Pattern* (in the Effect Controls panel). Then move the circle icon that appears in the Program Monitor panel to move the pattern. If you want, you can also click the word *Motion* and use the circle icon in the Program Monitor panel to move and change the size of both the pattern and the video clip.

You can change the look of the pattern by adjusting the Disperse, Size, and Offset controls. These controls change only the pattern; they do not affect the video clip. If you want, you can use the Motion controls to change both the pattern and the video clip. To do so, adjust the controls for the Position, Scale, Rotation, and Anchor Points options.

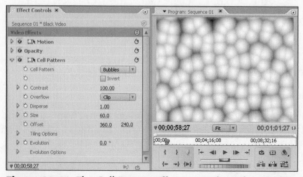

Figure 14-41: The Cell Pattern effect controls and a preview of its effect

For more or less contrast within the pattern, use the Contrast control. If you want, you can invert the pattern by clicking in the Invert check box.

Checkerboard

The Checkerboard effect can be applied to a black video or a color matte to create a checkerboard background or as a matte. The Checkerboard pattern can also be applied to an image and blended together to create an interesting effect. Figure 14-42 shows a preview of the Checkerboard effect in the Program Monitor panel. The effect was applied to the file, Highway.jpg.

In Figure 14-42, you can view the Checkerboard properties in the Effect Controls panel. To create the blending effect between the highway scene and the checkerboard, we chose Overlay in the Blending Mode drop-down menu. We changed the width size of the checkerboard by increasing the value of the Width control. To change the Height size, you first need to click the Size From drop-down menu and choose Width and Height Sliders. To blur the edges of the width and height, use the Width and Height Feather controls. You can change the color and opacity of the checkerboard by clicking the Color Swatch icon and changing the color in the Color Picker dialog box or by clicking one of the colors in the video clip with the Eyedropper icon. To move the pattern, use the Anchor control or click the word *Checkerboard* and move the circle icon in the Program Monitor panel.

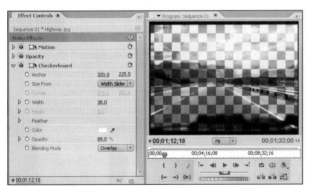

Figure 14-42: The Checkerboard effect controls and a preview of its effect

Circle

Apply the Circle effect to a black video or a solid color matte to create a circle or a ring. Try applying the Circle effect to the Highway.jpg file found in the Chapter 14 folder on the DVD that accompanies the book.

When you apply the Circle effect, the default settings are set to create a small white circle on a black background. To turn the circle into a ring, click the Edge drop-down menu from None to Edge Radius. Then increase the Edge Radius value. If you want, you also can change the Edge drop-down menu to Thickness or Thickness * Radius and then adjust the Thickness control. To soften the outer and inner edges of the ring, set the Edge drop-down menu to Thickness & Feather * Radius. Then increase the values of the Feather Outer Edge and Feather Inner Edge controls. To change the color of the ring or a circle, use the Color control. Increase the Feather Outer Edge value to feather the outer edge of a circle.

The circle or ring can be moved by using the Center controls in the Effect Controls panel. You can also move the circle by clicking the word *Circle* and moving the circle icon in the Program Monitor panel. To increase the size of the circle or ring, increase the value of the Radius control.

Switching the Circle effect's Blending Mode from None to Normal allows you to see the video clip to which the effect has been applied. To make the ring or circle mode translucent, reduce the value of the Opacity control. To invert the effect, click the Invert Circle check box.

To have the highway file appear as if it is on a record, set the Edge drop-down menu to Edge Radius. Then set the Edge Radius to 57. Make sure the Invert Circle check box is not selected. Set the Opacity value to 50 percent. Set the Blending Mode drop-down menu to Alpha Blending. Next, try using the Difference mode to create an interesting effect of blending the highway clip onto itself. For best results, have the Color swatch set to white.

Figure 14-43 shows how the Circle effect can be used to blend two images together. It shows the Circle properties in the Effect Controls panel used to create the effect seen in the Program Monitor panel. To create the effect seen in the Program Monitor panel in Figure 14-43, we used two clips, Highway.jpg and CloudySky.psd. Both files can be found in the Chapter 14 folder on the DVD that accompanies the book. The effect was applied to the highway file that was on the Video 2 track. Below the highway clip, in the Video 1 track was a clip of a cloudy sky. To blend the two clips together, we set the Blending Mode drop-down menu to Stencil Alpha.

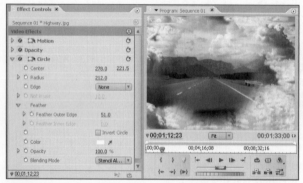

Figure 14-43: The Circle effect controls and a preview of its effect

Ellipse

The Ellipse effect makes ellipses in the form of a ring, with a hole in the center. The ellipse is created on a black background unless you have selected the Composite On Original control. Figure 14-44 shows the effects of the Ellipse effect with the Composite On Original option selected. The effect was applied to the Highway.jpg file.

The controls for the Ellipse effect, found in the Effect Controls panel, which is shown in Figure 14-44, can be used to move the ellipse or change the size and color of the ellipse. To adjust the size of the ellipse, use the Width and Height controls. To move the ellipse, use the Center control or click the word *Ellipse* (in the Effect Controls panel) and move the circle icon that appears in the Program Monitor panel. To increase the thickness of the ring of the ellipse, increase the value of the Thickness control. To soften the inner and outer edges of the ellipse, increase the Softness value. To change the color of the ellipse, use the Inside Color and Outside Color controls.

Figure 14-44: The Ellipse effect controls and a preview of its effect

Eyedropper Fill

The Eyedropper Fill effect selects a color from the clip to which the effect has been applied. To change the sample color, use the Sample Point and Sample Radius controls in the Effect Controls panel. Click the Average Pixel area drop-down menu to choose a method of choosing pixel colors. Increase the Blend with Original value to view more of the effected clip.

Grid

The Grid effect creates a grid that can be used as a matte or can be superimposed by using the Blending Mode options. Figure 14-45 shows the results of the Grid effect using the Add Blending Mode option. The effect was applied to the Sailing.psd file, which can be found in the Chapter 14 folder of the DVD that accompanies the book.

Figure 14-45 also shows the Grid effect properties in the Effect Controls panel. The width and height of the grid can be adjusted by using the Size From drop-down menu. When you click the drop-down menu, choose one of the three controls: Corner, Width, and Height. The thickness of the lines in the grid can be changed by adjusting the Border control. The edges of the lines can be softened by increasing the Feather values. The color of the lines in the grid can be changed by using the Color control. The grid can be inverted by clicking the Invert check box. To Blend the grid over the effected clip, click the Blending Mode drop-down menu and choose an option. To make the grid translucent, decrease the Opacity value.

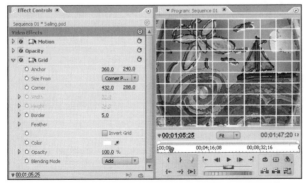

Figure 14-45: The Grid effect controls and a preview of its effect

Lens Flare

The Lens Flare effect creates a flaring light effect in your image. In the Lens Flare Settings dialog box, use the mouse to pick the image position of the flare in the Preview area. Click and drag the slider to adjust flare brightness, and pick a lens: Zoom, 35 mm, or 105 mm. Figure 14-46 shows the Lens Flare Settings dialog box.

Figure 14-46: The Lens Flare Settings dialog box

Lightning

The Lightning effect enables you to add lightning to a clip. With the Lightning setting, you can choose starting and ending points for the lightning. Moving the Segment slider to the right increases the number of segments the lightning has. Moving the Segment slider to the left decreases the number of segments. Conversely, moving the other Lightning effect sliders to the right increases the effect; moving the slider to the left decreases it. You can stylize your lightning bolt by adjusting the Segments, Amplitude, Branching, Speed, Stability, Width, Force, and Blending Mode options. Figure 14-47 shows a lightning bolt created using the Lightning effect.

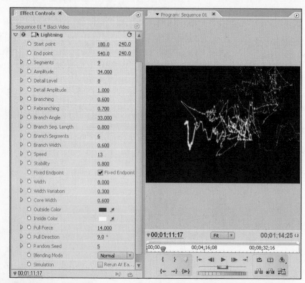

Figure 14-47: The image after applying the Lightning effect and Lightning options shown in the Effect Controls panel

Paint Bucket

The Paint Bucket effect can be used to colorize an image or used to apply a solid color to an area in an image. Note that the Paint Bucket effect works similarly to the way the Paint Bucket tool works in Photoshop. Figure 14-48 shows the Paint Bucket properties in the Effect Controls panel and a preview of the effect in the Program Monitor panel. The effect was applied to the Highway.jpg file. To blend the Paint Bucket color and the highway clip, we set the Blending Mode drop-down menu to Soft Light. To create the desired effect, we chose to invert the fill, so we selected the Invert Fill check box.

The color used to colorize the video clip is selected using the Color control property. The amount of color applied to the image is controlled by the Tolerance value. The Threshold control can be used as a form of retouching and color-correcting. It allows you to preview the clip and fill color in a black-and-white state. When spreading the Paint Bucket color onto your clip, click this control on and off to view the results in black and white. This makes it easier to see the results of the Paint Bucket color.

The Fill Point and Fill Selector controls are used to specify the area of the color effects. The Stroke drop-down menu determines how the edges of the color will work. To make the Paint Bucket color fill translucent, reduce the percent value for the Opacity control.

Figure 14-48: The Paint Bucket effect controls and a preview of its effect

Ramp

The Ramp effect allows you to create linear or radial blurs. Click the Ramp Shape drop-down menu to choose either Radial Ramp or Linear Ramp. You can set the start and end colors of the blur by clicking a color in your image and using the Eyedropper tool or by clicking the color swatch and using the Color Picker dialog box. Moving the Ramp Scale slider to the left creates a smoother blend. When the Blend Witness slider is set to 50, both the blend and image clip you are applying the effect to are set to 50 percent translucency. Moving the slider to the right makes the image clip more opaque. Moving the slider to the left makes the blend less opaque.

The Stylize bin

The effects found in the Stylize bin create a variety of effects that change images without creating major distortions. For example, the Emboss effect adds depth throughout your image, whereas the Tiles effect divides your image into mosaic tiles.

Alpha Glow

The Alpha Glow effect adds a glowing effect around alpha channel edges. In the Alpha Glow Settings dialog box, shown in Figure 14-49, use the Glow slider to control how far the glow extends from the alpha channel. Use the Brightness slider to increase and decrease brightness.

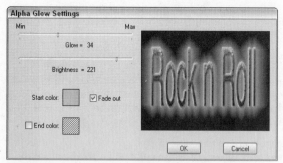

Figure 14-49: The Alpha Glow Settings dialog box

In the dialog box, the Start color swatch represents the glow color. If you want to change the color, click the color swatch and choose a color from Premiere Pro's Color Picker panel.

If you choose an End color, Premiere Pro adds an extra color at the edge of the glow. To create an End color, select the End color check box and click the color swatch to pick the color in the Color Picker panel. To fade out the Start color, click the Fade Out check box.

Brush Strokes

The Brush Strokes effect allows you to simulate the effect of adding brush strokes to a clip, as shown in Figure 14-50. The effect was applied to the Sailing.psd file.

Figure 14-50 also shows the Brush Strokes properties in the Effect Controls panel. Use the properties to control the effect. Start by picking a brush size and length using the Brush Size and Brush Length controls. Adjust the angle of the strokes by changing the value of the Brush Angle. How the strokes are applied is determined by the Stroke Density, Stroke Randomness, and Paint Surface drop-down menus. Use the Blend with Original control to determine how much of the original clip is viewed.

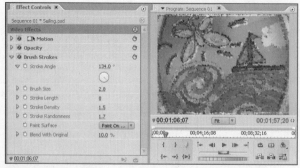

Figure 14-50: The Brush Strokes effect controls and a preview of its effect

Color Emboss

The Color Emboss effect creates the same effect as Emboss (described next), except that it doesn't remove color. Figure 14-51 shows the Color Emboss properties in the Effect Controls panel and a preview in the Program Monitor panel.

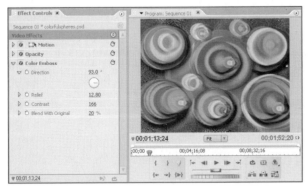

Figure 14-51: The Color Emboss effect controls and a preview of its effect

Emboss

The Emboss effect creates a raised 3D effect from image edge areas in a clip. In the Effect Controls panel, use the Direction slider to control the angle of the embossing. Drag the Relief slider to raise the emboss level to create a greater emboss effect. To create a more pronounced effect, add more contrast by dragging the Contrast slider to the right. Use the Blend with Original slider to blend shading of the embossing with the clip's original image. Figure 14-52 shows the Emboss properties in the Effect Controls panel and a preview in the Program Monitor panel.

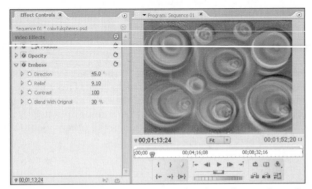

Figure 14-52: The Emboss effect controls and a preview of its effect

Find Edges

The Find Edges effect can make the image in a clip look as if it is a black-and-white sketch. The effect seeks out image areas of high contrast and turns them into black lines that appear against a white background, or as colored lines with a black background. In the Effect Controls panel, use the Blend with Original slider to blend the lines with the original image. Figure 14-53 shows a preview of the Find Edges effect.

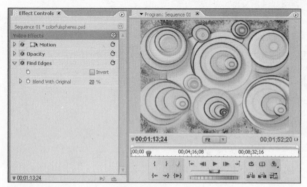

Figure 14-53: A preview of the Find Edges effect

Leave Color

The Leave Color effect turns an entire color image into grayscale with the exception of one color. When the Tolerance and Edge Softness controls are set to 0% and the Amount to Decolor control is set to 100%, an entire color image turns gray. To add color to the image, either reduce the percentage of the Amount to Decolor control or increase the Tolerance percentage value.

The Color To Leave swatch determines which color of your image will remain. Adjusting the Tolerance control determines how much of the swatch color is affected. For a smooth transition in color and gray areas, increase the Edge Softness control. Click the Match colors drop-down menu to pick either the RGB or Hue color model.

Mosaic

The Mosaic effect turns your image areas into rectangular tiles. In the Effect Controls panel, enter the number of mosaic blocks in the Horizontal/Vertical blocks field. This effect can be animated for use as a transition, where normally the average of the colors in the other video track is used to pick the tile color. However, if you choose the Sharp color option, Premiere Pro uses the pixel color in the center of the corresponding region in the other video track. Figure 14-54 shows a preview of the Mosaic effect.

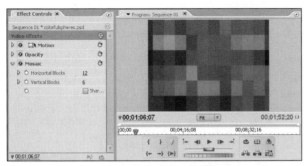

Figure 14-54: A preview of the Mosaic effect

Noise

The Noise effect randomly changes colors in a video clip to give your clip a grainy appearance. In the Effect Controls panel, use the Amount of Noise slider to designate how much "noise," or graininess, you want added to the clip. The more noise you add, the more your image disappears into the noise you create.

If you choose the Color Noise option, the effect randomly changes the pixels in the image. If Color Noise is turned off, the same amount of noise is added to each red, green, and blue channel in the image.

Clipping is a mathematical stopgap that prevents noise from becoming larger than a set value. When the Clipping option is not selected, noise values start at lower values after reaching a certain point. If you turn Clipping off, you may find that your image completely disappears into the noise.

Replicate

The Replicate effect creates multiple versions of the clip within the frame. The effect produces this replication effect by creating tiles and placing multiple versions of the clip into the tiles. Dragging the Replicate Settings Count slider in the Replicate Settings dialog box, shown in Figure 14-55, to the right increases the number of tiles onscreen.

Figure 14-55: The Replicate Settings dialog box

Roughen Edges

The Roughen Edges effect affects the edges of an image. It gives the edges a jagged look. Click the Edge Type drop-down menu to select a roughen style. If you choose a color option, you also need to select a color from the Edge Color control.

To customize the roughen edge, use the Border control to determine how large to make the roughen border. The Edge Sharpness control determines how sharp or soft the roughen edges appears. The Fractal Influence control determines how much of the roughen is controlled by fractal calculations. The Scale controls determines the size of the fractal used to create the roughen edges. The Stretch Width or Height control determines the width and height used to created the roughen edges. The Offset, Complexity, and Evolution controls are best used when animating the roughen edges.

Solarize

The Solarize effect creates a positive and a negative version of your image and then blends them together to create the solarizing effect. This can produce a lightened version of your image with darkened edges. In the Solarize Settings dialog box, shown in Figure 14-56, click and drag the Threshold slider to control the brightness level at which the Solarizing effect begins.

Figure 14-56: The Solarize Settings dialog box

Strobe Light

The Strobe Light effect creates the illusion of a strobe light flashing at regular or random intervals in your clip. In the Effect Controls panel, click the color swatch to choose a color for the strobe effect. Enter the duration of the strobe flash in the Duration field. In the Strobe Period field, enter the duration between strobe effects. (Duration is measured from the time the last strobe flashed — not when the flash ends.) If you want to create a random strobe effect, drag the Random Strobe Probability slider to the right. (The greater the probability setting, the more random the effect is.)

In the Strobe area of the Effect Controls panel, choose Operates on Color only if you want the strobe effect to be applied to all color channels. Choose Make Layer Transparent to make the track transparent when the strobe goes off. If you choose Operates on Color, you can select an arithmetic operator from the Strobe Operator drop-down menu that can further alter the strobe effect.

Note   If you set the strobe period longer than the strobe duration, the strobe will be constant — not flashing.

Texturize

The Texturize effect can create texture in a clip by applying texture, such as sand or rocks, found in one track to another track. To choose the video track supplying the texture, click in the Texture Layer drop-down menu in the Effect Controls panel and choose the track. Click and drag the Light Direction and Contrast slider to create the best effect. In the Texture Placement drop-down menu, choose Tile Texture to repeat the texture over the clip. Choose Center Texture to place the texture in the clip's center, and then choose Stretch Texture to stretch the text over the entire frame area.

Figure 14-57 shows Texturize properties in the Effect Controls panel and a preview in the Program Monitor panel. To create the effect seen in the Program Monitor panel, the Texturize effect was applied to an ocean beach scene (beach.psd) in the Video 1 track. In the Video 2 track, there was a graphic file called happy.jpg. (Both clips are found in the Chapter 14 folder on the DVD that accompanies the book.) The clip in the Video 2 track was hidden by clicking the Eye icon of that video track. The Texture Layer drop-down menu was set to Video 2. For the full effect of the texture, the Texture Contrast value was set to 2.0. Adjusting the Light Direction control changes the result of the texture. Use the Texture Placement drop-down menu to change the placement of the texture.

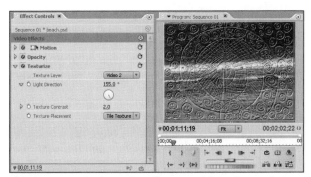

Figure 14-57: The Texturize effect controls and a preview of its effect

Write-on

The Write-on effect can be used to animate a colored brush stroke on a video clip, or it can be used with the effected clip to create brush strokes onto a clip beneath it. Here's how:

1. **Drag a clip into the Video 1 track.** Try using the beach.psd file located on the DVD.

2. **Directly below the clip in the Video 1 track, drag another clip into the Video 2 track.** Try using the Sailing.psd file located on the DVD.

3. **Apply the Write-on effect to the clip in the Video 2 track.** Use the controls in the Effect Controls panel to adjust the effect.

4. **Increase the Brush Size value to get a better look at the effect.** To change the color of the brush stroke, use the Color control. A small Brush Hardness percent value softens the edges of the brush stroke. To make the brush strokes translucent, reduce the percent value of the Brush Opacity.

5. **Use the Paint Style drop-down menu to determine what the brush strokes will use to paint with.** If you set the drop-down menu to On Original Image, the brush strokes paint on the Video 2 track (the clip to which the effect was applied) with the color selected in the Color control. If you set the drop-down menu to On Transparent, the brush strokes paint on the Video 1 track (the clip below the clip to which the effect was applied) with the color selected in the Color control. If you set the Paint Style drop-down menu to Reveal Original Image, the brush strokes paint on Video 1 Track using the Video 2 track as the brush strokes.

6. **To move the brush stroke, use the Brush Position controls or click the word *Write-on* (in the Effect Controls panel) and move the circle icon that appears in the Program Monitor panel.** To animate the movement of the brush strokes, move the current-time indicator to the beginning of the clip, and then click the Toggle animation icon that is in front of the Brush Position to create a keyframe. Continue moving the current-time indicator and adjusting the Brush Position controls to create keyframes for your brush stroke animation.

7. **Use the Stroke Length and Stroke Spacing, Part Time Properties, and Brush Time Properties controls to adjust the way the brush strokes are applied.**

The Time bin

The Time bin contains effects that specifically relate to different frames in the selected clip.

Echo

The Echo effect creates the visual version of an echo. In other words, frames from the selected clip are repeated again and again. This is effective only in clips that display motion. Depending on the clip, Echo can produce a repeated visual effect or possibly a streaking type of special effect. In the Effect Controls panel, use the Echo Time slider to control the time between the repetitions. Drag the Number of Echoes to designate how many frames to combine for the effect.

Use the Starting Intensity slider to control intensity of the first frame. A setting of 1 provides full intensity; .25 provides one-quarter intensity. The Decay slider controls how quickly the echo dissipates. If the Decay slider is set to .25, the first echo will be .25 of the starting intensity, the next echo will be .25 of the previous echo, and so on.

The Echo operator drop-down menu creates effects by combining the pixel values of the echoes. These are the drop-down menu choices:

✦ **Add:** Adds pixel values

✦ **Maximum:** Uses maximum pixels value of echoes

✦ **Minimum:** Uses minimum pixel value of echoes

✦ **Screen:** Similar to Add, but less likely to produce white streaks

✦ **Composite in Back:** Uses the clip's alpha channels and composites them starting at the back

✦ **Composite in Front:** Uses the clip's alpha channels and composites them starting at the front

Note   To combine an Echo effect with a Motion Settings effect, create a virtual clip and apply the effect to the virtual clip.

Posterize Time

The Posterize Time effect grabs control of a clip's frame rate settings and substitutes the frame rate specified in the Effect Controls frame rate slider.

The Transform bin

The Transform bin is filled with Transformation effects from Adobe After Effects that enable you to flip, crop, and roll a video clip and change the camera view.

Camera View

The Camera View effect simulates viewing the clip at a different camera angle. In the Camera View Settings dialog box, shown in Figure 14-58, use the sliders to control the effect. Click and drag the Latitude slider to flip the clip vertically. Use the Longitude slider to flip horizontally. The Roll slider simulates rolling the camera, thus rotating the clip. Click and drag the Focal Length slider to make the view wider or narrower. The Distance slider enables you to change the distance between the imaginary camera and the clip. Use the Zoom slider to zoom in and out. To create a fill color to use as a background, click the color swatch and choose a color in Premiere Pro's Color Picker panel. If you want the background area to be transparent, choose Fill Alpha Channel. (The clip must include an alpha channel to use this option.)

Figure 14-58: The Camera View Settings dialog box

Clip

The Clip effect hides the frame boundaries — similar to a Crop effect, except that the clip is not resized. The effect can be used to hide noise at image edges.

To use the Clip effect, drag the sliders in the Clipping Settings dialog box, shown in Figure 14-59, to clip the top, left, bottom, and/or right sides of the clip. Choose whether you want to clip according to pixels or percent. Click the Fill Color swatch to open Premiere Pro's Color Picker and choose a background color.

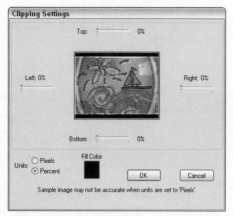

Figure 14-59: The Clipping Settings dialog box

Crop

The Crop effect provides the same settings as the Clip effect except that, with the Crop effect, Premiere Pro resizes the clip according to the dialog box settings.

The Edge Feather

The Edge Feather effect allows you to create a 3D feathered effect around the edge of the image clip you are working with. To apply a feathered edge, click Setup in the Effect Controls panel to display the Edge Feather Settings dialog box, shown in Figure 14-60. In the dialog box, move the Feather Value slider to the right to increase the size of the edge of the feather.

Figure 14-60: The Edge Feather Settings dialog box

Horizontal Flip

The Horizontal Flip effect flips the frame left to right.

Horizontal Hold

The Horizontal Hold effect is named after the horizontal hold knob found on a television set. As you might guess, the effect simulates turning the horizontal hold knob. In the Horizontal Hold Settings dialog box, shown in Figure 14-61, click and drag the slider to create the skewing effect.

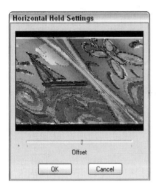

Figure 14-61: The Horizontal Hold Settings dialog box

Roll

The Roll effect provides a rotating effect. The Roll Settings dialog box, shown in Figure 14-62, enables you to roll the image left, right, up, or down.

Figure 14-62: The Roll Settings dialog box

Vertical Flip

The Vertical Flip effect flips your clip vertically. The result is an upside-down version of the original clip.

Vertical Hold

The Vertical Hold effect simulates turning the vertical hold knob found on a television set. Use the slider in the Vertical Hold Settings dialog box to create the effect you want.

The Transition bin

The effects found in the Transition bin perform effects similar to those performed by the transitions in the Video Transitions bin in the Effects panel.

Block Dissolve

The Block Dissolve effect can be used to have a clip disappear using random blocks of pixels.

Gradient Wipe

The Gradient Wipe effect blends the clip with the effect onto another clip (called the gradient layer) based upon luminance values. To use the effect, place a clip in the Video 1 track and apply the effect to the clip. Then place another clip in the Video 2 track, and use this clip as the gradient layer. Hide the clip in the Video 2 track by clicking the Eye icon in the Timeline panel. In the Effect Controls panel, set the Gradient Layer drop-down menu to the Video 2 track. Use the Transition Completion and Transition Softness controls to determine how much of the gradient layer is displayed. Use the Gradient Placement drop-down menu to choose how to position the gradient. If you want, you can click the Invert check box to invert the gradient.

Linear Wipe

The Linear Wipe effect allows you to wipe the effected clip away so that you can see the clip beneath it.

Follow these steps to use the Linear Wipe effect:

1. **Place a clip in the Video 1 track.** Try using Power.psd file found in the Chapter 14 folder on the DVD that accompanies the book.

2. **Directly below the clip in the Video 1 track, place another clip in the Video 2 track.** Try using the Sailing.psd files found in the Chapter 14 folder on the DVD that accompanies the book.

3. **Apply the Linear Wipe effect to the clip in the Video 2 track.**

4. **Use the controls for the effect in the Effect Controls panel to create the desired effect.** To wipe away the clip in the Video 2 track and see the clip below it in the Video 1 track, increase the Transition Completion percent value. To angle the linear wipe, adjust the Wipe Angle control. To create a smooth transition between the two clips, increase the Feather value.

Radial Wipe

The Radial Wipe effect can be used to wipe away a clip, revealing a clip below it using a circular wipe. Figure 14-63 shows the Radial Wipe properties in the Effect Controls panel and a preview of the effect in the Program Monitor panel. The Radial Wipe effect, shown in Figure 14-63, was applied to a file called Patchwork.psd. The Patchwork.psd file was placed in the Video 2 track, and in the Video 1 track was a file called Bariloche.psd. Both files can be found in the Chapter 14 folder on the DVD that accompanies the book.

Figure 14-63 displays the Effect Controls panel with the properties used to create the effect. To create a radial wipe, either increase the Transition Completion percentage or click the words *Radial Wipe* (in the Control Effects panel) and move the circle icon that appears in the

Program Monitor panel. To change the angle of the radial wipe, adjust the Start Angle control. To increase the radial wipe from its center out, you need to adjust the Center Wipe controls. Click the Wipe drop-down menu to choose whether you want to radial wipe to be clockwise, counterclockwise, or both. Increasing the Feather value gives a smoother blend between the two clips.

Figure 14-63: The Radial Wipe effect controls and a preview of its effect

Venetian Blinds

The Venetian Blinds effect can be used to wipe away the clip with the effect and display the clip below it using stripes. Figure 14-64 shows the Venetian Blinds properties in the Effect Controls panel and a preview of the effect in the Program Monitor panel.

The Venetian Blinds effect, seen in Figure 14-64, was applied to a file called RocknRoll.psd. Because the RocknRoll file was created in Adobe Photoshop using a transparent background, when we imported the file, the Import Layered File dialog box appeared. To take advantage of the transparent background of the file, we set the Layer Options to Choose Layer and set its drop-down menu to RocknRoll. Then we clicked OK. The file was imported with the text on a black background matte. The file was dragged from the Project panel to the Video 2 track of the Timeline panel. In the Video 1 track was a color matte clip that we create using the File ➪ New ➪ Color Matte command.

The RocknRoll.psd file is in the Chapter 14 folder on the DVD that accompanies the book.

To create Venetian Blinds, increase the Transition Completion percent value. Adjust the Direction control to change the angle of the Venetian Blinds. Use the Width control to determine how many Venetian Blinds you want and how wide you want them to be. Increase the Feather value if you want the blinds to have a soft edge.

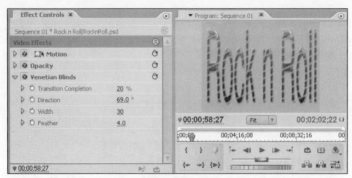

Figure 14-64: The Venetian Blinds effect controls and a preview of its effect

The Video bin

The effects found in the Video bin simulate electronic changes to a video signal. These effects need only be applied if you are outputting your production to videotape.

Broadcast Colors

If you are outputting your production to videotape, you may want to run the Broadcast Colors effect to improve color output quality. As we discuss in Chapters 11 and 18, the gamut, or range of video colors, is smaller than the color gamut of a computer monitor. To use the Broadcast Color effect, choose either NTSC for American television or PAL for European television in the Broadcast Locale drop-down menu. Then choose a method in the How to Make Colors Safe drop-down menu. These choices are available in this drop-down menu:

✦ **Reduce Luminance:** This option reduces pixels' brightness values, moving the pixel values toward black.

✦ **Reduce Saturation:** This option brings pixel values closer to gray, making the colors less intense.

✦ **Key out Unsafe:** Colors that fall beyond the TV gamut become transparent.

✦ **Key in Safe:** Colors that are within the TV gamut are transparent.

In the Maximum Signal Field, enter the IRE breakpoint value. (IRE measures image luminance.) Any levels above this value are altered. If you are unsure of what value to use, leave the default setting of 110.

Field Interpolate

The Field Interpolate effect creates missing scan lines from the average of other lines.

Reduce Interlace Flicker

The Reduce Interlace Flicker effect softens horizontal lines in an attempt to reduce interlace flicker (an odd or even interlace line that appears during video capture).

Note　　Choosing the wrong field settings in the Project Settings dialog box can increase flicker. To access the Project Settings dialog box, choose Project ➪ Project Settings ➪ General. These settings are covered in more detail in Chapter 5.

The Presets bin

Effects can be saved as presets so that they can be used on any clips in any project. When you save an effect as a preset, all the customized settings are saved. To save an effect as a preset, select the effect from the Effect Controls panel. Then choose Save Preset from the Effect Controls menu. In the Save Preset dialog box, you can name your preset and give a description. The Type options determine how Premiere Pro will handle keyframes. Click OK, and the preset appears in the Preset bin, within the Effect panel. If you want to organize all your custom preset effects into a bin, you can create new preset bin and drag them into the bin. To create a new preset bin, click the Effects menu and choose New Presets Bin. To rename the new preset bin folder, click and drag over the name and type a new name.

By default, the Presets bin consists of six bins with effects; Bevel Edges, Blurs, Mosaics, PIPS, Solarizes, and Twirls. The Blurs, Mosaics, Solarizes, and Twirls bins have In and an Out effects in their bins. Try applying one of these effects to a clip. Drag the In and Out effect to a video clip. Note that the effect is applied to the beginning and end of the clip. The middle of the clip is left untouched. The Bevel Edges bin preset contains a Bevel Edges Thick effect and a Bevel Edges Thin effect. The Bevel Edges Thick effect creates a thick bevel around the edge of the clip it is applied to, and the Bevel Edges Thin applies a thin bevel to the edge of the clip. The PIPS preset bin contains a 25% PIPS bin. Within the 25% PIPS bin are five bins: 25% LL, 25% LR, 25% Motion, 25% UL, and 25% UR. The effects in the LL bin decrease the size of the clip and put the clip in the lower-left corner of the Program Monitor panel. The effects in the LR bin decrease the size of the clip and put the clip in the lower-right corner of the Program Monitor panel. The effects in the UL bin decrease the size of the clip and put the clip in the upper-left corner of the Program Monitor panel. The effects in the UR bin decrease the size of the clip and put the clip in the upper-right corner of the Program Monitor panel. Within the Motion bin are effects that decrease the size of the clip and use keyframes to move the clip from the lower-left corner to the upper-right corner, and vice versa, or from the upper-left corner to the lower-right corner, and vice versa.

Summary

Premiere Pro's Video Effects provide dozens of special effects that can add interest to or correct video. This chapter covered the following topics:

✦ To add an effect to a clip, drag the effect from the Effects panel to the clip in the Timeline.

✦ Use the Effect Controls panel to specify settings for effects, to turn on and off preview, and to enable and disable keyframing.

✦ Set keyframes where effect settings change in the Timeline.

✦ Use Value and Velocity graphs to fine-tune the results of an effect.

✦   ✦   ✦

Superimposing

By telling a story or providing information using innovative effects, you can ensure that your message gets across. One of the best techniques for doing so creatively is to use superimposition options. Adobe Premiere Pro helps you create sophisticated transparency effects by enabling you to overlay two or more video clips and then blend the two together. For more sophisticated effects, the Premiere Pro 2 Video Effects Keying options provide a host of different effects that enable you to *key* out (hide) different parts of the image area in one track and fill them with the underlying video in the track beneath it.

This chapter provides a look at two powerful methods of creating transparency: the Premiere Pro Opacity option and the Premiere Pro keying options found in the Video Effects bin (folder) of the Effects panel. The Opacity option enables you to create blending effects by changing the opacity of one video track. The Keying bin in the Effects panel is home to 17 different keying options that enable you to create transparency based on color, alpha channels, or brightness levels. As you read through this chapter, think about all the different ways that you can apply the effects in your current or next project. Using transparency creatively will undoubtedly add to its success.

If you put a video clip or still in Video 2 track and another in Video 1 track, you see only the image that is in the top video track onscreen — in this case, Video 2 track. To see both images, you need to either fade Video 2 track or apply a keying effect to it.

Any video track higher than Video 1 track can be faded using Premiere Pro's Opacity option or superimposed using the keying options. Throughout this book, you find various examples of transparency effects. To review some of these examples, see Chapters 11, 14, 17, and 29.

Fading Video Tracks

You can fade an entire video clip or still image over a video clip or another still image. The top video clip or still image is faded over the bottom one. When you fade a video clip or still image, you are changing the opacity of the clip or image. Any video track, except for Video 1 track, can be used as a superimposed track and can be faded. Premiere Pro's fade option appears when you expand a video track. When a video track is expanded, you can display the Opacity by clicking the Show Keyframes icon and choosing Show Opacity Handles. The Opacity graph line is found underneath a clip when the track is expanded.

Cross-Reference Fading video tracks works similarly to fading sound tracks. For more information on fading sound tracks, see Chapter 8.

Follow these steps to fade a track:

1. **Choose File ➪ New ➪ Project to create a new project.** Make sure that you use the proper preset. If you are creating a high-resolution project, you may want to use a DV preset. If not, use a Non-DV preset. Instead of creating a new project you can also open a project that has two or more clips. If so, skip to step 3 or 4.

2. **Choose File ➪ Import to import two files.** Locate either two video clips or a video clip and a still image. Press and hold the Ctrl key to select more than one file. Click Open to import the files.

On the DVD-ROM If you want, you can use the two video clips that we used in our fade example, shown in Figures 15-1 to 15-5. On the DVD that accompanies this book, in the Digital Vision folder that is in the Chapter 15 folder, you will find two Digital Vision video clips that you can use, Electro 579018F.mov and Electro 579023F.mov, and a sound clip, City Life/Urban Moods 672015aw.wav.

3. **When the files appear in the Project panel, drag and drop one file to Video 2 track and the other to Video 1 track in the Timeline panel.** You will change the opacity of the clip in Video 2 track. Make sure that the files in the video tracks overlap each other. Select the clip in Video 2 track.

4. **To zoom into the Timeline, click and drag the time Zoom level slider to the right.** The time Zoom level slider is at the bottom of the Timeline panel. You can also click the Zoom In button or press the equal sign on your keyboard.

5. **To expand Video 2 track , click the Collapse/Expand Track icon to the left of the word Video.**

6. **Click the Show Keyframes icon, and choose Show Opacity Handles to reveal the Opacity graph line, shown in Figure 15-1.** Notice that a white line beneath the video clip is displayed.

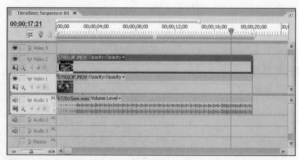

Figure 15-1: The Opacity graph line enables you to change the opacity of a video clip.

7. **To decrease the opacity of the file in Video 2 track, use either the Pen tool or the Selection tool in the Tools panel to click and drag the white Opacity graph line down.** As you drag, the Opacity percent value is displayed. The Opacity percent value is also displayed in the Effect Controls panel. To see the Opacity value, click the Collapse/Expand Track icon to display the Opacity percent value.

To slowly fade a video clip, you need to set the left side of the Opacity graph line so that it is at the top-left position and drag the far-right side down, as shown in Figure 15-2. To do so, you need to set two points (handles) on the Opacity graph line: one at the beginning of the clip and one at the end of the clip.

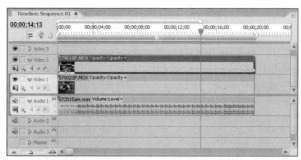

Figure 15-2: The Opacity graph line in the Timeline panel displays a gradual fade.

8. **To set the first point (handle), move the current-time indicator (Edit line) in the Timeline panel to the beginning of the clip and then click the Add/Remove Keyframes button.**

9. **To set the second point, move the current-time indicator (Edit line) in the Timeline panel to the end of the clip and click the Add/Remove Keyframes button.**

10. **Use the Selection or Pen tool to drag the last handle down.** The first handle should be at 100 percent. If it isn't, click the Go to Previous Keyframe button, and click and drag the handle up.

The fade in Figure 15-2 is gradual because the fade line gradually steps down. The top of the fade line indicates that the video clip is 100 percent opaque. When the fade line follows a long, slow, diagonal path from the top of the fade bar (100 percent opaque) to the bottom (100 percent transparent), the clip gradually fades out.

11. **Choose Window ➪ Effect Controls to display the Effect Controls panel.** To view the Opacity percent in the Effect Controls panel, shown in Figure 15-3, click the Collapse/ Expand Track icon in front of Opacity. Then click the Previous Keyframe or Next Keyframe button to move the current-time indicator (Edit line) to the Opacity keyframes on the Timeline. You can also drag the current-time indicator (Edit line) along the Effect Controls Timeline to see the percent values of the gradual fade. Figure 15-3 also shows the Value and Velocity graphs for the Opacity control. The Value and Velocity graphs can be used to adjust the Opacity control. For more information on using the Value and Velocity graphs, see Chapter 14.

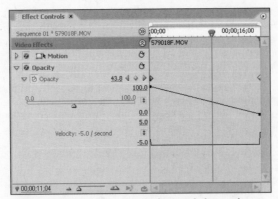

Figure 15-3: The Effect Controls panel shows the Opacity percentage value for the selected clip.

12. **To preview the fade effect, click the Play button in the Program Monitor panel.**

Note   You can also fade clips into one another using transitions. For more information on working with transitions, see Chapter 10.

13. **Before you save your work, you may want to import a sound clip into your project.** If the imported sound clip is too long, use the Razor tool to edit it. For more information on working with sound, see Chapter 8.

Adding opacity handles using the Pen tool and Selection tool

To create more sophisticated fades, you can add more handles to the Opacity graph line using either the Selection tool or the Pen tool. After you have handles, you can then drag different segments of the Opacity graph line. Here's how:

Note   To display the Opacity graph line, expand the Video track by clicking on the Collapse/Expand Track icon to the left of the word Video. Then click the Show Keyframes icon and choose Show Opacity Handles.

1. **With either the Pen tool or Selection tool selected, move the cursor over the Opacity graph line.** Move over to the area where you want to add a handle, and then press and hold Ctrl as you click to create a handle. A handle appears as a yellow diamond on the Opacity graph line.

2. **To create a few handles, press and hold Ctrl as you click the Opacity rubberband line a few times.**

3. **Now that you have a few handles on the Opacity graph line, you can move them, as shown in Figure 15-4.**

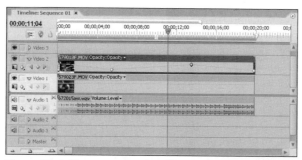

Figure 15-4: You can create handles on the Opacity graph line to create a fade.

4. **If you've created too many handles and want to delete one, just click a handle in the Timeline panel and press Delete.** You can also click a keyframe in the Effect Controls panel and press Delete.

Tip

To delete all the opacity keyframes from a Timeline, click the Toggle Animation icon in the Effect Controls panel. When the Warning prompt appears, click OK to delete all existing keyframes.

5. **Click and drag the handle to move up and/or down as shown in Figure 15-4.** When you click the handle, you should see a yellow diamond at the bottom of the Pen icon. A plus sign (+) indicates that you are going to add a handle when you click the Opacity graph line. Make sure you see the yellow diamond, and reposition the mouse more accurately over the handle you want to move.

Tip

Use the Go to Previous Keyframe and the Go to Next Keyframe buttons in the Timeline panel to move quickly from one keyframe to another.

6. **Use the Effect Controls panel to display the fade level percentage, as shown in Figure 15-5.** To display the Effect Controls panel, choose Window ➪ Effect Controls. Notice all the Opacity keyframes. Click a keyframe to view its percentage, or click and drag the Timeline to scroll through the different percentages. Figure 15-5 also shows the Value and Velocity graphs for the Opacity control. The Value and Velocity graphs can be used to adjust the Opacity control. For more information on using the Value and Velocity graphs, see Chapter 14.

   For a quick preview, click and drag the Edit line through the Timeline (of either the Timeline or the Effect Controls panel) to preview the fade effect in the Program Monitor panel. To display the Program Monitor panel, choose Window ➪ Program Monitor. You can also preview an effect by clicking the Play button in the Program Monitor.

7. **Choose File ➪ Save to save your work.**

Note

If desired, you can fade more video tracks. Just import more video clips and/or still images into the Project panel. Create new video tracks and drag the video clips and/or images into the new video tracks. Then use the Opacity graph line to fade the video tracks.

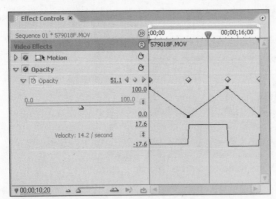

Figure 15-5: The Effect Controls panel displays the Opacity effect for the selected video clip.

Adjusting the Opacity graph line using the Pen tool and Selection tool

The Pen tool or Selection tool enables you to move either an entire Opacity graph line as a unit or move two handles simultaneously. Follow these steps to use either the Pen tool or the Selection tool to move two handles simultaneously.

Note

Before you proceed to Step 1, you should have a Premiere Pro project with a clip in Video 2 track. Video 2 track should be selected and expanded, and the Opacity graph line should be displayed. These steps are covered in the "Fading Video Tracks" section earlier in this chapter.

1. **Use the either the Selection tool or the Pen tool to create two handles on the Opacity graph line.** Make the handles so that they appear at the beginning and end of the Opacity graph line. With either the Pen tool or Selection tool, press and hold the Ctrl key as you click the Opacity graph line.

2. **Use either the Selection tool or Pen tool with the Ctrl key pressed to click the Opacity graph line to add two more handles.** Place the handles in the middle of the clip. Try to spread all the handles equally apart from each other.

3. **Move either the Selection tool or the Pen tool between the two middle handles.** When an up and down arrow icon appears next to the tool, click the Opacity graph line and drag down. When you click and drag between the two handles, the handles and the Opacity graph line between the two handles move as a unit. The Opacity graph line outside the handles gradually moves, as shown in Figure 15-6.

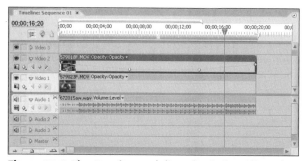

Figure 15-6: The Opacity graph line after being adjusted with the Pen tool

The Selection tool or the Pen tool also enables you to move just a section of the Opacity graph line completely separate from the rest. Here's how:

Note

Before you proceed to Step 1, you should have a Premiere Pro project with a clip in Video 2 track. Video 2 track should be selected and expanded, and the Opacity graph line should be displayed. These steps are covered in the "Fading Video Tracks" section earlier in this chapter.

1. **Start with an Opacity graph line that has two handles — one at the beginning of the Opacity graph line and another at the end.**

2. **Create two more handles.** They should be side by side in the middle of the Opacity graph line.

3. **Select either the Pen tool or Selection tool, if it is not selected.**

4. **Use either the Selection tool or the Pen tool to select the first handle.** Then press and hold the Shift key as you select the second handle.

5. **Now click and drag the Opacity graph line down.** Notice that only the line between the first handle on the Opacity graph line and second handle moves, as shown in Figure 15-7. The line moves at a constant percentage.

6. **Deselect the first and second handles.** Then use either the Pen tool or Selection tool to select the third handle. Press and hold the Shift key as you select the fourth handle.

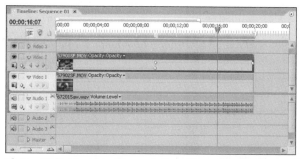

Figure 15-7: The Opacity graph line after using the Pen tool to move separate sections independently

7. **Now, click and drag the Opacity graph line down.** Notice that only the Opacity graph line between the third and fourth handles moves, as shown in Figure 15-7. The line moves at a constant percentage.

8. **Move either the Pen tool or the Selection tool to the right of the third handle and to the left of the last handle.** Then press Ctrl as you click the Opacity graph line. As you click, notice that you create a handle between the third and fourth handles. With this new handle selected, click and drag the Opacity graph line down in the shape of a V, as shown in Figure 15-8.

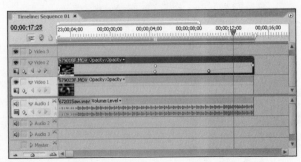

Figure 15-8: The Opacity graph line after using the Pen tool to create a V shape

Setting opacity keyframes using the Effect Controls panel and the Timeline panel

You can set opacity keyframes by using either the Effect Controls panel or the Timeline panel. Here's how to set keyframes using the Timeline panel.

Note Before you proceed to Step 1, you should have a Premiere Pro project with a clip in Video 2 track, and the track should be selected.

1. **Click the Collapse/Expand Track icon to expand Video 2 track.**

2. **Click the Show Keyframes icon, and choose Show Keyframes.**

3. **Click in the drop-down menu from the title bar of the clip in Video 2 track. and choose Opacity.**

4. **Move the current-time indicator (Edit line) to where you want to set a keyframe, and click the Add/Remove Keyframe icon to add a keyframe.**

5. **Repeat Step 4 as many times as you need.**

6. **Use either the Pen tool or the Selection tool to set the opacity for each keyframe.** With the Selection tool selected, click a keyframe and drag it either up or down on the Opacity graph line to where you want the opacity value to be.

Notice that the keyframes that you created using the Timeline panel now appear in the Effect Controls panel. You can continue editing the keyframes in either the Timeline panel or the

Effect Controls panel. You can also preview the effect of the opacity keyframes by moving the current-time indicator on the Timeline of either the Timeline panel or the Effect Controls panel.

Here's how to add keyframes using the Effect Controls panel.

Note   Before you proceed to Step 1, you should have a Premiere Pro project with a clip in Video 2 track, and the track should be expanded.

1. **Click the Collapse/Expand Opacity icon to display the Opacity options.**

2. **Move the current-time indicator (Edit line) in the Effect Controls panel to where you want to set a keyframe.**

3. **Adjust the Opacity percent value.**

4. **Click the Toggle Animation icon to set a keyframe.** The keyframe is set with the current Opacity value at the location of the current-time indicator.

5. **To set another keyframe, move the current-time indicator to the desired location.**

6. **Click the Toggle Keyframe button to create a keyframe at the position of the current-time indicator (Edit line).** Then adjust the Opacity value.

7. **Another way to create a keyframe on the Timeline in the Effect Controls panel is to move the current-time indicator (Edit line) to where you want to set a keyframe.** Then adjust the Opacity value. Notice that, as you adjust the Opacity value, a keyframe is created. As long as the Toggle Animation icon is on, Premiere Pro continues to record your actions. Every time you move the current-time indicator (Edit line) and adjust the Opacity value, Premiere Pro adds a keyframe to the Opacity Timeline.

8. **If you decide you want to delete all the keyframes and start all over again, just click the Toggle Animation icon.** When the warning prompt appears, click OK.

Superimposing Tracks Using the Keying Effects

You can superimpose a video clip and/or still image over another one using the Keying options, which are found in the Keying bin, which is in the Video Effects bin in the Effects panel. In the Keying bin, you have 17 key types to pick from. Using the key options is called *keying*. Keying makes part of the image transparent. The following sections cover how to use the different key options.

Displaying the Keying effects

To display and experiment with the Keying options, shown in Figure 15-9, you first need to have a Premiere Pro project onscreen. Either load an existing Premiere Pro project or create a new one by choosing File ➪ New ➪ Project. Import two video clips into the new project.

On the DVD-ROM   If you want, you can use one of the video clips found in the Chapter 15 folder that is located in the Tutorial Projects folder on the DVD that accompanies this book. Most of the images shown in this chapter are located on the DVD.

Figure 15-9: The Keying effects are in the Keying bin, which is in the Video Effects bin in the Effects panel.

To display the Keying bin, follow these steps:

1. **Drag a clip from the Project panel to Video 1 track.**

2. **Drag a clip from the Project panel to Video 2 track.**

3. **Click and drag the clip in Video 2 track so that it overlaps the clip in Video 1 track.**

4. **Select the clip in Video 2 track.** This is the clip to which you apply a key effect.

5. **Choose Window ➪ Effects.** In the Effects panel, click the Collapse/Expand triangle in front of the Video Effects bin. To display the Keying options, click the Collapse/Expand triangle in front of the Keying bin.

   In the Keying bin, you have 17 key types to choose from: Alpha Adjust Key, Blue Screen Key, Chroma Key, Color Key, Difference Matte Key, Eight-Point Garbage Matte, Four-Point Garbage Matte, Green Screen Key, Image Matte Key, Luma Key, Multiply Key, Non Red Key, RGB Difference Key, Remove Matte, Screen Key, Sixteen-Point Garbage Matte, and Track Matte Key.

6. **To apply a key effect, click and drag it onto the clip in Video 2 track or into the Effect Controls panel.**

   Each Keying effect has it own set of controls that you can adjust. The controls that are displayed are based on the key effect that you choose. To learn more about the key type effects and their controls, see the following sections.

7. **To preview the Keying effect, you can move the current-time indicator in the Timeline panel or the Effect Controls panel.** You can also click the Play button in the Monitor panel. By default, the preview quality is set to Automatic Quality. To change the preview quality, click the Program Monitor menu and choose Highest Quality or Draft Quality. To render the work area, choose Sequence ➪ Render Work Area.

8. **To preview the clip without the Keying effect, you can choose Effect Enabled from the Effect Controls panel menu, or you can click the Toggle the Effect On or Off button in front of the Keying effect.**

Applying Keying effects using keyframes

Premiere Pro allows you to animate a Keying effect control over time using keyframes. You can add keyframes using either the Effect Controls panel or the Timeline panel.

Follow these steps to animate a Keying effects control using the Effect Controls panel:

> **Note**
>
> Before you proceed to Step 1, you should have a Premiere Pro project with a clip in Video 2 track and another in Video 1 track.

1. **Click and drag a Keying effect to the clip in Video 2 track.**

2. **Select the clip in Video 2 track if it is not already selected.**

3. **Next click the Collapse/Expand triangle in front of the Keying effect to display its controls.**

4. **To animate a Keying effect control over time, move the current-time indicator (Edit line) to where you want to add your first keyframe.**

5. **Click the Toggle Animation icon in front of the control to add a keyframe.**

6. **Make the desired adjustments to the control.**

7. **To create a second keyframe, move the current-time indicator (Edit line) to a new location and adjust the control.** As you adjust the control, a keyframe is added to the control's Timeline. While the Toggle Animation icon is turned on, every time you move the current-time indicator and adjust the control, a keyframe is added to the control's Timeline.

> **Note**
>
> In the Effect Controls panel, you can click the Toggle Keyframe button to add keyframes. You can also move among keyframes by clicking the Next Keyframe and Previous Keyframe buttons.

8. **To move a keyframe, click and drag it to its new location.**

9. **To edit a keyframe, move the current-time indicator (Edit line) over the Keyframe and adjust the control.**

10. **To delete a keyframe, click the keyframe and press Delete.**

11. **To delete all the keyframes for a control and start all over again, click the Toggle Animation icon.** When the warning prompt appears, click OK.

Follow these steps to animate a Keying effects control using the Timeline panel.

Note Before you proceed to Step 1, you should have a Premiere Pro project with a clip in Video 2 track and another in Video 1 track. The clip in Video 2 track should have a Keying effect applied to it, and the track should be selected in the Timeline panel.

1. **Click the Collapse/Expand triangle in front of Video 2 track to expand the track.**

2. **Click the Show Keyframes icon, and choose Show Keyframes.**

3. **Click the video clip's drop-down menu in the title bar, and pick a Keying effect control.**

4. **Move the current-time indicator (Edit line) to where you want to add a keyframe, and click the Add/Remove Keyframe button to add a keyframe.**

5. **In the Effect Controls panel, make the adjustments to the control.**

6. **To add a second keyframe, move the current-time indicator (Edit line) to a new location and then adjust the control.** As you adjust the control, a second keyframe is applied.

7. **To edit keyframes, select the desired keyframe you want to edit by clicking either the Go to Next Keyframe or the Go to Previous Keyframe button.** Then edit the Keyframe.

Chroma Key

The Chroma Key option in the Keying bin enables you to key out a specific color or a range of colors. This key is often planned during preproduction so that the video is shot against one colored background. To select the color to key out, use the Eyedropper tool to click the background area of the image thumbnail. Alternatively, you can click in the color swatch (under the word *Color*) and choose a key color from the Premiere Pro color picker.

To fine-tune the key, click and drag the sliders and make adjustments to the following options:

✦ **Similarity.** Click and drag to the left or right to increase or decrease the range of colors that will be made transparent.

✦ **Blend.** Click and drag to the right to create more of a blend between the two clips. Dragging to the left produces the opposite effect.

✦ **Threshold.** Clicking and dragging to the right keeps more shadow areas in the clip. Dragging to the left produces the opposite effect.

✦ **Cutoff.** Clicking and dragging to the right darkens shadow areas. Dragging to the right lightens shadow areas. Note that if you drag beyond the level set in the Threshold slider, gray and transparent areas become inverted.

✦ **Smoothing.** This control sets anti-aliasing, which blends pixel colors to create smoother edges. Choose High for most smoothing, Low for some smoothing, or None for no smoothing. Choosing None is often the best choice when keying titles.

✦ **Mask Only:** Selecting the Mask Only option causes only the alpha channel of the clip to be displayed.

Figure 15-10 shows a few frames from a project using the Chroma Key type. The frames show an athlete jumping through a yellow-to-pink gradient. To create the project, we imported a video clip of the athlete into Video 1 track and imported a still image of a yellow-to-pink gradient into Video 2 track . The Timeline panel for the project is shown in Figure 15-11. In Audio 1 track, we placed Digital Vision's Acoustic Chillout 730006aw.wav. To apply the key effect, we selected the still image in Video 2 track and dragged the Chroma Key effect over it. In the Chroma Key settings, we set the Color to yellow and adjusted the Similarity, Blend, Threshold, and Cutoff values so that we could see the Athlete jumping through the gradient. The controls used to create the project (in Figure 15-10) are shown in Figure 15-12.

On the DVD-ROM You can use the files we used to create the Chroma Key project. The athlete clip is Digital Vision's Triangle Sports TRB05005.mov, Digital Vision's Acoustic Chillout 730006aw.wav, and the yellow-and-pink gradient is a Photoshop file (GRADIENT.psd). The clips are found in the Chapter 15 folder that is located in the Tutorial Projects folder on the DVD that accompanies this book.

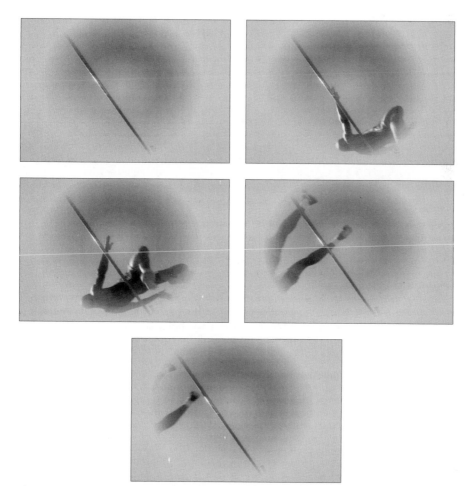

Figure 15-10: An athlete seen through a gradient, in a project using the Chroma Key type

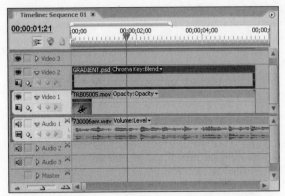

Figure 15-11: The Timeline used to create a project using the Chroma Key type

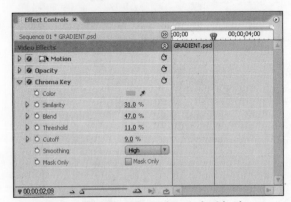

Figure 15-12: The Effect Controls panel with Chroma Key settings used to create the project shown in Figure 15-10

RGB Difference Key

The RGB Difference Key is an easy-to-use version of the Chroma Key option. Use this key when precise keying is not required or when the image being keyed appears in front of a bright background. As with the Chroma Key, the RGB Difference Key provides Similarity and Smoothing options but does not provide Blend, Threshold, or Cutoff controls.

Figure 15-13 shows a frame from the clip from the previous section with the RGB Difference Key type applied instead of the Chroma Key type (as was shown in Figure 15-10). Notice that the edges of the gradient do not slowly fade out into soft edges but rather end abruptly. Figure 15-14 shows the Effect Controls panel with the RGB Difference Key settings used in Figure 15-13.

Figure 15-13: A frame with the RGB Difference Key type applied to the clip from the project in the previous section

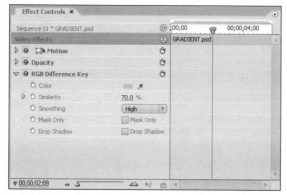

Figure 15-14: The Effect Controls panel with the RGB Difference Key type options

Color Key

The Color Key effect does a similar job to the Chrome Key effect. Both effects are used to key out a specific color or a range of colors. When you key out a color, it becomes translucent. Pick a color by using the Key Color swatch. The amount of transparency is controlled by the Color Tolerance control. The edge size and smoothness of a color can be adjusted by using the Edge Thin and Edge Feather controls. Figure 15-15 shows the Color Key controls in the Effect Controls panel. Use the clips from the Chroma Key section to experiment with the Color Key controls.

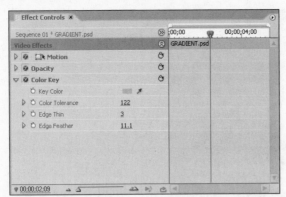

Figure 15-15: The Effect Controls panel with the Color Key options

Blue Screen and Green Screen keys

Blue and green are traditional keys used in broadcast television where announcers are often shown in front of a blue or green background. The Blue Screen keys out well-lit blue backgrounds. The Green Screen keys out well-lit green areas. These keys have the following options:

✦ **Threshold:** Start by dragging to the left to key out more green and blue areas.

✦ **Cutoff:** Click and drag to the right to fine-tune the key effect.

✦ **Smoothing:** This control sets anti-aliasing, which blends pixel colors to create smoother edges. Choose High for most smoothing, Low for some smoothing, or None for no smoothing. Choosing None is often the best choice when keying titles.

✦ **Mask Only:** This control allows you to choose whether to display the clip's alpha channel.

Normally when using the Blue Screen Key or Green Screen Key type, you would videotape a person or object against either a properly lit blue or green background. This way, you can import the video clip into Premiere Pro and use either the Blue Screen Key or Green Screen Key types to remove the background and replace it with any image your heart desires. In our example of a Green Screen Key type, we used two Digital Vision video clips: Working Numbers 577010f.mov and NightMoves 705014f.mov. The Working Numbers clip is pool balls falling onto a green pool top. Frames from this clip are shown in Figure 15-16. The NightMoves clip is of people playing pool on a red pool top. Frames from this clip are shown in Figure 15-17. Figure 15-18 shows a few frames from the Green Screen Key type project.

In Video 1 track, we placed the NightMoves 705014f.mov clip. We placed the Working Numbers 577010f.mov clip in Video 2 track and applied the Green Screen Key type. In order to see more of the clip in Video 1 track, we reduced the Green Screen Key type Threshold option to 44 percent. Figure 15-19 shows the Effect Controls panel with the Green Screen Key type options. In the Effect Controls window, you can see that we applied the Brightness & Contrast Video Effect. The final project was a little too dark, so we used a Video Effect to lighten it. In Audio 1 track, we placed Digital Vision's Acoustic Chillout 730006aw.wav. Figure 15-20 shows the Timeline panel we used to create the project. In Audio 1 track, we placed Digital Vision's Acoustic Chillout 730006aw.wav.

Figure 15-16: A few frames from the video clip in Video 2 track of the Green Screen Key type project

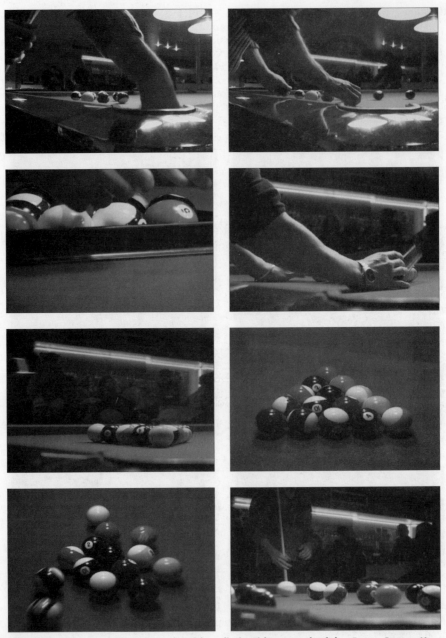

Figure 15-17: A few frames from the video clip in Video 1 track of the Green Screen Key type project

Figure 15-18: A few frames from a project created using the Green Screen Key effect to superimpose the video clips in Video tracks 1 and 2 (seen in Figures 15-16 and 15-17)

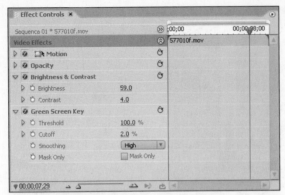

Figure 15-19: The Effect Controls panel with the Green Screen Key type options

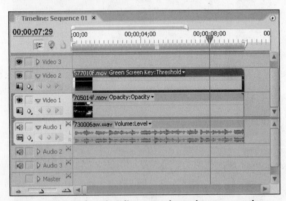

Figure 15-20: The Timeline panel used to create the Green Screen Key type project

On the DVD-ROM

If you want, you can load the clips used to create the Green Screen Key type project from the Chapter 15 folder that is in the Tutorial Projects folder on the DVD that accompanies this book.

Non Red Key

As with the blue and green screens, the Non Red Key is used to key out blue and green backgrounds, but does both at once. This key also includes a blending slider that enables you to blend two clips together.

Luma Key

The Luma Key type keys out darker image areas in a clip. Use the Threshold and Cutoff sliders to fine-tune the effect, as follows:

✦ **Threshold:** Click and drag to the right to increase the range of darker values that will be keyed out.

✦ **Cutoff:** This key controls the opacity of the Threshold range. Click and drag to the right to produce more transparency.

Figure 15-21 shows a few frames from a project using a Luma Key type. The frames show numbers counting down, superimposed over a video clip of two boxers fighting. Both clips are from Digital Vision. The numbers counting down clip is Working Numbers 577023f.mov, and the boxers fighting clip is Triangle Sports TRB05013.mov.

To create the Luma project, we imported the numbers counting down video clip into Video 1 track and imported the boxers fighting video clip into Video 2 track. We selected the video clip in Video 2 track and applied the Luma Key type option. We adjusted the Threshold and Cutoff values so that we could see both the numbers and boxers fighting. To fine-tune the effect, we reduced the opacity in the middle of the clip in Video 2 track. Figure 15-22 shows the Timeline used to create the project shown in Figure 15-21. In Audio 1 track, we placed Digital Vision's Acoustic Chillout 730006aw.wav. The Luma Key settings used to create the project appear in Figure 15-23. (For another Image Matte example, see Chapter 29.)

Figure 15-21: A few frames from the Luma Key type project

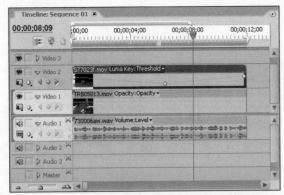

Figure 15-22: The Timeline panel used to create the Luma Key type project

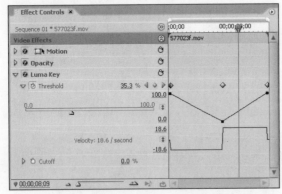

Figure 15-23: The Effect Controls panel with the Luma Key type settings used to create the project

On the DVD-ROM   You can load the clips used to create the Luma Key type project from the Chapter 15 folder that is in the Tutorial Projects folder on the DVD that accompanies this book.

Alpha Adjust

Use the Alpha Adjust Key to create transparency from imported images that contain an alpha channel (an image layer that represents a mask with shades of gray, including black and white, to indicate transparency levels). Premiere Pro reads alpha channels from such programs as Adobe Photoshop and three-dimensional software programs and also translates nontransparent areas of Illustrator files as alpha channels.

Note   Click on a file with an alpha channel in the Project panel. Then choose File ⇨ Interpret Footage. In the Interpret Footage dialog box, you can select the Ignore Alpha Channel to have Premiere Pro ignore the alpha channel of that file, or you can select the Invert Alpha Channel option to have Premiere Pro invert that file's alpha channel.

Figure 15-24 shows a few frames of an Alpha Adjust project. The project gives you the feeling that the guy is moving, when in reality the guy is not moving. The background clip is moving. To create the project, we imported a clip of a three-dimensional man that we created in Curious Labs' Poser and saved in Photoshop format with an alpha channel. The man is on a white background. To mask out the white background, we created an alpha channel of the man. The image of the 3D man was placed into Video 2 track. Then we applied the Alpha Adjust Key effect to the clip in Video 2 track. Video 1 track has a clip from Digital Vision's Working Numbers (577001f.mov). Figure 15-25 shows the Timeline used to create the project. Figure 15-26 shows the Alpha Adjust effect settings in the Effect Controls panel. The settings allow you to adjust how the alpha channel appears. Reducing the Opacity makes the image in the alpha channel more transparent. By selecting Ignore Alpha, Premiere Pro ignores the alpha channel. Selecting Invert Alpha causes Premiere Pro to invert the alpha channel, and choosing Mask Only displays only the mask of the alpha channel without the image.

Figure 15-24: Frames from an Alpha Adjust project

You can load the 3D man image (3Dguy.psd), the Digital Vision Working Numbers video clip 577001f.mov, and Digital Vision's Acoustic Chillout 730006aw.wav audio clip from the Chapter 15 folder that is in the Tutorial Projects folder on the DVD that accompanies this book.

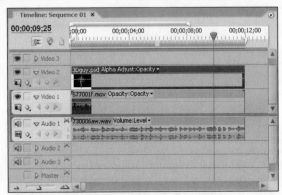

Figure 15-25: The Timeline panel from the Alpha Adjust project

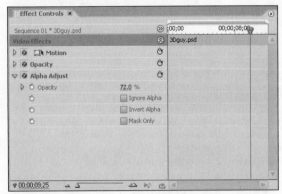

Figure 15-26: The Keying effects settings used in the Alpha Adjust project

Image Matte Key

The Image Matte Key is used to create transparency in still images, typically graphics. Image areas that correspond to black portions of the matte are transparent; areas corresponding to white areas are opaque. Gray areas create blending effects.

When using the Image Matte Key, click the Setup button (next to the Reset button in the Effect Controls panel) to choose an image. The final result depends upon the image you choose. You can create a composite using the alpha channel or the luminance of the clip. If you want to reverse the key effect, making areas that correspond to white transparent, areas corresponding to black areas will be opaque. The controls for the Image Matte Key effect are shown in Figure 15-27.

Figure 15-27 shows a project created using an Image Matte Key effect. To create the project (you can see a preview in the Monitor panel in Figure 15-27), we imported Digital Vision's SkyRide 652024f.mov video clip to Video 1 track. We selected Video 1 track and dragged the Image Matte Key effect over the clip. Next we clicked the Setup icon in the Effect Controls panel. In the Select a Matte Image dialog box, we selected an Adobe Illustrator file. To create the Illustrator file, we used the Brush tool to brush anchors. The anchor was selected from the Object Sample Brushes panel. The Timeline panel is shown in Figure 15-27. In Audio 1 track, we placed Digital Vision's Acoustic Chillout 730006aw.wav.

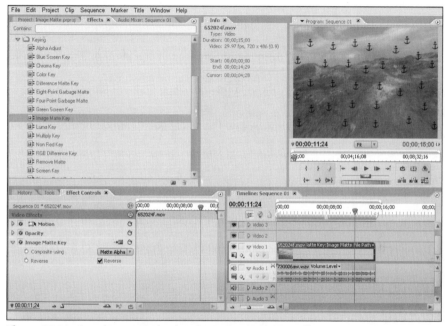

Figure 15-27: A project created using the Image Matte Key effect

You can load the files used to create the project in Figure 15-27 from the Chapter 15 folder that is in the Tutorial folder of the DVD that accompanies the book. The files used are Digital Vision's SkyRide 652024f.mov, Digital Vision's Acoustic Chillout 730006aw.wav, and anchors.ai.

Difference Matte Key

The Difference Matte Key enables you to key out image areas in one clip that match image areas in another clip. Whether you use the Difference Matte Key option depends upon the clips you use in your project. If your project has a background without motion over a clip that does, you may want to use the Difference Matte Key to key out image areas from the static clip.

Track Matte Key

The Track Matte Key enables you to create a moving or traveling matte effect. Often, the matte is a black-and-white image that is set in motion onscreen. Image areas corresponding to black in the matte are transparent; image areas corresponding to white are opaque. Gray areas create blending effects.

Cross-Reference For another example of the Track Matte Key effect, see Chapter 17.

Multiply and Screen Key

The Multiply and Screen Key effects are transparency effects in which the lower video track image exhibits a high degree of contrast. Use Multiply Key to create transparency in areas corresponding to bright image areas in the lower video track. Use Screen Key to create transparency in areas corresponding to dark image areas in the lower video track. For both key effects, adjust the Opacity and Cutoff percent values to fine-tune the effect.

Figure 15-28 shows a few frames from a Screen Key type project. To create the Screen Key project, we placed Digital Vision's Working Numbers 577025f.mov clip in Video 1 track, SkyRide 652022f.mov clip in Video 2 track, and a purple color matte that we created in Premiere Pro in Video 3 track. Figure 15-29 shows the Program Monitor panel with a frame from the clip in Video 1 track and a frame from the clip in Video 2 track.

We applied the Screen Key to the purple color matte in Video 3 track. This way, the entire project has a purple haze over the entire scene. The Screen Key controls are shown in Figure 15-29. The Opacity for the clip in Video 2 track was reduced so it would become translucent. Figure 15-30 shows the Effect Controls panel with the Opacity controls that were applied to the video clip in Video 2 track. Because the video clip in Video 1 track was longer than the clip in Video 2 track, we used the Opacity option to slowly fade the Video 1 track clip, shown in Figure 15-29. In Audio 1 track, we placed Digital Vision's Acoustic Chillout 730006aw.wav, also shown in Figure 15-29.

On the DVD-ROM You can load the clips used to create the Screen Key type project from the Chapter 15 folder that is in the Tutorial Projects folder on the DVD that accompanies this book.

Garbage Matte

A video clip may contain an object that you don't want to appear in your project. When this happens, you can create a Garbage Matte to eliminate (mask out) the unwanted object. Usually, the video clip in which you want to mask out an item goes on Video 2 track in the Timeline panel. Another clip that you want to use as a composite goes in Video 1 track.

The Keying bin has three different types of Garbage Mattes: Four-Point Garbage Matte Key, Eight-Point Garbage Matte Key, and Sixteen-Point Garbage Matte Key.

Note Sometimes, you may need to create a more sophisticated mask. When this happens, you may want to use Adobe After Effects. For more information on how to create a mask using Adobe After Effects, see Chapter 30.

A Garbage Matte Key can be used to create a split-screen effect that splits the screen between a clip in one track and a clip in another track, as shown in Figure 15-31. Notice that the video clip from Video 1 track is displayed on the left side of the preview and the video clip from Video 2 track is displayed on the right side. The clip in Video 1 track is Digital Vision's Working Numbers 577004f.mov, and the clip in Video 2 track is Working Numbers 577008f.mov. The Timeline used to create the split-screen effect is shown in Figure 15-31. In Audio 1 track, we placed Digital Vision's Acoustic Chillout 730006aw.wav.

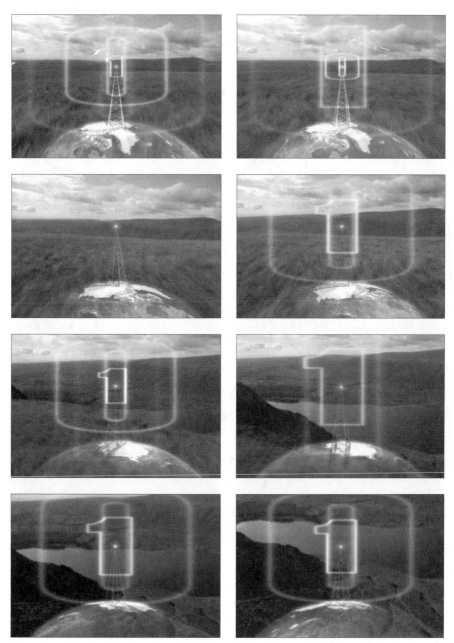

Figure 15-28: A few frames from a project using the Screen Key type

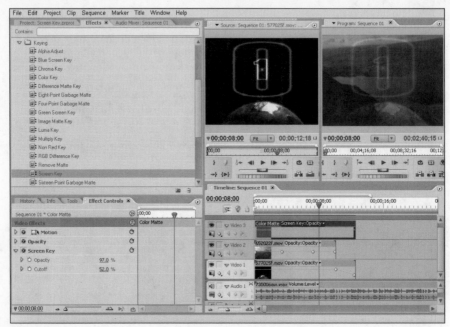

Figure 15-29: The Screen Key effect controls in the Effect Controls panel

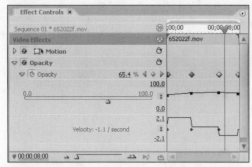

Figure 15-30: The layout of a Screen Key effect project

To create a split screen, follow these steps:

1. **Choose File ➪ New ➪ Project to create a new project.**

2. **Choose File ➪ Import to import two video clips.** Import a video clip in which you want to mask out an item, and import another clip (or a still image) that you want to use to composite.

On the DVD-ROM   You can load the clips used to create the split-screen project from the Chapter 15 folder that is in the Tutorial Projects folder on the DVD that accompanies this book.

3. **Drag the video clip that you want to split from the Project panel and into Video 2 track of the Timeline panel.**

4. **Drag the video clip that you want to use to composite from the Project panel into Video 1 track of the Timeline panel.**

5. **Select the video clip in Video 2 track.** Then click and drag either the Four-Point Garbage Matte Key or the Eight-Point Garbage Matte Key from the Effects panel to the video clip in the Timeline panel or to the Effect Controls panel. In Figure 15-31, we used the Eight-Point Garbage Matte Key.

6. **Click the Expand/Collapse triangle to display the Garbage Matte controls.** You can enter numbers in the fields to adjust the matte (by adjusting the first numbers in the left fields), or you can click the words *Garbage Matte* in the Effect Controls panel to display an outline around the clip, which is shown in the Program Monitor panel. Click one of the left points on the outline to adjust the matte. In Figure 15-31, we dragged the left center and corners to the middle of the clip's preview.

7. **Click the Play button in the Program Monitor panel to preview the effect.**

8. **Choose File ⇨ Save to save your project.**

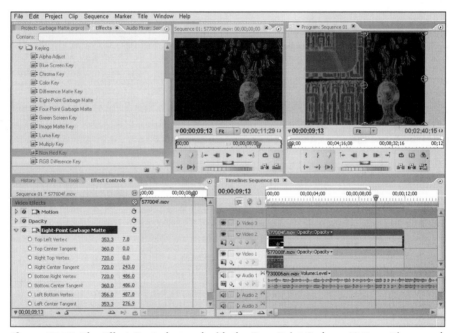

Figure 15-31: The Effect Controls panel with the Four-Point Garbage Matte settings used to create the split-screen project and the Program Monitor panel with an example of a split screen

Remove Matte

The Keying effects create transparency from alpha channels created from red, green, and blue channels, as well as the alpha channel. Normally, the Remove Matte Key is used to key out the black or white backgrounds. This is useful for graphics with solid white or black backgrounds.

Summary

Premiere Pro's superimposition options create interesting and attractive effects that blend video tracks together or make various areas of one track transparent. This chapter covered the following topics:

✦ Use the Premiere Pro Opacity options to blend a higher video track with the one beneath it.

✦ Click and drag the Opacity handles in the Opacity graph line to adjust the fading effect.

✦ To create key effects that make portions of a video track transparent, open Premiere Pro's Effects bin by choosing Window ➪ Effects. Then open the Video Effects bins so that you can open the Keying bin.

✦ Premiere Pro 2 provides 17 different keying effects: Alpha Adjust Key, Blue Screen Key, Chroma Key, Color Key, Difference Matte Key, Eight-Point Garbage Matte, Four-Point Garbage Matte, Green Screen Key, Image Matte Key, Luma Key, Multiply Key, Non Red Key, RGB Difference Key, Remove Matte, Screen Key, Sixteen-Point Garbage Matte, and Track Matte Key.

✦ Use the Blue Screen Key and Green Screen Key types to key out background image areas based on color.

✦ Use the Alpha Adjust Key to key out images based on an imported image's alpha channel.

✦ Use the Track Matte Key command to create traveling matte effects.

✦   ✦   ✦

Using Color Mattes and Backdrops

During the course of a video production, you may need to create a simple, colored background video track. You may need the track to be a solid color background for text, or you may need to create a background for transparency effects. This chapter looks at how to use colored background mattes and still-frame background images in Adobe Premiere Pro. You learn to create a color background in Premiere Pro and to export a still frame from a clip to use as a backdrop. This chapter concludes with tutorials on creating backdrops in three popular digital imaging programs — Adobe Photoshop, Adobe Illustrator, and Corel Painter.

Creating a Color Matte

If you need to create a colored background for text or graphics, use a Premiere Pro *color matte.* Unlike many of the Premiere Pro video mattes, a color matte is a solid matte that comprises the entire video frame. A color matte can be used as a background or as a temporary track placeholder until you've shot or created the final track.

Note   You may want to use a black video as a background matte. To create a black video, choose File ➪ New ➪ Black Video.

An advantage of using a colored background is its versatility. After you create the color matte, you can easily change its color with a few clicks of the mouse.

Follow these steps to create a color matte in Premiere Pro:

1. **With a project onscreen, choose File ➪ New ➪ Color Matte.** The Color Picker dialog box appears.

2. **Select a matte color.** If an exclamation mark appears next to the color swatches in the upper-right corner of the dialog box, as shown in Figure 16-1, you've chosen a color that is out of the NTSC color gamut. This color cannot be reproduced correctly in NTSC video. Click the exclamation mark to have Premiere Pro choose the next closest color.

 Cross-Reference   For more information on color gamuts, see Chapter 18.

Old color

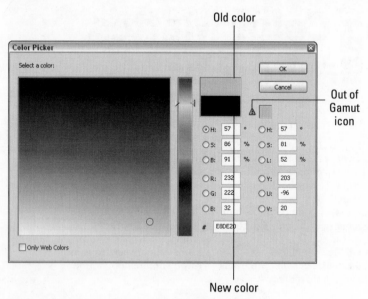

Out of
Gamut
icon

New color

Figure 16-1: The Premiere Pro Color Picker dialog box

3. Click OK to close the Color Picker dialog box.

4. In the Choose Name dialog box that appears, type a name for the color matte in the name field, as shown in Figure 16-2.

5. Click OK to place the matte in the Project panel.

6. To use the color matte, simply drag it from the Project panel into a video track.

Note   The default duration of a color matte is determined by the Still Frame setting in the General Preferences dialog box. To change the default setting, choose Edit ⇨ Preferences ⇨ General. In the Still Image Default Duration area, enter the number of frames that you want to use as the still image default.

Figure 16-2: The Choose Name dialog box

Creating a color matte from the Project panel

Follow these steps to use the Project panel to create a background matte using Premiere Pro:

Note   Before you begin, you must have a project onscreen.

1. **In the Project panel, click the New Item icon, which is located between the New Bin icon and the Trash icon, and choose Color Matte.**

2. **When the Color Picker dialog box appears, pick a color matte.**

3. **Click OK to close the Color Picker dialog box.** The Choose Name dialog box appears.

4. **Type a name for the color matte.**

5. **Click OK.** Instantly, the color matte appears in the Project panel, as shown in Figure 16-3, ready for you to drag it to the Timeline panel.

 Note   To change the duration of a matte, click it in the Project panel and choose Clip ⇨ Speed/ Duration. In the Clip Speed/Duration dialog box, click the Duration values to change them. Then click OK.

New Item icon

Figure 16-3: The Project panel with a color matte

Editing a color matte

The Premiere Pro color mattes have a distinct advantage over simply creating a colored background in the Title panel or creating titles in another program with a colored background. If you are using a Premiere Pro color matte, you can quickly change colors if the original matte color proves unsuitable or unattractive.

To change the colors of a color matte after you've placed it into the Timeline, simply double-click the matte clip in the Timeline. When Premiere Pro's Color Picker appears, pick a new color and then click OK. After you click OK, the color changes, not only in the selected clip but also in all the clips in the tracks that use that color matte.

 Note   You can create a color matte in Premiere Pro and then animate and incorporate it into a project. Chapter 16 provides two examples of creating color mattes and incorporating them into projects.

Creating a Backdrop from a Still Frame

As you work in Premiere Pro, you may want to export a still frame from a video clip and save it in a graphic format so that you can use it in another program as part of a background. Figure 16-4 shows a collage we created using four frames from Digital Vision's CityMix royalty-free video clip collection (clip 567001f).

On the DVD-ROM   Digital Vision's CityMix 567001f.mov clip is in the Digital Vision folder that is in the Chapter 16 folder on the DVD that accompanies the book.

To create the collage in Figure 16-4, we found four frames we liked from video clip 567001f. We then exported these frames from Premiere Pro as PICT files. Then we imported the four still frames into Photoshop. Using layers, we composited the collage. We added text and lines. The final collage, shown in Figure 16-4, can be used as promotional material, such as a poster for the actual video clip. The final collage can also be re-imported into Premiere Pro and used as a backdrop of the opening title of a video production.

Figure 16-4: A backdrop created by exporting a frame from a video clip in Premiere Pro into Photoshop

Follow these steps to export and save a portion of a video clip and use the still frame as a backdrop:

Note   Before we begin, open or create a project containing a video clip in one of the Timeline panel's video tracks.

1. **Double-click the clip from which you want to create a backdrop in the Project panel.** The clip opens in the Clip panel.

2. **Use the Scrubbing tool and/or Frame Advance icon to move to the frame that you want to export.**

Cross-Reference

For more information on using the Clip panel, see Chapter 7.

3. **Choose File ➪ Export ➪ Frame.** The Export Frame dialog box appears.

4. **In the Export Frame dialog box, click the Settings button.** The Export Frame Settings dialog box appears.

5. **In the Export Frame Settings dialog box, choose Windows Bitmap, GIF, Targa, or TIFF from the File Type format drop-down menu.** If you choose GIF, your image can contain a maximum of 256 colors. If you want, you can have the frame imported into the Project panel onscreen by selecting the Add to Project When Finished option. Click OK to apply the settings and close the Export Frame Settings dialog box.

6. **In the Export Frame dialog box, click Save to save the file.** You can now import the image into Photoshop by loading the program and choosing File ➪ Open. Photoshop enables you to enhance or manipulate your image. If you want, you can create a collage, as shown in Figure 16-4, by dragging and dropping all the files into one file. You may also want to import the final Photoshop image into Premiere Pro. To import the final Photoshop file into a Premiere Pro project, choose File ➪ Import. Locate and select the file. Then click Open.

Creating Background Mattes in Photoshop

Adobe Photoshop is an extremely versatile program for creating full-screen background mattes, or backdrops. Not only can you edit and manipulate photographs in Photoshop, but you can also create black-and-white or grayscale images to be used as background mattes. In this section, you create various different Photoshop projects. First, you learn how to create a simple backdrop, showing you how to create a textured backdrop to use as a backdrop when superimposing titles and graphics. Then you create more complicated examples that illustrate more of Photoshop's digital imaging power.

To create a Photoshop background file in Adobe Photoshop, load Adobe Photoshop. Then create a new file using the File ➪ New command. In the New dialog box, click in the Name drop-down menu and name your file. Then type in the dimensions of your file. We set the Width to 720 pixels and the Height to 480 pixels. Set the Resolution to 72 pixels, the Color Mode to RGB Color, and the Background Contents to White. Then click OK. To view Safe Action Margins and Safe Title Margins, you have to create them using Guides, as shown in Figure 16-5. To do so, first choose View ➪ Rulers. Then choose Edit ➪ Preferences ➪ Units & Rulers. In the Preferences Units & Rulers dialog box, set the Ruler drop-down menu to Picas and click OK.

Note

To have Premiere Pro create a Photoshop file with the same dimensions as the project you are working on, Choose File ➪ New ➪ Photoshop File. In the Save Photoshop File As dialog box, name the file and click Save. Adobe Photoshop is loaded with the new Photoshop file ready for you to work on. The changes you make to the Photoshop file are updated in Premiere Pro. The Photoshop file appears in the Project panel of your Premiere Pro project.

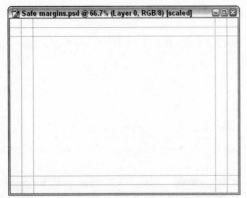

Figure 16-5: A Photoshop file created using guides as Safe Action Margins and Safe Title Margins

To make Safe Action Margins, click the Ruler on the left side and drag to the 3 pica mark. Again click the Ruler on the left side, and drag to the 57 pica mark. Next click the top Ruler, and drag to the 2 pica mark. Again click the top Ruler, and drag to the 38 pica mark. If you make a mistake, choose View ➪ Clear Guides. To lock the guides in place choose, View ➪ Lock Guides.

To make Safe Title Margins, click the Ruler on the left side and drag to the 6 pica mark. Again click the Ruler on the left side, and drag to the 54 pica mark. Next click the top Ruler, and drag to the 4 pica mark. Again click the top Ruler, and drag to the 36 pica mark. If you make a mistake, choose View ➪ Clear Guides. To lock the guides in place choose, View ➪ Lock Guides.

After you are finished editing the Photoshop background file, choose File ➪ Save. In the Save dialog box, save the file in Photoshop format. To import the Photoshop file into Adobe Premiere Pro, load Premiere Pro and choose File ➪ Import. In the Import dialog box, locate the Photoshop file that you want to import, click it, and choose Open. The Photoshop background appears in the Project panel. To apply the Photoshop background to your movie, click and drag it to a Video track in the Timeline panel.

Adobe Premiere Pro 2.0 allows you to create a new Adobe Photoshop file to be used as a background. To do so, choose File ➪ New ➪ Photoshop File command. In the Save Photoshop File As dialog box, click the File Name drop down menu and name your file. Make sure that the Add to Project (Merged Layers) check box is selected. That way, when you save the file, it is automatically saved in the current Premiere project's Project panel. When you click the Save button to save the file, Premiere Pro loads Photoshop with the saved Photoshop file onscreen. The Photoshop file onscreen appears with the Safe Action Margins and the Safe Title Margins. As you work on this Photoshop file, make sure to keep saving it (File ➪ Save) so that it keeps being updated in the Premiere Pro Project panel. To apply the Photoshop background file to the Premiere Pro project you were working on, first activate Premiere Pro and then drag the Photoshop background file from the Project panel to a Video track in the Timeline panel.

Creating simple backgrounds with the Gradient tool

In this section, you use create several Photoshop gradient backgrounds. You use the Adobe Premiere Pro File ⇨ New ⇨ Photoshop File command to create the Photoshop files. Start by loading Adobe Premiere Pro and creating a new project. Then choose File ⇨ New ⇨ Photoshop File command. In the Save Photoshop File As dialog box, click the File Name drop down menu and name your file. Then click Save. Now you are ready to create a Photoshop background file to use in your Premiere Pro project.

Creating a Photoshop background with the Gradient tool and image-editing tools

Create a new project in Premiere Pro by choosing the File ⇨ New ⇨ Photoshop File command. In the Save Photoshop File As dialog box, click the File Name drop-down menu and name your file. Then click Save.

In Photoshop, use the Gradient tool to create a green and white gradient. Then use the Smudge tool to give it a painterly effect. Then use the Dodge, Burn, and Sponge tools to give it dimension. Use the Sharpen and Blur tools to give it texture. Figure 16-6 shows the effects of applying various imaging tools to a gradient to create an interesting Photoshop background. (Be sure to save your work.)

To add the Photoshop background to your Premiere Pro project, activate Premiere Pro and drag the Photoshop file from the Project panel to the Timeline panel.

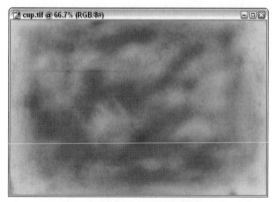

Figure 16-6: A Photoshop gradient background file created with Photoshop's Gradient tool and image-editing tools

Creating a Photoshop background with the Gradient tool and the Liquify filter

Create a new project in Premiere Pro by choosing the File ⇨ New ⇨ Photoshop File command. In the Save Photoshop File As dialog box, click the File Name drop-down menu and name your file. Then click Save.

In Photoshop, use the Gradient tool to create a black-and-white gradient. Then use the Filter ⇨ Liquify command to create an interesting background as shown in Figure 16-7.

To add the Photoshop background to your Premiere Pro project, activate Premiere Pro and drag the Photoshop file from the Project panel to the Timeline panel.

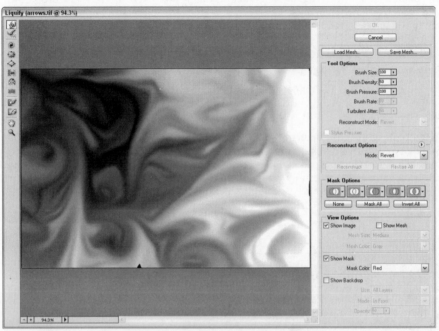

Figure 16-7: A Photoshop gradient background file created with the Photoshop Liquify filter

Creating a Photoshop background with the Gradient tool and the Elliptical Marquee tool

Create a new project in Premiere Pro by choosing the File ⇨ New ⇨ Photoshop File command. In the Save Photoshop File As dialog box, click the File Name drop-down menu and name your file. Then click Save.

In Photoshop, use the Elliptical Marquee tool to make a selection. Then use the Gradient tool with a radial gradient to create a radial gradient in the selection. Continue to create various elliptical selections and fill them with radial gradients with the Gradient tool until you have a background that looks similar to the one shown in Figure 16-8. To give the background a more painterly effect, as seen in the right side of Figure 16-8, apply the Filter ⇨ Artistic ⇨ Paint Daubs command, seen in Figure 16-9. To create the effect in Figure 16-9, we applied the Paint Daubs command a few times using different settings. If you want to conserve the Photoshop background file with the elliptical gradients before applying the Paint Daubs filter and after applying the filter, you need to use the File ⇨ Save As command to create a duplicate file. Do this before applying any filters to your background.

To add the Photoshop background to your Premiere Pro project, activate Premiere Pro and drag the Photoshop file from the Project panel to the Timeline panel. To add a duplicate Photoshop file to your Premiere Pro project, you must use the File ▷ Import command. We talk more about this in the next section.

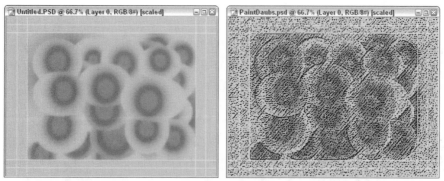

Figure 16-8: A Photoshop gradient background file created with Photoshop's Elliptical Marquee tool and Gradient tool (left), and after applying the Paint Daubs filter (right)

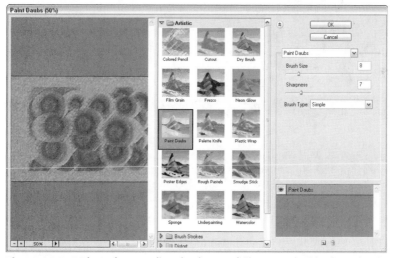

Figure 16-9: A Photoshop gradient background file created with Photoshop's Elliptical Marquee tool and the Gradient tool with the Paint Daubs filter dialog box

Creating a Photoshop background with the Gradient tool, Paintbrush tool, and layers

Create a new project in Premiere Pro by choosing the File ▷ New ▷ Photoshop File command. In the Save Photoshop File As dialog box, click the File Name drop-down menu and name your file Rainbow. Then click Save.

In Photoshop, use the Gradient tool to create a rainbow color gradient, as shown in Figure 16-10. Save the file. This file is automatically updated and saved into your Premiere Pro project. Then use the Save As command to create a copy of the file. Make sure to save the file in Photoshop format so that it can be saved with its layers. Call the file **RainbowLayers**. You'll import this file into Premiere as a Sequence file so that you can animate its layers, as shown in Figure 16-10.

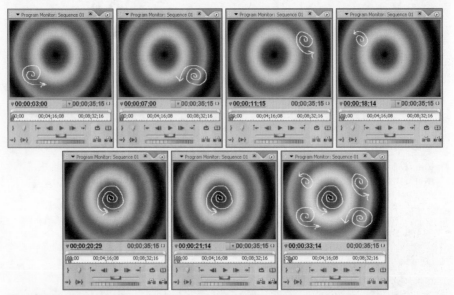

Figure 16-10: A Photoshop gradient background file created with layers using the Paintbrush tool, and then animated in Premiere Pro

In the RainbowLayers file, create a new layer by clicking the Create a New Layer icon in the Photoshop Layers panel. With white paint, use the Paintbrush tool to make a swirled arrow. Repeat this four more times so that you have five layers with five different swirled white arrows. Make sure you save your file in Photoshop format with its layers.

When you are finished, activate your Premiere Pro project. Notice that the RainbowLayers file is in the Project panel. Drag the RainbowLayers file from the Project panel to the Video 1 track of the Timeline panel.

To import the RainbowLayers file into your Premiere Pro project, choose File ⇨ Import to import the layered file. In the Import dialog box, locate the RainbowLayers file and click it. Click the Import As drop-down menu, choose Sequence, and click OK. Click the folder to view all the file's layers. Drag the RainbowLayers folder to the Video 3 track. To view the RainbowLayers file in the background of the entire RainbowLayers sequence, click and drag the left edge of the clip in the Video 1 track, as shown in Figure 16-11.

Save your Premiere Pro project by choosing File ⇨ Save. Then Preview it by clicking the Play button in the Program Monitor panel.

Figure 16-11: A Premiere Pro project with a Photoshop rainbow background and a Photoshop layer file imported as a sequence file

Orchid Flower Shop project

In this section, you create a project called Orchid Flower Shop. You use the Photoshop Gradient tool and several filters to create a background. Figure 16-12 shows the final background image created in Photoshop.

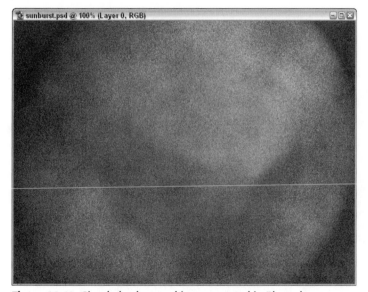

Figure 16-12: Simple background image created in Photoshop

After you create the background file, shown in Figure 16-12, for the Orchid Flower Shop project, you mask a flower from its background by using a transparent background, as shown in Figure 16-13. When this flower file is loaded into Premiere Pro, it reads the Photoshop file with a transparent background. Text appears on top of the two Photoshop images, created by using the Adobe Title Designer panel, as shown in Figure 16-14.

After you've created a background and isolated an image, you're ready to create the Orchid Flower Shop project. Figure 16-15 shows a frame from the Orchid Flower Shop project. In the frame, the orchid moves across the screen over the background from the far right to the far left.

Figure 16-13: Flower image with a transparent background

Figure 16-14: Orchid Flower Shop text created using the Adobe Title Designer

Figure 16-15: A frame from the Orchid Flower Shop project

Follow these steps to create the Orchid Flower Shop project:

1. **In Premiere Pro, choose File ⇨ New Project to create a new project.**

2. **In the New Project dialog box, set the preset to DV – NTSC Standard 48kHz.**

3. **Name your project, and click OK to create a new project.**

4. **Choose File ⇨ New ⇨ Photoshop File.** In the Save Photoshop File As dialog box, click the File Name drop-down menu and name your file. Then click Save.

If you want, you can import the images in Figures 16-12 (sunburst.psd) and 16-13 (orchid.psd) from the Chapter 16 folder, which is in the Tutorial Projects folder.

5. **Create a simple background in Photoshop (refer to Figure 16-12). Here's how:**

   a. **Set the foreground color to a light color, and set the background color to a darker shade of the same color.** To change the foreground and background colors, click the foreground and background swatches in the toolbox. In the Color Picker dialog box that appears, pick a color.

   b. **Click the Gradient tool in the toolbox.** Set the Gradient tool to use a Radial Gradient. The mode should be Normal, and the Opacity set to 100 percent.

   c. **With the Gradient tool selected, click and drag outward from the center of your image to create a gradient.**

   d. **With a radial gradient onscreen, choose Filter ⇨ Noise ⇨ Add Noise to add color to the gradient.**

   e. **Choose Filter ⇨ Render ⇨ Lighting Effects to add more depth and lighting variations.** Figure 16-16 shows the Lighting Effects dialog box.

   f. **Choose File ⇨ Save to save your file.** Save your file in Photoshop format. Then close the file.

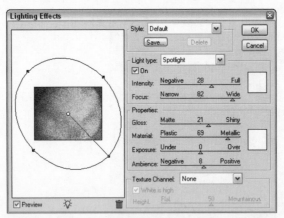

Figure 16-16: Use Photoshop's Lighting Effects filter to create a background.

6. **After you save your Photoshop background file, it is automatically updated in the Project panel of your Premiere Pro project. Activate your Premiere Pro project. Then drag and drop the Photoshop background image from the Project panel to the Video 1 track in the Timeline panel.**

7. **Now mask a flower from the background so you can import it into Premiere Pro with a transparent background. Here's how to isolate the orchid flower from its background:**

   a. **Choose File ➭ Open to open a file with flowers.** If you don't have a picture of flowers, you can load the orchid.psd file from the DVD that accompanies this book.

   b. **Double-click the Background layer in the Layers panel.**

   c. **In the New Layer dialog box that appears, rename the layer flower.** Click OK to close the dialog box.

   d. **Now mask the flower using one of Photoshop's masking tools.** You can use one of the Selection tools or the Select ➭ Color Range command to select the background. (For more information on using Photoshop's Color Range command, see Chapter 18.) When the background is selected, press Delete to have the flower appear on a transparent background. (By default, Photoshop represents a transparent background with a checkerboard.) You should now have a file with just a flower on a transparent background. Premiere Pro views an image on a transparent background the same way it does if the image had an alpha channel saved in the Channels panel.

Tip   If you are not familiar with Photoshop's masking features, you can use the Eraser tool to erase the background. If you make a mistake, either choose Edit ➭ Undo or File ➭ Revert. If you are familiar with Photoshop's tools, you may want to use the Pen tool to outline the flower and select it. If you use the Pen tool, you need to convert the path into a selection by choosing Make Selection from the Path drop-down menu. Next, reverse the selection by choosing Select ➭ Inverse and press Delete on your keyboard to erase the background and isolate the flower.

e. **Choose File ⇨ Save As to rename and save your file. In the Save As dialog box, name your file** OrchidLayer. **Then save your file in Photoshop format and have the Layers option selected.** This keeps the flower isolated from the background. Click Save, and close the file.

8. **Choose File ⇨ Import to import the Photoshop layer file (OrchidLayer.psd).** When you import a Photoshop file with a layer, the Import Layered File dialog box appears. In the Import Layered File dialog box, set the Import As drop down menu to Footage. Then click Choose Layer from the Layer Options. In the Choose Layer drop down menu, pick the layer you want. For the OrchidLayer.psd file, choose flower. Click OK to import the file. Drag the image with the masked (flower) in the Video 2 track.

Note   To extend the duration of either of the Photoshop clips that are in the Timeline panel, click the end of the clip and drag to the left.

9. **Select the image in the Video 2 track if it's not already selected.**

10. **Choose Window ⇨ Effect Controls.** The Motion controls appear in the Effect Controls panel, as shown in Figure 16-17.

11. **To create motion manually using the Program Monitor panel, first click on the transform icon that appears next to the word** *Motion* **in the Effect Controls panel.** Using the Program Monitor panel, drag the flower to the left, as shown in Figure 16-17.

Figure 16-17: The Motion settings in the Effect Controls panel allow you to add motion to a flower image that was created in Adobe Illustrator.

12. **To create motion from left to right, you need to create two keyframes.** First, click the Expand/Collapse icon to display the Motion controls. Then move the edit line to the beginning of the clip, and click the Position Toggle Animation icon to create the first keyframe. To create the last keyframe, move the edit line to the end of the clip. Then move the flower all the way to the right of the Program Monitor panel. The last (second) keyframe is created.

13. **Click the Play button in the Program Monitor panel to preview the motion.**

14. **Choose File ⇨ New ⇨ Title.** In the New Title dialog box that appears, name your title and click OK. The Adobe Title Designer panel opens.

15. **Create some text with the Type tool.** The Adobe Title Designer panel is shown in Figure 16-14.

16. **Save the title to make it appear in the Project panel.**

17. **Drag and drop the title clip from the Project panel to the Video 3 track in the Timeline panel, as shown in Figure 16-18.**

Figure 16-18: The Timeline panel for the Orchid Flower Shop project

18. **Choose File ⇨ Save to save the project.**

19. **Preview the file by clicking the Play button in the Program Monitor panel.** When the preview plays, you should see the text and flower visible over the background you created in Photoshop. To change the quality of the preview, click the Program Monitor menu and choose Highest Quality, Draft Quality, or Automatic Quality. By default, Premiere Pro sets the preview to Automatic Quality. To render the work area, choose Sequence ⇨ Render Work Area.

Creating background patterns with the Pattern command

This example shows you how to create a background pattern matte, shown in Figure 16-19, using the Pattern command in Photoshop 6.0 or greater. Using the Pattern command, you can quickly choose preset patterns and add 3D effects. The Pattern command creates a pattern on a new layer. After you save the pattern background in Photoshop, you can load it directly into Premiere Pro.

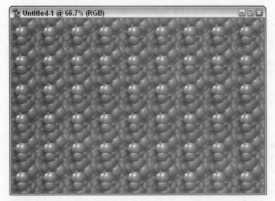

Figure 16-19: Background pattern matte created using Photoshop's Pattern command

Follow these steps to create a background pattern in Photoshop using the Pattern command:

1. **Create a new file in Photoshop by choosing File ⇨ New, and use the same pixel dimensions as you are using in your Premiere Pro project.** When you create the project, set the mode to RGB color and the background contents to Transparent.

2. **To create the pattern in a layer, choose Layer ⇨ New Fill Layer ⇨ Pattern.** The New Layer dialog box appears.

3. **In the New Layer dialog box, click OK.** The Pattern Fill dialog box opens, as shown in Figure 16-20. In the Pattern Fill dialog box, you can choose a pattern by clicking the pattern preview. When the drop-down menu of pattern thumbnails appears, make a selection. If you want, you can use the Scale option to scale the pattern.

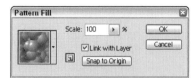

Figure 16-20: Photoshop's Pattern Fill dialog box.

4. **Click OK to create the pattern.**

5. **To add 3D or additional special effects to your pattern, choose Layer ⇨ Layer Style ⇨ Bevel and Emboss.** The Layer Style dialog box appears, as shown in Figure 16-21. To add more variation to the pattern, click the Contour drop-down menu and experiment with the contours. Notice that the Layer Style changes, as shown in Figure 16-22, when you click Contour. You can also click the Texture drop-down menu to add a texture to your image. Pick a pattern and experiment with the Scale and Depth sliders, which are shown in Figure 16-23. Use the Depth, Size, and Soften sliders to fine-tune the effect.

   The pattern is created with a mask. The layer mask thumbnail can be seen in the Layers panel.

6. **Choose Window ⇨ Layers to display the Layers panel.** The layer mask thumbnail appears next to the word *Pattern.*

7. **To use the pattern's mask to create special effects, select the Brush tool and pick a brush size. Set the painting color to black, and reduce the Opacity to 40 percent.** Then start drawing in the pattern. To erase your brushstrokes and start over, choose Edit ⇨ Fill. In the Fill dialog box, set the Use drop-down menu to White, the Mode to Normal, and the Opacity to 100 percent. Click OK.

Note   To remove the mask, choose Layer ⇨ Remove Layer Mask ⇨ Discard. Choosing this option removes the mask and discards any changes you may have made on the mask.

8. **When you've completed your background pattern, choose Layer ⇨ Flatten Image.**

9. **Save the file in Photoshop format.** The file can then be imported into any Premiere Pro project.

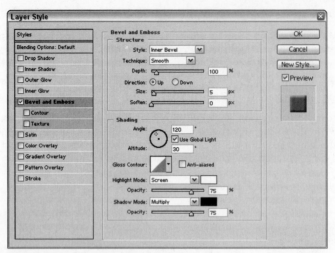

Figure 16-21: The Layer Style dialog box

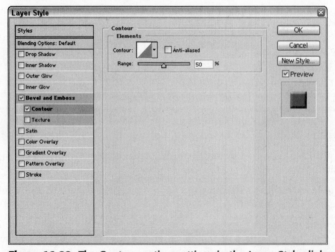

Figure 16-22: The Contour option settings in the Layer Style dialog box

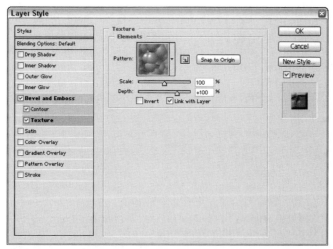

Figure 16-23: The Texture option settings in the Layer Style dialog box

Creating Background Mattes in Illustrator

In this section, you learn to create a project called Flowers Everywhere. To create this project, you use Adobe Illustrator to create a background matte, as shown in Figure 16-24.

Figure 16-24: Background matte
created in Adobe Illustrator

After you create an Illustrator background file, you take one of the elements (seen in Figure 16-25) from the Illustrator background file (seen in Figure 16-24) and copy it into a new file with a white background. Finally, after you've imported the Illustrator files into Premiere Pro, you use Premiere Pro's Adobe Title Designer panel to create text, shown in Figure 16-26, over the Illustrator background and image.

Figure 16-25: An Image from the Illustrator background file

Figure 16-26: Text created in Premiere Pro's Adobe Title Designer panel

Preparing a background matte to import

Follow these steps to create a background matte in Adobe Illustrator:

1. **Load Adobe Illustrator.**

2. **Choose File ➪ New to create a new file.** Pick an Artboard size. Make sure that the Color Mode is set to RGB Color and not to CMYK Color. (CMYK color is for print work.) Click OK to create a new file.

3. **To create the flowers shown in Figures 16-24 and 16-25, click the Polygon tool in the toolbox (which is located in the same place as the Rectangle tool).**

4. **With the Polygon tool selected, move to the center of the screen.**

5. **Alt-click to display the Polygon dialog box.**

6. **In the Polygon dialog box, set the Sides to 8.**

7. **Click OK to create a polygon.**

8. **Choose Filter ➪ Distort ➪ Punker & Bloat.**

9. **In the Punker & Bloat dialog box, drag the slider toward Bloat to about 100 percent.** Illustrator converts the polygon into a flower shape. To preview the effect before applying it, make sure that the Preview option is selected.

10. **Click OK to apply the effect.**

11. **Click the Ellipse tool in the toolbox.**

12. **Create a circle in the middle of the flower shape.** To create a perfect circle, press and hold the Shift key.

13. **Click the Select tool in the toolbox.**

14. **Click and drag over the flower and circle to select them.**

15. **Choose Edit ➪ Copy and Edit ➪ Paste to duplicate the flower.** Do this a few times, until you have a few flowers on the screen.

16. **Using the Color panel, pick colors for the flowers you created.**

17. **Use the Scale tool to scale some of the flowers.** Double-click the Scale tool in the tool-box. In the Scale dialog box, make sure that the Uniform option is selected. (Doing this prevents the flowers from being distorted when they are scaled.)

18. **Choose File ➪ Save to save the file in Illustrator format.** Now that you've created a background using Illustrator, you can easily pick one of the items from the background to use as a separate image in Premiere Pro.

19. **Before you close this file, select a flower for your image and choose Edit ➪ Copy.**

20. **While still in Illustrator, choose File ➪ New.**

21. **Paste the flower into the new file (with a white background) and save the file in Illustrator format.** In Figure 16-24, shown previously, we isolated a flower from the background and copied it into a new file to create the image shown in Figure 16-25.

Pulling together the Flowers Everywhere project

A great feature of using Adobe Illustrator with Premiere Pro is that Premiere Pro translates the blank areas of the Illustrator file as an alpha channel mask. You can now import the flower files that you just created into Premiere Pro and create the Flowers Everywhere project. In this project, the Bend video effect was applied to the background and the Bevel Alpha video effect was applied to the text in the top video track shown in Figure 16-27 (the Video 3 track). Figure 16-28 shows frames from the Flowers Everywhere project.

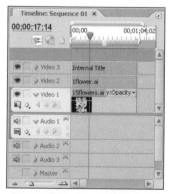

Figure 16-27: The Timeline panel used to create the Flowers Everywhere project

Figure 16-28: Frames from the Flowers Everywhere project

Follow these steps to create the Flowers Everywhere project:

1. **Open Adobe Premiere Pro.**

2. **Choose File ➪ New ➪ Project to create a new project.**

3. **In the New Project dialog box, choose a preset.**

4. **Click OK to apply the settings to the new project. The new project opens.**

5. **Choose Window ➪ Workspace ➪ Effects.** The Effects and Effect Controls panels are displayed.

6. **Choose File ➪ Import.**

On the DVD-ROM

If you want, you can load the images in Figure 16-24 (15flowers.ai) and Figure 16-25 (1flower.ai) from the Chapter 16 folder, which is in the Tutorial Projects folder on the DVD that accompanies this book.

7. **In the Import dialog box, locate and select the 15flowers.ai and 1flower.ai files.** Press and hold the Ctrl key to select more than one file.

8. **Click Open.** Premiere Pro imports the files into the Project panel.

9. **Drag the 15flowers.ai (background file) and 1flower.ai files to the Video 1 and 2 tracks, respectively.**

10. **Choose File ➪ New ➪ Title.** In the New Title dialog box that appears, name your title and click OK. The Adobe Title Designer panel opens.

11. **Create some text with the Type tool.**

12. **Close the Adobe Title Designer panel. Notice that it appears in the Project panel.**

13. **Drag and drop the title to the Video 3 track.**

Note   If you want, you can create two titles and set them side by side in the same video track. Then add a transition, such as the Cross Dissolve, to have a smooth transition between the two titles.

14. **Click the Video 2 track to reduce the opacity of the graphic.** Click the Expand/Collapse icon next to the Opacity option in the Effect Controls window. Then drag the Opacity value to the left.

Cross-Reference   See Chapter 15 to learn about fading clips and working with transparency.

15. **In the Effects panel, open the Video Effects bin (folder) to display the effects and open the Distort bin.**

16. **Drag the Bend effect from the panel, and drop it on the clip in the Video 1 track. In the Effects panel, click the Distort bin to display the Bend Effect.** Then click the Setup icon in the Effect Controls panel to display the Bend Settings dialog box. Figure 16-29 shows the Bend Settings dialog box.

17. **Save the file.**

18. **Click the Play button in the Program Monitor panel to preview the file to view the flowers and Bend effect.**

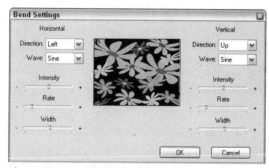

Figure 16-29: The Bend Settings dialog box with flower background file created in Illustrator

Creating Backgrounds with Corel Painter

You can use Corel Painter to create background mattes and QuickTime movies from graphics. Figure 16-30 displays the Timeline panel for a project called Summer Fun. The Video 1 track shows a background created in Painter. The Video 2 track features an animated horse created in Painter and imported in Premiere Pro as a QuickTime movie. The Video 3 track displays the text Summer Sun, which was created by using Adobe Premiere's Title Designer panel.

Here's how we created the project. To create the landscape background, we used Painter's shape tools and layers. To create the animated horse, we first created a new movie instead of a new canvas. Next we made a horse as a layer at the far right of the screen. We filled the horse with a gold color. Then we slowly moved the horse to the left in different frames. We saved the movie in QuickTime movie format.

Figure 16-30: The Summer Fun project Timeline panel

In Figure 16-31, you can see the frames for the Summer Fun project. In the frames, you can see a horse moving over a superimposed background. To add some interest to the text, we applied motion to it.

Figure 16-31: Frames from the Summer Fun project

Follow these steps to assemble the graphic elements in Premiere Pro to create the Summer Fun project:

1. **Create a new project.**

2. **Choose File ➪ Import.** Locate the Summer folder, and click the Import Folder button. The Summer folder appears in the Project window. Open the folder to view the clips (GoldHorse.mov, SummerFun.prtl, and Sunshine.psd).

On the DVD-ROM

You can find the files used to create the Summer Fun project in the Summer project folder that is in the Chapter 16 folder, which is located in the Tutorial Projects folder that is on the DVD that accompanies this book.

3. **Drag the GoldHorse.mov clip to the Video 1 track.**

4. **Drag Sunshine.psd (the background file) to the Video 2 track.**

5. **Choose Window ➪ Workspace ➪ Effects to display both the Effects and Effect Controls.**

6. **To superimpose both clips, use the Luma Key effect.** In the Effects window, click the Expand/Collapse icon to display all the effects. Open the Keying bin to display the Keying effects. Click and drag the Luma Key effect to the Video 2 track.

7. **In the Effect Controls panel, click the Expand/Collapse icon to display the Luma Key settings.** Click and drag the settings until the background from the video clip in the Video 2 track is removed. As you work, view the effects in the Program Monitor panel.

8. **Now you are ready to add some text to your project.** Choose File ➪ New ➪ Title. In the Adobe Title Designer panel, use the Type tool to create some text, as shown in Figure 16-32. When you are finished creating and stylizing your title, save it so that it appears in the Project window.

9. **Drag the title file to the Video 3 track.**

10. **Click the Title file icon in the Video 3 track.**

11. **To apply motion to the Title file, create two keyframes:**

   a. **Click the Expand/Collapse icon to display the Motion settings, and click the word *Motion*.**

   b. **Move the text to where you want your motion to begin, and move the edit line to the beginning of the Timeline.**

   c. **Click the Toggle Animation icon in front of the Position option.** A keyframe is created.

   d. **To create a second keyframe, move the edit line to the end of the Timeline and move the text in the Program Monitor panel to where you want the motion to end.**

   e. **Click the Add/Remove Keyframe to add the second keyframe.** Figure 16-33 shows the Effect Controls panel with the Motion settings.

12. **Click the Play button in the Program Monitor panel to preview the project.**

13. **Save your file.**

Figure 16-32: The Summer Fun Title Designer panel

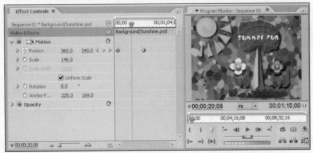

Figure 16-33: The Motion settings are found in the Effect Controls panel.

Summary

You can use Premiere Pro's color matte command to easily create solid-color backgrounds for text and graphics. This chapter covered these topics:

✦ You can use Adobe Photoshop, Adobe Illustrator, or Corel Painter to create your own backgrounds to use as background mattes.

✦ Photoshop and Illustrator files can be imported directly into Premiere Pro. All you need to do is save the Photoshop files in Photoshop format and the Illustrator files in Illustrator format.

✦   ✦   ✦

Creating Motion Effects in Premiere Pro

Motion creates interest and adds to the power of just about any presentation. In Adobe Premiere Pro, you can jazz up presentations by sending a title or logo spinning across the screen or bouncing a clip off the borders of the frame area. You can animate books by using a graphic with an alpha channel, or you can superimpose one moving object over another. You can also use traveling matte effects to create movies for the Web. A traveling matte effect has one image within a shape that moves across the screen over another image. This chapter not only shows you how to create traveling mattes, but it also shows you how to set titles and graphics in motion, including how to make them bend and rotate onscreen.

To create these motion effects, you use Premiere Pro's Motion effects controls, found in the Effect Controls panel.

Touring the Motion Effects Controls in the Effect Controls Panel

Premiere Pro's Motion effects controls allow you to scale, rotate, and move a clip. By animating the motion controls, you can wake up an otherwise boring image by setting it in motion over time using keyframes. You can make any clip move and jiggle or make a still frame move across the screen. (See Chapter 12 to learn how to use Premiere Pro's Motion effects controls to add motion to your titles.) The Motion effects are found in the Effect Controls panel, which is shown in Figure 17-1.

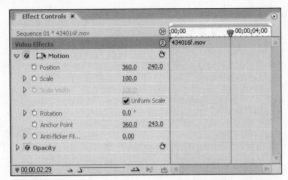

Figure 17-1: The Effect Controls panel and the Motion
effects controls

To use Premiere Pro's Motion effects controls, you need to have a project onscreen with a video clip selected in the Timeline panel. Follow these steps to create a new project, import two video clips, and display the Motion effect controls:

1. **Choose File ⇨ New ⇨ Project to create a new project. In the New Project dialog box, choose a preset, name the project, and click OK.**

2. **Load two video clips by choosing File ⇨ Import.** You can use your own video, or you can use Digital Vision's Ambient Space 434016f.mov and 434011f.mov files found on the DVD that accompanies this book. After you import the file into your project, it appears in the Project panel.

3. **If you want, load a sound clip by choosing File ⇨ Import. Locate a sound, and click Open.** (We used Digital Vision's Cool Lounge 666005aw.wav file.) Then drag the sound clip from the Project panel to Audio track 1 in the Timeline panel.

On the DVD-ROM

Digital Vision's Ambient Space 434016f.mov and 434011f.mov video clips and Digital Vision's Cool Lounge 666005aw.wav are found in the Digital Vision folder, in the Chapter 17 folder, which is in the Tutorial Projects folder on the DVD that accompanies this book.

4. **Next, click one of the video clips in the Project panel and drag it to Video 1 Track in the Timeline panel. Then drag the other video clip to Video 2 Track in the Timeline panel.** We dragged Digital Vision's Ambient Space 434011f.mov to Video 1 Track and Digital Vision's Ambient Space 434016f.mov to Video 2 track. The Timeline panel should now have two video clips, as shown in Figure 17-2.

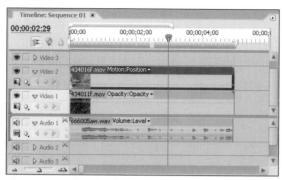

Figure 17-2: The Timeline panel with two video clips and a sound clip

> **Note**
>
> You can choose how a clip is displayed on the Timeline by clicking the Set Display Style icon and then clicking one of the options. To view the Set Display Style icon, you need to expand a video track by clicking the triangle in front of the word *Video*.

5. **With the clip in Video 2 Track selected, choose Window ➪ Effect Controls.** To display the Motion effects controls, click the triangle in front of the word *Motion.*

6. **To scale a clip's height and width in unison, make sure the Uniform Scale option is selected. Then click and drag over the value in the Scale section, or click the value, type a new value, and press Enter.** Acceptable ranges are from 0 to 700. Enter 0 to make the clip invisible; enter 600 to enlarge the clip seven times its normal size. We scaled our clip down to 42 percent, as shown in Figure 17-3.

> **Note**
>
> To scale the height of a clip separately from the width, remove the check mark from the Uniform Scale option in the Effect Controls panel.

Figure 17-3: The Effect Controls panel and Program Monitor panel after adjusting the Motion effects Scale option

7. **Use the Rotate option to rotate a clip around its center point.** To rotate, click and drag the Rotate degree value or enter a value in the Rotation degree field. To create one complete rotation, enter 360 degrees. We rotated the clip 90 degrees.

8. **To see a preview of how the Motion effects Scale and Rotation have changed the clip in Video 2 Track, open the Program Monitor panel by choosing Window ➪ Program Monitor, and then either click the Play button in the Program Monitor panel or click and drag the shuttle or jog slider.** You can also see a preview by moving the current-time indicator in the Effect Controls panel or the Timeline panel. Notice that the clip has been scaled and rotated and that it remains scaled and rotated throughout the duration of the clip.

Tip   To go back to the default motion settings, click the Reset icon to the left of the word *Motion* in the Effect Controls panel.

9. **To move the position of a clip, click and drag the Position values to change the values and move the clip on its X-axis and Y-axis.** To move the clip from its center point, click and drag the Anchor Point values.

10. **To move a clip manually, click the Transform icon, which is next to the word *Motion* in the Effect Controls panel.** Notice that in the Program Monitor panel, a wireframe appears around the clip, as shown in Figure 17-4. Click inside the wireframe, and move the clip. As you move the clip, the Position values change. You can also manually rotate and scale a clip. To scale a clip, move the cursor on either a corner or side handle. To keep the clip's proportions, press and hold the Shift key as you scale. To rotate a clip manually, move the cursor just outside of either a corner or side handle and drag in the direction you want to rotate.

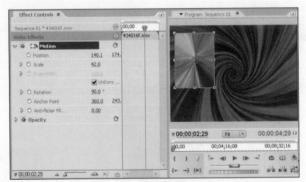

Figure 17-4: Notice that a wireframe appears around the active clip in the Program Monitor when you manually adjust a clip.

11. **Click the Play button in the Program Monitor panel to preview the effects of the Position settings.** To render a work area, choose Sequence ➪ Render Work Area. Notice that the clip starts at the new position and remains there throughout the duration of the clip. To move the clip's position to different places throughout the duration of the clip, you need to set keyframes. The next section explains more about working with keyframes.

Note By default, Premiere Pro displays a preview in Automatic Quality. To change the preview display, click the Monitor panel menu and choose Highest Quality or Draft Quality.

Setting Keyframes to Create Motion Effects Using the Effect Controls Panel

To create motion that moves in more than one direction or changes size or rotation throughout the duration of a clip, you need to add keyframes. You can use keyframes to create effects at specific points in time — for example, to create an effect using a graphic or video clip in motion simultaneously with another video clip. Using keyframes, the effect can occur at a specific point in your narration, and you can also add music to the effect. The motion path is displayed when the Transform icon is selected (it is next to the word *Motion*) in the Effect Controls panel. When the motion path is displayed, keyframes appear as points in the motion path and designate a change in position.

 Note You can also add keyframes to the motion path at specific points by clicking the Timeline. (The Timeline is described in the next section.)

Here's how to add keyframes to a motion path to create the effect of a clip moving diagonally from top left to bottom right:

1. **Choose File ➪ New ➪ Project to create a new project. In the New Project dialog box, choose a preset, name the project, and click OK.**

2. **Choose File ➪ Import. In the Import dialog box, locate and select a clip. Then choose Open to import a clip into the Project panel.** We used Digital Vision's Ambient Space 434006f.mov file.

 On the DVD-ROM If you want, you can use Digital Vision's Ambient Space 434006f.mov, which is found in the Digital Vision folder, in the Chapter 17 folder, which is in the Tutorial Projects folder on the DVD that accompanies this book.

3. **Drag the clip from the Project panel to Video 2 track of the Timeline.** This is the clip to which you will apply motion effects.

 Note At any time, you can import another clip into this project and use it as the background. After you import the clip, drag it into Video 1 track of the Timeline. You can also import a sound clip. After you've imported a sound, drag it into Audio 1 track.

4. **Click the clip that is in Video 2 track to select it.**

5. **Choose Window ➪ Workspace ➪ Effects to display both the Effect Controls panel and the Program Monitor panel. Then click the Effect Controls tab to display it.**

6. **In the Effect Controls panel, click the triangle in front of the word *Motion* to display the motion effects properties.**

7. **Move the current-time indicator in the Timeline of the Effect Controls panel to the beginning of the clip.**

Note Set the Timeline to show clips in one-second intervals by clicking and dragging the Time Zoom Level slider at the bottom of the panel.

8. **Reduce the size of the clip to 39 percent by using the Motion effects Scale property.** The clip is scaled 39 percent throughout its duration. If you want to rotate the clip, change the rotation value for the Rotation property.

9. **In the Effect Controls panel, click on the Transform icon, which is next to the word** *Motion,* **to be able to see the motion path as it is created.** Notice that the clip is selected with an outline around it.

10. **To create a starting point, move the clip in the Program Monitor panel to the top-left corner of the panel.**

11. **To create the first keyframe, click the Toggle Animation icon in front of the word** *Position* **in the Effect Controls panel.**

12. **To set a second keyframe, move the current-time indicator in the Effect Controls panel to the right. Then click in the middle of the clip, and move it to the center of the Program Monitor panel.** Notice that a second keyframe is automatically created and that a motion path is displayed from keyframe one to keyframe two, shown in Figure 17-5. Also notice that a Value and Velocity graph is created for the Position control. The Position control can be adjusted by using these graphs. To view the Position graph, click the triangle in front of the word *Position.*

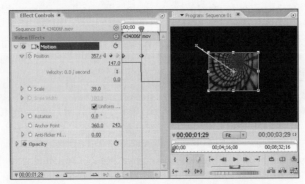

Figure 17-5: The motion path is between keyframes one and two.

13. **To set a third keyframe (the last keyframe), move the current-time indicator in the Effect Controls panel to the right (toward the end of the clip). Then in the Program Monitor panel, click in the middle of the clip and move it to the bottom-right side.** Notice that a third keyframe is automatically created and that the motion path is showing a specific point for each keyframe, as shown in Figure 17-6. Notice also the change to the graphs.

First Keyframe

Show/Hide Timeline View

Show/Hide Fixed Effects

Currently selected video clip

Display Outline and Motion Path

Timeline ruler

Clip's name

Current-time indicator

Collapse/Expand triangle | Reset | Last Keyframe | Motion F

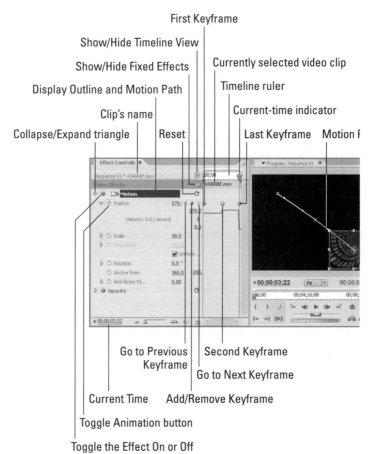

Go to Previous
Keyframe

Second Keyframe

Go to Next Keyframe

Current Time | Add/Remove Keyframe

Toggle Animation button

Toggle the Effect On or Off

Figure 17-6: The motion path is between keyframes two and three.

14. **Move the current-time indicator to the beginning of the clip, and click the Play button in the Program Monitor panel to preview the motion effect.** To preview specific segments of the motion effect, click and drag the current-time indicator in the Timeline of the Effect Controls panel.

Note

For more motion path contolrs, you may want to try using Adobe After Effects. For more information on using After Effects, see Chapters 27, 30, and 31.

Using the Timeline Panel to Preview and Add Keyframes

The Timeline panel allows you to view, add, and edit motion keyframes very much as you do using the Effect Controls panel.

Follow these steps to preview keyframes in the Timeline panel:

1. **Onscreen you should have a project with a video clip in the Timeline panel.**

2. **Click the Collapse/Expand Track triangle next to the name of the video track with the video clip. Then click the Show Keyframes icon, and click Show Keyframes.** Notice that a line appears in the area below the clip's name. If the video clip has any motion effect keyframes applied to it, you see white diamonds representing the keyframes on the line, as shown in Figure 17-7. To the right of where the clip's name appears is a drop-down menu displaying the Motion Effect controls.

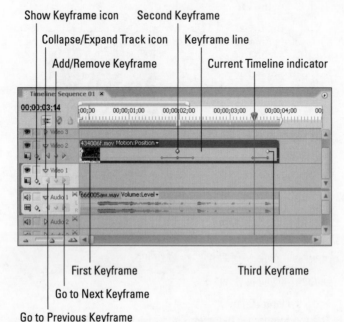

Figure 17-7: A preview of motion keyframes in the Timeline panel

3. **Click and drag the current-time indicator in the Timeline panel to see the preview of the motion in the Monitor panel.** To see a preview of the motion path, make sure that the Transform icon is selected in the Effect Controls panel (it is next to the word *Motion*).

Adding keyframes using the Timeline panel is the same as adding keyframes using the Timeline in the Effect Controls panel. Here's how to add keyframes in the Timeline panel:

1. **Move the current-time indicator in the Timeline panel to where you want to add a keyframe.**

2. **Click the Motion drop-down menu, and choose the control you want to affect.**

3. **Either numerically make the Motion effect change to one of the Motion effect controls you choose, or manually adjust the clip in the Monitor panel.**

4. **Click the Add/Remove Keyframe icon in the Timeline panel to add a keyframe.**

For more information on editing keyframes, see the next section.

Editing Motion Paths

To edit motion paths, you can move, delete, or add keyframes, or even copy and paste them. Sometimes, by adding keyframes you can create smoother motion paths.

Follow these steps to add a keyframe:

1. **Select the clip you want to animate.**

2. **Move the current-time indicator to where you want to add a keyframe.**

3. **To add a keyframe, use the Effect Controls panel or the Timeline panel.**

4. **To add a keyframe using the Effect Controls panel, turn on the Toggle Animation stopwatch.** If the Toggle Animation stopwatch is already activated, click the Add/Remove Keyframe icon to add another keyframe.

5. **To add a keyframe using the Timeline panel, click the Add/Remove Keyframe icon or press and hold the Ctrl key as you use the Pen tool or the Selection tool to add a keyframe to the motion line.**

Moving a keyframe point

After you add a motion keyframe, you can return to it at any time to move it. You can move a motion keyframe point using either the Effect Controls panel or the Timeline panel. You can also move a keyframe point using the motion path that is displayed in the Monitor panel. When you move the keyframe point in the Effect Controls or Timeline panel, you change when the motion effect occurs on the Timeline. When you move the keyframe point in the motion path, you affect the shape of the motion path.

Follow these steps to move a keyframe point using the Effect Controls or Timeline panel:

1. **Move the current-time indicator to where you want to move the keyframe.** As you move the current-time indicator, use the Info panel to find the correct location.

2. **Select the keyframe point that you want to move by clicking it with the mouse.** When you click a keyframe point in the Timeline panel, the cursor displays its position on the Timeline.

Note   To select more than one keyframe at a time, press and hold the Shift key as you select the keyframe point.

3. **Click and drag the selected keyframe point to the new location.**

Follow these steps to move a keyframe point using the motion path displayed in the Monitor panel:

1. **To display the motion path in the Program Monitor panel, select the Transform icon, which is next to the word *Motion* in the Effect Controls panel.**

2. **Select the keyframe point that you want to move by clicking it with the mouse.**

3. **Click and drag the selected keyframe point to the new location.**

These tips help you make intricate edits on the motion path:

✦ To move a keyframe on the motion path one pixel at a time, press one of the directional arrow keys on your keyboard.

✦ To move the motion path five pixels at a time, hold down the Shift key and press a directional arrow key on your keyboard.

✦ Click in the Info box below the Timeline, and enter a specific coordinate for the point on the path. When you select a point, the point number appears in the Info box. For example, if you want to center the clip in the middle of the screen, enter 0,0 in the box. If you enter a positive number in the first box, the clip moves to the right. If you enter a negative number, the clip moves to the left. If you enter a positive number in the right box, the clip moves down; entering a negative number makes the clip move up. For example, if you enter –10,10, the clip moves ten pixels to the left and ten pixels down from the middle of the screen.

Deleting keyframe points

As you edit, you may want to delete a keyframe point. To do this, simply select the point or points and press the Delete key. If you want to delete all the keyframe points for a Motion effect option, click the Toggle Animation icon in the Effect Controls panel. A warning prompt appears asking whether you want to delete all existing keyframes; if so, click OK.

Copying and pasting keyframe points

Follow these steps to copy a keyframe point and paste it in another place in the Timeline:

1. **To copy a keyframe point, you first need to select it by clicking it.**

2. **Choose Edit ➪ Copy.**

3. **Move the current-time indicator to the new location.**

4. **Choose Edit ➪ Paste.**

Adding keyframes to change a motion path's speed

Premiere Pro determines motion speed by the distance between keyframes. To increase the speed of motion, set keyframes further apart. To slow the speed of motion, create keyframes that are closer together.

Note The speed of a motion can also be adjusted by moving the handles of a keyframe using a Bezier interpolation. See the next section for details.

Follow these steps to change the speed of motion:

1. **If you don't already have keyframes, create keyframes on the Timeline by using either the Effect Controls panel or Timeline panel (see the steps earlier in this chapter).**

2. **To increase motion speed, drag keyframes further apart. To decrease motion speed, drag keyframes closer together. To move a keyframe, click the keyframe to select it, and then click and drag the keyframe point and move it on the Timeline.**

Note You can also use the Clip ⇨ Speed/Duration command to change the speed and/or duration of a clip.

Changing a keyframe's interpolation method

Premiere Pro interpolates the data between one keyframe and another. The interpolation method used has a dramatic effect on how the motion effect is displayed. By changing the interpolation method you can change the speed, smoothness, and shape of a motion path. The most common keyframe interpolation methods used are Linear interpolation and Bezier interpolation. To view the different interpolation methods for a keyframe, right-click a keyframe in the Timeline panel. When the Interpolation menu appears, as shown in Figure 17-8, you can pick a new interpolation method.

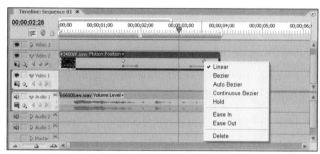

Figure 17-8: Right-click on a keyframe in the Timeline panel to display the Interpolation menu.

Following are different interpolation methods:

✦ Linear interpolation creates a uniform rate of motion change.

✦ The Bezier interpolation methods (Bezier, Auto Bezier, and Continuous Bezier) allow for smoother motion changes.

✦ Hold interpolation creates abrupt motion changes. It can be used to create a strobe effect.

✦ Ease In and Ease Out interpolation allows you to have a slow motion change or a fast motion change. It also allows a gradual start and finish.

Linear interpolation versus Bezier interpolation

The motion effect results of a animating the Motion Position property controls are determined by various factors. The effect that a Position's motion path has is determined by how many keyframes are used, what type of interpolation method a keyframe uses, and the shape of the Position's motion path. Both the number of keyframes used and the interpolation method greatly affect a motion path's speed and smoothness. Figure 17-9 shows a Position motion path in the shape of a V, and Figure 17-10 shows a Position motion path in the shape of a U. Both paths were created using three keyframes. The three keyframes were created by animating the

Motion Position's property. The V shape was created by applying the Linear interpolation method on the second keyframe in Figure 17-9. The U shape was created by applying the Bezier interpolation method on the second keyframe in Figure 17-10.

A motion path is displayed in the Program Monitor panel, as shown in Figures 17-9 and 17-10. The motion path is made up of tiny white dots. Each dot represents a frame in the clip. Each X on the white path represents a keyframe. The spacing between the dots determines how fast or slow the motion occurs. The farther apart the dots are spaced, the faster the rate of motion. Therefore, the closer together the dots are, the slower the rate of motion. If the dots vary in spacing, the motion rate varies. The dots represent Temporal Interpolation because it has to do with how fast or slow a motion path works over time. The shape of the motion path has to do with Spatial Interpolation because it has to do with how the shape of the motion path is displayed in its spatial surroundings.

In the Effect Controls panel, the motion path is displayed by a graph, as shown in Figures 17-9 and 17-10, and the keyframes are different icons depending upon the interpolation method used. Notice that in Figures 17-9 and 17-10, the second keyframe icons in the Effect Controls panel are different. The keyframe icon in Figure 17-9 looks like a diamond. This shows it is using Linear interpolation. The second keyframe icon in Figure 17-10 looks like an hourglass. This shows it is using Bezier interpolation. An Auto Bezier interpolation icon is represented by a circle icon. Also notice in Figure 17-9 and 17-10 that the graph in the Effect Controls panel is different for a keyframe with a Linear interpolation and a keyframe with a Bezier interpolation.

Tip　　Right-click a keyframe in the Timeline panel, Program Monitor panel, or Effect Controls panel to view or change interpolation methods. Ctrl-click a keyframe in the Timeline panel to automatically change from one interpolation method to another.

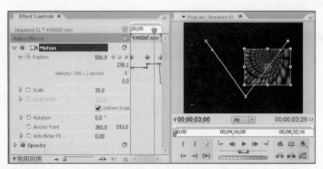

Figure 17-9: The Program Monitor panel and Effect Controls panel show the middle keyframe of the Position Motion path using Linear interpolation.

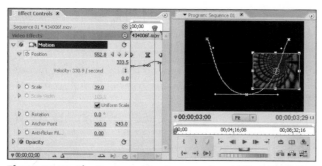

Figure 17-10: The Program Monitor panel and Effect Controls panel show the middle keyframe of the Position Motion path using Bezier interpolation.

Using Bezier interpolation to adjust the smoothness of a motion path

To adjust the smoothness of a Bezier curve, you use Bezier handles. Bezier handles are two-directional lines that control the shape of the Bezier curve. The directional lines for both the Bezier and Continuous interpolation can be adjusted. For Auto Bezier, the Bezier curve is created automatically. The Auto Bezier option does not allow you to adjust the curves shape. The advantage of using Bezier interpolation is that the two Bezier handles can be manipulated independently of one another. This means that the incoming handle and the outgoing handle can have different settings.

Dragging the Bezier handles up accelerates the change of motion. Dragging the handles down decelerates the change of motion. Increasing the length of the directional lines (dragging away from the center point) increases the size of the curve and spreads the tiny white dots farther apart, making the motion effect faster. Decreasing the length of the directional lines (dragging toward the center point) decreases the size of the curve and brings the tiny white dots closer together, making the motion effect slower. You can make more dramatic motion effects by varying the angle and length of directional lines. The Bezier handles can be adjusted in the Program Monitor panel or by using the Effect Controls panel.

Try it!

The best way to understand how the interpolation method works is to try it! Here's how:

1 **Create a new project.**

2. **With a project onscreen, drag a clip from the Project panel to a Video track in the Timeline panel.** We used the same clip we used in the previous sections of this chapter: Digital Vision's Ambient Space 434006f.mov.

3. **In the Effect Controls panel, click the triangle in front of the word** *Motion* **to display the Position, Scale, Rotation, and Anchor Point properties.**

4. **Set the Motion Scale property to 39 percent.**

5. **Use the Timeline panel or the Effect Controls panel to move the current-time indicator to the beginning of the clip.**

6. In the Program Monitor panel, click the clip and move it to the top-left hand corner of the panel.

7. Click the Position Toggle Animation icon to create a Position keyframe.

8. Using the Effect Controls panel, move the current-time indicator to the middle of the clip. Then move the clip in the Program Monitor to the bottom-middle of the panel to create a second keyframe.

9. Using the Effect Controls panel, move the current-time indicator to the end of the clip. Then move the clip in the Program Monitor to the top-right corner of the panel to create a third keyframe. Notice the motion path in the Program Monitor panel.

10. In the Effect Controls panel, click the triangle in front of the word *Position* to display the Position graph.

11. Try different interpolation methods. To change interpolation methods for the second keyframe, Ctrl-click it in the Timeline panel, Program Monitor panel, or the Effect Controls panel. Try also adjusting the Bezier handles to change the shape of the Bezier curve. Alternate from Bezier to Linear interpolation, and vice versa. Slowly ease in and out keyframes. Use the Hold interpolation to animate the clip rotating at a specific point in time.

12. Try experimenting with the effects of changing the shape of the motion path.

Adding Effects to Motion paths

After you've animated an object, title, or clip you may want to apply some other effects to it. Change the moving object's opacity to make it translucent. Apply one of the Image Control video effects or one of the Color Correcting video effects if you want to color correct the moving object. Use some of the other video effects to create some interesting special effects.

Changing opacity

In the Fixed Effects section of the Effect Controls panel, you find the Motion Effect controls and the Opacity controls. By reducing the opacity of a clip, you make the clip more translucent. To change the opacity of a clip throughout its duration, click and drag to the left on the Opacity percent value. You can also change the Opacity percent field by clicking in the field and then typing a number and pressing Enter. Alternatively, you can expand the Opacity controls by clicking the triangle in front of the Opacity name and then clicking and dragging the Opacity slider.

To set keyframes for the Opacity using the Effect Controls panel, follow these steps:

1. Activate the Toggle Animation icon.

2. Change the Opacity field, and click the Toggle Keyframe icon to set a keyframe.

To set keyframes for the Opacity using the Timeline panel, follow these steps:

1. Click the Show Keyframes icon.

2. Choose Opacity from the clip's title drop-down menu, and click the Add/Remove Keyframe icon to add a keyframe.

To change the Opacity field, use the white line below the clip's name. Click and drag down on the white line to reduce the opacity of the clip. For more information on using the Opacity controls, see Chapter 15.

Applying special effects

After you've animated a clip using the Fixed Effects controls (Motion and Opacity) in the Effect Controls panel, you may find that you want to add a few more effects to your clip. You can find various effects in the Video Effects bin (folders) of the Effects panel. To adjust an image's color, try using one of the Image Control video effects or one of the Color Correcting video effects. For more information on adjusting color using video effects, see Chapter 18. If you want to distort a clip, try using one of the Distort video effects. For more information on using the video effects, see Chapter 14. Follow these steps to add effects to a clip:

1. **Start by moving the current-time indicator on the Timeline in the Effect Controls panel or in the Timeline panel to the place where you want to add an effect.**

2. **Pick an effect from the Effects panel, and drag it to the Effect Controls panel or the Timeline panel.**

3. **Adjust the settings for the effect, and then click the Toggle Animation icon to create a keyframe.** If you want the effect to change over time, you need to create various keyframes.

Using a Clip with an Alpha Channel

If you create motion effects with text or logos, you may want the text or logo to appear as though it were on a sheet of clear acetate to enable a background video track to show through. The standard digital method of creating this effect is to use an alpha channel.

If the image you set in motion includes an alpha channel, Premiere Pro can mask out the background and substitute the background area with visuals from another video track.

What's an Alpha Channel?

Essentially, an alpha channel is an extra grayscale image layer that Premiere Pro translates into different levels of transparency.

Alpha channels are typically used to define the transparent areas of a graphic or title. They enable you to combine a logo or text in one video track with a background video track in another. The background track surrounds the logo or text and is seen through the letters in the text. If you viewed an alpha channel of text, it might appear as pure white text on a black background. When Premiere Pro uses the alpha channel to create transparency, it can place colored text in the white area of the alpha channel and a background video track in the black area.

Alpha channels can be created in image-editing programs, such as Adobe Photoshop and Corel Painter. Most 3D programs create alpha channels as well. When you create titles in the Title Designer, Premiere Pro automatically creates an alpha channel for the text. (For more information about alpha channels, see Chapter 16. Chapter 28 provides detailed instructions for creating alpha channels in Photoshop.)

The following steps explain how to apply the Motion to a clip with an alpha channel. Figure 17-11 shows a 3D still image over a sky background. The 3D image was created using Strata StudioPro. The image was saved with an alpha channel in Photoshop format. The sky background is from Digital Vision's Drifting Skies 386009f.mov file.

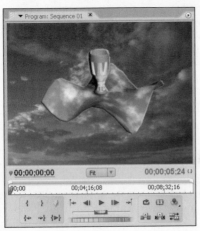

Figure 17-11: An image with an alpha channel over a background in the Monitor panel

Follow these steps to apply motion to a clip with an alpha channel:

1. **Choose File ➪ New ➪ Project to create a new project. In the New Project dialog box, choose a preset, name the project, and click OK to create a new project.**

2. **Choose File ➪ Import to import two clips into the Project panel.** To see the transparency effects of an alpha channel, you need two images in two different video tracks, one on top of the other. One image should be a file that has an alpha channel; the other clip will be used as the background. If you want, you can use the images from Figure 17-8, or you can use the text tools in the Title Designer to create a title with an alpha channel. You can also use the graphic tools in the Title Designer to create a background.

Note

When you import a file with an Alpha Channel into Premiere Pro, the Import Layered File dialog box appears. In this box, click Choose Layer from the Layer Options section. Then click the Choose Layer menu, and select the layer with the alpha channel. Click OK to import the file.

On the DVD-ROM

The 3D image (StillLife.psd) and background file (Digital Vision's Drifting Skies 386009f.mov), shown in Figure 17-8, are found in the Digital Vision folder in the Chapter 17 folder, which is in the Tutorial Projects folder on the DVD accompanying this book.

Cross-Reference

To review how to create titles and graphics using the Title Designer, see Chapter 11.

3. **Drag the background image to the Video 1 track in the Timeline panel.**

4. **Drag the file with the alpha channel (either the title clip or graphic file) from the Project panel to the Video 2 track in the Timeline panel.**

5. **Change the duration of the image in the Video 2 track to match the background clip in the Video 1 track.** The clip in the Video 2 track should be selected. If it isn't, select it now.

6. **To apply motion effects to the clip in the Video 2 track, use the Effect Controls panel or the Timeline panel.**

7. **Press Enter to render the project. To preview the motion effects in the Program Monitor panel, click the Play button.**

8. **To add a sound clip, choose File ⇨ Import. In the Import dialog box, select a sound clip and click Open.** We used Digital Vision's CityMix 576009s.mov, which is in the Digital Vision folder, in the Chapter 17 folder, in the Tutorial Projects folder on the DVD.

9. **Choose File ⇨ Save to save the project.**

Creating Traveling Mattes

A traveling matte (or mask) is a special effect that combines motion and masking. Typically, the matte is a shape that moves across the screen. Within the matte is one image; outside the mask is a background image.

Figure 17-12 shows a frame of the traveling matte effect. Notice that one image is seen through a star-shaped graphic pattern, which is the mask. The matte is simply a star-shaped white graphic created against a black background.

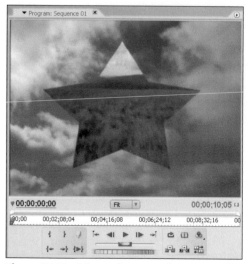

Figure 17-12: A frame for a traveling matte effect

To create a traveling matte effect, you need two video clips: one for the background and another to travel within the matte. You also need a graphic image for the matte itself. Figure 17-13 shows the clips in the Timeline used to create the traveling matte effect shown in Figure 17-12. In the Video 3 track is a star image. In the Video 2 track is a landscape video clip, and in the Video 1 track is a video clip of a sky.

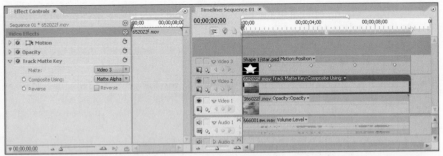

Figure 17-13: Timeline tracks used to create the traveling matte effect in Figure 17-12

Follow these steps for creating a traveling matte effect:

1. **Choose File ⇨ New ⇨ Project to create a new project. In the New Project dialog box, choose a preset.** If you are using the images from the DVD, choose the DV-NTSC Standard 48 kHz preset. Name the project, and click OK to create a new project.

2. **Choose File ⇨ Import to import two clips: one to use in the background and one to use as the element to appear in the mask.** In Figure 17-9, we used a sky video clip as the background and a landscape clip to appear in the mask. Both clips shown in Figure 17-9 are from Digital Vision. The landscape clip is file 65022f.mov from the Sky Ride CD, and the sky clip is file 386022f.mov from the Drifting Skies CD.

On the DVD-ROM

The Digital Vision clip Sky Ride 65022f.mov clip and Drifting Skies 386022f.mov clip, shown in Figure 17-9, are found in the Digital Vision folder, in the Chapter 17 folder, which is in the Tutorial Projects folder on this book's companion DVD. If you prefer, you can use any two video clips located in the DVD's Tutorial Projects folder.

3. **Drag the image that you want to use as your background to the Video 1 track.**

4. **Drag the image that you want to appear within the matte into the Video 2 track.**

5. **Choose File ⇨ Import to import a graphic image to use as a matte.** We used the star.psd image, which is on this book's DVD. In the Import Layered File dialog box, leave the Import As drop-down menu set to Footage and select the Choose Layer option. In the Choose Layer drop-down menu, choose the appropriate layer; we chose Shape 1. Click OK to import the star shape into the Project panel.

On the DVD-ROM

The star.psd image used in Figure 17-9 is found in the Chapter 17 folder, which is in the Tutorial Projects folder on the DVD that accompanies this book.

Note

If you want, you can create a white image against a black background to use as a matte. (We used Photoshop's Shape tool to create the star. When creating the file, set the pixel dimensions to be the same as those you want to use for your project. For more information on using Adobe Photoshop, see Chapter 28. For more information on using Adobe Illustrator, see Chapter 29.) You can also use the tools in the Title Designer to create a matte shape. To use the Title Designer, choose File ➪ New ➪ Title. (For more information on creating shapes in the Title Designer, see Chapter 11.) Remember that after the traveling matte is complete, one clip appears within the white area. A background image appears in the black area.

6. **Drag the graphic image you want to use as a matte from the Project panel into the Video 3 track.** In Figure 17-9, we used the star graphic as the matte graphic.

7. **Extend the duration of the image in the Video 3 track by clicking and dragging the left side of the clip. Extend the duration so that it is the same as the clip in the Video 1 and Video 2 tracks.**

8. **Select the matte in the Video 3 track by clicking it with the Selection tool.**

9. **To apply motion to the matte graphic, use the Motion controls in the Effect Controls panel or Timeline panel.**

10. **Select the Video 2 track, which is the track sandwiched between the matte and the background image.**

11. **Choose Window ➪ Effects to display the Effects panel.**

12. **Click the triangle in front of the Video Effects bin (folder) to display the video effects. Then click the triangle in front of the Keying bin (folder). Select the Track Matte key option, and drag it over the clip in the Video 2 track.** The Track Matte Key controls are displayed in the Effect Controls panel. Set the Matte drop-down menu to Video 3 track. (For a detailed discussion of the Keying effects, see Chapter 15.)

13. **Hide the Video 3 track by clicking the eye icon in the Timeline panel.**

14. **Press the Enter key to render the project. Preview the project in the Program Monitor panel by clicking the Play button.**

15. **If you want, add a sound clip to the project. Make sure to save your file by choosing File ➪ Save.**

Creating Motion Projects

The following projects provide the steps for integrating graphics with alpha channels to create motion effects. In the first example, a coffee cup and text move across a chart of coffee bean sales. The second example is an animated book cover — an idea that booksellers may start using on their Web sites.

Creating a presentation

You can use the Motion properties to create an animated presentation. Figure 17-14 shows the frames used to create a sample Coffee Bean Sales presentation. As you view the frames, notice the motion applied to the coffee cup and text clips.

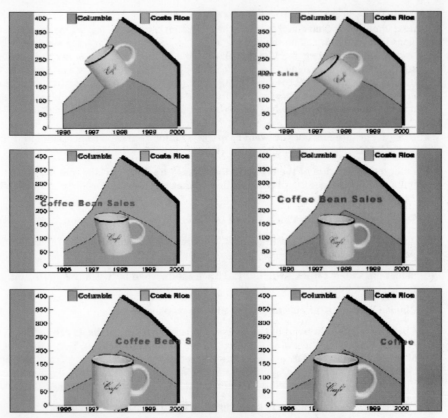

Figure 17-14: Frames from the sample Coffee Bean Sales presentation

We created the sample chart shown in Figure 17-15 using Adobe Illustrator and then saved it in Illustrator format. The coffee cup, shown in Figure 17-16, was scanned and manipulated using Adobe Photoshop. We used the Paintbrush and Eyedropper tools to fine-tune the edges and insides of the coffee cup. Then a selection of the coffee cup was created using the Polygonal Lasso tool. To soften the edges of the selection, a two-pixel feather was applied to the selection (Select ⇨ Feather). The selection was saved as an alpha channel (Select ⇨ Save Selection). To save the coffee cup and alpha channel, we saved the file in Photoshop format (you can also save in PICT or TIFF formats). We created the text using Premiere Pro's Title Designer. All the images were imported into a new project. To make the coffee cup and text overlap, we placed them into different video tracks. We set the coffee cup and text into motion, using Motion controls.

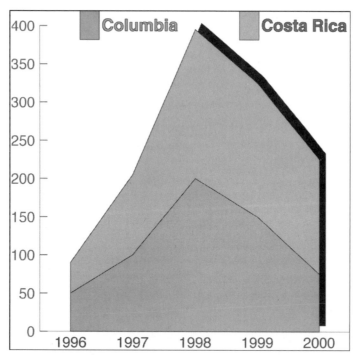

Figure 17-15: Coffee bean chart

Figure 17-16: Coffee cup

On the DVD-ROM

All the graphics used in this example can be found in the Chapter 17 Coffee folder, in the Tutorial Projects folder on the DVD that accompanies this book.

If you want to create your own graphics for a presentation, you need the following three production elements:

✦ **A background image.**

✦ **A title.** You can create a title in the Title Designer, which is covered extensively in Chapter 11.

✦ **A graphic with an alpha channel.** Create this in a program that enables you to create alpha channels or save masks, such as Adobe Photoshop, Corel Painter, or a 3D program.

Follow these steps to create an animated presentation:

1. **Create a new project by choosing File ➪ New ➪ Project.**

2. **In the New Project dialog box, choose your project settings.** Name your file, and click OK to create your new project.

3. **To import the sample graphic files from the DVD that accompanies this book, choose File ➪ Import. In the Import dialog box, locate the Coffee folder from the Chapter 17 folder on the DVD and click Import Folder button.** The Coffee Cup was created in Photoshop using a transparent background, so when you import it into Premiere Pro, the Import Layered File dialog box appears. In the dialog box, select the Choose Layer option and click OK to import the coffee cup with a transparent background. After you've imported the files, they appear in the Project panel, as shown in Figure 17-17.

4. **If you are importing your own files, choose File ➪ Import.** To import more than one file at a time, press and hold the Ctrl key, select the files that you want to import, and then import them. After you've imported the files, they appear in the Project panel.

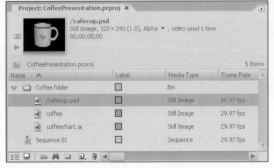

Figure 17-17: The Project panel with the files needed for the Coffee Bean Sales presentation

5. **Drag the background file from the Project panel to the Video 1 track in the Timeline panel. To create the Coffee Bean Sales presentation, drag the Chart file to the Video 1 track.**

6. **Drag the image with the alpha channel from the Project panel to the Video 2 track in the Timeline panel. To create the Coffee Bean Sales presentation, drag the coffee cup image to the Video 2 track.**

7. **Drag and drop the title (Coffee Bean Sales) that you imported from the DVD that accompanies this book to the Video 3 track.** If you want to create your own title, proceed to Step 8; otherwise, skip to the next set of steps in this section to apply motion to your images. The Timeline used to create the Coffee Bean Sales project is shown in Figure 17-18.

Figure 17-18: The Timeline panel with the files used for the Coffee Bean Sales presentation

8. **To create your own title, choose File ➪ New ➪ Title.** In the New Title dialog box that appears, name the title and click OK. In the Title Designer, make sure that the Show Video option is selected if you want to see the image in the Video 2 track. Then use the Text tool to type some text. Stylize the text using the commands in the Title menu or the options in the Properties section of the Title Properties panel. After you've stylized the title, drag the title to the Video 3 track.

9. **The Title is saved automatically with the project. To export the title, click it in the Project panel and choose File ➪ Export ➪ Title.** The title is saved to your hard disk.

Now you're ready to apply motion to the images in the Video 2 and Video 3 tracks:

1. **Click the clip in the Video 3 track in the Timeline panel, and use the Motion properties in the Effect Controls panel or the Timeline panel to edit the motion using the techniques described in this chapter.** We set three points on the Motion Timeline: a starting point, a middle point, and a finish point. The text moves from left to right. At the middle point, we created a delay so that the text would stop moving long enough for the viewer to read it. The size of the text was decreased at the Start and Finish points and increased in the middle point.

2. **Press Enter to render the project. To preview the Motion effect, click the Play button in the Program Monitor panel.**

3. **Apply your own Motion properties to the image in the Video 2 track by clicking the clip in the Video 2 track and then using the Motion properties in the Effect Controls panel.** We made the cup move from the top down. The cup drops to the middle of the chart and then spills into the text. We added left rotations to points on the Motion Timeline. On the points in the middle of the Motion Timeline, we also added a delay for both the coffee cup and text. We also decreased and increased the coffee cup size. We used the clip's alpha channel option so that the white background is removed from the image.

4. **Press Enter to render the project. Preview the motion by clicking the Play button in the Program Monitor panel.**

Next, you need to add the audio clip to your presentation:

1. **Choose File ➪ Import. Locate Digital Vision's Cool Lounge 666001aw.wav audio file from the Digital Vision folder in the Chapter 17 folder on the DVD that accompanies this book.** When the audio file appears in the Project panel, drag it to the Audio 1 track in the Timeline panel. (For more information on working with audio, see Chapter 8.)

2. **Export the current video settings by choosing File ⇨ Export ⇨ Movie.** If you want to change the export settings, click the Settings button. Otherwise, enter a filename and click Save.

Animating a book cover

In the following steps, you create an animated book cover. You can see a frame from the book cover project in Figure 17-19. Here, an angel image moves from the top left of the screen down to the bottom center of the screen. The angel starts on her side and as she moves, she slowly rotates to the right, then to the left, and eventually ends in an upright position. When the angel reaches the bottom of screen, she halts for a moment while the text (Angel Stories) appears over a sky background in the middle of the screen. To create the motion for the angel, we used the Motion Settings dialog box. To create the background, we scanned a sky image and saved it in JPEG format. We used Premiere Pro's Title Designer to create the text. We used both Adobe Illustrator and Adobe Photoshop to create the angel image.

On the DVD-ROM

All the graphics for this example can be loaded from the Angel folder in the Chapter 17 folder, which is in the Tutorial Projects folder on the DVD that accompanies this book.

If you want to create your own graphics for an animated book cover, you need these three production elements:

✦ **A background image.**

✦ **A title.** You can create this in Premiere Pro's Title Designer, which is discussed earlier in this chapter and covered extensively in Chapter 11.

✦ **A graphic with an alpha channel.** Create this in a program that enables you to create alpha channels or save masks, such as Adobe Photoshop or MetaCreations Painter. Most 3D programs also create alpha channels.

Figure 17-19: A frame of the book cover project

Follow these steps for creating the angel with an alpha channel:

1. **Create a pencil sketch of an angel image.**

2. **Scan it into Photoshop, or using your scanning software, save it in TIFF format.**

3. **Next, load the pencil sketch into Adobe Illustrator, and use the Pen tool to outline the object and fill it with color.**

4. **Open the angel image in Photoshop.** When the image of the angel opens in Photoshop, it opens against a transparent background called Layer 1. The transparent background enables you to easily create the alpha channel.

5. **To add depth to the angel, apply a filter such as Texture (Filter ➪ Texture) or use the Layer ➪ Layer Style ➪ Bevel and Emboss command.**

6. **To begin creating the alpha channel, you need to select only the angel onscreen. To do this, press and hold Ctrl as you click in the middle of Layer 1 in the Layers panel.** A selection appears around the angel image.

7. **With the selection onscreen, choose Select ➪ Save Selection. In the Save Selection dialog box, enter a name for the selection and click OK.** You should now have an alpha channel in the Channels panel.

8. **To save the file with the alpha channel, choose File ➪ Save As. In the Save As dialog box, save in TIFF, PICT, or Photoshop format, making sure that the Save Alpha Channels option is selected.**

Follow these steps to create the animated book cover:

1. **Create a new project by choosing File ➪ New ➪ Project. Pick a preset, name your file, and click OK to create your new project.**

2. **Choose File ➪ Import. Locate and select the Angel folder that is located in the Chapter 17 folder on the DVD that accompanies this book. Then choose Import folder.** To import your own images, choose File ➪ Import to import files needed for the project. In the Import dialog box, press and hold the Ctrl key to select more than one item at a time. Click Open to import the files into the Project panel.

3. **Drag and drop the background image (the sky image) from the Project panel to the Video 1 track.**

4. **Drag and drop the graphic image with the alpha channel (Angel) from the Project panel to the Video 2 track.**

5. **Drag and drop the title (Angel Stories) to the Video 3 track.** To create your own title, choose File ➪ New ➪ Title. In the New Title dialog box, name your title and click OK. In the Title Designer (shown in Figure 17-20), create the desired type effect.

Figure 17-20: The Title Designer allows you to create type effects.

6. **With the graphic alpha channel image (the angel image) in the Video 2 track selected, use the Motion properties to apply motion to the angel image.** We made the angel move from the top-left side to the middle and then downward.

7. **Use the Selection tool to select the title (Angel Stories) in the Timeline.**

8. **Use the Motion properties to make the text move from the top left to the top right.**

9. **Press Enter to render the project. Preview your project by clicking Play in the Program Monitor panel.**

10. **To export your project according to your project presets, choose File ➪ Export ➪ Movie. Name your file, and click Save.**

Summary

Premiere Pro's Motion enables you to create motion effects from graphics and video clips. This chapter covered the following topics:

✦ You can change motion speed and direction with the Motion properties.

✦ You can rotate and scale images with the Motion properties.

✦ Use the Motion control with clips that have alpha channels to create motion effects where image backgrounds are transparent.

✦ Use the Track Matte Key Type to create a traveling matte effect.

✦   ✦   ✦

Enhancing Video

When shooting video, you occasionally may have little control over the locale or lighting conditions. This can result in video clips that are too dark or too bright or that display a color cast onscreen. Fortunately, Premiere Pro's Video Effects panel provides a number of effects specifically designed to coax rich colors out of stubbornly dull or poorly lit video. Using Premiere Pro's color effects, you can adjust image brightness, contrast, and colors. All the effects can be previewed onscreen in the Program Monitor or in Premiere Pro's Reference Monitor while you adjust controls in the Effect Controls panel. Although there is no substitute for high-quality video shot with well-planned lighting, Premiere Pro's Video Effects may be able to boost the overall tonal and color quality of your production.

This chapter looks at the Premiere Pro effects that can be used to enhance colors. It starts with an overview of the RGB color model and then proceeds to review the color enhancement effects in the Video Effects panel's Color Correction, Adjust, and Image Control bins.

Tip   You also may be able to enhance a scene by using a matte, and then keying one scene behind another. See Chapter 17 for information about using key effects.

The RGB Color Model

Before you begin to correct color, lightness, brightness, and contrast in Premiere Pro, you should review a few important concepts about computer color theory. As you'll soon see, most of Premiere Pro's image-enhancement effects are not based on the electronics of video color. Instead, they're based on the fundamentals of how a computer creates color.

When you view images on a computer display, colors are created from different combinations of red, green, and blue light. When you need to choose or edit colors, most computer applications allow you to choose from 256 levels of red, 256 levels of green, and 256 levels of blue. This results in over 17.6 million color possibilities (256 × 256 × 256). In both Premiere Pro and Photoshop, each red, green, and blue color component of an image is called a *channel*.

Premiere Pro's Color Picker provides an example of how red, green, and blue channels create color. Using the Color Picker, you can choose colors by specifying red, green, and blue values. To open

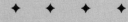

Premiere Pro's Color Picker, you must first have a project onscreen and then choose File ➪ New ➪ Color Matte. In the Color Picker dialog box, shown in Figure 18-1, notice the Red, Green, and Blue entry fields. If you click a color on the color area, the numbers in the entry fields change to show how many levels of red, green, and blue are used to create that color. To change colors, you can also enter a value from 0 to 255 into each of the Red, Green, and Blue fields.

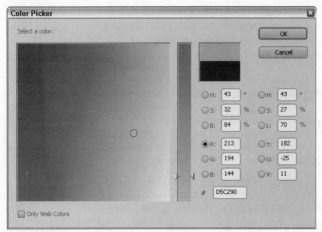

Figure 18-1: Premiere Pro's Color Picker enables you to choose colors by specifying red, green, and blue color values.

If you will be using Premiere Pro to color correct, it's helpful to have a basic understanding of how the red, green, and blue color channels interact to create red, green, and blue color, and their complements (or opposites), cyan, magenta, and yellow. The following list of color combinations can help you understand how different channels create colors. Note that the lower numbers are darker and the higher numbers are brighter. The combination 0 red, 0 green, 0 blue creates black — the absence of light. If red, green, and blue values are set to 255, white is created — the most amount of light. If you add equal values or red, green, and blue, you produce a shade of gray, with lower red, green, and blue values producing dark gray, and higher values producing lighter gray.

> 255 red + 255 green + 255 blue = white
>
> 0 red + 0 green + 0 blue = black
>
> 255 red + 255 green = yellow
>
> 255 red + 255 blue = magenta
>
> 255 green + 255 blue = cyan

Notice that adding two of the RGB color components produces cyan, magenta, or yellow. These are the complements of red, green, and blue. Understanding this relationship is helpful, because it can help provide some direction as you work. From the preceding color calculations, you can see that adding more red and green to an image produces more yellow; adding more red and blue produces more magenta; adding more green and blue produces more cyan.

The preceding calculations also provide a basis for the results of adding or subtracting one of the red, green, or blue channels from an image:

Add red = less cyan

Reduce red = more cyan

Increase green = less magenta

Reduce green = more magenta

Add blue = less yellow

Reduce blue = more yellow

The HSL Color Model

As you'll see from the examples in this chapter, many of Premiere Pro's image enhancement effects utilize controls that adjust red, green, and blue color channels. Those effects that don't use the RGB color model utilize Hue, Saturation, and Lightness controls. If you are new to color correcting, you may wonder why you would use HSL instead of RGB — since RGB is the computer's native method of creating colors. The answer is that many artists find creating and adjusting colors using HSL to be more intuitive than using RGB. In the HSL color model, colors are created in much the same way as color is perceived. *Hue* is the color, *Lightness* is the brightness or darkness of the color, and *Saturation* is the color intensity.

Using HSL, you can quickly start your correction work by choosing a color on a color wheel (or slider representing a 360-degree wheel) and adjusting its intensity and lightness. This technique is generally quicker than trying to add and subtract red, green, and blue values to fine-tune colors.

The YUV Color System

If you are exporting to videotape, realize that the color gamut (the range of colors that make up an image) displayed on a computer screen is greater than the color gamut of a television screen. Your computer monitor creates colors using red, green, and blue phosphors. American broadcast television uses the YCbCr standard (often abbreviated as YCC). YCbCr utilizes one luminance channel and two chroma or chrominance channels.

Note   Luminance values are the brightness values of an image. If you view the luminance values of an image, you see it as a grayscale image. Chrominance is often described as the combination of hue and saturation, or color subtracted from luminance.

YCbCr is based upon the YUV color system (although the term is often used synonomously with YUV). YUV is the color model used by Premere Pro and PAL analog television systems. The YUV system is composed of a luminance channel (Y) and two color chroma channels: U and V. The luminance channel was, and still is, based on the luminance value used for black-and-white television. This value was kept so those viewers with black-and-white television could view the television signal when color was adapted.

Like RGB and HSL, YUV color values are displayed in the Adobe Color Picker. YUV color can be derived from RGB color values. For example, the Y (luminance) component is derived from percentages of Red, Green, and Blue. The U component is derived by subtracting the Y luminance value from the Blue RGB value and multiplying it by a constant. The V component is derived by subtracting the Y luminance value from the Red RGB value and multiplying it by another constant. This is why the term *chrominance* essentially means a signal based upon color subtracted from a luminance value. See `http://en.wikipedia.org/wiki/YUV` for more details.

If you are working on a high-definition project, you can choose between 8-bit and 16-bit YUV color in the Video Rendering section of the Project Settings dialog box (Project ⇨ Project Settings ⇨ Video Rendering). Most project presets also allow you to access a Maximum Bit depth checkbox, which allows a color bit depth up to 32 bits, depending upon the project's preset Compressor setting. Selecting Maximum Bit Depth can improve the quality of video effects but is more taxing on your computer system.

Note   The term *YUV 4:2:2* appears as a choice for Video Rendering when using a High Definition preset. 4:2:2 is a color down-sampling ratio from analog to digital. The value 4 represents Y (luminance), and the 2:2 indicates that the chroma values are sampled at half the rate of luminance. This process is called *chroma subsampling*. This subsampling of color is possible because the human eye is much less sensitive to changes in color than luminance.

Starting a Color Correcting Session

Before you start correcting video, you can improve the results with a few minor workspace changes. You may want to start by setting your workspace to Premiere Pro's Color Correction workspace by choosing Window ⇨ Workspace ⇨ Color Correction.

✦ **Use a Reference Monitor.** Using a Reference Monitor is similar to working with another Program Monitor opened onscreen. Thus, you can view two different scenes from a video sequence simultaneously: one in the Reference Monitor and one in the Program Monitor. You can also view Premiere Pro's Video scopes in the Reference Monitor while viewing the actual video that the scopes represent in the Program Monitor.

If you choose to use the Color Correction Workspace, the Reference Monitor opens automatically. If the Reference Monitor is not open, you can display it by choosing Reference Monitor from the Program Monitor panel menu. By default, the Reference Monitor is *ganged* to be in play in sync with your Program Monitor. You can also set the Reference Monitor loose (so you can view one scene in the Reference Monitor and another in the Program Monitor) by deselecting Gang to Program Monitor in the Reference Monitor panel menu. You can also *ungang* the Reference Monitor by clicking the Gang to Program Monitor button in the Reference Monitor.

✦ **View the highest quality output.** You can change the output quality of Premiere Pro's Source, Program, and Reference Monitors. When making color adjustments, you'll want to be viewing the highest quality output so you can accurately judge colors. To set a monitor to highest quality, click the Monitor's panel menu, and choose Highest Quality.

✦ **Use the Maximum bit depth.** To obtain the highest quality output, you can set Premiere Pro's video rendering to for the maximum color depth allowed by the Projects preset Compressor. Choose Preference ➪ General ➪ Video Rendering. In the Video Rendering section, select Maximum Bit depth.

✦ **Use Premiere Pro's Video Scopes.** If your project will be viewed on a video monitor, use Premiere Pro's scopes to help ensure that your video levels don't stray beyond target levels for professional video. The next section discusses Premiere Pro's video scopes.

Using the Video Scopes

Premiere Pro's video scopes provide a graphic representation of color information. They simulate video scopes used in professional broadcast studies and are most important to Premiere Pro users who are outputting NTSC or Pal video. Several of the scopes output graphic representations of a video signal's chroma (the color and intensity) and luminance (brightness values — essentially black, white, and gray values).

To view a scope readout for a clip, double-click the clip in the Project panel or move the current-time indicator to the clip in a sequence on the Timeline. Then pick the scope or group of scopes from the Source, Program, or Reference Monitor's menu.

The Vectorscope

The Vectorscope displays a graphic representation of a clip's chroma in relation to hue. The Vectorscope, shown in Figure 18-2, displays hues along a color wheel with Red, Magenta, Blue, Cyan, Green, and Yellow (R, MG, B, Cy, G, YL) markers. Thus, the angle of the readout indicates hue properties. Readings toward the outer edges of the Vectorscope indicate highly saturated colors. Moderately saturated colors appear between the center of the circle and its outer edges. Black and White portions of the video appear at the center.

The tiny target boxes in the Vectorscope indicate upper levels of saturation. NTSC video levels should not go beyond these boxes.

The top of the scope displays controls allowing you to change the intensity of the Vectorscope display. You can click a different intensity, or you can click and drag to change the intensity percentage. These intensity options do not change chroma levels in the video; they only change the scope's display. The 75% option above the Vectorscope changes the display to approximate analog chrominance; the 100% option displays digital video chrominance.

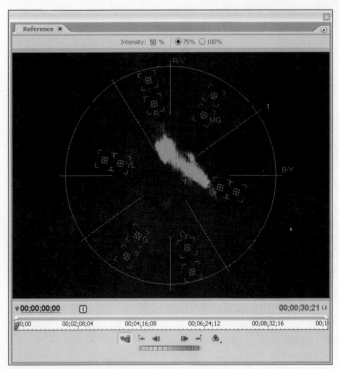

Figure 18-2: The Vectorscope charts video chroma.

YC Waveform

The YC Waveform scope, shown in Fiugre 18-3, provides a waveform representation of video signal intensity. (Y represents luminance, and C represents chrominance.) In the YC Waveform, the horizontal axis represents the video clip itself, while the vertical axis charts signal intensity measured in IRE (for Institute of Radio Engineers).

The green waveform pattern in the scope represents video luminance. The waveform for brighter video appears at the top of the chart; the waveform for darker video appears at the bottom of the chart. Chroma is indicated by a blue waveform. (In general, luminance and chroma overlap, and their IRE values should be about the same level.)

In the United States, acceptable Luminance levels for NTSC Video range from 7.5 (black level, referred to as pedestal level) to 100 IRE (White level); for Japan, the values range from 0 to 100.

To aid you in interpreting the scope, you can turn the Chroma display on and off by clicking in the Chroma check box. Like the Vectorscope, you can click and drag the over the Intensity percentage to change the intensity of the scope display. By default, the YC Waveform attempts to display waveforms as they would appear as if output to analog video. To view the waveform for digital video, deselect the Setup (7.5 IRE) check box.

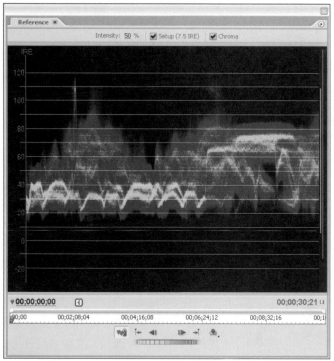

Figure 18-3: The YC Waveform Scope displays Luminance and Chrominance.

YCbCr Parade

The YCBCr Parade scopes, shown in FIgure 18-4, provide a "parade" of waveforms that indicate the luminance and color differences in a video signal. The order of the parade is as follows:

✦ Y: The first waveform is the Y or luminance level.

✦ Cb: The second waveform is Cb (blue minus luma).

✦ Cr: The third waveform is Cr (red minus luma).

✦ The vertical bars at the end of the chart indicate the range of signal of the Y, Cb, and Cr waveforms.

You can control the intensity of the display by clicking and dragging over the intensity readout.

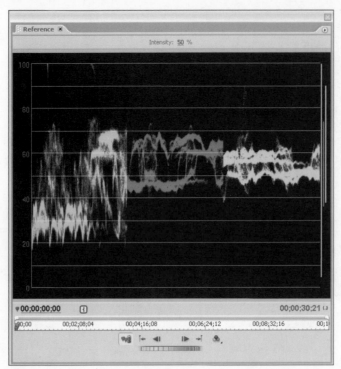

Figure 18-4: The YCbCr Parade displays luminance and color differences.

RGB Parade

The RGB Parade, shown in Figure 18-5, displays waveforms for red, green, and blue levels in a video clip. The RGB Parade scope can be helpful in indicating how color is distributed throughout a clip. In the scope, red is the first waveform, green is the second, and blue is the last. The vertical bars at the right of the RGB Parade scope represent the range of each RGB signal.

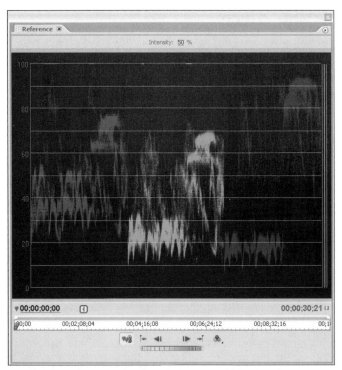

Figure 18-5: The RGB Parade red, green, and blue levels

Color Enhancement Effects

Premiere Pro's color enhancement ools are dispersed among three bins in the Video Effects panel — Color Correction, Adjust, and Image Control. Not surprisingly, you can find the most powerful effects in the Color Correction Bin. The Color Correction effects provide the most precise and quickest options for correcting color. This section covers all the Color Correction effects, as well as several found in the Adjust and Image Control bins.

Color Correction effects are applied in the same manner as other video effects. As discussed in Chapter 14, to apply an effect, you can simply click and drag the effect over a video clip in the Timeline. After you've applied the effect, you can adjust it using controls in the Effect Controls panel. As with other video effects, click the Show/Hide Timeline button to view a Timeline in the panel. To create keyframes, click the Toggle Animation button before moving the current-time indicator and making adjustments. You can also click the Reset button to cancel the effect. See Chapter 14 for detailed instructions on using the Video Effects panel and applying keyframes.

On the DVD-ROM

Before you begin exploring Premiere Pro's color enhancement commands, start by creating a new project. Import a color clip into Premiere Pro, and drag it into the Video 1 track. If you don't have a video clip to use, you can use one of the clips found in the Chapter 18 folder, which is in the Tutorial Projects folder that is on the DVD that accompanies this book.

The Color Correction effects

Premiere Pro's most powerful color correcting tools reside in the Color Correction folder in the Video Effects panel. You can use these effects to fine-tune chroma (color) and Luminance (brightness values) in video. As you make adjustments, you can view the effects in the Program Monitor, in the video scopes, or in Premiere Pro's Reference Monitor. The effects in this section are grouped according to similarity, to make it easier for you to compare the different features.

When using the Color Correcting effects, you'll see that many share similar features. For example, each effect option allows you to choose how you will view the scene you are correcting in the Program or Reference Monitor. These commands include the following:

✦ **Output:** The Output drop-down menu controls what is displayed in the Program or Reference Monitor. These are the choices:

   • **Composite:** Displays the composite image as it normally is displayed in the Program or Reference Monitor.

   • **Luma:** Displays luminance values (a grayscale image displaying lightness and darkness values).

   • **Mask:** When correcting using the Secondary Color Correction controls, the Mask option displays a black and white version of the image. White areas indicate image areas that will be affected by color adjustments; black areas will not be affected.

   • **Tonal Range:** Several Color Correction effects include the Tonal Range Definition bar, which allows you to specify a tonal range of shadows, midtones, and highlights to correct. When you choose Tonal Range in the Output drop-down, the target tonal range is displayed in the Program or Reference Monitor.

✦ **Show Split View:** Select to split the screen so that you can compare the original (uncorrected) video and live adjustments.

✦ **Layout:** Choose between a vertical or horizontal split view. This option allows you to view corrected and noncorrected areas as a vertical split screen or horizontal split screen.

✦ **Split View Percent:** Choose the percentage of corrected video to be seen in the split screen view.

Note   Because the controls described above appear in most of the Color Correction effects, they are not repeated in the individual effect descriptions.

Fast Color Corrector

The Fast Color Corrector, shown in Figure 18-6, allows you to quickly adjust a clip's color and luminance. You can also remove color casts from white areas using the Fast Color Corrector's White Balance control. To use the Fast Color Corrector, start by setting the Output options (described above), and then begin correcting color using the Hue Balance and Angle color wheel. To correct brightness and contrast, use the Levels sliders located below the color wheel.

On the DVD-ROM

The short ColorCorrect.avi clip on the DVD needs color correction. As you read through this section. Click with the white eyedropper on the cat's tail in the image to control the color cast, and then use the Gamma control to help adjust color in the midtones. To practice changing hues, load the QuickTime 750259.mov and change the background hue from twilight to day by changing the hue from yellow-orange to blue.

Show/Hide Timeline

Balance Gain   Toggle Effect on/off

Hue Angle   Balance Angle

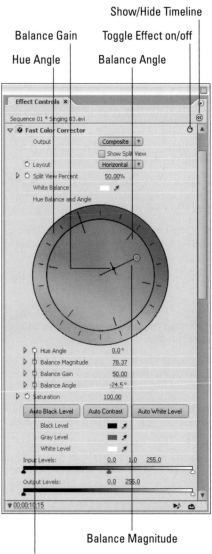

Figure 18-6: The Fast Color Corrector wheel controls

Balance Magnitude

Toggle Animation (for Keyframes.)

White Balance

Use the White Balance controls to help remove color casts. Select the White Balance Eyedropper and click an imae area that should be white. When you click, Premiere Pro adjusts the colors throughout the image.

Hue Balance and Angle color wheel

The Hue Balance and Angle color wheel allows you to quickly choose hue and adjust hue intensity. You can click and drag the outer wheel to change hue — which changes the Hue Angle values — and then click and drag the circle in the middle of the wheel to control color intensity — which changes the Balance Magnitude values. Changing angles alters the color toward the direction you point it; clicking and dragging the bar or handle in the middle fine-tunes the adjustment.

To see a graphic representation of using the wheel, view the Vectorscope in the Reference Monitor. The following list describes the color wheel controls. For most of these adjustments, you can click and drag within the color wheel or click and drag the sliders beneath the wheel:

✦ **Hue Angle:** Click and drag the outer wheel to adjust the hue. Clicking and dragging the outer wheel left spins to green colors, clicking and dragging right spins to red colors. As you drag, the Hue angle readout indicates the degree on the wheel.

✦ **Balance Magnitude:** Click and drag the circle in the middle of the wheel toward a hue to control the intensity of the color. As you drag outward, the color becomes more intense (you can easily see this in Premiere Pro's Vectorscope).

✦ **Balance Gain:** Use this handle to fine-tune the Balance Gain and Balance Angle controls. Dragging the handle outward creates a coarser effect; keeping the handle near the center creates a more subtle effect.

✦ **Balance Angle:** Clicking and dragging the Balance Angle alters the color in the direction in which you point the handle.

✦ **Saturation:** Click and drag the saturation slider to adjust color intensity. Dragging the slider left toward 0 removes or desaturates colors (turning it into a grayscale version display luminance values). Dragging to the right intensifies saturation.

✦ **Auto Black Level:** Click Auto Black Level to boost black levels above 7.5 IRE. This effectively clips or cuts off darker levels and proportionally redistributes pixel values, which usually lightens shadow areas.

✦ **Auto Contrast:** Clicking Auto Contrast has the same effect as applying both Auto Black Level and Auto White Level. The shadow areas are lightened, and highlight areas are darkened. This may help add contrast to some clips.

✦ **Auto White Levels:** Click Auto White Levels to lower white levels so that no highlight areas are above 100 IRE. This effectively clips or cuts off white levels. When the pixel values are redistributed proportionally, the effect usually darkens highlight areas.

✦ **Black Level, White Level, Gray Level:** These controls provide similar adjustments as the Auto Contrast, Auto White Level, and Auto Black Level, except that you can choose the level by clicking in your image or by clicking the swatch and choosing a color from the Adobe Color Picker. By setting black and white points, you can specify which areas should be the brightest and darkest image areas; thus, you can expand an image's tonal range. When you set a white or black point, you should click the lightest or darkest area that you want to maintain in the image. After you click, Premiere Pro adjusts the tonal range of the image based upon the new white point. For example, if you click a white area in your image, Premiere Pro makes all areas lighter than the white point white and then remaps the pixels proportionally.

> **Note**
>
> In the United States, acceptable Luminance levels for NTSC Video range from 7.5 to 100 IRE; for Japan, the range is 0 to 100. As discussed earlier, the YC Waveform scope measures luminance using an IRE scale.

✦ **Levels:** Use the Levels controls to adjust contrast and brightness. The outer markers on the Input and Output sliders indicate Black and White points. The Input sliders designate white and black points in relationship to the Output levels. Input and Output levels range from 0 (black) to 255 (white). You can use the two sliders together to increase or decrease contrast in an image. For example, if you drag the white Input slider left to 230, pixels that were 230 become 255 (white); highlights are brightened and the number of highlighted pixels increases. However, if you drag the white Output slider to the left to 230, you remap the image so that 230 is the lightest value in the image (Premiere Pro also remaps other pixels values in the image accordingly).

As you might expect, dragging the black Input and Output sliders reverses the effects of the white Input and Output sliders. Drag the black Input slider to the right, and you darken the image. If you drag the black Output slider to the right, you lighten it.

To change midtones with little effect on the highlights and shadows, click and drag the Gamma Input slider. Drag to the right to lighten midtones; drag to the left to darken midtones.

> **Note**
>
> Premiere Pro's Adjust bin includes a Levels effect. This effect also provides a Histogram, or graphic chart of pixel values in your image. To learn more about levels, see the Levels effect in the Adjust effects section of this chapter.

Three-Way Color Corrector

The Three-Way Color Corrector is Premiere Pro's Swiss Army knife of color adjustment. The Three-Way Color Corrector provides an assortment of controls for correcting colors as well as shadows (darkest image areas), midtones, and highlights (brightest image areas). As you can see from Figure 18-7, in many respects, the Three-Way Color Corrector is an extended version of the Fast Color Corrector. It extends the functionality of the Fast Color Corrector because it allows you to target specific color ranges and provides a Secondary Color Correction group, which allows you to further specify a tonal range for your adjustments. The following is a review of the options.

The Balance commands can remove color casts from an image by neutralizing white black and grays. They can also be used to add a color cast. For example, you may want a red warm color cast in a scene that takes place around a burning fire in a fireplace. If you do not want neutral blacks, whites, or grays and **do** want a color cast, you can set the color in the Adobe Color Picker by clicking the white, black, or gray tile adjacent to the eyedropper. Note that the balance commands can affect all colors in a clip.

✦ **White Balance:** Select the White Balance Eyedropper, and click an image area that should be white.

✦ **Gray Balance:** Select the Gray Balance Eyedropper, and click an image area that is supposed to be gray.

✦ **Black Balance:** Click an area that is supposed to be black.

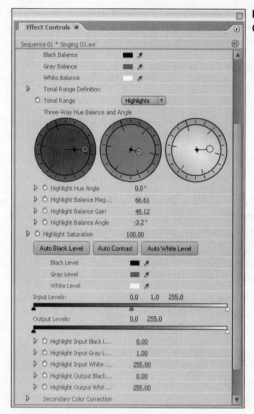

Figure 18-7: The Three-Way Color Corrector controls

Hue Balance and Angle color wheels

The Three-Way Color Corrector's Hue Balance and Angle color function is similar to the wheel in the Fast Color Corrector. However, the Three-Way Color Corrector allows you to use a Master wheel (one wheel), or you can use three wheels. To view the three wheels, as shown in Figure 18-7, choose Shadows, Midtones, or Highlights from the Tonal Range drop-down menu. The first wheel represents shadows, the second wheel midtones, and the third wheel represents highlights.

The following list describes the color wheel controls. For most of these adjustments, you can click and drag on or within the color wheel (see the callouts on the wheel in Figure 18-6), or click and drag the sliders beneath the wheel.

✦ **Hue Angle:** Click and drag the outer wheel to adjust the hue. Clicking and dragging the outer wheel left rotates the wheel toward green; clicking and dragging right rotates the wheel toward red. As you drag, the Hue angle readout indicates the degree on the wheel.

✦ **Balance Magnitude:** Click and drag the circle in the middle of the wheel toward a hue to control the intensity of the color. As you drag outward, the color becomes more intense (you can easily see this in Premiere Pro's Vectorscope).

✦ **Balance Gain:** Using this handle, you can fine-tune the Balance Gain and Balance Angle controls. Dragging the handle outward creates a less subtle, coarser effect; keeping the handle near the center creates a more subtle effect.

✦ **Balance Angle:** Clicking and dragging the control alters the color in the direction to which you point the handle.

✦ **Saturation slider:** Click and drag the saturation slider to adjust color intensity for the overall image or shadows, midtones, and highlights. Dragging the slider left toward 0 removes or desaturates colors (turning it into a grayscale version display luminance values). Dragging to the right intensifies saturation.

✦ **Auto Contrast:** Clicking Auto Contrast has the same effect as applying both Auto Black Level and Auto White Level. In general, shadow areas are lightened and highlight areas are darkened. Clicking Auto Contrast can help add contrast to image areas.

✦ **Auto Black Level:** Click Auto Black Level to boost black levels above 7.5 IRE. This effectively clips or cuts off darker levels and proportionally redistributes pixel values, which usually lightens shadow areas.

✦ **Auto White Level:** Click Auto White Level to lower white levels so that no highlight areas are above 100 IRE. This effectively clips or cuts off white levels. When the pixel values are redistributed proportionally, the effect usually darkens highlight areas.

✦ **Black Level, White Level, Gray Level:** These controls provide adjustments similar to Auto Contrast, Auto White Level, and Auto Black Level, except that you can choose the level by clicking in your image or by clicking the swatch and choosing a color from the Adobe Color Picker. By setting black and white points, you can specify which areas should be the brightest and darkest image areas; thus, you can expand an image's tonal range. When you set a white or black point, you should click the lightest or darkest area that you want to maintain in the image. After you click, Premiere Pro adjusts the tonal range of the image based upon the new white point. For example, if you click a white area in your image, Premiere Pro makes all areas lighter than the white point white and then remaps the pixels proportionally.

✦ **Levels:** Use the Levels controls to adjust contrast and brightness. Levels change the overall image or the shadows, midtones, and highlights depending upon which Tonal Range you select in the Tonal Range drop-down menu.

To change middle areas with little affect on the brightest and darkest image areas, click and drag the Gamma Input slider. Drag to the left to darken the middle range area; drag to the right to lighten.

As discussed in the Fast Color Corrector section, the Input and Output sliders indicate black and white points. The Input Sliders designate white and black points in relationship to the Output levels, which can range between 0 and 255. You can use the two sliders together to increase or decrease contrast in an image. For example, you can darken your image by dragging the black point Input slider to the right. If you reset the black point Input slider to 25, pixels that were 25 become 0 (black); shadows are darkened, and the number of shadow pixels increases. However, if you drag the black Output slider to the right to 25 or higher, you remap the image so that the new Output value is the darkest value in the image, thereby lightening it, as Premiere Pro remaps the pixels in the image accordingly.

Secondary Color Correction

The Secondary Color Correction tools provide controls to restrict color correction to a specific range or specific color in a clip. These controls, shown in Figure 18-8, allow you to pinpoint a specific color or tonal range to correct, without worrying that other ranges will be affected. Using the Secondary Color Corrector, you can restrict color correction by specify a hue, saturation, and luminance range. The Secondary Color Correction option appears in the Three-Way Color Corrector, Luma Correct, Luma Curve, RGB Color Corrector, and RGB Curves effects.

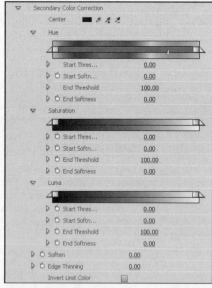

Figure 18-8: The Secondary Color Correction controls

Follow these steps for using the Secondary Color Correction controls:

1. **Click the eyedropper, and select the color area in the image in the Program or Reference Monitor that you want to change.** You can also pick a color by clicking the color swatch and choosing a color in the Adobe Color Picker.

2. **Adjust the color range using one of the following techniques:**

   • To extend the color range, click the eyedropper with the plus (+) sign.

   • To subtract the color range, click the eyedropper with the minus (–) sign.

   • To expand the Hue control, start by clicking the Hue triangle to open the Hue slider. Then click the Square Start and End Threshold sliders to specify the color range. Note that you can add to the colors visible in the Hue slider itself by clicking and dragging the colored area.

3. **To soften the difference between the color range to correct and the adjacent areas, click and drag the Start and End Softness sliders.** You can also click and drag the triangles in the Hue slider.

4. **Adjust Saturation and Luminance ranges by clicking and dragging these controls.**

5. **Use Edge Thinning to fine-tune the effect.** Edge thinning can thin the edges of the color from a thin –100 to a very thin 100.

6. **If you want to adjust all colors except the color range selected, choose Invert Color.**

7. **To view a mask (flat black, white, and gray area) representing the color change, choose Mask in the Output drop-down menu.** A mask can make seeing just what image areas you are adjusting easier. When Mask is chosen, these things are true:

   - Black represents image areas completely changed by the color correction.

   - Gray represents partially changed image areas.

   - White represents the area not changed (masked out).

Luma Corrector

The Luma Corrector allows you to adjust a clip's luminance or brightness values. The Luma Corrector is shown in Figure 18-9. When using the Luma Corrector, start by isolating the tonal range that you want to correct. Then use the Luma Corrector's Definition controls to adjust brightness and contrast.

Tip   To help you conceptualize the tonal range, you can click Tonal Range in the Output drop-down menu. This causes the Program or Reference Monitor to display the tonal range that will be affected by the Luma Corrector. After you've established the tonal range to correct, then switch the Output drop-down menu to either Composite or Luma.

These are the controls in the Luma Corrector:

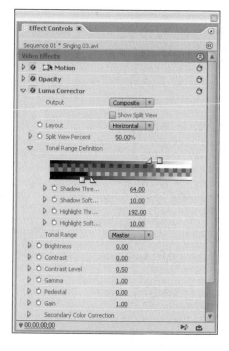

Figure 18-9: Use the Luma Corrector to adjust luminance values.

✦ **Tonal Range Definition:** Click the triangle to view the Tonal Range Definition bar, and then click and drag to set the range of shadows, midtones, and highlights that you want to adjust. Clicking the squares controls Shadow and Highlight Thresholds — the upper and lower limits of Shadow and Highlight areas. Clicking the triangles controls Shadow and Highlight softness — the drop-off between the affected and nonaffected areas. The softness sliders essentially allow a softer adjustment range. You can also use the sliders (described below) to set the tonal range for the correction.

The following slider controls can be used to adjust the tonal range if you do not want to click and drag in the Tonal Range Definition bar to adjust the image areas to be affected by the Luma Corrector:

- **Shadow Threshold:** Specifies the tonal range of shadows (darker areas).

- **Shadow Softness:** Specifies the shadow tonal range with a soft edge.

- **Highlight Threshold:** Adjusts the tonal range of highlights (bright image areas).

- **Highlight Soft:** Determines the highlight's tonal range with a soft edge.

✦ **Tonal Range drop-down menu:** Choose whether to apply the correction to the composite Master image, Highlights, Midtones, or Shadows.

The Definition controls allow you to set brightness and contrast:

✦ **Brightness:** Sets the black level in the clip. If blacks do not appear as black, try raising contrast.

✦ **Contrast:** Adjusts contrast based on the contrast level (described next).

✦ **Contrast Level:** Sets the contrast level for adjusting previously discussed Contrast control.

✦ **Gamma:** Primarily adjusts midtone levels. Thus, if an image is too light or too dark, but shadows and highlights are not too dark or too light, use the Gamma control.

✦ **Pedestal:** Adds a specific offset pixel value. The Pedestal combined with Gain (described next) can be used to brighten an image.

✦ **Gain:** Adjusts brightness values by multiplying pixel values. The result is to change the ratio of lighter to darker pixels; but this has more of an effect on lighter pixels.

Luma Curve

Luma Curve allows you to make adjustments to a clip's luminance values by clicking and dragging a curve representing the clip's brightness values. The curve's x-axis represents the original image values, and the y-axis represents the values that are changed. Because all points are equal when you begin, the Luma Curve opens by displaying a straight diagonal line. The left-end of the horizontal axis represents darker areas of the original image; brighter areas are represented on the right side of the horizontal axis.

To adjust midtones, click and drag in the middle of the curve. Click and drag up to lighten the image; click and drag down to darken. To darken highlight areas, drag down on the top right of the curve. Dragging the bottom left of the curve up lightens shadows. Creating an S-shaped curve, as shown in Figure 18-10, can add contrast to an image.

To fine-tune adjustments, you can click to create up to 16 anchor points on the curve by clicking on it. Then you can click and drag the anchor points or click and drag the area between anchor points. To remove an anchor point, click and drag it off the curve.

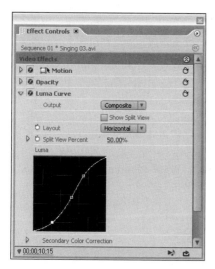

Figure 18-10: Use the Luma Curve to adjust luminance values by clicking and dragging a curve.

RGB Corrector

The RGB Color Corrector allows you to make adjustments to color and luminance using RG B values. As you can see from Figure 18-11, the RGB Corrector provides many of the same controls as the Luma Corrector, but adds RGB color controls:

✦ **Tonal Range Definition:** Click the triangle to view the Tonal Range Definition bar, and then click and drag to set the range for shadows, midtones, and highlights that you want to adjust. Clicking the squares controls Shadow and Highlight Thresholds — the upper and lower limits of Shadow and Highlight areas. Clicking the triangles controls Shadow and Highlight softness — the drop-off between the affected and nonaffected areas. The softness sliders essentially allow a softer adjustment range. You can also use the sliders (described below) to set the tonal range for the correction.

The following slider controls can be used to adjust the tonal range if you do not want to click and drag in the Tonal Range Definition bar to adjust the image areas to be affected by the RGB Corrector:

- **Shadow Threshold:** Specifies the tonal range of shadows (darker areas).

- **Shadow Softness:** Specifies the shadow tonal range with a soft edge.

- **Highlight Threshold:** Adjusts the tonal range of highlights (bright image areas).

- **Highlight Softness:** Determines the highlight's tonal range with a soft edge.

✦ **Tonal Range:** Click in the Tonal Range drop-down menu depending upon whether you want to apply the correction to the composite Master image, Highlights, Midtones, or Shadows.

The Definition controls allow you to set brightness and contrast:

✦ **Brightness:** Sets the black level in the clip. If blacks do not appear as black, try raising the contrast.

✦ **Contrast:** Adjusts contrast based on the contrast level (described next).

✦ **Contrast Level:** Sets the contrast level for adjusting previously discussed Contrast control.

✦ **Gamma:** Primarily adjusts midtone levels. Thus, if an image is too light or too dark, but shadows and highlights are not too dark or too light, use the Gamma control.

✦ **Pedestal:** Adds a specific offset pixel value. The Pedestal combined with Gain (described next) can be used to brighten an image.

✦ **Gain:** Adjusts brightness values by multiplying pixel values. The result is to change the ratio of lighter to darker pixels, but it has more of an effect on lighter pixels.

✦ **RGB:** Click the RGB triangle to expand and view the RGB sliders. The sliders are Gamma, Pedestal, and Gain sliders for the Red, Green, and Blue color channels in the clip.

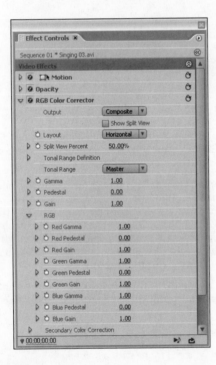

Figure 18-11: Use the RGB Color Corrector to specify a tonal range and correct using RGB controls.

RGB Curves

The RGB Curves effect allows you to adjust RGB Color values using Curves.

In the Curves effect, shown in Figure 18-12, the x-axis of the dialog box represents the original image values, and the y-axis represents the values that are changed. Because all points are equal when you begin, the Curves dialog box opens by displaying four diagonal lines.

The left side of the horizontal axis of each curve represents darker areas of the original image; brighter areas are represented on the right side of the horizontal axis.

To lighten an image area, click and drag up on a curve; to darken an area, click and drag down. As you drag, the curve shows how the rest of the pixels in the image change. To prevent part of the curve from changing, you can click the curve to establish anchor points. As you click and drag, the anchor points lock down the curve. If you want to delete an anchor point, drag it off the curve.

If you click and drag a curve representing a channel, dragging upward increases that channel's color in the image, whereas dragging downward reduces it and adds that color's complement. For example, dragging up on the Green channel adds more green, and dragging down on the curve adds more magenta.

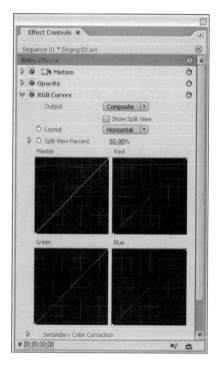

Figure 18-12: Use the RGB Curves effect to adjust RGB values by clicking and dragging a curve.

Video Limiter

Use the Video Limiter effect after color correcting to ensure that the video falls within specific limits. You can set limits for a clip's overall signal, chroma alone, or luminance and chroma. Like the Luma Corrector and RGB Corrector, the Video Limiter effect allows you to target the effect to a specific Tonal Range. The Video Limiter, shown in Figure 18-13, provides the following options:

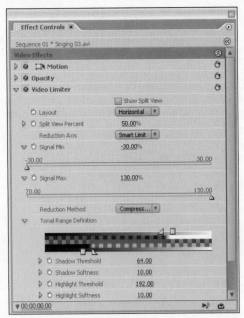

Figure 18-13: Use the Video Limiter to set limits for a clip's overall signal, chroma, or luminance.

✦ **Reduction Axis:** Use the reduction axis to choose which part of the video signal to limit: Luminance, Chroma, Chroma and Luminance, or overall video Signal (Smart Limit).

✦ **Signal Min and Signal Max:** After you choose a Reduction Axis, the Signal Min and Signal Max sliders change based upon the Reduction Axis. Thus, if you choose Luminance in the Reduction Axis, you can set minimum and maximum values for Luminance.

✦ **Reduction Method:** Use Reduction Method to choose a specific tonal range to compress: Highlights, Midtones, Shadows, or Compress all. Choosing a Reduction Method can help keep images sharp in specific image areas.

✦ **Tonal Range Definition:** Click the triangle to view the Tonal Range Definition bar, and then click and drag to set the range for shadows, midtones, and highlights that you want to adjust. Clicking the squares controls Shadow and Highlight Thresholds–the upper and lower limits of Shadow and Highlight areas. Clicking the triangles controls Shadow and Highlight softness — the drop-off between the affected and nonaffected areas. The softness sliders essentially allow a softer adjustment range. You can also use the sliders (described below) to set the tonal range for the correction.

The following slider controls can be used to adjust the tonal range if you do not want to click and drag in the Tonal Range Definition bar to adjust the image areas to be affected by the Luma Corrector:

- **Shadow Threshold:** Specifies the tonal range of shadows (darker areas).
- **Shadow Softness:** Specifies the shadow tonal range with a soft edge.
- **Highlight Threshold:** Adjusts the tonal range of highlights (bright image areas).
- **Highlight Softness:** Determines the highlight's tonal range with a soft edge.

The Adjust effects

The video effects in the Adjust folder are Brightness & Contrast, Channel Mixer, Convolution Kernel, Extract, Levels, Posterize, and ProAmp.

Changing brightness and contrast

The Brightness and Contrast effect is one of the easiest image effects to use. Brightness controls the light levels in your image, while contrast is the difference between the brightest and darkest levels. As with other effects, to use Brightness and Contrast, drag the effect from the Video Effects panel over the clip that you want to adjust. Take a moment to try out each of the Brightness & Contrast settings:

✦ **Brightness:** To increase overall brightness in your clip, click and drag the Brightness slider to the right. As you drag, the entire image lightens. To decrease Brightness, click and drag to the left. As you drag, the entire clip gets darker.

✦ **Contrast:** To see the effect of the Contrast slider, first click and drag the slider to the right. As you drag, you add contrast, increasing the difference between the lightest and darkest areas of your image. This also tends to create a sharper image. To decrease sharpness, click and drag to the left. As you drag, the entire clip begins to fade out.

Changing levels

The Levels effect can be used for fine-tuning shadows (dark image areas), midtones (mid-level image areas), and highlights (light image areas). Using Levels, you can correct the red, green, and blue channels simultaneously or individually. The Levels effect in the Adjust bin is virtually identical to the Levels command found in Adobe Photoshop. To see the Levels Settings dialog box, as shown in Figure 18-14, click the Setup button in the Effect Controls panel (the setup button looks like a tiny dialog box).

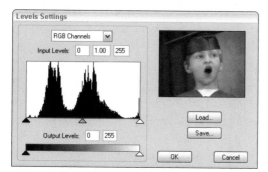

Figure 18-14: Premiere Pro's Levels Settings dialog box enables you to adjust shadows, midtones, and highlights.

In the Levels Settings dialog box, Premiere Pro displays a histogram of the image. The histogram is a chart that provides a graphical representation of the brightness levels of the pixels in your image. Darker pixel levels are represented at the left end of the histogram, and brighter levels are represented at the right side of the histogram. The taller the level line in the histogram is, the larger the number of pixels that occur at that brightness level. The lower the level line is, the fewer the number of pixels that occur at that brightness level.

Use the Levels controls to adjust contrast and brightness. The outer markers on the Input and Output sliders indicate black and white points. The Input sliders designate white and black points in relationship to the Output levels. The Input and Output range is from 0 to 255. You can use the two sliders together to increase or decrease contrast in an image. If you want to lighten a dark image, click and drag the white Input slider to the left. Here's how it works: If you reset the white Input slider to 230, pixels that were 230 (as well as those lighter than 230) become 255 (white); highlights are brightened, and the number of highlight pixels increases. However, if you drag the white Output slider to the left you darken the image. If you drag this slider to 230, any pixels that were white (255) are now 230 and the image is remapped accordingly. Thus, any pixels that were 230 are darker as well.

If you drag the black Input slider right to 25, pixels that were 25 become 0 (black); shadows are darkened, and the number of shadow pixels increases. If you drag the black Output slider to the right to 25 or higher, you remap the image so that the new Output value is the darkest value in the image, thereby lightening it, and Premiere Pro remaps the pixels in the image accordingly.

To change midtones with little effect on the highlights and shadows, click and drag the Gamma Input slider. In general, it's often best to start correcting using the Midtone slider: Drag to the right to lighten midtones, and drag to the left to darken midtones.

Changing channel levels

The Levels Settings dialog box also enables you to change levels for individual Red, Green, and Blue channels. For example, to add contrast to the Red channel, choose Red from the pop-up menu in the Levels Settings dialog box. When you pick a channel, the histogram displays changes to show you the pixel distribution of colors for only that channel. As you click and drag the highlight slider, you can increase contrast in the Red channel. By clicking and dragging the Output slider, you can reduce contrast in the Red channel.

 Note   If you frequently use the same Levels settings, you can save them to disk by clicking the Save button in the Levels Settings dialog box. You can reload your settings by clicking the Load button.

Using other Adjust effects

These other commands in the Adjust bin affect a video clip's color:

✦ **Channel Mixer:** Use the Channel Mixer video effect to create special effects, such as sepia or tinted effects.

✦ **Posterize:** The Posterize effect enables you to reduce the number of gray levels in your image.

✦ **Convolution Kernel:** Use Convolution Kernel to change the brightness and sharpness of your image.

✦ **Extract:** The Extract video effect enables you to convert your color clip to black and white.

✦ **ProAmp:** The ProAmp video effect enables you to adjust the hue, saturation, and luminance of a clip.

For more information about these effects, see Chapter 14.

The Image Control effects

Adobe Premiere Pro provides even more color effects in the Image Control folder. The effects in the Image Control folder are Black & White, Change Color, Change To Color, Color Balance (HSL), Color Balance (RGB), Color Match, Color Offset, Color Pass, Color Replace, and Tint. This section covers the Image Control effects used for correcting colors. (For more information on other Image Control effects, see Chapter 14.)

Change Color

The Change Color effect, shown in Figure 18-15, allows you to change the hue, saturation, and lightness of a specific color or color area. In general, follow these steps to correct using Change Color:

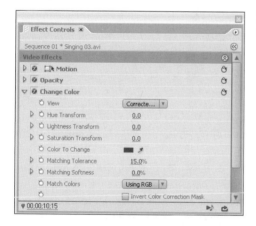

Figure 18-15: Change Color changes colors in a specific area.

1. **Select the Color To Change eyedropper, and click in the image to take a sample of the color area that you want to change.**

2. **Choose Color Correction Mask in the View menu to view the area that will be affected when you adjust colors.**

3. **Adjust the colors range in the mask using the Matching Tolerance and Matching Softness sliders.**

4. **Use the Hue Transform, Lightness Transform, and Saturation Transform sliders to adjust the colors in your clip.**

Here is an overview of the Change Colors controls:

✦ **View:** Choose either Corrected Layer or Color Correction Mask. Corrected Layer displays your image as you correct. Color Correction Mask displays a black-and-white mask representing the area to be corrected. White areas are the areas that will be affected by color adjustments. Figure 18-16 shows the mask.

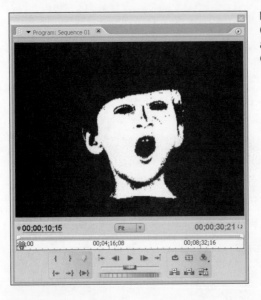

Figure 18-16: The Color Correction Mask displays image areas that will be altered by the Change Color effect.

✦ **Hue Transform:** Click and drag to adjust the hue of the colors to be applied. The degree slider simulates a color wheel.

✦ **Lightness Transform:** This control boosts or decreases color lightness. Use Positive values to brighten and negative to darken.

✦ **Saturation Transform:** This control increases and decreases color intensity. You can achieve some interesting effects by desaturating only a specific image area (drag the Saturation slider to the left), which can make a portion of your image gray and the rest color.

✦ **Color To Change:** Use the eyedropper to click in your image to choose the color that you want to change, or click the swatch to pick a color using the Adobe Color Picker.

✦ **Matching Tolerance:** This item controls the similarity of colors (based on the Color To Change) that will be adjusted. Choose a low tolerance to affect colors similar to the Color To Change. If you choose a high tolerance value, larger areas of the image will be affected.

✦ **Matching Softness:** Clicking and dragging to the right generally softens the Color Correction Mask. This control can also soften the look of the actual correction.

✦ **Match Colors:** Choose a method for matching colors in this drop-down menu. The choices are: Using RGB, Using Hue, and Using Chroma. RGB matches RGB values; Hue matches Hue, which means shades of a specific color will be affected; Chroma matches using saturation and hue, and thus ignores lightness.

✦ **Invert Color Correction Mask:** Click this check box to reverse the mask. When the mask is reversed, black areas in the mask are affected by the color correction, rather than the lighter areas of the mask.

Change To Color

The Change To Color effect allows you to quickly change a selected color to another using hue, saturation, and lightness. When you change a color, other colors are not affected. Here is a review of the Change To Color options, shown in Figure 18-17:

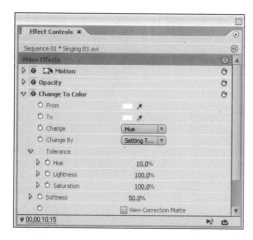

Figure 18-17: Use the Change To Color effect to change a selected color to another color.

✦ **From:** Click the From eyedropper to select the color area that you want to change, or click the swatch to choose a color using the Adobe Color Picker.

✦ **To:** Click the area in the image that you want to use as the final, corrected color, or click the swatch to choose a color using the Adobe Color Picker.

✦ **Change:** Choose which combination of HSL values to affect. Your choices are Hue; Hue and Lightness; Hue and Saturation; and Hue, Lightness, and Saturation.

✦ **Change By:** The Change By choices are Setting to Color or Transforming to Color. Choose Setting to Color to change the color directly without any interpolation. Choose Transforming to Color to base the color change on the difference between the From and To pixel values, as well as the Tolerance value.

✦ **Tolerance:** Expanding the Tolerance slider allows you to control the color range that will be changed based upon Hue, Lightness, and Saturation values. Higher values expand the image range that will be changed, and lower values reduce the range. You can see the range to be changed by clicking View Color Correction Matte.

✦ **Softness:** Click and drag to the right to create smoother transitions between the From and To colors.

✦ **View Correction Matte:** Click to display a black-and-white mask in the Program or Reference Monitor. This allows you to clearly see which image areas will be affected by the Change To Color effect. White areas are affected, black areas aren't, and gray areas are partially affected.

Color Match

The Color Match effect, shown in Figure 18-18, allows you to match colors, highlights, midtones, or shadows in one clip with the color in another. The effect allows you to copy the color or color tones in one clip to another so that the two match when edited together. You can match two colors within the Program monitor or match a color in the Source Monitor with a color in the Program Monitor. Before applying the effect, select the clip that you want to adjust in the Timeline, and then drag the Color Match effect over it. If you will be matching a color in a Source clip, display it in the Source Monitor. Follow these steps for using Color Match in the Effect Controls:

1. **Start by choosing a selection in the Method menu.** The choices include HSL, RGB, and Curves. HSL allows you to apply the effect to different HSL values, RGB allows you to apply the effect to one or a combination of color channels, and Curves allows you to match color using brightness and contrast.

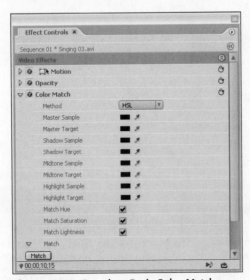

Figure 18-18: Premiere Pro's Color Match allows you to match the colors in one clip with colors in another.

2. **Select the Sample color (the color you want to match) by selecting a Sample eyedropper and clicking in the Source or Program Monitor.** You can pick a Master Sample, or you can choose to match Shadows, Midtones, Highlights, Hue, Saturation, or Lightness.

3. **Select the Target color (the color you want to change or correct) by selecting a Target eyedropper and clicking in the Source or Program Monitor.** You can pick a Master Target, or you can choose to match Shadows, Midtones, Highlight, Hue, Saturation, or Lightness. Note that the Target control you select should correspond with the Sample control. For instance, if you pick a Highlight Sample pick a Highlight Target.

4. You can also choose to include or exclude any combination of HSL or RGB values by selecting or deselecting in the HSL and RGB check boxes.

5. When you are ready to match colors or color components, display the Match button by clicking the triangle in the Match section and then clicking the Match button.

Balancing colors

The Color Balance (RGB) effect enables you to change the balance of a clip's red, green, and blue color channels. As you work with this effect, you put into practice the RGB color theory. Here's how the Red, Green, and Blue sliders work:

✦ Click and drag the red slider to the right. As you drag, you gradually pump red into your image. Drag the slider to the left to decrease red. Note that as you reduce red, you increase cyan. Cyan is added because you now have more green and blue in your image. To increase cyan, click and drag both the green and blue sliders to the right.

✦ Click and drag the green slider to the right. As you drag, you increase green in your image. Drag to the left to decrease green. As you reduce green, you add magenta. Magenta is added because you have more red and blue in your image than green. To add more magenta, click and drag both the red and blue sliders to the right.

✦ Click and drag the blue slider to the right. As you drag, you increase blue in your image. Drag to the left to decrease blue. As you reduce blue, you add yellow. Yellow is added because you have more red and green in your image. You add even more yellow by clicking and dragging both the red and green sliders to the right.

Using HSL Color Balance

Although the RGB color model is used by computer displays to create colors, it's not very intuitive. Many users find the HSL color model more intuitive. As discussed earlier, *Hue* is the color, *Lightness* is the brightness or darkness of the color, and *Saturation* is the color intensity.

To use the HSL Color Balance effect, start by clicking and dragging the Hue circular control (or drag over the numerical readout) to choose a color, as shown in Figure 18-19.

Figure 18-19: The HSL Color Balance effect enables you to adjust color balance using Hue, Saturation, and Lightness controls.

Note If you want to enter a precise number for a slider, click any numeric value above the slider. Doing so opens a dialog box in which you can enter a specific value.

The best way to see the effect of the changing hues is to add saturation to your image. Click and drag the Saturation slider to the right. To see the effect of the Lightness slider, click and drag to the right to add more light to the image, and then drag to the left to reduce the amount of light.

Gamma Correction

The Gamma Correction filter changes midtones with little or no effect on shadows and high-lights. In the Gamma Correction Settings dialog box, simply click and drag the slider. As you click and drag to the right, you increase gamma, thereby darkening your image. By clicking and dragging to the left, you lighten midtones as you decrease gamma.

The Video folder effects

The effects in the Video folder are designed to improve clips that will be exported to video-tape. The effects in the Video folder are Broadcast Colors, Field Interpolate, and Reduce Interlace Flicker. For more information on video effects, see Chapter 14.

Broadcast Colors

To use the Broadcast Colors effect, click and drag the effect from the Video Effects folder from the Effects window over a clip in a video track in the Timeline window.

Note If you are exporting your Premiere Pro production to videotape, you can add color bars to the beginning of your production. Color bars enable a video production facility to calibrate colors when duplicating or broadcasting video. Adding color bars is discussed in Chapter 2.

The sliders and controls for the effect appear in the Effect Controls window. To use the effect, choose either NTSC for American television or PAL for European television in the Broadcast locale pop-up menu. Then choose a method in the How to Make Colors Safe pop-up menu. Here is an explanation of the choices:

✦ **Reduce Luminance:** Reduces pixel brightness values. As the values are reduced, colors become darker.

✦ **Reduce Saturation:** Brings pixel values closer to gray. This makes the colors less intense.

✦ **Key out Unsafe:** Colors that fall beyond the TV gamut become transparent.

✦ **Key in Safe:** Colors that are within the TV gamut are transparent.

In the Maximum Signal Field, use the slider to enter the maximum IRE (or image luminance) breakpoint value. Any levels above this value are altered. If you are unsure of what value to use, use the default setting of 110.

Note In some video cameras, black and white stripes appear in the viewfinder when an image's brightness surpasses 100 IRE. This indicates that the image luminance is too bright.

Field Interpolate and Reduce Interlace Flicker

Two other image-enhancing effects appear in the Video folder: Field Interpolate and Reduce Interlace Flicker.

✦ **Field Interpolate:** This effect creates missing scan lines from the average of other lines.

✦ **Reduce Interlace Flicker:** This effect softens horizontal lines in an attempt to reduce interlace flicker.

Note   Adobe After Effects includes many of the same color-correcting techniques as Adobe Premiere Pro. However, After Effects enables you to mask or isolate areas onscreen. After you mask an area, you can choose to color correct the masked area only.

Timecode

The Timecode effect is not used to enhance colors. Instead it is used to "burn" timecode into footage so it is visible in the Program Monitor. When you apply this effect you can choose position, size, and opacity options in the Effect Controls panel. You can also choose among timecode formats and apply a frame offset.

You can also use the Timecode effect to place timecode in transparent video in a track over your footage. This allows you to view timecode without affecting the actual program footage. To create Transparent Video, choose File ➪ New Transparent Video. Then drag the Transparent Video from the Project panel into a track above your footage in the Timeline. Next, apply the Timecode effect by dragging it over the transparent video.

Summary

If your video clips need color correction or if they need brightness or contrast enhanced, you can use Adobe Premiere Pro's Video Effects. The Adjust, Image Control, and Video folders all contain effects that can enhance video. This chapter covered these topics:

✦ You can view Premiere Pro scopes in a Reference Monitor while you correct video clips.

✦ To quickly adjust hue and luminance, use the Fast Color Corrector in the Color Correction bin.

✦ To correct Luminance, use the Luma Corrector or Luma Curves in the Color Correction bin.

✦ Use the Video Limiter effect to ensure that the video falls within specific limits.

✦ To match a color in one clip with another, use the Color Match effect.

✦   ✦   ✦

Outputting Digital Video from Premiere Pro

◆ ◆ ◆ ◆

Exporting to DVD, MPEG, AVI, and QuickTime

After you've completed the finishing touches on your Adobe Premiere Pro project, you're ready to export the production as a digital movie. When you export the file, you can output it to DVD, CD-ROM, or videotape, or you can export it to disk for viewing on another computer system. If you export your Premiere Pro project as a QuickTime, Video for Windows (AVI), or MPEG file, you can easily view it on most Macs and PCs by simply double-clicking the exported video movie. Movies saved in QuickTime or Video for Windows can be integrated into other multimedia programs, such as Adobe After Effects, Macromedia Director, or Macromedia Flash. MPEG-1 files can be used on the Web. The Hollywood movies and music videos you see on DVD are encoded in MPEG-2 format before the DVD is burned. Because DVD is becoming the most popular vehicle for viewing film and video productions, video producers and editors will undoubtedly be most interested in using Premiere Pro's DVD creation capabilities — particularly because the program's DVD markers and templates makes the process efficient and easy.

This chapter explains how to export Premiere Pro projects to DVD, MPEG format, QuickTime, and Video for Windows. It covers the simple steps you need to execute to begin the export process and then focuses on export settings, such as choosing a compressor, keyframes, and data rates.

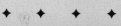

Note   In this book, we divide the exporting procedure into different chapters — this chapter, which covers exporting DVD, MPEG, QuickTime, and Video for Windows, and Chapter 20, which covers Web file formats. Later, Chapter 21 discusses how to export your Premiere Pro project using the Advanced Windows Media and RealVideo Export plug-ins. Chapter 22 covers exporting to videotape.

Creating DVDs in Premiere Pro

Although Premiere Pro is not a sophisticated DVD-authoring program like Adobe Encore, it does provide templates that allow you to quickly create interactive menus and buttons. The menus and buttons are linked to and named by DVD markers created in Premiere Pro's Timeline. Although templates provide the most sophisticated method of creating DVDs, it can be helpful to evaluate all of Premiere Pro's DVD exporting capabilities. The following is a summary of commands that allow you to prepare and/or burn a DVD:

✦ **File ➪ Export ➪ Adobe Media Encoder:** Adobe Media Encoder allows you to export Premiere movies as MPEG-2 files, the file format used by DVDs. Adobe Media Encoder provides presets for exporting in NTSC and PAL standards for standard and widescreen DVD formats.

✦ **File ➪ Export to DVD:** This command allows you to export the selected sequence in the Timeline to DVD. You can burn a DVD, or save a DVD file to disc, or save it as an ISO image file. You can also change encoding settings by accessing the Adobe Media Encoder.

Note   An ISO image file uses the ISO 9660 standard to create an image file that can later be used to burn a DVD. Many DVD burner software packages can read ISO image files. ISO stands for International Organization for Standardization.

✦ **Window ➪ DVD Layout:** This command allows you to create a DVD with menus and buttons based on Premiere Pro template files. The template's menu items and buttons are based upon DVD markers created in Premiere Pro. From the DVD Layout panel, you can preview and burn your DVD. Before burning your DVD, you can change encoding settings by accessing the Adobe Media Encoder. Using File ➪ DVD Layout, you can also create an auto-play DVD, which also uses DVD markers, but does not use graphic templates. Auto-play DVDs use DVD markers as navigational landmarks accessed through the DVD player's Next Scene and Previous Scene buttons.

Using DVD Markers and Templates

Premiere Pro's templates streamline the process of authoring interactive DVDs. Because the templates provide predesigned graphics, menus, and buttons, they can save you hours of design time. But the templates go further than just providing graphic templates; they automatically create navigation links tied to DVD markers created in Premiere Pro.

As you finish your Premiere project, you can set three types of DVD markers in the Timeline panel: Scene Markers, Main Movie Markers, and Stop Markers. When you choose a template, the template automatically links its buttons based on the different markers you've created. Figure 19-1 displays a DVD screen created with Premiere Pro templates.

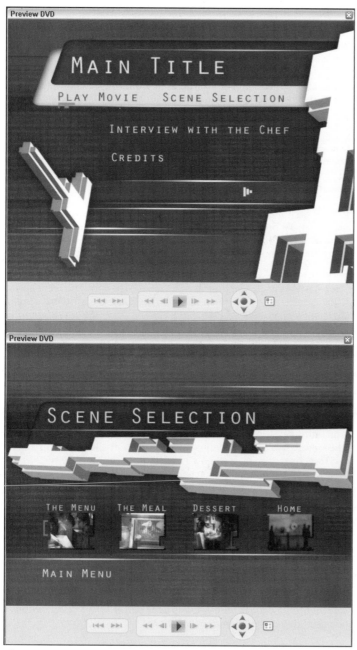

Figure 19-1: DVD Menu created with Premiere Pro templates

Here's how markers work:

✦ **Scene marker:** Scene markers are used for creating links to different scenes within a movie. If you create a scene marker, Premiere Pro creates a scene selection button in the template. This button links to a menu screen with different buttons allowing you to navigate to different scenes. In Figure 19-1, the Scene buttons were created using scene markers. The template automatically loaded a frame from the video into the button. Scene markers can also be used if you are creating an autoplay DVD, which displays no templates. If you create an auto-play DVD, the viewer can jump to different scenes based upon scene markers created in Premiere Pro. In the Timeline, scene markers appear with a blue triangle beneath them.

✦ **Main menu marker:** Main menu markers link to different movies on a DVD from buttons on the main menu. For example, on one DVD, you could have a main movie, a movie showing how the production was made, and another movie of credits. If you create a movie marker, Premiere Pro creates buttons on its main screen that navigate to each movie. Note that you do not need to create a movie marker for the main movie. Premiere Pro automatically creates a button that jumps to the first frame in your movie. In Figure 19-1, the Interview with the Chef and the Credits buttons were automatically added to the templates based on main menu markers. On the Timeline, main menu markers appear with a green triangle beneath them.

✦ **Stop marker:** Stop markers indicate the end of a movie. When the DVD reaches a stop marker, navigation is returned to the main menu. In the Timeline, stop markers appear with a red triangle beneath them.

Understanding Premiere Pro DVD types

After you understand the role that markers play in DVD production, you can begin to conceptualize the type of DVDs you can create with templates. The three basic types of DVD you can create with DVD markers are:

✦ **Scene Selection DVD:** Scene Selection templates provide a Main Menu, Play Movie, and a Scene Selection button as shown in the first panel of Figure 19-1. The Scene Selection button sends the viewer to a second menu with buttons that allow him or her to choose scenes. The scenes that play when you click these buttons are specified by placing Scene markers at specific points on the Timeline. The second panel in Figure 19-1 shows buttons created from Scene markers.

✦ **Movie Selection DVD:** A movie selection DVD provides buttons that link to different movies on a DVD. Use Main Menu markers at different self-contained sections on the DVD to generate Movie Selection buttons, and then use stop markers to send the DVD navigation back to the main menu. Figure 19-2 shows a DVD template with Movie Selection buttons. Movies start from the beginning of the Timeline, so you do not need to place a Main Menu marker at the start of the time ruler.

✦ **Auto-play DVD:** Auto-play DVDs play without menus. You can place scene markers in movies that you want to play automatically. The DVD player's Next and Previous buttons can then be used to jump from marker to marker.

Note   Premiere Pro's templates and DVD markers provide basic DVD navigation. To create more sophisticated links and buttons, you probably need to use a DVD-authoring program, such as Adobe Encore, which is discussed in Chapters 25 and 26.

Figure 19-2: A DVD template with Movie Selection buttons

Creating DVD markers

In order to use DVD templates to create an interactive DVD in Premiere Pro, you must set DVD markers along the Timeline of your project. Because you don't want to keep resetting your DVD markers, creating DVD markers when you have completed your production is most efficient. You can create DVD markers both manually and automatically. The manual method is the slowest, but it provides the most flexibility. As you create markers, note that they can be edited easily, and Premier Pro allows you to preview your production before you burn the DVD.

Creating manual markers

If you create markers manually, you can choose to create scene, main movie, or stop markers, and you can name the markers. The marker names later appear in template buttons. Follow these steps for manually creating DVD markers:

1. **Open the Timeline panel.**

2. **In the Timeline, move the current-time indicator to where you want to create a DVD marker.** Then click the DVD icon in the Timeline. This opens the DVD Marker dialog box, show in Figure 19-3. Alternatively, click and drag the DVD icon to the location where you want to place the DVD marker. When you release the mouse, the DVD Marker dialog box opens.

Tip   You can also create a DVD marker at the current-time indicator by choosing Marker ⇨ Set DVD Marker, and then choosing Scene, Main Menu, or Stop from the list of choices. This creates a DVD marker without opening the DVD Marker dialog box, so it's a quick technique for adding stop markers.

3. **Enter a short name for your marker.** The template eventually uses the marker name as a button name. The button name can be edited, so don't spend too much time pondering an appropriate a marker name.

4. **In the Marker Type, choose a marker type: Scene Marker, Main Menu Marker, or Stop Marker.** As discussed earlier in this section, use scene markers to indicate a link to specific scenes; use main menu markers to specify a link to self-contained clips; use stop markers to stop the DVD and send it back to the main menu.

5. **If you want to change the image that appears in a template's thumbnail button, drag the mouse over the timecode readout.** Stop when you reach the frame that you want to appear as a thumbnail in the button. This does not change the marker location, only the frame that appears in the template. Note that not all templates display images in buttons.

6. **If you want to create an animated button from the video footage at the marker location, select the Motion Menu button.** Templates that do not display images do not display Motion buttons.

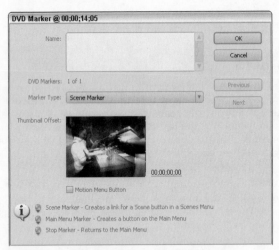

Figure 19-3: Use the DVD Marker dialog box to create navigational links.

Creating automatic markers

The quickest way to create scene markers in a production is to use Premiere Pro's Auto Generate DVD Marker command. This command can create markers at every edit, or it can distribute them throughout a production. This command is probably most useful if you are creating an auto-play DVD because auto-play DVDs do not use menus or buttons; they jump from scene to scene when the Next Scene and Previous Scene buttons are pressed on the DVD control.

To automatically generate DVD markers, select the Timeline panel and then choose Marker ⇨ Auto-Generate DVD Markers. This opens the Automatically Set DVD Scene Markers dialog box, shown in Figure 19-4.

Figure 19-4: Use the Automatically Set DVD Scene Markers dialog box to create automatic markers.

The following options are provided for automatically generating DVD markers:

✦ **At Each Scene:** This option creates a scene marker at each edit.

✦ **Every __ Minute:** This option creates a scene marker at specific time intervals.

✦ **Total Markers:** Choose this option to create a specific number of markers equally distributed throughout the Timeline.

✦ **Clear Existing DVD Markers:** Checking this box clears all current markers before auto-generating new markers.

Moving, editing, and deleting markers

If you want to later move the DVD button, simply click and drag it to the position where you want it on the Timeline. If you want to edit the button, double-click the marker on the Timeline. This opens the DVD Marker dialog box.

If you want to delete a marker, you have several options. Perhaps the easiest is to right-click on the marker and choose Clear DVD Marker or Clear All DVD Markers from the menu that appears. Alternatively, move the current-time indicator to the marker, and choose Marker ⇨ Clear DVD Marker ⇨ Marker at Current Time Indicator. If you simply want to delete all DVD markers, you can right-click on the Timeline and choose Clear All DVD Markers, or choose Marker ⇨ Clear DVD Markers ⇨ All DVD Marker.

Using DVD Templates

The fastest and easiest way to turn your Premiere Pro project into an interactive DVD is to use templates. Premiere Pro provides a variety of custom-made templates with background menus and buttons. The templates are divided into categories such as Corporate, Education, Entertainment, and Sports. The templates also include prebuilt buttons, some of which display thumbnail frames from marker positions on the Timeline. The text of the buttons and their specific layout is based upon DVD marker names and whether you've placed scene markers or main menu markers on the Timeline. For example, if you created main menu markers in your production, your template provides one main screen with navigational buttons for the DVD movie markers, but it does not include a Scene Selection button.

Follow these steps for picking a template:

1. **Select the sequence in the Timeline panel that contains your DVD markers. Then choose Window ➪ DVD layout.**

2. **In the DVD Layout dialog box, shown in Figure 19-5, click Change Template.** This opens the DVD Templates dialog box, shown in Figure 19-5.

Figure 19-5: DVD Layout dialog box before choosing a template

Note   If you want to create an auto-play DVD, you can click Preview to preview the DVD or Burn to burn the DVD.

3. **Click Apply a Template for a DVD with menus.**

4. **Choose a theme in the Theme drop-down menu.**

5. **Click a template image to choose the template, as shown in Figure 19-6, and then click OK.** Premiere Pro returns to the DVD Layout dialog box displaying the template customized to reflect your DVD marker choices.

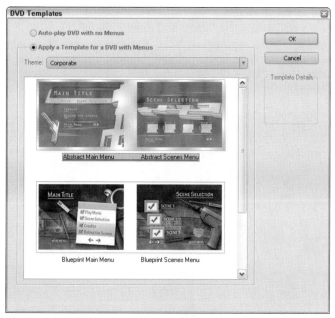

Figure 19-6: Choose a template in the DVD Templates dialog box.

Customizing DVD templates

Premiere Pro's DVD templates undoubtedly save you design and authoring time, however, you may want to customize the templates. If desired, you can move the position of text and buttons and change background and button images. You can make simple edits directly on the DVD templates; however, you make changes to fonts and images in the Effect Controls panel.

Moving buttons and editing text

When editing a template, you'll find that you may need to use the DVD Layout, DVD Marker dialog box, and the Effect Controls panel. Before you begin to edit, make sure that the Effect Controls panel is open onscreen. If it isn't, choose Window ➪ Effect Controls. If the DVD Layout is not open, choose Window ➪ DVD Layout. If you haven't chosen a template, click Change Template and select a template.

Follow these steps to move objects and edit text that appears in a template in the DVD Layout panel:

✦ **To move a text object or button on a template, click it with the Selection tool and drag it to a new location.**

✦ **To resize an object on a template, click it with the Selection tool and drag on a handle.**

✦ **To edit text of a button on a template created from a DVD marker, double-click it.** This opens the DVD Marker dialog box. Edit the text in the Name field. To use multiple lines, press Ctrl+Enter at the end of each line. You can also open the DVD Marker dialog box clicking the button in the template and then clicking Edit in the Effect Controls panel. For more information about editing buttons, see the section "Editing DVD Buttons."

✦ To edit the text of items not created from DVD markers, double-click the text. This opens the Change Text dialog box, where you can edit words in the text.

✦ **To change the typeface, size, or color of text, click the text in the template.** In the Effect Controls panel, click the Type or Size or Color drop-down menu. Click the "T" icons for underlining or bold. Figure 19-7, shows the Type and Size drop-down menus in the Effect Controls panel.

Figure 19-7: Editing a Template with the Effect Controls panel

Editing and creating motion backgrounds

Although most template backgrounds are attractive, you may want to replace a template with your own corporate design or use video as the background for a DVD menu. To edit a background, you need to have a custom template selected and the Effect Controls panel open. If you don't have a template selected, choose Window ➪ DVD Layout and select Change Template. After you select a template, you can change the background using these options:

✦ **To replace a background in a DVD template, click and drag a graphic or clip from the Project panel to the selected template (in the top area of the DVD Templates dialog box).**

✦ **In the Effect Controls panel, you can choose options for controlling the background.** Figure 19-8 shows the Effect Controls panel background editing options. If these options don't appear, click the background in the DVD Layout panel. The video options can be accessed only if you're replacing the template background with a video clip. Here are is a description of the options:

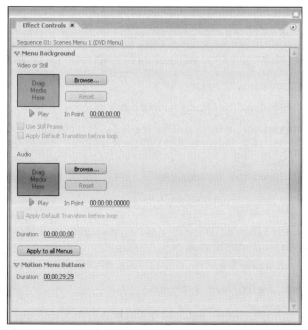

Figure 19-8: Use the Effect Controls panel to edit DVD menu backgrounds.

- **Reset:** This option resets the background to the original template.

- **Play:** This option allows you to preview the video clip background as a thumbnail. After the clip starts playing, the Play button turns to a Pause button.

- **In Point:** Click and drag over the timecode area to set the in point for the frame where you want the video clip background to start.

- **Use Still Frame:** This option freezes a still frame at the video in point for the background.

- **Apply Default Transition:** Click to use the default transition set in the Effects panel as the transition to play when the video begins.

- **Duration:** Use this option to set the duration of background video or audio (timed from the in point).

- **Apply to all Menus:** This option applies the background to all template menus.

- **Duration (Motion buttons):** This option allows you set the duration of all motion buttons. The Motion button option must be selected in the DVD Marker dialog box.

Editing DVD buttons

If you want to change a button on a DVD template, you can easily edit its text or change it into a motion button based on video in the Timeline. To edit a button, you need to have a DVD template selected and the Effect Controls panel open. If you don't have a template selected, choose Window ➪ DVD Layout and select Change Template. After you select a template, you can change the background following these steps:

1. **Select the button on the template.** The Effect Controls panel displays the button.

2. **If you want to edit the marker text, click Edit.** This opens the DVD Marker dialog box where you can change the text. Changes here affect only one button. The following options are available:

   • To rename a button, type a new marker name.

   • If the template allows you to create motion buttons, you can turn the button into a Motion button by clicking Motion Menu Button.

   • To pick a frame for the button display, click and drag the timecode display and stop when you reach the desired frame.

   • To delete a button, click Delete. Both the marker and the button are deleted.

   Click OK to save changes in the DVD Marker dialog.

3. **If you want to change button settings, you can also use options in the Effect Controls:**

   • If you to create Motion button, and you didn't set the button to be a Motion button in the DVD Marker dialog, you can click Motion Menu Button in the Effect Controls panel.

   • If you want to revise the In Point of the motion button, click and drag in the In Point timecode display to change it.

   • To apply Motion effects to all Marker Buttons, click Apply to All Marker buttons.

   • To edit text, choose a typeface, a type size, and styles. To apply text changes to all buttons, click Apply to all Marker Buttons in the Text Area.

Previewing a DVD

Before you burn your DVD, you'll undoubtedly want to preview the buttons and menus, particularly because burning a DVD can be quite time-consuming. To preview a DVD, open the template by choosing Window ➪ DVD Layout and then clicking the Preview button. The Preview DVD window shown in Figure 19-9 shows the buttons and their functions.

Burning a DVD

If you want to export your Premiere Pro project to DVD, you can burn the DVD directly from Adobe Premiere Pro. Premiere Pro supports DVD+R, DVD+RW, DVD-R, and DVD-RW. You can record on single-sided 4.7GB discs. If your DVD recorder is not compatible with Premiere Pro, you can use one of the Burn options to save to a disc folder, and then use your DVD recorder's software to burn the DVD.

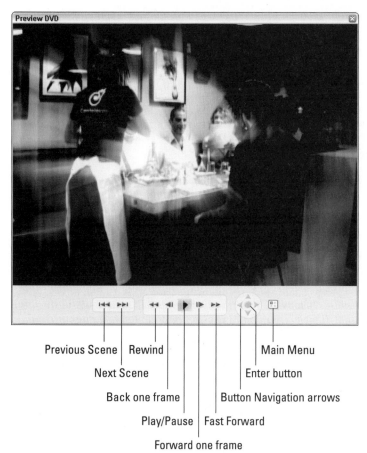

Figure 19-9: Use the Preview DVD window before you burn a DVD.

> **Note** DVD+R and DVD-R are competing DVD recording formats. DVD+RW and DVD-RW are competing rewritable DVD formats.

Follow these steps for burning a DVD from Premiere Pro:

> **Note** If you have an external DVD Recorder, it must be started before you open Premiere Pro. If your DVD recorder is not on, start it and then restart Premiere Pro.

1. **If you created a template for the DVD, choose Window ⇨ DVD Layout, then click Burn DVD.** This opens the Burn DVD dialog box, shown in Figure 19-10.

> **Note** If you didn't create DVD markers, you can burn a DVD by choosing Export ⇨ Export to DVD.

2. **At this point, you can burn the DVD disk or save a file or a folder for burning later.** To burn a disk, proceed to Step 3. To save to a folder or an ISO image:

   - If you want to burn to a specific folder, click Folder, Name your folder in the Folder Name field, and then click Browse. Navigate for where you want your folder to be created. If you want to create another folder, click Make a New Folder and then name the folder. Next click OK. In the Burn DVD dialog box, click Burn.

   - If you want to burn to an ISO image, name the file in the File name field and click Browse. Navigate to where you want the ISO image created. Next click Make a New Folder. Name the folder, click OK, and then click Burn.

3. **To burn to a disc, click Disc.**

4. **Enter a name for the disc in the Disc Name filed.**

5. **Choose the Burner location if needed.**

6. **If a disc is not in the Drive, insert it and click Rescan make to have Premiere Pro examine the media.**

7. **If you want to burn more than one copy of the DVD, enter the number of copies that you want to burn.**

8. **If you want to change quality settings or change from NTSC to PAL or vice versa, click Settings; otherwise click Burn.** This opens Adobe Media Encoder, where you can change encoding settings. (Using Adobe Media Encoder is discussed in the next section.)

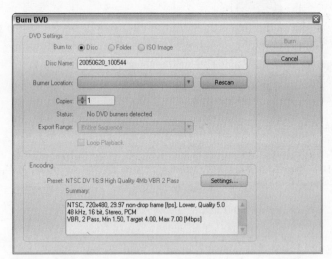

Figure 19-10: Use the Burn DVD dialog box to burn a DVD to disc or to save the DVD file.

Using the Adobe Media Encoder

Adobe's Media Encoder provides an efficient means of choosing MPEG2 settings before burning a DVD or for creating MPEG files. Although most Premiere Pro users will choose the MPEG2-DVD format to prepare files for DVD creation, other MPEG formats exist. The different MPEG formats described in this section are options available in software that burn DVDs. The different formats allow for different screen sizes and different data rates. Some enable subtitles, links, and menus to be integrated into the DVD production.

Using the Adobe Media Encoder is quite simple: Follow these steps to set options in the Adobe Media Encoder before creating an MPEG file or before burning a DVD from the Burn DVD dialog box:

1. **If you did not click the Settings button in the Burn DVD dialog box, click the sequence in the Timeline panel that you want to export and choose File ⇨ Export ⇨ Adobe Media Encoder.** This opens the Export Settings dialog box, shown in Figure 19-11.

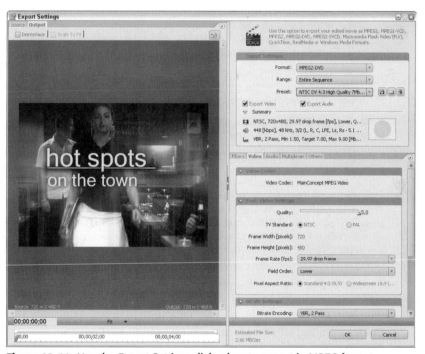

Figure 19-11: Use the Export Settings dialog box to export in MPEG format.

2. **If you are creating an MPEG file, choose an MPEG format from the Format drop-down menu.** (If you opened the Export Settings dialog box from the Burn DVD dialog box, the MPEG2-DVD format is chosen automatically.) When you pick a format, the Presets and Audio and Video CODECS are automatically chosen for you. The following list describes the Format choices:

   - **MPEG1:** This option creates a generic MPEG1 file at 720 × 480 pixels with a frame rate of 29.97 frames per second. The default bit rate is 1.7MB per second.

   - **MPEG1-VCD:** This format uses MPEG1 encoding and provides a frame size of 352 × 240 (NTSC). VCD discs can be played in standard CD-ROM drives, yet they can play as much as 74 minutes of audio and video.

   - **MPEG2:** This option creates a generic MPEG2 file. The default bit rate for the generic MPEG2 file is 4.2MB per second — more than twice the rate of an MPEG1 file. If you click in the Basic Video Settings section, you can change a variety of settings for the generic file.

   - **MPEG2-DVD:** This option is the Hollywood standard for creating DVDs. This format utilizes a full frame of 720 × 480 pixels. When the file is exported, audio and video are separated into two MPEG2 files. The video file extension is .m2v; the audio file extension is .wav (NTSC) or .mpa (for PAL systems).

   - **MPEG2-SVCD:** This format uses MPEG2 encoding and provides a frame size of 480 × 480. This format can provide titles and links. It's supported by major electronics companies such as Sony, Phillips, Matsushita, and JVC.

3. **Next click the Range menu to choose what portion of the Premiere project you want to export — either Work Area from the Timeline panel or the Entire Sequence.**

4. **Change the Preset if desired.** These provide different bit rates and types of encoding: two-pass encoding or one-pass encoding. Although the preset chosen by the Format should be suitable for most work, you may want to experiment to see which presets provide the best results. Note that there are presets for Progressive Scan DVDs. If you are working with progressive scan footage and the DVD will be viewed on a progressive scan DVD player, you will obtain high-quality results with one of these presents. The default calls for High Quality Variable bit rate and two passes. Figure 19-12 shows many of the presets available when you choose the MPEG2-DVD option. Note that some are low-quality and others high-quality and that the choices provide different aspect ratios.

5. **Deselect Export Video or Export Audio if you do not want to export either video or audio.**

6. **If you want to change audio settings, click the Audio Tab. You can choose from Dolby stereo and MPEG code and choose PCM.** (Pulse Code Modulation is an uncompressed format that can produce CD Audio Quality.) Note that Premiere Pro allows you to export three times using Dolby Surround Sound before you must pay a license fee. Figure 19-13 displays MPEG-2 DVD audio options.

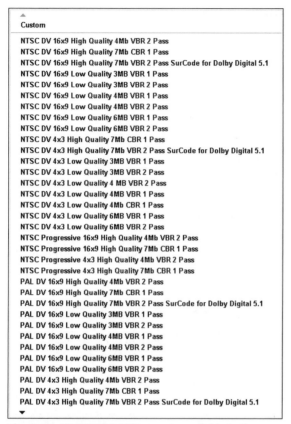

Figure 19-12: MPEG2-DVD presets available in the Export Settings dialog box

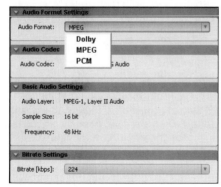

Figure 19-13: MPEG2-DVD presets audio options

7. **Change quality settings if desired.** To lower video quality, click and drag the Quality slider to the left. Why lower the quality? The MPEG compresses faster. Thus, if you're testing or viewing rough edits only, you can save yourself time by lowering quality.

8. **Choose either NTSC or PAL.** NTSC standard is used in North America and Japan. Europe uses PAL.

9. **If desired, change the Frame Rate and Field Order.** The Field Order drop-down menu does not appear if you are using the Progressive scan preset, which does not use video fields. For more information about progressive scanning, see Chapter 4.

10. **If desired, apply a noise reduction filter.** The noise reduction filter is applied before the file is encoded. Noise reduction can reduce file size and reduce video noise. To apply the filter, click the Filters tab and then select the Video Noise Reduction checkbox. Click and drag the Noise Reduction slider to specify the amount of noise reduction.

11. **Switch aspect ratios if needed.** If you chose a preset, either Standard or Widescreen is chosen automatically, so you shouldn't need to change this.

12. **Review the "Adobe Encore Optional features" in the next section. Then finish the DVD burning or MPEG exporting process by following the instructions in the "Completing the MPEG Export" section.**

Understanding Encoding and Bit Rates

The Adobe Media Encoder's presets include a variety of technical encoding terms. Although many Premiere Pro users prefer not to change MPEG settings, here is a review of some of the encoding terms you encounter if you choose to change settings:

✦ **Variable bit rate (VBR)** varies the bit rate of a clip as it plays back. When a high-action scene needs more bits or bandwidth, the encoding process delivers the extra bits; in areas that don't require high bandwidth, it lowers the bit rate. Thus, for clips that vary in action, VBR can provide better quality than constant bit rate (CBR), which does not vary the bit rate of the clip as it plays back. Although VBR generally provides higher quality, it requires more processing power than CBR. Since the MPEG file may be played back on different systems, be aware that a file exported at a constant bit rate may play back more reliably on older computers and playback systems.

If you select CBR, you can select the bitrate (in megabits per second) for the file. If you select VBR, you can select a Target, Maximum, and Minimum bit rate. You also specify the number of passes used to analyze the file.

✦ **Two-pass encoding** increases the digital quality of exported video. When two-pass encoding is used, the video is processed twice. The first time, the encoder analyzes the video to determine the best way to encode it. On the second pass, the encoder uses the information gathered in the first pass to encode the video. As you might guess, two-pass encoding takes longer than one-pass, but it increases the quality of the encoded video.

If you are exporting using MPEG-2 format, you can also change several intra-frame compression options. When MPEG-2 files are compressed, Groups of Pictures (GOP) are analyzed and compressed into one frame. For example, in MPEG-2, as many as 15 frames may be grouped together (12 frames in PAL). The GOP consists of *I frames, B frames,* and *P frames*. An *I frame* is a keyframe of the entire frame data, and a *P frame* is a predictive frame that can be a small percentage of the size of the I frame. A *B frame* is a frame that can use a portion of the I frame and the P frame. When exporting to MPEG-2, Adobe Media Encorder provides these options. Most users do not need to change the default settings for these options:

- **M Frames:** Choose the number of B frames (between consecutive I and P frames) in the drop-down menu. The default setting is 2.

- **N Frames:** Choose the number of frames between I frames in the drop-down menu. The N frames value must be a multiple of M Frames. The default setting is 12.

- **Closed GOP Every:** Enter the number of repeated Closed Group of Pictures. The Closed GOP does not process frames outside of the Group of Pictures. (This option does not appear in the MPEG2-DVD preset.)

- **Automatic GOP Placement**: Leave this option selected to allow Automatic GOP placement. (This option does not appear in MPEG2-DVD preset.)

Adobe Encoder optional features

During the export process, the Adobe Media Encoder allows you to create custom presets and to crop, preview, and deinterlace video.

Previewing

The Adobe Media Encoder provides a preview of your source file and a preview of the final video output. The following list describes options for previewing Source and Output video:

✦ **To preview the source file, click the Source tab.**

✦ **To preview the video based upon the settings in the Adobe Media Encoder, click the Output tab.**

✦ **To scrub through video in either the Source or Output tab, click and drag in the Time Ruler at the bottom of the preview area.**

Cropping and scaling

Before you export your file, you can crop the Source video. Cropped areas appear as black in the final video. Follow these steps to crop your video:

1. **Click the Source tab.** This opens the Source view of your video

2. **Select the Crop tool, shown in Figure 19-14.**

3. **To crop precisely using pixel dimension, click and drag over the Left, Top, Right, or Bottom numerical fields.** Clicking and dragging right reduces the cropping area. As you click and drag, the cropping area is displayed onscreen. Alternatively, click and drag a corner over the area of the video that you want to retain. As you click and drag, a readout appears displaying the frame size in pixels.

4. **If you want to change the aspect ratio of the crop to 4:3 or 16:9, click in the crop proportions drop-down menu and choose the aspect ratio.**

5. To preview the cropped video, click the Output tab.

6. If you want to Scale your video frame to fit with in the crop borders, select the Scale to Fit check box (next to the Interlace check box).

Figure 19-14: Use the crop icon to crop the video frame.

Deinterlacing video

To deinterlace video, click the Output tab and then click the Deinterlace check box. Deinterlacing removes one field from a video frame to prevent blurring artifacts, which can occur when video is output on a computer. This blurring is most likely to occur during scenes that exhibit motion. The blurring results from the difference in frame information between the odd or upper video field and the even or lower video field that comprise a video frame.

Saving Metadata

If you are creating an MPEG file, you can embed metadata with the file by choosing XMP Info in the Export Settings panel menu. This opens the XMP dialog box where you can enter information copyright and descriptive information about the file. XMP is Adobe's Extensible Metadata Platform. XMP data can be shared with other applications that support this format.

Saving, importing, and deleting presets

If you make changes to a preset, you can save your custom preset to disk so that you can use it later. After you save presets, you can import or delete them. Here are the options:

✦ **Saving presets:** If you edit a preset and want to save it to use later, or use as a basis for comparing export quality, click the Save Preset button (the disk icon). Then enter a name in the Choose Name dialog box. If you want to save the Filter tab settings, click the Save Filter Settings check box. To save cropping and Deinterlace settings, select the Save Other Tasks check box.

✦ **Importing presets:** The easiest way to import a custom preset is to click the Preset drop-down menu and choose it from the top portion of the list. Alternatively, you can click the Import Preset button (the folder icon) and then load the presets from disk. Presets have a *.vpr* file extension.

✦ **Deleting presets:** To delete a preset, load the preset and then click the Delete Preset button (the trash icon). An alert appears, warning you that the deletion process cannot be undone.

Completing the MPEG export

After you've chosen and perhaps fine-tuned settings in the Export Settings dialog box, you can simply click OK to return to the Burn DVD screen or to start the process of creating an MPEG file. After clicking OK, click Burn if you are returning to the DVD Layout screen, or name your file in the Save File dialog box and choose a folder and drive location.

Exporting in AVI and QuickTime

If you don't choose to export your movie as a DVD or in MPEG format, you may want to export in either Windows AVI or QuickTime. If you export a movie in Video for Windows (called Microsoft AVI in the Export Movie Settings dialog box) format, your movie can be viewed on systems running Microsoft Windows. Mac users can also view AVI movies by importing them into the latest version of Apple's QuickTime Movie player. On the Web, Microsoft has switched from AVI format to Advanced Windows Media format (covered in Chapter 21). However, AVI format is still accepted as a format that can be imported into many multimedia software programs. Video-editing programs such as Premiere Pro capture movies using Microsoft's DV AVI format.

After you edit your work and preview your production, you can export your project by selecting the sequence you want to export in the Timeline and choosing File ⇨ Export ⇨ Movie. Doing so opens the Export Movie dialog box, shown in Figure 19-15. At the bottom left of the screen, Premiere Pro displays the current video and audio settings. If you want to export using these settings, simply name the file and click Save. The length of time Premiere Pro takes to render the final movie depends on the size of your production, its frame rate, frame size, and compression settings.

Figure 19-15: The Export Movie dialog box displays the current video and audio settings for your Premiere Pro project.

 Note   You can export a frame by moving the current-time indicator to it and choosing File ➪ Export ➪ Frame.

 Note   Video for Windows files are saved with an .avi (audio video interleave) file extension. Video for Windows files are often referred to as *AVI files*.

Changing Export settings

Although the video and audio settings used during the creation of a Premiere Pro project may be perfect during editing, they may not produce the best quality for specific viewing environments. For example, a digital movie with a large frame size and high frame per second rate may stutter playing back in a multimedia program or on the Web. Thus, you may want to change several configuration settings before exporting your Premiere Pro project to disc. To change export settings, click the Settings button in the Export Movie dialog box. (If the Export Movie dialog box is not onscreen, you can display it by selecting a sequence in the Timeline panel and choosing File ➪ Export ➪ Movie.)

After you click Settings, the Export Movie Settings dialog box, shown in Figure 19-16, appears. When this dialog box opens, it is automatically set to the General setting.

Figure 19-16: The Export Movie Settings dialog box

Following is a description of the choices available in the Export Movie Settings dialog box:

✦ **File Type:** If you want to switch file types, use this menu. Apart from picking a QuickTime or AVI format, you can also choose to save your digital movie as a series of still frames in different file formats, such as GIF, TIF, or Windows Bitmap.

✦ **Range:** Here, you can choose to export the Entire Sequence or the Work Area specified in the Timeline.

✦ **Export Video:** Deselect this option if you do not want to export the video.

✦ **Export Audio:** Deselect this option if you do not want to export the audio.

✦ **Add to Project When Finished:** This option adds the exported movie to the Project panel.

✦ **Beep When Finished:** This option causes your computer to beep when the project is finished.

✦ **Embedding Options:** This option allows you to create a link between the Premiere and the exported movie. To create the link, choose Project in the Embedding Options drop-down menu. After the link is created, you can open the original project by choosing Edit ➪ Edit Original in another Adobe Application. Note that this option isn't available for all export choices.

Changing Video settings

To review or change video settings, choose Video in the Export Movie Settings dialog box. The video settings reflect the currently used project settings. When choosing settings, you must understand that choices you make may affect quality. For example, if you are exporting to the Web, you want to reduce the frame size of DV projects and change from non-square to square pixels. Consider the following options when exporting to the Web or multimedia applications:

✦ If you change the frame size, make sure the aspect ratio matches that of your project. For example, you can change a DV image from 720 × 480 to 320 × 240 or 160 × 120, and the pixel aspect ratio changes from 4:3 to 3:2. Switching the pixel aspect ratio to square pixels before exporting maintains the 4:3 image aspect ratio.

✦ Reducing the frame rate for Web and multimedia export usually produces smoother playback. Several codecs provide better quality if the exported frame rate is a multiple of the original frame rate. Thus, you can choose 15 frames per second for footage recorded at 30 frames per second.

Choosing a QuickTime compressor

When creating a project, capturing video, or exporting a Premiere Pro project, one of the most important decisions you can make is to choose the correct compression settings. A compressor or *CODEC* (COmpression/DECompression) determines exactly how the computer restructures or removes data to make the digital video file smaller. Although most compression settings are designed to compress files, not all of these settings are suitable for all types of projects. The trick is to choose the best CODEC for your Premiere Pro project to produce the best quality with the smallest file size. One CODEC may be better for Web digital video, and another may be best suited to a project that contains animation created in a painting program.

The settings that appear in the Compressor pop-up menu are based upon the file type chosen in the Export Movie Settings dialog box. The QuickTime CODECs, shown in Figure 19-17, are different from the Video for Windows CODECs. Furthermore, depending on the compressor, the options in the Video section of the Export Movie Settings dialog box change.

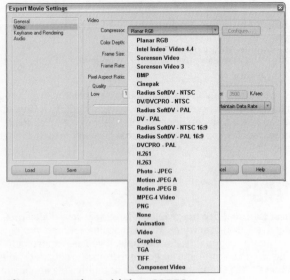

Figure 19-17: The QuickTime CODECs

Following is a brief review of some of the QuickTime CODEC choices available in the Export Movie Settings dialog box:

✦ **Animation:** This setting is can be useful for storing two-dimensional animation, particularly animated titles with flat colors. Using this compressor, you can set the bit depth to Millions+ (of colors), which enables exporting an alpha channel with the movie. If you choose the 100% option, Animation provides *lossless* compression, which can produce large file sizes. The CODEC is generally not suitable for "real-life video" footage. It is generally considered to be a CODEC used for storage and authoring, rather than a delivery CODEC.

✦ **Cinepak:** This format was one of the most popular for Web and multimedia work. Although it can still be used for playback on slower computer systems, this CODEC has largely become a relic of the past, supplanted by the Sorenson CODEC. When exporting, you can also set the data rate using Cinepak, but be aware that setting the data rate below 30K per second can lower the quality of the video.

✦ **MJPEG-A, MJPEG-B:** These formats are used for editing and capturing video. These CODECs can provide very good results when quality is set to 100%. Both CODECs use spatial compression, so no keyframe control is available. Also, MJPEG usually requires a hardware board for playback.

✦ **Sorenson 3:** This format is used for high-quality desktop video for the Web and for CD-ROM. This CODEC provides better compression than Cinepak. Sorenson 3 can reduce file sizes by three to four times as much as Cinepak does. Note that, when exporting from a DV project to Web or multimedia, this CODEC allows you to change the pixel aspect ratio to square pixels. Sorenson 3 provides better quality and is the forbearer to Sorenson 2, and should be used instead of Sorenson 2.

Note Sorenson also sells a high-end version of the Sorenson CODEC that provides better quality and more features. For example, Sorenson Pro provides temporal stability, which essentially allows the video frame rate to slow down for slower systems.

✦ **Planar RGB:** This is a lossless CODEC good for animation created in painting and 3D programs and is an alternative to the Animation CODEC.

✦ **Video:** This is an outdated CODEC and generally should not be used.

✦ **Component Video:** Generally, this is used for capturing analog video. When you capture video, this may be your only choice, depending on the video capture board installed in your computer.

✦ **Graphics:** Used for graphics with 256 colors or less, it is generally not used in desktop video.

✦ **Photo-JPEG:** Although this CODEC can create good image quality, slow decompression makes this CODEC unsuitable for desktop video.

✦ **H.263:** This option is used for video conferencing and provides better quality than the H.261 CODEC. This CODEC is not recommended for video editing.

✦ **PNG:** This option generally is not used for motion graphics. This CODEC is included in QuickTime as a means of saving still graphics in PNG Web format or flat RGB animation.

✦ **TIF:** Short for Tagged Information File Format, this is a printing format for still images.

✦ **BMP:** This is a Windows-compatible graphics format for still images.

✦ **DV-PAL and DV-NTSC:** These digital video formats for NTSC and PAL (choose the format that applies to the geographic region for your intended audience) are used for transferring digitized data from DV camcorders or from camcorders into Premiere Pro. They are useful formats for capturing video that is transferred to another video-editing system.

Note

The QuickTime CODECs list may contain hardware-specific CODECs supplied by computer and board manufacturers. For example, Sony Vaio computer owners see a Sony DV format in the QuickTime CODEC list. Follow the instructions provided with your capture board or computer when choosing one of these CODECs.

Choosing a Video for Windows compressor

If you are exporting a Video for Windows file, the compressor choices are different from the QuickTime choices. Following is a brief review of several AVI CODECs:

✦ **Cinepak:** Originally created by Radius, this option provides the same features as QuickTime's Cinepak. This CODEC is primarily used for multimedia output on older systems. Compression can be time-consuming, but image quality is generally good.

✦ **Indeo Video 5.10:** Created by Intel (makers of the Pentium computer chip), this CODEC provides good image quality. It's often used for capturing raw data. Quality is similar to desktop video produced using the Cinepak CODEC.

✦ **Microsoft RLE (Run Length Encoding):** The bit depth for this CODEC is limited to 256 colors, making it suitable only for animation created in painting programs with 256 colors or images that have been reduced to 256 colors. When the Quality slider is set to High, this CODEC produces lossless compression.

Changing bit depth

After you choose a CODEC, the dialog box changes to show the different options provided by that CODEC. If your CODEC enables you to change bit depth, you can choose another setting in the Bit Depth pop-up menu. For example, the Sorenson CODEC does not enable you to switch bit depths. However, the Cinepak CODEC enables you to choose 256 colors. Because the Cinepak CODEC allows 256 colors, clicking the Palette button enables you to load a palette or have Premiere Pro create a 256-color palette from the clips in the movie. However, be aware that reducing the palette to 256 colors can result in poor picture quality. Unless you are working with an animation created in a painting program, you probably don't want to reduce the colors in your video project to 256.

Choosing quality

The next option controlled by the selected CODEC is the Quality slider. Most CODECs enable you to click and drag to choose a quality setting. The higher the quality is, the larger the file size of the exported movie.

Choosing a data rate

Many CODECs enable you to specify an output data rate. The *data rate* is the amount of data per second that must be processed during playback of the exported video file. The data rate changes, depending on which system plays your production. For example, the data rate of CD-ROM playback on a slow computer is far less than the data rate of a hard disk. If the data rate of the video file is too high, the system cannot handle the playback. If this is the case, playback may be garbled as frames are dropped. Following are a few suggestions for different playback scenarios:

✦ **World Wide Web:** Choose a data rate that accounts for Web connection speeds. Remember that even though a modem may be capable of 56Kbps (kilobits per second), the actual connection speed is probably slower. Also remember that the data rate field accepts data in kilobits per second, rather than bits per second. For Sorenson and Cinepak CODECs, try a data rate of 50. Adobe recommends trying a data rate of 150K per second for movies with a frame size of 240 × 180. Note that when uploading to the Web, smaller file size is more important than data rate. See Chapter 20 for more information about exporting video to the Web, especially if you are using a streaming media server.

✦ **Videotape editing:** If you are exporting video files for further editing, the data rate should be set so that the computer editing system can handle it. To export for further editing, use a CODEC that does not reduce video quality, such as a DV CODEC.

✦ **CD-ROM:** For CD-ROM playback, specify a data rate consistent with the data rate of the CD-ROM drive. The data rate setting is especially important for older CD-ROM drives. For example, a double-speed CD-ROM has a data rate at 300K per second. Typical data rates for double-speed CD-ROMs are between 200K and 250K per second. For older compressors, such as Cinepak, Adobe recommends data rates for a 12-speed (12X) CD-ROM drive to be 1.8MB per second; for a 24X CD-ROM, 3–3.6MB. If you are using the Sorenson 3 CODEC, you can set the data rate at 200KB per second or below. Sorenson recommends this formula as a starting point: height × width × frames per second ÷ 48000. Thus, if exporting a 320 × 240 video at 15 frames per second, you can limit the data rate to 24KB per second as a starting point; at 30 frames per second, you can limit the data rate to 48KB per second. (For high-action clips, you generally need a higher data rate.)

✦ **Intranets:** The data rate speed depends upon the actual speed of the network. Because most intranets use high-speed connections, you can generally set the playback to 100K or more.

✦ **Hard disk:** If you are creating a production for playback on a computer system, try to ascertain the data rate of the audience's hard disk. The data rates for most modern hard disks are in excess of 33 million bits per second.

Note   Adobe's Support Knowledgebase document "Applying Data Rate Limits in Premiere Pro" is available online at www.adobe.com/support/techdocs/a60a.htm.

Setting recompression

If you specify a data rate, select the Recompress check box. Doing this helps guarantee that Premiere Pro keeps the data rate beneath the one specified in the data rate field. If you want Premiere Pro to recompress every frame, whether or not it is below the data rate, choose Always in the Recompress pop-up menu. Better quality is produced, however, if you choose the Maintain Data Rate setting. This recompresses only the frames that are higher than the specified data rate.

Changing frame rates and frame size

Before exporting video, you may want to reduce the frame rate or reduce the frame size to reduce the file size of your production. The frame rate is the number of frames Premiere Pro exports per second. If you change frame size, be sure to specify the horizontal and vertical dimensions in pixels. If your video was captured at a 4:3 aspect ratio, be sure to maintain this ratio to avoid distorting clips. As noted earlier, to maintain the aspect ratio, you may need to change the pixel aspect ratio.

Specifying keyframes

Another video export setting that can control export file size is the Keyframe setting in the Export Movie Settings dialog box's Keyframe and Rendering section (see Figure 19-18).

Figure 19-18: The Keyframe and Rendering section of the Export Movie Settings dialog box

Keyframe settings can be changed when choosing CODECs, such as Cinepak and Sorenson video, with temporal compression. As discussed in Chapter 4, the keyframe setting specifies how many times to save the complete video frame. If the keyframe setting for the codec is specified in frames, a setting of 60 creates a keyframe every two seconds at 30 frames per second. As the CODEC compresses, it compares each subsequent frame and saves only the information that changes in each frame. Thus, using keyframes can significantly reduce the file size of your video.

Before creating keyframes you should research the selected CODEC, if possible. For example, the Sorensen 3 CODEC creates keyframes automatically every 50 frames. Sorenson documentation recommends setting a keyframe every 35 to 65 frames. When experimenting, try to keep as few keyframes as possible. However, note that images displaying motion generally require more keyframes then those without much motion.

To help ensure smooth transitions, you may want to force Premiere Pro to create a keyframe at transitions and edits. To set keyframes at Edit points, select the Add Keyframes at Edits option in the Export Movie Settings dialog box. To set keyframes at specific points in your production, set markers at points where you want Premiere Pro to create a keyframe and then select the Add Keyframe at Markers option in the Export Movie Settings dialog box.

Tip   To view of the number of the keyframes in a clip, select it in the Project panel and choose File ➪ Get Properties for Selection. In the Properties dialog box, scroll down to view the number of keyframes in the clip.

Changing Audio settings

When you export your final project, you may want to change the audio settings. To access the audio options, choose Audio in the Export Movie Settings dialog box. The settings in the Audio section of the Export Movie Settings dialog box, shown in Figure 19-19, are as follows:

Figure 19-19: The Audio section of the Export Movie Settings dialog box

✦ **Compressor:** In the compressor pop-up menu, choose a compressor if desired. (The audio CODECs are reviewed at the end of this section.)

✦ **Sample Rate:** Lower the rate setting to reduce file size and to speed up the rendering of the final production. Higher rates produce better quality and increase processing time. (CD-ROM quality is 44kHz.)

✦ **Sample Type:** Stereo 16-bit is the highest setting; 8-bit mono is the lowest setting. Lower bit depths produce smaller files and reduce rendering times.

✦ **Channels:** Choose either Stereo (two channels) or Mono (one channel).

✦ **Interleave:** This option determines how frequently audio is inserted into the video frames. Choosing 1 frame in the pop-up menu tells Premiere Pro to load the audio for the frame until the next frame is processed. However, this can cause the sound to break up if the computer cannot handle lots of audio data quickly.

Choosing QuickTime audio CODECs

Following is a brief review of several QuickTime audio CODECs. You must specify a CODEC only if you want to add compression to sound. For each CODEC, the compression ratio appears next to its name:

✦ **ULaw 2:1:** Used as a common audio format on Unix platforms, ULaw is used for digital telephony in both North America and Japan.

✦ **16-bit Endian and 16-bit Little Endian:** This format is not used for video editing, but it is used by hardware engineers and software developers.

✦ **24-bit integer and 32-bit integer soft:** This format is not used for video editing, but it is used by hardware engineers and software developers.

✦ **IMA Designed by the Interactive Multimedia Association:** This cross-platform format can be used to compress audio for multimedia.

✦ **32-bit floating point and 64-bit floating point:** This format it not used for video editing, but it is used by hardware engineers and software developers.

✦ **Alaw:** This format is used for European digital telephony.

✦ **Qdesign Music CODEC:** This format can be used for high-quality Web output and can provide CD-ROM quality over a modem.

✦ **Qualcomm Pure Voice:** This speech format shouldn't be used at an audio rate higher than 8kHz.

✦ **MACE 3:1 and MACE 6:1:** This Macintosh audio CODEC can be used for QuickTime movies for PCs and Macs. MACE 3:1 provides better quality because it uses less compression.

Choosing Video for Windows audio CODECs

Premiere Pro offers the following audio compression options when exporting a project as a Video for Windows file:

✦ **Indeo audio software:** This option is good for Web output of music and speech. It was created for use with Indeo video CODECs.

✦ **Truespeech:** This option is used for speech over the Internet. It works best at low data rates.

✦ **Microsoft GSM 6.10:** This option is for speech only and is used for telephony compression in Europe.

✦ **MS-ADPCM:** Microsoft's version of an Adaptive Differential Pulse Code Modulation compressor, this option can be used for CD-ROM quality sound.

✦ **Microsoft IMA ADPCM:** This option, used for cross-platform multimedia, was developed by the Interactive Multimedia Association.

✦ **Voxware CODECs:** This option can be used for speech output on the Web. It's best at low data rates.

Summary

Premiere Pro movies can be output to DVD directly from Premiere Pro. If you want to create an interactive DVD, you can set DVD markers that will be used to create menus and buttons in Premiere Pro DVD templates.

To view a Premiere Pro movie on a CD-ROM or the Web or to view it on a computer system that does not have Premiere Pro installed, you can export the Premiere Pro file in QuickTime, AVI, or MPEG format.

This chapter covered the following topics:

✦ Place DVD markers on the Timeline if you want to create interactive DVDs using Premiere Pro's DVD Templates.

✦ Change DVD templates in the DVD Layout panel.

✦ Click Preview in the DVD Layout panel to preview a DVD.

✦ To export your movie as an MPEG file, choose File ➪ Export ➪ Adobe Media Encoder.

✦ To burn a CD directly from Premiere Pro, choose File ➪ Export ➪ Export to DVD.

✦ To change export settings when exporting to AVI or QuickTime, click the Settings button in the Export Movie dialog box.

✦ When exporting, you can change Video, Keyframe and Rendering, and Audio settings.

✦ Choosing the correct CODEC and reducing frame rates and frame size reduces file size of the exported production.

✦   ✦   ✦

Outputting to the Web and Intranets

If you're a video producer or Web designer the day will undoubtedly come when you want to showcase one of your Premiere Pro video productions on a Web page, or on a company intranet. Before you start creating digital movies for the Web, it can be helpful to know exactly how a browser loads a digital movie onto a Web page and what options are available to you. For example, when a QuickTime movie is displayed on a Web page, you can have it play immediately or you can add controls to have the user start and stop the movie. This chapter provides an overview of the movie file formats for the Web and discusses how to add a digital movie to the Web and the QuickTime HTML options available.

Understanding Your Web Delivery Options

You don't need to be a Webmaster or Java programmer to play a Premiere movie on a Web or intranet page. To get started, all you need to know is a little HTML. As you'll discover from reading this chapter, movies can be displayed by using a simple HTML *embed* tag, as illustrated in this example:

```
<EMBED SRC="mypremiere.mov", WIDTH=320, HEIGHT=240>
```

In this case, the name of the movie is my mypremiere.mov. Its frame size is 320 ¥ 240 pixels. The embed command tells the browser to load the movie from a Web server and use a plug-in to play the movie. Although this technique works, it can lead to poor playback. Unless the movie is saved so that it can stream or use progressive playback, the viewer needs to wait until the entire movie is downloaded to his hard drive before he can view it. It's almost like having to wait for a VCR to play the entire program once before you can view it. If you want to display digital movies on a Web or intranet page, you should investigate two delivery choices designed to enhance playback quality: *streaming video* and *progressive download*.

Streaming video

If you can afford it, streaming is the best vehicle for delivering digital video over the Web or an intranet. In many ways, streaming is similar to cable TV. You see the program as it arrives at your home or office. No portion of the file is downloaded to disk before or during playback. Instead, it is *buffered* to memory first and then displayed onscreen. Typically, the video is streamed at different data rates: a data rate for modems (narrow band connections) as well as data rates for faster connections (broadband).

Note　Streaming video does not use the Web standard HTTP (Hypertext Transfer Protocol). HTTP determines exactly the formatting, transmittal method, and responses that Web servers and browsers use when responding to commands issued over the Internet. Instead of HTTP, streaming media uses Real Time Streaming Protocol (RTSP), which not only allows streaming media, but can also provide users with the power to interact with the streaming server. For example, RTSP allows viewers to rewind video and jump to different chapters in QuickTime movies.

Often, viewers click an onscreen button to request a data stream based upon whether they have a slow or fast connection. This "on-demand" Web broadcasting comes at a price. To handle the streams of video and audio, a high-speed connection, such as a DSL, cable modem, or T1, is required.

Furthermore, special server software is needed to stream the video. Often, the server software and video content are on a separate computer that just handles video streaming.

The three primary producers of streaming media software are Apple, Microsoft, and Real Networks. Apple's QuickTime streaming software (www.quicktime.com) is part of its OS X server package. Apple also provides QuickTime streaming software for Linux and Windows NT. Microsoft provides Windows Media server software (www.microsoft.com/windows/ windowsmedia/default.asp) with its Windows 2000 server package. Real Networks server software must be purchased from RealMedia (www.realnetworks.com).

Progressive download

For short video clips, progressive download often can provide a suitable alternative to streaming media. Although progressive download doesn't provide video and audio quality as high as that in streaming media, it allows the beginning of the video clip to be played before it is downloaded. For most producers, this is the key to preventing viewers from surfing away while the video downloads. However, unlike streaming media, the video is actually down-loaded to the viewer's hard drive. A further drawback is that playback can become distorted if the data rate of the Web connection slows. In contrast, streaming media removes portions of the video to keep the playback consistent (often, the viewer doesn't notice).

Note　For an in-depth discussion of streaming media, see www.adobe.com/smprimer. For the latest on streaming media as well as a few streaming media tutorials, check out www.streamingmedia.com. If you're looking for a job in the streaming media industry, click the careers link on the aforementioned Web page.

Choosing the Right Web File Format

Before you begin planning to output your digital movies to the Web or an intranet, you should be familiar with the different movie file formats that can be viewed in a browser connected to the Web or an intranet. The file formats listed here all require some form of plug-in to be installed in the browser software. Saving QuickTime Windows Media and RealVideo files for the Web is covered in Chapter 21.

✦ **QuickTime (MOV):** Apple's QuickTime format is one of the most popular Web video file formats. It is cross-platform and provides good quality. QuickTime provides numerous HTML options that can change how the movie appears on the Web. Different QuickTime tracks (discussed later in this chapter) can also be added to Web-based movies.

Although not a requirement for Web playback, for the best results, QuickTime movies should be streamed by Apple's QuickTime streaming software. This software is included with Apple's Mac OS X server package. As mentioned earlier, Apple Computer has created QuickTime Streaming Server versions for Windows NT and Linux. Premiere Pro users can quickly create QuickTime streaming-ready movies by exporting their movies using Adobe's Media Encoder (File ⇨ Export ⇨ Adobe Media Encoder).

✦ **Windows Media format (WMV):** Video created in Windows Media format is loaded on a Web page into Microsoft's Window's media player. In Premiere Pro, you can output projects in Windows Media format by choosing File ⇨ Export ⇨ Adobe Media Encoder. The current version of Windows provides compression improvements from 15 to 50 percent over previous versions. Microsoft's Web page claims that it provides the "highest fidelity audio and best quality video at any bit rate from dial-up to broadband."

✦ **RealVideo (RM):** RealNetworks' streaming video format is probably the most popular format available. For true high-quality video, the RealVideo encoded movies must be created with RealNetworks streaming software CODEC. Premiere Pro's File ⇨ Export ⇨ Adobe Media Encoder command enables you to export Premiere Pro movies in RealVideo format.

✦ **Flash Video (FLV):** Movies saved in FLV (Flash Video) format can be viewed in Macromedia's Flash player. FLV files can be loaded from a Web server for progressive downloading, or streamed using Macromedia's Flash Communications Server. The combination of Flash Video and Flash Communications Server has quickly grown in popularity, largely because the Flash player is used in over 90 percent of the world's browsers. When video is played within Flash, it can be controlled by Actionscript, Flash's versatile scripting language that provides powerful interactive features. Premiere Pro's Export Timeline ⇨ Adobe Media Encoder command enables you to export Premiere Pro movies in FLV format for use in Flash Video. Using Flash Video is covered in Chapter 23.

✦ **Audio Video Interleave (AVI):** All Windows computers are equipped to read Microsoft AVI files; however, because AVI is not cross-platform, it is not often used on the Web. For Web use, Microsoft has dropped the format and replaced it with the more sophisticated Windows Media Format.

Understanding HTML

If you plan to output digital video to the Web, you should have an understanding of how digital movies are loaded onto a Web page. With this knowledge, you can control how your movie is displayed and when it begins to play. Your first step is to understand how Hypertext Markup Language (HTML) can be used to load text and images on a Web page.

How a movie is loaded onto a Web page

When you see a digital movie on a Web page, it appears because the HTML code instructs the browser to load the movie from a Web server. HTML is a series of text codes or tags that tell the browser what to do. Although numerous programs exist that can write HTML code for you, you could construct an entire Web page using a simple text editor. For example, the following HTML code snippet tells the Web browser to put the words **Premiere on the Web** on a page in bold type:

```
<b>Premiere on the Web</b>
```

As examples, we created a simple Web page displaying in Windows Media. To create the Windows Media page, we used Adobe GoLive, which created most of the following HTML instructions. (Loading a movie into GoLive is covered later in this chapter.)

```
<html xmlns="http://www.w3.org/1999/xhtml">

    <head>
        <meta http-equiv="content-type"
content="text/html;charset=utf-8" />
        <meta name="generator" content="Adobe GoLive" />
        <title>Web Movie Center</title>
    </head>
    <body>
    <div align="center">
    <h1>WEB MOVIES</h1>
    <object id="MediaPlayer" classid="clsid:6BF52A52-394A-11D3-
B153-00C04F79FAA6" type="application/x-oleobject" standby="Loading
Microsoft Windows Media Player components..." height="240" width="320">
            <param name="enabled" value="true" />
            <param name="fullscreen" value="false" />
            <param name="url" value="PremiereMovie.wmv" />
            <param name="autostart" value="false" />
            <param name="uimode" value="full" />
        </object></p>
    </body>

</html>
```

If you are using QuickTime, you could use the following snippet of HTML to load a QuickTime movie into a Web page without the QuickTime controller.

```
<embed src="mymovie.mov" width="320" height="240"
type="video/QuickTime" controller="false" autoplay="true">
```

Figure 20-1: A sample Web page that contains a Windows Media movie

To those unfamiliar with HTML, the code may look complicated. However, after you become familiar with the syntax, you will find HTML coding quite easy. If you scan through the code, you'll see several HTML *tags*, such as `<head>` and `<body>`. Each tag designates a specific area or formatting section in the page. Most tags begin with a word, such as `<title>`. At the end of the section, the tag is repeated with a / (forward slash) in front of it. For example, the end tag of `<title>` is `</title>`.

Here's a review of the some of the more important elements in the HTML code, shown previously:

✦ `<html>`: This tag simply tells the browser that the HTML coding system will be used.

✦ `<head>`: The "head" area of the page provides the browser with information concerning the character set used (within the meta tag). If scripting languages such as JavaScript will be used, this information normally appears in the "head" area as well.

✦ `<title>`: The window title of the browser page appears within the title tag.

✦ `<body>`: The main elements of a Web page are found within the body area. Notice that the body tag ends just above the ending `</html>` tag. Within the body is the information that loads the QuickTime movie.

✦ `<object>`: In the Windows Media example, the object tag is used to load the player and the movie. The ID option's player name allows you to assign a word to the player so that it can be referred to in a Web scripting language. The CLASSID is a unique hexadecimal code for the ActiveX control defining the Windows Media player. The URL attribute specifies the path and filename of the movie to be loaded. The `height` and `width` sections show the width and height of the movie on the page.

✦ `<embed>`: In the QuickTime example, the embed tag loads the digital movie plug-in. The src section provides the name of the digital movie that will be loaded from the Web server. The height and width sections show the width and height of the movie on the page. The type attribute tells the browser that a QuickTime movie is being loaded. controller="false" tells the browser not to place the QuickTime controller. autoplay="true" tells the browser to start playing the movie as soon as the page loads.

To enable the movie to be seen on the Web, the page must be named. If you name the page Index.htm, most Web servers will load this as the home page for a Web site. For the page and movie to appear, both must be copied to the Web server that hosts the Web site.

QuickTime settings for Web pages

Because QuickTime is one of the more popular digital video Web formats, we've provided a list of HTML tags that enable you to customize how a QuickTime movie appears on a Web page. Many of the tags are simple true/false statements, such as Loop=True or Loop=False. These tags, described next, are easily inserted using a word processor that saves files in standard text format. However, using a Web-page layout program, such as Adobe GoLive, to insert these tags is easiest.

✦ `Bg color`: Background color for the movie. Example: bg color="#FF0000". (Colors are created in hexadecimal code when assigned in HTML. FF0000 displays red.)

✦ `Cache=True/False`: Caches the movie. (Netscape browsers read the cache setting; Internet Explorer does not.) This allows the movie to be loaded faster if the user returns to the page.

✦ `Controller=True/False`: Adds the QuickTime controller, which enables the user to start and stop the movie.

✦ `Hidden=True/False`: Hides the QuickTime movie but plays the audio.

✦ `HREF`: Enables you to enter a clickable link. When the user clicks the QuickTime movie, the browser jumps to the specified Universal Resource Locator (URL) or Web address. (Example: HREF=http//:myhomepage.com/Page-3.com)

✦ `Target=`: This option is related to the HREF tag. When the movie jumps to a URL, it tells the movie which frame to play in. (Note that frame is an HTML frame, not a digital video frame.) You can include a frame name or common frame tags, such as _self, _parent, _top, or _blank. (Example: target = _ top)

✦ `Loop=True/False`: Plays the movie nonstop. You can also choose Loop=Palindrome, which plays the move from beginning to end, then from end to beginning.

✦ `Play every frame=True/False`: Forces every frame to be played. If this option is activated, every frame of the movie is played. This option is usually not turned on, primarily because it could slow movie playback and throw the soundtrack out of sync or turn it off entirely.

✦ `Scale`: Enables you to resize the movie. (Example: Scale=2 doubles the movie size.)

✦ `Volume`: Enables you to control the volume. Uses values from 0 to 256. By default, the value is set to 256. To turn off the sound, use Volume=0.

Loading Streaming Video onto a Web Page

Setting up video to be streamed over a Web page is slightly more involved than setting up a digital movie to progressively download from a Web page. Although differences exist for setting up files in Windows Media Server, RealNetworks' Helix Server, and Apple's QuickTime Streaming Server, they all require the creation of a pointer or *metafile*. Typically, the pointer or metafile is a small file saved on a Web server. When a user clicks a link on a Web page, the metafile causes the streaming media plug-in to load and provides instructions as to which movie to load off the streaming media server.

The following sections provide brief, general summaries of the steps involved for setting up streaming files for Windows Media Server, RealMedia Helix Server, and QuickTime Media Server. For specific instructions, consult user documentation.

In all cases, you save your clip to a directory on your streaming media server. The Web server will contain HTML code that points to the Web server.

Windows Media

Windows Media Server requires you to set up a metafile on your Web server. This is a file that the browser uses to load the Windows Media plug-in, which in turn instructs the streaming media server to play the movie. General steps for setting up the process are described next. For more information, see `www.microsoft.com/windows/windowsmedia/default.aspx`.

1. **Export your Premiere Pro project as a Windows Media file using Adobe Media Encoder (File ⇨ Export ⇨ Adobe Media Encoder).** Assume that the name of this movie is MyWindowsMovie.asm.

2. **Upload the exported movie to the correct directory on your media server.**

3. **Create a metafile in a text editor. The metafile includes instructions as to the location of the actual movie file.** The text of the metafile could be as simple as this:

   ```
   <ASX version="3.0"
   <Entry>
   <Title>My Movie Title</Title>
   <ref HREF="mms://ServerName/Path/MyWindowsMovie.wmv>
   </Entry>
   </ASX
   ```

4. **Name the file MyWindowsMovie.asx. Note that the filename of the movie is the same as the actual exported Windows media file, but uses an .asx file extension.** Save the file on your Web server.

5. **On your Web page, write HTML that creates a link to the .asx file.** The HTML might look something like this:

   ```
   <A HREF="myWindowsmove.asx">Click to play movie</A>
   ```

RealVideo streaming

The process of loading a streaming movie for a RealNetworks streaming media server requires setting up a metafile or *ram* file on your Web server that includes the path to the digital movie. When a user clicks a link, the browser instructs the RealMedia plug-in to load and sends the URL of the movie to the plug-in. Here's an overview of the steps involved. For more information about RealNetworks streaming products, see `http://realnetworks.com`.

1. **Export your Premiere project as a RealMedia file using the Adobe Media Encoder (File ⇨ Export ⇨ Adobe Media Encoder).** Assume that the name of this movie is MyRealMovie.rm.

2. **Upload the exported movie to the correct directory on your media server.**

3. **Create a metafile in a text editor.** The metafile includes instructions as to the location and name of the actual media file. The text of the metafile could be as simple as this:

   `Rtsp: //servername/path/MyRealmovie.rm`

4. **Name the file MyRealMovie.ram. Note that the filename includes the name of the exported RealMedia file, but uses the .ram file extension.** Save the file on your Web server.

5. **On your Web page, write HTML that creates a link to the .ram file.** The HTML might look something like this:

   `<A HREF ="myRealMovie.ram">My movie is here/A>`

QuickTime streaming

When setting up a movie for QuickTime streaming, you must create a "reference movie" on your Web server. The reference movie is a small file that contains reference information about the movie or movies to be loaded from the QuickTime Streaming Media Server. Within the reference movie is the URL of the QuickTime movie that must be loaded. If the media stream contains alternate files for different connection speeds, the URLs of those movies are also included in the reference movie. For detailed information, see Apple's QuickTime Web site, which provides detailed step-by-step information: `www.apple.com/quicktime/products/qtss/`.

1. **Export a QuickTime streaming movie file using the Adobe Media Encoder (File ⇨ Export ⇨ Adobe Media Encoder).** By default, this movie will seek a "hinted" track. The hinted track contains information about the server, packet size, and the protocol needed for streaming. If you are not using the Adobe Media Encoder, but are using QuickTime Pro, make sure you create the movie as a hinted movie. Assume the name of your movie is MyQTmovie.mov.

2. **Create a reference movie for the clip and its alternatives.** A reference movie is a movie on the Web server that points to the actual movie. The easiest way to create a reference movie is to use Apple's MakeRef movie, which you can download from Apple's QuickTime Web site. When creating the reference movie, you name the URLs of the Web server. You must also do this for all alternate movies that might be loaded at different connection speeds. The URL in the movie might be something like this:

   `rtsp://qtmedia.mywebsite.com/MyQTmovie.mov`

3. **Save the movie using a filename such as refMyQTMovie.mov.**

4. **Create a link for your movie, such as the following:**

```
<A HREF="refMoviemypremieremovie.mov">my movie</A>
```

You could also embed the movie with a command such as this:

```
<EMBED SRC="ref.mov" WIDTH="pixels" HEIGHT="pixels" AUTOPLAY="true"
CONTROLLER="true" LOOP="false"
PLUGINSPAGE="http://www.apple.com/quicktime/download/">
```

Placing a Movie onto a Web Page with Adobe GoLive

If you want to add video movies to your Web page, your best bet is to use a Web-page layout program such as Adobe GoLive or Macromedia Dreamweaver.

Adobe GoLive is one of the best Web-page layout programs for QuickTime movie producers. GoLive even features a QuickTime tab, which enables you to edit the tracks of a QuickTime movie and add special effects. GoLive's panels allow you to quickly and easily place a QuickTime movie on a page.

On the DVD-ROM   A trial version of Adobe GoLive is included on the DVD that accompanies this book.

Follow these steps to add a QuickTime, Flash, Windows Media, or Real movie to a Web page and edit its attributes with Adobe GoLive:

1. **Create a new window in GoLive for the Web page by choosing File ⇨ New.**

2. **In the New dialog box click Web ⇨ Pages ⇨ HTML Page, and then click OK.**

3. **If the Objects panel is not opened, open it by choosing Window ⇨ Objects.**

4. **Click the QuickTime, Windows Media, or Real Icon in the panel, shown in Figure 20-2, and drag it to the page.** GoLive provides a placeholder for the digital movie. The position of the placeholder determines where the movie appears on the page. You can click and drag the placeholder to specify the size of the movie when it appears on the Web page.

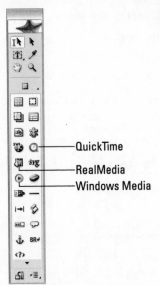

Figure 20-2: The Adobe GoLive Objects panel includes icons for different Web movie formats.

QuickTime

RealMedia

Windows Media

5. **To specify the filename and attributes, open the Inspector panel (if it isn't already open) by choosing Window ⇨ Inspector.**

6. **In the Inspector panel, click the Basic tab, shown in Figure 20-3.**

Figure 20-3: The Inspector panel's Windows Media Basic tab

7. **To select the QuickTime/Windows Media or RealMedia movie you want to load, click the folder icon in the Basic tab section.** Doing this opens a dialog box in which you can choose the movie from your hard disk. (Alternatively, if you have a Web site already designed, you can drag the Point-and-Shoot icon directly to the file in your Adobe GoLive site window on your computer's desktop.)

After the movie is placed in a Web page, you can adjust its frame size in the width and height fields to match your movie's frame size.

8. **Click the More tab in the Inspector panel, shown in Figure 20-4.**

9. **If you want to enter a name for your movie (for Web scripting use only), type a name in the Name field.** The QuickTime version of this page also enables you to designate a page from which to download the QuickTime plug-in. If you want to add padding between the movie and surrounding text, enter a value in pixels in HSpace, for horizontal space, and/or VSpace, for vertical space. To hide the movie and play back audio only, QuickTime users can select the Is Hidden check box in the QuickTime More tab.

10. **To view or change attributes for the HTML object tab, click Attribs.** Here you can enter a name for the player, change the URL of the source media and specify whether you want the user interface windows controller and buttons to appear (uimode="full"). If you don't want the Windows media controls to appear, you set change uimode to "none."

Figure 20-4: The Inspector panel's Windows Attributes tab

11. **To specify more HTML attributes, click the QuickTime Windows Media or RealMedia tab, shown in Figure 20-5.** For example, you can set whether the movie automatically plays upon opening or whether you can right-click to access a context menu to control the movie. After you've clicked the Windows Media tab, you can also click the Windows Media URL button, which allows you to reset the URL and reset the uimode by selecting from a drop-down menu. For QuickTime users, clicking check boxes in the QuickTime movie tab automatically creates the attributes described in the section "QuickTime Settings for Web pages."

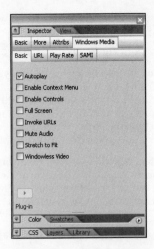

Figure 20-5: The Inspector panel's Windows Media tab

12. **If you want to preview a QuickTime movie while in GoLive, click the Open Movie button at the bottom of the QuickTime tab.** When the movie appears, the Basic tab provides track, size, and data rate information about the movie.

Creating a Web Link in Premiere Pro

Adobe Premiere Pro enables you to add an HREF track in a QuickTime movie. Using the HREF track, you can make the user's browser jump to another Web location while the movie plays. In Premiere Pro, this feature is called a *Web link*.

You set up a Web link within Premiere Pro using Markers. A Marker adds a visual clue on the Timeline for specific important points in a movie. Follow these steps for adding a Marker to the Timeline. (Before following these steps, you should have at least one clip in the Timeline.)

1. **Activate the Timeline panel by clicking it.**

2. **If a clip is selected in the Timeline, deselect it.**

3. **Click and drag the current-time indicator in the Timeline panel to move to the frame where you want to set the Web link.**

4. **Choose Marker ➪ Set Sequence Marker ➪ Unnumbered.** The marker appears on the Timeline.

Note   You can also create a Marker by clicking and dragging a Marker icon in the Timeline to a specific frame in the current sequence or double-clicking the Marker icon in the Timeline.

5. **Now that you've created a Marker, double-click it in the Timeline window to open the Marker dialog box, shown in Figure 20-6, to specify the URL you want to jump to.**

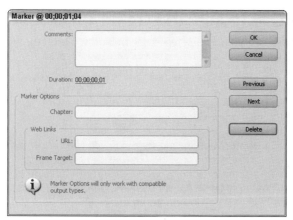

Figure 20-6: Premiere Pro's Marker dialog box allows the movie to open a Web page at a specific point in the movie.

6. **In the Marker dialog box, enter a URL in the URL field, such as** `http://myhomepage`
   `.com/page_2.htm`. You can enter a frame in the Frame Target field if you are using HTML framesets. Frames are handy tools if you want to create an effect in which the QuickTime movie opens a frame in a Web page. To create this effect, you need to enter the name of the URL and the filename for the frame in the Frame Target area.

Note   Web links can be created only from Timeline Markers. You cannot create a Web link from a clip marker.

Using QuickTime Tracks for the Web

QuickTime provides several hidden movie tracks that can add to the versatility of the Web and intranet movies. For example, QuickTime enables you to create an *HREF track* that can make the browser jump to another Web page at a specific point in the movie. QuickTime also provides a *chapter track*, which enables a user to click a chapter name and jump to that section of the movie. Perhaps the most unusual QuickTime track is the *sprite track*. The sprite track enables you to add graphics and provide interactivity to the QuickTime movie. For example, by using a sprite track, you can add a button that is assigned an action to your QuickTime movie. When the user clicks the button, the action occurs, such as restarting the movie, going to another Web page, or turning up the volume.

The following sections show you how to add tracks to a QuickTime movie. The first section shows how to add an HREF track with Adobe Premiere Pro. The sections that follow show you how to create chapter and sprite tracks with Adobe GoLive.

Using Adobe GoLive to edit and create QuickTime tracks

Adobe GoLive provides extensive support for QuickTime tracks for use on the Web. Using GoLive, you can add HREF links as well as chapter tracks and sprite tracks.

The following sections show you how to create and edit QuickTime video tracks in Adobe GoLive. Before you begin, here are the basic steps for loading a QuickTime movie and viewing its tracks so that you can edit them. (For a complete explanation of GoLive's QuickTime editing options, see the online help manual or the GoLive users' guide.)

Note   GoLive also enables you to create QuickTime movies and to add effect tracks to them.

1. **To open a QuickTime movie in GoLive to edit tracks, choose File ➪ Open.** In the Open dialog box, use the mouse to navigate to the QuickTime movie you want to open and click OK. The movie opens in GoLive's Preview tab.

   To edit or add tracks to use on the Web, you must view the QuickTime movie in a Timeline. Figure 20-7 shows a Timeline with HREF, chapter, and sprite tracks. To view the Timeline for the QuickTime movie, choose Movie ➪ Show Timeline Editor.

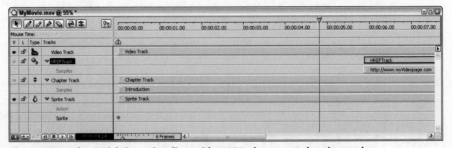

Figure 20-7: The QuickTime Timeline with HREF, chapter, and sprite tracks

2. **Select QuickTime in the Objects panel by clicking the tiny triangle toward the top of the panel to access the QuickTime icons.** The different icons that appear enable you to edit and add tracks, as shown in Figure 20-8.

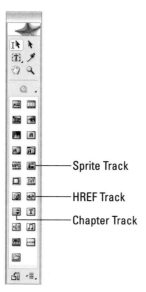

Figure 20-8: The QuickTime Objects panel with track icons

Sprite Track

HREF Track

Chapter Track

Adding an HREF track

You can use QuickTime's HREF track to create Web links. Unlike Premiere Pro, GoLive enables you to create clickable Web links.

You can use this feature in a page with HTML frames. When the movie plays, you can send it to the URL of the frame and specify that it play in the top part of a frame or in a new window.

Here's how to add a QuickTime HREF track and to specify a Web link with Adobe GoLive:

1. **To create a new HREF track, click and drag the HREF icon from the QuickTime section of GoLive's Object panel to the Tracks section of the Timeline.**

2. **Activate the New Sample tool (Pencil icon), and click the triangle next to the HREF track to open the samples track.**

3. **Create a new samples track by clicking and dragging with the New Sample tool in the blank sample HREF area of the Movie Timeline (which is beneath the background track).**

4. **Position the HREF track in the area where you want to have the Web link occur.** To shorten or lengthen the track, click and drag the edge of the track.

5. **Open the Inspector panel, shown in Figure 20-9, by choosing Window ➪ Inspector.** The time readout in the Inspector panel shows the start and stop times for the Web link action.

6. **If desired, use the Divide Sample tool to divide the track into the specific number of HREF segments you want.** (Do this only if you want to create multiple clickable links.)

7. **Select the sample area of the track that you want to assign to the URL. In the Inspector panel, enter the linking HREF.** You can use the GoLive Point-and-Shoot icon to link to a Web site. If you are using frame sets, enter the frame that you want to use in the target box. You can click the Target pop-up menu to open a list of standard frame set locations, such as _top, _parent, _self, and _blank. For example, _top loads the movie into a full browser window and replaces any framesets, and _blank opens the movie into a blank browser window.

Figure 20-9: The Inspector panel

8. **If you want to have the URL load automatically so that the user does not have to click the QuickTime movie, select Autoload URL.**

Creating a chapter track

QuickTime chapter tracks enable Web page visitors to jump to different areas of a QuickTime movie. When a chapter track is created, QuickTime adds a pop-up menu with the different chapters in it. All the Web page visitor needs to do is click the pop-up menu to move to that segment of the movie.

Follow these steps to add a chapter track to your QuickTime movie:

1. **To create a new chapter track, click and drag the Chapter icon from the QuickTime section of the Objects panel (choose Window ➪ Objects to open the Objects panel) to the Tracks section of the Timeline.**

2. Activate the New Sample tool (Pencil icon), and click the triangle next to chapter track to open the samples track.

3. Create a new samples track by clicking and dragging with the New Sample tool in the blank samples area of the movie Timeline (which is beneath the background track).

4. Open the sample area of the chapter track, and then click and drag in the Timeline area in the sample track to create the new sample.

5. To create multiple chapters, activate the Divide Sample tool and click along the sample track to divide it into different segments.

6. Choose Window ➪ Inspector to open the Inspector panel.

7. Activate the Arrow Selection tool, and then select each chapter. After you select the chapter, enter a name in the Chapter Title field in the Inspector panel, as shown in Figure 20-10. Do this for each segment in the chapter samples track.

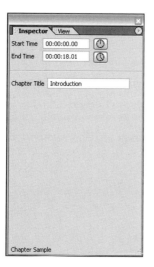

Figure 20-10: Entering a chapter name in the Inspector panel

8. To edit the time for each track, use the Arrow tool to click and drag the position of the sample or edit the track length by clicking the edge. As you click and drag, the time readout in the Inspector panel changes.

Creating interactivity with sprite tracks

Interactive sprites are the most sophisticated effect that you can add to a QuickTime movie in Adobe GoLive. (The term *sprite* is often used to represent a graphic or object that can be used repeatedly.) After you add a sprite track to a QuickTime movie, you can import graphics and use the graphics for added visual effect or even as interactive buttons.

You can use sprites and interactive behaviors in countless ways. Following is a short example to give you an idea of the possibilities. This example shows you how to import a graphic into a QuickTime movie and have the image change when the user moves the mouse over it. We also show you how to assign an action to the graphic. Because creating and using sprites can be a time-consuming process, we've broken the project into three short sections.

Adding sprite tracks

The following simple steps show you how to create a sprite track that can be used to add graphics and interactivity to a QuickTime move:

1. **To create a new sprite track, click and drag the Sprite icon from the QuickTime section of the Object panel (choose Window ➪ Objects to open the Objects panel) to the Tracks section of the Timeline.**

2. **If you want to rename the track, double-click it and enter a new name.**

Importing graphics

You can import graphics to use as sprites in the sprite track of a QuickTime movie. For example, you can create tiny buttons or characters that appear and disappear while the QuickTime movie plays. After the graphics are imported, you can load them into the sprite track and create interactivity. In this example, you'll import two graphics into the sprite track. However, after the graphics are added to the sprite track, they do not appear until you place them into a sprite subtrack. (Creating sprite subtracks is discussed later in this section.)

Note   You can load the following graphic formats into sprite tracks: JPEG, GIF, PICT, BMP, and PSD (Photoshop native format).

1. **Select the sprite track in the Tracks section of the Timeline.**

2. **If the Inspector panel is not opened, open it by choosing Window ➪ Inspector panel.**

3. **Click the Images tab in the Inspector panel, as shown in Figure 20-11.**

Figure 20-11: The Images tab in the Inspector panel

4. **Before importing graphics, deselect multiple layers (otherwise, you might import layers with nothing in them).** To import graphics, click the Import button in the Images tab. When the Open dialog box appears, select the graphics you want to add and then click Add for each graphic. Click Done when you're finished.

5. **Importing graphics opens the Compression Settings dialog box, shown in Figure 20-12. If desired, change the Quality settings and the Compressor.**

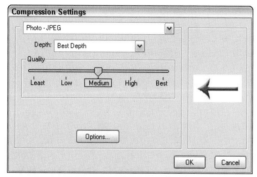

Figure 20-12: You can change compression settings in the Compression Settings dialog box.

Creating sprite subtracks

Importing sprites adds them to the Tracks sprite pool. Now they can be used as many times as desired in sprite subtracks. In a sprite subtrack, you can control sprite positioning and switch from one sprite to another.

1. **Select the sprite track in the Tracks section of the Timeline.**

2. **Click the Sprites tab in the Inspector panel.**

> **Note**
>
> You can change the background color of the sprite track by clicking the background color check box in the Sprites tab and then clicking the color swatch. (By default, the sprite track is black.) You can also set a blending mode for the track by clicking the Basic tab in the Inspector panel.

3. **Click in the Add New Sprites field, as shown in Figure 20-13.** Enter the number of sprite subtracks that you want to add, and press the Tab key. If you want to create a simple rollover effect or a simple action, type **1**. Doing this adds a sprite subtrack to the Timeline and creates a keyframe for the sprite. (A diamond in the subtrack area of the Timeline represents the keyframe.)

Figure 20-13: Type the number of subtracks that you want to add in the Add New Sprites field.

Changing location and creating simple behaviors

If you want the sprites to switch sprite images or sprite positions in the subtrack as the movie plays, you must create more keyframes and then use the Inspector to switch images or locations. Here's how:

1. **In the Timeline, select the keyframe for the subtrack.**

2. **If you want to change the positions of the sprite, enter the new coordinates in the position section of the Basic tab in the Inspector panel.**

You can also make a sprite invisible at a keyframe by deselecting the Visible check box in the Basic tab of the Inspector panel.

3. **If you want to switch graphic images, select the image from the Image pop-up menu in the Basic tab of the Inspector panel.**

4. **To create a new keyframe, press Option/Alt, click and drag the keyframe in the Timeline track to the right, and then release the mouse button.**

    After creating a keyframe, you can change images or image positions.

5. **If you want to create interactivity or a rollover effect, click in the Over swatch (for a rollover) or in the Click Inside or Click Outside boxes in the Basic tab of the Inspector panel.** Then choose the image that you want to switch to when the mouse rolls over or clicks inside or outside of the image. A Click Inside effect is shown in Figure 20-14.

Figure 20-14: Switching images with a mouse-click in the Basic tab

Assigning actions to a sprite

GoLive enables you to assign an action when the user clicks or moves the mouse over a sprite. For example, when the user clicks a sprite, you can have the movie increase volume, return to its beginning, or jump to another Web page. While assigning actions, remember that actions only occur at keyframes. Therefore, you may need to create many keyframes to give the user enough time to click the sprite.

Follow these steps to assign actions to a sprite:

1. **Select the keyframe where you want the action to occur.**

2. **Click the Action tab in the Inspector panel.**

3. **Choose an event in the event list, such as Mouse Down, Mouse Click, or Mouse Enter.**

4. **Click the New Action icon (dog-eared page icon).**

5. **In the pop-up menu at the bottom of the screen, choose an action, such as Movie Set Volume, Movie GoTo Time, or Movie GoTo Beginning, as shown in Figure 20-15.**

6. **Click the Apply button.**

Previewing and saving your work

When you are finished creating sprites and assigning actions to them, you can preview your work by clicking the Play icon (triangle) at the bottom of the Timeline. You can also slowly preview your sprite work by clicking and dragging the Edit line Marker over the Timeline.

At this point, you can save your movie by choosing File ➪ Save. Then choose Movie ➪ Export Movie. In GoLive's Save Exported File dialog box, click the Options button to review or change the QuickTime video settings and then click OK to save the movie.

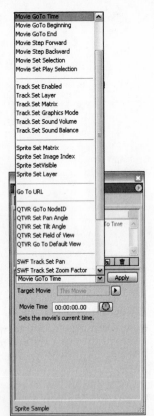

Figure 20-15: Assigning an action to a sprite

Summary

If you will be exporting a movie to the Web or to an intranet, knowing the HTML options available to you can help you add features to your movies. A program such as Adobe GoLive can simplify the task of loading a digital movie onto a Web page and the task of writing the HTML code. QuickTime movies enable you to add many features that can be utilized on the Web. This chapter covered these topics:

✦ Streaming and progressive downloading are two common techniques for displaying video on Web pages.

✦ Common Web video file formats include Flash Video, QuickTime, RealMedia, and Windows Media.

✦ You can add a clickable HREF track to a QuickTime movie.

✦ You can add a chapter pull-down menu that appears on a Web page. When a user clicks the chapter name, the movie jumps to that section.

✦ You can add sprite graphics to a QuickTime movie and add interactivity.

✦   ✦   ✦

Exporting Video to the Web

Now that more and more Internet users log on to the Web using speedy broadband connections, video producers undoubtedly will be exporting their Web files with streaming media in mind.

Streaming media enables users to view a video program as it downloads. Before the advent of streaming media, Web users had to wait for an entire clip to download before the video actually started to play. When media is streamed, information packets are sent by special streaming server applications such as RealNetworks RealVideo server, Microsoft's Windows Media Server, or Apple's QuickTime Streaming Media Server.

Fortunately, Premiere Pro users can easily export video for streaming media projects or for slower modem connections. Premiere Pro's Adobe Media Encoder provides a consistent and straightforward tool for outputting video files in streaming and non-streaming formats. This exporting module, installed within Premiere Pro, takes the guesswork out of choosing the appropriate output settings for Web viewing. You can export your Premiere Pro projects in Windows Media, RealVideo, or QuickTime formats. Furthermore, presets built into the Encoder enable you to easily export a video sequence optimized for multiple bandwidths. In other words, you can export a high-quality file to the Web or an intranet and have the Encoder create versions for users with either high- or low-bandwidth connections. When you output to an intranet or the Web, the Adobe Media Encoder presets can save you time and help ensure quality playback for users who view your videos.

 Note   Exporting movies in FLV format for Flash and Macromedia's Streaming media application, Flash Media Server, is covered in Chapter 23.

Encoding Terms

This chapter provides an overview of choosing Web encoding formats using the Adobe Media Encoder. As you choose different formats, you see a variety of arcane encoding terms such as two-pass encoding, variable bit rate, and constant bit rate. These terms appear regardless of whether you are exporting to Windows Media,

RealMedia, or QuickTime format. Fortunately, Adobe Media Encoder provides exporting presets, and you may never have to change encoding settings. Nevertheless, before continuing, you may want to review some brief definitions:

✦ **Two-pass encoding:** Two-pass encoding can improve the digital quality of exported video. When two-pass encoding is used, the video that is processed is actually processed twice. The first time, the encoder analyzes the video to determine the best manner to encode it. On the second pass, it uses the information gathered in the first pass to encode it. As you might guess, two-pass encoding takes longer than single-pass.

✦ **Variable bit rate:** Bit rate defines how much data is transferred per second. Variable bit rate (VBR) varies the bit rate of a clip as it plays back. When a high-action scene needs more bits or bandwidth, the encoding process delivers the extra bits; in areas that don't require high bandwidth, it lowers the bit rate. Thus, for clips that vary in action, VBR can provide better quality than constant bit rate (CBR), which does not vary the bit rate of the clip as it plays back. For Windows Media, the Adobe Media Encoder's Bitrate Mode drop-down menu allows you to choose between Constrained and Unconstrained VBR.

  • **Unconstrained VBR** encoding allows you to specify an average value for the bit rate. This encoding process strives to provide the highest quality while still attempting to sustain the average bit rate. Despite its attempts, the bit rate may vary widely from the specified average. Thus, Unconstrained VBR tries to provide high quality within the confines of bandwidth constraints.

  • **Constrained VBR** is similar to unconstrained except that it adds Maximum bit rate values and a Buffer time to the equation. Controls for maximum buffer rate are in the Advanced Video section.

Note   For more information about how Windows Media Variable Rate encoding works, see `http://msdn.microsoft.com/library/default.asp?url=/library/en-us/wmcodecs/htm/encodingmethods.asp`.

✦ **Keyframe:** When some CODECs compress video, they can compare each frame with subsequent frames and can save only the information that changes. When the information changes, the CODEC saves a full frame of video only when it needs to. This frame is often called a *keyframe*. So CODECs that use keyframes can reduce the file size of exported video. The number of keyframes needed depends upon the CODEC and the amount of motion in the video. For Web work, the fewer keyframes the better, because fewer keyframes result in smaller file sizes. Presets for Windows Media and RealMedia specify keyframe distance in seconds; presets for QuickTime are in frames. For example, the Sorenson 3 Codec used by QuickTime has a preset of one keyframe every 50 frames.

✦ **Deinterlace:** Deinterlacing removes one field from a video frame to prevent blurring artifacts that can occur when video is output on a computer. This blurring is most likely to occur during scenes that exhibit motion. The blurring results from the difference in frame information between the odd or upper video field and the even or lower video field that comprise a video frame.

✦ **Video Noise Reduction:** All formats include a Filters tab that allows you to apply a video noise reduction filter. The filter is applied before compression and can reduce file size by removing noise artifacts from source video.

✦ **Metadata:** Metadata for Web video clips is text data about the clip that can be searched for on the World Wide Web or read by computer applications. Often, metadata information includes information such as title, date, and creator. The Adobe Media Encoder allows you to add metadata to MPEG and QuickTime files.

Using the Adobe Media Encoder

Premiere Pro's Adobe Media Encoder provides a consistent interface for exporting to the major streaming media formats. Whether you are exporting to Windows Media, RealMedia, or QuickTime format, the basic steps for exporting are the same. All exporting starts at the Adobe Media Encoder's Export Settings dialog box, which provides video and audio settings, as well as presets and options for exporting multiple streams with one file. Follow these basic steps for exporting:

1. **Select the Timeline or Program Monitor panel that includes the footage to be exported.**

2. **Choose File ⇨ Export ⇨ Adobe Media Encoder.** This opens the Export Settings dialog box, shown in Figure 21-1.

Figure 21-1: Use the Export Settings dialog box to export video for the Web.

3. **In the Export Settings dialog box, choose an export format such as Windows Media, RealMedia, or QuickTime in the Format drop-down menu.**

4. **In the Range pop-up menu, choose whether you want to export the Entire Sequence or the Work area.**

5. **Choose a Preset in the Preset drop-down menu.** Choose the best preset for your intended audience. The presets are descriptions of the type of Web connection that you expect your audience to be using. Figure 21-1 displays the Windows Media 256K-download preset. This choice indicates the approximate amount of data sent each second, measured in kilobits per second.

6. **Choose whether you want to include Video or Audio in the Export by de-selecting or selecting the Export Video or Export Audio check boxes.**

7. **Review the video settings in the Video tab.** Make changes if needed. For example, you may want to change the frame size or frame rate. Because you are exporting to the Web, you should leave the pixel aspect ratio set to square pixels (available in Windows Media and QuickTime formats). Because you are exporting to a computer screen and not a video screen that uses interlacing, the field order settings should be set to Progressive.

8. **Review the Audio settings by clicking the Audio tab.** Make changes if needed.

9. **Review the different streams associated with the preset by clicking the Filters/ Video/Audio/Audiences/Others panel menu, shown later in Figure 21-5.** If desired, add or subtract video streams (called Audiences when exporting in Windows Media or RealMedia format; referred to as Alternates when exporting in QuickTime format). Note that not all presets include more than one video stream.

10. **If you wish to add a filter to reduce video noise before the file is compressed, click the Filters tab.** In the Filters tab click the Video Noise Reduction checkbox, and then drag the slider to set the Noise Reduction value.

11. **If you want to send the exported file to an FTP site, click the Others tab, and then enter FTP server and log-in information.**

12. **To start the Export process, click OK.** A Save dialog box appears allowing you to name and save your file, or you can click a Settings button, to return to the Export Settings Dialog box.

Adobe Encoder optional features

During the export process, the Adobe Media Encoder allows you to create custom presets and to crop, preview, and deinterlace video.

Previewing

The Adobe Media Encoder provides a preview of your source file and a preview of the final video output. The following list describes options for previewing Source and Output video:

✦ **To preview the source file, click the Source tab.**

✦ **To preview the video based upon the settings in the Adobe Media Encoder, click the Output tab.**

Note The Source/Output panel menu allows you choose to view the Source and Output screens displayed with pixel aspect ratio correction, or in square pixels. The Aspect Ratio Corrected choice adjusts the display so that source pixels are viewed properly on a computer display. The 1:1 Pixel Preview choice displays the source image with square pixels, which can result in image distortion.

✦ **To scrub through video in either the Source or Output tab, click and drag in the Time Ruler at the bottom of the preview area.**

Cropping and scaling

Before you export you file, you can crop the Source video. Cropped areas appear as black in the final video. Follow these steps to crop your video:

1. **Click the Source tab.** This opens the Source view of your video, shown in Figure 21-2.

Figure 21-2: Source view with Crop tool

2. **Select the Crop tool.**

3. **To crop precisely using pixel dimension, click and drag over the Left, Top, Right, or Bottom numerical fields.** Clicking and dragging right reduces the cropping area. As you click and drag, the cropping area is displayed onscreen. Alternatively, click and drag a

corner over the area of the video that you want to retain. As you click and drag, a read-out appears displaying the frame size in pixels.

4. **If you want to change the aspect ratio of the crop to 4:3 or 16:9, click in the crop proportions drop-down menu and chose the aspect ratio.**

5. **To preview the cropped video, click the Output tab.**

6. **If you want to Scale your video frame to fit with in the crop borders, select the Scale to Fit check box (next to the Interlace check box).**

Deinterlacing video

To deinterlace video, click the Output tab and then click the Deinterlace check box.

Saving, importing, and deleting presets

If you make changes to a preset, you can save your custom preset to disk so that you can use it at a later time. After you save presets, you can import or delete them.

✦ **Saving presets:** If you edit a preset and want to save it to use at a later time or use it as a basis for comparing export quality, click the Save Preset button (disk icon). Then enter a name in the Choose Name dialog box, shown in Figure 21-3. If you want to save Filters tab settings, click the Save Filter Settings check box. To save cropping and Deinterlace settings, select the Save Other Tasks check box.

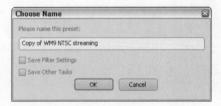

Figure 21-3: Choose a Name for a Preset in the Choose Name dialog box.

✦ **Importing presets:** The easiest way to import a custom preset is to click the Preset drop-down menu and choose it from the top portion of the list. Alternatively, you can, click the Import Preset button (folder icon) and then load the presets from disk. Presets have a *.vpr* file extension.

✦ **Deleting presets:** To delete a preset, load the preset and then click the Delete Preset button (trash icon). An alert appears warning you that the deletion process cannot be undone.

Viewing help on screen

The Adobe Media Encoder provides brief information messages that describe the different fields in the Adobe Media Encoder. To view an information statement, move your mouse over a field such as bit rate. In the information line (toward the bottom of the screen), the following message appears: "Data Rate for Video in Kilobits per Second."

Exporting to Windows Media Format

Premiere Pro's Adobe Media Encoder allows you to export movies in Windows Media format, Microsoft's newest audio and video format. Windows Media movies can play in Internet Explorer and can be streamed from Microsoft's Streaming Media server. Windows media files are recognizable by their .wmv file extension. WMV files can be read by Windows Media Player version 7 and higher.

To export in Windows Media format, open the Adobe Media Encoder and then choose a Windows Media preset. Many of the presets are shown in Figure 21-4.

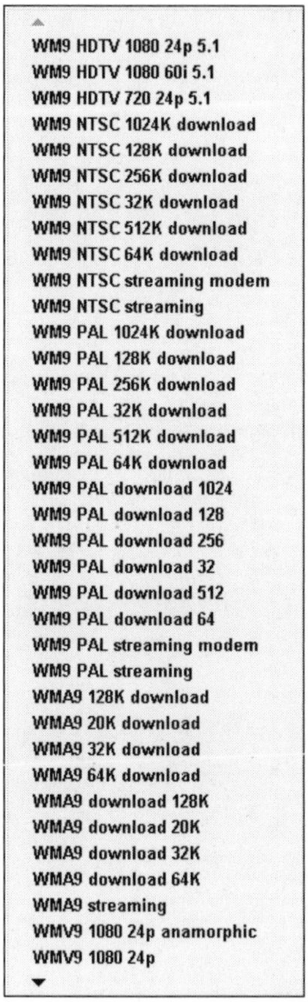

▲
WM9 HDTV 1080 24p 5.1
WM9 HDTV 1080 60i 5.1
WM9 HDTV 720 24p 5.1
WM9 NTSC 1024K download
WM9 NTSC 128K download
WM9 NTSC 256K download
WM9 NTSC 32K download
WM9 NTSC 512K download
WM9 NTSC 64K download
WM9 NTSC streaming modem
WM9 NTSC streaming
WM9 PAL 1024K download
WM9 PAL 128K download
WM9 PAL 256K download
WM9 PAL 32K download
WM9 PAL 512K download
WM9 PAL 64K download
WM9 PAL download 1024
WM9 PAL download 128
WM9 PAL download 256
WM9 PAL download 32
WM9 PAL download 512
WM9 PAL download 64
WM9 PAL streaming modem
WM9 PAL streaming
WMA9 128K download
WMA9 20K download
WMA9 32K download
WMA9 64K download
WMA9 download 128K
WMA9 download 20K
WMA9 download 32K
WMA9 download 64K
WMA9 streaming
WMV9 1080 24p anamorphic
WMV9 1080 24p
▼

Figure 21-4: Windows Media presets

The options for Windows Media files allow for multiple bit rate encoding, in which one file provides multiple streams at different bit rates. Thus, the file includes streams for different "audiences." When a browser sends the signal to start streaming the video, Windows Media Server uses "intelligent streaming" to decide which bit rate to use. The server can choose this bit rate when the stream starts, or it can choose a slower bit rate if the bandwidth decreases. (You should understand even though you can connect to the Internet at a specific bit rate, you may not be able to connect at this bandwidth all the time.)

Viewing audience settings

To use a preset with multiple bit rates for different audiences, you can choose WM9 NTSC Streaming. To view the multiple streams, click the panel menu, as shown in Figure 21-5. Note that the bit rates range from a 28.8 Kbps modem to a stream for broadband and cable modem. The frame sizes for the different streams begin at 128 × 96 and jump to 510 × 384. To see the video and audio settings for any stream, click it in the panel menu. After you click a stream, the Video, and Audio settings for the stream appear in their respective tabs.

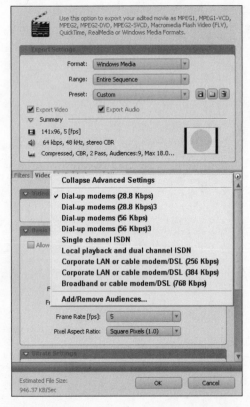

Figure 21-5: Multiple streams for different audiences

Adding and removing audiences

If you want to change the number of streams in a preset, you can add or remove preset bit rates for different target audiences. To add an audience, choose Add/Remove Audiences from the panel menu. In the Target Audience dialog box, click Add. This opens the System Audiences dialog box, shown in Figure 21-6. Here, you can see the list of target audience streams and the data rates in kilobits per second. To add an audience, simply click the check box for stream that you want to add. Then click OK.

If you want to remove a target audience from a preset, click Delete in the Target Audience dialog box.

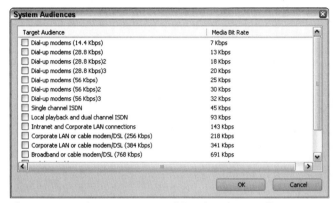

Figure 21-6: Select a stream to add to the target audience.

Using QuickTime Streaming

The Adobe Media Encoder provides exporting options for creating QuickTime streaming media files. As discussed in Chapter 20, QuickTime is Apple's cross-platform digital media format. QuickTime streaming files can be streamed from Apple's Streaming Media Server as well as RealNetworks RealMedia Streaming server. Not only are QuickTime files cross-platform, but Apple's Streaming Media Server is also available on Windows NT and UNIX platforms. The Adobe Media Encoder also includes presets for progressive downloading of files. In a progressive download, the entire video clip is downloaded before it can be viewed.

Note You can also prepare a QuickTime movie for streaming by exporting a Premiere Pro movie by choosing File ➪ Export ➪ Movie and choosing QuickTime as a setting. You can then use Apple's QuickTime Pro to export the file for Apple's QuickTime Media server.

When you choose a QuickTime preset, the standard video CODEC selected is Sorensen 3. To choose a format with multiple streams, choose QT alternate NTSC streaming. To view the streams (called Alternates), click the flyout menu, as shown in Figure 21-7. The alternate streams range from one for a 28.8 modem to a stream for a 1 Mbps cable modem. To view the video and audio specifics of a stream, simply click the Alternate stream name in the panel menu. After you click the stream, the video and audio options update to reflect your choice.

Unlike Windows Media, which packs its audience streams into one file, QuickTime exports a separate file for each stream. QuickTime streaming also requires a "hint" file, which can be contained in the target stream. If desired, you can set a prefix for all the stream files and a separate file location. These options are shown in Figure 21-7 in the Alternates tab, which also allows you to specify that the streams automatically loop or autoplay when loading. Also shown in Figure 21-7 is the XMP Info menu choice. It allows you to add metadata to your QuickTime files using Adobe's Extensible Metadata Platform.

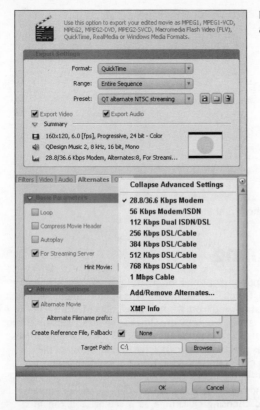

Figure 21-7: QuickTime streaming alternate settings

Exporting to Advanced RealMedia Format

The Adobe Media Encoder's RealMedia export formats enable you to create digital movies in RealMedia format, one of the most popular streaming video formats used on the Web. RealMedia quickly became popular because it was one of the first true streaming video formats. As the data streams, the RealPlayer (or newer RealOne Player) software and the RealMedia server communicate to ensure that the data is sent at the best data rate. The RealMedia options in the Export Settings dialog box enable you to create one video clip for multiple audiences. When the clip is downloaded, RealMedia switches to either the faster stream for faster connection users or the slower stream for slower dial-up modem users.

When you choose a RealMedia preset, the Export Settings section of the Export Settings dialog box allows you to pick a bit rate setting. You can choose Frame rate and Keyframe Interval settings in the Video tab. Unlike Windows Media or QuickTime, RealMedia provides Video Content choices, as shown in Figure 21-8.

✦ **Normal Motion Video:** Use this option for clips that include some motion and stills.

✦ **Smoothest Motion Video:** Select this option for clips that feature limited motion.

✦ **Sharpest Image Quality:** Use this option for sporting events and other action clips.

✦ **Slide Show:** This makes your video appear as a series of still frames.

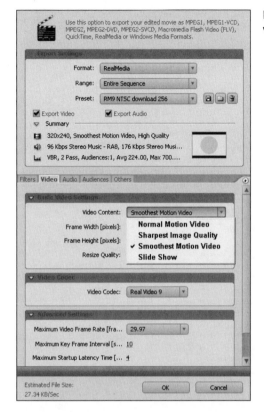

Figure 21-8: RealMedia preset with video content choices

Like the Windows Media format, RealMedia allows you to add or subtract target audiences by clicking Add/Remove Audiences in the panel menu to the right of the Others tab. (See the "Adding and removing audiences" section earlier in this chapter.)

Summary

Slow Web connection speeds can make downloading digital video a time-consuming task. Premiere Pro's Adobe Media Encoder takes advantage of video streaming and helps optimize download times. This chapter covered these topics:

✦ Use the Windows Media Format to export files for different target audiences in Windows media format.

✦ Use the QuickTime format to export files for Apple's Streaming Media server.

✦ Use the RealMedia format to export files for RealNetwork's RealMedia Media Server.

✦   ✦   ✦

Exporting to Videotape

Despite the excitement generated by outputting video to the World Wide Web, videotape still remains one of the most popular mediums for distributing and showing high-quality video productions. Provided you have the right hardware, Adobe Premiere Pro enables you to export clips and complete projects to videotape.

Professionals who demand high-quality output can also have Premiere Pro export their projects to an Advanced Authoring Format (AAF) file. An AAF file is a multimedia file format that allows Premiere Pro users to send data to other digital video editing systems.

This chapter discusses the steps you need to take to output your Premiere Pro files to videotape or to an AAF file.

Preparing to Export Video

In order to precisely export your Premiere Pro project to videotape, your system must support device control, which enables you to start and stop a videotape recorder or camcorder directly from Premiere Pro. If you have a DV camcorder and your computer has an IEEE 1394 port, chances are good that you can use device control. If you have professional videotape recording equipment and a capture board in your computer, you may be able to export video to your videotape recorder using serial device control. Before you get started, you may want to add black video or bars and tones to the beginning of your project.

Adding black video, color bars, and tone

If you are sending your Premiere Pro project to a video production facility, you may want to add black video to the beginning of your project. The extra black video provides the production facility more time to get its equipment rolling before your project begins. Follow these steps to create black video:

1. **Click the New Item button at the bottom of the Project panel.**

2. **In the pop-up menu, shown in Figure 22-1, choose Black Video.** This adds five seconds of black video to the Project panel.

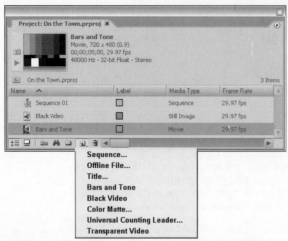

Figure 22-1: Click the New Item button to add black video and bars and tone.

3. **To add the black to the Source Monitor, double-click the Black Video in the Project panel.** You can then insert the Black Video into a sequence by moving the current-time indicator to the front of the time ruler in the Timeline panel and then clicking the Insert button in the Source Monitor panel.

In order to calibrate color and audio, production facilities set their electronic equipment to color bars and a 1 kHz tone. If you are working with a video production facility, you can easily add bars and tone to your Premiere Pro project. Follow these steps:

1. **Click the New Item button at the bottom of the Project panel.**

2. **In the drop-down menu, shown in Figure 22-1, choose Bars and Tone.** This adds five seconds of color bars and a tone to the Project panel.

3. **To increase the duration of the bars and tone, select Bars and Tone in the Project panel (or right-click the bars and tone in the Project panel) and then choose Speed/Duration in the drop-down menu.** In the Clip Speed/Duration dialog box, add the desired time in frames.

4. **To add the bars and tone to the Monitor panel, double-click the bars and tone in the Project panel.** You can then insert the bars and tone into a sequence by moving the current-time indicator to the front of the time ruler in the Timeline panel and then clicking the Insert button in the Source Monitor panel.

Checking project settings

Before exporting to videotape, review your production's project settings by choosing Project ➪ Project Settings ➪ General. Review the Video, Audio, and Keyframe and Rendering sections. As you view the settings in these dialog boxes, make sure that they are set to the highest-quality output, because Premiere Pro uses these settings when exporting to videotape.

Note The video settings in Premiere Pro are explained in several chapters in this book (see Chapters 4 and 19), so we do not repeat them here. You may, however, want to review the Fields setting in the General options of the Project Settings dialog box, as shown in Figure 22-2.

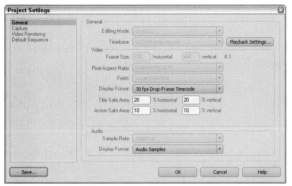

Figure 22-2: The General options in the Project Settings dialog box.

Fields are relevant only when exporting to videotape. The NTSC, PAL, and Secam standards divide each frame into two fields. In NTSC video, where the frame rate is approximately 29.97 frames per second, approximately 30 video frames appear each second. Each frame is divided into two fields that appear for a 60th of a second. PAL and Secam display a video frame every 25 frames, and each field is displayed for a 50th of a second.

When the field is displayed, it displays alternating scan lines. Thus, the first frame may scan lines 1, 3, 5, 7, and so on. After the first field is scanned, the frame then scans lines 2, 4, 6, 8, and so on. So, in some respects, you may conceptualize a video frame to be like a child's puzzle with the video fields being two zigzagging, interlocking pieces. If you view only one of the pieces, you don't get a sharp picture. In fact, if you could freeze a field onscreen, you would see an image with blurry lines.

When setting export settings, you can choose Upper Field First or Lower Field First, depending on which field your system expects to receive first. If this setting is incorrect, jerky and jumpy video may result. The default setting for a DV project is Lower Field First.

Note If you don't know in what order your equipment expects fields, run a quick export of a project that includes motion. Export the project set to Upper Field First, and then export it set to Lower Field First. The correct field setting should provide the best playback. Use this setting when you export your video project.

Checking device control settings

Before you begin exporting your project to videotape, check to be sure that your device control options are properly installed. These settings appear in Premiere Pro's Preferences dialog box. To open the Preferences dialog box and access the Device Control section directly, choose Edit ➪ Preferences ➪ Device Control.

Click the Device pop-up menu, and choose the Device Control option for your equipment. Next, click the Options button. Doing so opens the DV Device Control Options dialog box, where you can choose your output device, as shown in Figure 22-3.

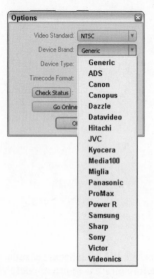

Figure 22-3: Choose your camcorder in the Device Brand drop-down menu.

In the DV Device Control Options dialog box, choose the correct video standard (NTSC or PAL). Choose a Device Brand and a Device Type. Next, pick the timecode format you want to use in the Timecode Format menu. If your camcorder is off, turn it on and click the Check Status button. If all connections are properly set, the Offline readout should change to Online. If you are connected to the Internet, to check the compatibility of your camcorder with Premiere Pro, click Go Online for Device info. This command brings you to a Web page that lists camcorders and their compatibility with Premiere Pro.

Setting digital video playback options

After you've checked your video and device control settings, your next step is to establish playback options. The choices are different, depending upon the hardware you are using.

If you are using digital video equipment, start by connecting the IEEE 1394 cable from your camcorder or tape deck to your computer.

Now, set the playback to your camcorder by following these steps:

1. **Turn on your camcorder or recording device.** If you are using a camcorder, make sure it is set to the VCR or VTR setting.

2. **To set the playback to a digital video recording device, choose Project ➪ Project Settings.** In the General options panel, choose DV Playback in the Editing Mode pop-up menu.

3. **Click the Playback Settings button.**

If you choose DV Playback in the Editing Mode field, the \ Playback Settings dialog box, as shown in Figure 22-4, appears.

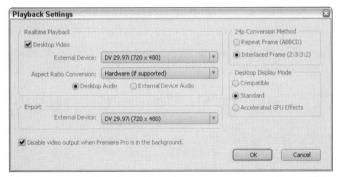

Figure 22-4: Setting playback options to a DV camcorder or VCR

You have these options in the DV Playback Settings dialog box:

✦ In the Realtime Playback section:

- **Desktop Video:** Select this to view your video on your desktop computer system.

- **External Device:** If you wish to view playback on an external device such as a camcorder, select it in the External Device drop-down menu.

- **Aspect Ratio Conversion:** This option allows you to choose whether pixel aspect ratio conversion is handled by hardware or software. In the Aspect Ratio Conversion drop-down menu, choose None for No conversion, choose Hardware if your hardware supports Aspect Ratio Conversion, or choose Software to allow Premiere to handle the aspect ratio conversion.

- **Desktop Audio/External Device Audio:** Choose whether you want to play back audio on your desktop computer system or on an external device such as a camcorder.

✦ In the Export section, choose your external device in the External Device drop-down menu.

Exporting with Device Control

The following section describes how to export to videotape with device control for DV hardware.

Before starting the export session, make sure that you have set the DV control options in the DV Playback Settings dialog box and that you have reviewed your video settings.

To export to videotape using DV device control, follow these steps:

1. **Turn on your videotape deck, and load the tape on which you are recording into your tape deck.** To record using DV device control, you must insert a tape pre-striped with timecodes into your tape deck; then write down the timecode location at which you want to begin recording.

Note

To pre-stripe video tape, place an unused tape (without any timecode) in your camcorder. Place the lens cap on and begin recording until the tape runs out.

2. **Select the Sequence that you want to export by clicking it in the Project panel.**

3. **Choose File ⇨ Export ⇨ Export to Tape.**

4. **In the Export to Tape dialog box, shown in Figure 22-5, select Activate Recording Device.** This tells Premiere Pro to take control of the recording device.

Figure 22-5: The Export to Tape dialog box instructs Premiere Pro to take control of the recording device.

5. **If you don't want the recording to begin at the current location, choose Assemble at timecode and enter the timecode where you want recording to begin.**

6. **In the Delay Movie Start field, enter a delay in quarter-frames.** (Some devices need this delay to sync the recording device with the movie after starting the recording process.)

7. **In the Preroll field, enter the number of frames you want to back up before the specified timecode.** This enables the tape to attain the proper speed before recording. Five seconds (150 frames) is usually sufficient.

8. **In the Option section, choose whether you want Premiere Pro to Abort After Dropped Frames, Report Dropped Frames in a text report, or whether you wish Premiere to Render Audio Before Export.** This last option can help prevent dropped frames due to complicated audio.

9. **Click Record.**

Exporting without Device Control

If your hardware setup does not allow device control, you can still record to videotape by manually controlling your video recording device. Before you start, make sure you can play back video on your recording device or camcorder. If not, review the Playback Settings. Follow these steps:

1. **Make sure that your camcorder or recording device is connected properly.**

2. **Turn on your videotape deck, and load the tape onto which you are recording into your tape deck.**

3. **Select the sequence that you want to export by clicking it in the Project window.** You should be able to see the sequence on your video display.

4. **Cue the tape recorder to the position where you want to begin recording.**

5. **Move the current-time indicator to the start of your Premiere Pro movie.**

6. **Press the Record button on your recording device.**

7. **Press the Play button in the Monitor window.**

8. **After you are finished recording, click the Stop button in the Monitor window and then press the Stop button on your recording device.**

Exporting with Serial Device Control

Adobe Premiere allows you to control video to professional VTR equipment through your computer's serial communications (COM) port. The computer's serial port is often used for modem communication and printing. Serial control allows transport and timecode information to be sent over the computer's serial port. Using serial device control, you can capture, play back, and record video. Because serial control exports only timecode and transport signals, you need a hardware capture card to send the video and audio signals to tape. Premiere supports the following standards: nine-pin serial port, Sony RS-422, Sony RS-232, Sony RS-232 UVW, Panasonic RS-422, Panasonic RS-232, and JVC-232.

Serial device control setup

Before you can export using serial device control, you must set up Premiere's Serial Device Control preferences. Before you begin, read your equipment manuals and connect your recording equipment to your computer's com port. Then follow these steps in Premiere:

1. **Open the Device Control Preferences dialog box by choosing Edit ➪ Preferences ➪ Device Control.**

2. **In the Device Control dialog box, choose Serial Device Control in the Control Device drop-down menu.**

3. **In the Options dialog box, shown in Figure 22-6, choose from the following options:**

   - **Protocol:** In the Protocol drop-down menu, choose the serial protocol specified by your recording equipment manufacturer.

   - **Port:** Choose your com port from the Port drop-down menu.

   - **Use VTRs Internal Cue:** This may be necessary if your equipment cannot properly cue to specific timecode numbers. (It should be not necessary if you are using high-end equipment.)

   - **Use 19.2 Baud for RS-232:** This is a high-speed communication option that can improve editing accuracy. This option is available only for RS-232 mode equipment.

   - **Time Source:** Choose the Time Source used by your source videotape. If you want your equipment to choose, select the LTC+VITC choice. Otherwise, choose LTC (Longitudinal Timecode) or VITC (Vertical Interval Timecode).

   - **Timebase:** In the Timebase drop-down menu, select the Timebase that matches your source videotape.

Figure 22-6: Set serial device options in the Serial Device Control dialog box.

Calibrating for serial export

To help ensure accuracy when exporting with serial control, you may want to use Premiere's Time Code video effect to help calibrate your VTR. Premiere's Time Code effect allows you to superimpose a timecode over a video effect. You can use the superimposed timecode to match the desired exported video in point with the in point on the tape.

To calibrate, follow these steps:

1. **Start by applying the Timecode video effect to a short video sequence.** The Timecode effect is in the Video bin within the Video Effects bin in the Effects panel.

2. **Put a timecode striped videotape in your videotape recorder.**

3. **Export the tape using an Assemble or Insert edit.**

4. **Use the controls in the Export to Tape dialog box to move to the in point of the sequence.**

5. **Use the Play and Frame Forward buttons to move to the tape in point. Look for black or duplicate frames.** If duplicate or black frames appear before the desired in point, count the frames.

6. **Click Options in the Export to Tape dialog box, and enter the number of duplicate or black frames in the Delay Start Movie field.**

7. **Export again and repeat Step 5 until the first frame of the exported video matches the in point of the tape.**

Exporting using serial device control

When you export to tape using serial device control, you set the in and out points in the Export to Tape dialog box. Before you begin, make sure that you have correctly set the preferences in the Serial Device Control Preferences dialog box (see the section "Serial device control setup" earlier in this chapter). You should also have a good understanding of the capabilities of your videotape recorder. Before you get started, your VTR must be powered up and a tape must be in the VTR. Follow these steps to export using serial device control:

1. **Select the sequence to be exported in the Timeline panel.**

2. **Choose File ➪ Export ➪ Export to Tape.**

3. **In the Export to Tape dialog box, click Options.** Set options specific to your videotape recorder. You may also want to change the following fields:

   • **Sync Record:** Use this option to set the tape timecode to the in point entered in the Set In field in the Export to Tape dialog box. This option is dependent upon the VTR capabilities.

   • **Delay Movie Start:** This option allows you to delay starting the export so that you can sync up properly with your tape machine. This allows you to delay exporting after the record command is sent to the VTR. In the Delay Movie Start field, enter the number of frames to use to create the delay duration.

   • **Preroll:** Preroll backs up the videotape recorder so that it is up to speed when recording starts. Enter the time in seconds to preroll before the designated time-code starting point.

   • **Hard Record Frame Control:** Choose either Drop-Frame or Non-Drop-Frame. This setting is used only when exporting using Hard Record.

4. **In the Export to Tape dialog box, choose Assemble or Insert.** Note that when executing an Assemble or Insert edit, if you are not recording to striped tape, you must have 15 seconds of black and timecode on the tape to which you are recording.

Note If you will be executing a Hard or Crash edit, you will choose this option in Step 7.

5. **Set the in and out points on the tape using the transport controls in the Export to Tape dialog box.** Cue the tape using the transport controls, and click the In Point and Out Point buttons at the desired frame locations. The transport control icons are similar to those in the Source Monitor window.

6. **If you are executing an insert edit with VTRs that support RSS-422 or RSS-232, click the Preview button to preview the export to tape.**

7. **To begin exporting to tape, choose one of the following options depending upon whether you are executing an Assemble, Insert Edit, or Hard Record:**

   • For Assemble and Insert edits, click Auto Edit. This send a signal for the VTR to begin its preroll and start recording at the in point specified in the Export to Tape dialog box.

   • To execute a Hard Record, click the Record button. The VTR immediately begins recording.

Exporting an EDL File

Rather than export to tape, some video producers may want to export an Edit Decision List (EDL) so that their Premiere edits can be reconstructed on high-end video editing systems. An EDL file is a text-based file that contains the names of clips, reel numbers, and transitions, as well as the in and out points of all edits. Premiere allows you to create an EDL file for CMD 3600 format. To create an EDL, first select the video sequence in the Timeline panel and then choose File ⇨ Export ⇨ Export to EDL to open the EDL Export Settings dialog box. The EDL Export Settings dialog box, shown in Figure 22-7, provides the following options, which you may edit. After you change settings, simply click OK. You can then choose a name and location for the file. You can view the file in WordPad and most word processors.

✦ **EDL Tile:** Enter the Title that appears in the first line of the EDL file.

✦ **Start Timecode:** Enter the starting timecode for the first edit.

✦ **Drop Frame:** Enter whether you want drop-frame or non-drop-frame on the master tape.

✦ **Include Video Levels:** Leave the check box selected to include Video Level comments.

✦ **Include Audio Levels:** Leave the check box selected to include Audio Level comments.

✦ **Audio Processing:** This option allows you to choose whether you want audio processing to occur. Choices are Audio Follows Video, Audio Separately, and Audio at the End.

✦ **Tracks to Export:** This option allows you to choose which tracks to export to the EDL file. One video track and four mono tracks are allowed. If you have a track above the video track, EDL uses this track as a track for superimposing key effects.

Figure 22-7: Use the EDL Export Settings dialog box to export an EDL file.

Exporting to AAF

In your day-to-day work as a digital video editor or producer, you may find the need to re-create your Premiere Pro project on another video system, perhaps a high-end system. Re-creating your project from scratch on another system could prove to be costly and time-consuming. Fortunately, you can export your Premiere Pro project in Advanced Authoring Format (AAF). This standard industry format, which was created in the late 1990s, has been embraced by a variety of high-end video systems. Theoretically, you should be able to export your Premiere Pro project in AAF and later import the file into another system. After the import, you should be able to work with all your files and footage. But, realistically, how accurately the high-end system reads the AAF file may vary from system to system.

Exporting to AAF is quite easy. Simply select the Project window and choose Project ➪ Export Project as AAF. In the Save As dialog box that appears, enter a name for the AAF file. After you save, a dialog box appears allowing you to specify whether you want to save the file as Legacy AAF or Embed audio. If you choose legacy AAF, you cannot embed audio information in the file. Click OK to complete the export.

Note For details about which Adobe Premiere Pro effects are supported when exporting to AAF, open the AAF plug-in.doc file found in the Adobe Premiere Pro folder.

Summary

Premiere Pro allows you to output your movies directly to videotape. You can output with or without device control. This chapter covered these topics:

✦ Premiere Pro uses File ➪ Export ➪ Export to Tape to export to videotape.

✦ Premiere Pro uses the settings in the Project Settings dialog box when outputting to videotape.

✦ If you want to create an AAF file, choose Project ➪ Export Project as AAF.

✦   ✦   ✦

Outputting to CD-ROM, Macromedia Flash, and Macromedia Director

Macromedia Flash is responsible for livening up more Web pages than any other computer application. It doesn't take many mouse clicks in a Web browser to land in a Flash-centric site. In fact, throughout the world, Flash movies appear on thousands of Web sites. Flash is used for virtually everything that moves on animated logos, full-featured cartoons, and interactive games. Many Web producers even use Flash to create interactive forms that post data to databases and display the results as animation. Fortunately, Premiere Pro users can take advantage of the millions of Web users who can view Flash movies because Flash can progressively download and stream video files.

This chapter also looks at how to use video files in Flash as well as Macromedia's other multimedia program, Director. Unlike Flash, Director is primarily used for kiosk and CD-ROM projects. This chapter provides an overview of how to load a digital movie into Director, as well as how to export a movie from Premiere for CD-ROM viewing in multimedia programs.

Macromedia Flash

Macromedia Flash is a program designed to provide efficient delivery of animated graphics over the Web. Unlike images created in graphics programs like Photoshop, those created in Flash are not based on pixels; they are based on vectors. *Vector images* are based on mathematical coordinates. Vector images are the foundation of programs like Adobe Illustrator and Macromedia Freehand. In Illustrator and Freehand, you can click and drag the mouse to create an image and move it and bend it with ease. The image transformations are quickly processed by mathematical computations. To display the image on a computer screen, Flash renders the vector-based data to a screen image. When a Flash movie is viewed in a Web browser, the vector graphics scale to fit the user's window.

Flash features a rich set of drawing tools, but if you need graphics created in other programs, such as Photoshop or Illustrator, you can easily import them. Images are animated in a time-line interface, somewhat similar to Premiere Pro's. Instead of video tracks, however, Flash supports a multitude of superimposition effects using layers. Interactivity is provided by Flash's powerful scripting language, Actionscript. Using Actionscript, you can program not only navigation and interactive buttons, but you can load video from Flash Media Server, Macromedia's streaming media server.

When you've finished creating graphics, animation, and interactivity, you publish the Flash movie as an .swf file that can be saved to a Web server.

During the publishing process, Flash can create an HTML file containing the scripting code that loads Flash onto a Web page. The movie appears in a Web browser courtesy of a Flash plug-in that must be installed in the user's browser. Fortunately for Flash developers, the Flash plug-in is one of the most popular in the world. According to Macromedia, it is installed in over 90 percent of the computers that can access the Internet.

Creating Flash Video files

The current version of Flash allows you to play video for progressive downloading or stream video from Macromedia's Flash Media Server. In order to use either progressive downloading or streaming video in Flash, you first need to convert your video into a Flash video (.flv) file. If you have Flash Professional 8 installed on your computer, you can create an .flv file directly from Premiere Pro using the Adobe Media Encoder. When you export an .flv file from Premiere Pro, you can choose to export files for either the Flash 7 or Flash 8 player. The Flash 7 CODEC uses the Sorensen Spark CODEC. The Flash 8CODEC uses On2 Technology's On2VP6 CODEC, which provides higher quality video with smaller file sizes than the Sorensen Spark CODEC. Note that .flv files created with the On2VP6 CODEC cannot be viewed in browsers with the Flash 6 or Flash 7 player installed.

Note On2Technology also sells Flx Exporter, a standalone video exporter that can export video in Flash 8 .flv format. See www.on2.com for details. Sorenson Media sells Sorenson Squeeze for Macromedia Flash, a standalone video exporter that can export video for Flash 7 players. See www.sorensonmedia.com.

To export a Flash Video file from Premiere Pro, follow these steps:

1. **Select the sequence in the Timeline panel that includes the footage you want to export.**

2. **Choose File ➪ Export ➪ Adobe Media Encoder.**

3. **In the Adobe Media Encoder, choose Macromedia Flash Video in the Format drop-down menu.**

4. **Choose a Flash Video preset in the Preset drop-down menu, as shown in Figure 23-1.** Choose Flash 7 if your target audience is using Flash Player 7 or Flash Player 6; choose Flash 8 if your target audience is using Flash Player 8. The High Quality Settings are for streaming video.

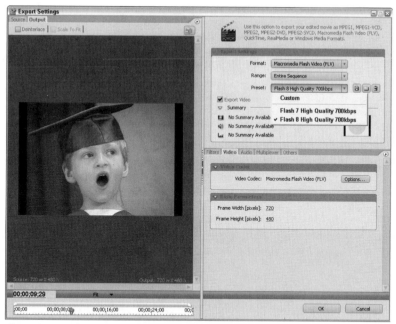

Figure 23-1: Choosing a Flash Video preset

5. **If you do not want to export audio with audio, deselect Audio in the Export Setting section.**

6. **If you wish to apply a video noise reduction filter before exporting, click the Filters tab.** Then Select the Video Noise Reduction Filter. Adjust the slider to control the amount of noise reduction. Reducing noise can improve quality and reduce file size.

7. **If you do not want to change video settings, click the Video tab and set the frame size for the exported file.** Otherwise, proceed to step 8.

8. **If you want to change quality or other settings, click Options.** This opens the Flash Video Encoding dialog box shown in Figure 23-2. Here you can change quality settings, specify keyframe settings, change frame size, as well as other standard video options. After making changes, click OK to return to the Adobe Media Encoder Export Settings dialog box.

9. **To start the export process, click OK in the Adobe Media Encoder. Name your file, and then click Save.**

Note   Flash Professional 8 also provides a standalone exporting application that allows you to export multiple files to .flv format.

After you've created an .flv file, you can save it to your Web server and have Flash download it progressively, or you can stream the video from Macromedia's Flash Media Server.

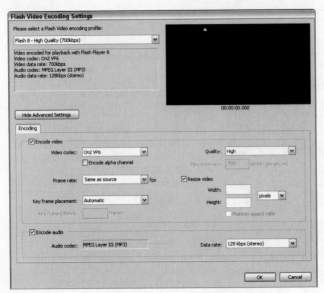

Figure 23-2: Advanced Settings for the On2VP6 codec

Note   In early versions of Flash, multimedia producers sometimes embedded a video into a Flash movie, rather than load it from a Web server or streaming media server. Embedded video provides poorer playback than streaming or progressive video, and the frame rate of the video always played at the frame rate of the animation, which provided further constraints on using video in Flash. When video is streamed, it is loaded in sections into a Web browser and thus consumes less memory than video embedded in a Flash movie.

Integrating digital video into Flash

After you've created an .flv file, you can access it for playback quite easily using prebuilt components within Flash. These components allow you to quickly display and control video from within Flash. The components allow you to drag objects onstage to speed your production work. View the components by choosing Window ➪ Development Panels ➪ Components. Flash 8 Professional includes the FLVPlayback Component, which provides a prebuilt video player, and custom components that allow you to build your own video player.

Using the FLVMedia component

The fastest way to set up and play external video for progressive downloading from Flash is to use the FLVPlayback Component, which allows the viewer to start, stop, and pause video displayed onscreen. To use the FLVPlayback Component and link it a Flash Video file, follow these steps:

1. **Create a new document in Flash.** Specify a document size appropriate for your project.

2. **If you don't see the components onscreen, choose Window ➪ Development Panels ➪ Components.**

3. **Drag the FLVPlayback component into the Flash main screen.** Figure 23-3 shows the Component Panels open with the MediaPlayback component onscreen.

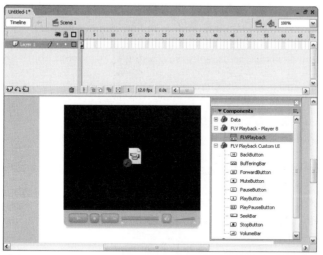

Figure 23-3: Use the FLVPlayback component to display and control video in Flash.

4. **Now use the component inspector to tell Flash where to find your video file. Choose Window ➪ Development Panels ➪ Component Inspector.**

5. **In the component inspector, set options for video. In the contentPath field, enter the location of your video, such as http://mystreaming.com/flv/mymovie.flv.** If the video is in the same directory as your movie, you can simply enter a relative path. You can also click the Magnifying Glass icon, which automatically enters the path to the file after you navigate to it on disk, as shown in Figure 23-4. The Content Path dialog box allows you to match the component's dimensions to the source video dimensions.

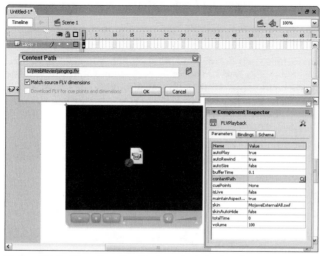

Figure 23-4: Choosing the Content Path in the Component Inspector

6. **If you want to change "skins" for the video player, click the skin field, and choose a different skin.**

7. **Test your movie by choosing Control ⇨ Test Movie.** Figure 23-5 shows an .flv file playing in a Flash movie displayed using the FLVPlayback Component.

Figure 23-5: Video from Premiere Pro playing in Flash

8. **When you complete all your design work, publish the movie by choosing File ⇨ Publish.** This creates the .swf file that can be stored on your Web server.

Using Actionscript to load an FLV movie

If you want to customize the video controls for a Flash movie, you can use Actionscript to load a movie and then create your own buttons that play, stop, and rewind the movie. A full tutorial of Actionscript is beyond the scope of this book, but here are a few steps to get you started. The steps described show how to use Actionscript to load video into Flash for a project that uses progressive downloading.

1. **Create a new document in Flash.** Specify a document size appropriate for your project.

2. **Create a new embedded video library object by choosing New Video in the Library panel menu.**

3. **Drag the embedded video object onto the main movie display area.**

4. **Set the size of the video object by changing dimensions in the Properties panel.**

5. **Name your embedded video object in the property panel: myonscreenflv.**

6. **Create an Actionscript in frame 1 layer 1, by clicking in frame 1, layer 1 of the Timeline, and then enter the Actionscript code in the Actions panel.** The Actionscript in this example creates a new netstream object for playing the video that attaches the object to the onscreen video object. The last line plays the video from the same directory that includes the Flash animation file:

```
netConn.connect(null);
myNetStream = new NetStream(netConn);
myonscreenvideoobject.attachVideo(myNetStream);
mynetStream.play("Myvideofile.flv");
```

Using Actionscript to stream an FLV movie

If you want to stream video using Flash, you need to use Macromedia's Flash Communication Server. When you set up Flash Media Server, you create an application folder for your Flash project. In order to stream video, you need to connect to "register" the applications location on Flash Video Server with Actionscript. This is accomplished using the Actionscript `connect` command, which connects to the server using Macromedia's RTMP (Real Time Messaging Protocol) communications protocol. The following script provides the basics of connecting to Flash Media Server and playing the Flash movie. Like the previous Actionscript example, this also attaches the NetStream object to the video object in the Flash main window. Note also that when issuing the play command, you do not use the .flv file extension.

```
Mync=new NetConnection();
Mync.connect("rtmp://mydomain/myappfolder");
MyNetStream=new NetStream(my_nc);
MyonscreenvideoObject.attachVideo(MyNetStream);
MyNetStream.play("myflvfile");
```

Note   If you don't want to set up a streaming media server, you can still use Flash Media Server by paying a monthly hosting charge to an Internet Service Provider such as Vitalstream (www.vitalstream.com).

Working with Flash Media Server

If you want to work with Flash streaming media files, you should start by downloading a trial version of Flash Media Server (FMS) from Macromedia's Web site (www.macromedia.com). Next, try developing some of the sample applications provided with the FMS, as well as the examples in the Flash Development Center area of Macromedia's Web site.

Exporting to CD-ROM

Although more and more video continues to appear on the Web, one of the most widely used mediums for distributing digital movies is CD-ROM. Virtually every computer sold today can play CD-ROM discs. A standard CD-ROM holds 650MB of data, usually enough space for at least 30 minutes of compressed digital video. CD-ROMs also are among the cheapest and most durable digital media available.

Many multimedia producers who distribute their work on CD-ROM find that to truly take advantage of the medium, they need to add interactivity to their Adobe Premiere Pro presentations. A popular interactive multimedia program is Macromedia Director. If you import a Premiere Pro movie into Director, you can create buttons that start, stop, and rewind your Premiere Pro movie. You can also put several Premiere Pro movies into different Director frames and create buttons that enable the viewer to move from one movie to another.

This section guides you through the steps for exporting your Premiere Pro movie to CD-ROM. It also includes an overview of how to use Macromedia Director to create interactive behaviors to control digital movies.

Exporting Premiere Pro Movies to CD-ROM

Before Premiere Pro turned "pro," earlier versions of the program actually provided the multimedia project presets for both QuickTime and AVI movies. The presets created a square pixel project at 320×280 at 15 frames per second with audio set at 16-bit mono, with a sampling rate of 22050 Hz. Today's multimedia producer is more likely to work in a DV project at 720×480, at 29.97 frames per second. In order to use the file for multimedia purposes, the producer would then export the video at a smaller frame size, lower frame rate, and with square pixels. Follow these steps for exporting for CD-ROM:

1. **Complete your editing.**

2. **Select the Timeline panel that you want to export, and choose File ⇨ Export ⇨ Movie.** Click the Settings button in the Export Movie dialog box. If you want to export using RealMedia, Windows Media, or an MPEG format (MPEG1 is suitable for CD-ROM), select the sequence to export in the Timeline panel and choose File ⇨ Export ⇨ Adobe Media Encoder.

3. **Change settings as desired in the General, Video, Keyframe and Rendering, and Audio sections.** If you're exporting QuickTime movies, you may want to choose Sorensen Video 3 as your compressor (in the Video settings section). Sorensen can provide higher-quality movies in smaller file sizes. Figure 23-6 shows the Sorenson Video settings in the Export Movie Settings dialog box. One of the most important options in this dialog box is the Data Rate. The value entered in this dialog box limits the flow of data so that the video doesn't pour out at a rate the CD-ROM can't handle. Typical data rates for double-speed CD-ROMs are between 200K and 250K per second. For older compressors, such as Cinepak, Adobe recommended data rates for a 12-speed (12X) CD-ROM drive to be 1.8MB per second; for a 24X CD-ROM, 3–3.6MB See http://www.adobe.com/support/ techdocs/315097.html for more details. However, if you are using the Sorenson 3 CODEC you set the data rate anywhere from 200KB per second or lower. Sorenson recommends this formula as a starting point: height × width × frames per second ÷ 48000. Thus, if exporting a 320×240 video at 15 frames per second, you could limit the data rate to 24KB per second as a starting point. At 30 frames per second, you could limit the data rate to 48KB per second. (Of course, for high-action clips, you generally need a higher data rate.)

Tip   If you reduce the number of frames per second in the Frame Rate menu, you can usually increase the data rate.

4. **After editing settings in the Export Movie Settings dialog box, click OK.**

5. **In the Export Movie dialog box, name your file.**

6. **Click Save.** The CODEC starts compressing your movie.

7. **If you are importing your Premiere Pro movie into Director or another multimedia program, such as Macromedia Authorware, import the Premiere Pro movie into the program.** Then complete the final production in Director or Authorware.

8. **Save the final production to a CD-ROM using a CD-ROM recorder.** Most Mac CD-ROM recording software enables you to partition the CD-ROM to create a Mac version and a Windows version.

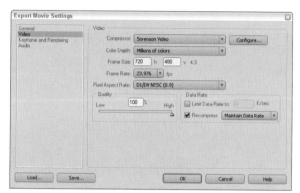

Figure 23-6: The Sorenson Video settings in the Export Movie Settings dialog box

Using Macromedia Director

Macromedia Director is a powerful and widely used multimedia-authoring program. Like Premiere Pro, Director enables you to import graphics files from such programs as Adobe Photoshop and Adobe ImageReady. It also enables you to import source images from Macromedia FireWorks and Macromedia Flash.

Although Director is often used for creating animated sequences, to Premiere Pro users it offers the power of adding interactivity to digital movies. Unlike Premiere Pro, Director features a powerful programming language called Lingo. Using Lingo, you can create scripts or behaviors that enable the user to jump from frame to frame or to start and stop digital movies imported into Director. For example, using both Premiere Pro and Director, you can create educational productions that enable users to choose what areas they want to learn and what video segments they want to see.

Note   Director can import AVI, QuickTime, RealMedia, and Windows Media files. Thus, you need to export your Premiere Pro movie in one of these formats in order to use it in Director. You can export in AVI and QuickTime formats, using File ➪ Export ➪ Movie. To export in RealMedia or Windows Media format, choose File ➪ Export ➪ Adobe Media Encoder.

Director overview

To understand how Premiere Pro movies can be integrated into a Director presentation, you should become familiar with the various elements of the Director interface. Director uses three primary screen areas: the Stage, the Score, and the Cast windows, as shown in Figure 23-7. The *Stage* is where all animation and activity take place. You may view this as equivalent to Premiere Pro's Program Monitor. The *Score* is somewhat similar to Premiere Pro's Timeline.

In the Director score, each frame is represented by a tiny rectangle. Each track in Director is called a *Channel*. All program elements imported or created in Director are automatically added to its *Cast*. To start the process of creating a production, cast members are dragged from the cast window to the stage. Cast members can include graphics such as buttons, digital movies, text, audio, and behaviors.

Figure 23-7: The Director Stage, Score, and Cast windows

Importing Premiere Pro movies into Director

For Premiere Pro users, one of Director's most valuable features is that it enables you to import and control video files. Before you can use a Premiere Pro movie in Director, you must first import it into the program.

To import a movie into Director, follow these steps:

1. **If you have multiple casts in Director, start by selecting the cast you want to import the digital movie into and then choose File ⇨ Import.**

2. **In the Import Files dialog box, select the digital movie that you want to import.**

3. **If you are importing only one file, click the Import button.** Otherwise, select another digital movie and click Add.

4. **When you are finished adding movies, click Import.** After the movie is imported, it is loaded as a cast member in the Cast window.

Changing movie properties

Although you most likely will control digital movies in Director using Lingo, you can easily change settings that affect playback in the Cast Member Properties windows. To open the Property Inspector window shown in Figure 23-8, select the digital movie in the Cast tab and then click the Info button. The digital movie's properties window (in the Property Inspector) enables you to choose to play back both video and sound, or one or the other. Perhaps the most important choice in the dialog box is the Paused check box. This enables you to prevent the movie from playing as soon as the viewer enters the frame that contains the video. If you select the Paused button, you can use Lingo to have the user start and stop the movie. If you select Loop, the digital video movie plays continuously.

Figure 23-8: The Property Inspector window

QuickTime movies enable the QuickTime controller to appear onscreen as a device for starting and stopping QuickTime movies. Many multimedia producers choose not to show the controller, preferring to create their own interface and controlling it with Lingo.

Usually, the Sync to Soundtrack option is selected. The other choice in the pop-up menu — Play Every Frame — can result in video playing without audio. If the Director to Stage option is selected, you can place other cast members over QuickTime movies.

Placing the movie onstage

For a digital movie to be viewed in Director, it must be positioned in Director's Stage window. Before dragging the movie from the Cast window to the Stage window, most Director users select the frame where the QuickTime, RealMedia, and Windows Media will reside. Typically, the background and buttons are created in Director or Adobe Photoshop. After the frame in the Score window is selected, clicking and dragging the movie from the Cast window to the Score window puts the movie on that frame.

At this point, the Director producer must decide whether he or she wants the movie to play in one Director frame or whether the movie should play over multiple Director frames. Projects are often easier to manage if the movie plays in one Director frame. When movies play in one frame, Director must stop its own playback head and turn the processing over to the video movie.

Pausing the playback head with the Tempo channel

If you set up Director to play a movie in one frame, you must tell Director to halt and wait for the end of the QuickTime movie or wait for a button to tell it to move off the frame. The easiest way to tell Director to wait for the end of a movie is to specify this in Director's Tempo channel.

To access the Tempo channel controls for the movie, simply double-click the Tempo channel frame directly above the movie frame. In the Tempo channel dialog box, shown in Figure 23-9, select Wait for Cue Point and then click {End} in the Cue Point pop-up menu.

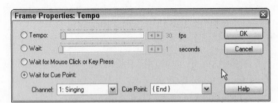

Figure 23-9: Director's Tempo channel dialog box enables you to pause the playback head while a digital video movie plays.

Pausing the playback with a behavior

Although the Tempo channel provides a quick way of stopping Director's playback head, most experienced Director users don't use it because it does not provide as much power as does Lingo. To pause the playback head while a digital movie plays, you can use a Lingo behavior instead of the Tempo channel. Fortunately, for nonprogrammers, Director comes packaged with prewritten behaviors. You can use a prewritten behavior to pause the playback head by dragging the Hold on Current Frame behavior from Director's Behavior Library (in the Navigation section) into the Score channel frame that appears directly above the digital movie frame. (The Score channel appears above channel 1.)

Using Lingo

Although playing QuickTime and AVI windows from within Director is quite easy, learning a few Lingo commands to control navigation and start and stop QuickTime movies is helpful. Director provides a simple interface to get you started creating Lingo scripts. The following section shows you how to create a simple navigational script using Director's Behavior Inspector. After you learn how to use the Behavior Inspector, you can create scripts that control QuickTime movies.

Creating behaviors

Director *behaviors* are Lingo scripts that can be used to control navigation and to control QuickTime movies. After you create a behavior, you can click and drag it over an onscreen object such as a button. If the behavior includes commands for mouse events, you can program the behavior to execute when the user clicks the mouse on the object that contains the behavior.

Follow these steps for creating a simple navigational behavior:

1. **Choose Window ➪ Inspectors ➪ Behavior.**

2. **To create a new behavior, click the plus (+) button and choose New Behavior.**

3. **In the New Behavior dialog box, enter a name for your behavior and click OK.**

4. **To utilize the Behavior Inspector window's automatic scripting features, click the arrow in the middle of the dialog box to expand it.** The dialog box is shown in Figure 23-10.

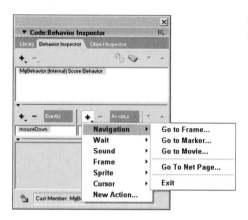

Figure 23-10: Create behaviors in the Behavior Inspector dialog box.

5. **In the Events section in the Behavior Inspector dialog box, click the plus (+) button and choose an event to trigger your behavior.** For most button-triggered programs, choose Mouse Up or Mouse Enter. Choose Mouse Up instead of Mouse Down to enable the user to release the mouse. If a Mouse Down triggers the event, the user cannot cancel after clicking the mouse. If you use a Mouse Up event, the user can cancel the event by moving the mouse off the button before releasing the mouse.

6. **In the Actions section, select an Action category.** For example, if you are creating a navigational button, choose Navigation.

7. **In the menu that appears, pick a specific action such as Go To Frame.** If you choose Go To Frame, enter the frame number you want to go to.

8. **Click OK.**

9. **If you want to see the Lingo script that was created, click the Script window icon.**

10. **Close the Behavior Inspector window by clicking the Close icon.**

11. **To use your behavior, drag it from the Cast window and release it over an object such as a button graphic in the Stage window.**

Creating your own Lingo

When you know the basics of creating behaviors, you can begin using Lingo to control QuickTime and AVI movies. Most of the Lingo that controls QuickTime and AVI movies refers to the movie by the channel the movie is in or its cast member name or number. When you drag a movie from the Cast window to the stage, the movie becomes known as a *sprite*. Lingo addresses different sprites according to the channel the sprite is in. Thus, if you dragged a digital video movie into channel 1, you refer to it as *Sprite 1*.

To create your own behaviors that control QuickTime movies, you can use the Behavior Inspector dialog box to get you started and then enter the Lingo commands that control digital video movies by opening the Script Window dialog box and entering them there. The following sections review some commonly used Lingo commands that control digital video movies.

Playing movies with Lingo

If you want to create Lingo buttons that start, stop, and reverse QuickTime movies, you can set and change the sprite's movieRate property and the movieRate function. The following are common movie rate values:

Play   1

Stop   0

Reverse   –1

Note   You can slow down the movie by setting the movie rate to .5.

Here's a simple script that starts a QuickTime movie in channel 3 when the user clicks the mouse on an object containing the following behavior:

```
On mouseUp
Set the movieRate of sprite 3 to 1
End mouseUp
```

Or, in Director 7 and later versions, you can use "dot syntax":

```
On mouseUp
sprite(3).movieRate=1
End mouseUp
```

Checking movie duration

Director's movieTime and duration commands are more helpful Lingo utilities. Use movieTime to check how much of a QuickTime movie has played. Duration measures the length of a QuickTime movie. Both duration and movieTime are measured in *ticks* (one tick equals one-sixtieth of a second), not frames. By constantly comparing the movieTime property of a QuickTime movie to its duration, you can tell when the movie actually stops playing. When the movie stops playing, you can then send Director's playback head to another frame. The following Lingo is an example. A movie script that is executed when the production starts puts the duration of a QuickTime movie into a *variable* called gmovduration. In this example, the QuickTime movie is in Director's third channel (like a video track). In Lingo, this is designated as Sprite 3.

```
Global gmovduration
Put the duration of sprite 3 into gmovduration
```

Another script, executed when the playback head exits a frame, compares the current MovieTime of the QuickTime movie to its duration. If the movieTime is less than the duration, then the movie hasn't ended yet. Thus, the Lingo script keeps Director playback on the current Director frame. The Lingo command "go to the frame keeps the playback head in the current frame. When the QuickTime movie finishes, its movieTime is no longer less than its duration. At this point, the "go to the frame" section of the code is not executed, so Director's playback moves on to the next frame in the Director production.

```
Global gmovduration
On Exit Frame
Put the movieTime of sprite 3 into myMovieTime
If myMovieTime < gmovduration then go to the frame
```

```
End
```

You can also change the `MovieTime` of a digital movie with a script like this:

```
Set the movieTime of sprite 3 to 360
```

The dot syntax version would be as follows:

```
sprite(3).movieTime=360
```

The preceding Lingo code results in the playback of the QuickTime movie jumping to the new time position you have assigned.

Changing digital movie settings

The movie settings in the Cast Properties window that controls looping and whether the movie pauses when the playback head enters the frame are easily controlled with Lingo commands.

For example, at the beginning of a movie or at a certain point in a movie, you can turn off looping with the following line of Lingo code:

```
Set the loop of member "Mymovie" =True
```

Or you can stop the movie from playing when the playback head enters the frame with this Lingo:

```
Set the pausedAtStart of member "Mymovie"=TRUE
```

Playing a portion of a digital movie

Director also enables you to start and stop a digital video movie from any point in the movie using its `startTime` and `stopTime` commands. Using these Lingo commands, you can create a button labeled Show intro or Show interview. When the user clicks the button, only the specified segment is played. `startTime` and `stopTime` are measured in ticks. For example, this Lingo snippet tells Director to start the digital movie one minute into the digital movie:

```
Set the startTime of sprite 1=360
```

Or

```
sprite(1).startTime=360
```

To set the stop point of the movie, you could use this Lingo snippet:

```
Set the stopTime of sprite 10=720
```

Or

```
sprite(10).stoptime=720
```

Other Lingo commands

Director includes numerous Lingo commands that work with QuickTime movies. For example, Lingo includes commands that can turn QuickTime soundtracks on and off. Lingo can determine whether QuickTime or Video for Windows is installed on a computer, and it can tell the video producer when keyframes occur. Lingo commands are well documented in Director's Lingo dictionary. However, if you are a Director beginner, be forewarned: You won't become a Lingo expert overnight.

Summary

The most widely used medium for distributing digital movies is CD-ROM. Many Premiere Pro movies are imported into interactive multimedia programs such as Macromedia Director before the project is saved to CD-ROM. When exporting a movie that will play on CD-ROM, your export settings should be based on the system that will be playing your movie. This chapter covered the following topics:

✦ If you want to add interactivity to a Premiere Pro movie, you can export your movie into Macromedia Director or Macromedia Flash. For progressive downloading and streaming in Flash, you must convert your Premiere Pro movie to .flv format.

✦ If you have Flash Professional 8 installed on you computer, you can export your Premiere Pro in .flv format.

✦ The Sorenson Video CODEC is commonly used for exporting movies for CD-ROM.

✦ Macromedia Director's programming language, Lingo, features many commands that enable onscreen clickable buttons that can start and stop digital video movies.

✦　　✦　　✦

Premiere Pro and Beyond

◆ ◆ ◆ ◆

◆ ◆ ◆ ◆

Editing Audio with Adobe Audition

Although Premiere Pro includes audio-editing, mixing, and recording tools, it does not include tools for intricate audio editing. Premiere Pro users who need more audio-editing power should examine the features provided by Audition, Adobe's professional audio production application. Audition's tools allow you to precisely zoom in, pinpoint, and select audio data, and then cut, copy, and paste it. Audition features tools that can extend, hunt down, and remove silence from an entire audio clip. It can also automatically recognize and select beats in an audio rhythm. When copying and pasting in Audition, you can even mix the audio as you paste.

As part of the Adobe Video Collection, Audition allows you to import an audio clip directly into Premiere Pro. After you edit it and save it in Audition, the changes are updated in Premiere. Audition also allows you to export a mixing sessions, and re-edit the mix even after you've already imported it into Premiere.

If you own Audition, or if you're considering purchasing it, this chapter provides you the basics for exploring its audio-editing capabilities. As you read through this chapter, you'll see how Audition's selection, zooming, and editing controls can enhance the sound of music and narration in Premiere Pro.

Note   This chapter focuses on audio-editing features not found in Premiere Pro, particularly in regard to audio waveform editing. Because Premiere Pro provides mixing and audio effects (covered in Chapters 9 and 10), those areas of Audition are not discussed in detail.

Understanding Audition

To work efficiently with Adobe Audition, you should first become familiar with the program's menus and panels. Although Audition's interface is quite different from Premiere's, there are several similarities. Like Premier Pro, Audition's workspace, shown in Figure 24-1, is divided into different panels that can be resized, moved, docked, and separated. Furthermore, you can choose different workspaces and save workspaces using options in the Window menu. Figure 24-1 shows the Editing workspace. When the Editing workspace opens, it switches the Main Panel and menus to *Edit View* with this view set to display an audio waveform. The following sections provide an overview of the main panels you use to edit audio in Audition.

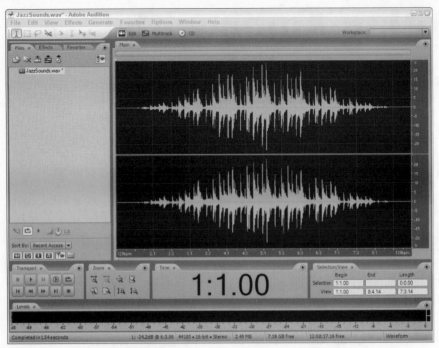

Figure 24-1: Audition in Edit View

Becoming Familiar with the Main Panel

The Main panel is Audition's timeline work area for audio production. The contents of the main panel change according to whether you are working in Edit View, Multitrack View, or CD View. You can switch from one view to another by choosing one of these views in the View menu. When you change views, Audition changes the tools and menu commands to correspond with the chosen view. For example, you can import video with audio into Multitrack View, but you cannot import video into Edit View, which displays only one audio at a time.

✦ **Edit View:** Edit View provides editing options and menus for cutting, copying, and electronically splicing audio data together. If you need to remove narration flubs or extraneous noise or add silence to a clip, you use Edit View. In Edit View, you can view and edit the waveform of an audio clip. You can also view audio data in a spectral frequency display, which allows you to cut, copy, and paste according to audio frequency. You can also select a portion of the audio and apply an audio effect from Audition's Effects or Favorites menus.

In Edit View, the default vertical scale format is decibels, and the default horizontal scale is beats per minutes. To change either of these options, choose View ➪ Vertical Scale Format or View ➪ Horizontal Scale Format. After you have completed editing in Edit View, you can save your file in standard audio formats such as .wav, .aif, or .wma.

Note After you switch to Edit View, the View menu contents change to provide you with different Edit View options. For example, to change to waveform or spectral frequency display, choose View ⇨ Waveform Display or View ⇨ Spectral Frequency Display.

✦ **Multitrack View:** Shown in Figure 24-2, Multitrack View is primarily used as a timeline view for mixing. In this view, you can drag audio clips from the File panel and drop them into different tracks. Using this view, you can also sequence one audio clip after another. Like Premiere Pro's Audio Mixer panel, Multitrack View provides volume, panning, and automation controls. (Audition's Mixer window provides even more sophisticated mixing options.) While in Multitrack View, you can also apply audio effects to tracks. If you need to edit a clip while in Multitrack View, you can quickly switch to Edit View by double-clicking the clip in one of the tracks.

Figure 24-2: The Audition Main panel in Multitrack View

While working in Multitrack View, you save your work in a *session* file. When finished mixing, you can then export your file into a stereo or mono track in a variety of standard audio formats.

✦ **CD View:** Use CD View for producing audio CDs. In CD View, you can change track order and burn a CD.

Transport panel

Use the transport to play, stop, and rewind audio. Figure 24-3 shows the different buttons and their functions. Unlike Premiere Pro, Audition does not provide a scrubbing transport control. To scrub audio in Audition, you must activate the scrubbing tool and then click and drag. Note that you can also play audio from the current cursor position by pressing the spacebar.

Play from cursor to end of file

Play from cursor to end of view

Stop | Pause | Play Looped

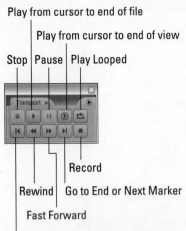

Record

Rewind | Go to End or Next Marker

Fast Forward

Go to Beginning or Previous Marker

Figure 24-3: Transport panel controls

Zoom panel

When editing audio, use the Zoom panel to zoom into waveforms so you can edit more precisely. As shown in Figure 24-4, Audition's Zoom tools allow you to zoom horizontally, vertically, and to the edges of selections. When you zoom in horizontally to a waveform, the waveform becomes stretch out, often allowing you to work more precisely.

Zoom Out Horizontally   Zoom Out to Normal Size

Zoom In Horizontally   Zoom to Selection

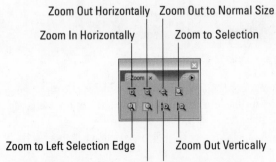

Zoom to Left Selection Edge   Zoom Out Vertically

Zoom to Right Selection Edge   Zoom In Vertically

Figure 24-4: Audition provides several Zoom tools for zooming into audio data.

Time panel

The Time panel provides a time readout of the currently selected audio sequence. Time can be viewed in different audio formats, such as SMPTE drop-frame, non-drop-frame, audio samples, and bars and beats. As audio plays, the time readout displays the sample or frame being played. If you click within an audio clip, the Time panel readout changes to show the point in the audio sequence that you clicked.

You can change display formats by View ➪ Display Time Format.

Selection/View panel

The Selection/View panel is divided into to sections: the Selection area displays the start and length of a selection; the View section displays what portion of the audio clip appears in the Main panel. As you click and drag to create a selection, the selection section of this panel automatically changes to reflect the selection.

Levels panel

The levels panel displays audio levels in dbfs (decibels below full scale). Stereo clips display two bars; mono tracks display one bar. When you play audio, vertical lines at the far right of the panel indicate peak levels. If the amplitude level peaks above 0, clipping or distortion can occur. Clipping is indicated by red lights at the right of the levels gauge.

Tools panel

The Tools panel shown in Figure 24-5 provides tools for selecting and scrubbing audio. Activation of tools depends upon whether you are in Edit View or Multitrack View. For example, you can create a selection by clicking and dragging the Time Selection tool in Edit View, but in Multitrack View, you must click and drag with the Multitrack's Time Selection tool. To use the Marquee and Lasso tools while in Edit View, choose View ➪ Spectral Frequency Display. Use the Marquee tool to create rectangular selections; use the Lasso tool to create polygonal and rounded selections.

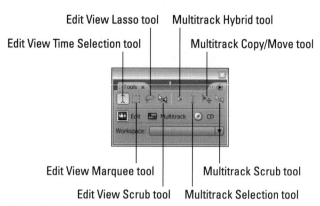

Figure 24-5: Tools panel for Edit View and Multitrack View

In both Edit View and Multitrack View, you can scrub audio by clicking and dragging with the Scrub tool. If you click and drag slowly, you will hear the sound in slow motion; click and drag faster, and Audition plays the selected sound at a faster rate.

In Multitrack View, you can select and move audio blocks by clicking in the middle of a clip and dragging with the Move/Copy tool. In Multitrack View, the Hybrid tool often can be used as a selection tool or in place of the Move/Copy tool.

Files panel

The Files panel displays files that have been opened in Audition. In both Edit View and Multitrack View, you can drag audio clips directly into the Main panel. Icons at the bottom of the panel allow you to restrict the display in the Panel to audio, loop, video, midi files, or markers.

Effects panel

Audition's Effects panel provides access to a variety of audio effects, many similar to those found in Premiere Pro. Unlike Premiere, Audition's effects are grouped according to category, such as Amplitude, Delay Effects, and Restoration. In Audition, effects can be applied to audio by selecting audio data and by clicking and dragging the effect over the audio in Multitrack View. You can also apply effects from Edit View by selecting audio data and choosing an effect from the Effects menu. You store effects and settings for effects in the Favorites menu where you can quickly access them when needed. (Using the Effects in the Favorites menu is covered later in this chapter, in the section "Applying and Creating Custom Effects.")

Importing Audio and Video

After you become familiar with Audition's panels and workspace, you can import audio and begin editing. Audio and video files can be imported into Audition in several ways. You can load an audio file directly into Audition, or you can load an audio clip into Audition directly from Premiere Pro. If you create a mix in Audition, you can also link the file so you can return to Audition and edit the mix, if necessary.

Opening audio files

Audition can read all major audio file formats, such as .wav, .aif, and .mp3. The steps are quite similar to opening a file in Premiere:

1. **In Edit View, choose File ⇨ Open.**

2. **In the Open dialog box, navigate to the file you want to open.** To open more than one file, press Ctrl and then click the files you want to open.

3. **To preview the audio before opening, click Play.**

4. **To open the audio file, click Open.**

Tip

If you choose File ⇨ Open as instead of File ⇨ Open, Audition allows you to convert the file from stereo to mono (and vice versa) and to change its sample rate and resolution. If you want to change audio attributes of a file that is already loaded, choose Edit ⇨ Adjust Sample Rate or Edit ⇨ Adjust Sample Type.

Linking an Audition Mix with Premiere Pro

If you prefer to mix audio in Audition rather than Premiere Pro, you can create a link between the two programs. This allows you to freely return and edit the audio in Audition. In Audition, follow these steps:

1. Choose View ➪ Multitrack.
2. After you are finished mixing, choose File ➪ Export Audio Mix down to export the mix-down file.
3. In the Export Audio Mix down dialog box, select Embed Edit Original link data.

If you need to return to Audition after importing the file into Premiere Pro, follow these steps in Premiere:

1. Select the Audio clip in the Timeline or Project panel.
2. Choose Edit ➪ Edit Original.

Opening audio from video

Audition allows you to import audio from Premiere Pro, separate audio from a video clip, and import video. Here are several techniques for importing audio when working on a video project:

✦ **Edit in Audition from Premiere:** If you've placed audio into a sequence in Premiere Pro and want to edit it in Audition, your best bet is to use Premiere's Edit in Audition command. This automatically loads the audio into Audition. After you've edited the clip and saved it in Audition, the changes appear in Premiere Pro.

To use Edit in Audition, first select the audio clip in Premiere's Timeline panel and then choose Edit ➪ Edit in Audition. After Audition loads, edit the clip as desired and then save the clip. When you return to Premiere Pro, the changes are intact.

✦ **Importing Audio from Video:** In Audition's Edit View, you can import audio from a video clip — without the video. To import audio from a video clip, choose File ➪ Open Audio From Video. Navigate to the video file, and then click Open to open the audio file.

✦ **Importing Video with Audio:** Like Premiere Pro, Audition allows you to view video with audio so that you can synchronize sound with picture. To load a video file into Audition, switch to Multitrack View by choosing View ➪ Multitrack View. Next click in a track to establish a starting time for the video and audio. To import the video and audio into the track, choose Insert ➪ Video. Navigate to an AVI, MOV, WMA or MPG file, and then click Open. The video is loaded into a video track and the audio into an audio track, with a video monitor window displaying the video, as shown in Figure 24-6. You can use the Move/Copy Clip tool to move the video and audio in sync. To separate audio from video, select the audio or video and choose Clip ➪ Group Clips. (After you choose Group Clips, the check mark in the menu disappears indicating that the clips are no longer grouped.)

Figure 24-6: Video with audio inserted into Audition

Playing Audio and Scrolling

To play an audio clip that you've opened in Audition, simply press the spacebar or click the Play button in the Transport panel. (The transport controls are shown in Figure 24-3.) When you need to jump to another area of an audio clip, you can click and drag Audition's current-time indicator (also referred to as a cursor). To scroll, click and drag the scrolling control in the horizontal colored bar above the time display in Edit View or Multitrack View.

As mentioned earlier, unlike Premiere Pro, Audition provides no scrubbing transport control. To scrub, you must use the Scrub tool. To select the scrub, click it in the Tools panel. Then click and drag slowly in the waveform in Edit View or over an audio clip in Multitrack View. As you click and drag, the audio plays.

Selecting Audio

Before you can execute most of Audition's audio-editing options, you must first select the audio data that you want to edit. Because pinpointing the precise sound you want to edit can sometimes be difficult with a mouse, Audition provides numerous utilities to aid in selecting audio. For example, Audition can find silence and beats, and it can extend or reduce a selection based on the audio waveform.

Here are the major ways to select audio in Audition:

✦ **Range Selection:** Click and drag with the Selection tool over the audio waveform. If you did not select the proper area, press Shift and click in the waveform to extend or reduce the selection. Figure 24-7 shows a waveform selection in Edit View.

Tip

You can extend a selection by clicking and dragging the yellow triangles at the top of the selection area at the top of the waveform.

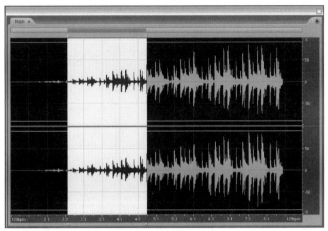

Figure 24-7: Waveform selected in Edit View

✦ **Visible Range:** To select only the visible portion of the waveform that appears onscreen, double click the waveform.

✦ **Channel Selection:** You can select only one channel by dragging the mouse near the top of the top channel or bottom of the lower channel. As you drag, the cursor changes either to an R or an L, indicating whether you are selecting either the Right or Left channel.

Note   To restrict editing to a specific channel, choose Edit ➪ Edit Channel and then choose the channel in the submenu.

✦ **Spectral Selection:** Audition allows you to edit audio by selecting a frequency range. For example, if you want to edit high frequencies from an audio clip, you can click and drag over a spectral frequency display with the mouse. (To view audio frequencies, choose View ➪ Spectral Frequency Display.) To create a rectangular selection, click and drag with the Marquee tool. To create a polygonal or rounded selection, click and drag with the Lasso tool. When you release the mouse, the Lasso tool closes the selection. After you create a selection, you can then resize the selection by clicking and dragging an edge. To move the selection, position the cursor over the selection and then click and drag to move it.

Using zero crossing points

When editing audio, often the best point to edit is where the waveform crosses zero on the waveform display, at the *zero crossing point*. By selecting and editing at zero crossing points, you avoid hearing a click or pop when Audition automatically splices audio edits together. (Selecting a zero crossing point is somewhat similar to selecting the blank space between words in a text document.) To edit using a zero crossing point, start by selecting the audio with one of the Selection tools. Then choose Edit ➪ Zero Crossing. In the Zero Crossing sub-menu, choose one of the following options:

✦ **Adjust Selection Inward:** Adjusts inward to the closest zero point

✦ **Adjust Selection Outward:** Adjusts outward to the closest zero point

✦ **Adjust Left Side To Left:** Adjusts left to the closest zero point

✦ **Adjust Left Side To Right:** Adjusts the left selection border to the closest zero point to the right

✦ **Adjust Right Side To Left:** Adjusts the right selection border to the closest zero point to the left

✦ **Adjust Right Side to Right:** Adjusts the right selection border to the closest zero point to the right

Snapping selections

Like Premiere Pro, Audition provides an invisible magnetic-like force that can help you work more precisely. Audition's snapping option can make selections snap to the current-time indicator, markers, ruler ticks, and zero crossing points. By default, Snapping is enabled, though it can be easily disabled if desired.

To activate or deactivate snapping, choose Edit ➪ Snapping and then choose from the following options:

✦ **Snap To Marker:** This option enables the cursor to snap to makers.

✦ **Snap To Ruler (Coarse):** This option enables the cursor to snap to major ruler divisions or to snap only to the major numeric divisions.

✦ **Snap To Ruler (Fine):** This option enables the cursor to snap to each ruler subdivision.

✦ **Snap To Clips:** This option allows the cursor to snap to clip edges.

✦ **Snap To Loop Endpoints:** This option allows the cursor to snap to endpoints of loops.

✦ **Snap To Frames (Always):** When Audition's time format is set to frames, this option allows snapping to frames.

Finding beats

As you edit music, you may want to select between one beat and another. Often, a beat is evident by a regular peak in the waveform display. However, you may be able to save yourself editing time by having Audition find the beat or by having Audition select the beat.

To automatically find the beginning of the beat, click in the waveform and then choose Edit ➪ Find Beats ➪ Find Next Beat (Left Side). If you want to find the next beat after that, choose Edit ➪ Find Beats ➪ Find Next Beat (Right Side).

Deleting, Trimming, Copying, and Pasting

After you've selected the audio data that you want edit, you often want to delete or copy the selection. Before making a selection, decide whether you want to edit the audio data in waveform or spectral data display. If you want to edit an audio clip's waveform, choose View ➪ Waveform Display in EditView. If you want to edit by selecting a frequency, choose View ➪ Spectral Frequency Display in Edit View.

In Edit View, you can cut, copy, and paste in Waveform Display or Spectral Display. When pasting in Audition, you can choose to simply paste audio data at the current-time indicator, or you can paste and mix. Follow these steps:

1. **Select the data that you want to cut.** Using one of the Zoom tools can help you make your selection more precise.

2. **To cut the data, choose Edit ⇨ Cut or Edit ⇨ Delete Selection.** After executing the Delete Selection or Cut command, the selection is removed and audio is spliced together.

Note   Edit ⇨ Cut places the cut selection in the Clipboard; Delete Selection does not.

Note   You can delete audio in Multitrack View by selecting audio in a track and choosing Edit ⇨ Insert/Delete Time.

Tip   When you cut, copy, or paste, Audition allows you to use up to five clipboards. To use one of the Audition clipboards, choose Edit ⇨ Set Current Clipboard. In the submenu that appears, select one of the five Audition clipboards, or select the Windows clipboard and then proceed to cut, copy, or paste.

To copy audio, follow these steps:

1. **Select the data that you want to copy.**

2. **To copy the data, choose Edit ⇨ Copy.**

Trimming audio removes everything but the selected area. To trim audio, follow these steps:

1. **Select the audio data that you want to retain.**

2. **Choose Edit ⇨ Trim.**

When pasting data, you can choose to paste audio into the current time area, or you can paste and mix audio at the same time. Paste mix allows you to blend audio levels and modulate sound for special effects. Follow these steps:

1. **Copy or cut the data that you want to move.**

2. **Click or click and drag in the waveform area where you want to paste.**

3. **Choose Edit ⇨ Paste or Edit ⇨ Mix Paste.** If you choose Mix Paste, the Mix Paste dialog box opens, as shown in Figure 24-8. Choose among these options when pasting, and then click OK:

   • **Volume:** This option allows you to change volume levels before pasting.

   • **Invert:** This option inverts the pasted waveform, pasting in an upside-down version.

   • **Lock Left/Right:** This option locks the volume sliders in the dialog box so that they move simultaneously.

- **Insert:** This option inserts audio at the current-time indicator. If a selection was made, pasted audio replaces the selection.

- **Overlap:** This option mixes the audio data at current volume level while pasting.

- **Modulate:** This option creates a special effect by multiplying waveform values together when pasting.

- **Crossfade:** This option fades-in audio when pasting. Enter a value in milliseconds for the fade duration.

- **From Clipboard:** This option pastes from the specified clipboard number.

- **From Windows Clipboard:** This option pastes from the standard Windows clipboard.

- **From File:** This option allows pasting from an audio file on disk.

- **Loop Paste:** This option pastes audio based upon a number specified in the Loop Paste field.

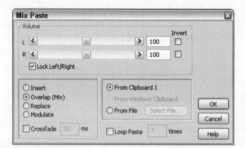

Figure 24-8: The Mix Paste options

Deleting silence

When editing, you may want to delete silence to remove narration dull spots or to make the narration move quicker. Audition's Delete Silence command provides a fast and easy method of deleting silence. When you execute Delete Silence, Audition removes the silences and shortens the audio clip.

To remove silence from a selected area, select it first with a Selection tool. If you do not make a selection, the Delete Silence command deletes silence from the entire audio clip. To delete silence, follow these steps:

1. **Choose Edit ➪ Delete Silence.**

2. **In the Delete Silence dialog box, shown in Figure 24-9, set options for deleting silence.** If desired, change the values in the "Silence is defined as" and "Audio is defined as" sections. If desired, change the duration of Continuous Silence in milliseconds. To scan for silence, click Scan for Silence Now. To automatically set levels for the Signal fields, click Find Levels. This causes Audition to analyze the waveform or selected range and set an appropriate starting dB level.

3. **To remove the Silence, click OK.**

Figure 24-9: Delete Silence dialog box options

Creating silence

When editing, you may find that you need to create a little breathing room in a narration or between audio clips by creating silence. Adobe Audition provides two methods for creating silence in Edit View. Audition's Mute command mutes or turns sound into silence in a selected area.

To mute audio, follow these steps:

1. **Select the range that you want to mute.**

2. **Choose Effects ➪ Mute.**

To insert silence into an audio clip, follow these steps:

1. **Click the point in the waveform where you want to create silence.** If you want to replace audio with silence, select the area with a Selection tool.

2. **Choose Generate ➪ Silence.**

3. **Enter the number of seconds of silence you want to create.** Use decimal numbers (for example, .5 for a half a second).

4. **Click OK to insert the silence.** This extends the audio clip's duration.

Applying and Creating Custom Effects

Although Audition users can apply effects in Multitrack View or in the Mixer window, you can apply, edit, and create your own audio effects in Edit View. To apply an effect, simply click and drag over a clip area and choose an effect from the Effects menu. You can also customize and store selected effects using Audition's Favorites menu.

Effects such as fade-ins and fade-outs can be applied to the selected area of a waveform by simply clicking Favorites ➪ Fade In or Effects ➪ Favorites Fade Out. You can use the Favorites ➪ Vocal Remove effect to remove male or female voice frequencies from audio data.

If you want to add an audio effect to the Favorites menu, choose Favorites ➪ Edit Effects. In the Favorites dialog box, click New. Next, name your effect. In the Audition Effect drop-down menu, choose an effect, as shown in Figure 24-10. After you choose the effect, click Edit Settings to adjust the settings for the effect. When you return to the Favorites dialog box, click Save to save your effect.

Figure 24-10: Choose from Audition effects to create a new favorite effect.

To view settings for a favorite effect or to edit Favorites, choose Edit ➪ Favorites. In the Favorites dialog box (refer to Figure 24-10), select an effect and then click Edit. Next, click Edit Settings to open the settings for the effect you want to edit. The settings for the Smooth Fade In effect are shown in Figure 24-11.

After you edit the settings, click OK. Then click Save in the Favorites dialog box.

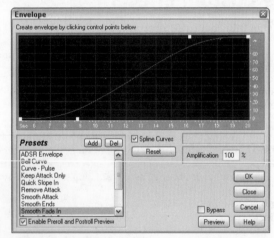

Figure 24-11: Fade In settings

Generating Audio

Although you'll primarily utilize Audition for editing audio, it can be used to generate sounds that can be used as sound effects or background tones. Audition's Generate command allows you to generate Noise that could be used as a waterfall sound. Audition's Generate Tones command can be used to create different electronic sounds.

Generating noise

Audition's Generate Noise command allows you to generate Brown, Pink, or White Noise. The categories provide noise at different frequencies: Brown noise is low frequency noise, such as thunder; Pink noise is noise at frequencies often found in nature, such as rainfall; white noise is a higher frequency noise that can create hissing sounds. Generating noise and experimenting with the results is quite simple.

To generate noise, follow these steps:

1. **Click in the waveform area where you want the noise to appear.** If you want noise to replace audio, select the audio.

2. **In Edit View, choose Generate ➪ Noise.**

3. **In the Generate Noise dialog box, shown in Figure 24-12, choose a noise option: Brown, Pink, or White.** Choose values for intensity and duration. And select a style: Spatial stereo creates a surround-sound sense.

Figure 24-12: Noise generating options

4. **Click OK to generate the noise and add it to the waveform.**

Generating tones

Audition's Generate Tones command allows you to generate tones by controlling frequency, phase options, and wave shapes. Using Generate Tones, you can create a variety of tones. The dialog box provides a few presets, such as Bell, Chord, and Out of Control.

Follow these steps to generate tones:

1. **In Edit View, click in the waveform area where you want the noise to appear.** If you want noise to replace audio, select the audio.

2. **Choose Generate ➪ Tones.**

3. **In the Generate Tones dialog box, click a Preset if desired.** Change settings in the Initial Settings tab, click the Final Settings, and change Settings again. Click OK to create the tones.

Saving Audio Files

After you've finished editing audio in Edit View, you can choose to save your file, rename it, or revert to the last saved version using standard commands in Audition's File menu. As mentioned earlier, Audition saves in all standard audio application formats. If you are working in Multitrack View, you save work as a session file by choosing File ➪ Session. If you want to export the session in an audio format that can be read by Premiere Pro, choose File ➪ Export.

Summary

Adobe Audition provides more extensive audio-recording and audio-editing features than Premiere Pro. To edit audio clips, use Audition's Edit View, where you can edit an audio clip's waveform, or use Audition's Spectral Frequency Display. If you want to layer audio into different tracks to create a mix, use Audition's Multitrack View and its Mixer window (Window ➪ Mixer). This chapter covered these topics:

✦ To export audio from Premiere Pro for editing in Audition, choose Edit ➪ Edit in Audition.

✦ To import video into Audition, choose Import ➪ Video in Multitrack View.

✦ To create silence, choose Effects ➪ Mute or Generate ➪ Silence.

✦ To apply an effect in Edit View, select the audio waveform, and then choose an effect from Audition's Effects or Favorites menu.

Using Adobe Encore to Create DVDs

Adobe Encore DVDII is a high-end DVD authoring program that allows you to create interactive DVDs. As part of the Adobe Video Collection, Encore DVD allows you to import audio and video exported from Premiere Pro. Using Encore DVD, you can create menus and navigational buttons that add sophisticated interactivity to your Premiere Pro projects. Because many of Encore's navigational links are created automatically by dragging and dropping graphics onscreen, it probably won't take Premiere Pro users long to get up and running in Encore DVD. Although the interface is different from Premiere Pro's, most users will probably find themselves right at home in Encore's Project and Timelines panels. This chapter provides an overview of the basics of DVD authoring in Encore DVD. So follow along, and you'll see how to integrate Premiere Pro footage into a DVD authoring program that provides more graphics and navigational features than those provided by Premiere Pro.

Note This chapter leads you through the steps of creating a simple interactive DVD in which Encore DVD automatically creates links to multiple video files. Chapter 26 shows you how to create DVD chapters and link to chapter files

Note A downloadable version of Adobe Encore DVDII is available at www.adobe.com. If you want to create a DVD project using this chapter as a guide, you can use a Premiere Pro project as your video source footage. However, in order to import it into Encore DVD, you must export the project in one of these formats: MPEG-2, DV AVI, or QuickTime DV formats.

Creating a New Project

To get started working in Encore DVD, you must create a project and specify whether it will be NTSC or PAL. After you create a project, you can then use the Encore DVD panel utilities to begin the DVD authoring process. To create a new project, follow these steps:

1. **Click New Project in the Encore DVD opening splash screen, or choose File ➪ New Project.** The New Project Settings dialog box appears, as shown Figure 25-1.

Figure 25-1: Choose a video standard in the New Project Settings dialog box.

2. **Choose whether you want to use the NTSC (US Standard) or the PAL (European) video standard, and click OK.**

Navigating the Encore DVD Panels

The following sections provide a brief overview of the Encore DVD panels. The process of opening, closing, and docking panels in Encore is virtually identical to working with panels in Premiere Pro. Like Premiere Pro, you can also choose a workspace from the Window menu as well.

After you create a new project, you're ready to start examining Encore's most important panels: Project, Menu, Timelines, and Disc. These four panels allow you to perform most major tasks related to a project. To access any of the panels, click its tab or choose a panel name from the Encore DVD Window menu. Like the Premiere Pro Project panel, the Encore DVD Project panel allows you to view the project assets (video, audio, and graphics) that comprise your project. The Menus Panel allows you to manage menus where you'll place navigational buttons. The Timelines Panel lists timelines, and the Timeline Viewer provides a bird's eye overview of your project, also allowing you to set chapter markers. The Disc tab is used for burning DVDs.

After you have a project open onscreen, Encore's other panels provide options for DVD navigation and graphics. As mentioned earlier, like Premiere Pro's panels, the Encore DVD panels can be dragged apart and reunited in different combinations. The following sections describe panels that help you create buttons, menus, and navigation.

The Properties panel

Encore's Properties panel is a multipurpose info panel that provides details about what is selected in other panels. Figure 25-2 shows the Properties panel displaying information about an Encore DVD menu. The information in the panel changes to reflect different items that you click in the Project panel or in the Menu Viewer. For example, if you click a video clip in the Project tab, the Properties panel displays information about the clip's location and duration.

The Layers panel

The Layers panel allows you to manipulate layers used in menus. You can select, show, hide, and change the stacking order of objects on menu screens. The Layers panel is shown in Figure 25-3. Typically, layers displayed in Encore DVD are created in Adobe Photoshop. Encore reads Photoshop layer sets preceded with (+) as menu button sets. Layers with button graphics and colors in the button set for a subpicture (used to highlight buttons) are named with a (=1), (=2), or (=3) prefix. (Each of these special layers can be used to create a different color or can include different shapes that appear as part of the button. The button colors displayed when the DVD plays are based upon a Color Set within Encore DVD.)

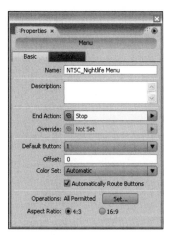

Figure 25-2: The Properties panel provides information about different Encore DVD production elements.

Figure 25-3: The Layers panel displays information about graphic elements on a menu page.

The Character panel

Use the Character panel to specify type options for characters created for buttons and menus. The Character panel drop-down menus access choices for changing typefaces, type size, and style. The Character panel is shown in Figure 25-4.

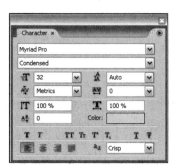

Figure 25-4: Use the Character panel to change type settings.

The Library panel

Encore's Library comes stocked with templates for menus, buttons, and various backgrounds. Use the Library panel to quickly load graphics from the Library or add graphics to the Library. In the section "Using menu templates," later in this chapter, you see how to use a menu screen from the Library panel as the basis for an interactive menu. The icons in the middle of the panel allow you to change views so that you can see Only Menus, Only Buttons, or Only Backgrounds.

Menus panel and Menu Viewer

Encore's Menus panel displays menus and their buttons. You can drag a menu from the Library directly into the Menus panel. Double-clicking a menu in the Menus panel opens it in the Menu Viewer where you can edit the graphics and the links to the menu's button.

Timelines panel and Timeline Viewer

The Timelines panel provides an overview of your DVD media sources in sequential order. You can also use the Timeline viewer to divide your DVD into chapters, add subtitles to tracks, and choose the language for subtitles. As you see later in this chapter, you can place video into different timelines and link the timelines to buttons on DVD menus.

Importing source video and audio

Encore DVD allows you to import MPEG-2, DV AVI files, QuickTime DV, and WAV files, as well as graphics files. In Encore DVD, source material such as video clips, graphics, and sound files are called *assets*. Adobe Photoshop users will be happy to learn that Encore DVD is fully compatible with Photoshop; you can load Photoshop layers in as separate buttons in a menu. To load an asset into Encore, choose File ⇨ Import as Asset. In the Import as Asset dialog box, select the file you want to import and click Open.

If you want to create a practice project, load the AVI file from the Chapter 26 folder of the Adobe Premiere Pro or another file using the File ⇨ Import as Asset, and then continue following the sections to choose a menu, link buttons, and burn or preview as DVD.

If you export one of your Premiere projects as an AVI movie (choose File ⇨ Export ⇨ Movie), you can import it into Encore DVD. Encore also can import MPEG video files. Like Premiere Pro, all imported source material appears in the Project panel, as shown in Figure 25-5.

Note   Encore DVD can import MPEG-2 files, which are considered DVD-compliant (meaning that they meet DVD recording standards). Encore DVD can also import some non-DVD-compliant files, such as NTSC AVI and QuickTime files — which must have a frame size of 720 × 480, 720 × 486, or 404 × 480 with a frame rate of 24 frames per second or 29.97 frames per second. PAL files must have a frame size of 720 × 576 or 704 × 576 with a frame rate of 25 frames per second. Files that are not DVD-compliant are transcoded by Encore to make them DVD-compliant. Working with DVD-compliant files saves time, because Encore DVD does not need to transcode them when you burn a DVD or import files. DVD-compliant file types include .wav files (48 kHz, 16-bit or 24-bit) and .aif files (though not .aif-c files). Also note that when you import AVI files, Encore DVD automatically imports audio. If you import MPEG files, you need to import the audio separately.

Figure 25-5: Encore's Project panel with video and graphics files

Using menu templates

To most computer users, the term *menu* refers to a drop-down list of choices that appear at the top of a computer application. In the world of DVD development, a menu is a screen with interactive buttons. Typically, the first screen you see when viewing a DVD production is a menu screen. Clicking a button on the menu typically ushers you to another menu or to the start of the production. In this section, you choose a menu from a list of pre-designed templates to use for your project.

You use the Encore DVD Library panel to load a background and preset buttons to get you started creating your opening DVD screen. Follow these steps:

1. **Click the Library panel to access it.** Figure 25-6 shows the Library panel with a list of templates.

2. **In the Set drop-down menu, choose a category, such as General, Corporate, or Education.**

3. **Note the buttons in the middle of the panel, and click the first on the left to display the menus.**

4. **Choose a menu from the list by clicking it.** Note that the submenus in the list can be used to link additional menus to the main menu.

5. **Now create a new menu based upon the template by clicking the New Menu button (not the New Item button).** Alternatively, you can drag the menu from the Library into the Menus panel. The new menu appears onscreen in the Menu Viewer, as shown in Figure 25-7. The menu is now listed in the Project and Menus panels.

6. **Select the menu in the Menus panel.** After you select the menu, its buttons appear in the bottom portion of the Menus panel.

Editing the menu

Now you can customize the menu by changing the text and placement of buttons. You can edit the menu using the menu-editing tools shown in Figure 25-8.

Display Backgrounds   Display Layer Sets

Display Graphics   Display Text Items

Display Buttons   Display Shapes

Display Menus   Display Replacement Layers

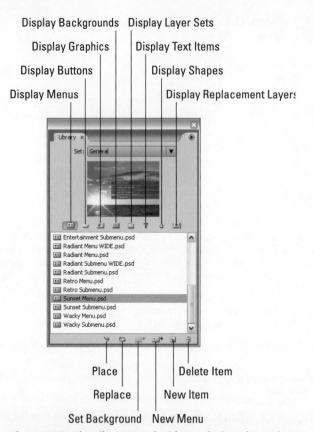

Place   Delete Item

Replace   New Item

Set Background   New Menu

Figure 25-6: The Library panel with pre-designed templates

Figure 25-7: Use the Menu Viewer screen to edit text and buttons on the menu.

Selection tool

Move tool   Zoom tool

Text tool   Preview

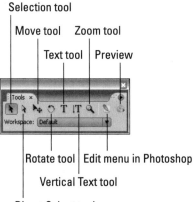

Rotate tool | Edit menu in Photoshop

Vertical Text tool

Direct Select tool

Figure 25-8: Menu-editing tools

Here's a review of the tools:

✦ **Selection tool:** Use to select a button set, which can include the button, its text and its subpictures. Once you select a button set with the Selection tool, you can click and drag to move it.

✦ **Direct Select tool:** Use to select, move, and resize individual objects on a menu screen.

✦ **Move tool:** The Move tool is handy for moving objects that you select in the Layers panel. After you select an object in the Layers panel, the object is selected in the Menu Viewer. You can then click and drag on it with the Move tool.

Tip

To move an object among stacked objects in layers, right-click the object with a selection tool. In the drop-down menu that appears, choose Select. In the Select drop-down menu, choose the object you want to move. You can then move the object with the Move tool.

✦ **Rotate tool:** Use the Rotate tool to rotate text and graphics. Click and drag in a circular motion. You can also rotate using the Selection or Direct Select tool by clicking and dragging the corner handle of an object. To rotate at 45-degree angles, press Shift while rotating.

✦ **Text tool:** Use the Text tool to create and edit text.

✦ **Vertical Text tool:** Use the Vertical Text tool to create and edit vertical text.

✦ **Zoom tool:** Use the Zoom tool to zoom in and out.

✦ **Edit menu in Photoshop:** Use to open the selected menu in Photoshop.

✦ **Preview:** Use to preview the DVD in the Preview panel.

Along with the Encore DVD layout tools, you can also use the Arrange, Align, and Distribute commands found in the Object menu. These commands allow you to quickly move and align objects onscreen. Figure 25-9 shows an expanded view of this menu.

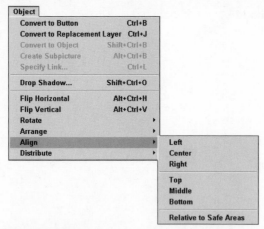

Figure 25-9: Use Arrange, Align, and Distribute as you edit a menu.

Creating button links and Timelines

In this section, you link the video files to buttons on your menu page. These links trigger the video to play when the user clicks a button. Set up the Encore window so that you can see the Project panel and the Menu Viewer. (If you don't have a video file in the Project panel, you can import one by choosing File ⇨ Import as Asset.) To create a link to a button, follow these steps:

1. **Click a video file in the Project panel, and drag it over the button to which you want to link.** When the mouse is correctly positioned over the button, a rectangle appears over the button. Release the mouse after the rectangle appears, and the button name changes to indicate Chapter 1 or the name of the video file.

Caution   If you don't release the mouse over a button, Encore creates a new button on the menu page.

2. **With the Selection tool activated, click the linked button.** Observe the Properties panel. Note that the Link field displays the link to the button, as shown in Figure 25-10.

3. If desired, change the name of the button by editing the text of the Name field in the Properties panel.

4. **Observe the Timeline.** Click the Timelines tab, and note that Encore DVD created a Timeline listing for the video file.

Note   If you want to view the Timeline in the Timeline Viewer, double-click the Timeline in the Timelines panel.

5. **Repeat Steps 1 and 2 to create more links to buttons to different video files as needed.**

Note   You can also create a timeline by choosing Timeline ⇨ New Timeline and then dragging video files to the Timeline. This technique is covered in Chapter 26.

Figure 25-10: A linked button listed in the Properties panel

Examining the Timeline

Encore's Timeline Viewer provides a graphic display of the video and audio in your project. The Timeline Viewer can display a track for video as well as for audio and subtitles. (As discussed earlier, to view a Timeline in the Timeline Viewer, double-click the Timeline listing in the Timelines panel.) As in Premiere Pro, you can place different video clips into the Timeline. Figure 25-11 shows a Timeline in the Timeline Viewer with an AVI video file and its audio file.

Note   If you import a DV AVI with audio, the audio file is imported automatically with it. If you import MPEG-2 files rather than AVI files, you need to import the audio separately.

Click the Timeline in the Project panel, and then view the Properties panel. The End Action field in the Properties panel displays the name of the linked video, which indicates that, after the video is over, the original menu will be displayed.

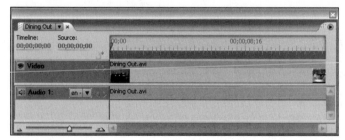

Figure 25-11: Encore's Timeline provides a graphical representation of audio and video files.

Viewing the Flowchart

As the links to your DVD gets more complicated, you may want to refer to Encore DVD's Flowchart panel, which provides you with a graphical view of your project workflow. To view a flowchart, shown in Figure 25-12, simply click the Flowchart tab. (If the tab isn't open onscreen, choose Window ➪ Flowchart.) When viewing the flowchart, you can use the Selection tool to create links; the Direct Select tool to drag objects onto the flowchart; and the Move tool to move objects. Unlinked objects appear at the bottom of the flowchart. These objects can be dragged into the main area of the flowchart and can be linked using the Selection tool. To create a link, simply click and drag from one object to another.

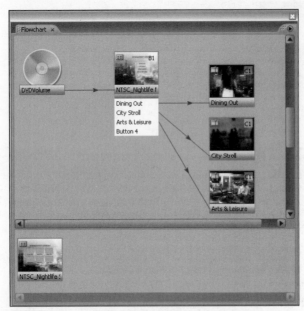

Figure 25-12: The flowchart provides a graphical representation of your DVD project.

Previewing the DVD

After you've created your menus and button links, you're ready to preview your DVD project. When you run the preview, Encore DVD creates a simulation mode where you can test the button links. Follow these steps to preview:

1. **Choose File ⇨ Preview.**

2. **When the project switches to Preview mode, click the menu screen buttons to check that all the links work properly.**

3. **If you need to fix a link, click the button in the Project tab and correct the link in the Properties panel.**

Burning the DVD

After you've previewed your work and tested the button links, you're ready to burn a single layer or dual layer DVD. You'll find burning options for the DVD on the Disc tab. Here are the steps:

1. **Insert a blank DVD into your DVD burner.**

2. **Select the Disc panel, shown in Figure 25-13.**

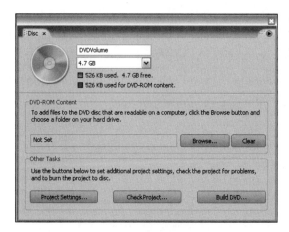

Figure 25-13: Use the Disc panel to start the process of burning a DVD.

3. **In the first field at the top of the panel, name the DVD.**

4. **In the drop-down menu, specify the DVD size that you are using. If you are burning a dual layer DVD, set the size to 8.54 GB.**

5. **If you want to check project links, click Check Project and then click Start in the Check Project dialog box.**

6. **Click the Build DVD button.**

7. **At this point, you should see your DVD recorder listed in the Destination area of the Build DVD panel.**

8. **If you are creating a dual layer DVD, choose Automatic in the Setting section to have Encore DVD set the layer break automatically.** If you want Encore to try to use an existing break, select If Possible, Use Existing Layer Break. Otherwise, Encore attempts to use the last available chapter point. If it can't find a chapter point, the program uses a midpoint based on timecode. If you choose Manual, a dialog box opens allowing you to choose a timecode location or chapter point as the break location.

9. **To burn the DVD, click Build. If the Save alert appears, save your project.** The progress indicator displays an alert when the DVD is complete.

Encore DVD provides other options for creating DVDs. You can access all the following options by choosing File ➪ Build DVD:

✦ **DVD Folder:** This option creates a directory on your hard drive of the DVD structure. You can play back the DVD from the stored disk structure for testing purposes.

✦ **DVD Image:** This option creates an image of the DVD on your hard drive that can be used to master the DVD with a third-party mastering program.

✦ **DVD Master:** This option creates a DVD on digital linear tape (DLT). DLTs are used for mass duplication of DVDs.

Summary

Encore DVD is a DVD production application. Using Encore DVD, you can design DVD menus with interactive buttons and preview and burn DVDs. This chapter covered these topics:

✦ Use File ➪ Import as Asset to load source material into Encore DVD.

✦ The Library panel provides numerous pre-designed buttons and menus.

✦ You can create linked buttons by dragging a video file from the Project panel on to a button in the Menu Viewer.

✦ Preview your DVD by choosing File ➪ Preview.

✦   ✦   ✦

Customizing DVD Screens and Navigation in Adobe Encore DVD

CHAPTER

26

This chapter takes you into the world of DVD creation with Encore DVDII. The previous chapter covered how to quickly create a DVD project with a menu screen and interactive buttons. This chapter focuses on customization. It covers how to create menus and buttons using your own graphic images and how to customize links from buttons to menus, from buttons to DVD chapters, and from buttons to the Timeline.

This chapter provides a step-by-step look at how to create a custom DVD presentation in Encore DVD (see the sidebar "Custom DVD Presentation" later in this chapter). After you read through this chapter, you are ready to enter the world of DVD production.

 On the DVD-ROM   A sample video, graphic button, and background are included in the Chapter 26 folder on the *Adobe Premiere Pro 2* Bible DVD

Creating Menus and Buttons from Still Images

Although Encore DVD's menu templates provide a quick means for making menus and buttons, multimedia and design professionals will undoubtedly want to create their own based upon digitized images or backgrounds. This section shows you how to create menus from scratch. Before you begin, you should plan your entire menu structure. Design your menu on paper, and use flow charts to plan navigation. After you've created all your source material or assets, you're ready to start.

Custom DVD Presentation

These are the general steps for creating a custom DVD presentation (we cover many of these steps in this chapter):

1. **Create the video and audio in Premiere Pro.**

   Note that markers in .avi files exported from Premiere Pro can be used as chapters in Encore DVD. Create markers by moving the current-time indicator in Premiere Pro, then double-clicking the Marker icon in the Timeline panel. Enter text into the Chapter field in the Marker dialog box. Encore uses this text to name chapters in its Timeline. Export the avi file using File ⇨ Export ⇨ Movie. To ensure the markers are exported, click Settings. In the Export Movie Settings dialog box, click Compile Settings, and make sure the Chapters checkbox is selected.

2. **Plan the navigation for the DVD production.**

3. **Create the buttons and background screen for the menus in Photoshop or another graphics application.**

4. **Import audio, graphics, and other assets into Encore DVD.**

5. **Create a custom menu in Encore DVD.**

6. **Place the background screen and buttons into Encore.**

7. **Create a Timeline or Timelines.**

8. **Create chapters in Timelines.**

9. **Link buttons to chapters.**

10. **Create disc navigation.**

11. **Preview the DVD project, and burn a disc.**

Creating menus from scratch

Encore DVD works hand-in-hand with Adobe Photoshop. Although Encore DVD can read TIFF, JPEG, and BMP graphics, your best is to create images in Photoshop and import them directly into Encore DVD, particularly because Encore DVD can interpret a Photoshop layer as a button.

Note   In order for Encore DVD to correctly interpret Photoshop layers as DVD highlight elements, layer-naming prefixes are required in Photoshop. For example, a layer set for buttons requires a "(+)" prefix. Subpicture colors must be named with prefixes such as (=1), (=2), (=3) (Subpictures can be used to highlight buttons. All colored shapes in subpicture layers in Photoshop appear in the button; but the final color and opacity seen in the DVD are controlled by menu color sets in Encore DVD).

If you want to create a menu from scratch, the steps are quite simple. For standard DVD 4:3 aspect ratio, create an image at 720×534 pixels (PAL 768×576). The default aspect ratio in Encore DVD is 4:3. (You can change this to the DVD Widescreen format of 16:9.)

1. **If you haven't created a new project, create the project by choosing File ⇨ New Project. Click the NTSC or PAL choice, and click OK.**

2. **Import the Photoshop background screen that you want to use for your menu by choosing File ⇨ Import as Menu.** In the Import as Asset dialog box, select your file and click Open.

   The menu now appears in the Menus panel and in the Menu Viewer, as shown in Figure 26-1.

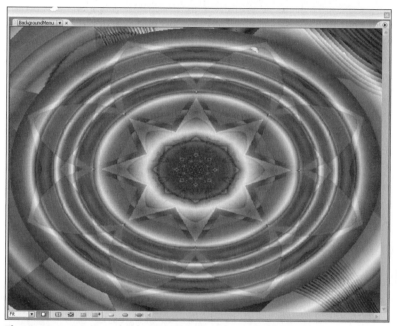

Figure 26-1: A custom background loaded into the Menu Viewer

3. **To rename the menu, right-click the menu listing in the Project panel or Menus panel and enter a new name in the Rename Menu dialog box.** Alternatively, you can rename the menu in the Name field of the Properties panel.

Adding buttons to the menu

After you've created your custom menu, you may want to add buttons you've created in Photoshop or another graphic application to your DVD screen. If you didn't create buttons in Photoshop, you can add a graphic as a button by following these steps:

1. **Import graphic elements into your project by choosing File ⇨ Import as Asset.**

2. **Drag the button graphic or button graphics to the Menu Viewer panel.**

3. **Select the graphic with the Direct Select tool, and then choose Object ⇨ Convert to Button.**

4. **If you want all the buttons on the menu to be similar, drag the same button object to the menu screen as many times as you want; then repeat Step 3 so that Encore recognizes them as different buttons.** Figure 26-2 shows button graphics created in Photoshop added to a menu.

Figure 26-2: Buttons created in Photoshop imported into Encore DVD

Menu Viewer controls

When working in the Menu Viewer, use the Object menu to align and distribute your buttons. You can also press the arrow directional keys to move selected objects right, left, up, and down. In the Menu Viewer, the buttons at the bottom of the screen provide the following utilities:

✦ **Correct Menu pixels for TV Display:** This option rescales the menu to proper height and width for video display.

✦ **Show Safe Area:** This option displays the title and action-safe zones — zones that help ensure that text and graphics are not cut off from the TV monitor. If your production will be viewed on a television monitor, don't place text beyond the inner title safety zone and don't place crucial visual objects outside of the outer action safety zone.

✦ **Show Button Routing:** Routing buttons are menu buttons that can be used as DVD remote control buttons. If you turn off the Automatically Route button option in the Menu panel, remote control routing for buttons are displayed in the menus.

✦ **Show Guides:** This option displays guides to aid in graphic design of the menu screen.

✦ **New Guide:** This option creates a new vertical or horizontal guide.

✦ **Show Normal Subpicture Highlight:** Subpictures allow you to create different color button states for activated buttons. This option displays the unselected state for buttons.

Note   To use subpictures for buttons, choose Object ➪ Convert to Subpicture. Setting highlight colors for subpictures is discussed in the next section.

✦ **Show Selected Subpicture Highlight:** This option displays the selected or highlighted state for buttons.

✦ **Show Activated Subpicture Highlight:** This option displays the activated state for buttons. (Activation requires selecting a button with the remote control and pressing Enter. However, buttons can be set to Auto Activate when simply clicked by the mouse. To set a button to Auto Activate, select the button and choose Auto Activate from the Properties panel.)

Using Color Sets for Menus and Buttons

When you click a DVD button in a menu or move the mouse over the button, it typically changes colors. In order to help you maintain a consistent color scheme in your production, Encore stores menu highlight colors in a color set. When you import a menu into Encore DVD, it creates a color set from subpictures in Photoshop layers. (As mentioned earlier, subpictures are used for highlighting buttons.) Fifteen colors comprise each color set, and each menu can use only one specific color set. Because you can have many different menus in a DVD production, you can use multiple color sets. However, to help ensure a consistent look throughout a project, you may want to use only one color set or Encore's default color set.

By default, Encore DVD creates one predefined default color set. If you import a menu from Photoshop, Encore DVD creates a color set named Automatic. (If you want to alter the colors and opacities of this color set, you must duplicate it and rename it.) If desired, you can switch from one color set to another, or you can create your own color set from scratch. You can save color sets and use them in other projects. To view the color set for a menu, select a menu in the Menu Viewer and choose Menu ➪ Edit Menu Color Set. This opens the Menu Color Set dialog box, shown in Figure 26-3.

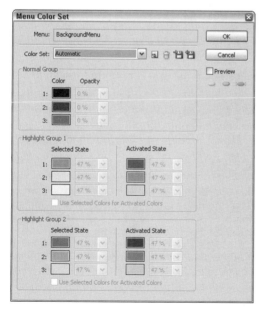

Figure 26-3: The Menu Color Set dialog box controls the highlight color for buttons.

At first, the layout of the Menu Color Set dialog box may look confusing. The grouping in the dialog box shows three different colors for normal states, three different colors for selected states, and three different colors for activated states. Each set of three colors is called a *highlight group*. Thus, you could use one highlight group for buttons labeled part 1, part 2, and so on, and another highlight group for buttons labeled "next chapter" or "previous chapter." If you want to change colors for any color set, simply click the color swatch and adjust the colors in the Color Picker dialog box that appears. If you want to create a new color set, click the New Color Set button (the page icon to the left of the disc icon).

You can also change the opacity for colors in the Menu Color Set dialog box to create rollover effects. For example, suppose you created a menu with a button set in Photoshop. The button set includes a colored shape in the (=2) layer. You want this shape to appear in the button when it is activated. To accomplish this, import the menu with the button set into Encore DVD. In order to adjust opacity for the automatic menu color set created from this menu, duplicate the menu color set and rename it (by clicking the New Color Set button in the Menu Color Set dialog box). Now you can create a rollover effect by adjusting opacity in the Menu Color Set dialog box. If your button uses Highlight Group 1, you can set the opacity for color 2 to 0% for the Selected State in this highlight group. You can then raise color 2's opacity to 100% for the Activated State in Highlight Group 1. The result: when the button is activated in the DVD menu, the subpicture shape, originally created in the Photoshop (=2) layer, appears.

Note You can choose a highlight group for a button by selecting the button in the Menu Viewer and choosing a highlight group in the Highlight drop-down menu in the Properties panel. By default, buttons are assigned Highlight Group 1.

Changing menu color sets

You can easily change color for a menu using the Menus tab and Properties panel. Follow these steps:

1. **Select the menu whose color set you want to set or change.** Shift-click to add to other menus to the selection.

2. **If the Properties panel isn't open, choose Window ➪ Properties to open it.**

3. **Click the Color Set drop-down menu, and select a color set.** Choose Automatic to keep the menu's color set, or choose Menu Default to switch to the default color set for your project.

Creating and Using Timelines

After you've planned your navigation and created your menus and buttons, you need to create a Timeline for your DVD production. Like Premiere Pro's Timeline, Encore's Timeline provides a visual representation of source footage and sound. Figure 26-4 shows a Timeline with the current-time indicator and a chapter marker. For NTSC productions, the Timeline frame rate is 29.97 frames per second; for PAL, the frame rate is 25 frames per second. If you don't have a video file in your Encore DVD project, you can add one by choosing File ➪ Import as Asset. Encore DVD can import MPEG-2, QuickTime, and .AVI files (NTSC: 720 × 480 or 720 × 486; PAL: 720×576 or 704×576).

Note The default length in the Timeline for still images is 6 seconds. To change the default length, choose Edit ➪ Preferences ➪ Timelines.

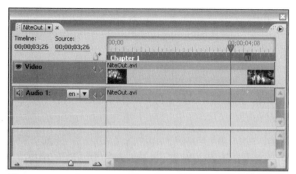

Figure 26-4: The Encore Timeline with video and audio tracks and chapter points

Follow these steps to create a Timeline in Encore DVD and add video or still images to it:

1. **Create a new Timeline by choosing Timeline ➪ New Timeline.**

2. **Drag the video or still image from the Project panel into the video track in the Timeline.** Video clips are automatically positioned at the start of the Timeline and assigned to be Chapter 1. If you place still images on the Timeline instead, chapter entries are created at the beginning of each still image.

3. **Right-click a Timeline in the Project panel, and choose Rename in the pop-up menu to assign a name to the Timeline.** The Rename Timeline dialog box opens, where you can enter a name for the Timeline. You can also rename the Timeline by editing the name in the Properties panel.

Tip

You can create a Timeline automatically and place video on it by selecting the video in the Project panel and choosing Timeline ➪ New Timeline.

Adding a chapter point to the Timeline

In DVD movie productions, chapter points typically are used as a means for jumping to specific scenes. In Encore DVD, you can mark a frame on the Timeline as a chapter point and then link menus, buttons, or other Timelines to it. To keep organized, you can assign names to chapter points and even write notes about specific chapter points. (You can write descriptive notes in the Properties panel when creating chapter points.)

Follow these steps to create chapter points on the Timeline:

1. **If the Timelines panel is not onscreen, open it by Choosing Window ➪ Timelines.**

2. **If you want to preview the video as you add chapter points, open the Monitor panel by choosing Window ➪ Monitor.**

3. **Click and drag the current-timeline indicator to the frame where you want to create the chapter point.**

Note

If you have placed an MPEG-2 video in the Timeline, you can click the Skip Forward or Skip Backward button to move to a GOP header (a *GOP* is a continuous groups of pictures and is usually 13 frames long), which is indicated by the white vertical lines at the bottom of the ruler. Chapter points for MPEG-2 files must start at the nearest prior GOP header. If you are working with AVI videos, Adobe recommends that chapter points be at least 15 frames apart to ensure best quality.

4. **To create a chapter point, choose Timeline ⇨ Add Chapter Point or click the Add Chapter button in the Timeline panel.**

Naming chapter points

After you've created a chapter point, you can assign it a descriptive name and provide a description of the chapter point in the chapter point's Properties panel. Follow these steps to create chapter point names and chapter point descriptions:

1. **If the Timelines panel isn't open, open it by choosing Window ⇨ Timelines.**

2. **Click the Timelines tab, and select the desired Timeline.** At the bottom of the frame, Encore displays the chapter points, as shown in Figure 26-5.

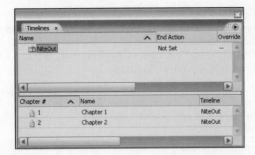

Figure 26-5: Chapter points appear in the Timeline tab.

3. **Select the desired chapter point in the Timeline panel.**

4. **If the Properties panel is not open, choose Window ⇨ Properties.** The Properties panel displays the chapter point's attributes.

5. **In the Properties panel, edit the Name field for the chapter.**

6. **To add a description, click in the Description box and type a description of the chapter point.**

Customizing Navigation

After you've assembled your buttons in the Menu Viewer, picked your subpicture colors, and added chapters, your next step is to ensure that the buttons lead your viewers in the right direction. The following sections provide details about looping menu buttons, menu navigation, first-play options, the duration the menu stays onscreen, and button navigation.

Setting First Play disc links

By default, your completed DVD begins to play when it displays the first menu you create. From this menu, you can direct navigation to go to any menu or chapter. Follow these steps to set First Play options for the disc:

1. **Choose Window ➪ Disc to open the Disc panel.**

2. **Choose Window ➪ Properties to load the Properties panel, or click the Properties panel tab to activate it.**

3. **Activate the First Play pop-up menu by clicking the Arrow icon.** Choices for First Play appear in the submenus, as shown in Figure 26-6. Choose the chapter or the menu you want to use as your First Play location. You can also click and drag the Pick Wick icon (the curlicue icon in the pop-up menu) to the chapter or menu.

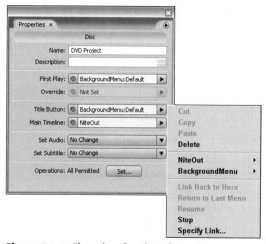

Figure 26-6: Changing the First Play setting

4. **If you want to use the Pick Wick icon (the curlicue icon), make sure that the Project tab is visible onscreen and then drag the First Play Pick Wick icon to any of the following destinations:**

   - To a menu or Timeline in the Project tab

   - To the chapter in the Timeline

   - To the menu or button in the Menus tab

Note   The Override options specify the end action for the First Play link, overriding the default end action of the menu or Timeline. In the Override field, you can designate a menu and the button to highlight or a Timeline and starting chapter point.

Setting menu display time and looping

If you're planning to have your DVD displayed at a kiosk or at a public locale such as a museum, you may want to use Encore DVD's menu display settings to control navigation if nobody clicks a button. Menu-timing choices are controlled in the Menus panel. Activate the menu by first clicking the menu name in the Menus Panel and then clicking the Motion tab in the Properties panel. These are the timing choices:

✦ **Hold Forever:** The menu is displayed until an action is taken. This is the default setting.

✦ **Duration:** Set the duration in time. For a motion menu, the Duration should be the time multiplied by the Loop setting.

✦ **Loop #:** Use the Loop setting to choose how many times the menu repeats itself.

✦ **Loop Point:** Use the Loop Point setting for animated buttons. Click the Animate Button check box, and enter the time in the Loop Point field.

Setting button navigation

Without question, the most common interactive navigational tool in DVD productions is the button. When linking buttons in Encore DVD, you must link to another menu or to a chapter point in a Timeline. When linking a button, the most versatile means is to use the button's Property panel.

These steps explain how to create a link from a menu button to a menu or chapter point. When creating the link, you can link directly from the button in the Menu Viewer or you can create a link from the button via the Menus tab.

1. **If the Menus panel isn't activated, choose Window ➪ Menus.**

2. **In the Menus panel, click the menu that contains the buttons that you want to link or double-click the menu, which opens the menu in the Menu Viewer.**

3. **Select the button from which you want to create a link.** If you are working in the Menu Viewer, select a button with the Selection tool, which selects the button set.

4. **If the Properties panel isn't open, choose Window ➪ Properties.**

5. **Click the Link pop-up menu, and choose the button or chapter point from the submenu, as shown in Figure 26-7. Alternatively, click the Pick Wick icon, and drag it to a Timeline or menu in the Project panel.** Note that if you are linking to a Timeline, you link to a chapter point within the Timeline, setting a specific point as to where the video should begin to play.

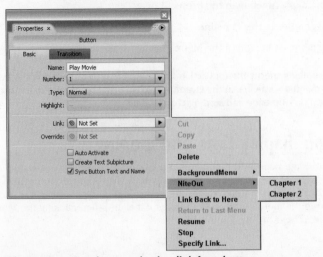

Figure 26-7: Creating a navigation link for a button

Setting Timeline Navigation

When you activate the Timeline tab in the Project panel, Encore DVD provides two navigation choices. You can set an end action for the Timeline, or you can set a menu remote link. An end action specifies where the navigation heads when the Timeline finishes playing. The menu remote choice creates a destination for the DVD navigation when the user clicks the remote control. Normally, when the viewer clicks the remote control, navigation returns to the last menu used. Follow these steps for setting these Timeline navigation choices:

1. **Select a Timeline in the Project panel.**

2. **If the Properties panel isn't open, open it by choosing Window ⇨ Properties.** The Properties panel now shows properties for the selected Timeline.

3. **In the Properties panel, select a destination for End Action by clicking the pop-up menu down arrow and choosing an option from the submenu, as shown in Figure 26-8.** Notice that Figure 26-8 shows another Timeline as a possible navigational link. If doing so is more convenient, you can also create the link by clicking and dragging the Pick Wick icon to an asset in the Project panel.

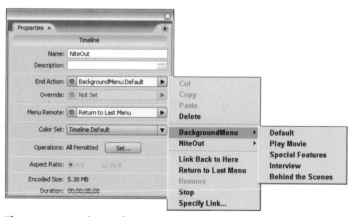

Figure 26-8: Setting end action navigation

4. **In the Properties panel, select a destination for Menu Remote by clicking the pop-up menu down arrow and choosing an option from the submenu.** If doing so is more convenient, you can also create the link by clicking and dragging the Pick Wick icon to an asset in the Project panel.

Summary

Encore enables you to import custom-made graphics and buttons to use for a DVD production. You can also customize button links. This chapter covered these topics:

✦ Import a menu into Encore DVD by choosing File ⇨ Import as Menu.

✦ Use Object ⇨ Convert to Button to designate a graphic object as a button.

✦ Change color settings for activated buttons by setting the highlight group in the Properties panel.

✦ Create new chapters in the Timeline Viewer.

✦ Use the Properties panel to set links for button.

✦   ✦   ✦

Trimming Clips in After Effects

CHAPTER

27

Adobe Premiere Pro features a complete set of video-editing tools. However, from time to time, you may need to make a few quick edits in Adobe After Effects. Adobe After Effects is another digital-video-editing application created by Adobe Systems. It provides certain functionality that Premiere Pro does not, such as creating Bezier masks in the Composition panel (see Chapter 30), creating motion paths, and creating composite projects (see Chapter 31). We've included a trial version of After Effects 6.5 on the DVD that accompanies this book. You can go to www.adobe.com for the latest tryout and details on purchasing the product. If you want to create masks or special effects in After Effects, you may find it more convenient to import the video clips into After Effects and trim clips (change the clips' in and out points) while you work in After Effects.

Cross-Reference See Chapter 31 to learn how to create special effects in After Effects; Chapter 30 covers creating masks in After Effects.

AVI movies, QuickTime movies, and Premiere Pro projects can be imported into After Effects for more video editing and compositing. After editing in After Effects, the work can be exported and saved as a Premiere Pro project and re-imported into Premiere Pro or exported from After Effects and saved in some other format. After Effects 7.0 allows you to export your work and save it as an AVI movie, QuickTime movie, MPEG-4, DV Stream, 3G, Macromedia Flash (SWF), or as a Premiere Pro project. You can also export your After Effects work as a sequence of separate graphic files. Later, you can import the sequence folder into Premiere Pro.

Many digital video producers use both Premiere Pro and After Effects to create a project. This chapter introduces you to trimming a video clip in After Effects using the Layer panel, as well as trimming in the Timeline panel. The chapter also shows you how to export clips from After Effects as Premiere Pro projects, AVI movies, QuickTime movies, and graphic sequences.

Cross-Reference For information on editing video clips using Adobe Premiere Pro, refer to Chapters 7 and 13.

Trimming in After Effects: What's It All About?

In Adobe After Effects, you can use either the Layer panel or the Timeline panel to trim a video clip. If you want, you can trim a clip from a Premiere Pro project. You can trim a clip at the beginning or at the end of a video clip. When you trim at the beginning, you change the clip's *in point*. When you trim at the end of the video clip, you change the clip's *out point*. As in Premiere Pro, even though the in and out points change after editing, the original in and out points are always accessible. You can re-edit the clip at any time.

Note   When you trim the in point in the Layer panel, the clip is edited in the Timeline panel, but its starting time in the composition doesn't change. Also, when you trim a still image, only the duration of the still image changes, not the actual still image.

Creating a new After Effects project

Trimming video clips in the After Effects Timeline panel is easy. To trim a video clip using the After Effects Timeline panel, you need to have an After Effects project onscreen with at least one video clip in the Timeline panel.

Follow these steps to create a new After Effects project and import video clips:

1. **Load After Effects. Choose File ➪ New ➪ New Project to create a new project.**

2. **Choose Composition ➪ New Composition.** The Composition Settings dialog box appears, as shown in Figure 27-1.

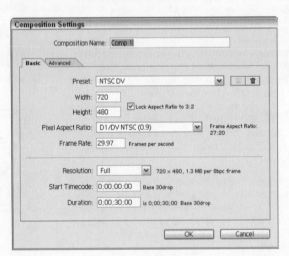

Figure 27-1: The Composition Settings dialog box enables you to set the frame size of your project.

3. **In the Composition Settings dialog box, you can set the Frame Size to the same size as that of the project.** Choose a preset, and notice that the Width and Height values automatically change. If you want, you can change the Frame Rate and Resolution settings. If you are working with a project that uses a Non-DV preset, select the appropriate Non-DV preset from the Preset drop down menu in the Composition Settings dialog box. For DVD output, choose a DV preset.

4. **Click OK to close the Composition Settings dialog box.**

5. **Choose File ⇨ Import ⇨ File. Locate a video clip to use, and click Open. If you need to select more than one file, press and hold the Ctrl key. To import various files, choose File ⇨ Import ⇨ Multiple Files. Locate clips, and select them.** When you have selected all the video clips, still images, and sound clips you are going to use in the project, click the Done button.

If you want, you can follow along using the video clips found in the Chapter 27 folder on the DVD that accompanies this book. The video clips are Digital Vision's 800052f.mov and 800063f.mov from the Flux CD-ROM.

You can also load an Adobe Photoshop layered file into After Effects by choosing File ⇨ Import ⇨ File. In the Import File dialog box, to import the Photoshop file with all its layers, choose Composition from the Import Kind drop down menu. Then pick a footage dimension, and click OK. A folder appears in the project panel of After Effects with all the layers. You can also import a Photoshop layered file with just one layer. In the Layer Options section of the Import dialog box, you can select the Merged Layers option to have the Photoshop layers merged together or you can select the Choose Layer option to choose which Photoshop layer you would like to import. After you've made your selection, choose a footage dimension and click OK. Only one layer is imported into the Project panel in After Effects. For more information on working with Adobe Photoshop, turn to Chapter 28. Chapter 28 also shows you how to export a frame from After Effects as a Photoshop file with layers.

6. **Drag the clips from the Project panel to the Composition panel.** The items appear in layers in the Timeline panel. To change the order of the clips, just drag one layer above another. Figure 27-2 shows the After Effects panels.

Creating a new After Effects project and importing a Premiere Pro project

A Premiere Pro project can be imported into After Effects and then trimmed in After Effects. After the work is done in After Effects, the Premiere Pro project can be re-imported into Premiere Pro or exported as a movie.

Follow these steps to import a Premiere Pro project into an After Effects project:

1. **Load After Effects. Choose File ⇨ New ⇨ New Project to create a new project. Then choose Composition ⇨ New Composition to choose the settings for the project.**

2. **To load a Premiere Pro project into After Effects, choose File ⇨ Import ⇨ File.**

3. **In the Import File dialog box, locate the Premiere Pro project you want to import and click Open.**

4. **In the Import Project dialog box, seen in Figure 27-3, click the Select Sequence drop-down menu and make a selection. Leave the Import Audio check box selected to import audio.**

5. **In the Import Project dialog box, click OK.** After Effects imports the Premiere Pro project, which appears in the After Effects Project panel.

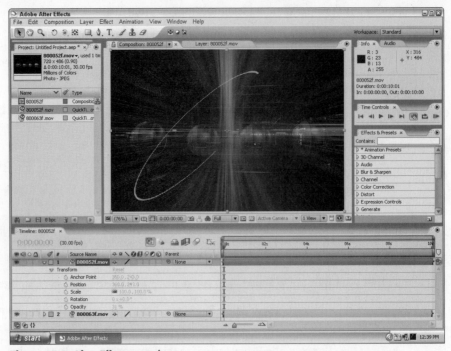

Figure 27-2: After Effects panels

Figure 27-3: The Import Project dialog box allows you to choose which Premiere Pro sequence you want to import into After Effects 7.0.

6. **Double-click the Premiere Pro project Sequence file to have all the Premiere Pro files displayed in the Timeline panel and Composition panel.** The Timeline panel appears with layers. The layers are the video and sound tracks from the Premiere Pro project. The items in the layers can be viewed in the Composition panel.

Trimming Using the Timeline Panel

When you have an After Effects project with the items you need in the Timeline panel, you can trim them using the Timeline panel. Trimming using the Timeline panel is easy. You can trim using the Timeline panel either by dragging the in and out points in the layer duration bar or by using the current-time indicator.

Trimming with the layer duration bar

A video clip's duration in the Timeline panel is displayed as a layer duration bar. Figure 27-4 shows the layer duration bar before trimming. Figure 27-5 shows the layer duration bar after trimming. Also notice that the changes are updated in the Info panel.

Here's how to trim a video clip using the layer duration bar:

✦ **To trim the in point:** Click at the beginning of a clip and drag to the right to change the in point and trim the video clip.

✦ **To trim the out point:** Click at the end of a clip and drag to the left to change the out point and trim the video clip.

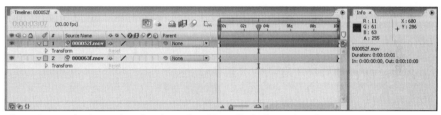

Figure 27-4: The layer duration bar of a video clip before trimming

Figure 27-5: Trimming the in point and out point with the Timeline panel with the results seen in the Info panel

Trimming with the current-time indicator

Follow these steps to trim a clip at the current-time indicator:

1. **Click the layer in which your video clip resides.**

2. **Move the current-time indicator to the point you want to trim.**

3. **Trim the in or out point:**

   • To trim the in point, press Alt+[.

   • To trim the out point, press Alt+].

Trimming Using the Layer Panel

Trimming in the After Effects Layer panel is similar to trimming in Premiere Pro's Monitor panel except that trimming a clip's in point in the After Effect's Layer panel doesn't affect the clip's relative starting position in the Timeline panel. In other words, no gap appears in front of it when you remove frames from the clip's in point.

Follow these steps to trim using the Layer panel:

1. **Choose File ➪ New ➪ New Project to create a new project. You also can choose to load a project.**

2. **Choose Composition ➪ New Composition.** The Composition Settings dialog box appears.

3. **Set the Frame Size to be the same size as the size of the project.** Choose a preset, and notice that the Width and Height values automatically change. If you want, you can change the Frame Rate and Resolution values.

4. **If you want to import a Premiere Pro project into After Effects, skip Steps 5 and 6, and jump to Step 7.**

5. **To import multiple clips into After Effects, choose File ➪ Import ➪ Multiple Files.** When the Import Multiple Files dialog box appears, select a file. Click Open to import the selected file. Continue selecting files and choosing Open until you've imported all the files you need. To close the dialog box, click Done.

   Note   You can choose File ➪ Import ➪ Capture in Adobe Premiere Pro to capture, save and then import some new footage into your After Effects project. To import the captured video from Premiere Pro to After Effects, select the clip from the Project panel in Premiere Pro and then copy it. After you've copied the clip, activate the Project panel in After Effects and paste the captured clip into the Project panel of After Effects. To use the clip in your After Effects project, just drag it from the Project panel to the Timeline panel.

6. **Drag the imported items from the Project panel to the Composition panel.** The items appear in the Timeline panel.

7. **To import a Premiere Pro project into After Effects, choose File ➪ Import ➪ File. When the Import File dialog box appears, select a Premiere Pro file. In the Import Project dialog box that appears, pick a Premiere Pro sequence to import and then click OK.** The Premiere Pro project appears in the After Effects Project panel.

8. **Double-click the Premiere Pro Sequence file in the Project panel to display the Premiere Pro project Sequence files in the Composition panel and the Timeline panel.** The Timeline panel appears with layers representing the video and sound tracks from the Premiere Pro project.

9. **To display the Layer panel, shown in Figure 27-6, either double-click the layer in the Timeline panel or select the layer and choose Layer ➪ Open Layer.** The Layer panel opens.

10. **Click the In and Out buttons, shown in Figure 27-6, to trim the clip.** Just move the current-time indicator to where you want to set the in or out point, and then click the In or Out button in the Layer panel.

The trimmed portion of your video footage appears in the Timeline panel as outlines, as shown in Figure 27-7.

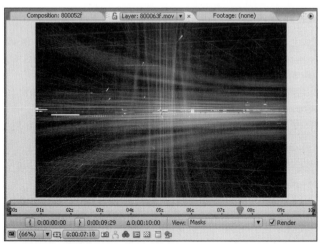

Figure 27-6: Trimming a clip using the In and Out buttons in the Layer panel in After Effects

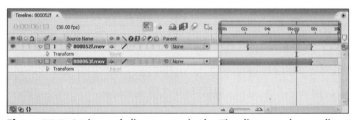

Figure 27-7: A trimmed clip appears in the Timeline panel as outlines.

Exporting Your Adobe After Effects Files

If you want to export your After Effects work so that you can import it into Adobe Premiere Pro, you can save the After Effects file in Adobe Premiere Pro Project format, as an AVI movie or QuickTime movie, or as an *image sequence,* which is a series of separate graphic files, rather than a stream of video frames.

To export your After Effects projects and save them in Adobe Premiere Pro Project format, choose the File ➪ Export ➪ Adobe Premiere Pro Project. In the Export As Adobe Premiere Pro Project dialog box that appears, name your file and click Save.

To export your After Effects projects and save them in a movie format, choose the File ➪ Export command or the Composition ➪ Make Movie command.

Note

You can choose to export the entire After Effects project, or you can just export a section of the After Effects project. To export a portion of your After Effects work, click the Timeline panel and move the work area bar (this bar appears where the current-time indicator is located) over the area you want to save.

Exporting a QuickTime movie from After Effects

Almost any machine can read QuickTime and AVI movies. To quickly save your After Effects project as either a QuickTime or AVI movie, follow these steps:

1. **Click the Timeline panel to activate it, if necessary.**

2. **Choose File ➪ Export ➪ AVI or File ➪ Export ➪ QuickTime Movie.** When exporting an AVI movie, the AVI Settings dialog box, shown in Figure 27-8, appears. When exporting a QuickTime movie, the Movie Settings dialog box, shown in Figure 27-9, appears.

Figure 27-8: The AVI Settings dialog box allows you to choose compression settings for an AVI movie.

Figure 27-9: The Movie Settings dialog box allows you to choose compression settings for a QuickTime movie.

3. **In the settings dialog box, click the Settings button in the Video section.** The Compression Settings dialog box appears.

4. **In the Compression Settings dialog box, click the top drop-down menu to choose a type of compression.**

5. **Set any desired options in the Movie Settings dialog box that appears when export-ing a QuickTime movie.**

   • Click the Filter button to apply a filter (video effect) to your work.

   • Click the Size button to apply a custom size to your work.

   • Click the Sound Settings button to change the sound settings.

6. **Click OK to set the compression settings and close the dialog box.**

7. **In the Save As dialog box, name your movie and then click Save.**

Exporting an image sequence from After Effects

A quick way to save your After Effects work in a sequence format is to use the File ⇨ Export command. You can save your sequence file in Photoshop format. A Photoshop sequence file can be imported into Premiere Pro or Adobe Photoshop for more editing.

Follow these steps to save your work as an image sequence using the File ⇨ Export command:

Note Before you begin, create a new folder on your hard disk and name it. You will use this folder to save your sequence files.

1. **Click the Timeline panel to activate it, if necessary.**

2. **Choose File ⇨ Export ⇨ Image Sequence.** The Save As dialog box appears.

3. **Save your sequence image in the new folder you created.** All the sequence files are saved in the folder.

4. **Click Save.** The Export Image Sequence Settings dialog box, shown in Figure 27-10, appears.

5. **Select a format option type (BMP, JPEG, MacPaint, Photoshop, PICT, PNG, QuickTime Image, SGI, TGA, or TIFF).** You can also set the frames per second. By default, the Frames per second option is set to Best. If you want to use a different option, click the menu.

Tip For best results, save your image sequence in Photoshop format if you will be importing it into Adobe Premiere Pro.

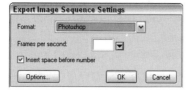

Figure 27-10: The Export Image Sequence Settings dialog box

6. **Click the Options button in the Export Image Sequence Settings dialog box to view and set the compression and color options.** Click OK to exit compression and color options and return to the Export Image Sequence Settings dialog box.

7. **In the Export Image Sequence Settings dialog box, click OK to create a sequence.**
The Export dialog box displays how long the sequence will take and how many frames will be created in the sequence.

Note   Turn to the end of this chapter to learn how to import the sequence into Adobe Premiere Pro.

The Make Movie command

The Make Movie command offers precise control of your rendering options. For better quality files, use this command to save your After Effects project as a movie file or an image sequence file.

Follow these steps to save your work using the Make Movie command.

Note   If you are outputting to a sequence, create a new folder in which to save your sequence frames before naming and saving your file.

Note   You can choose to export either the entire After Effects project or just a section of the After Effects project. To export a portion of your After Effects work, click the Timeline panel and move the work area bar (this bar appears where the current-time indicator is located) over the area you want to save.

1. **Click the Timeline panel to activate it.**

2. **Choose Composition ⟹ Make Movie or Composition ⟹ Pre-Render.** The Render Queue panel appears, as shown in Figure 27-11, and enables you to change the Render Settings and the Output Module.

3. **To view and change the Render Settings, click the current Render Settings to display the Render Settings dialog box.**

4. **In the Render Settings dialog box, choose the resolution with which you want your work to be saved by clicking the Resolution menu.** Be careful not to use a resolution higher than what you are working with, because your work will appear blurry. You can choose a resolution lower than what you are working with. You may want to reduce the resolution of your work if you want to reduce the file size of the final movie, which may be an issue if you are outputting to the Web or e-mailing your movie to someone.

5. **In the Render Settings dialog box, click the Time Span drop-down menu to specify whether you want to output a designated work area, an entire composition, or a custom area.**

6. **Click OK to close the Render Settings dialog box.**

7. **Double-click Output Module to view and change the Output Module settings.**

8. **In the Output Module Settings dialog box, click the Format drop-down menu to pick a format in which to save your work.**

9. **In the Output Module Settings dialog box, click the Channels and Depth drop-down menus to select how many colors you want your movie to be saved with.**

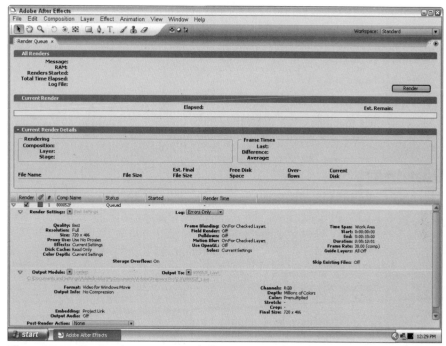

Figure 27-11: The Render Queue panel allows you to adjust the render output settings.

10. **In the Output Module Settings dialog box, click the Audio Output section to select the audio output you want.**

11. **In the Output Module Settings dialog box, click OK to close the dialog box.**

12. **When you are ready to output your After Effects work, click the Render button in the Render Queue panel.**

Importing After Effects Files into Premiere Pro

To import an After Effects file that was saved in Premiere Pro Project format into Premiere Pro, simply choose File ➪ Open.

To load an After Effects file that was saved in movie format or image sequence file into Premiere Pro, you need to create a new Premiere Pro project and import the file. Follow these steps to import a file:

1. **In Adobe Premiere Pro, choose File ➪ New ➪ New Project to create a new Premiere Pro project.**

2. **Choose File ➪ Import.**

3. **Locate the AVI file or QuickTime file.**

4. **Click Open.** The file appears in the Project panel, ready for you to drag it to a video track in the Timeline panel.

Follow these steps to import a Photoshop sequence file (that was created in After Effects) into Premiere Pro:

1. **In Adobe Premiere Pro, choose File ➪ New ➪ New Project to create a new Premiere Pro project.**

2. **Choose File ➪ Import.**

3. **In the Import dialog box, locate the sequence folder.**

4. **Click the Import Folder button.** The Sequence folder appears in the Project panel. You can now drag it to a video track in the Timeline panel.

Summary

If you import clips into After Effects to create special effects, you also may want to edit the in and out points of the clips while you are in After Effects. Later, you can import the clips into Adobe Premiere Pro as AVI movies, QuickTime movies, or a sequence of separate graphic files. This chapter covered the following topics:

✦ In After Effects, you can trim clips in the Timeline panel or the Layer panel.

✦ Clips can be trimmed by clicking the edge of a clip and then dragging or pressing a keyboard command. To trim the in point, press Alt+[. To trim the out point, press Alt+].

✦ To import a sequence of graphics created in After Effects into Premiere Pro, choose File ➪ Import. In the Import dialog box, locate the file and click the Import Folder button.

✦   ✦   ✦

The Photoshop Connection

During video production, you may want to export still frames from your Adobe Premiere Pro project for use on a Web page or in a print document, such as a brochure. If you export the still frames to Adobe Photoshop, you can prepare them for print and optimize them for the Web. You can even export an entire Premiere project with all its video tracks into After Effects. Once in After Effects, each track appears as a separate layer. A frame exported from After Effects to Photoshop retains its layers. A frame exported from Premiere Pro to Photoshop does not.

Photoshop can also be used as an image data source. You can use Photoshop to create backgrounds, titles, or images with alpha channels. These images can then be integrated into a Premiere Pro project.

Exporting a Premiere Pro Frame to Photoshop

Although Premiere Pro is primarily used for creating desktop video projects, you can easily export a video frame from your project to use as a still image. The frame can be any individual frame from a clip, or it can display a frame from a transition or video effect.

In addition to using the still frame for print purposes, you can use the still frame to create or enhance a Web site or to create a background scene in an interactive presentation. After the frame is in Photoshop, you can edit the clip's colors, convert the clip to grayscale or black and white, and even add or delete items or people from a clip.

To learn how to export an entire video clip as a QuickTime or AVI movie, see Chapter 19. To learn how to export a Premiere Pro video clip to Photoshop as a Filmstrip file, see Chapter 18.

Follow these steps to export a frame from Adobe Premiere Pro:

1. **Open or create a Premiere Pro project.**

To have Premiere Pro create a Photoshop file with the same dimensions as the project you are working on, Choose File ➪ New ➪ Photoshop File. In the Save Photoshop File As dialog box, name the file and click Save. Adobe Photoshop is loaded with the new Photoshop file ready for you to work on. The changes you make to the Photoshop file are updated in Premiere Pro. The Photoshop file appears in the Project panel of your Premiere Pro project.

2. **Locate the frame of your project that you want to export.** Start by opening the Program Monitor panel. To display the Program Monitor panel, choose Window ⇨ Program Monitors ⇨ Sequence 01. **Use the Frame Forward and Frame Back buttons in the Program Monitor panel to locate the frame you want to export.** Figure 28-1 shows the frame that we want to export in the Program Monitor panel.

Figure 28-1: This still frame will be exported.

3. **After you have chosen the frame you want to export, choose File ⇨ Export ⇨ Frame.**

4. **In the Export Frame dialog box, name your frame.** Also notice that below the File name field, the frame's make and video size appear. Click the Settings button if you need to change the file format and image size.

5. **In the Export Frame Settings dialog box, shown in Figure 28-2, General is selected by default. To choose a file format, click the File Type drop-down menu.** You can choose Windows Bitmap, GIF, Targa, or TIFF. If you are going to use the still frame for print, you probably want to save your file in TIFF format. Use the Targa format if you are going to import this frame into a 3D program. If you are going to use this frame for multimedia purposes, choose Windows Bitmap.

   If you are going to use the frame for the Web and want to reduce the number of colors in the image to 256, use the GIF format. When you pick the GIF format, a Compile Settings button appears. You can click this button and choose whether you want your GIF file to be dithered and whether you want the image to contain a transparent background.

The Export Frame Settings dialog box Video settings enable you to change the color depth and choose a compressor and frame size for the exported still frame.

Figure 28-2: The Export Frame Settings dialog box's General settings enable you to export a still frame as a Windows BMP, GIF, Targa, or TIFF file.

Note   If you are going to use this frame for multimedia purposes, you may want to import the still frame into Macromedia Director. To learn more about using Premiere Pro and Macromedia Director, see Chapter 23.

6. **When you finish adjusting the General and Video settings, click OK to return to the Export Frame dialog box.**

7. **In the Export Frame dialog box, click Save to save the frame in the format chosen.** The frame just saved appears onscreen. If this is the right frame, you can close the file and export another frame or quit Premiere Pro and load Photoshop to import the frame.

Importing a still frame from Premiere Pro into Photoshop

After you've exported a still frame from Premiere Pro, you probably want to import it into Photoshop to color-correct it or incorporate it into a collage or other project.

Follow these steps to import a still frame from Premiere Pro into Photoshop:

1. **Load Adobe Photoshop.**

2. **Choose File ➪ Open.**

3. **In the Open dialog box, locate and select the Premiere Pro file you saved as a still image. Then click the Open button to import the Premiere Pro file into Photoshop.**

4. **When the Premiere Pro still image file opens in Photoshop, you see all the tracks flattened into one layer.**

If you want to load a Premiere Pro frame into Photoshop and have the tracks appear as separate layers, you must export the frame to Adobe After Effects first, which is discussed in the following section.

Exporting a Frame to After Effects and Then to Photoshop

You can use After Effects to export a frame from a Premiere Pro project to Photoshop. If you want to export a frame (containing all its video tracks) from a Premiere Pro project, you need to first import the Premiere Pro project into After Effects. In After Effects, the video tracks from a Premiere Pro project appear as separate layers. Then in After Effects, you can export the frame with all its video layers into Photoshop. Each video layer appears as a Photoshop layer.

Follow these steps to import a Premiere Pro project into After Effects and then export the frame from the Premiere Pro project that is in After Effects to Photoshop:

1. **Load Adobe After Effects.**

2. **Choose File ➪ New ➪ New Project.**

3. **Choose File ➪ Import ➪ File.** In the Import File dialog box that appears, locate the Premiere Pro project you want to import. Then set the Import As drop down menu to Composition. Click Import to import the Premiere Pro project into the After Effects project.

4. **Double-click the Composition file in the Project panel to display the Timeline panel and Composition panel.** In the Timeline panel, all Premiere Pro tracks appear as layers. In the Composition panel, you see the layers as a composite.

5. **Move the current-time indicator in the Timeline panel to the frame you want to export.**

6. **Choose Composition ➪ Save Frame As ➪ Photoshop Layers to save the still frame with all its layers.** To save a still frame as a composite without the layers, choose Composition ➪ Save Frame As ➪ File.

7. **To open the file in Photoshop, load Adobe Photoshop and choose File ➪ Open to open the file.** When the file opens, the video tracks from Premiere Pro appear in different Photoshop layers.

Creating a Photoshop Layer File and Importing It into Premiere Pro as a Photoshop Sequence

In this section, you learn how to create a presentation by first exporting four frames from Adobe Premiere Pro into Adobe Photoshop. In Photoshop, create a layer document from all four frames. In Photoshop, each Premiere Pro frame becomes a layer. Text is added to each of the layers (frames). Afterward, the Photoshop layer file is imported into Premiere Pro as a sequence file where sound is added to create a presentation. Figure 28-3 shows four frames of a Premiere Pro project created using a Photoshop sequence file.

Figure 28-3: Frames from a presentation (FashionShow) created using an Adobe Photoshop sequence file and Adobe Premiere Pro

To create a Photoshop layer file from exported frames from a Premiere Pro video clip, and then import the Photoshop file as a sequence into Premiere Pro, follow these steps:

1. **Open a Premiere Pro project with a video clip that you want to use to create a presentation.** If you want to use the video clip that was used to create the presentation shown in Figure 28-3, create a new Premiere Pro project and then choose File ⇨ Import. Locate the file (Digital Vision's 567026f.mov CityMix video clip) and click Open.

2. **Drag the video clip from the Project panel to Video 1 track in the Timeline panel.**

On the DVD-ROM

Digital Vision's 567026f.mov CityMix video clip (used to create the frames in Figure 28-3) is found in the Chapter 28 folder (which is in the Tutorial Projects folder) on the DVD that accompanies this book.

3. **Export four frames.** To export each frame, move the Timeline Marker to the frame you want to export. Then choose File ⇨ Export ⇨ Frame. Click the Settings button. In the Export Frame Settings dialog box, click the File Type drop-down menu and choose TIFF. Click OK. In the Export Frame dialog box, name your frame and click Save to export the frame.

   The first frame we exported was at 00:00 on the Timeline, the second frame was at 01:07 on the Timeline, the third frame was at 12:26 on the Timeline, and the fourth frame was at 21:16 on the Timeline.

4. **Load Photoshop. Create a new Photoshop file with the same dimensions as the Premiere Pro video clip, and name it Fashion.**

5. **Use Photoshop to open all the exported frame files.**

6. **Drag and drop each exported frame file into the Fashion file.** Each frame should now be a layer in the Layers palette in the Photoshop Fashion file.

   The bottom layer should be the frame that you want to appear first and the top layer should the frame you want to appear last.

7. **To rearrange the layers, click and drag them up or down in the Layers palette.**

8. **Close all the files except the Fashion file.**

9. **Click the eye icon to hide all the layers except the bottom layer.**

10. **Use the Horizontal Type tool to create type in the bottom layer.**

Note   In Adobe Photoshop CS, you can create text on a path.

11. **Move the mouse to the place on the image where you want the text to appear, and click the mouse once.** Begin typing.

12. **With the text selected, select a font and size.** You can also add tracking (spacing between the letters). To do so, use the Character palette. Choose Window ➪ Character to display the Character palette.

13. **To add interesting effects to your text, choose Layer ➪ Layer Style and then choose an effect.** To create the text effect shown earlier in Figure 28-3, we used the Drop Shadow, Inner Shadow, Outer Shadow, Color Overlay, and Pattern Overlay Layer Style options. After you apply the effects, the effects appear in the Layers palette. We also used the Warp Text option on the text. This option is found just the below the menu bar.

14. **To move the text onscreen, drag it with the Move tool.**

Note   You may be wondering why we didn't just use Premiere Pro to create the text. We used Photoshop to create the text, and not Premiere Pro, because Photoshop has powerful layer style features that enable you to create 3D text effects.

15. **Now that you've created some text and stylized it, you can duplicate it and then edit it to use on another layer.** To do so, follow these steps:

    a. **To duplicate the text layer, click and drag the text layer over the Create a New Layer icon in the Layers palette.**

    b. **Click the eye icon above the bottom layer to display the next layer.**

    c. **Drag the duplicated text layer above the displayed layer.**

    d. **Now use the Move tool to move the text into the desired location.**

    e. **Use the Horizontal Type tool to edit the text.**

16. **To add text to the third layer from the bottom, first display the layer by clicking the eye icon in the Layers palette.** Next, you need to duplicate, move, and edit the text as

you did in the preceding step. After you've done that, repeat this process to add text to the fourth layer from the bottom.

17. **Merge the text down to the frame below it by selecting the text layer and choosing Merge Down from the Layers palette drop-down menu.** Do this for each text layer. This way, you have only four layers, rather than eight.

18. **Choose File ➪ Save to save your work.** Be sure to save your work in Photoshop format with all its layers.

Now you are ready to import the Photoshop sequence file into Premiere Pro to create a presentation:

1. **Choose File ➪ New ➪ Project to create a new project. In the New Project dialog box, pick a preset that matches the dimensions of the Photoshop file.**

2. **Choose File ➪ Import, locate the Photoshop file, and click Open.** When the Import Layered File dialog box appears, click the Import As drop-down menu and choose Sequence, as shown in Figure 28-4. Click OK to import the Photoshop file as a sequence.

Figure 28-4: Premiere Pro's Import Layered File dialog box allows you to import sequence files.

The Photoshop sequence file appears in the Project panel as a folder with the layers within the folder, as shown in Figure 28-5.

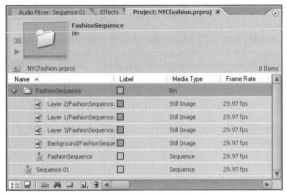

Figure 28-5: When you import a Photoshop sequence file into Premiere Pro, the contents of the file appear in a folder in the Project panel.

3. **Open the sequence folder if it is not already open; in the folder, double-click FashionSequence.** Notice that all the layers of the sequence appear in separate video tracks in the Timeline panel, shown in Figure 28-6. The Photoshop files appear in the Project panel and the Timeline panel in the same order as they did in the Layers palette in Photoshop. The file FashionSequence is in the Chapter 28 folder, which is in the Tutorial Projects folder that is on the DVD that accompanies the book.

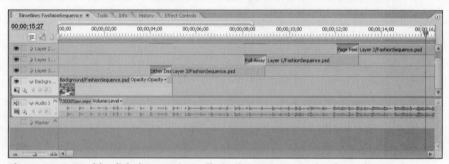

Figure 28-6: Double-click the sequence file in the Project panel to have the sequence appear in the Timeline panel.

4. **Use the Selection tool to move the clips in the Timeline panel so that they appear as shown in Figure 28-6.** The end of the first clip should overlap the beginning of the second clip. The end of the second clip should overlap the beginning of the third clip, and the third clip should overlap the beginning of the fourth clip. If you want, you can extend the length of the clips.

5. **Now add transitions to the overlapping areas between the clips.** We added the Dither Dissolve transition (located in the Dissolve bin in the Video Transitions bin that is in the Effects panel) to the overlapping areas of the first and second clips. To the overlapping areas of the second and third clips, we used the Roll Away transition (located in the Page Peel bin). To the overlapping areas between the third and fourth clips, we used the Page Peel transition (located in the Page Peel bin).

6. **To complete your presentation, add some sound to it by choosing File ➪ Import.** Locate and select a sound file. Then click Open to import the file. We used Digital Vision's 730005aw.wav Acoustic Chillout clip. If you want, you can cut the audio clip to match the length of the video clips.

On the DVD-ROM You can find Digital Vision's 730005aw.wav Acoustic Chillout clip in the Chapter 28 folder (which is in the Tutorial Projects folder) on the DVD that accompanies this book.

7. **To preview the presentation, click the Play button in the Program Monitor panel.** Be sure to save your work when you are finished.

Preventing Distorted Graphics

If you create a graphic at 720 × 480 (or 720 × 486) in a square pixel program such as Adobe Photoshop 7 and import it into a Premiere Pro NTSC DV project, the graphic may appear distorted in Premiere Pro. The graphic is distorted because Premiere Pro automatically converts it to a non-square 0.9 pixel aspect ratio. You can convert the imported Photoshop graphic file back to square pixels. First, select the graphic in the Project panel. Then choose File ⇨ Interpret Footage. In the Pixel Aspect Ratio section of the Interpret Footage dialog box, click Conform to, choose Square Pixels (1.0) in the drop-down menu, and click OK. Although this technique works, it may result in a reduction in graphic quality. If you are using Photoshop 7, your best bet is to create full-screen graphics for DV projects at 720 × 534 or 720 × 540 (768 × 576 for PAL). After creating your graphics, choose Edit ⇨ Preferences ⇨ General. In the dialog box, select the Default scale to frame size option before you import the graphics into Premiere Pro. You can also choose to import a graphic, then select it in the Project panel and choose Clip ⇨ Video Options ⇨ Scale to Frame Size. This squeezes the graphic to fit into your DV project frame size.

If you are creating full-screen graphic files in Photoshop CS for a Premiere Pro DV project, create them in Photoshop CS using the 720 × 480 DV preset. This preset (which sets the Photoshop pixel aspect ratio to 0.9), can help you prevent distortion because you can preview graphics in Photoshop before importing them into a Premiere Pro DV project.

Creating a Photoshop File with an Alpha Channel

To have the bird.psd file (shown in Figure 28-7) appear in Premiere Pro without its background, you must select the bird and then save the selection to an alpha channel. When you load the file into Premiere Pro, the alpha channel enables you to use Motion to animate the bird, without its background appearing.

Figure 28-7: Photoshop file of a bird before creating an alpha channel

After you load Photoshop, follow these steps to select an image and save the selection to an alpha channel:

1. **Open the file with the image you want to isolate.**

On the DVD-ROM

To use the bird image (shown in Figure 28-7), load the bird.psd file found in the Chapter 28 folder (which is in the Tutorial Projects folder) on the DVD that accompanies this book.

2. **Use a Photoshop Selection tool (the Pen tool, the Magic Wand, or the Lasso tool) to select the image you want to isolate from the background.** We used the Polygonal Lasso tool to select the bird. For a soft-edged selection, we set the Lasso tool to have a feather radius of 1.

3. **With the selection onscreen, choose Select ⇨ Save Selection.** In the Save Selection dialog box, shown in Figure 28-8, we clicked the Channel drop-down menu and set it to New and left the Operation radio button set to New Channel. Then we clicked Save to save the selection to an alpha channel.

Figure 28-8: The Save Selection dialog box enables you to save a selection to an alpha channel.

Note   To load a saved selection, choose Select ⇨ Load Selection.

4. **To see the alpha channel, choose Window ⇨ Channels.** In the Channels palette, you see a Red, a Green, a Blue, and an Alpha channel, as shown in Figure 28-9. Click Alpha 1 in the Channels palette to display the alpha channel. The alpha channel shown in Figure 28-10 displays the white area as the selected area. The white area is the only area that Premiere Pro reads. The black area represents the area that Premiere Pro won't read. (This happens only if the Color Indicates option, in the Channel Options dialog box, is set to Masked Areas — the default setting. To display the Channel Options dialog box, double-click Alpha 1 in the Channels palette.)

Figure 28-9: The Channels palette with its channels

Figure 28-10: The Photoshop file with the alpha channel displayed

5. **To import this file into Premiere Pro with the alpha channel, save the alpha channel with the file by choosing File ⇨ Save As.** In the Save As dialog box, click the Format drop-down menu and choose Photoshop format. In the Save section, only the Alpha Channel option should be selected. Click Save to save the file.

Placing a Photoshop alpha channel file into a Premiere Pro project

Now that you've created a Photoshop file with an alpha channel, you are ready to import it into Premiere Pro. After it's in Premiere Pro, you use the bird image to create a project called Freebird. Figure 28-11 shows a few frames from the Freebird Premiere Pro project.

Figure 28-11: Frames from the Freebird project

To create the Freebird project, we used two Photoshop files — a background file (3dwindow.psd) and an alpha channel file (bird.psd) — and and created some text using Premiere's Adobe Title Designer. Follow these steps to import a Photoshop file with an alpha channel into a Premiere Pro project:

1. **Load Adobe Premiere Pro, and then choose File ⇨ New ⇨ Project to create a new project.** In the New Project dialog box, pick a preset, name your project, and click OK.

2. **In a new Premiere Pro project, choose File ⇨ Import.**

3. **In the Import dialog box, locate the Photoshop file with an alpha channel (bird.psd) and click Open. In the Import Layered File dialog box, set the Import As drop-down menu to Footage and the Layer Options to Merged Layers, as shown in Figure 28-12. Click OK.** Premiere Pro stores the file in the Project panel, as shown in Figure 28-13.

Figure 28-12: The Import Layered File dialog box used to Import a Photoshop file

Figure 28-13: The Project panel with a Photoshop Alpha Channel file

4. **Choose File ⇨ Import to import a background video clip or image.** We used the file 3dwindow.psd for the background.

On the DVD-ROM

The bird image (bird.psd) and the background image (3dwindow.psd) are located in the Chapter 28 folder (which is in the Tutorial Projects folder) on the DVD that accompanies this book.

5. **Drag the bird file from the Project panel to Video 2 track in the Timeline panel.**

6. **Drag the background file (3dwindow.psd) from the Project panel to Video 1 track in the Timeline panel.** In Video 3 track, you'll place some text created using the Adobe Title Designer. Figure 28-14 shows the Timeline panel for the Freebird project.

7. **Choose File ⇨ New ⇨ Title.** In the Adobe Title Designer, shown in Figure 28-15, make sure the Show Video option is selected so that you can see the background image. Select the Type tool, move the cursor to the black area of the background, and type the text **Freebird.** Choose a font. We used Matisse ITC.

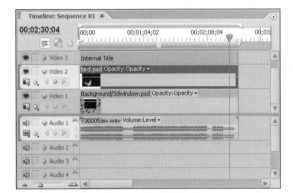

Figure 28-14: The Timeline panel used to create the Freebird project

Figure 28-15: Use the Adobe Title Designer to create the text for the Freebird project.

To animate the bird image, we used Premiere Pro's Motion settings, shown in Figure 28-16. The Motion controls are found in the Effect Controls panel. The bird in the Freebird project moves from the top-right corner down to the bottom-left side.

8. **To start the Bird animation, first select the clip in Video 2 track of the Timeline panel. Then move the Edit line to the beginning of the clip. Click the word *Motion* in the Effect Controls panel. Move the bird to the top-left corner. Now click the triangle next to the Motion effect to display the effects controls. Click the Position Toggle Animation icon to create a keyframe. Keep moving the Edit line and the bird to create more keyframes.**

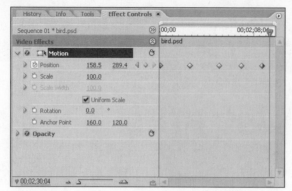

Figure 28-16: The Effect Controls panel shows the key frames used to animate the bird in the Freebird project.

9. **To preview the Freebird project, click the Play button in the Program Monitor panel.** By creating an alpha channel for the bird file, you can have the bird image move without having the background move with it. In order to create the alpha channel, we had to create and save a selection around the bird (refer to the previous section to learn how). When you save a selection, Photoshop saves the selection as a mask in an alpha channel. Because the bird image is in Video 2 track, between the text that is in Video 3 track and the background image that is in Video 1 track, when you add motion to the bird, the bird moves from behind the text to in front of the text.

10. **Choose File ➪ Import to import a sound clip.** We used Digital Vision's 730005aw.wav Acoustic Chillout clip.

On the DVD-ROM

Digital Vision's 730005aw.wav Acoustic Chillout clip is found in the Chapter 28 folder (which is in the Tutorial Projects folder) on the DVD that accompanies this book.

11. **Choose File ➪ Save to save your work.**

Summary

You can easily export a frame from Premiere Pro to Photoshop or export Photoshop files into Premiere Pro. This chapter covered these topics:

✦ If you want to load a Premiere Pro frame into Photoshop and have a Premiere Pro frame appear as a layer, export the Premiere Pro project to After Effects first.

✦ Premiere Pro automatically reads the background transparency of Photoshop layers. It does not convert Photoshop transparency into a white background.

✦ Premiere Pro can use Photoshop alpha channels to create transparency effects.

Using Adobe Premiere Pro and Adobe Illustrator

Adobe Illustrator is one of the most powerful desktop illustration programs available for personal computers. Using Adobe Illustrator, graphic designers can place text on a curve or bend and reshape the letters in a word. Illustrator, which is a *vector-based* program, provides designers with the power they need to create virtually any shape that can be drawn. In vector-based programs, shapes are defined mathematically and easily can be moved and reshaped. In Adobe Illustrator, shapes appear as *paths* filled or outlined with color. Onscreen, a path resembles a wireframe outline with tiny squares called *anchor points*. Editing the anchor points edits the path.

For Adobe Premiere Pro users, Adobe Illustrator opens up a new world of possibilities. Adobe Illustrator type and shapes can be imported directly into Adobe Premiere Pro. When Premiere Pro opens an Illustrator file, it automatically converts it from Illustrator's vector format to Premiere Pro's *raster* format and appears with transparent backgrounds. This conversion enables you not only to use the Illustrator text but also to use shapes created in Illustrator as masks.

Working with Illustrator Type

You can create type effects in Adobe Illustrator and then import them into Adobe Premiere Pro for use as title effects, logos, credits, and more. You can also import Illustrator type into Premiere Pro, use the type as a mask, and have a video clip run through the shape of the text, as described later in this chapter.

Note   For creating title effects and logos, you may want to use Adobe Illustrator CS's new 3D shapes and Type tool features. Adobe Illustrator CS also allows you to wrap artwork around shapes.

Adobe Illustrator features six tools with which to create type.

The Type tool enables you to create text that reads horizontally, from left to right.

The Area Type tool is used to create type inside a shape. You can select the Ellipse, Polygon, Star, or Rectangle tools to create a shape. To create more elaborate shapes, you can apply one of Illustrator's Effect commands to a shape, such as the Punker & Bloat command (Effect ⇨ Distort & Transform ⇨ Punker & Bloat). With a shape onscreen, click inside the shape with the Area Type tool and start typing. Your text appears onscreen in the shape of the path shape and reads from left to right.

The Path Type tool creates text on a path. To use the Path Type tool, you first need to create a path. You can create a path using the Pen, Pencil, Paintbrush, or Ellipse tools. You can also use the Arc or Spiral tools to create an arc or spiral path on which the text can appear, as shown in Figure 29-1. These tools are found in the same place as the Line tool in the Toolbox.

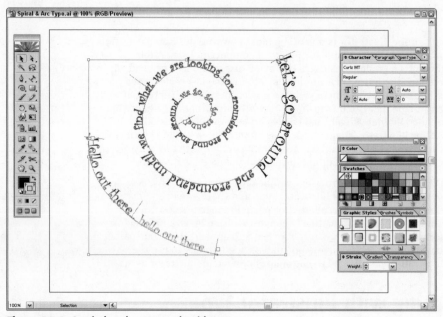

Figure 29-1: A spiral and an arc path with text

After you've created a path, click it with the Path Type tool and start typing. The text appears on the path as you type (refer to Figure 29-1). In some cases, the font size may be too big to appear on the path. In this case, you may need to scale down the font size. To do so, click and drag over the text with the Path Type tool to select it. Then choose Type ⇨ Size, and pick a size or click the Font Size drop-down menu in the Character palette. To display the Character palette, choose Window ⇨ Type ⇨ Character.

The Vertical Type tool flows text from top to bottom (vertically), rather than from left to right (horizontally) as the Type tool does. To create vertical text, click the Vertical Type tool in the Toolbox, click in the document where you want the type to appear, and then start typing.

The Vertical Area Type tool works like the Area Type tool. Both type tools create type within a path. When type appears while using the Vertical Area Type tool, it appears from top to bottom (vertically) inside the path rather than from left to right (horizontally) as it does when using the Path Area Type tool.

The Vertical Path Type tool works similarly to the Path Type tool. Both type tools create type on a path. However, instead of the type appearing left to right (horizontally) as it does when using the Path Type tool, it appears top to bottom (vertically).

Follow these steps to learn how to use Illustrator's type tools:

1. **Load Adobe Illustrator, if it is not already loaded.**

2. **Choose File ⇨ New to create a new document.** The New Document dialog box appears, as shown in Figure 29-2.

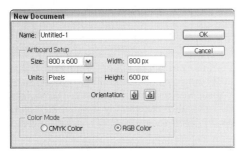

Figure 29-2: Adobe Illustrator's New Document dialog box

3. **Set the Artboard Size to 800 × 600 pixels (or the frame size that you will be using in Premiere), set Color Mode to RGB Color, and click OK.** A new document appears.

4. **Select either the Type Tool or Vertical Type tool in Illustrator.**

5. **Move the cursor to the middle of the document.**

6. **Click the document, and type a word or two.**

7. **Choose Window ⇨ Type ⇨ Character or Window ⇨ Type ⇨ Paragraph to display the Character or Paragraph palette.**

8. **Click and drag over the area you want to stylize.** You can stylize an entire word or just a letter or two in the word.

9. **With the Type tool selected, set the Fill color to the desired type color.** Double-click either the Fill swatch in the Tools palette (the top, overlapping square toward the bottom of the Tools palette) or the Fill swatch in the Color palette (the top, overlapping square at the top-left side of the Color palette). The Color Picker dialog box appears.

Tip By default, Illustrator uses the Fill color as the type color. If you set the Fill color to the color you want the text to be, you won't have to worry about changing it later.

10. **Click a color in the Select Color area or on the color slider next to it.** If you are creating a project for the Web, be sure to select the Only Web Colors option.

11. **Click OK.** The Fill color changes to the newly selected color. If you decide to change the Fill color, the easiest way to pick a new color is to use the color bar in the Color palette. To display the Color palette, choose Window ⇨ Color. In the Color palette, click a color in the color bar at the bottom of the palette to change the fill color. To create a new color, move the sliders in the middle of the palette.

12. **To apply a stroke to the text, click the Stroke swatch (which is below the Fill swatch) and pick a color.** Select a color either by using the Color Picker dialog box—accessed by double-clicking the Stroke swatch in the Tools or Color palette—or by dragging the sliders and/or color bar in the Color palette. To set the size of the stroke, click the Weight menu in the Stroke palette and pick a size. To display the Stroke palette, choose Window ➪ Stroke.

13. **Set the Fill color to black.** Click the Default Fill and Stroke Color icon, which is below the overlapping Fill and Stroke swatch in the Tools palette. This sets the Stroke swatch to black and the Fill color to white. Next, click the Swap Fill and Stroke icon (the curved arrow next to the Fill and Stroke swatch) to set the Fill to black and the Stroke to white. To use the Illustrator text as a mask with a video clip run through the shape of the text, you must set the Fill color to black. Now you are ready to use a Type tool to start creating some type.

For a more interesting text effect, you can use one of the Effect commands to alter the text path. The Effect ➪ Distort & Transform ➪ Transform command allows you to scale, move, and rotate, as seen in Figure 29-3. Figure 29-4 shows the Effect ➪ Distort & Transform ➪ Free Distort command when applied to text. To create a 3D effect, you can use Adobe Illustrator's 3D Effect commands. Figure 29-5 shows the Effect ➪ 3D ➪ Extrude & Bevel dialog box options applied to a text path outline.

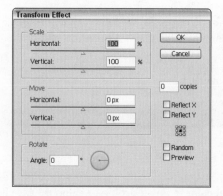

Figure 29-3: The Transform Effect dialog box can be used to scale, move, and rotate text paths.

Converting Illustrator type to path outlines

You may want to convert your Illustrator type into outline paths so that you can manipulate it further. Illustrator type path outlines can be manipulated just like graphic path outlines. To manipulate path outlines, click the type path's anchor points using the Direct Selection tool (the white arrow) and move the anchor points to alter the type path and the type itself. Essentially, this enables you to create your own type designs.

Note   When you convert text to outline format, it is no longer considered a font. The outline paths now appear as art, not text. So, if you send an Illustrator file to another person, that person won't need to have the font on their machine.

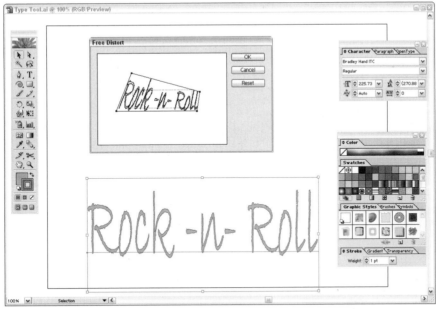

Figure 29-4: The Free Distort dialog box can be used to distort text paths.

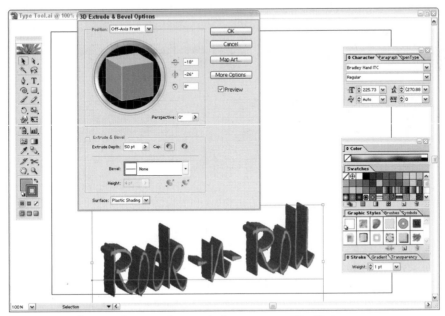

Figure 29-5: The Extrude & Bevel command can create a 3D effect.

Follow these steps to convert your type into outline type paths:

1. **Create text either Illustrator's Type tool or the Vertical Type tool.**

2. **Use the Selection tool to select the type.**

3. **Choose Type ➪ Create Outlines to convert the text from type to art.**

Editing path outlines

After you have converted your text into outlines, Illustrator views the text as art (a path that is in the shape of text). You'll probably manipulate, distort, or enlarge the text so that when you import it into Premiere Pro, you can run a video clip through the text, as shown later in this chapter. You can also run video clips through graphic path outlines. Type graphic path outlines can be enlarged with the Scale tool, rotated with the Rotate tool, and moved with the Selection tool. With Adobe Illustrator, type path outlines can be manipulated using the Reflect, Shear, and Free Transform tools. They can be distorted using the Warp, Reshape, and Twist tools.

Note   To select an entire path, use the Selection tool. To select a portion of a path, use the Group Selection tool. To select a point on a path, use the Direct Selection tool.

Here's how to scale, rotate, and move path outlines:

✦ **Enlarging path outlines:** Make sure that the path outline is selected (use the Selection tool, the black arrow). To use the Scale dialog box, double-click the Scale tool in the toolbox. When the Scale dialog box appears, as shown in Figure 29-6, make the adjustments you want and click OK to scale the text.

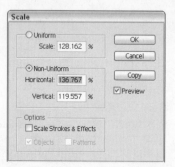

Figure 29-6: The Scale dialog box enables you to scale paths.

✦ **Scaling a single path outline:** Click the outline path with the Group Selection Type tool (the white arrow with the plus sign). Next, select the Scale tool in the toolbox, and click once in your document. Now click and drag the letter with the Scale tool selected to scale the letter.

✦ **Rotating type:** Select the path outline of the letter you want to select. Next, click the Rotate tool in the toolbox (next to the Scale tool in the toolbox) and click in your document. Next, click and drag the letter to rotate it. If you want to display the Rotate dialog box, press and hold the Alt key while you click the text with the Rotate tool.

✦ **Moving path outlines:** Click inside the path using the Group Selection tool and drag the path to where you want to move it. You can also use the arrow keys on your keyboard to move the letter onscreen. By default, the arrow keys are set to move in 1-pixel increments. You can change the increments in the Keyboard Increment section of the General Preferences dialog box. To access this dialog box, choose Edit ➪ Preferences ➪ General.

Editing with anchor points

Type outlines can be manipulated so that you can create new typefaces. You manipulate type path outlines by moving either anchor points or directional lines. Figure 29-7 shows a type path outline anchor points and directional lines.

Figure 29-7: Path type outline with anchor points and directional lines

To move an anchor point, click it with the Direct Selection tool (the white arrow) and then drag. Illustrator also enables you to move multiple anchor points at one time. To select more than one anchor point, press and hold the Shift key as you select anchor points. You can also click and drag over the anchor points you want to select.

Tip   You can also press the arrow keys on your keyboard to move a selected anchor point. Anchor points move keyboard increments that are set in the General Preferences dialog box. To display the General Preferences dialog box, choose Edit ➪ Preferences ➪ General.

Editing with directional lines

Curves on a path are created from a *curve anchor point*. Curve anchor points have *directional lines*, which determine the size and arc of your curve. Clicking and dragging a directional line changes the form of the curve.

Other ways to adjust the type path outline include using the Pen + tool, Pen – tool, and the Convert tool. Use the Pen + tool to click the path to add an anchor point. This anchor point can then be manipulated. Clicking an anchor point with the Pen – tool deletes it. Use the Convert tool to click on a corner anchor point to convert the corner anchor point to a curve anchor point, and vice versa.

Adobe Illustrator enables you to create some interesting distortions with the Warp tool. You can convert plain path outlines into interesting and unusual ones.

Using an Illustrator Text Shape in a Premiere Pro Project

Earlier in this chapter, you learned how to use Illustrator to create type and then convert the type into type shapes. This section shows you how to use Illustrator's Type tool to create text, convert it into a type shape, and then import it into a Premiere Pro project that uses the text shape as a mask. The Premiere Pro project in this chapter's examples feature a video clip playing through and behind the Illustrator text shape. Figure 29-8 shows frames from a Premiere Pro project that has a video clip running inside and behind an Illustrator text shape.

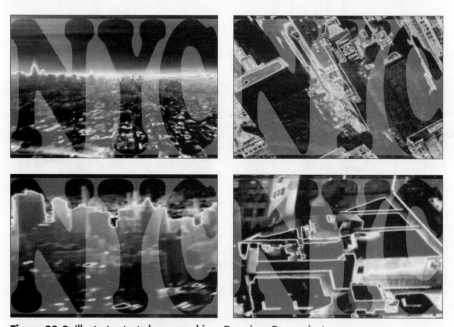

Figure 29-8: Illustrator text shape used in a Premiere Pro project

The following steps show how to create an Illustrator text shape, import it into a Premiere Pro project, and use it as a mask:

On the DVD-ROM

The images shown in Figure 29-8 are on the DVD that accompanies this book. The images are an "NYC" text shape created in Illustrator, a black-and-white video clip of New York City from Digital Vision's CityMix collection (567005f.mov), and a sound clip from Digital Vision's City Life/Urban Moods collection (576002s.aif).

1. **Load Adobe Illustrator and create a new document.** The document should be the same size as your Premiere Pro project. If you don't have access to Adobe Illustrator, skip Steps 1–7.

2. **Select either Illustrator's Type tool or Vertical Type tool.**

3. **Choose a font and type size.**

4. **Set the foreground color to black so that the text you create is black.** The black text is used later as a mask in Premiere Pro.

5. **Create some text.**

Cross-Reference

To learn about using the different Illustrator Type tools, see the section "Working with Illustrator Type" earlier in this chapter.

6. **Manipulate the text in Illustrator.** Choose Effect ➪ Distort & Transform, or convert the type into outlines using the Direct Selection tool. To convert the type into outlines, select it with the Selection tool and choose Type ➪ Create Outlines. Figure 29-9 shows the Illustrator text shape we created for the project shown in Figure 29-9. We converted the NYC text into outlines and then manipulated the text by using the Direct Selection tool.

Figure 29-9: An Illustrator text shape created in Illustrator

7. **After you've created an Illustrator text shape, save your file in Illustrator format.** Premiere Pro can then read the Illustrator file information. If you want, you can quit Adobe Illustrator.

8. **Load Premiere Pro, and create a new project.**

9. **Import an Illustrator text shape, a video clip, and a sound clip.** Choose File ⇨ Import to import the files needed for this project. If you want, you can import the files we used to create the frames shown in Figure 29-10. You can find them in the Chapter 29 folder (which is in the Tutorial Projects folder) on the DVD that accompanies this book. They are NYC.ai and Digital Vision's video clip 567005f.mov (from the CityMix CD-ROM); the sound clip 576002s.aif is from Digital Vision's City Life/Urban Moods collection.

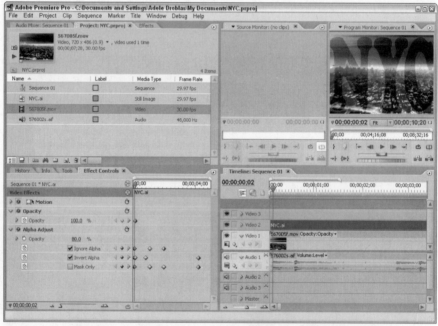

Figure 29-10: The Premiere Pro panels used to create the project in Figure 29-8

10. **Drag the video clip to Video 1 track, the Illustrator text shape to Video 2 track, and if you want, a sound clip to Audio 1 track.** If the text shape is not as long as the video clip, you can click the end of the text shape in the Timeline panel and drag to the right until it's the same duration as the video clip. (For more information on basic editing, refer to Chapter 7.) If the sound clip is longer than the video clip, you can use the Razor tool to cut it. (For more information on editing sound clips, turn to Chapter 8.)

11. **Select the text shape in Video 2 track.**

12. **Choose Window ⇨ Workspace ⇨ Effects.** In the Effects panel, open the Video Effects bin (folder).

13. **In the Effects panel, open the Keying bin and drag the Alpha Adjust Key effect over the text shape in Video 2 track.**

14. **In the Effect Controls panel, use the Alpha Adjust settings to create transparency with the clip in Video 1 track.** Use the Alpha Adjust Opacity setting to reduce the Opacity of the text shape so that you can see more of the video clip in Video 1 track. Drag the Opacity slider to the left to make the text shape in Video 2 track more transparent and see more of the background. Drag the Opacity slider to the right to have the text shape in Video 1 track more opaque. Click the Invert Alpha and/or Mask Only to alter the effect. If you want, you can click the Toggle Animation icon (before the Effects option) to change the options setting over time.

Note
> Choosing the Keying Video options results in different effects. Using the Keying Video Effects and options enables you to run video clips inside or behind the text and graphic shapes. For more information on using Keying effects, refer to Chapter 15.

15. **To soften the edges of the text shape, you may want to blur it by using the Gaussian Blur video effect.** To do so, select the text shape in Video 2 track. In the Effects panel, open the Blur & Sharpen bin and drag the Gaussian Blur video effect over the text shape in Video 2 track. The Effect Controls panel appears onscreen if it is not there already. Drag the Blurriness slider a little to the right. Figure 29-10 shows all the panels used to create the frames for the NYC project.

16. **Choose File ⇨ Save to save your project.**

17. **Press Enter on the keyboard to Render the project. Click the Play button in the Program Monitor panel to preview the project.** If you want, you can make a movie by choosing File ⇨ Export ⇨ Movie. Click the Settings button if you want to change the settings of your movie. For more information on outputting your Premiere Pro projects to movies, turn to Chapter 19.

Working with Illustrator Graphics

Illustrator graphic shapes can be used in the same way as Illustrator text shapes for use in creating logos, special effects, and masks. Figure 29-11 shows a variety of different types of graphics that can be created in Illustrator CS. Illustrator CS allows you to create 3D shapes, like those shown seen in Figure 29-11. In Illustrator CS, to create a 3D graphic, you simply click an icon from the 3D Effects palette and drag it to your document. To display the 3D Effects palette, choose Window ⇨ Graphic Style Libraries ⇨ 3D Effects. Illustrator CS also contains a palette of 3D symbols. To display the 3D Symbols palette, choose Window ⇨ Symbol Libraries ⇨ 3D Symbols. Other interesting Symbol libraries include: Arrows, Artistic Textures, Buildings, Charts, Communication, Decorative Elements, Document Icons, Food, Hair and Fur, International Currency, Logos, Maps, Nature, Networking, Occasions, Office, People, Science, Web Buttons and Bars, and Web Icons. In Figure 29-11, the butterfly, fish, bumble bee, fire, and envelope are all created by using symbols from the Symbol Libraries.

Note
> Here is how to bring objects in font of or behind another object: Select the object, and choose Edit ⇨ Cut. Then select Edit ⇨ Paste In Front or Edit ⇨ Paste In Back.

Another way of creating interesting graphics is by first using one of the basic shape tools: the Rectangle tool, Rounded Rectangle tool, Ellipse tool, Polygon tool, or Star tool. Then fill the shape with one of the graphic style effects from the Graphic Style Library. In Figure 29-11 we created a rounded rectangle shape and filled it with the Stained Glass style, which is located in the Textures Graphic Style Library. To create the flare seen in the middle of the rounded rectangle shape, we used the Flare tool.

Figure 29-11: Illustrator CS allows you to easily create 3D and interesting symbols and graphics.

Many Graphic Style Libraries can be used to apply interesting fills to graphics. To create button and rollover graphics, use the Window ➪ Graphic Style Libraries ➪ Buttons and Rollovers library. All the styles in this library create interesting fills with no stroke. Only the Red Coils Normal style includes a fill and a stroke. All the effects in the Scribble Effects library include strokes and no fills. The styles in the Special Effects, Artistic Effects, and Image Effects libraries include a variety of effects. Some of the effects include a fill or a stroke, and others include a stroke with no fill. Creating graphics with a stroke and no fill allows you to see through the background of the graphic. Another library that allows for some interesting strokes with no fill (transparent background) is the Window ➪ Graphic Style Libraries ➪ Neon Effects library.

Note   You can use an Illustrator graphic shape that has a stroke with no fill (a transparent fill) as a mask in Premiere Pro. To do so, import the Illustrator graphic into Premiere Pro and place it in a Video track above a background clip. When you play the project, you will see the background clip through the transparent fill of the Illustrator shape.

Creating Illustrator Graphic Shapes as Masks for Use in Premiere Pro

The Illustrator drawing capabilities make it the perfect place to create intricate masks for Premiere Pro. This example shows you how to create a simple shape in Illustrator that can be used as a mask in Premiere Pro. In the following section, you learn to use Illustrator graphic shapes as masks in Premiere Pro (see Figure 29-14).

Follow these steps to create a simple mask:

1. **Load Adobe Illustrator, if it isn't running already.**

2. **Choose File ➪ New to create a new document.** In the New Document dialog box, set the Artboard Size and choose RGB Color for the Color Mode.

3. **Select the Rectangle, Ellipse, Polygon, or Star tool, as shown in Figure 29-12, from the toolbox.**

 Figure 29-12: Illustrator's Rectangle, Ellipse, Polygon, and Star tools

4. **Click and drag to create a shape, or Alt-click to display the tool's dialog box.** In the dialog box that appears, make your adjustments.

5. **Click OK to create the shape.** Create at least one rectangle, ellipse, polygon, and star shape. The shapes you create are filled with whatever the Fill and Stroke colors are in the toolbox. If you want, you can change the Fill and Stroke colors by double-clicking the Fill or Stroke swatch in the toolbox. When the Color Picker appears, make your adjustment and click OK. Figure 29-13 shows the Star dialog box and a star created using it.

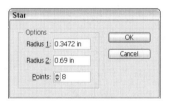

Figure 29-13: The Star dialog box allows you to create stars. At right, you see a star created using the Star dialog box.

 Note Experiment with using different fill shades. Filling with black, white, and different shades of gray and colors will result in different effects in Premiere Pro.

6. **When you have a star shape onscreen, experiment with a few of the Effect ➪ Distort & Transform commands.** The Effect ➪ Distort & Transform commands create interesting transformations, such as these:

   • To transform the star shape into a flower shape, use the Pucker & Bloat command.

   • To convert the star shape into a blob shape, use the Roughen command.

   • To convert the star shape into abstract art, use the Tweak command.

   • To twirl the star shape, use the Twist command.

   • To convert the star shape into a snowflake, use the Zig Zag command.

7. A star shape can be converted to a rectangle, rounded rectangle or an ellipse. **Try using the Effect ➪ Convert to Shape ➪ Ellipse command to convert the star into an ellipse.**

8. You can also transform simple shapes created in Adobe Illustrator into more elaborate shapes by bending and distorting them using the Effect ➪ Warp ➪ Arc command. **With a graphic selected, choose the Arc command.** By using the options in the Style drop down menu in the Warp Options dialog box you can arch, bulge, shell, flag, wave, fish, rise, fisheye, inflate, squeeze, or twist a graphic.

9. The Effect ⇨ Stylize commands (Drop Shadow, Inner Glow, Outer Glow, and Feather) allow you to add drop shadows, glows, or feathers to your graphic. The Effect ⇨ Stylize ⇨ Round Corners command allows you to make round corners. The Effect ⇨ Stylize ⇨ Scribble command creates a scribble effect inside your graphic. Try experimenting with these styles.

Using Illustrator Shapes as Masks in Premiere Pro

After you know how to use Illustrator to create graphic shapes and manipulate the shapes, you can import the shapes into Premiere Pro and use them as masks, as shown in Figure 29-14. Follow these steps:

1. **Choose File ⇨ New ⇨ Project.**

2. **Choose File ⇨ Import, locate a video clip, and click Open.** We used Digital Vision's Ambient Space 434023f.mov video clip.

On the DVD-ROM

Digital Vision's Ambient Space 434023f.mov clip is located in the Chapter 29 folder on the DVD that accompanies this book.

3. **Drag the video clip from the Project panel to the Video 2 track in the Timeline panel.**

4. **Click the video clip in the Video 2 track.**

5. **Choose Window ⇨ Workspace ⇨ Effects to display the Effects panel and the Effect Controls panel.**

6. **Drag the Image Matte Key effect (located in the Keying bin) from the Effects panel to the video clip in the Video 2 track.** The Image Matte Key option is a good choice to use when you would like a video clip to be seen through an Illustrator shape.

7. **Click the Image Matte Key Setup button in the Effect Controls panel.** When the Select a Matte Image dialog box appears, choose an Illustrator shape file. We used the Startwirl.ai file. Click Open to view the star in the Monitor panel. Notice that the white areas on the outside of the star don't show up in the preview. Only the black areas show through. The video clip shows through the black areas. If you want, you can reverse the effect by clicking the Reverse check box or by changing the Composite Using option. These options are found within the Image Matte key in the Effect Controls panel.

On the DVD-ROM

You can find the Startwirl.ai file in the Chapter 29 folder on the DVD that accompanies this book.

8. **Choose File ⇨ Import to import a clip to appear in the background.** Import a video clip, a Photoshop file, or an Illustrator file. We imported an Illustrator file that we created to use as a background. This file (surplus.ai) is on the DVD that accompanies this book. Figure 29-14 shows the surplus background with the twirl star image matte applied to a video clip. Drag the clip from the Project panel to the Video 1 track. In the next section, you learn how to create Illustrator background files and how to import them into Premiere Pro and animate them.

Figure 29-14: A frame of a video clip through an Illustrator twirled star shape with an Illustrator background

Creating, Importing, and Animating Illustrator Backgrounds

In this section, you learn to create Illustrator background files and import them into Premiere Pro, where you animate them using Premiere Pro's Motion effect. Figure 29-15 shows the Illustrator background files in the Monitor panel of Premiere Pro. Follow these steps to create background files in Adobe Illustrator CS and then import them into a Premiere Pro project (Figure 29-18 shows the panels used to create the Premiere Pro Background project.):

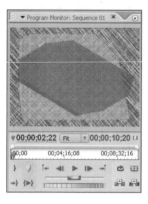

Figure 29-15: A frame of a Premiere Pro project using Illustrator background

1. Load Adobe Illustrator CS.

2. Choose File ➪ New.

3. **In the New Document dialog box, in the Name field, name your document Background. Set the Size drop down menu to 800 × 600 pixels and the Color Mode to RGB Color. Then click OK to create a new document.**

4. **Select the Rectangle tool from the toolbox, and create a rectangle a little smaller than the size of your document.**

5. **To fill the rectangle, use one of the effects from one of the Graphic Style Libraries.** We filled the rectangle in the Background file with the Scribble 3 effect from the Window ⇨ Graphic Style Libraries ⇨ Scribble Effects library.

6. **Choose File ⇨ Save.** Save the file in Illustrator format in the Background Project folder.

7. **Repeat Steps 2 through 6 twice to create two more backgrounds.** Name one of the files **Background1** and the other **Background2**. To fill the rectangle in the Background1 file, we used the Tissue Paper Collage 2 effect from the Artistic Effects library. To fill the rectangle in the Background2 file, we used the Side View effect from the 3D Effects library.

8. **Load Adobe Premiere Pro.**

9. **Choose File ⇨ Import to import the background clips.** In the Import dialog box, locate the background files. Press and hold the Shift key as you select the background files so that you can import all the files at the same time.

The background files used in this section are located in the Chapter 29 folder on the DVD that accompanies this book.

10. **Drag the Background file from the Project panel to the Video 1 track. Drag the Background1 file from the Project panel to the Video 2 track. Drag the Background2 file from the Project panel to the Video 3 track. Have the clips aligned so that they appear above the Background clip in the Video 1 track.**

11. **To animate the background clips, you can use the Motion and Opacity options in the Effect Controls panel. To do so, move the Edit line to the beginning of the background clip, and then click the Toggle animation icon in front of the option you want to adjust. Make the desired adjustment, and then move the Edit line and continue making adjustments.** Notice that marks are being created on the keyframe line. This is used to animate the background clip. Animate as many options as you like in the Effect Controls panel. For Background2, we applied and animated the Four-Point Garbage Matte (found in the Keying bin within the Video Effects bin in the Effects panel). For Background1, we applied and animated the Eight-Point Garbage Matte (found in the Keying bin within the Video Effects bin in the Effects panel). Figure 29-16 shows the Effect Controls panel with the Eight-Point Garbage Matte effect. Figure 29-17 shows the Effect Controls panel with the Four-Point Garbage Matte effect. If you want, try using the Sixteen-Point Garbage Matte effect.

For more information on using the Garbage Matte effects, turn to Chapter 15.

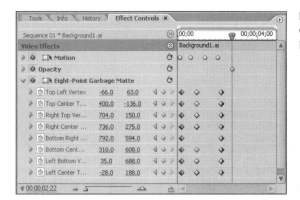

Figure 29-16: The Effect Controls panel with the Eight-Point Garbage Matte effect

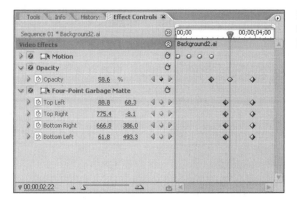

Figure 29-17: The Effect Controls panel with the Four-Point Garbage Matte effect

Note   For more information on adjusting and animating the opacity of a clip, see Chapter 15. In Chapter 15, you also find more information on using and animating the Keying Video effects. For more information on using different Video Effects, turn to Chapter 14. For more information on using and animating the Motion effect, see Chapter 17.

12. **To view the transparency effect of an Illustrator shape over the background files in the Background project, we imported a shape created in Illustrator CS.** The Shape.ai file was created with the Polygon tool. The polygon was filled with the Neon Type effect from the Window ➪ Graphic Style Libraries ➪ Default_RGB library. After the Shape file was imported to the Background project, a new Video Track was added to the Timeline. To add a new Video Track, click the Timeline panel and choose Sequence ➪ Add Tracks. Then drag the Shape file from the Project panel to the Video 4 track in the Timeline panel, shown in Figure 29-18. If you want, you can animate the Motion and Opacity effects of the Shape clip, as shown in Figure 29-18.

On the DVD-ROM   The Shape.ai file is located in the Chapter 29 folder on the DVD that accompanies this book.

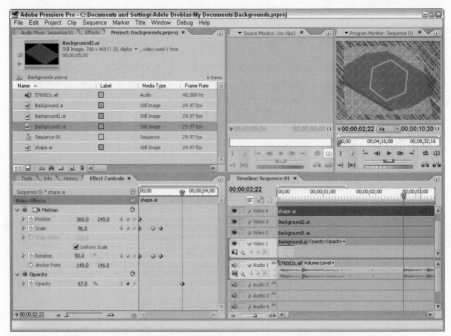

Figure 29-18: The panels used to create the Premiere Pro Background project

13. **Choose File ➪ Save to save your file.**

Note   If you want, you can import a sound clip and add it to your project.

On the DVD-ROM   A sound clip from Digital Vision's City Life/Urban Moods collection (576002s.aif) is located in the Chapter 29 folder on the DVD that accompanies this book.

14. **Press Enter to render the project.** The Rendering dialog box appears with render details. Choose Play from the Program Monitor panel to preview the project.

15. **To make a more interesting Background project, copy and paste the video clips in the Timeline.** Then edit the clips' color and add transitions. Replace the Shape clip with a Title clip. Figure 29-19 shows the Timeline panel used to extend the length of the Background Premiere Pro project. Figure 29-20 shows frames from extending the Background project. To do it, press and hold the Shift key as you select all the clips in the four Video tracks. Choose Edit ➪ Copy. Then move the Edit line to the end of the video clips, and choose Edit ➪ Paste. Delete the second Shape clip and replace it with a Title clip. Create a new Title clip.

16. **Add transitions between the clips in the Video tracks.** We added the Cross Dissolve transition to the clips in the Video 4 track, the Cube Spin transition between the clips in the Video 3 track, the Curtain transition between the clips in the Video 2 track, and the Flip Over transition between the clips in the Video 1 track.

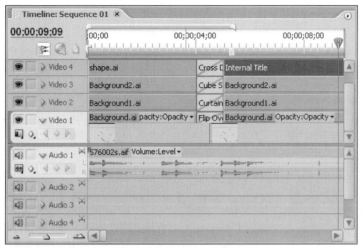

Figure 29-19: The Timeline panel used to extend the Premiere Pro Background project

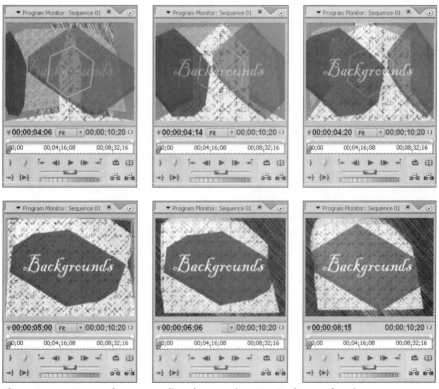

Figure 29-20: Frames from extending the Premiere Pro Background project.

17. **Alter the copied clips by using Video Effects.** We altered the colors in the clips by using the Adjust Effects. To change the second clip in the Video 3 track, we applied the Channel Mixer effect. To change the second clip in the Video 2 track, we applied the Extract effect. To change the second clip in the Video 1 track, we applied the Lighting Effects.

18. **Resave your work every time you make changes to your project. Press Enter to render your project.**

19. **To export your project as a movie, choose, File ⇨ Export ⇨ Movie.** In the Export Movie dialog box, name your movie and save it in AVI format. The final AVI file for the Background project can be found in the Chapter 29 folder of the DVD that accompanies this book.

Creating a Mask Using Photoshop and Illustrator

Combining the strengths of Adobe Photoshop and Adobe Illustrator, you can create elaborate masks. Start by using Photoshop to save a scanned photograph, an image captured with a digital camera, or a stock image. Then load the file into Illustrator, and use one of the path-creating tools to create a path around the area in the photo that you want to import into Adobe Premiere Pro. In Figure 29-24, we used Illustrator's Paintbrush tool to create a path. After the path is in Premiere Pro, you can have a video clip running in the background, as shown in Figure 29-25.

Follow these steps to create a complex mask using both Adobe Photoshop and Adobe Illustrator:

1. **Scan or capture an image into Adobe Photoshop with a scanner, digital camera, or digital camcorder.**

2. **Save the file in either Photoshop or TIFF format.** Many photo-finishing labs can develop your film as well as archive the pictures on a DVD, CD-ROM, or floppy disk.

3. **Load Adobe Illustrator, and create a New File.**

4. **Choose File ⇨ Place.** Locate the digitized Photoshop image, and place it. Figure 29-21 shows the sample image we used in this section.

Figure 29-21: Sample photo used to create a mask in Photoshop and Illustrator

If you want, you can load the sample image shown in Figure 29-21 (girl.psd) from the Chapter 29 folder on this book's DVD.

5. **If the Layers palette is not onscreen, choose Window ⇨ Show Layers.**

6. **In the Layers palette, double-click the layer.** The Layer Options dialog box appears, as shown in Figure 29-22.

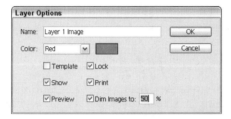

Figure 29-22: The Layer Options dialog box enables you to lock and dim a layer.

7. **Click both the Lock and Dim image options to lock and dim the layer.** Make sure that the Dim option is set to 50%.

8. **Click OK for the effects to take place.**

9. **Click the New Layer menu in the Layers palette to create a new layer.** In the Layer Options dialog box that appears, name the layer **Image** and click OK.

10. **Select the Pen, Pencil, or Paintbrush tool.**

11. **Trace the dimmed image's outline.** If you use the Pen tool, a small circle appears next to the tool when the starting and finishing points meet. When this happens, click to close the path, if you want to create a closed path. Figure 29-23 shows the Layers palette with the sample image dimmed in a layer and a few path strokes created with the Paintbrush in another layer.

Figure 29-23: The Layers palette with the dimmed image on one layer and the Paintbrush paths in another layer

When you are drawing, it's easier to see the image you are tracing if you trace with a stroke and no fill, as shown in Figure 29-24. If you draw with a fill, you won't see the image in the layer below. To set the Fill to none, click the Fill swatch (the top overlapping square) in the toolbox and then click the third small square (the one with the dialog line) below the Fill swatch. Click the Stroke swatch (behind the Fill swatch), and then click the first small square to set the stroke color to black. Choose Window ⇨ Stroke to display the Stroke palette. The Stroke palette enables you to choose the width of your stroke.

12. **After you've created a few black strokes, you may want to hide the bottom layer with the image in it to see how your path strokes are appearing.** Click the eye icon next to the layer you want to hide.

Figure 29-24: The traced image created in Illustrator

13. **After you have a path, fill it with black if you want to use it as a solid mask in Premiere Pro.** You may want to fill the path with a shade of gray to create a translucent mask.

14. **When you finish tracing over the dimmed image, you can delete it.** You may, however, first want to use the File ⇨ Save As command to duplicate the file.

15. **Save your final file in Illustrator format.**

16. **Load Adobe Premiere Pro, and create a new project.**

17. **Choose File ⇨ Import.** Locate the Illustrator file you want to import, and click Open.

The screen shots in this section feature the traced image created in the preceding section. If you want, you can load the girl.ai file from the Chapter 29 folder on this book's DVD. Or, if you prefer, you can import an Illustrator or Photoshop file that has text.

18. **Drag the Illustrator file from the Project panel to the Video 2 track in the Timeline panel.**

19. **Choose File ⇨ Import.** Locate a video clip, and click Open. We used an Illustrator file (RouchenParchment.ai) that we created by filling a rectangle with RGB Parchment effect (Window ⇨ Graphic Style Library ⇨ Textures). Then we applied the Effect ⇨ Distort &Transform ⇨ Rouchen command.

You can find the RouchenParchment.ai file in the Chapter 29 folder on the DVD that accompanies this book.

20. **Drag the Illustrator background file or video clip from the Project panel to the Video 1 track in the Timeline panel.** You should now have a background clip in the Video 1 track and an Illustrator file in the Video 2 track. To make the background more interesting, we applied the Color Balance (HLS) effect and animated the effect over time by changing the Hue. Press Enter to render the project.

21. **Click the Play button in the Program Monitor panel to preview the project.** Figure 29-25 shows a frame of the project.

Figure 29-25: An Illustrator mask over a background

Summary

You can use Adobe Illustrator to create text and masks for Premiere Pro projects. This chapter covered the following topics:

✦ Illustrator features six Type tools: Type tool, Area Type tool, Path Type tool, Vertical Type tool, Vertical Area Type tool, and Vertical Path Type tool. Illustrator text can be converted into art to create your own custom text to be used in a Premiere Pro project.

✦ You can create shapes in Illustrator using the Rectangle, Ellipse, Polygon, and Star tools. You can alter the shapes using some of the Effect commands. You can convert these shapes into backgrounds and import them in Premiere Pro and animate them using Motion, Opacity, and/or other Video Effects.

✦ When creating masks using Illustrator, the Alpha Adjust, Screen, or Multiply keys are best used when you only want the black or colored areas of the mask to appear.

✦ The Image Matte Key Type option is the best option when you want a video clip to be seen through an Illustrator image.

✦ You can create complex masks by using both Adobe Photoshop and Adobe Premiere Pro.

✦　　　✦　　　✦

Working with Masks in Adobe After Effects

Matte effects are undoubtedly one of the more interesting spe-cial effects provided by Adobe Premiere Pro. In Chapters 15 and 16, you learned how mattes can be used to hide portions of one video clip in a track behind the masked area of a shape in another video track.

If you want to create a matte effect in Premiere Pro, one technique is to create a shape in another program to use as a mask and import it into Premiere Pro. Although this is a rather straightforward and sim-ple process, it does not enable you to create the mask at the same time as previewing the clip with which it will be used. Nor does it enable you to change the matte's shape as the clip runs.

If you need to create sophisticated matte effects, you can turn to Adobe After Effects. In After Effects, you can create masks using the After Effects Pen tool, edit them, and animate them over time. You can also import Adobe Illustrator and Adobe Photoshop files into After Effects to be used as masks. After Effects also enables you to import Illustrator and Photoshop paths or Photoshop alpha channels to be used as masks.

This chapter looks at Adobe After Effects' masking options. It also discusses the features that Premiere Pro lacks but which you still may want to use to add interesting and unusual matte effects to Premiere Pro. To do this, you can import a Premiere Pro project into After Effects and use After Effects' masking capabilities to add pizzazz to your clips.

Understanding After Effects Masks

In Adobe After Effects, you can load a video clip or an entire Premiere Pro project into After Effects and isolate an area by using a mask so that the viewer sees only a portion of the video clip or project. In After Effects, masks can be created using *paths*. A path is similar to a wire-frame line onscreen that can be used to create anything from shapes with sharp corners to flowing waves created from perfect curves. After Effects allows you to create three types of masks: Rectangular, Elliptical, and RotoBezier. To create a rectangular-shaped mask, use the Rectangular Mask tool in the Tools palette. To create an elliptical-shaped mask, use the Elliptical Mask tool in the Tools panel. If you are creating any other shaped mask, you work with either a Bezier or RotoBezier mask. To create a Bezier mask, you can use the Pen tool, which is found in the Tools panel. Note that when you use the Pen tool in After Effects, you can also click the RotoBezier option. The RotoBezier option enables you to more easily create curves.

The Pen tool in After Effects is quite similar to the Pen tool in Adobe Illustrator and Adobe Photoshop. You can edit the path using the Pen +, Pen –, and Convert tools. These tools reside in the same location in the Toolbox as the Pen tool. You can use the Selection tool (arrow tool) in the Tools panel to edit a point on the path by clicking the point and dragging it to the position you want. If you double-click the path with the Selection tool, you can move, scale, or rotate the path as a whole. The effects of a mask are displayed in the Composition panel. Masks are edited in either the Composition panel or Layer panel. Masks can be altered over time by using the Timeline panel.

Creating Oval and Rectangular Masks

You can have lots of fun creating interesting effects with masks. A quick way to create a mask in After Effects is to use either the mask tools (the Elliptical Mask tool or the Rectangular Mask tool) in the toolbar or to use the Layer ➪ Mask ➪ New Mask command.

Figure 30-1 shows a frame with a video clip before applying a mask. We placed a still image in the background. For an added effect, we applied the Twirl command (Effect ➪ Distort ➪ Twirl) to the background still image.

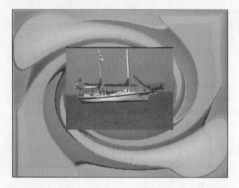

Figure 30-1: An After Effects fra002.tifme before using a mask

Figure 30-2 shows the same frame from Figure 30-1, after an oval mask was used on the video clip's perimeter. The mask in Figure 30-2 was created using the Layer ➪ Mask ➪ New Mask command.

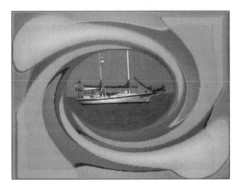

Figure 30-2: An After Effects frame created using an oval mask

Here's how to create an oval or rectangular mask in After Effects using the Layer ➪ Mask ➪ New Mask command:

1. **Load After Effects.**

2. **Choose File ➪ New ➪ New Project to create a new project.**

3. **Choose Composition ➪ New Composition to create a new composition.**

4. **In the New Composition dialog box, set the frame size.** Click OK.

5. **Choose File ➪ Import ➪ File.**

On the DVD-ROM

When creating a mask in After Effects for the first time, you may want to use just a simple video clip for the mask and a still image as the background. If you want, you can use the video clip of the sailboat.mov and the shapes.psd we used in this section. The sailboat.mov video clip and the shapes.psd still image are found in the Chapter 30 folder on the DVD that accompanies this book.

6. **Choose File ➪ Import ➪ File to import a clip to use in the background or import a still image to use as the background.** When creating a mask, it is easier to view the effects of a mask if you have a background that you can see through the transparent areas of the mask. Locate the still image or video clip that you want to import. When importing the shapes.psd file, click Footage from the Import Kind drop-down. Select Merged Layers in the Layer Options. Click OK.

Note

If you want, you can copy a clip from the Project or Timeline panel in Premiere Pro and paste it into either the Project or Timeline panel of After Effects.

7. **When the imported background clip appears in the Project panel, drag it to the Timeline panel.**

8. **To apply an effect to the background clip, choose a command from the Effect menu.** In Figure 30-2, we applied the Effect ➪ Distort ➪ Twirl command. After you've applied an effect to the background, click the lock column that is next to the triangle in front of the background clip, so that the background clip is accidentally affected when you begin working with the video clip you are masking.

Note   If you want, you can create your own background using the commands in the Effect menu.

9. **Choose File ⇨ Import ⇨ File to import a video clip you want to mask.**

10. **In the Import File dialog box, select a file that you want to mask and then set the Import As menu to Footage.** Click Open. The imported video clip appears in the Project panel.

    You can use one of the video clips found on the DVD that accompanies this book. The video clip used in Figure 30-1 is called sailboat.mov and is found in the Chapter 30 folder on the DVD that accompanies the book. Also in the Chapter 30 folder is a video clip from Digital Vision that you can use. The Digital Vision clip is from the CityMix CD-ROM (576004p.mov).

11. **Click and drag the imported video clip that you will mask to the middle of the Composition panel.** Not only does the video clip appear in the Composition panel, but it also appears in the Timeline panel. This clip should appear on top of the background clip.

12. **In the Timeline panel, click the triangle in front of the name of the video clip to display its options.** Notice that the Mask option is not currently available.

13. **To add a mask in the shape of the selected video clip, choose Layer ⇨ Mask ⇨ New Mask.**

Note   You can use the Rectangular Mask tool in the toolbar to create a rectangular-shaped mask. To create an elliptical-shaped mask, use the Elliptical Mask tool in the Tools panel. See the following step-by-step instructions to learn how.

    Notice that in the Timeline panel, the selected video clip now has a Masks option.

14. **Click the triangle in front of the word Masks in the Timeline panel. Then click the triangle in front of the word Mask 1 to reveal the Mask 1 options.** The options are Mask Shape, Mask Feather, Mask Opacity, and Mask Expansion.

15. **To change the shape of the mask, either click Shape (next to Mask Shape in the Timeline panel) or choose Layer ⇨ Mask ⇨ Mask Shape.** The Mask Shape dialog box appears, as shown in Figure 30-3.

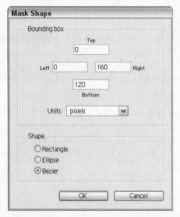

Figure 30-3: The Mask Shape dialog box enables you to pick a shape for your mask.

16. **To convert the mask to an ellipse, click Ellipse, in the Mask Shape dialog box.** Don't change the Bounding box values and leave the Units menu set to pixels. Click OK to see the effects of the mask in the Composition panel.

17. **To preview the effect of the mask over time, move the current-time indicator along the Timeline.**

18. **Save your file by choosing File ⇨ Save.**

    If you want, you can continue editing the mask. The mask can be edited by using the Mask 1 options. For more information on editing a mask, proceed to the next section.

Here's how to create an oval or rectangular mask in After Effects using the Elliptical Mask tool or the Rectangular Mask tool:

1. **Load After Effects.**

2. **Choose File ⇨ New ⇨ New Project to create a new project.**

3. **Choose Composition ⇨ New Composition to create a new composition.**

4. **In the New Composition dialog box, set the frame size.** Click OK.

5. **Choose File ⇨ Import ⇨ File to import a video clip you want to mask.**

6. **In the Import File dialog box, select a file that you want to mask and then set the Import As menu to Footage. Click Open.** The imported video clip appears in the Project panel. Try using the Digital Vision CityMix clip 576004f.mov, which you can find in the Chapter 30 folder of the DVD that accompanies the book.

7. **Drag the clip from the Project panel to either the Composition panel or the Timeline panel.**

8. **To create an elliptical mask, click the Elliptical Mask tool and click and drag the clip in the Composition panel. To create an elliptical mask, click the Rectangular Mask tool and click and drag the clip in the Composition panel. To edit the mask, click the points on the edge of the mask with the Selection tool.** For more information on editing mask, turn to the next section.

9. **Choose File ⇨ Import ⇨ File to import a clip to use in the background or import a still image to use as the background. After you've imported the background clip, remember to drag it from the Project panel to the Timeline panel. The background clip must be below the mask clip in order to view the mask.**

If desired, you can create your own background using the After Effects 7.0 Brush tool. To use the Brush tool, start by choosing Layer ⇨ New ⇨ Solid. In the Solid Footage Settings dialog box, name the solid and set the presets. Then click OK. When the solid appears in the Timeline panel, double-click it to display the solid in the Layer panel. Then select the Brush from the Tools panel and begin painting. Use the Paint panel to change the painting color and brush size.

Editing a Mask

After you've created a mask (see the preceding section to review creating simple elliptical and rectangular masks), you can edit the mask by using the Layer menu and either the Layer panel or the Composition panel, along with the Selection tool in the Tools panel. You can also edit a mask by using the Mask options in the Timeline panel.

Here are a few mask-editing tips:

✦ **To edit the mask, the mask must be selected.** If the mask isn't selected, you can select it by double-clicking the name of the clip you are working on in the Timeline panel. In the Layer panel that appears, click the path to select it. You can also select a mask by clicking it in the Timeline panel.

✦ **The mask can be edited in the Layer panel or the Composition panel.** If you change the path in the Layer panel, you can see the effect of the mask on the video clip in the Composition panel. Figure 30-4 shows the path and the mask in the Layer panel.

✦ **A mask can be edited by using the Mask options in the Timeline panel.** In the Timeline panel, click the triangle in front of the clip with the mask that you want to edit. When the masks for that clip appear, click the triangle in front of the Mask that you want to edit. The mask options allow you to invert the mask, edit the shape, change the opacity, or expand the mask. It also allows you to soften the edges of the mask.

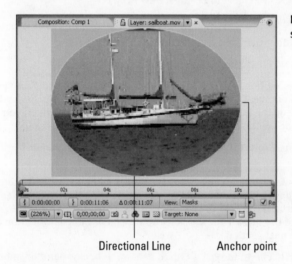

Figure 30-4: The Layer panel shows the mask as a path.

Directional Line   Anchor point

Here's how to edit a mask:

1. **Start by selecting in the Timeline panel the mask that you want to edit.** The mask should be displayed in the Composition panel.

2. **With the mask selected in the Timeline panel, you can choose Layer ⇨ Mask ⇨ Free Transform Points to transform the mask.** Notice that in the Composition panel, the mask appears with a bounding box with handles around it. In the Composition panel, click and drag one of the handles to increase or decrease the size of the mask. Move the mouse over one of the handles, and wait for the cursor to change to a curved line with arrows at either end. Then drag in the direction you want to rotate the mask. To activate the changes, double-click inside the mask shape in the Composition panel.

Tip

If you want to cancel the changes you made to your mask, choose Layer ⇨ Mask ⇨ Reset Mask to reset the mask to its original state. If desired, you can remove the mask by choosing Layer ⇨ Mask ⇨ Remove Mask and then choosing Layer ⇨ Mask ⇨ New Mask to create a new mask and start over again.

3. **To resize a mask using the Selection tool, choose the Selection tool from the toolbar. Then click and drag one of the four corners of the mask in either the Composition panel or Layer panel.** To display the mask in the Layer panel, double-click the clip in the Timeline panel. To keep the proportions of the mask as you change the size of the mask, press and hold the Shift key as you drag.

4. **To increase or decrease the expansion of a mask, click and drag the Mask Expansion values.** The Mask Expansion values are found in the Timeline panel in the Mask section of the selected video clip.

5. **To change the shape of a mask, use the Layer ⇨ Mask ⇨ Mask Shape command or the Mask Shape option in the Timeline panel.**

6. **To display the mask's path in the Layer panel, double-click the video clip's name in the Timeline panel or double-click inside the mask.** The mask appears as a path in the Layer panel. To display the anchor points, you may need to click the path with the Selection tool found in the Tools panel.

7. **To edit the path, click an anchor point, shown in Figure 30-5, using the Selection tool. Then press an arrow key on your keyboard to move the anchor point up, down, right, or left.** As you edit the path, the mask in the Composition panel is affected. Clicking and moving the directional line in the oval path changes the shape of the curve.

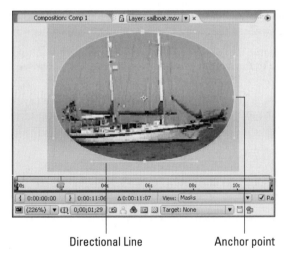

Directional Line   Anchor point

Figure 30-5: You can edit an oval path by moving anchor points and directional lines.

8. **To display the mask's path in the Composition panel, double-click Comp 1 in the Project panel.** Click the mask with the Selection tool to select it.

9. **Click and drag inside the mask with the Selection tool to move the mask.** Click the edge of the mask to display the path of the mask.

10. **With the Selection tool, click either an anchor point or directional line to edit the path.**

11. **With the mask in the Timeline panel, change the opacity of the mask by choosing Layer ⇨ Mask ⇨ Opacity.** In the Opacity dialog box, set the opacity you want. Click OK, and notice the change in the Composition panel. You can also change the opacity of a mask by using the Mask Opacity option in the Timeline panel.

12. **To soften your mask's edges, you can apply a feather by choosing Layer ⇨ Mask ⇨ Mask Feather. In the Feather Mask dialog box, type a small value to create a small feather.** A large value results in a large feather. You can also feather a mask by using the Mask Feather option in the Timeline panel.

13. **To adjust the colors of the clip, you can use any of the Effect ⇨ Color Correction commands.** After you apply a command, use the Effect Controls panel to adjust the controls for that effect.

14. **To stroke the mask, choose Effect ⇨ Generate ⇨ Stroke. Use the Effect Controls panel to set the stroke color, width, and opacity.** You can also set a fill color by choosing Effect ⇨ Generate ⇨ Fill. Again, use the Effect Controls panel to set the fill color and opacity, and use a fill mask.

15. **Choose Effect ⇨ Perspective ⇨ Basic 3D to swivel and tilt the mask in 360 degrees. To apply a shadow to the mask, choose Effect ⇨ Perspective ⇨ Drop Shadow or Radial Shadow. To apply a bevel to the mask, choose Effect ⇨ Perspective ⇨ Bevel Alpha or Bevel Edges.** The controls for the Perspective commands can be adjusted using the Effect Controls panel.

16. **Use the Effect ⇨ Distort ⇨ Bezier Warp command to warp the mask using Beziers. Use the Beziers and the controls in the Effect Controls panel to adjust the warp.**

17. **To invert the mask (reverse the effect of the mask), choose Layer ⇨ Mask ⇨ Inverse. To bring the mask back to the state it was before you inverted it, choose Layer ⇨ Mask ⇨ Inverted.**

18. **To change how the mask is displayed over the background, choose Layer ⇨ Mask ⇨ Mode and then choose a mode.** By default, the mode is set to Add.

Creating a Bezier Mask

The Pen tools used in programs such as Illustrator, Photoshop, Freehand, and CorelDRAW provide digital artists with the power to draw virtually any shape imaginable. The After Effects Pen tool provides similar power — except instead of using the Pen tool to create works of art, After Effects users can use the Pen tool to create masks.

Figure 30-6 shows the first frame of a video clip without a Bezier mask. Figure 30-7 shows the same frame with a Bezier mask applied to the chipmunk in the clip. In order to isolate the chipmunk from the background, we used a Bezier mask — because using an oval or rectangle obviously wouldn't provide the desired effect. After we isolated the chipmunk from its background by applying the mask, we added a background still image. To make the background image more interesting, we applied the Effect ⇨ Stylize ⇨ Mosaic command. Finally, we added text on a path by using the After Effects Effect ⇨ Text ⇨ Path Text command.

Cross-Reference   To use the After Effects Path Text command, you first need to create a New Solid by using the Layer ⇨ New Solid menu command. For more information on creating and animating text in After Effects, see Chapter 31.

Figure 30-6: A frame from a video clip without a Bezier mask

Figure 30-7: A frame from a video clip with a Bezier mask

Here's how to create a simple Bezier mask using the After Effects Pen tool:

1. **In After Effects, create a new project by choosing File ➪ New ➪ New Project.**

2. **Choose Composition ➪ New Composition to create a new composition.**

3. **In the New Composition dialog box, specify a frame size. Click OK.**

4. **Choose File ➪ Import ➪ File to import a video clip you want to mask.** In the Import File dialog box, choose a file and then set the Import As menu to Footage. Choose Open to import the selected video clip. The imported video clip appears in the Project panel.

On the DVD-ROM

If you want to use the video clip of the chipmunk.mov shown in Figure 30-6, you can find it in the Chapter 30 folder on the DVD that accompanies this book.

5. **Drag the imported video clip to the middle of the Composition panel.** The video clip not only appears in the Composition panel, but it also appears in the Timeline panel. Notice that the current-time indicator is at the beginning of the clip. Any changes you make to the clip will affect only where the current-time indicator is positioned.

6. **Double-click the video clip's name in the Timeline panel to display the video clip in the Layer panel.**

7. **Select the Pen tool in the toolbar. After you have selected the Pen tool, you can click the RotoBezier option from the toolbar.** The RotoBezier option facilitates making Bezier paths that contain many curves.

8. **Create a path around the image.** Click in the image you want to isolate. Keep clicking the perimeter of the image with the Pen tool to create a path around the image. When the first and last points meet, a tiny circle appears next to the Pen icon. Click the mouse to close the path. As you create a Bezier path in the Layer panel, the effect of the mask appears in the Composition panel. Figure 30-8 shows the chipmunk without a mask. Figure 30-9 shows the mask path in the Layer panel and the effect of the mask.

Figure 30-8: The chipmunk before the mask

Figure 30-9: The mask path in the Layer panel and the mask effect

Editing Paths with the Pen Tool

You can edit a path in After Effects by using the Selection tool to select an anchor point and move it, or you can click on a directional line with the Selection tool to change the shape of a curve. You can use the Convert tool, which is found in the same location as the Pen tool, to convert a curve to a corner point, or vice versa. If you need more anchor points, select the Pen + tool and click the path to add a point at that location. To omit a point, click it with the Pen tool.

Note
If you find the Pen tool difficult to use, you can start by using the Elliptical Mask tool or Rectangular Mask tool to create a path and then use the Pen and Selection tools to edit the path.

9. **To see the effects of the mask over a background, choose File ⇨ Import ⇨ File to import a file. Import either a still image or video clip to use as the background.** In the Import File dialog box, locate a file and click Open. In Figure 30-9, we used the file 12squares.psd as the background. This file is located in the Chapter 30 folder in the DVD that accompanies the *Adobe Premiere Pro 2 Bible*.

10. **When the background clip appears in the Project panel, drag it below the clip in the Timeline panel.** To make the background image more interesting, we applied the Effect ⇨ Stylize ⇨ Mosaic command. To lock the background so that it doesn't move, click the Lock column (next to the triangle icon) in the Timeline panel.

11. **To see a preview of your work, click the Composition panel and then choose Composition ⇨ Preview ⇨ RAM Preview.**

12. **To add text on a path, choose Layer ⇨ New ⇨ Text and then choose Effect ⇨ Text ⇨ Path Text. In the Path Text dialog box that appears, type** Chipmunk Software.

    Use the Font drop-down menu to choose a font. Click OK to apply the text to your project. Use the Effect Controls panel to edit the path text. To have the text appear around a circle, click the Shape Type drop-down menu in the Effect Controls panel and choose Circle. Notice that when you work with text in After Effects, a new layer is created in the Timeline panel.

Note
To add horizontal text to your project, click the Horizontal Type tool in the Tools panel. Next move the cursor to the Composition panel, and then click the mouse button and begin typing. Use the Character panel to change the font and font size. To convert horizontal type into a path outline, select the type with the Selection tool. Then choose Layer ⇨ Create Outlines. The path outline of the text can be edited with the Selection tool. The path outline can also be used as a mask.

13. **Save your file by choosing File ⇨ Save.**

Animating a Mask with the Timeline Panel

You can edit a mask's shape, location, feather, and opacity over various time intervals using After Effects Timeline panel, Composition panel, and Layer panel. Figure 30-10 shows the effects of animating a mask at different points in time. Notice that the mask shape changes as the video progresses.

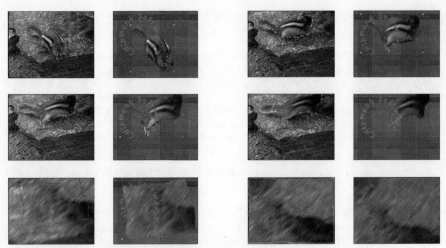

Figure 30-10: The frames show that the mask shape changes over time.

To use the Timeline panel to edit a mask over time, follow these steps:

Note   Before you begin, you should have a clip in the Timeline panel. That clip should also have a mask.

1. **Click the triangle next to the video clip's name in the Timeline panel.**

2. **Click the triangle in front of the word Masks to display the mask.**

3. **Click the triangle in front of the mask you want to edit to show the mask options.** The Mask options are as follows:

   - **Mask Shape:** This option allows you to set the shape to Rectangle, Oval, or Bezier.

   - **Mask Feather:** This option allows you to apply a horizontal or vertical feather to the edges of a mask.

   - **Mask Opacity:** This option allows you to change the opacity. To make the mask translucent, set the Opacity to less than 100 percent.

   - **Mask Expansion:** This option allows you to expand the mask using pixels values.

   - **Mask mode:** By default, the mode is set to Add. (Next to the modes, After Effects provides an area that you can click if you want to invert the mask.)

4. **Move the current-time indicator to the beginning of the clip in the Timeline panel.**

5. **Click the stopwatch next to the mask option that you want to animate.** In Figure 30-10, we changed the mask's shape so that it would follow the chipmunk as it moved over time. To animate the mask shape, click the stopwatch in front of Mask Shape. Notice that a keyframe is created in the Timeline panel. To animate a mask, you need to create keyframes.

6. **To create another keyframe, move the current-time indicator to the right just a bit and edit the mask shape.** To follow an image the way we did in Figure 30-10, you need to move and edit the mask path in the Composition panel or Layer panel using the Selection tool or Pen tool.

7. **When you've finished editing the mask path in the current time location, move the current-time indicator to the right again.**

8. **Edit the mask shape again.** As you edit the mask shape, notice that another keyframe is created. Continue moving the current-time indicator and editing the mask until you've reached the end of the clip in the Timeline panel. You can also edit a mask option from a point other than the beginning. For Figure 30-10, we started editing the opacity at the middle of the Timeline.

Follow these steps to edit the opacity of a mask:

1. **Move the current-time indicator to the beginning of the clip in the Timeline panel.**

2. **Click the stopwatch in front of the Opacity option.** Notice that a keyframe is created. A keyframe is created with the Opacity's default settings, 100 percent.

3. **Move the current-time indicator to the middle of the clip in the Timeline panel.**

4. **Change the mask opacity option by clicking and dragging the Mask Opacity value in the Timeline panel.** Note that you can also use the Mask Opacity command (Layer ⇨ Mask ⇨ Mask Opacity). When the Mask Opacity dialog box appears, type a number and click OK. In Figure 30-10, we changed the Opacity setting to 50 percent.

5. **Preview the project by choosing Composition ⇨ Preview ⇨ RAM Preview.** When the current-time indicator reaches the keyframe in the middle of the Timeline, the opacity changes to the value you entered in Step 4.

6. **Make the opacity (mask option) gradually change from the middle of the clip to the end of the clip.** Move the current-time indicator to the end of the clip. Next, set the desired opacity option.

Importing Masks from Illustrator or Photoshop

You can import a black-and-white Illustrator or Photoshop file into After Effects to use as a mask. The Illustrator or Photoshop file can be used to isolate areas in a video clip, as shown in Figure 30-11. Figure 30-12 shows the black-and-white Illustrator file used as a mask.

Figure 30-11: The effect of an Illustrator file used as a mask on a video clip in After Effects

Figure 30-12: The black-and-white Illustrator file used as a mask

Here's how to use Adobe Illustrator and Adobe Photoshop to create a mask in After Effects:

1. **In Adobe Illustrator CS, create a shape using the Rectangle, Oval, Star, or Polygon tool. Fill the shape with black. To distort the shape, use the Warp tool. Apply a filter or effect to the shape to create a more interesting shape.** Do not rasterize the shape. When you are finished creating the shape, choose File ➪ Save. In the Save dialog box, set the Save as type drop-down menu to Illustrator and click Save.

2. **In Adobe Photoshop CS, choose File ➪ New to create a new file. In the New dialog box, choose a preset, set the Mode to RGB Color, and make the background transparent.** Click OK to create a new file.

   In Photoshop, you can use various tools to create a shape. Try using the Brush tool or the Custom Shape tool. Before using one of these tools, set the Foreground color in the toolbox to black. Then pick a brush size and shape. You can also use the Lasso tool to create a selection.

   After you've created the selection, fill it with black by choosing Edit ➪ Fill. In the Fill dialog box, set the Use drop-down menu to Black, the Mode to Normal, and the Opacity to 100 percent. The Preserve Transparency option should not be selected. Click OK. To deselect the selection, choose Select ➪ Deselect.

   To create a more unusual shape, you can apply one of Photoshop's filters. After you've created a shape, choose File ➪ Save. In the Save dialog box, set the Format drop-down menu to Photoshop and click Save.

3. **After you have created a black shape in Adobe Illustrator or Adobe Photoshop, load After Effects and create a new project by choosing File ➪ New ➪ Project and a new composition by choosing Composition ➪ New Composition.** When importing the Adobe Photoshop file, make sure to choose a shape or layer from the Choose Layer drop-down menu that appears.

4. **Import the Photoshop or Illustrator file, as well as a video clip, into the project by choosing File ➪ Import ➪ Multiple Files.**

On the DVD-ROM

In the Chapter 30 folder on the DVD that accompanies this book, you can find Photoshop shape files (puzzle.psd and balloon.psd) and Illustrator shape files (starfish.ai and roughen.ai). In the Digital Vision folder in the Chapter 30 folder is a video clip from Digital Vision that you can use. The Digital Vision clip is from Digital Vision's CityMix CD-ROM (567004f.mov).

5. **Drag the video clip from the Project panel to the middle of the Composition panel.**

6. **Drag the Photoshop or Illustrator black-and-white file below the video clip in the Timeline panel.**

7. **Click the video clip in the Timeline panel.**

8. **Choose Layer ➪ Blending Mode ➪ Silhouette Luma.**

9. **Experiment with the other Blending modes, such as Hard Light, Soft Light, Overlay, Difference, Multiply, Lighten, Pin Light, and Luminosity.** Figure 30-13 shows the effect of applying the Overlay Blending mode to a puzzle mask (Photoshop file). In the Timeline panel, note that the puzzle mask is in a layer above another layer. In the bottom layer is a Photoshop file that is used as the background layer.

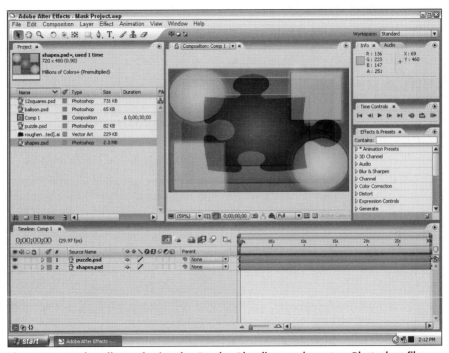

Figure 30-13: The effects of using the Overlay Blending mode on two Photoshop files.

10. **Choose Layer ➪ Blending Mode ➪ Normal to remove the blending mode.**

11. **Click the mask file's name in the Timeline panel.**

12. **Choose Layer ➪ Track Matte ➪ Luma Inverted Mask.**

13. **Choose Layer ➪ Track Matte ➪ No Track Matte to discard the matte effect.**

Note

If desired, you can copy a clip from the Project or Timeline panel in After Effects and paste it into either the Project or Timeline panel of Premiere Pro.

Using Illustrator Paths as Masks

Hardcore Adobe Illustrator users most likely prefer to create their masks in Illustrator, which provides more path-editing commands than does After Effects. Fortunately, importing an Illustrator file into After Effects is a simple copy-and-paste operation. Here are the steps:

1. **In Illustrator CS, choose File ➪ Preferences ➪ File Handling & Clipboard. In the Clipboard on Quit section of the Preferences dialog box, the Copy As option should be set to AICB, Preserve Paths. Click OK.**

2. **In Illustrator, create a path with the Pen tool, or use the Rectangle, Ellipse, Polygon, or Star tool to create a path.**

3. **Use the Selection tool to elect the path and all its anchor points, and then choose Edit ➪ Copy.**

4. **Switch to After Effects, open the Layer panel for the target layer (a layer with a video clip), and then choose Edit ➪ Paste.**

Summary

Although Adobe Premiere Pro provides numerous matting effects, it does not enable you to create sophisticated masks or edit masks over time as you can it Adobe After Effects. This chapter covered the following topics:

✦ After Effects enables you to create oval, rectangular, and Bezier masks.

✦ In After Effects, you can edit masks in both the Layer and Composition panels using the Pen tool and the Selection tool and by using the commands in the Layer menu.

✦ After Effects masks can be edited over time using the Timeline panel.

✦   ✦   ✦

Adding Special Effects in Adobe After Effects

Although Adobe Premiere Pro is packed with powerful video effects, at times you may want to create composite motion or text effects; that may not be possible within the confines of Premiere Pro's panels. If your project requires a bit more pizzazz than Premiere Pro can produce, consider using Adobe After Effects.

After Effects can create dozens of effects that aren't possible in Premiere Pro. For example, you can fine-tune a motion path's shape as you would a curve in Adobe Illustrator or Photoshop. You can also rotate text 360 degrees along a curve over time. You can animate in 3D. After Effects enables you to run multiple clips simultaneously in the video frame — creating a three-ring circus of video effects.

This chapter's goal is not to persuade you to use After Effects over Premiere Pro, but to show you how the two can work together to create the ultimate video production. Both programs have their strengths, and you can use this to your advantage.

Note   If you have the Adobe Production Studio, you can create a Dynamic link between After Effects and Premiere Pro so that you can take advantage of the strengths of both programs. You can also add a Dynamic link to Adobe Encore DVD.

How After Effects Works

After Effects combines some of the features of Photoshop and Premiere Pro. To start a project in After Effects, first create a new project and then create a new *composition*. A composition determines the type of movie you create. In the Composition Settings dialog box, you pick your settings for width, height, and frame rate. Then you import all the images, sounds, titles, and video clips you need to create your video production. Like Premiere Pro, After Effects stores all these imported items in a Project panel. As you need footage items, you drag them from the Project window into the Timeline panel. Unlike Premiere Pro, the items in the Timeline panel are not stored in video or sound tracks. Video and sound clips don't appear in different tracks; instead, they are organized as layers. In this way, Adobe After Effects works like Adobe Photoshop. In both programs, you also can apply transformations (scale, rotate, and so on), effects, and masks to the layers. Adobe After Effects, however, enables you to animate the transformation, effects, and masks over time and in 3D; in Adobe Photoshop, each layer's properties remain static.

 Cross-Reference   If you import a Photoshop file into Adobe ImageReady, you can make animation frames from your layers and output the file as a QuickTime movie. See Chapter 12 for an example of how to do this.

Importing Premiere Pro Projects

You can import an entire Premiere Pro project along with its transitions and effects directly into After Effects to take advantage of the program's powerful features, such as animating transformations and masks over time.

Follow these steps to import a Premiere Pro project into After Effects:

1. **In After Effects, create a new project and new composition. Then choose File ⇨ Import ⇨ File.** The Import File dialog box appears.

2. **Select the Premiere Pro project you want to import, and click Open.** If you created the Angel Stories Premiere Pro project in Chapter 17, you can select it and import it into After Effects so that you can apply some interesting effects to it.

3. **In the Import Project dialog box, select a sequence and click OK.** After Effects 7.0 imports the Premiere Pro project into the Project panel.

4. **Double-click the Premiere Pro sequence file that is in the Project panel.** The video and sound tracks now appear in the Composition panel and as layers in the Timeline panel. The first layer in the Timeline panel is the first video or sound track that appears in the Premiere Pro Timeline panel.

5. **If needed, you can now click a layer and animate it over time, using the Layer ⇨ Transform commands or by using the Transform options in the Timeline panel.** To reveal the Transform options for a layer, click the triangle in front of that layer's name. The Transform options can be animated over time using keyframes — similar to the way Premiere Pro uses keyframes with video effects.

   Effects and Masks can be applied to a layer in the Timeline panel and animated over time.

6. **To apply an effect to a layer, first select the layer in the Timeline panel and then use one of the Effect commands found in the Effect menu or in the Effects & Presets panel.** When working with various effects, you should use the Effects workspace. To do so, choose Window ⇨ Workspace ⇨ Effects.

7. **To apply a mask to a layer, select the layer and then use the Layer ⇨ Mask commands.** For more information about working with masks using After Effects, turn to Chapter 30.

 Note   Not only can you import a Premiere Pro project into After Effects, but you also can output your Premiere Pro project as a QuickTime movie or AVI movie format and then import the movie into After Effects by choosing File ⇨ Import ⇨ File.

Importing and Animating Photoshop Files

To animate a Photoshop file in After Effects, you can have two choices: (1) You can create a folder and place all the Photoshop files in it and import it as a Photoshop Sequence, or (2) you can import a Photoshop file with layers like the one shown in Figure 31-1. When you import a Photoshop file with layers as a composition, a folder is created in the Project panel with the layers inside the folder.

Figure 31-1: The "It's a Party" file in Photoshop with its layers

Follow these steps to use Photoshop to create a Photoshop file with layers and then import it into an After Effects project:

Note

You can create a Photoshop file from within After Effects. To do so, choose File ⇨ New ⇨ Adobe Photoshop File. When the Save Layered File As dialog box appears, name your file and click Save. The new Photoshop file is loaded into Adobe Photoshop ready for you to work on. After you make changes to the file, save it so that the changes are updated in After Effects. If you create your new layers in this file, the layers do not show up in the After Effects project unless you import it as a composite file. To do so, choose File ⇨ Import ⇨ File. In the Import File dialog box, locate the Photoshop file with layers and click Open. In the dialog box that appears, set the Import Kind drop-down menu to Composition and click OK. Double-click the Photoshop Composition icon in the Project panel to have all the Photoshop layers appear in the Timeline panel.

1. **Create a Photoshop file that has layers, as the image in Figure 31-1 does, and save it in Photoshop format.** Follow these steps to create layers in Photoshop:

    a. **Load Photoshop.**

    b. **Choose File ⇨ New to create a new file.**

    c. **In the New dialog box, set the width and height to the size you want your After Effects movie to be. Set the Mode to RGB Color and the Contents to Transparent. You can also click the Preset drop-down menu and make a selection. Then click OK.**

    d. **In the transparent background, use the painting tools from the Tools panel and the filters from the Filter menu to create some abstract art to use as the background.**

    e. **Click the Create New Layer icon in the Layers panel, or choose New Layer from the Layers panel drop-down menu.** To open the Layers panel, choose Window ⇨ Layers.

    f. **Create an image in the new layer.** You can scan or digitize an image with a digital camcorder. Use one of the Selection tools to select an item in the image, and then copy and paste the digital image into the new layer. Be sure to select only a portion of the image so that you can see the background in the layer below. If you want, you can copy the Clown.psd file that is in the Chapter 31 folder on the DVD that accompanies the book.

    g. **Create another new layer.** Keep creating layers until you have all the layers needed. If you want, you can also use Photoshop's Horizontal Type tool to create text in a layer.

    h. **Choose File ⇨ Save to save the file in Photoshop format.**

    i. **Quit Photoshop.**

2. **Load After Effects.**

3. **In After Effects, choose File ⇨ New ⇨ New Project.** The Project panel appears.

4. **Choose File ⇨ Import ⇨ File.** The Import File dialog box appears.

5. **Locate the Photoshop layer file that you want to import, and click Open. In the dialog box that appears, set the Import Kind drop-down menu to Composition and then click OK.**

6. **In the Project panel, a folder and a composition icon appear, as shown in Figure 31-2.** You can find the Photoshop file (Party.psd) shown in Figure 31-2 on the DVD that accompanies the book.

    • **To see the Photoshop layers, either double-click the folder or click the triangle.**

    • **To view the layers in the Composition panel and Timeline panel, either double-click the file icon at the top of the Project panel or double-click the composition icon, which is above the Photoshop layers folder in the Project panel.** Notice that the layers appear in the Composition panel and the Timeline panel. The layers also appear in the Timeline panel in the same order as they did in Photoshop's Layers panel. You don't have to drag each layer to the Timeline panel. After Effects automatically places them there.

    • **To decrease or increase the view of the Composition panel, first select the panel and then choose Zoom out or Zoom in from the View menu.**

Click triangle to expand folder

Composition icon

Folder icon

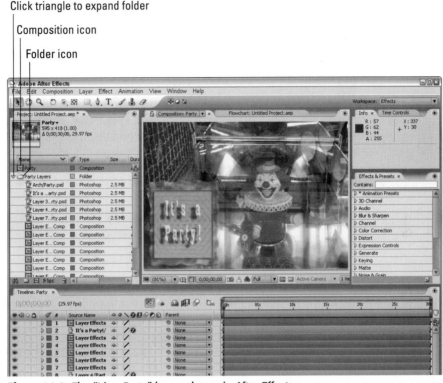

Figure 31-2: The "It's a Party" layers shown in After Effects

> **Note**
>
> To import various Photoshop files as a sequence, create a folder and place the Photoshop files in the folder. Then, in After Effects, choose File ➪ Import ➪ Multiple Files. When the Import Multiple Files dialog box appears, click the first Photoshop file of the sequence; then click the Photoshop Sequence option and click Open. Continue to select files, select the Photoshop Sequence option, and click Open until you have selected all the files. When you are finished, click Done.

After importing a Photoshop file, you can *animate* its layers. When you animate a layer, you do one of three things: transform it (scale, rotate, or change opacity and/or position), apply an effect (such as distortion), or apply a mask to the entire layer or just a portion.

> **Note**
>
> In Adobe Photoshop, you can use the Modes menu to create composite effects between layers. To display the modes, click the Switches/Modes option at the bottom of the panel until you see the word Mode next to the Source Name column.

Follow these steps to animate Photoshop layers in After Effects:

1. **Click the triangle beside one of the layers in the Timeline panel.** When you expand the layer, the Transform option appears.

2. **Click the triangle next to Transform.** Notice that the Anchor Point, Position, Scale, Rotation, and Opacity options are visible. You can animate the layer's anchor point, position, scale, rotation, or opacity.

3. **To animate the layer's position, first move the current-time indicator to the beginning of the clip and click the stopwatch icon in front of the word Position.** A keyframe is created.

4. **Move the current-time indicator to the right.**

5. **Change the position of the layer either by adjusting the Position values in the Timeline panel or by moving the layer in the Composition panel.** After changing the layer position, a new keyframe is created.

6. **To continue animating the position of the layer over time, continue moving the current-time indicator to the right and then move the layer in the Composition panel.** Another keyframe is created.

7. **To preview your work, choose Composition ➪ Preview ➪ RAM Preview.**

8. **To animate a layer using an effect, choose a layer in the Timeline panel.**

9. **Move the current-time indicator to the beginning of the clip.**

10. **Click the Effect menu, and choose an effect.**

11. **Click the Effects triangle in the Timeline panel.** The name of the effect you choose appears onscreen. In front of the effect name is a stopwatch icon. Click the stopwatch icon to create a keyframe.

12. **Move the current-time indicator to the right. Then alter the effect in the Effect Controls panel.** Notice that another keyframe is created.

13. **Again move the current-time indicator, and alter the effect.** Another keyframe is created.

14. **To preview your work, choose Composition ➪ Preview ➪ RAM Preview.**

15. **If you want to add sound to your file, import a sound clip. Then drag it from the Project panel to the Timeline panel.**

16. **When you are finished, choose File ➪ Save to save your work as an After Effects project.**

To export your work as a Premiere Pro Project, choose File ➪ Export ➪ Adobe Premiere Pro Project. Name your project, and click Save. After you've saved your work as a Premiere Pro file, you can open it in Premiere Pro as you would any other Premiere Pro project.

To export your work in either QuickTime or AVI movie format, choose File ➪ Export ➪ QuickTime Movie or AVI. In the settings dialog box that appears, make the necessary adjustments and click OK. In the Save As dialog box, name the file and then click Save to save the file. After you've saved your work in a movie format, if you want, you can import it into a Premiere Pro project as you would any other file.

Importing Photoshop Files with Adjustment Layers

In this section, you learn how to create a Photoshop file with Adjustment Layers and then import it as a composition file into After Effects. By importing the Photoshop Adjustment

Layer into After Effects as a Composition, each Adjustment Layer along with the background layer is imported.

In Photoshop, you can use Adjustment Layers to change the color of an image in a separate layer from the background. This way the Adjustment Layers can be edited or removed without affecting the original image. You can also create Adjustment Layers in After Effects. You learn more about this in the next section.

Follow these steps to create a Photoshop file with Adjustment Layers:

1. **Load Photoshop and create a new file or load a file that already has a background.** If you create a new file, you need to create a background. You can use the Paint tools and the Filter menus to create a background.

2. **Choose Window ➪ Layers to display the Layers panel.**

3. **Choose Layer ➪ New Adjustment Layer and pick a command.** When the New Layer dialog box appears, you can name your layer. Click OK to create a new layer. A dialog box may appear, depending upon which command you picked. If it does, make the necessary adjustments and click OK.

4. **Notice that a new Adjustment Layer appears in the Layers panel.** Create as many Adjustment Layers as you need.

5. **Choose File ➪ Save to save your file.** Name your file and save it in Photoshop format.

Follow these steps to load a Photoshop file with Adjustment Layers into After Effects:

1. **Load After Effects and either create a new project or load a project.**

2. **Choose File ➪ Import ➪ File.** In the Import File dialog box, locate the Photoshop Adjustment Layer file and click Open. In the dialog box that appears, set the Import Kind drop down-menu to Composition. Leave the Footage Dimension drop-down menu set to Document. Click OK to import the Photoshop Adjustment Layer file as a composition.

3. **When the Photoshop composition file appears in the Project panel, double-click on it.** A new Composition is created in the Timeline panel with all the Adjustment Layers and the Background Layer used to create the Photoshop file.

4. **If you want to turn off one of the Adjustment Layers, click the Effect icon in the Timeline panel.** It is the round circle with an *f* in the middle of it. To turn off an Adjustment Layer and make the layer appear white, click the Adjustment Layer icon. This icon appears as a circle, half white and half black.

5. **Choose Window ➪ Workspace ➪ Effects.** The Effect Controls panel appears.

6. **Click on one of the Adjustment Layers in the Timeline panel.** Notice that the controls for that Adjustment appears in the panel. If you want, you can make adjustments to the controls. When you make changes you can view them in the Composition panel.

7. **If you want, you can import a new background and apply the Adjustment Layers to the new background.** Once you've imported the new background, move it into the Timeline panel above the old background layer.

8. **Either save your project in After Effects format or export as a movie or an Adobe Premiere Pro project.**

Creating an Adjustment Layer In After Effects

In this section, you use After Effects to create an Adjustment Layer and apply effects in this layer. These effects affect the layers behind the Adjustment Layer but are not permanent. The Adjustment Layer can always be deleted.

Follow these steps to create an Adjustment Layer in After Effects:

1. **Load After Effects and either create a new project or load a project.** If you create a new project, you need to import a file to use as a background.

2. **Drag a file from the Project panel to the Timeline panel to use as a background.**

3. **Choose Layer ⇨ New ⇨ Adjustment Layer.** An Adjustment Layer appears above the background layer in the Timeline panel.

4. **Choose Window ⇨ Workspace ⇨ Effects.**

5. **Pick an effect from the Effects & Presets panel and drag it to the Adjustment Layer in the Composition panel.** Apply as many effects as you like.

6. **Use the Effect Controls panel to change the effect's controls.**

7. **If you want, you can apply the Adjustment Layer to another background.** To do so, just drag a clip from the Project panel to the Timeline panel. Place the clip above the background clip that is already in the Timeline panel.

8. **Either save your project in After Effects format or export it as a movie or an Adobe Premiere Pro project.**

Importing and Animating Illustrator Files

In this section, you learn how to import an Illustrator file with layers into After Effects and animate it. We used this technique to create a project filled with butterflies.

Follow these steps to import an Illustrator file with layers into After Effects:

1. **Using Illustrator CS, create a file with layers, like the one shown in Figure 31-3, and save it in Illustrator format.** Here are the steps:

   a. **Load Illustrator.**

   b. **Choose File ⇨ New to create a new file.** In the New dialog box, name the file and set the Color mode to RGB Color.

   c. **In the New Document dialog box, set the artboard width and height to your After Effects project size pixel dimensions. Click OK.**

   d. **To create the Butterfly project, click the Paintbrush tool in the toolbox.**

   e. **Choose Window ⇨ Brush Libraries ⇨ Animals_ Insects.**

   f. **Click the Butterfly 1 shape.**

   g. **Click in the artboard area to create a butterfly.** Click again and again. If you want, you can click and drag to create a few butterflies.

   h. **Choose Window ⇨ Layers to open the Layers panel.**

i. **To create a new layer, click the Create New Layer icon in the Layers panel or choose New Layer from the Layers panel drop-down menu.**

j. **In the new layer, click the artboard to create a butterfly in the new layer.** Then create another new layer, and create another butterfly. Repeat the process until you have nine layers with butterflies, as shown in Figure 31-3.

k. **Create another new layer.** This should be your tenth layer. In this layer, use the Pencil tool to create a curve.

l. **Using the Path Type tool, create some text on the curve that you created with the Pencil.** We typed "Summer time brings butterflies" for the image in Figure 31-3.

m. **Save your file in Illustrator format, and then quit Illustrator.**

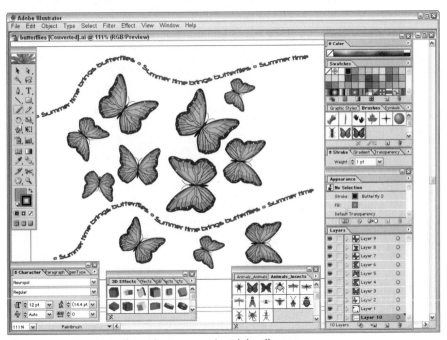

Figure 31-3: The Butterfly project as seen in Adobe Illustrator

2. **Load After Effects, and create a new project. To import the Illustrator file, choose File ➪ Import ➪ File. In the dialog box that appears, set the Import Kind drop-down menu to Composition and click OK.**

On the DVD-ROM

The Adobe Illustrator file (butterflies.ai) seen in Figure 31-3 can be found in the Chapter 31 folder that is on the DVD that accompanies the book.

Notice that a folder icon and a composition icon appear in the Project panel as shown in Figure 31-4.

Figure 31-4: The Butterfly project as seen in Adobe After Effects

3. **To see the Illustrator layers, either double-click the folder or click the triangle in front of the folder. To view the layers in the Composition and Timeline panels, double-click the Composition preview in the Project panel.** Notice that the layers appear in the Composition panel and the Timeline panel.

4. **To decrease or increase the view of the Composition panel, choose Zoom out or Zoom in.** The layers also appear in the Timeline panel in the same order as they appeared in Illustrator's Layers panel. You don't have to drag each layer to the Timeline panel—After Effects automatically places them there.

5. **To animate the Illustrator layers, click the triangle of one of the Timeline panel's layers.** You can choose to animate that layer's masks or effects or to transform the layer itself.

6. **Try animating the butterflies by rotating, moving, and scaling them and applying effects over time.**

7. **Choose File ⇨ Save to save your work. Choose File ⇨ Export ⇨ Adobe Premiere Pro Project to save for work in Premiere Pro project format. A Premiere Pro project file can be opened in Premiere Pro by choosing File ⇨ Open.**

Creating and Animating Type Using After Effects

In After Effects, you create text either by directly using the Horizontal Type tool in the Composition panel or by choosing Layer ⇨ New ⇨ Text. After Effects recognizes three different types of text: Basic Text, Numbers, and Path Text. When you select the Basic Text option, you can create horizontal or vertical text. You can also use the Basic Text option to animate one letter of a word at a time. The Numbers option enables you to create numbers. Path Text creates text on a path.

Because you cannot create text on a path or around a circle in Premiere Pro, the following example covers creating path text. Figure 31-5 shows the panels used to create Path Type project. We used the Rotate option, found in the Timeline panel, to animate text around the curve to create the text in this example.

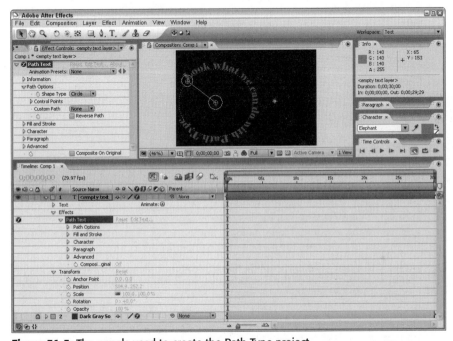

Figure 31-5: The panels used to create the Path Type project

Following the Path Type project example, you find an example on how to animate horizontal text using After Effects' Animate Text command.

Follow these steps to create and animate path text in After Effects:

1. **Choose File ➪ New ➪ New Project.** Instantly, the Project panel appears.

2. **Choose Composition ➪ New Composition.** The Composition Settings dialog box appears, as shown in Figure 31-6.

3. **Name your composition, and choose the width and height that you want to use.**

4. **Click OK to create a new composition and display the Timeline panel.**

Note   If you want to change the settings in the composition, choose Composition ➪ Composition Settings.

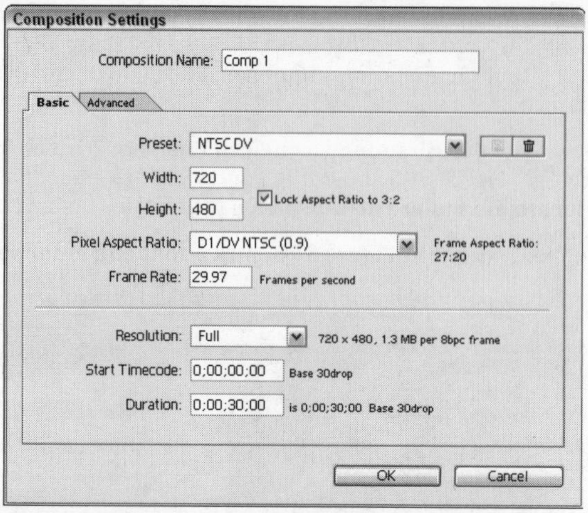

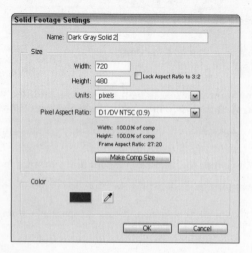

Figure 31-6: The Composition Settings dialog box

5. **To import a background clip, choose File ➪ Import ➪ File to import a file that will work as a background for the path text.**

To create your own background, you need to create a new solid layer.

6. **Choose Layer ➪ New ➪ Solid. When the Solid Footage Settings dialog box appears, shown in Figure 31-7, type a name for your layer in the Solid Footage Settings dialog box. Leave the width and height alone, and click OK to create a new solid.** (Usually the width and height are the same as the composition.)

Notice that a new solid layer appears in the Timeline panel. The new solid layer also takes up the entire size of the Composition panel. After creating a new solid layer, you can apply different effects. We applied the Effect ➪ Noise & Grain ➪ Fractal Noise command and the Effect ➪ Stylize ➪ Mosaic command to create a background for our project.

Figure 31-7: The Solid Footage Settings dialog box

7. **If you imported a background file, drag the background file from the Project panel to the Timeline panel.** The background file immediately turns into a layer.

8. **Move the current-time indicator to the position in the Timeline in which you want to apply path text.**

9. **Choose Layer ⇨ New ⇨ Text to create new text layer.**

10. **Choose Effect ⇨ Text ⇨ Path Text to create text on a path.**

11. **In the Path Text dialog box, shown in Figure 31-8, pick a font and enter some text in the text field.**

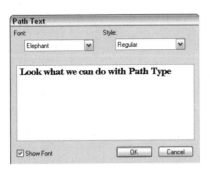

Figure 31-8: Type some text in the Path Text dialog box

12. **Click OK to close the dialog box and view your text on a curve in the Composition panel.** The Effect Controls panel, shown in Figure 31-9, appears at the same time as the text on the curve appears in the Composition panel.

Note

If you can't see the text, you may need to click the background file and drag it below the text icon in the Timeline panel.

13. **Use the Effect Controls panel to change the size, tracking (letter spacing), fill, and stroke color or to edit the text you just wrote.**

   - **To change the size of the text, click and drag the Size slider in the Effect Controls panel.**

   - **To edit the text, click the words Edit Text at the top of the Effect Controls panel, across from the word Path Text.** When the Path Text dialog box appears, you can edit the text. Click and drag over the letters you want to change.

   - **To choose whether you want your text to be filled, stroked, or filled with a stroke surrounding it, click the Options drop-down menu in the Fill and Stroke section.** To change the fill or stroke color, click the color swatch next to the words Fill Color or Stroke Color. When the Color dialog box appears, pick a color and click OK. You can also use the Eyedropper tool to change a color. To change the fill or stroke color to the color you've selected with the Eyedropper, click the Eyedropper next to either Fill Color or Stroke Color and then click a color from the background file. To change the stroke color's width, click the Stroke Width option and type a number.

   - **Clicking the Shape Type drop-down menu lets you choose whether you want the shape of the text to be on a Bezier, Circle, Loop, or Line.** Click the circles in the Composition panel to adjust the type path shape.

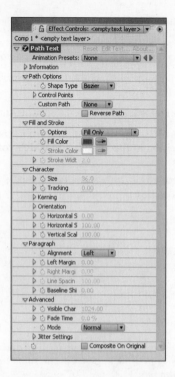

Figure 31-9: You can use the Effect Controls panel to adjust the text in the composition.

Note   If the Effect Controls panel is not onscreen, you can display it by first clicking a layer you want and then choosing Effect ⇨ Effect Controls.

14. **Choose Circle from the Shape Type drop-down menu in the Effect Controls panel to have the text appear on a circle.**

15. **To rotate text around a curve and animate it, you can click the triangle in front of the Path Text layer in the Timeline panel to display its features and click the Transform triangle to display the Rotation option.** Then follow these steps:

    a. **Move the current-time indicator to the Timeline's beginning, and click the stopwatch icon next to the Rotation option to create your first keyframe.**

    b. **Then move the current-time indicator over on the Timeline, and click the degree amount next to the Rotation option.**

    c. **When the Rotation dialog box appears, type a degree amount and click OK to create another keyframe.**

    d. **Continue moving the current-time indicator on the Timeline and changing the Rotation degree to create keyframes.** Continue until you have a number of keyframes or until you've created a complete rotation.

16. **Choose File ⇨ Save to save your work. To preview your work, choose Composition ⇨ Preview ⇨ RAM Preview.**

17. **To import this project into Premiere Pro, choose File ⇨ Export ⇨ Adobe Premiere Pro Project.** In the Export As Adobe Premiere Pro dialog box that appears, name the file and click Save to save the file.

Follow these steps to create horizontal text and animate it using After Effects 7.0 Animate Text command:

1. **Move the current-time indicator to the position in the Timeline in which you want to apply horizontal text.**

2. **Select the Horizontal Type Tool from the Tools panel, and start typing in the Composition panel.** As soon as you add text to the Composition panel, a text layer appears in the Timeline panel. Use the Character panel to change the font and font size.

3. **Move the current-time indicator to the position in the Timeline in which you want animate the horizontal text.**

4. **Choose Animation ⇨ Animate Text, or click the word Animate in the Timeline panel.** Then choose the option you want to animate. You can animate the text's position, you can scale the text, and you can rotate it or change its color. After you've chosen an animation option, the Animator option appears in the Timeline panel. Click the stopwatch next to the Animator option to create a keyframe.

5. **Move the current-time indicator to the right, and adjust the Animator option.** Another keyframe is created. Continue this step as many times as you need to.

6. **To animate in 3D space using X, Y, Z coordinates, click the 3D Layer icon at the top of the Timeline panel** (the cube that is next to the word Parent).

Working with Motion Paths

After Effects provides more control of motion effects than does Premiere Pro. In After Effects, you can create motion along a path by moving an object along the object's anchor point. When moving an object along its anchor point, you are essentially using a path similar to Illustrator and Photoshop paths. Figure 31-10 shows a butterfly that's been animated in After Effects using its anchor point. Notice that the path is visible in the Layer panel.

 Cross-Reference   For more information on using the Motion controls in Premiere Pro, refer to Chapter 17.

Animating with anchor points

Follow these steps to animate an object in After Effects using its anchor point:

1. **Choose File ⇨ New ⇨ New Project to create a new project.** Then choose Composition ⇨ New Composition. In the Composition Settings dialog box, set the presets and then click OK. If you prefer, you can choose File ⇨ Open to load an After Effects project.

2. **Choose Window ⇨ Workspace ⇨ Standard.**

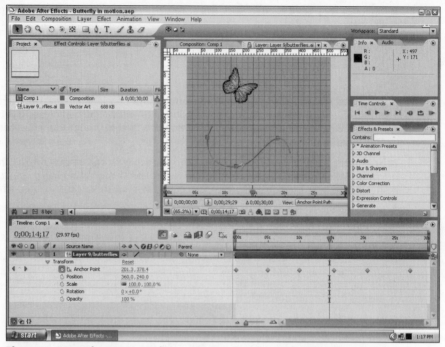

Figure 31-10: In the Layer panel, you can see a motion path created.

3. **Choose File ➪ Import ➪ File to import a Photoshop or Illustrator object.** If you want, use the butterflies.ai file from the companion DVD's Chapter 31 folder. When importing the file, select Footage from the Import Kind drop-down menu in the dialog box that appears. Select Choose Layer, and then choose the layer you want to import from the drop-down menu. We imported layer 9. That way, only the layer you want to work with is imported, not all the layers.

4. **Click and drag the imported file from the Project panel to the Timeline panel. The layer not only appears in the Timeline panel but also in the Composition panel. To change the background color of the Composition panel, choose Composition ➪ Background Color. Click the swatch, and pick a color; then click OK.** We changed the color of the background from black to a vibrant light blue color.

5. **Expand the layer by clicking the triangle next to the layer's name in the Timeline panel.**

6. **Click the Transform triangle to display the Transform options.** The Transform options are displayed.

7. **Move the current-time indicator to the Timeline's beginning or to where you want to start animating your object.**

8. **Click the stopwatch icon next to the words Anchor Point.**

9. **Double-click the layer in the Timeline panel to display the Layer panel.**

10. **In the Layer panel, choose Anchor Point Path from the View drop-down menu.**

11. **Choose View ➪ Show Grid and Choose View ➪ Show Ruler to have a ruler and a grid appear in the layer panel where you are working.**

12. **In the Layer panel, click the circle and move it to where you want the path to begin.**

13. **Move the current-time indicator to a new position in the Timeline, and then move the circle again to start creating the motion path.** Continue moving the current-time indicator, and move the circle in succession until you've finished creating your motion path. To edit the motion path, you can move the layer keyframe, direction handles, or direction lines.

    Depending upon the path you've created, you may want to use the Layer ➪ Transform ➪ Auto-Orient Rotation command. In the Auto-Orientation dialog box, choose Orient Along Path and then click OK. The Auto-Orient Rotation command enables you to rotate an object along a path so that the object is facing a different direction.

    To manually adjust the path, use the handles and vector points to control the size and shape of the paths curves.

14. **To preview the motion you just created, click the Composition panel. Then choose one of three commands:**

    • Composition ➪ Preview ➪ Motion with Trails (fastest)

    • Composition ➪ Preview ➪ Wireframe Preview

    • Composition ➪ Preview ➪ RAM Preview (slowest)

15. **If you want to keep your work, choose File ➪ Save to save it.**

Animating with Sketch a Motion

The Sketch a Motion option enables you to draw your path freehand.

Follow these steps to animate using Sketch a Motion:

1. **Choose File ➪ New ➪ New Project to create a new project. Then choose Composition ➪ New Composition. In the Composition Settings dialog box, set the presets and then click OK. If you prefer, you can choose File ➪ Open to load an After Effects project.**

2. **Choose File ➪ Import ➪ File to import a Photoshop or Illustrator object.** If you want, use the butterflies.ai file from the companion DVD's Chapter 31 folder. When importing the file, select Footage from the Import Kind drop-down menu in the dialog box that appears. Select Layer Options, and then choose the layer you want to import. We imported layer 7. That way, only the layer you want to work with is imported, not all the layers.

3. **Click and drag the imported file from the Project panel to the Timeline panel.** The layer not only appears in the Timeline panel but also in the Composition panel.

4. **Move the current-time indicator to the Timeline's beginning or to where you want to start animating your object.**

5. **Move the object you are animating to the place from where you want it to start.**

6. **Choose Window ➪ Workspace ➪ Animation to display the animation workspace, including the Motion Sketch panel.**

7. **Click the Start Capture button in the Motion Sketch panel.**

8. **Move the cursor to the Composition panel.**

9. **Press and hold the mouse button while you draw your motion path.** As soon as you let go of the mouse button, After Effects stops creating the motion sketch. The motion sketch is displayed in Figure 31-11.

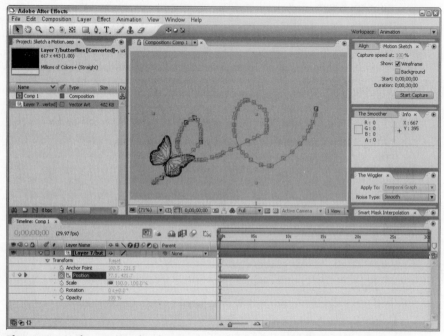

Figure 31-11: The motion sketch appears in the Composition panel; motion sketch is created with the Motion Sketch panel.

10. **Click the triangle in front of the layer you have selected in the Timeline panel.**

11. **Click the triangle in front of the word Transform.** Notice that the Motion Sketch command has created keyframes in front of the Position section of the Timeline panel.

12. **Preview the motion.** Choose the Composition ➪ Preview ➪ Motion with Trails command, the Composition ➪ Preview ➪ Wireframe Preview command, or the Composition ➪ Preview ➪ RAM Preview command.

Creating a Composite Video Clip

You can use After Effects to create a *composite video clip*. A composite video clip consists of a few video clips displayed side by side on the screen at the same time, as shown in Figure 31-12. To create the Venice project illustrated in Figure 31-12, we placed two video clips side by side and then added some text below the two clips. If your project calls for it, you can have three or four video clips. The video clips that you use to create a composite clip can be Premiere Pro projects, video captured from your digital camcorder, or even stock video clips.

Figure 31-12: The Venice project is an example of a composite clip.

Follow these steps to create a composite video clip in After Effects:

1. **Choose File ➪ New ➪ New Project.**

2. **Choose Composition ➪ New Composition.** The Composition Settings dialog box appears.

3. **In the Composition Settings dialog box, name your composition.** Pick the correct frame size for your project's width and height.

4. **Click OK to create a new composition.**

5. **Choose File ➪ Import ➪ Multiple Files.** The Import Multiple File dialog box appears.

6. **In the Import Multiple Files dialog box, set the Import As option to Footage.**

7. **Select the video clips, and then click Open.** If you want, you can use the clips shown in Figure 31-12 (gondola.mov and cruising.mov), which are found in the Chapter 31 folder on the DVD that accompanies this book. When you have finished importing files, click Done.

8. **Drag the video clips you imported from the Project panel to the Composite panel.** If you want your composite to appear as it does in Figure 31-12, place the video clips so that they are diagonally across from each other. You can also place two clips side by

side or on top of each other on the left side of the Composition panel and place text to the right of the video clips. You can also fill the Composite panel video clips and have no text.

9. **If you want your composite to include text, as shown in Figure 31-12, first select the Horizontal Type tool. Then click the Composition panel, and type some text.** Using the Horizontal Type tool in the Composition panel creates a new text. Another way to create a new text layer is to choose Layer ➪ New ➪ Text.

10. **Use the Character panel to change text size and pick a font.**

11. **To bevel and add a drop shadow to your text, choose Effect ➪ Perspective ➪ Bevel Alpha and also choose Effect ➪ Perspective ➪ Drop Shadow.**

12. **To bevel and add a drop shadow to the video clips, first select one of the clips in the Timeline panel. Then choose Effect ➪ Perspective ➪ Bevel Edges and choose Effect ➪ Perspective ➪ Drop Shadow. You may also want to adjust the colors of the video clips; to do so, use the Color Correction effects.**

13. **To create the background that appears behind the text, as shown in Figure 31-12, you first need to create another solid layer.** Choose Layer ➪ New ➪ Solid. In the Solid Footage Settings dialog box, click the Eyedropper tool and pick a color from one of the video clips. This is the color that appears in the solid. Leave the other settings as they are. If you want, name the solid. Click OK to create the new solid. When the new solid appears in the Timeline panel, it appears in front of the text you just created.

14. **To see the text, click the new solid layer in the Timeline panel, and drag it below all the other layers.** Figure 31-12 shows the layers in the Timeline panel.

15. **If you want to create a special effect for the background, use one of the commands found in the Effect menu.** We used the Effect ➪ Generate ➪ 4-Color Gradient option, the Effect ➪ Generate ➪ Lens Flare option, the Effect ➪ Stylize ➪ Posterize option, and the Effect ➪ Distort ➪ Liquify option.

16. **To preview your work in RAM, choose Composition ➪ Preview ➪ RAM Preview.**

17. **Choose File ➪ Save to save your work.**

Tip   You can save a frame of your After Effects project as a Photoshop file, either with or without layers. Choose Composition ➪ Save Frame As ➪ Photoshop Layers or Composition ➪ Save Frame As ➪ File.

18. **To export your work as an Adobe Premiere Pro Project, choose File ➪ Export ➪ Adobe Premiere Pro Project. In the dialog box that appears, name your file and then click Save. The After Effects file saved in Adobe Premiere Pro Project can be opened in Premiere Pro for further editing.**

19. **To export your work as a QuickTime movie, choose File ➪ Export ➪ QuickTime Movie.** When the Movie Settings dialog box appears, click the Video Settings button to set the compression, color depth, and frames per second. Click the Filter button if you want to apply a filter to your clip. Beware of changing the Size button. Either leave the size as is, or if you change your movie's size, make it smaller rather than larger. Making your movie size larger causes the clip to become pixilated and blurry. You can also adjust

sound settings and choose whether you want to stream for the Web. Make the necessary adjustments, and click OK. When the Save As dialog box appears, name your movie and click Save to create a QuickTime movie. After you've created a QuickTime movie, you can import the QuickTime movie into a Premiere Pro project for further editing.

Note

To export your movie in a different format, choose Composition ➪ Make Movie. In the Render Queue panel, click the triangle in front of the Composition being rendered. Next, click Lossless, which is next to the Output Module option. In the Output Module Settings dialog box, click the Format drop-down menu and choose a format. Available format options include Animated GIF, BMP Sequence, Cineon Sequence, ElectricImage IMAGE, FLC/FLI, Filmstrip, IFF Sequence, JPEG Sequence, MP3, MPEG2, MPEG-2DVD, OMF, OpenEXR Sequence, PCX Sequence, PICT Sequence, PNG Sequence, Photoshop Sequence, Pixar Sequence, QuickTime Movie, Radiance Sequence, Real Media, SGI Sequence, TIFF Sequence, TARGA Sequence, Video for Windows, WAV, and Windows Media.

Summary

Although Adobe Premiere Pro features many video effects, Adobe After Effects provides more motion and compositing effects. This chapter covered these topics:

✦ You can import a Premiere Pro movie directly into After Effects.

✦ You can export an After Effects project as an Adobe Premiere Pro Project.

✦ You can animate text on a curve in After Effects.

✦ You can animate in 3D space using X, Y, and Z coordinates in After Effects.

✦ You can open multiple QuickTime movies into After Effects.

✦   ✦   ✦

Appendixes

What's on the DVD

This appendix provides you with information on the contents of the DVD that accompanies this book. For the latest and greatest information, please refer to the ReadMe file located at the root of the DVD.

System Requirements

Make sure that your computer meets Adobe Premiere Pro's minimum system requirements listed in this section. If your computer doesn't match up to most of these requirements, you may have a problem using the contents of the DVD.

For Windows XP:

- ◆ PC with Intel Pentium 4, 1.4GHz processor or faster.

- ◆ At least 512MB of RAM installed on your computer; for best performance, 1GB or more is recommended.

- ◆ Microsoft Windows XP Professional or XP Home Edition with Service Pack 2 installed.

- ◆ 800MB of available hard-disk space for installation. Additional hard-disk space is required for project files and to install all software on the DVD.

- ◆ A DVD drive is required for installation. (A DVD recordable drive—DVD+R—is required to burn DVDs using Premiere Pro.)

- ◆ QuickTime 6 is required to load the QuickTime tutorial files.

Using the DVD with Windows XP

To install the items from the DVD to your hard drive, insert the DVD into your computer's DVD drive. A window appears with the following options: Tutorial Files, Explore, PDFs, Links, and Exit.

- ◆ **Tutorial Files:** Allows you to copy Tutorial Files from the DVD to your hard disk.

- ◆ **Explore:** Allows you to view the contents of the DVD in its directory structure.

✦ **PDFs:** Lets you access the electronic version of this book.

✦ **Links:** Opens a hyperlinked page of Web sites.

✦ **Exit:** Closes the autorun window.

If you do not have autorun enabled or if the autorun window does not appear, follow these steps to access the DVD:

1. **Click Start⇨Run.**

2. **In the dialog box that appears, type** *d*:\start.exe, **where** *d* **is the letter of your DVD drive.** This brings up the autorun window previously described.

3. **Choose the Tutorial Files, Explore, PDFs, Links, or Exit option from the menu (see preceding list for description of these options).**

What's on the DVD

The following sections provide a summary of the software and other materials you'll find on the DVD.

Tutorial files

In the Tutorial Projects folder are still images, video, and sound clips for following along with the exercises in the book. You can click Explore from within the DVD interface to browse these images on the DVD. The still images are in Photoshop, Illustrator, JPEG, and PICT file formats. The digital video clips are in AVI or QuickTime file format. Many of the files used are from Digital Vision, providers of royalty-free still and moving images. The sound files are in AIFF or WAV format. The files are divided into chapter folders that are associated with the chapters in the book. Please note that the images in the Tutorial Projects folder are for instructional purposes only. They are not for commercial use.

Software trials

On the DVD are various software tryouts from Adobe Systems. They are Adobe Encore DVD 1.5, Adobe After Effects, Adobe Photoshop, Adobe Premiere Pro 1.5, Adobe Illustrator, Adobe GoLive, and Adobe Acrobat Reader. Note that Adobe does not provide technical support for the software tryouts. Also included on the DVD are Macromedia Director MX 2004 and Macromedia Flash MX 8.

For more information on these software trials, go to these Web sites: www.adobe.com, and www.macromedia.com.

Note   We have included the tryout version of Adobe Premiere Pro 1.5 (Adobe Systems, Inc.). Use Adobe Premiere Pro to edit and manipulate your video clips. See www.adobe.com for a try-out version of Adobe Premiere Pro 2.

✦ **Adobe After Effects (Adobe Systems, Inc.):** The tryout version of Adobe After Effects is a 30-day tryout version. Use Adobe After Effects to create digital video special effects.

✦ **Adobe Encore DVD 1.5 (Adobe Systems, Inc.):** The tryout version of Adobe Encore DVD is a 30-day tryout version. Use Adobe Encore DVD for DVD authoring. See www.adobe.com for a tryout version of Adobe Encore Pro 2.

✦ **Adobe GoLive CS2 (Adobe Systems, Inc.):** The tryout version of Adobe GoLive CS2 is a 30-day tryout version. Use Adobe GoLive to create content for the Web.

✦ **Adobe Illustrator CS2 (Adobe Systems, Inc.):** The tryout version does not allow you to save, print, or export your work. Use Adobe Illustrator to create vector graphics.

✦ **Adobe Photoshop CS2 (Adobe Systems, Inc.):** We have included the tryout version of Adobe Photoshop CS2. Use Adobe Photoshop CS2 to edit digital images.

✦ **Macromedia Director MX 2004 (Macromedia, Inc.):** The trial version of Macromedia Director is a 30-day trial version. Use Macromedia Director to author your presentations.

✦ **Macromedia Flash 8 (Macromedia, Inc.):** The trial version of Macromedia Flash is a 30-day trial version. Use Macromedia Flash to create interactive Web experiences.

✦ **Macromedia Dreamweaver 8 (Macromedia, Inc.):** The trial version of Macromedia Dreamweaver 8 is a 30-day trial version. Use Macromedia Dreamweaver 8 to create content for the Web.

Shareware programs are fully functional, trial versions of copyrighted programs. If you like particular programs, register with their authors for a nominal fee and receive licenses, enhanced versions, and technical support. *Freeware programs* are copyrighted games, applications, and utilities that are free for personal use. Unlike shareware, these programs do not require a fee or provide technical support. *GNU software* is governed by its own license, which is included inside the folder of the GNU product. See the GNU license for more details.

Trial, demo, or evaluation versions are usually limited either by time or functionality (such as being unable to save projects). Some trial versions are very sensitive to system date changes. If you alter your computer's date, the programs will "time out" and will no longer be functional.

PDF files

Each chapter in the book has been converted to a PDF file. You can load the files onto your computer and search for specific topics as you work with Premiere Pro. You need to install a copy of Adobe's Acrobat Reader (also included on this DVD) to view these files.

Troubleshooting

If you have difficulty installing or using any of the materials on the companion DVD, try the following solutions:

✦ **Turn off any antivirus software that you may have running.** Installers sometimes mimic virus activity and can make your computer incorrectly believe that it is being infected by a virus. (Be sure to turn the antivirus software back on later.)

✦ **Close all running programs.** The more programs you're running, the less memory is available to other programs. Installers also typically update files and programs; if you keep other programs running, installation may not work properly.

✦ **Reference the ReadMe file.** Please refer to the ReadMe file located at the root of the DVD for the latest product information at the time of publication.

If you still have trouble with the DVD, please call the Customer Care phone number: (800) 762-2974. Outside the United States, call (317) 572-3994. You can also contact Customer Service by e-mail at http://support.wiley.com. Wiley Publishing, Inc., provides technical support only for installation and other general quality control items; for technical support on the applications themselves, consult the program's vendor or author.

✦   ✦   ✦

Places to Visit on the Web

You can use the following list of Web resources as a guide to digital video software and hardware manufacturers and distributors. Also included are a variety of resources that should prove valuable to digital video producers.

Software

www.apple.com

This site offers access to Apple's QuickTime site as well as useful information about MPEG-4 (www.apple.com/mpeg4).

www.adobe.com

Check Adobe's site for Premiere upgrades and tech support. The site also includes Premiere tutorials, as well as samples from professionals in the digital video field. Be sure to sign up for an e-mail newsletter that provides updates and important Premiere technical information.

www.corel.com

Go to this Web site to find out more about Corel Painter, discussed in Chapter 16.

www.discreet.com

Find out more about Discreet Cleaner as well as other Discreet programs for editing and creating special effects and animation.

www.macromedia.com

This site is maintained by Macromedia, the makers of Director, Authorware, and Flash. Many Premiere Pro movies find homes in Director and Flash projects. Download free trial software at this site, which includes lots of tech notes for Macromedia products.

www.maincept.com

Produces MPEG encoders and MPEG decoders, DV filters, and CODEC.

www.microsoft.com/windows/windowsmedia

Get updates on the latest Microsoft Windows Media and streaming video products.

www.quicktime.com

Download the latest version of QuickTime or upgrade to QuickTime Pro. The site includes developer and licensing information as well as links to many sites using QuickTime.

www.realnetworks.com

Find out about RealNetworks audio and video streaming products. Download the latest plug-ins.

www.sorensonmedia.com

Sorenson creates compression software for QuickTime and Flash. Find out about Sorenson Squeeze and other products at this site.

General Resources

www.adobe.com/support/forums/main.html

Here you can find a users group forum for Adobe products. You can ask questions or scroll through other users' questions and answers.

www.aftra.com

This is the Web site for the American Federation of Television and Radio Artists. Here you can find out about using union talent, contacts, and industry news.

www.creativecow.com

This site provides a forum and news for digital media professionals. The site includes a Premiere Pro forum.

www.dmnforums.com

DMN Forums has forums for various products, including Adobe Premiere Pro. On this site, you can also find newsletters that contain information about digital media.

www.dv.com

This is the digital video Web magazine, an excellent source of hardware and software information, as well as technical articles. It features news, tutorials, and a buyer's guide. The site enables you to search back issues for product information and technical articles.

www.dvpa.com

This is the Web site for the Digital Video Producers Association. Membership enables access to thousands of stock clips available online for instant download.

www.ieee.com

This is the Web site for the Institute of Electrical and Electronics Engineers. It contains information on products and services for engineers.

www.videomaker.com

This is the Web site for Videomaker magazine. You can find articles on video as well as online workshops.

Hardware

www.adstech.com
Check out this site for info on the ADS Pyro video card. Here you can purchase products and download drivers.

www.apple.com
Virtually all new Macs include FireWire ports for transferring digital video directly to desktop or laptop. Purchase a Mac here or find out the latest from Apple's tech support library.

www.aja.com
At this site, you can find information about the Xena PCI card for HD production.

www.boxxtech.com
Boxx makes workstations for HD editing and other graphics intensive applications.

www.canon.com
At this site, you can find out about Canon DV cameras and other products.

www.dell.com
Several Dell computers include digital video cards. Purchase a computer or video board for your computer.

www.hewlett-packard.com
Find out more about Hewlett-Packard's products, from desktops and workstations to monitors and from projectors to printers.

www.epson.com
Learn more about Epson's color printers.

www.harman-multimedia.com
Learn more about powered satellite speakers and subwoofers for your computer.

www.hp.com
At this site, you can learn more about Hewlett-Packard's color printers.

www.jvc.com
Details about JVC professional and consumer video equipment are available at this site.

www.matrox.com
Matrox is the creator of video boards and video capture boards (Millennium, Marvel, and so on). Obtain specifications and compatibility information here.

www.olympus.com/digital
At this site, you can learn more about Olympus's digital cameras.

www.pinnaclesys.com

Find out about tech specs for Pinnacle's PC video boards, editing systems, and broadcast-quality equipment.

www.shure.com

This site includes information on Shure's audio products as well as downloadable technical guides.

www.sony.com

Most Sony laptops include i.LINK digital video ports that conform to the IEEE 1394 standard. Find out about the latest Sony computers, monitors, digital camcorders, and professional video equipment.

Stock Image, Sound, and Video Clips

www.gettyimages.com

Many of the video and sound clips in this book are from Digital Vision, a division of Getty Images. At its site, you can learn more about its products.

www.smartsound.com

Visit this site to learn more about stock sound clips.

✦   ✦   ✦

The Digital Video Recording Studio

Setting up a small studio to create desktop digital video movies often involves the purchase of computer, video, and sound equipment. For digital video producers, editors, and graphic designers without a technical background, evaluating hardware can be a frustrating and confusing undertaking.

This appendix provides a hardware overview, describing some of the hardware you may consider purchasing. The sections here are meant to provide you with a general idea of the hardware components that you may need to purchase or rent when shooting a video production. For a thorough analysis of using digital video hardware, you may check several resources: Web sites of hardware manufacturers (such as www.sel.sony.com, www.canon.com, or www.dell.com, magazine Web sites (www.DV.com), or publishers of books specializing in DV and file production (www.focalpress.com). Another good resource is your local library. Many video books written over the past 20 years include video shooting, sound, and lighting chapters that are still relevant today. Finally, you may want to investigate television production workshops and classes provided by local colleges and universities.

Computers

For most Premiere Pro users, the most important element in their digital studio is their computer. The general rule for running Premiere Pro is to get the fastest system you can afford. Digital video typically consumes 13GB per hour of footage, so you not only want a fast system, but one with lots of storage capacity.

If you're in the market for a video system, you may start by checking preconfigured systems designed for video editing. Both Dell and Sony manufacture systems configured for video work. For high definition production, you may want to investigate a Boxx high-end workstation. Boxx (www.boxxtech.com) sells workstations designed for both high-end video and 3D graphics.

These are the minimum system requirements for Premiere Pro.

Windows requirements

✦ Intel Pentium 4 processor, 1.4GHz

   • For HDV: Intel Pentium 4, 3.0GHz processor with Hyper-Threading

   • For HD: Dual Intel Xeon 2.6GHz processors

✦ Microsoft Windows XP Pro or XP Home Edition with Service Pack 2

✦ 512K RAM or more recommended

   • For HDV: 2GB of RAM Intel Xeon 2.6GHz processors

✦ 7200RPM hard disk

   • For HD: Striped disk array (RAID 0)

✦ 800MB of available hard-disk space for installation, 6GB for additional content

✦ For DV: 1394 interface and dedicated large-capacity 7200 RPM UDMA 66 IDE or SCSI hard disk or disk array

✦ DVD-ROM drive required for installation

✦ DVD+R required to export to DVD

✦ OHCI compatible IEEE 1394 interface for DV I/O

   • For HD: AJA Xena HS for SD/HD SDI I/O

✦ Microsoft DirectX-compatible sound card

✦ Optional: ASIO audio compatible sound card required for Surround Sound.

✦ QuickTime 6 or greater required to import and save QuickTime files

Processing speed

A computer system's central processing unit (CPU) and the speed of its hard drive (or disks) determine its overall speed when working with multimedia projects.

Many consider the computer's CPU to be the brains of the system. Modern processors, such as the Pentium Xeon, are faster and more sophisticated than the Pentium 4 chips. Chip speed is measured in *megahertz* (MHz) — a million clock cycles per second — where a higher number indicates a faster chip. Thus, a 1.6MHz chip is faster than a 1.4MHz chip. As this book goes to press, 3-gigahertz (GHz) processors and higher are the state of the art in processors.

Coprocessors

Two CPUs are better than one. Premiere Pro, unlike many computer programs, takes full advantage of computer systems with two or more processors. If you are working with HD footage, dual processors are required. Preview rendering speeds should be dramatically increased with multiple processors.

Hard-drive speed

Hard-drive speed is generally evaluated by the revolutions per minute, seek speed, and data transfer rate. Most of the faster hard drives provide a rotational speed of at least 7200 RPM (revolutions per minute). Some high-capacity drives have a rotation speed of 10,000 RPM.

Seek speed essentially measures the time it takes to seek out the section of the hard drive that it needs to read to or write to. Seek time is measured in milliseconds (ms). Thus, a seek time of 8.5ms is faster than 9.5ms. A hard drive's transfer rate determines how fast the drive can transfer data. A High Capacity UltraSCSI (Small Computer Systems Interface) drive may be able to support a transfer rate of 320MB per second. The actual sustained transfer rate of the hard drive (how long it takes a hard drive to save data to its platters) will be slower. For instance, the sustained data rate of Maxtor's Atlas 19K III Ultra 320 is 55MB/sec — certainly fast enough for video capture. (To capture video, Adobe recommends a minimum sustained transfer rate of 3MB per second, and preferably a sustained transfer rate of 6MB per second.) Note that the actual video transfer rates are probably about half the maximum transfer rates of a hard drive.

If you are capturing video, experts also recommend that you maintain a separate hard disk just for video capture and keep the disk defragmented. If you're interested in finding more about hard-drive storage and hard-drive storage rates, go to www.storagereview.com.

IEEE boards

Most high-end PCs are now sold with built-in IEEE 1394 cards. The IEEE standard has been pioneered by Apple computer, which calls the IEEE 1394 standard FireWire (Sony calls it iLINK). IEEE 1394 ports enable you to copy digitized audio and video from a DV camcorder or DV tape recorder directly to your computer. The actual digitization process takes place in the camera. The IEEE 1394 port enables the transfer of data at high speeds from the camcorder to the computer or from computer to hard disk. The top transfer rate for the IEEE 1394/FireWire standard is a blistering 400MB per second. FireWire supports up to 63 connected devices and cables up to 14 feet long.

If your computer does not have an IEEE port, you may be able to purchase an add-in IEEE card for $50, and sometimes less. The IEEE 1394 port can also be used to attach a hard disk or CD-ROM recorder. Prices of IEEE 1394/FireWire peripherals have dropped steadily.

Companies such as Pinnacle Systems and Miro sell high-end IEEE 1394 video boards, which can cost over $1,000. High-end DV cards usually enable you to export files in MPEG-2 format. MPEG-2 is a high-compression video format that provides extremely high-quality output. Most MPEG-2 boards enable you to export your files to DVD-ROM format. A further benefit of high-end cards is that most processing chips are built into the cards and, therefore, can create and/or render digital effects at high speeds.

Xena HD cards

AJA's Xena HS for SD/HD SDI I/O is a PCI card that provides uncompressed audio and video input and output. The Serial Device Interface (SDI) card is a required for HD editing with Premiere Pro. For more information and to download manuals for Xena HD cards, see www.aja.com.

Video cards

A third-party video card can speed the display of video effects in real time and often improve image quality. While you're taking a break from your video production work, these cards also speed the processing of 3D games. Newer, faster GPUs (Graphics Processing Units) are PCI-Express cards, which can deliver high-performance graphics to Pentium-based mother-boards. PCI-Express cards are faster than older AGP cards that delivered four times the bandwidth of the PCI bus. PCI-Express cards can transfer data at rates of over 4GB per second. (The PCI — peripheral component interconnect — is a high-performance system that handles the transfer of data from the CPU to expansion slots. It is standard on most computers.) These cards reduce bottlenecks between the computer's CPU and RAM, providing very high transfer of graphics data.

If you're interested in high-end graphics cards, check out ATI's FireGL cards (www.ati.com), such as the FireGL V7100, and PNY's NVidia Quadro cards, such as the Quadro FX 4400 (see www.pny.com).

RAID arrays

To help attain extremely high transfer rates, many multimedia producers have installed RAID array systems, in which data is shared among several hard drives. RAID (Redundant Array of Independent Disks) systems can split the data transfer over two or more hard disks in a procedure known as *striping*. Striping is a requirement for HD video editing in Adobe Premiere Pro. (Raid arrays that provide basis striping are referred to as Raid 0 or Raid Level 0.) Because the computer can read and write from multiple drives, transfer rates are increased. Many RAID systems use Ultra-SCSI connections (IDE-RAID systems are also available), which provide faster transfer than standard PC ATA connections or standard SCSI connections.

Peripheral Storage Devices

As you work with digitized video and sound, you consume large amounts of storage space. Where do you store clips and sounds that you no longer need to access directly from your hard disks? One of the most common storage solutions is to use a DLT (Digital Linear Tape) or Super DLT drive. DLT drives can store several gigabytes of data to over a 100GB. For example, Quantum's DLT1 stores 40GB at 3MB per second. Quantum's SDLT 220 can store 110GB at a transfer rate of 11MB per second. (If compression is used, it can store approximately twice is much data.) Apart from using DLT drives as backup drives, they can also be used to master DVDs. Quantum, IBM, Hewlett-Packard, and Dell all sell DLT drives.

For long-term storage, yet slower recording and slower loading, you can use a CD/DVD recorder to record directly onto a CD-ROM or a DVD drive. Most high-end computer models include DVD drives that allow you to record on DVD rewritable DVD-ROMs, which can store about 4.7GB on a single drive. CD-ROMs store about 650MB.

Analog Capture Boards

Analog capture boards accept an analog video signal and digitize video to a computer's hard disk or other storage device. On the PC, most analog boards are add-in boards that must be purchased separately from the computer system. If you are not shooting video using a DV system, you may consider purchasing an analog board. The three formats used by analog boards are *composite video*, *S-video,* and *component* video.

✦ **Composite video:** Composite video provides fair to good quality capture. In this system, the video brightness and color components are combined into one signal. Most composite boards have three cables: one video and two sound cables. Many of the older DV camcorders that are still on the market enable you to place analog tape in them and transfer data using composite signals. Many VHS tape recorders allow input from composite video.

✦ **S-video:** S-video provides a higher quality video signal than composite video because luminance and color are separated into two different signals. Most analog boards that provide S-video also allow composite output. S-video is considered better quality than VHS. Most VHS tape recorders allow input from S-video. (Many DV cameras provide an S-video port to enable you to transfer DV footage to VHS tape decks.)

✦ **Component:** Component video provides broadcast quality video. In component video, two channels handle color and one channel handles luminance. Although composite and S-video boards enable connections to camcorder and consumer tape decks, component boards enable a connection to broadcast quality Beta SP tape decks.

Digital Video Cameras

With the introduction of HDV cameras, the process of choosing a camcorder has become more complicated. As discussed in Chapter 4, HDV cameras output at 1280×720 pixels and 1440×1080, storing data in MPEG-2 format. HDV cameras such as Sony's HDR-FX1 can output progressive scanned video, which provides a more film-like look than traditional interlaced video. (See Chapter 4 for a discussion of the differences between progressive and interlaced video.) Like DV cameras, which output at a resolution of 720×480 digitized, HDV cameras record to mini-DV tapes. Both formats allow you to capture video using an IEEE 1394 port. At the time of the publication of this book, many video producers are starting the transition from DV to HDV. But before you take the leap, realize that HDV camcorders are more expensive than DV camcorders, and you need more RAM and a faster processor to edit HDV footage in Premiere Pro.

Better DV camcorders usually create pictures with more pixels. For example, several Canon Elura models feature a ¼-inch CCD (charge coupler device, responsible for converting the image into a signal that can be digitized) that provides over 600,000 pixels; however, some cameras — such as the Canon XLS, Canon GL1, Sony TVR900, and Sony DCR-VX2000 — provide three CCDs with 270,000 pixels per CCD, which provide a sharper image. (High-end camcorders typically feature three CCDS.)

Another consideration is accessories. Some cameras enable you to change lenses and have more control for changing exposure and shutter speed. If audio is important, you may want to check whether your camera can connect to a wireless microphone or to an audio mixer. Another feature to consider is whether you want to be able to use older analog tape formats. Some models can take a Hi-8 or 8mm tape and digitize the video right in the camera, so it can be transferred to the computer's IEEE 1394 port (rather than to an analog capture board). Most models feature an S-video port so that the digital video data can be transferred to a consumer VHS tape recorder.

If you're interested in purchasing a DV or HDV camcorder, start by surveying the Web pages of camcorder manufacturers such as Sony, Canon, and JVC. Look at the features listed and compare prices. (Canon's Web page currently allows you to download user manuals, which can help you understand the camera's features.) Usually, the higher the cost, the better the camera and the more features you get. You may also want to view Web sites of DV magazines such as eventdv.net or camcorder-specific Web sites such as www.camcorderinfo.com.

Lenses

Most casual users of video equipment simply purchase a camera and use whatever lens is mounted on the camera. If you keep working with video equipment, you should learn a bit about lenses. Virtually all camcorders sold today include zoom lenses. For example, Canon's XL1S, one of the more expensive pro-consumer cameras on the market, features a 16x zoom. The modifier *16x* indicates that the camera can zoom in to make the focal length 16 times greater. This enables you to alter the built-in focal length of the XL1S from 5.5mm to 88mm. (This lens is interchangeable with other lenses.)

The focal length is the middle of the lens to the point where an image begins to appear, usually measured in millimeters. The focal length indicates exactly what image areas can appear in the lens. If the focal length is low, the viewing area is large; if the focal length is large, the viewing area is correspondingly smaller. Thus, if you focus on a subject with a smaller focal length, such as 10mm (a wide angle lens), you see more of the subject than at 50mm (telephoto). At 10mm, you may see an image of a person from head to toe; at 50mm, only the person's face is seen in a closeup.

Many cameras provide digital zooms of up to 50x. Although this provides further zooming capabilities, the picture quality usually isn't as good as optical zooming. When viewing the specs of high-range cameras, you frequently see the f-stop range. The f-stops control the iris opening of the camera. The lower the f-stop, the greater the amount of light allowed in. Higher f-stops allow less light in. Canon's XL1 provides a range of 1.6–16. (You can adjust the shutter speed on this camera as well.) This enables you to set manual exposure and provides greater control over depth-of-field.

Depth-of-field is typically defined as the area from the nearest point in focus to the furthest point in focus. Having sufficient depth-of-field is especially important if a subject you are shooting is moving. You don't want the subject moving in and out of focus. The focal length of the lens, the distance of the subject from the camera, and the f-stop setting all determine depth-of-field.

Microphones

Although most camcorders feature a built-in microphone, you may want to purchase an external microphone to capture better quality audio. For sophisticated audio recording, you may want to purchase a mixer that enables you to accept multiple sound inputs and enables you to monitor and set recording levels. Behringer, Shure, Sony, and Soundcraft are among the manufacturers of mixers designed for live-event recording.

If you are purchasing a microphone, you want to become familiar with several common audio terms. The first one is *frequency response*, which describes the pick up or sensitivity range of sound for the microphone, from low to high sounds. Sound waves are measured in cycles per second (Hz). The human ear is sensitive to a range from 20Hz to 16,000Hz. A microphone frequency response determines the range of sounds it can record. An expensive studio microphone can have a range from 20Hz to 20,000Hz.

Microphones are divided into different categories, according to the inner electronics that control the capture of sound. The primary categories are *condenser*, *dynamic*, and *crystal*.

Condenser mics are generally used as studio mics. They are usually expensive. But you get what you pay for. They are sensitive and provide a broad frequency response. Electret condensers are a subcategory of condenser microphones, which can be powered with a small battery provider. They are good for reproduction of narration. Because these microphones are especially sensitive to heat and humidity, care must be taken when using and storing them.

Dynamic microphones are often used as external mics for camcorders. They are inexpensive and usually quite durable. Although the sound quality recorded from dynamic microphones is not excellent, it is generally good enough for most DV taping sessions.

Crystal mics are the least expensive. They do not record a large frequency range and should generally be avoided.

Another basic audio concept to understand about microphones is that they utilize different pick-up patterns. Mics can be omnidirectional or unidirectional.

✦ **Omnidirectional:** These mics pick up sounds from all directions. If you are not recording in a noisy area and want to capture all sounds from the recording site, you probably want to use an omnidirectional microphone.

✦ **Unidirectional:** These microphones pick up sound primarily from one direction. If you are recording in a noisy room and want to record someone speaking, a unidirectional can help eliminate background sounds.

To further specify how microphones pick up sounds, microphone manufacturers provide polar graphs showing the response of a microphone. A polar graph is plotted over 360 degrees, with the center of the graph depicting the center of the microphone. The round curves depict the area from which the microphone picks up sound. The graph patterns are described as cardioid and bidirectional.

✦ **Cardioid:** Picks up sounds primarily from the front of the mic. They eliminate sounds from the back of the mic and can pick up some sounds from the side. If you stand in front of the mic, most cardioids accept a 30-angle range.

✦ **Bidirectional:** Picks up sounds primarily from the front and back of the microphone.

On a more technical level, mics are considered either high or low *impedance*. Measured in ohms, impedance is an electrical term indicating resistance in the circuit. Most professional (and thus high quality) audio/video equipment and studio equipment is low impedance. Low impedance equipment is often called Low-Z. Less expensive equipment is generally high impedance (called Hi-Z). Generally, short-cabled microphones are Hi-Z, and long-cabled microphones are Low-Z (15 feet or longer).

As you work with audio, you also see the terms *balanced* and *unbalanced* to describe audio cabling. Short cables with high impedance equipment using RCA mini-plugs are using unbalanced lines. Most non-broadcast camcorders provide unbalanced lines. Balanced lines feature XLR and cannon plugs (shielded cables), which eliminate buzzing sounds and other electronic noise. Expensive pro-consumer camcorders, such as the Cannon l XL1, provide a connection to a CLR plug for hookup to an audio mixer.

Tip   You may also want to visit audio equipment manufacturer Shure's Web site, which includes technical publications such as "Guide to Audio Systems for Video Production" by Shure engineer Christopher Lyons. This publication — which reviews microphones and mixers, and covers topics such as "Connecting a Mixer to a Camcorder" and "How to Handle Some Common Miking Situations" — can be downloaded from Shure's Web site at www.shure.com (follow these links: Knowledge > Contractor's Corner > Educational material).

Lighting

Lighting is one of the crucial factors determining video quality. If you are shooting indoors, you should investigate lighting equipment and learn the basics of setting up lights. If you're new to video, you may take a basic studio production course or read a book on television lighting. (The Focal press offers a variety of books on this subject.)

If you are primarily going to be shooting interior scenes and want to produce high-quality video, you should investigate purchasing a lighting kit, along with lighting utilities, such as scrims and barn doors, which can limit and control lights.

Although this appendix is not designed to serve as a lighting guide, to properly light a scene, you typically include a key light and a fill light, with a backlight added to provide more depth. The key light is the main source of illumination. Often, the key light is set at a 45-degree angle between the camera and the subject. The fill light, often placed on the opposite side of the camera from the key, helps lighten shadow areas produced by the key.

If you are setting up lights on-location, be wary of blowing out a fuse. A typical U.S. consumer circuit is a 15-amp line and does not handle more than 1,800 watts (multiply total amps times voltage to obtain the total watts used, $120 \times 15 = 1800$). It's a good idea to add up all the watts you are using, including any camera equipment, before you start plugging in electrical equipment. Also remember that other electrical equipment may be using the circuit as well.

✦   ✦   ✦

Index

Wiley Publishing, Inc.
End-User License Agreement

READ THIS. You should carefully read these terms and conditions before opening the software packet(s) included with this book "Book". This is a license agreement "Agreement" between you and Wiley Publishing, Inc. "WPI". By opening the accompanying software packet(s), you acknowledge that you have read and accept the following terms and conditions. If you do not agree and do not want to be bound by such terms and conditions, promptly return the Book and the unopened software packet(s) to the place you obtained them for a full refund.

1. **License Grant.** WPI grants to you (either an individual or entity) a nonexclusive license to use one copy of the enclosed software program(s) (collectively, the "Software" solely for your own personal or business purposes on a single computer (whether a standard computer or a workstation component of a multi-user network). The Software is in use on a computer when it is loaded into temporary memory (RAM) or installed into permanent memory (hard disk, CD-ROM, or other storage device). WPI reserves all rights not expressly granted herein.

2. **Ownership.** WPI is the owner of all right, title, and interest, including copyright, in and to the compilation of the Software recorded on the disk(s) or CD-ROM "Software Media". Copyright to the individual programs recorded on the Software Media is owned by the author or other authorized copyright owner of each program. Ownership of the Software and all proprietary rights relating thereto remain with WPI and its licensers.

3. **Restrictions On Use and Transfer.**

   (a) You may only (i) make one copy of the Software for backup or archival purposes, or (ii) transfer the Software to a single hard disk, provided that you keep the original for backup or archival purposes. You may not (i) rent or lease the Software, (ii) copy or reproduce the Software through a LAN or other network system or through any computer subscriber system or bulletin- board system, or (iii) modify, adapt, or create derivative works based on the Software.

   (b) You may not reverse engineer, decompile, or disassemble the Software. You may transfer the Software and user documentation on a permanent basis, provided that the transferee agrees to accept the terms and conditions of this Agreement and you retain no copies. If the Software is an update or has been updated, any transfer must include the most recent update and all prior versions.

4. **Restrictions on Use of Individual Programs.** You must follow the individual requirements and restrictions detailed for each individual program in the "What's on the DVD" appendix of this Book. These limitations are also contained in the individual license agreements recorded on the Software Media. These limitations may include a requirement that after using the program for a specified period of time, the user must pay a registration fee or discontinue use. By opening the Software packet(s), you will be agreeing to abide by the licenses and restrictions for these individual programs that are detailed in the "What's on the DVD" appendix and on the Software Media. None of the material on this Software Media or listed in this Book may ever be redistributed, in original or modified form, for commercial purposes.

5. Limited Warranty.

(a) WPI warrants that the Software and Software Media are free from defects in materials and workmanship under normal use for a period of sixty (60) days from the date of purchase of this Book. If WPI receives notification within the warranty period of defects in materials or workmanship, WPI will replace the defective Software Media.

(b) WPI AND THE AUTHOR OF THE BOOK DISCLAIM ALL OTHER WARRANTIES, EXPRESS OR IMPLIED, INCLUDING WITHOUT LIMITATION IMPLIED WARRANTIES OF MERCHANTABILITY AND FITNESS FOR A PARTICULAR PURPOSE, WITH RESPECT TO THE SOFTWARE, THE PROGRAMS, THE SOURCE CODE CONTAINED THEREIN, AND/OR THE TECHNIQUES DESCRIBED IN THIS BOOK. WPI DOES NOT WARRANT THAT THE FUNCTIONS CONTAINED IN THE SOFTWARE WILL MEET YOUR REQUIREMENTS OR THAT THE OPERATION OF THE SOFTWARE WILL BE ERROR FREE.

(c) This limited warranty gives you specific legal rights, and you may have other rights that vary from jurisdiction to jurisdiction.

6. Remedies.

(a) WPI's entire liability and your exclusive remedy for defects in materials and workmanship shall be limited to replacement of the Software Media, which may be returned to WPI with a copy of your receipt at the following address: Software Media Fulfillment Department, Attn.: *Adobe Premiere Pro 2 Bible*, Wiley Publishing, Inc., 10475 Crosspoint Blvd., Indianapolis, IN 46256, or call 1-800-762-2974. Please allow four to six weeks for delivery. This Limited Warranty is void if failure of the Software Media has resulted from accident, abuse, or misapplication. Any replacement Software Media will be warranted for the remainder of the original warranty period or thirty (30) days, whichever is longer.

(b) In no event shall WPI or the author be liable for any damages whatsoever (including without limitation damages for loss of business profits, business interruption, loss of business information, or any other pecuniary loss) arising from the use of or inability to use the Book or the Software, even if WPI has been advised of the possibility of such damages.

(c) Because some jurisdictions do not allow the exclusion or limitation of liability for consequential or incidental damages, the above limitation or exclusion may not apply to you.

7. U.S. Government Restricted Rights. Use, duplication, or disclosure of the Software for or on behalf of the United States of America, its agencies and/or instrumentalities "U.S. Government" is subject to restrictions as stated in paragraph (c)(1)(ii) of the Rights in Technical Data and Computer Software clause of DFARS 252.227-7013, or subparagraphs (c) (1) and (2) of the Commercial Computer Software - Restricted Rights clause at FAR 52.227-19, and in similar clauses in the NASA FAR supplement, as applicable.

8. General. This Agreement constitutes the entire understanding of the parties and revokes and supersedes all prior agreements, oral or written, between them and may not be modified or amended except in a writing signed by both parties hereto that specifically refers to this Agreement. This Agreement shall take precedence over any other documents that may be in conflict herewith. If any one or more provisions contained in this Agreement are held by any court or tribunal to be invalid, illegal, or otherwise unenforceable, each and every other provision shall remain in full force and effect.